Ancient Mexico

An Enthralling Guide to the Aztec Empire, Maya Civilization, Olmecs, Toltecs, and Teotihuacan

Free limited time bonus

Stop for a moment. We have a free bonus set up for you. The problem is this: we forget 90% of everything that we read after 7 days. Crazy fact, right? Here's the solution: we've created a printable, 1-page pdf summary for this book that you're reading now. All you have to do to get your free pdf summary is to go to the following website:

https://livetolearn.lpages.co/enthrallinghistory/

Once you do, it will be intuitive. Enjoy, and thank you!

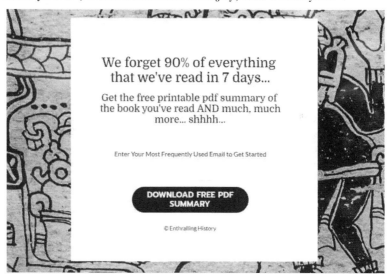

Table of Contents

Part 1: The Aztec Empire

An Enthralling Overview of the History of the Aztecs, Starting with the Settlement in the Valley of Mexico

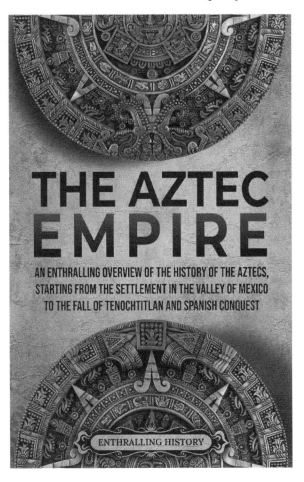

THE AZTEC EMPIRE

AN ENTHRALLING OVERVIEW OF THE HISTORY OF THE AZTECS, STARTING FROM THE SETTLEMENT IN THE VALLEY OF MEXICO TO THE FALL OF TENOCHTITLAN AND SPANISH CONQUEST

ENTHRALLING HISTORY

Introduction

They saw it! They finally saw it. Right there, in front of them, was an eagle, perched on a cactus, eating a snake. The prophecy was fulfilled! The "people from Aztlan" had found the place where they would settle down after countless years of wandering the barren wastelands.

The year was AD 1325, almost 200 years before the first Europeans set foot on the shores of Mexico. A nomadic tribe called the *Mexica* built their city on a small swampy island, an unlikely location for what would become the capital of a great empire. From unpromising origins, the extraordinary Aztec Empire would soon form and expand into a civilization renown for military skills, market exchange, fascinating culture, and extensive and sophisticated agricultural endeavors. Through conquest and alliances with other powerful city-states, the Aztecs developed a vast, organized, densely populated empire that encompassed much of today's Mexico.

This overview of the Aztec Empire will reveal many of the captivating mysteries of this vast nation. What civilizations existed in the area before the Mexica gained supremacy? Where did the Mexica come from? How did they gain ascendency over other civilizations and form their extensive network of power? What was the mythology and religion of the Aztecs, and how was their art a reflection of their belief system? How was their agricultural and market system distinct from surrounding cultures? How did their social order function?

Aztec Calendar[1]

This comprehensive and detailed guide to the Aztec Empire will answer these questions and many more about this intriguing nation and its culture. It will explain the distinctive features of this great empire, what made it exceptional, and how the Aztec culture has had a lasting impact on the modern world. Readers will gain in-depth insight into who the Aztecs were – not just what they did, but how they lived, what they believed, and how they interacted.

Many books have been written about the Aztec Empire, so why is another one needed? Existing books tend to fall into several categories: some are missing information gleaned from the more recent archaeological finds and scholarly studies, some are dry and dusty and overly academic, some focus only on one aspect of the Aztec Empire, and some are simplistic and limited in scope – geared for a child audience.

The objective of this book is to provide a well-researched and broad presentation of the Aztec Empire in an easy-to-understand

[1] https://www.needpix.com/photo/892953/aztec-calendar-aztec

and interesting format that keeps the reader fascinated and engaged. History buffs and those simply curious about the Aztecs will appreciate the depth of information and insight woven into this authoritative work, accompanied by striking illustrations that clarify the narrative and bring the Aztec and other Mesoamerican cultures to life.

This guide is divided into four sections, starting with the primary cultures that existed in the area before the Aztec Empire: the Olmecs and Epi-Olmecs, the Toltecs, and the Chichimeca. We will explore how they flourished, what they were famous for, and who were some of their important leaders. We will consider the factors which led to each civilization collapsing, fading into oblivion, or being assimilated by later cultures.

Part Two, The Rise of the Aztec Civilization, focuses on the rise of the Aztec Empire, diving into the origins of the Aztec people and how they defined themselves. This section explores the mystery of the Aztec's home country: Aztlan, in the Lake of the Moon. We will probe theories regarding where it was located and what the word *Aztlan* means. We will investigate who the Mexica tribe were and how they rose to become the dominant tribe of the Aztecs in early settlements in the Valley of Mexico.

The Mexican coat of arms depicts the Mexica-Aztec legend of the eagle eating a rattlesnake while perched on a cactus.[2]

[2] https://en.wikipedia.org/wiki/Aztecs#Mexica_migration_and_foundation_of_Tenochtitlan

And what's this legend about an eagle eating a snake while perched on a prickly pear cactus? What does this symbolize, and how did it lead to founding a capital city in the middle of a swamp?

We will analyze the key elements of the establishment of the Aztec dynasty, how the city-states were organized and connected to each other, and how the Aztecs controlled other Mesoamerican city-states. We will study how the Triple Alliance was formed and what was their successful strategy of conquest.

Part Three, the Spanish Conquest, will explore what happened when the Europeans showed up. How did the Aztecs respond when they first spotted strange ships in the Gulf, like nothing they had ever seen? How did the Spanish conquistador Hernán Cortés cunningly form alliances with the Tlaxcala people, rivals of the Aztecs? This section will probe the events leading up to Emperor Moctezuma being held prisoner in his own palace and the revolt of the Aztecs against the Spaniards following the massacre in the Great Temple.

In this section, we will see how the clash played out between two great empires, formerly divided by a great ocean and unknown to the other. How did the Spaniards organize the siege on Tenochtitlan, the Aztec capital? What factors led to the fall of the great city and the Spanish invaders gaining the upper hand? We will examine what happened when the Spaniards took control, how the Aztecs and other indigenous people adapted to Spain's rule and a new way of life, as they were pressured to abandon their idols and convert (on the surface, at least) to Catholicism.

Part Four - Art, Culture, & Legacy - reviews the fascinating Aztec culture and their continuing impact, beginning with the Aztec religion and who their gods were. Did they really practice human sacrifice? What were their religious rituals like? We will also examine how their market system worked, analyzing the relationships and trade of the Aztecs with other peoples, as well as their education system. And how did the common people live? We will explore what marriage was like in the Aztec culture and intriguing aspects of family and everyday life.

Did you know the Aztecs had a writing system? Their written communication was a form of art, combining pictograms and ideograms. Art was central to Aztec culture, and in Part Four, we will explore the breathtaking beauty of Aztec architecture, sculptures, mosaics, poetry, ceramics, metalwork, and their exquisite featherwork used to dress warriors, priests, and idols. We will examine how their art and other cultural artifacts were influenced by surrounding groups and how they themselves influenced the area around them - even modern-day Mexico and the rest of Mesoamerica.

Let's step back in time and begin following the fascinating journey of a people of mysterious origins who built a city in a swamp and proceeded to develop the vast and breathtaking Aztec Empire.

SECTION ONE:
BEFORE THE AZTECS

Chapter 1: The Olmecs and the Epi-Olmecs

What do rubber balls, chocolate, colossal heads, *werejaguars* (like a werewolf, but jaguar and human), and a pyramid all have in common? They were all cultural distinctions of the Olmecs, the first major civilization or "mother culture" of Mesoamerica, the region extending from central Mexico down to northern Costa Rica.

Formal agriculture in the Americas, especially the widespread growing of maize (corn), goes back to at least the 4th millennium BC, advancing most rapidly in what is now Mexico and Guatemala, as well as the Andes region of South America. Among these farming cultures, the Olmec civilization emerged around 1600 B.C in the swampy tropical lowlands close to the Gulf of Mexico, to the south and east of what is now Mexico City.

The rich and well-watered soil in this area supported productive farming, which provided food for a dense population, and the Olmec established three settlements overlooking the Coatzacoalcos River. We don't know the original Olmec name, but their chief settlement is known today as San Lorenzo Tenochtitlán, in what is now the state of Veracruz. To avoid getting confused with the different Mexica-Aztec city named Tenochtitlán, we will refer to the Olmec city as just *San Lorenzo*.

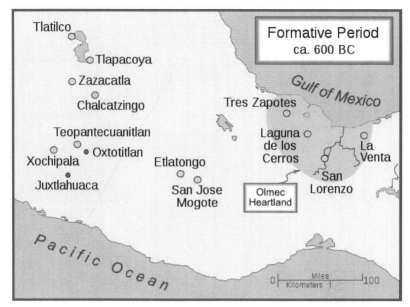

Olmec Region[3].

San Lorenzo, a ceremonial center for surrounding agricultural villages, was built on a manmade plateau of 140 acres, which would have required toiling laborers carrying in tons of earthen fill in baskets. Archeologists were amazed to discover an elaborate drainage system with water-storage cisterns, sophisticated for this time period, even in advanced civilizations on the opposite side of the globe. An engineering masterpiece, the aqueduct of San Lorenzo featured covered water channels formed from basalt, providing fresh water for the citizens.

The settlements flourished over time, and by 1200 BC, San Lorenzo was at its peak. The city proper could have housed 5000, with a possible population of 13,000 in the entire area, the first true city in Mesoamerica. This large population generated a hierarchy, with an elite class ruling the city, skilled artisans carving semi-precious minerals, and laborers for the building projects and for farming crops of corn, sweet potato, beans, squash, and cassava, and growing avocado and cacao trees. These foods provided the core diet of the Olmec, along with domesticated dog

---

(their main source of protein) and fish and wild game.

Some of the jade and obsidian used in carvings came from as far as Guatemala, made possible by trade on the Coatzacoalcos River system. Because of their extensive trade system, the Olmec had a cultural influence on a wider area than where they lived. Olmec artifacts have been found as far north as present-day Mexico City and as far south as Guatemala City. Many aspects of Olmec culture were also passed down to future civilizations, including the Aztec.

Archaeologists discovered a palace in San Lorenzo made of earthen walls and floors with a plaster finish, colored with red ochre, made from the iron oxide hematite. Carved from basalt, 13-foot columns supported the roof of the "red palace." This palace would have housed the ruling elite, while commoners lived on the slopes around the city in "wattle and daub" houses: a framework of wood (wattle) covered with wet earth or clay (daubing).

The word *Olmec* comes from an Aztec word meaning "rubber people," and there's a good reason they were called that! The Panama rubber tree is native to tropical areas of Mexico and Central America. The Olmec harvested the sap from this tree and mixed it with sap from morning glory vines to make it supple, so it could be used to form objects. They would press the rubber sap around stones and make rubber balls. Yes! Rubber balls for ball games. The Olmec invented the first rubber balls!

Rubber balls have also been found in Olmec sacrificial pits, indicating they might have been sacrificed to deities. They might have also used them under heavy objects, to roll them from one place to another, as the Olmec were also known for huge stone figurines that would have needed to be transported somehow.

Altar at La Venta[4].

Around 900 BC, the city of San Lorenzo declined for unknown reasons, but most likely because rivers in the area changed course during that period. The city would have depended on the rivers for trade and for transporting basalt from the mountains. About the same time, another city emerged as the center of Olmec culture. La Venta, settled around 1200 BC, was about 300 years old at the time of San Lorenzo's decline. It rose to dominance as the leading city of the Olmec and remained so for 500 years.

La Venta was in what is now the Mexican state of Tabasco, about ten miles from the Gulf of Mexico and on the Río Palma, a tributary of the Tonalá River. The city was constructed on an island in the middle of a swamp (a recurring theme of cultures in the area), which may have provided natural protection. La Venta's population grew to perhaps 20,000 people, about twice the size of San Lorenzo.

Archaeological examination reveals several distinct sections within the city of La Venta, with a temple complex at the north end of the site and a great pyramid just south of the temple. Curiously, the city is aligned 8 degrees west of north, with almost identical east

[4] Ruben Charles, (http://www.rubencharles.com), CC BY 2.0
<https://creativecommons.org/licenses/by/2.0>, via Wikimedia Commons
https://commons.wikimedia.org/wiki/File:Altar_4_La_Venta_(Ruben_Charles).jpg

and west sides. A great deal of planning went into this city!

The La Venta pyramid was once thought to be the earliest known pyramid of the Americas. However, we now know the Caral civilization in Peru built pyramids predating the Egyptian pyramids by 100 years and the La Venta pyramid by over 1000 years. Could the Peruvians have somehow influenced the Olmec culture? Scholars believe a trading system by raft, extending from Peru to Mexico, existed about 1000 years after the Olmec. They believe this is how civilizations in Mexico suddenly adopted metallurgy around AD 800. It's conceivable that a raft trade could have existed much earlier, in the Olmec era, or at least there may have been an occasional traveler between the two areas. Regardless of where they got the idea, the La Venta pyramid ushered in a trend of pyramid building throughout Mesoamerica by various civilizations following the Olmec.

La Venta pyramid [5]

What did this pyramid of La Venta look like? It was rectangular, with steps at the sides going up to the top. Today, even after thousands of years of erosion, it stands 112 feet in height. About 100,000 cubic meters of clay was used in the construction.

---

[5] https://commons.wikimedia.org/wiki/File:La_Venta_Pir%C3%A1mide_cara_poniente.jpg

Like other American pyramids, it was built of packed clay and faced with stone.

Art was a hallmark of Olmec culture. The Olmec made exceptional carvings in jade (using jadeite jade rather than the nephrite jade used in China). These carvings depicted what is believed to be supernatural creatures, such as the part-human and part-jaguar mythological werejaguar.

Olmec Colossal Head [6]

An astonishing art form distinctive to the Olmec were the colossal heads. These awe-inspiring carvings have been found mostly in San Lorenzo, with some in La Venta and a couple in other settlements. These heads were gigantic – up to 11 feet high! Weighing several tons, they were carved from massive volcanic basalt boulders from Cerro Cintepec in the Tuxtlas mountains, over fifty miles away. Another source of basalt used in the colossal heads was the San Martin Volcano.

How did the Olmec move these enormous stones over all those miles? The mysterious transportation of these massive carved heads is mind-boggling. They would have had to have been dragged – perhaps on a platform rolled over rubber balls. They

[6] https://pixabay.com/sv/photos/olmec-chef-tabasco-rean-mexico-619120/

could have been transported by raft on the river system, but that would have required exceptional raft-making skills to float an object weighing several tons. It would have taken over 1000 men, laboring for months, to get them to their destination.

Archaeological evidence indicates the colossal heads were covered with plaster painted in bright colors. Each head is different, and their faces feature full lips, wide noses, and almond-shaped eyes, some with an epicanthic fold (common in Asians and Polynesians). Some people feel they are African in appearance, or perhaps Asian or Polynesian.

Is this what the Olmec looked like? What were the origins of the Olmec? Some have theorized that the Olmecs were originally from Africa, but DNA studies on two Olmec remains indicate they had DNA consistent with the indigenous populations of the Americas. No specific DNA link has been found between the Olmec and Polynesia or Africa.

Interestingly though, a DNA study published in *Nature* in July 2020 links the ancient Zenú, who lived on the Caribbean side of the country of Columbia, to Easter Island and Fatu Hiva (in Polynesia). Researchers believe this happened around AD 1200, which would have been long after the Olmec civilization, but it does set the imagination racing. Perhaps future archaeological finds and DNA studies will tell us more.

Because the colossal heads can be found at both La Venta and San Lorenzo, we know that producing these massive carvings continued over several centuries. What did they represent? Perhaps each head was that of an Olmec ruler. The heads are carved with some type of head gear, such as a helmet, suggesting an association with the military. Others speculate that the colossal heads represent athletes in the rubber ball games who wore helmets.

The Olmec not only invented rubber balls; they were also known for ball games played by two teams with the rubber ball in a sunken pit. The apparent object of the game was to get the ball to the other end of the court without using their hands (like modern soccer). Depictions in Olmec carvings indicate protective equipment was worn, including helmets. The game was likely an ancient form of the ball game *Ulama*, also played by Aztec and

Maya civilizations, and still played today in Mesoamerica. In Ulama, the ball is hit with the hip, upper thigh, or forearm. About 2000 ancient ball courts have been found in Mesoamerica.

Olmec figurine presenting an infant (who appears to be a werejaguar). [7]

Little is known about the religion and myths of the Olmec, other than what can be gleaned from artifacts. Sacrifice is part of virtually every culture, and it was practiced by the Olmec. Olmec carvings of a person "presenting" an inert baby or small child hints at child sacrifice; partial and complete infant skeletons (found in what are believed to be sacrifice pits) seem to confirm this practice. Other items in the pits suggest sacrifices of metal jewelry, rubber balls, grain, produce, and livestock. Bloodletting, common in later Mesoamerican cultures, is believed to have been part of the sacrificial system, using real and ceramic stingray spikes and shark teeth.

Olmec rulers, priests, and shamans all probably had a part in leading religious activities. They had a jaguar god, along with other

[7] Madman2001, CC BY 3.0 <https://creativecommons.org/licenses/by/3.0>, via Wikimedia Commons
https://commons.wikimedia.org/wiki/File:Olmec_Figurine_holding_infant_(Met).jpg

supernatural beings that they worshiped. The werejaguar were part of the ancient mythology of the Mesoamericans, including the Olmec. Actual jaguars were at the top of the food chain and had a wide range in ancient times. The werejaguar was probably an Olmec deity representing supremacy and strength. Werejaguar figures had almond eyes, a cleft head, and an open mouth turned downward in a sort of grimace.

Werejaguar sculpture from the Museum of Anthropology at Xalapa, Vera Cruz, Mexico.[8]

A werejaguar image is sometimes depicted as an infant in the arms of a human man, possibly a shamanic practice of harnessing the fierce power of the jaguar or possibly the mythological offspring of a jaguar mated with a human. Olmec artifacts include jade masks of a jaguar, usually found at shrines, cemeteries, and temples, obviously carrying significant spiritual meaning.

---

[8] https://en.wikipedia.org/wiki/Werejaguar#/media/File:Jaguarbaby.jpg

Other deities thought to be worshiped by the Olmec included a dragon or earth monster, depicted in their art as having fangs, eyebrows of fire, and a split tongue. Carvings show a maize deity, with corn growing from his cleft head. The Olmec may have had a rain spirit, and carvings on bowls show what may be some sort of banded-eye god. A feathered serpent, a common deity in many Mesoamerican religions, was found on a stele carving and in a cave painting. Lastly, the Olmec appeared to have had a fish or shark deity.

Recent archeological finds show the Olmec apparently developed an early, very primitive writing system. In the late 1990s, workers building a road in what was the Olmec heartland discovered a block of stone in a pile of bulldozer debris, which also included clay figurines that dated back to the San Lorenzo Olmec period. On the block are 62 glyphs, or elemental symbols, resembling maize, pineapple, fish, and insects, as well as more abstract glyphs. The symbols run horizontally, while other forms of Mesoamerican writing or proto-writing were all vertical, like ancient Chinese writing.

This slab, with its carvings of symbols, generated a lot of controversy. Some scholars hailed it as irrefutable evidence of an early writing system in the Olmec culture. Other scholars felt the slab wasn't as genuinely old as believed or that the symbols weren't a type of writing.

In 1997 and 1998, at an archeological site three miles north of La Venta, three artifacts were uncovered that also appear to point to an Olmec writing system. They dated to about 650 BC, when the Olmec civilization at La Venta was active. One was a cylinder seal, which, when rolled out, showed a bird "speaking" words (or glyphs). Two fragments of a plaque were found that each contained a glyph similar to glyphs used in later Mesoamerican cultures.

Now, let's move on to what many of us might consider the most interesting aspect of Olmec culture – chocolate! An article in the May 2011 edition of *Proceedings of the National Academy of Sciences* reported on 156 potsherds collected from an archeological dig at San Lorenzo. Residue in the bowls, cups, and bottles was analyzed at the University of California. Testing revealed that 17% of the potsherds had residue containing theobromine, an alkaloid chemical primarily found in the cocoa plant. The Olmec were drinking chocolate! So, the Olmec not only invented rubber balls, but we can also thank them for figuring out how to make chocolate from cacao beans.

As noted earlier, the Olmec culture first emerged in the San Lorenzo area around 1600 BC. In 900 BC, San Lorenzo abruptly declined, and the Olmec city of La Venta rose to prominence as the cultural center or capital city. La Venta developed and dominated until around 400 BC when it also was suddenly evacuated and abandoned. For the next 2000 years, the eastern half of the Olmec heartland was sparsely inhabited. A large segment of the Olmec seemed to have suddenly died out.

La Venta Stela 19, the earliest known representation of the Feathered Serpent in Mesoamerica.[9]

What caused their eventual extinction? Archeologists believe their depopulation resulted from abrupt and serious changes in the environment to the extent that the area could no longer support a

[9] Audrey and George Delange
https://commons.wikimedia.org/wiki/File:La_Venta_Stele_19_(Delange).jpg

dense population requiring immense agricultural production and a good river system for trade and transport.

We've already speculated on changes to the river courses that likely caused the decline of San Lorenzo. What about La Venta? Tectonic upheaval and shift could have caused earthquakes and volcanic eruptions in the area, as well as further disruption of the river system that the Olmec depended on. Mexico sits on three of the Earth's largest tectonic plates, and earthquakes are common. The soft soil of the marshy Olmec heartland would have amplified the effects of the tremors.

Mexico is the fourth most hazardous country in the world for volcanoes. The San Martin volcano was close to La Venta and erupted as recently as 1796. The El Chichón volcano was also not far away and is still active, last erupting in 1981. The Olmecs lived in the marshy lowlands; even if a volcano isn't erupting, it can leak lethal carbon dioxide, which can collect in low-lying areas, killing humans, animals, and plant life.

The Epi-Olmec

Within a century of the abrupt decline of the Olmec culture, a new culture succeeded it. We refer to them as Epi-Olmec: "epi," meaning "post" or "after." As previously mentioned, the eastern part of the Olmec heartland became a virtual wasteland. However, two cities, Tres Zapotes and Cerro de la Mesas gained prominence in the western part of what was once the Olmec heartland.

The Epi-Olmec culture endured for about 550 years, from 300 BC to AD 250, and seemed to be a gradual transformation from the Olmec culture, rather than a completely new culture gaining dominance. Although not as large and organized as the Olmec, the Epi-Olmecs developed a sophisticated calendar and writing system. However, their trade system did not equal the Olmec, and their art lacked the Olmec refinement.

La Mojarra Stela 1 showing the "Harvester Mountain Lord," AD 156[10]

Several artifacts found in the Epi-Olmec region depict a writing system known as Isthmian script, which may have descended from the Olmec glyphs. In 1986, the *La Mojarra Stela* was unearthed, an extremely important discovery! This carved monument dates to

[10] From the Museum of Anthropology at Xalapa, Vera Cruz, Mexico.
https://en.wikipedia.org/wiki/Epi-Olmec_culture#/media/File:Harvestermountainlord.jpg

AD 156 and has 535 glyphs. On the right side of the stone is a carving of a man wearing an elaborate headdress with a hook-beaked bird deity and sharks. This – along with his feathered cape – indicate he is a ruler, deity, or priest. Over him are twelve columns of glyphs, and on his right side are eight more columns of glyphs.

In 1997, two linguists, John Justeson and Terrence Kaufman, published a paper saying they had deciphered the script. They reported that the man is the Harvester Mountain Lord and that the writings tell of a solar eclipse and appearances of Venus, how the Mountain Lord came to power, his wars, his own bloodletting, and the sacrifice of his brother-in-law. Some archeologists dispute this translation.

The stone also contained two dates in the form of the Mesoamerican Long Count Calendar, which correspond to the months and years of May AD 143 and July AD 156. The Long Count Calendar was a system that emerged in the Epi-Olmec era and was found in areas influenced by Olmec cultures. It measured time by calculating the number of days from what they considered their creation date, which would have been 3114 BC in our calendar.

Earlier, in 1902, the Tuxtla Statuette was discovered by a farmer in the foothills of the Tuxtlas mountains. The statuette is in the shape of a man with a duck mouth and wings. On it are carved 75 glyphs (known as Isthmian script and corresponding to the La Mojarra Stela) and a Long Count Calendar date which corresponds to AD 162.

The oldest artifact of the Epi-Olmec, containing calendar entries and glyphs, was Stela C. The bottom half of this monument was discovered in 1939 at the Tres Zapotes archeological site (and the location of one of the two leading cities of the Epi-Olmec), and the top half was found in 1969. A Long Count calendar date was carved on this monument that corresponds to September 3, 32 BC. On the back of the stela were carved glyphs in the Epi-Olmec Isthmian script.

We are fortunate to have these glimpses into the Epi-Olmec culture. Everyday life and homes for the common people did not seem to change much in the transition from Olmec to Epi-Olmec.

The Epi-Olmec don't seem to have had the centralized hierarchy of the Olmec. By AD 250, their culture gave way to the Classic Veracruz culture, situated a little further north on the Gulf Coast.

Chapter 2: The Toltecs

The Toltec Kingdom, known for legendary sculptors and artists as well as ferocious warrior conquerors, followed the Olmecs as a great Mesoamerican civilization thriving between AD 600 to 1200. The Toltecs were infamous for regularly practicing human sacrifice of adults and children and collecting their skulls on a rack in their ceremonial plaza. They were zealous in spreading the Cult of Quetzalcoatl, the feathered-serpent deity of Mesoamerica and the name their most beloved emperor assumed. The Mexica-Aztecs greatly revered the Toltecs, collected their sculptures and other relics from the Toltec's abandoned city, and claimed to be descended from Toltec royalty.

What were the origins of these warriors and artists? They are believed to have descended from a wild, nomadic people, called the Toltec-Chichimeca, from the deserts of northwestern Mexico and perhaps southern California. In the 9th century, some of these people migrated southward toward the Valley of Mexico: the area encompassing present Mexico City and eastward to the Gulf of Mexico. In their wanderings, the Toltecs picked up cultural influences from the Olmec, the Maya, and, most importantly, the Teotihuacan people.

Pyramid B in Tula.[11]

According to the oral and pictograph tradition of the Aztecs, some of these nomads settled in Tlachicatzin in the territory of the Hue-Tlapallan people, who called them *Tolteca*, meaning artisan or architect, for their renown as craftsmen and artists. Led by two chiefs, Chalcaltzin and Tlacamihtzin, the Toltecs rebelled against their overlords in AD 544. The Toltecs fought for thirteen years, lost the war, and were exiled.

The exiles traveled to Tlasiculiacan, where they reunited with part of their clan that had fled Tlachicatzin earlier. Together they pressed on, reaching a place called Tlapallanconco, where they lived for three years. But they feared being so close to the Hue-Tlapallan people, so their council of chieftains decided to migrate further.

Their astrologer-priest, Huematzin (the man with the long hand), gave them a prophecy of an uninhabited land in the east where they could live. Hearing this, the Toltecs left part of their clan in Tlapallanconco, and the rest would migrate east. They made a solemn vow they would abstain from sexual relations during the migration, so they could travel without the complications of pregnancies and small children.

They marched east, arriving at Xalisco (Jalisco), where they lived eight years. Leaving some of their people there, they migrated to Chimalhuacan Ateneo. At this point, they decided they'd gone long enough without sex, so they celebrated a conjugal feast, enjoyed relations with their wives, and eventually started having children again. They built boats and settled in the islands of the area, then later lived all together in one large wooden building in a place called Tulantzinco. Finally, in AD 648, after 104 years of nomadic living, they moved to what would be their final home, which they named Tollan (Tula), which literally means *place of the reeds*, indicating abundance.

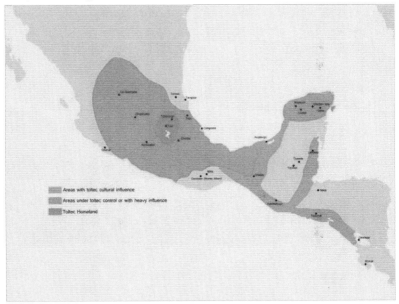

Map of Toltec Influence[12]

The Toltec core area of Tula was in the region immediately northwest of what is now Mexico City. The extent of Toltec artifacts and architectural influences stretched from the Pacific Ocean to the Gulf of Mexico. Additionally, significant numbers of Toltecs migrated to the Yucatan peninsula in several waves, where

[12] Mabarlabin, CC BY-SA 3.0 <https://creativecommons.org/licenses/by-sa/3.0>, via Wikimedia Commons
https://commons.wikimedia.org/wiki/File:Toltec_influence_cities_marked1.jpg

they influenced Mayan culture.

Ixtlilcuechahua was one of the earliest Toltec kings, son of Chalchiuhtlanetzin, the chief that founded Tula. Ixtlilcuechahua became king in AD 771, about the age of 37. From his father, he received a legacy of wisdom and good judgment and was loved by his subjects. His greatest task was to establish his once-nomadic people into a civilized society.

Ixtlilcuechahua ruled under the guidance of Huematzin, the priest-prophet who had accompanied the Toltec through their wanderings. The Aztecs said Huematzin chronicled the journeys of the Toltec in the *Teoamoxtli* (Book of the Gods), which also contained the laws, astrology, division of time, sacred rites, and science of the Toltec people. Some scholars question the existence of this book, as no form of writing has been found on Toltec artifacts. Huematzin died at the remarkable age of 300, according to a later Aztec account.

Ixtlilcuechahua made no attempts to conquer peaceful neighboring territories. However, he would fiercely protect Tula from anyone foolish enough to attack the city and then set out to conquer the cities of the attackers, eliminating future threats. This expanded the Toltec territory to include other people and cultures. Ixtlilcuechahua reigned 52 years, apparently resigning in AD 823.

Interestingly, the chronicles of the rulers of Tula show most of them reigned for 52 years, which coincides with the ancient Mesoamerican calendar cycle of 52 years. Some historians question the reliability of the chronicles, concluding they are legendary in nature. However, a mandatory 52-year reign could be a stroke of genius, something like term limits for presidents today. It would help avoid issues like kings with dementia or rulers too feeble to lead their warriors into battle.

The most important Toltec ruler was the priest-king Ce Acatl Topiltzin Quetzalcoatl, believed to have lived from AD 895-947, during the golden age of Tula. One cannot tell the story of the Toltecs without telling the story of Quetzalcoatl. But first, we must mention the Teotihuacan culture flourishing to the east of Tula, which had a strong influence on Toltec culture. Before the Toltecs arrived, the Teotihuacan were worshiping their Lord of Creation, a feathered serpent named Quetzalcoatl.

The story of the man named Quetzalcoatl began when the Toltec king Mixcoatl was out hunting one day and was confronted by a naked woman, Chimalma, whose name meant *hand shield*. For whatever reason, Mixcoatl began shooting arrows at Chimalma, but she was *hand shield*, so she deflected the arrows. This aroused admiration within Mixcoatl, and he fell in love with Chimalma and married her.

After swallowing a precious jade stone, Chimalma became pregnant and gave birth to a son. He was named Ce Acatl Topiltzin, which means *our prince from the year one reed*, because he was born in the first year of the 52-year cycle of the Mesoamerican calendar. Chimalma died in childbirth, and Mixcoatl was assassinated by his own brother, leaving Ce Acatl Topiltzin an orphan. He was raised by his maternal grandparents, who taught him to revere the Teotihuacan god Quetzalcoatl. The prince eventually took on the name Quetzalcoatl out of admiration for the feathered serpent.

After avenging his father's death, Ce Acatl Topiltzin Quetzalcoatl became Emperor of the Toltecs, bringing in new knowledge, including advanced agricultural methods for corn and cacao beans (chocolate). Topiltzin Quetzalcoatl ruled over an orderly and harmonious city of wealth and brilliant artistry. During Quetzalcoatl's reign, the city of Tula built a new district for the major religious and political buildings, known today as *Tula Grande* (Great Tula).

Ce Acatl Topiltzin Quetzalcoatl.

Fragment of a mural by Diego Rivera in the Palacio Nacional (Mexico City)[13]

Seeking to transform Toltec society, Quetzalcoatl outlawed human sacrifice. Beloved by his people as a peaceful, merciful, and just priest-ruler, he never sacrificed humans, but only birds, snakes, and butterflies. Migrants from several ethnic groups began flooding the city, perhaps drawn by the wise and benevolent ruler Quetzalcoatl.

Quetzalcoatl's idyllic reign ended when Tezcatlipoca, the *smoke and mirrors god,* tricked him with a mirror which made Quetzalcoatl look deformed. Tezcatlipoca then handed Quetzalcoatl a drink: "Just swallow this, and you will look young and handsome again!" Quetzalcoatl invited his sister to drink the "medicine" with him. Unknown to them, the drink held hallucinogens, and they ended up behaving disgracefully. The next morning, they were found naked, lying next to each other.

Ashamed and humiliated, Quetzalcoatl abdicated his priesthood and crown. For the next year, he wandered from village to village, trying to purge his sin by continuous bloodletting. Finally, he arrived at the Gulf of Mexico, built a funeral pyre, and

---

[13] O.Mustafin, CC0, via Wikimedia Commons
https://commons.wikimedia.org/wiki/File:Topiltzin.jpg

set himself on fire. Legend says thousands of quetzal birds flew out of the fire. After his death, he descended into the underworld, where he outwitted Mictlantecuhtli, god of the dead, and then ascended into the heavens to become Venus, the morning star.

In a different and more popular version of the story, Quetzalcoatl sailed out to sea on a raft of serpents, vowing that one day he would return in the *year of one reed*. This refers to the 52-year calendar cycle, which had a reed for each year. He was born in the year of one reed, left the earth 52 years later in a year of one reed, and would come back in another year of one reed. Quetzalcoatl promised he would return to the same spot from which he was leaving to overthrow Tezcatlipoca and restore his utopian kingdom. Legends say that just as his raft reached the horizon, it exploded, and Quetzalcoatl shot up into the sky to become Venus.

According to some historians, this alternative version played a pivotal role when, in AD 1519, the Spanish conquistador Cortés sailed in from the Gulf of Mexico. This was *a year of one reed* in the Aztec calendar. The Aztec king Moctezuma apparently believed Cortés was Quetzalcoatl returning to claim his kingdom, according to some. However, as we will learn later, Moctezuma didn't exactly welcome Cortés with open arms.

At any rate, once Quetzalcoatl was out of the way, the trickster Tezcatlipoca usurped the city of Tula, demanding human sacrifice. The golden age was no more, and a pronounced decline of the Toltec empire ensued. Thousands of Toltecs left Tula around AD 981, mostly heading to the Yucatan Peninsula and the city of Uxmal.

The myth likely has a basis in fact. When the Toltecs first arrived at Tula, they favored a peaceful theocracy led by a righteous priest-king. The legend of Quetzalcoatl being outwitted by Tezcatlipoca probably represents an actual military coup that overturned the theocracy and set up a more violent military dictatorship, as the Toltecs eventually became infamous for brutal conquest and human sacrifice.

Another intriguing royal Toltec was Empress Xochitl, who rose from peasant to power. Her father, Papantzin, invented *pulque*, a favorite Mesoamerican drink made from the fermented syrup of the maguey (agave) plant. His daughter Xochitl carried a bowl of pulque as a gift to Emperor Tecpancaltzin, who was enchanted with Xochitl and enjoyed the unusual beverage.

Xochitl with father Papantzin offering pulque to Emperor. (Obregón, 1869) [14]

Xochitl would occasionally bring the emperor more bowls of pulque, and her charm won him over. He elevated Papantzin to land-holding nobility, and Xochitl became his concubine. Xochitl gave birth to a son named Meconetzin, meaning *child of maguey*, who became crown prince, as Tecpancaltzin's first wife, Maxio, had only daughters. After Maxio died, Xochitl became Empress.

During Tecpancaltzin's reign, an ethnic-religious civil war erupted between the mostly Nonoalca worshipers of Quetzalcoatl and the Chichimeca, who worshiped his archrival Tezcatlipoca. The conflict centered on human sacrifice, which Quetzalcoatl had forbidden, but which Tezcatlipoca's followers believed was intrinsic to keeping the gods happy.

When the war broke out, Xochitl called her fellow women out to battle, leading an entirely female battalion. Both Xochitl and her

[14] Mabarlabin, CC BY-SA 3.0 <https://creativecommons.org/licenses/by-sa/3.0>, via Wikimedia Commons
https://commons.wikimedia.org/wiki/File:El_descubrimiento_del_pulque_Jos%C3%A9_Mar%C3%ADa_Obreg%C3%B3n.jpg

husband died on the battlefield, and the battle was lost. Most followers of the Cult of Quetzalcoatl fled to the Yucatan, where they were welcomed by their clansmen, descendants of those who had previously emigrated from Tula after Quetzalcoatl had abdicated.

Chac Mool[15]

The Toltecs were well-known for their beautiful carvings and artwork. One intriguing example, distinctive to Toltec culture, are *Chac Mool* stone figurines reclining back on their elbows and holding a bowl on their chests. The Toltecs made exquisite gold and turquoise jewelry such as nose rings, elegant masks of jade, and carved human and jaguar standard-bearers. They created fine metalwork and stunning architectural features such as serpent columns and massive porticoes.

Along with their artistry, the Toltecs were noted for warfare. In the latter part of their civilization, warfare was essentially a religion, and the warrior class was viewed with honor and distinction. Warriors were highly trained, fierce, and formidable. The higher ranks of the thoroughly organized and efficient Toltec military wore padded cotton armor to deflect spears and arrows. The soldiers carried round shields and swords into battle. Their

[15] Gary Todd, CC0, via Wikimedia Commons
https://commons.wikimedia.org/wiki/File:Toltec_Chac_Mool.jpg

helmets were decorated with quetzal plumes, they wore nose rings as a sign of their nobility, and some had beards.

Quetzalcoatl the Feathered Serpent[16]

The Toltecs had several major deities. Quetzalcoatl, worshiped by many other Mesoamerican people, was considered the wisest of all beings, creator of the universe, and god of wind, air, and learning. In Toltec art, Quetzalcoatl was depicted as the feathered serpent or as a man with a beard. Quetzalcoatl's beard is somewhat curious, as bearded men were uncommon among the indigenous Mesoamericans. Perhaps the Toltecs had more facial hair, as carvings and paintings of Toltec warriors also show some with beards.

Tlaloc was the cloud deity, both the benevolent giver of rain and the destructive god of storms. He was married to Xochiquetzal, the goddess of beauty, love, and youth. She could be erratic, doing things like seducing a priest, then turning him into a

[16] Cangadoba, CC BY-SA 4.0 <https://creativecommons.org/licenses/by-sa/4.0>, via Wikimedia Commons.
https://commons.wikimedia.org/wiki/File:Quetzalcoatl_isolated.png

scorpion.

Tezcatlipoca, Quetzalcoatl's nemesis but sometimes considered to be his brother, had the nickname *Smoking Mirror* due to tricking Quetzalcoatl with the magic mirror. He was the god of the night, of time, and of memory. He was also a creator God.

Centeotl was Lord of the Maize, the predominant crop in Mesoamerica. Corn, or maize, was gifted to humans by Quetzalcoatl, but Centeotl was the maintainer of the crop's growth and fertility. He held the key to successful agriculture, which he taught to humans.

The ceremonial plaza at Tula contained temples and pyramids where Toltec deities were worshiped, ballgames played, and people sacrificed. The partially excavated Pyramid C, the Temple of the Sun, is probably a temple of Quetzalcoatl. Pyramid B is the temple of Tlahuizcalpantecuhtli, or Venus, an incarnation of Quetzalcoatl.

Atlantes of Pyramid B at Tula[17]

[17] AlejandroLinaresGarcia, CC BY-SA 3.0 <https://creativecommons.org/licenses/by-sa/3.0>, via Wikimedia Commons
https://commons.wikimedia.org/wiki/File:TulaSite81.JPG

Astonishing columns, carved to represent warriors, are called the *Atlantes of Tula*, the most dominant architecture associated with the Toltecs. Just as the Olmecs are known for their colossal heads, the Toltecs are defined by the Atlantean columns. They are called Atlanteans (or Atlantes) because they carry at their side the *atlatl*, a spear-throwing tool that leverages a spear's velocity. The Atlanteans are close to 15 feet high and held up the roofs of the great rooms of the temples.

The Toltec Temple B was decorated with carvings, depicting a row of jaguars, under which were carvings of Venus, followed by a row of coyotes, followed by a row of eagles, each devouring a heart. These symbols represented the ranks of the military. Next to the Temple of Venus are pillared hallways for festive occasions.

In the temple complex of Tula are two ball courts. The Toltecs loved ball games as much as the Olmecs. On the side of one ball court is a sweat lodge, where players would purify themselves before and after the games. Benches are found throughout the temple complex with carved images of the Feathered Serpent over a procession of warriors. In the middle of the temple complex is a small altar, with a skull rack next to it, another Toltec distinctive.

Chichén Itzá Pyramid[18]

The influence of Toltec migrants in the Yucatan area is clearly seen in the ruins of Chichén Itzá. Archeology suggests that the Itzá people were either Toltec or strongly influenced by the Toltec people. The pyramid in Chichén Itzá is a temple to Quetzalcoatl (Kukulkan) that showcases the Toltec influence. The Temple of the Warriors in Chichén Itzá mirrors Temple B in Tula, with all its colonnades and a Chac Mool figurine in front of two images of

[18] Daniel Schwen, CC BY-SA 4.0 <https://creativecommons.org/licenses/by-sa/4.0>, via Wikimedia Commons. https://commons.wikimedia.org/wiki/File:Chichen_Itza_2.jpg

Quetzalcoatl. The largest ballcourt in Mesoamerica is found in the temple complex of Chichén Itzá, with the Toltec skull rack just next to it.

The Toltec capital city of Tula (Tollan) was one of the largest cities in pre-Columbian Mesoamerica, with an estimated population of 85,000. Large apartment complexes housed most of the urban population, with the ruling elite living in palaces. Distinct sections separated citizens of different classes. Most structures were of stone covered with adobe mud.

Tula society was ruled by an aristocracy of warriors and priests. The cherished artisans, who gave the Toltecs their name, formed the middle class, along with merchants. Tula was dependent on agriculture to feed the large population, so farmers were given special rights and privileges. The many immigrants likely served in the working class. Accounts speak of Toltec warriors carrying the weeping Huastec people and others into Tula; the captives were likely facing slavery, or worse yet, human sacrifice.

What caused the artistic yet warlike Toltec civilization to be assimilated by other kingdoms and fade away? One element was the ongoing internal conflict between the two dominant ethnic groups: the Nonoalca worshipers of Quetzalcoatl and the Chichimeca worshipers of Tezcatlipoca. A seven-year drought, from AD 1070 to 1077, caused a collapse in the agricultural system, and the population was decimated by starvation. Many survivors migrated to more fertile areas.

Tula was invaded by the Chichimeca people from the north in AD 1115. War raged for a year, each side sacrificing their prisoners-of-war to their deities, ending with the Toltec defeat. Huemac, king of Tula, fled with his citizens, creating a Toltec diaspora across Mexico. Most of Tula was abandoned, with the Toltec remnant ruled by surrounding city-states.

The *Codex Boturini*, an ancient Aztec manuscript written soon after the Spaniards arrived, depicts the early migration of the Aztec-Mexica people through Tula, where they stopped for twenty years. This would have been about AD 1250, and by this time, most Toltecs had abandoned Tula. The Mexica spent twenty years among the remnant of the population, surrounded by the Toltec architecture and artifacts, soaking in the Toltec culture they so deeply admired.

Desiring to claim descendancy from the Toltecs, the Mexica married their princesses to the remaining Toltec nobility. The Mexica not only absorbed Toltec culture during their stay in Tula, but they also appropriated many Toltec relics, which later showed up in their own cities.

Chapter 3: The Chichimeca

Children of the Wind was what they called themselves; when running or climbing, it appeared these people were carried by the wind. Other cultures called them *Chichimeca*, carrying the idea of *barbarian*. That's how these roaming tribes were regarded by other civilizations of Mesoamerica: the ones who had built cities with majestic temples and palaces and developed advanced agriculture and written languages. And yet, the untamed Chichimeca remained undefeated by the Spanish invaders, to whom more civilized cultures swiftly fell. Several Chichimeca tribal groups still exist today, speaking their ancient languages and maintaining elements of their primeval cultures.

Chichimeca is an umbrella term for multiple groups of nomadic and semi-nomadic people belonging to the larger Nahuatl language group who originally lived in the deserts of northern Mexico. Although usually painted with a broad brush, they were individual cultures of around seven to ten tribes. They shared the same language group, but they spoke distinct dialects, often unintelligible from one another. We might think of the Nahuatl language group as something like the Romance language group, with the differences between Spanish, Italian, French, Romanian, and Portuguese. The main similarities shared by the Chichimeca tribes were the harsh living conditions of the lands they inhabited and their nomadic lifestyle.

Images from a 1580 map of San Miguel and San Felipe in the Chichimeca region

Juan Carlos Fonseca Mata.[19]

Most of what we know about the Chichimeca tribes is what other civilizations recorded about them, such as the Aztecs and eventually the Spaniards. The Chichimeca had no written language of their own, and they didn't build temples or other permanent structures that could later be studied by archaeologists. Their lifestyle was so simple that they left almost no historical imprint, other than observations by others and what is left of their culture in the remnant Chichimeca tribes of today.

The great Toltec civilization had its origins in one Chichimeca tribe, the Tolteca-Chichimeca, which drifted south and eventually settled down and built a great city. More waves of Chichimeca migrations infiltrated their ranks until the Toltecs struggled in an internal war between the earlier and later cultures. Eventually, attacked by another Chichimeca tribe, the Toltecs lost the war and fled their great city. Thus, it could be said that the Chichimeca gave birth to the Toltecs and later served as their executioners.

---

[19] Juan Carlos Fonseca Mata, CC BY-SA 4.0 <https://creativecommons.org/licenses/by-sa/4.0>, via Wikimedia Commons
https://commons.wikimedia.org/wiki/File:Mapa_de_San_Miguel_y_San_Felipe_de_los_Chichimecas_(1580)_-_Chichimecas_2.jpg

The Mexica-Aztecs were probably another Chichimeca tribe. While the Olmecs and Toltecs were building great temples and pyramids, the Mexica were subsisting in the northern wilderness. Finally, they migrated south, learned from the Toltec and other civilizations, developed their own written language and astounding Aztec culture, and became the chroniclers of previous cultures as well as their own Chichimeca origins.

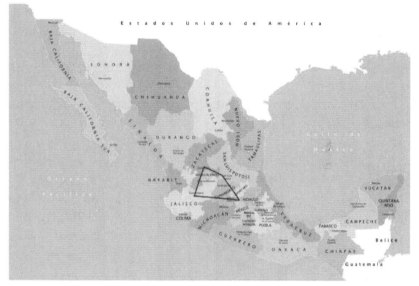

Bajio region of Mexico[20]

As hunters and gatherers, the Chichimeca roamed the harsh deserts of northern Mexico that extended into Arizona and California until some of the tribes migrated in several waves into the rugged mountains and arid areas of central Mexico. A sizeable population of Chichimeca established themselves in the lowland Bajio region of central Mexico, in today's states of Aguascalientes, Jalisco, Guanajuato, and Querétaro. Their region encompassed about 62,000 square miles. In the days before the Spanish invasion, few permanent settlements existed in this area.

Before the arrival of the Spaniards, most tribes were nomadic or semi-nomadic desert dwellers. They hunted game and gathered

[20] Juan Carlos Fonseca Mata, CC BY-SA 4.0 <https://creativecommons.org/licenses/by-sa/4.0>, via Wikimedia Commons
https://commons.wikimedia.org/wiki/File:Baj%C3%ADo_Mx.png

cacti fruit, agave plants, berries, roots, and mesquite beans for food. The tribes who lived in the southernmost area of the broad Chichimeca heartland, closest to the Aztec civilization, engaged in primitive farming, mostly raising squash and maize.

They went mostly naked, covering only their genitals with animal skins or cloth woven from the maguey plant. As many as 60,000 Chichimeca roamed the plains of central and northern Mexico, living in caves or temporary shelters, while the more sedentary lived in small settlements (*rancherias*). The Chichimeca did not build temples and generally had no idols. They were more animistic, believing in spirits connected to nature and attached to specific locations. They sacrificed plants and animals to their deities, and some tribes practiced human sacrifice. The ones closest to the Aztec region adopted some of the Aztec deities and worship practices.

In the 16th century, Sahagún, a Franciscan friar, recorded his ethnographic research in the *Florentine Codex.* He reported that the Chichimeca were seldom ill and lived remarkably long lives. He said they could run long distances without tiring. Their women would give birth and then rejoin the group's activity without pausing to rest.

Four of the Chichimeca nations, with decentralized governments and overlapping territories, became a great irritant to the Spanish conquistadors. These tribes – the Guachichiles, the Pames, the Guamares, and the Zacatecos – formed a loose alliance to successfully defeat the Spaniards' attempts to subjugate them and colonize their lands. Although there were several other Chichimeca tribes, we know more about these four from Spanish accounts.

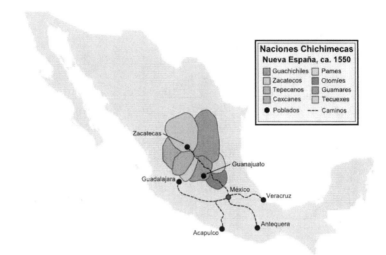

Territory of Chichimeca Nations[21]

What is now the city of San Luis Potosí is roughly at the center of the large area around which the Guachichiles tribal group roamed. The largest of the four groups, they assumed leadership of the Chichimeca Confederation. Their name comes from their fondness for the color red; they dyed their hair, skin, and clothing red. They delighted in collecting scalps of Spanish men with red hair, and they enjoyed kidnapping or purchasing red-haired European women to be their wives. Even today, a red-haired child is occasionally born to their descendants.

The Guachichiles were fierce fighters and expert hunters, extremely skilled in archery. Children learned to use a bow when they began walking. The velocity, strength, and sharpness of their arrows were incredible, able to penetrate the Spaniards' metal armor. They could easily survive in the cacti-filled terrain they called home, knowing where to find food and water. They battled their rivals with cunning and subterfuge rather than direct attacks. They employed spies to assess their adversaries' strengths and weaknesses and to follow their movements. They would ambush their enemies, striking fear by suddenly jumping out wearing animal heads and red paint and howling and shrieking – they even

[21] Elmer Homero CC BY-SA 3.0 <http://creativecommons.org/licenses/by-sa/3.0/>, via Wikimedia Commons https://commons.wikimedia.org/wiki/File:ChichimecNations.png

scared the horses!

The Pame people were more docile than the neighboring Guachichiles and more likely to assimilate the religion and culture of the developed civilizations. They were traders, so it was to their advantage to get along with everybody and learn the dialects of those around them. Their adaptability aided their survival into our modern world as a Chichimeca tribe whose culture endures today.

The Pames were enigmatic, outwardly complying with the Spanish requirement to live clustered around missions and submit to Catholic indoctrination while quietly worshiping their own deities, following the guidance of their shamans, and practicing their traditional dances. Even today, the 10,000 Pame-language-speaking people living in Santa Maria Acapulco are syncretistic: nominal Catholics who continue to practice their traditional religion.

The Guamare tribe called themselves *Children of the Wind* for their tradition of cremating their dead and throwing their ashes into the wind. Living in the mountains of what today is Guanajuato state, they were shrewd, fearless, and known for double-crossing others. Like the Guachichiles, they enjoyed coloring their hair and bodies – sometimes red, sometimes white, and sometimes other colors, depending on their clan. They tattooed their bodies, and both men and women wore their hair down to their waists.

The fourth tribe in the Chichimeca Confederation were the Zacatecos, living in what is now the states of Durango and Zacatecas, where they overlapped with the Guachichiles. Descendants of this tribe still live in the area, but they have largely abandoned their culture and traditions. In days of old, some were nomads, while others cultivated maize. They wore animal-skin shin-guards to protect themselves from the thorny bushes and cacti, and they sometimes wore leather sandals.

Member of Chichimeca Jonaz tribe[22]

Juan Bautista de Pomar, a 16th-century mestizo historian, wrote that the Zacatecos were "graceful, strong, robust, and beardless" and "the best archers in the world." The Zacatecos deities were celestial: the sun, moon, and several stars. They did not practice human sacrifice but worshiped with flowers, herbs, and dancing.

When the Spaniards arrived in Mexico, far to the south of the Chichimeca lands, their initial concern was conquering the Aztecs, which they did two years later. Most of the other civilizations in Mexico quickly submitted to Spanish rule or were conquered after a few battles. The Spaniards' main interest was collecting and mining gold and other precious minerals and establishing colonies in fertile areas.

The Chichimeca were of scant interest to the Spaniards initially, as their lands were generally unsuitable for farming, and they had nothing the Spaniards considered valuable. In a 1526 letter, Hernán Cortés wrote that the uncivilized Chichimeca might be useful as slave labor in the mines. The Spaniards apparently did not tap this potential labor source; if they tried, the Chichimeca probably proved too difficult to tame.

Then, in AD 1546, the Spaniards learned that silver-rich ore existed close to the Zacatecas territory. Excited by this discovery and eager for quick wealth, hundreds of Spaniards migrated north to the Chichimeca heartland, which they called *La Gran Chichimeca*. They began digging silver mines, building roads, and establishing towns. The Chichimeca tribes resented this intrusion on their sacred, ancestral lands and retaliated with guerilla warfare, attacking caravans of goods moving through their territory.

The conflict in the Bajio region became the forty-year Chichimeca War (1550-1590), the lengthiest and most costly military campaign in the history of the Spanish Empire in Mesoamerica. The Chichimeca raided and pillaged Spanish settlements and caravans, and the Spaniards attempted to vanquish them with a strategy of *fire and blood*, but the Chichimeca proved undefeatable.

Portrait of Chichimeca Jonaz dancers at Ceremonial Center, Mision Chichimecas; live direct descendants of Chichimeca[23]

Primarily nomads, the Chichimeca had few settlements for the Spaniards to target, and they were adapted to the rough terrain. They knew how to live off the land, but the Spanish invaders depended on livestock, agriculture, and imported supplies. By

[23] Francisco del Valle, CC BY-SA 4.0 <https://creativecommons.org/licenses/by-sa/4.0>, via Wikimedia Commons
https://commons.wikimedia.org/wiki/File:Centro_Ceremonial_Chichimeca.jpg

ambushing the Spanish caravans and raiding their settlements, the Chichimeca effectively cut off the Spaniards' food and weapons supply while enriching themselves with the Spanish livestock and goods. The four tribes in the Chichimeca Confederation had joined forces to fight the Spaniards, but even the more distant tribes came to raid the Spaniards, lured by the loot.

The Chichimeca legendary archery skills were a force to reckon with. Their lethal arrowheads of volcanic obsidian, sharper than razors, penetrated the chain-mail armor of the Spaniards. Even when outnumbered four to one, the Chichimeca defeated the Spaniards in battle. Before attacking a Spanish town, they would first send in spies to gather strategic details and then steal their horses to slow down the Spaniards. At first, the Chichimeca ate the horses they stole but quickly learned to ride them, which made them swift in their ongoing raids on the Spaniards.

In desperation, the Spaniards began building forts, hiring mercenaries, and training their indigenous slaves to fight. Eleven years into the war, the Chichimeca had killed over 4000 Spaniards and their Mesoamerican allies. The Spanish policy of *fire and blood* threatened to kill, enslave, or mutilate every Chichimeca warrior. Yet the Chichimeca dominated the struggle. The Chichimeca Confederation used their combined numbers and diverse skills to cut off roads, raid towns, and damage mines.

Spain dug into the royal treasury to fund military forces, weapons, and materials for forts, but the Chichimeca continued attacking with even greater ferocity, essentially shutting down the silver mines and destroying the royal roads and all the Spanish forts within the Guachichiles territory. The Spaniards were no match for the Chichimeca Confederation. The war of fire and blood was a failure, and the Spanish royal treasury was decimated. The Spaniards were confounded; they had conquered the Aztecs with only 500 or 600 men but could not conquer the Chichimeca even with thousands of soldiers.

Artwork from 1580 map of Chichimeca areas of San Miguel and San Felipe Juan Carlos Fonseca Mata[24]

Some Spanish clerics had become appalled by Spanish mistreatment of Chichimeca women and children and by the killings or mutilations of their captive warriors. The clergy pointed out that Spanish callousness and cruelty had stirred up the initial conflict and was perpetuating the antipathy of the Chichimeca. The Dominicans declared in 1574 that the war against the Chichimeca was unjust and that continued aggression would only further inflame the Chichimeca's hostility and prolong the conflict. Could there be a different, more gentle way to bring peace with the Chichimeca while still permitting the Spaniards to mine the land?

The Bishop of Guadalajara came up with a proposal in 1584, which he called a "Christian remedy." Instead of conquering or killing the Chichimeca, his plan was to Christianize them. He suggested establishing peaceful villages throughout the Chichimeca heartland, inhabited by indigenous people who would be friendly with the Chichimeca and by priests who could teach the Catholic faith. To end the conflict, the bishop recommended that the Spaniards change their policy to purchasing peace and gently assimilating the Chichimeca into Spanish culture.

In 1585, Álvaro Manrique de Zúñiga became Viceroy of *New Spain* (the Spanish colonies in the Americas and the Pacific islands). He liked the bishop's proposal and decided to implement it. His first step was to remove most of the Spanish military from the Chichimeca area. They weren't proving effective against the Chichimeca, and he felt their presence was an affront to the indigenous people, provoking violence rather than stemming it. Manrique de Zúñiga then began negotiations with the Chichimeca leaders. He promised an end to Spanish military operations and offered land, food, farm animals, clothing, and tools in exchange for peace.

Captain Miguel Caldera, who was part-Chichimeca, of Spanish and Guachichiles descent, was a key negotiator in implementing the *Purchase for Peace* program. He negotiated peace treaties between the Spaniards and the tribal groups. Large quantities of food, clothing, goods, plows, hoes, and livestock were sent north to the Chichimeca to persuade them to end the raids. They were also promised freedom from taxes and forced service.

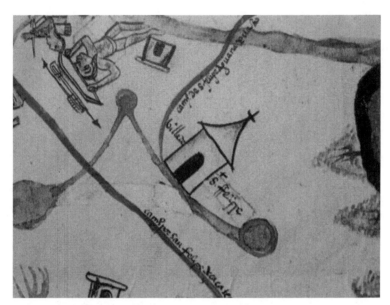

Late 1500's map showing settlements around a mission church. Juan Carlos Fonseca Mata.[25]

The next step was to move 400 families of the indigenous Tlaxcala people into the area to establish eight settlements. The Tlaxcala were old allies of the Spaniards from the south, who had helped them bring down the Aztecs. The plan was for the Tlaxcala to befriend the Chichimeca, teach them how to raise crops and livestock, serve as Christian examples, and gently persuade the Chichimeca tribes to settle in villages. The Tlaxcala people agreed to move into the area in exchange for land grants, tax freedom, two years of food, and the right to bear arms.

Another important step was to end the slave-raids of the Chichimeca people by arresting the guilty parties (including Spanish soldiers). As the Chichimeca gradually settled into villages, Franciscan and Jesuit missionary-priests who had learned the tribal dialects were sent to the settlements to convert the Chichimeca to Christianity. Over time, more Chichimeca abandoned their nomadic lifestyle to become farmers and ranchers. Gradually, the

[25] Juan Carlos Fonseca Mata, CC BY-SA 4.0 <https://creativecommons.org/licenses/by-sa/4.0>, via Wikimedia Commons
https://commons.wikimedia.org/wiki/File:San_Felipe,_Guanajuato_-_Mapa_de_San_Miguel_y_San_Felipe_de_los_Chichimecas_(1580).jpg

Chichimeca were integrated into "civilized" society and adopted nominal Catholicism. By 1590, the roads in the Zacatecas region were finally safe; after forty years of warfare, peace had come.

When military conquest had failed, the new Spanish policy of peace with the Chichimeca was based on four pillars: 1) negotiating peace treaties by providing food and other goods and removing soldiers and slave-traders that were provoking the Chichimeca; 2) encouraging conversion to the Catholic faith; 3) moving indigenous allies to the Bajio region to serve as examples and teachers, and 4) providing the means (including livestock and tools) for the Chichimeca to settle into villages. The new policy succeeded in ending the war, and the Spaniards continued to use this strategy on other frontiers of New Spain.

The new Spanish policy of Purchase for Peace worked well for the Spanish; they reopened the silver mines, safely travel on the roads in Le Grande Chichimeca, and no longer feared the tribal people. Fourteen monasteries were scattered through the area. However, for most of the Chichimeca, it was the end of their culture. They no longer roamed free and wild, living off what the land offered them.

Now, they were working the fields and mines, along with the Aztecs, Tlaxcala, and other indigenous people with more developed cultures. The Chichimeca began to absorb this Mestizo culture, with a blend of Spanish and indigenous traditions, as their own way of life faded away. Most tribes lost their languages, their lifestyle, and their traditions until they each became virtually extinct as a culture. A few groups struggled on into modern society, but they have been forced into small reservations on inhospitable land, making survival difficult. The mighty and untamed children of the wind were bribed into abandoning their identity.

SECTION TWO:
THE RISE OF THE AZTEC CIVILIZATION

Chapter 4: Aztec Origins and Mythical Aztlan

About 850 years ago, a nomadic people wandered into the highlands plateau of the Valley of Mexico. Great civilizations had risen and fallen in this area for over a thousand years: Cuicuilco, buried under the lava of the Xitle volcano, Teotihuacan, and the Toltec Empire. Now the stately pyramids, majestic temples, and impressive carvings of past civilizations were largely abandoned, but new settlements were rapidly springing up.

The newcomers were the Nahuatl-speaking Mexica, also called Aztec, after their mysterious home country of Aztlan they had left over 100 years earlier. Who were these people, and where did they come from? How did they define themselves? Was their ancestral home of Aztlan mythical or a real place?

Based on their language group (Nahuatl) and their descriptions of their wanderings through the northern area full of cacti spines, thistles, and poisonous lizards, the Mexica were likely a branch of the Chichimeca tribes, subsisting in the desert before they settled in the Valley of Mexico. The Mexica-Aztecs themselves presented their origins as Chichimeca but also Toltec.

The hunter-warrior aspect of the Chichimeca likely resonated with them. The Chichimeca represented virality, strength, skill in battle, the ability to thrive in harsh conditions, cunning, and fearlessness – all characteristics of the perfect warrior the Aztecs strove to become.

The Mexica-Aztecs also admired the once-nomadic Toltecs, who rose from their own Tolteca-Chichimeca origins to develop a great civilization. They were role models for the Mexica, who aspired to emulate their rise to power and take it to a higher plane. The Mexica-Aztecs prided themselves on being an evolving people, always advancing, always rising to the next level.

The Aztecs defined themselves as descendants of fierce nomads who had risen to fulfill their destiny as warriors, conquerors, and empire builders. They considered their history as an extended military campaign of making war on provinces and cities and subjugating them. The Mexica-Aztec claimed they were following the prophecy of their chief god, Huitzilopochtli, the enemy of tranquility and friend of contention. They considered the concepts of peace and maintaining the status quo as impediments to achieving what was foreordained.

And yet, there was a time when they weren't nomads or empire builders. There was a time when, according to their legends, they once lived a peaceful life as agriculturalists and fishermen in their idyllic island of Aztlan. What can we know about this mysterious land and its location?

Page 3 of Codex Boturini showing the journey of Aztecs from Aztlan to the Valley of Mexico[26]

---

[26] https://commons.wikimedia.org/wiki/File:Codex_Boturini,_page_3.jpg

We can glean some understanding about the origins of these people from several Aztec manuscripts written in the 16th century, either just before or after the Spanish conquistadors arrived. They include the *Codex Boturini,* the *Crónica Mexicáyotl,* the *Codex Ramirez,* the *Codex Aubin,* and *Los Anales de Tlatelolco.* We also have histories written by early Spanish chroniclers, based on their study of Aztec documents and interviews with the Aztec people. These include *Monarquía Indiana (Indian Monarchy),* written in 1615 by Friar Juan de Torquemada, and *Historia de las Indias de Nueva España (History of the Indians of New Spain)* by Friar Diego Durán (ca.1537-1588).

The Mexica-Aztecs said they came from an idyllic place called Aztlan. Where was Aztlan? Can we find any linguistic clues from the meaning of the name? In the Nahuatl language, the suffix *lan* or *tlan* means *the place of,* and the suffix *tec* means *people from.* So, *Aztec* means *people from Az* or *Azt,* and *Aztlan* means *place of Az* or *Azt.* What does the prefix *Az* or *Azt* mean? Linguists and historical documents have presented several options.

The Aztec chronicle *Crónica Mexicáyotl* says Aztlan means *place of herons.* The Nahuatl word *aztatl* means *heron or egret,* putting together the Nahuatl prefix *azt,* which frequently refers to a heron or heron plumage or a bird, with the suffix *atl* for *water.* This would fit with the description of Aztlan as an island on a lake filled with waterfowl.

Some linguists say that Aztlan means *white place* because the Nahuatl word *aztapiltic* means something very white. However, this word for white takes us back to the idea of *heron;* it basically means *heron color* by combining the prefix for heron with the suffix *iltic* that carries the idea of color. Many Nahuatl words for colors end with *ic, itc, ltic, or iltic.*

A third idea is that Aztlan means *place of tools.* The rationale for this meaning is that in the Nahuatl language, *āz* (or *huaztli*) is a *morpheme* (word part) that changes a noun into a different noun that could be used to produce something. For instance, the word *log* in Nahuatl is *tepontli,* but inserting *āz* into the word changes it to *teponāztli,* meaning *drum.* Linguistically, this is a bit of a stretch because one must have a noun to insert *āz* into for this to work. With *Aztlan,* we don't have a noun – just the suffix *tlan* or *lan,* meaning *place of.*

In summary, the strongest definition for Aztlan from a linguistic standpoint is *place of (white) herons.* This is what the Aztecs themselves said it meant in the *Crónica Mexicáyotl,* and it also fits with the description of the island paradise that would have herons along the shore. Furthermore, herons and heron plumage played an important part in Aztec culture – they formed elaborate headdresses from the plumes of this bird and decorated their ceremonial areas and sacred objects with heron feathers.

According to their history, the Mexica left their home of Aztlan around AD 1168 and wandered almost two centuries before reaching the island on the swampy lake where they would build their city. They were led by their chieftain Tenoch, the son of Iztac Mixcoatl. Mixcoatl had two wives and seven sons and may have been a real person, but in both Toltec and Aztec mythology, he is identified as the god of the hunt. You might remember him in the earlier chapter on the Toltecs as the hunter and king who married Chimalma and became father to Ce Acatl Topiltzin, who later called himself Quetzalcoatl.

Tenoch, Mexica chieftain, from the Codex Mendoza[27]

[27] https://commons.wikimedia.org/wiki/File:Tenoch.jpg

Even though of royal birth as the son of Mixcoatl, Tenoch was elected chieftain by a council of elders and was held in great respect by the people he led on their great southern migration. Throughout their history, the Mexica nobility and priests elected their leaders. When the Mexica finally reached their ultimate destination at Lake Texcoco, they named their island settlement Tenochtitlan in honor of this esteemed chieftain. Another name for the Mexica was Tenochca, people of the great chieftain who guided them to the place where they would soon build an empire.

Leaving Aztlan, from the Codex Boturini.[28]

The first page of the *Codex Boturini* has a picture of the island of Aztlan with a pyramid. The picture indicates that a priest led the Mexica and their ancestress Chimalma from Aztlan on a boat. Interestingly, the Mexica-Aztecs claimed both Mixcoatl and Chimalma as their ancestors. These two were the parents of Emperor Ce Acatl Topiltzin Quetzalcoatl in Toltec history. Were the Mexica trying to claim legitimacy by adopting this couple as their own ancestors? Or were they really from the same clan and just migrated several centuries later?

The rest of the *Codex Boturini* chronicles the migration of the Mexica and their history from AD 1168 to 1355. It doesn't give much information about Aztlan itself, except that it mentions that

[28]https://commons.wikimedia.org/wiki/File:MA_D037_From_the_Boturini_MS_showing_the_commencement_of_the_Aztec_migration.jpg

after the Mexica left Aztlan, their god Huitzilopochtli taught them how to sacrifice blood and that they first offered human sacrifice. From that, we can infer that human sacrifice and blood sacrifice were not a part of the Aztlan culture.

An interesting trend in Mesoamerica was building cities on an island in a lake or swampy area. Ancient sources say Aztlan was an island in a lake called *Metztliapan* or *Lake of the Moon,* with a great hill called *Colhuacan* (or *Coatepec).* The people of the island were said to enjoy all they needed to live. The waters around Aztlan were filled with waterfowl, including herons and ducks. The people caught beautiful large fish from their canoes and tended floating *Chinampas* gardens of peppers, tomatoes, and maize. Exquisite red and yellow birds fluttered in the shade trees that lined the banks of the island, filling the air with song.

Seven tribes emerging from seven caves[29]

---

[29] https://commons.wikimedia.org/wiki/File:ToltecaChichimeca_Chicomostoc.jpg

In the hill called Colhuacan on the island (or near the island) were located seven caves from which seven tribes emerged: the Xochimilca, Tlahuica, Acolhua, Tlaxcalteca, Tepaneca, Chalca, and Mexica. Each tribe left, one by one, to migrate and settle in different areas. The Mexica were the last tribe to leave. Perhaps these seven tribes were the seven sons of Iztac Mixcoatl, father of the Mexica chieftain Tenoch. Since they all came from Aztlan, all seven tribes can be collectively called Aztec.

Where was Aztlan located? The answer is shrouded in mystery. One clue, from tracing their linguistic lineage, is that the Aztec tribes were from the lands north of Mexico City. The Aztecs spoke the Nahuatl language, which has given us words in English, including coyote, tomato, chocolate, avocado, and chili. Nahuatl is from the Uto-Aztecan language family, which extends from Mexico to the southwestern United States, leading to speculation that the Aztecs may have come from north of the border.

Their description of floating gardens in the waters surrounding Aztlan is fascinating. Did the Aztecs carry this custom with them? The Xochimilca, another Nahuatl-speaking culture said to be among the seven tribes from Aztlan, were well-known for *chinampas* or floating gardens constructed from reed rafts covered with mud from the lake. On these rafts, the people grew vegetables, fruit, and flowers, which they shipped two miles to the Aztec capital Tenochtitlan. The research of anthropologist and archaeologist Richard Blanton dates the chinampa settlements on Lake Xochimilco to AD 1100, meaning they were there before the Mexica arrived, but the Xochimilca were another Aztec tribe who may have imported the technology from Aztlan.

A confusing aspect of the Aztec origins is what or who *Chicomoztoca* was. Some accounts say Chicomoztoca was the cave from which the seven tribes were birthed. Others say the Chicomoztoca were a people who preceded the seven tribes and were less civilized. The *Codex Aubin* says the Aztecs left Aztlan because of the tyranny of a ruling elite called Azteca Chicomoztoca. Other accounts mention Chicomoztoca as being a place near Aztlan, but not on Aztlan itself. Were the Mexica of Aztlan perhaps vassals of a nearby nation? Had they been conquered by a people called Chicomoztoca? Or was it a place of refuge after leaving Aztlan?

Why did the Mexica and other Aztec tribes leave their idyllic Aztlan? Perhaps some internal struggle or attack from another tribe or overlord forced them to leave their blissful island. They could have also been affected by some natural disaster, such as a great drought, volcanic eruption, flooding, or an earthquake. Something traumatic may have forced them to suddenly transition from sedentary farmers and fishermen into nomads.

The Mexica reported that when they left Aztlan, their life of ease was replaced by thorns, thistles, sharp rocks, snakes, and poisonous lizards in a land turned against them. This characterizes the harsh deserts they migrated through in their long journey to the Valley of Mexico. It also provides further hints to the location of Aztlan as being a fertile place but close to desert areas. The northwestern terrain of Mexico is mostly arid or semi-arid, but swathes of tropical wetlands extend up the western part of the country toward the northern border.

La Quemada Pyramid overlooking lake Marisol Narváez Quiroz[30]

One proposed location for Aztlan (or for Chicomoztoca) is La Quemada, an archeological site in the Chichimeca lands in the state of Zacatecas, about 450 miles northwest of Mexico City. Some say the ruins there are from the mysterious Chicomoztoc culture. La Quemada, with a view of a large lake to its east, is on a high hill with trees and green grass, overlooking the desert. Friar Juan de Torquemada, in his *Monarquía Indiana* (Indian Monarchy), recorded that La Quemada was a stopping-off place for the Aztecs in their migration to the Valley of Mexico. He said the Aztecs stayed there for nine years, then left their elderly people and children there and continued their migration.

La Quemada site, AD 300-1200[31]

La Quemada, the city on a hill, has masonry construction of terraces, statuesque pillars, a majestic pyramid standing 40 feet high, a ball court, and a residential site. The pyramid is unique in that most Mesoamerican pyramids are formed by a core of rubble and packed earth held in place with retaining walls faced with limestone-covered adobe bricks. The La Quemada votive pyramid is solid and much steeper than other Mexican pyramids, albeit smaller.

It's rather surprising to find a site with such grand architecture in the wilderness this far north. What was this sophisticated city doing out in Chichimeca territory, so far from the Valley of Mexico? Archeological evidence suggests La Quemada was not influenced by the Mesoamerican civilizations to the south, such as the Toltec, but built by a people who independently developed their own techniques and styles.

La Quemada[32]

Radiocarbon dating places the construction as beginning in AD 300 and extending to 1200. This would place the earlier history of the city long before the Toltec culture but would coincide with when the Aztecs lived in Aztlan and with the time they said they left their island around AD 1168. La Ciudad Quemada means *burnt city*, because the ruins show evidence of a massive fire that apparently destroyed the city. La Quemada has some similarities to the Chalchihuites culture that flourished about 100 miles west of La Quemada from about AD 100 – 1250.

Items that make La Quemada a possible fit with Aztlan include the age of the city, its situation on a high hill in a fertile area surrounded by desert, the pyramid, and destruction by a fire that may have precipitated a migration at about the same time the Mexica left Aztlan. It's not an island in a lake, but a lake is within view. That lake was formed by damming a river on the eastern side of the city. Along the western side of the hill is a jagged ravine, probably a stream bed. Perhaps, centuries ago, before the dam was built, the city was a sort of island surrounded by the river and stream. Alternatively, maybe La Quemada was not Aztlan itself but Chicomóztoc, which, by Friar Torquemada's account, was an area near Aztlan where the Aztecs stopped to regroup, staying nine years before their migration south.

Another clue for the location of Aztlan is the name *Colhuacan* for the great hill on the island of Aztlan. Colhuacan (or *Culhuacan)* is also the name of a pre-Colombian city-state founded by the Toltecs under Mixcoatl (and remember Mixcoatl is also supposed to be an ancestor to the Mexica). It is believed to be the first settlement of the Toltecs in the area, even before they built Tula. Colhuacan was in the Valley of Mexico on the shores of Lake Xochimilco, which connected to Lake Texcoco, where the Mexica later established their city of Tenochtitlan on an island. Colhuacan was also known for having floating gardens. It survived the fall of Tula and continued into the Aztec era.

In the Colhuacan region is a hill called Chapultepec (meaning grasshopper) located on an island in Lake Texcoco, close to where the Mexica-Aztec capital city of Tenochtitlan was built. When the Mexica first arrived in the Valley of Mexico, it was populated by the remnant of the Toltecs, by the Chichimeca who had migrated there earlier, by other tribes from Aztlan, and by other cultures. There wasn't much room for the Mexica, and the local people didn't like these newcomers.

However, after years of subservience to other cultures and struggling to survive, the Aztecs managed to take control of Chapultepec, an island on the west side of Lake Texcoco. In the center of this island was a small, extinct volcano rising above a shoreline with freshwater springs. For about twenty years, they lived on this island with a high hill on a lake with the culture of floating gardens. Chapultepec island bore an uncanny resemblance to Aztlan!

Could Chapultepec be the mythical Aztlan? What if the Aztecs were always desert nomads up to this point? What if their life in Aztlan occurred in far more recent history but was "adjusted" in time to build credibility? Alternatively, could later descriptions of Aztlan been clouded by memories of Chapultepec?

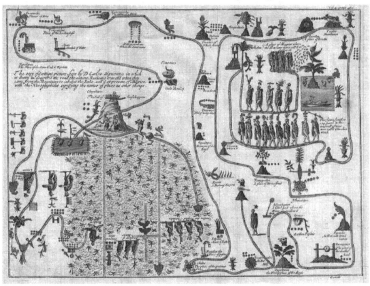

1704 Gemelli Map of the Aztec Migration from Aztlan (upper right corner lake & palm tree) to Chapultepec, in the left middle, a hill with a grasshopper on top)[33]

Even after founding the city of Tenochtitlan, the Mexica had a soft spot in their hearts for Chapultepec Island. It became a sacred place for them, where they built a religious center and a retreat for their emperors. The hill on the island is believed to be where the ashes of cremated Aztec emperors were buried.

Was Aztlan real or mythical? This is a mystery for which we have no definite answer. Were the Aztecs always hunters and gathers before settling in Tenochtitlan, or did they have origins as

[33]https://commons.wikimedia.org/wiki/File:1704_Gemelli_Map_of_the_Aztec_Migration _from_Aztlan_to_Chapultapec_-_Geographicus_-_AztecMigration-gemelli-1704.jpg

agriculturalists? We can glean clues from their legends, from archeology, and from linguistics, yet the beginnings of the people that would build a great empire are shrouded in mist.

Chapter 5: The Early Settlements and Tenochtitlan

Assuming Aztlan was a real place, one can imagine the disorientation and bewilderment of the Mexica-Aztecs when they left their ancestral home. Some cataclysmic event, perhaps warfare or natural disaster or the voice of their god, had forced the exile. What would happen to them? Where would they go?

According to their own accounts, they were soon comforted by the singing of the hummingbird god Huitzilopochtli, who told them he had adopted them as his people and would lead them to a new home. He promised them he would provide them with the tools they needed for their journey and that they would be great and prosperous. In return, he demanded sacrifice, gory sacrifice.

A hummingbird seems a strange manifestation for a deity who was the god of war and the god of the sun. Huitzilopochtli's name literally meant *hummingbird of the left (left was south to the Mexica)*. The Mexica believed that warriors were reincarnated as hummingbirds. Night after night, this reincarnated warrior Huitzilopochtli sang to them, instructing them where to go and what to do.

After the Mexica-Azteca crossed the lake from Aztlan, they encountered the other tribes who, like the Mexica, had each come out of the seven caves of Aztlan: the Xochimilca, Tlahuica, Acolhua, Tlaxcalteca, Tepaneca, and Chalca. These tribes, who had left Aztlan earlier, asked to join the Mexica, and they journeyed together for some time.

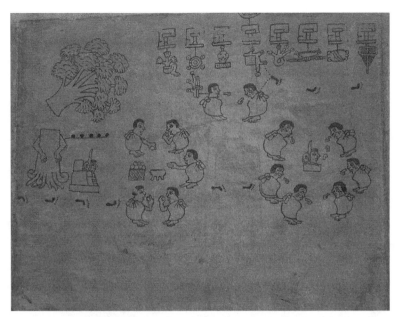

Broken tree, a symbol of the split of the Mexica from other Aztec tribes. To the right of the picture, six men are gathered around Huitzilopochtli, pictured as a man in a hummingbird mouth. From the Codex Boturini.[34]

After arriving at a place called Tlatzallan Texcaltepetzallan, the Mexica's god Huitzilopochtli ordered them to separate from the other tribes; this division is pictured in the *Codex Boturini* as the top of a tree cut off from the trunk. Over 100 years later, the Mexica did meet up again with their kinsmen Aztec tribes from Aztlan, who got to the Valley of Mexico before them. The other Aztec tribes did not give the Mexica a warm welcome.

Following their separation from the other tribes, their god announced that they were now to be called Mexica, not Aztec. The people we know today as Aztecs mostly called themselves Mexica throughout their history. The name Aztec was an inclusive term for all the seven tribes from the seven caves of Aztlan. This can get confusing because in more recent history, the Mexica tribe has often been called *Aztec.*

Today, the term *Aztec* is sometimes used exclusively for the Mexica tribe who eventually settled in Tenochtitlan. The name *Aztec* is more accurately used to designate the three main tribes of

---

[34] https://commons.wikimedia.org/wiki/File:Boturini_Codex_(folio_3).JPG

the Triple Alliance who formed the Aztec Empire: the Mexica, Acolhua, and Tepanec. These three tribes all came from Aztlan, so collectively, they are correctly called Aztec. The name *Aztec* also can refer to all the citizens of the city-states that were loosely part of the Empire and spoke Nahuatl as a common language. Many tribes of these city-states were among the seven tribes from Aztlan, so of Aztec heritage.

For clarity, this book uses the term *Mexica* or *Mexica-Aztec* when referring to the specific tribe that settled Tenochtitlan. It uses *Aztec* when speaking of the seven tribes of Aztlan, the Triple Alliance tribes, and when speaking of the Empire as a whole.

First Human Sacrifice by Mexica, as depicted in Codex Boturini.[35]

Getting back to the long migration, the Mexica remained under the broken tree for four years after their breakup with the other Aztec tribes. It is at this point that they began the grisly practice of human sacrifice. The *Codex Boturini* depicts Huitzilopochtli guiding them through the slaughter of three victims, two men and a woman of the Chicomóztoc-Mimixcoa tribe. In this picture, you can see the fourth man from the left carrying the hummingbird god

---

[35] https://commons.wikimedia.org/wiki/File:Boturini_Codex_(folio_4).JPG

Huitzilopochtli on his back; the god has the head of a bird with a long beak combined with a human head.

The *Crónica Mexicayotl* says that the Mexica-Aztecs continued journeying south, living off the land for many decades. They would stop for a season when they came to a more fertile place, remaining long enough to plant and then harvest a crop, which they could carry with them. This indicates that the Mexica were not completely hunters and gatherers; they must have had an agricultural background to know how to grow crops.

Huitzilopochtli's sister Malinalxoch was traveling with them, a beautiful sorceress who dealt in witchcraft with snakes, scorpions, and other poisonous creatures. Huitzilopochtli thought his sister was evil – incongruous, as he was the one commanding his followers to rip the hearts out of living people as tribute to him. He warned the Mexica that she was a grave threat to them.

"Sorcery is not my way," Huitzilopochtli explained. "My way is war."

Huitzilopochtli went on to tell them the rewards of their conquest under his guidance: "This will bring us jade, gold and colored feathers to decorate my temple. You will have corn and chocolate and cotton. Together, we will have everything."

One day while the sorceress was sleeping, Huitzilopochtli and the Mexica quietly crept away, leaving her behind. Years later, Malinalxoch's son Copil attempted to avenge the abandonment of his mother by attacking the Mexica in their cherished island of Chapultepec. That did not go well for Copil. The Mexica killed him, and following Huitzilopochtli's instructions, cut out his heart and threw it into Lake Texcoco. Mexica myth says that the island that would later become Tenochtitlan grew from Copil's heart.

After decades of nomadic wandering, the Mexica arrived at Tula (Tollan), the ghost town of the Toltecs. They walked about Tula's dramatic ruins, learning from the remaining locals of how the Toltecs ruled the area. They settled in Tula for twenty years, perhaps scheming how they would one day establish an empire of their own. Later, when they arrived in the Valley of Anahuac (Valley of Mexico), they would seek alliances with the Colhuacan people, a branch of the Toltecs, intermarrying with them to establish a Toltec lineage.

Following their twenty-year sojourn in the ruins of Tula, the Mexica resumed their migration south, entering the Valley of Anahuac sometime around AD 1220 to 1240. The new world they encountered was an advanced civilization, more densely populated than what they'd experienced before and politically organized into city-states. Fertile soil and dependable rainfall promoted extensive agriculture, primarily of corn.

Location of major city-states around Lake Texcoco.[36]

Who was there, in the Valley of Anahuac, when they arrived? They encountered four of the Aztec tribes they'd split off from over a century before: the Xochimilca, Acolhua, Tepaneca, and Chalca. Their kinsmen and other people in the valley shunned

[36] File:Lago de Texcoco-posclásico.png: YavidaxiuFile:Valley of Mexico c.1519-fr.svg: historicair 13:51, 11 September 2007 (UTC)derivative work: Sémhur, CC BY-SA 4.0 <https://creativecommons.org/licenses/by-sa/4.0>, via Wikimedia Commons https://commons.wikimedia.org/wiki/File:Basin_of_Mexico_1519_map-en.svg

them, not wanting competition for the land, the resources, and the political power each group was striving to build.

The powerful Colhuacan-Toltecs ruled the southern part of the valley, and the Tepanec city of Azcapotzalco was rapidly forming an empire to the west. Other Chichimec tribes had migrated in, living in the periphery. The Mexica had to contend with these other civilizations as they tried to make a place for themselves.

The Mexica sought to establish themselves in the mainstream of the active valley culture by hiring themselves out as stone cutters, construction workers, and mercenary soldiers. These vocations enhanced their knowledge of architecture and honed their military skill. They initiated alliances with various city-states through marriage. Finally, they worked toward establishing their own settlements; the first was the village of Huixachtitlan, settled in 1240.

Their employment as mercenary warriors proved immediately beneficial when war broke out between the *altepetl* (city-state) of Tenayocan and the altepetl of Colhuacan. Seeking to ingratiate themselves with the Toltec Colhuacan, the Mexica allied with them to successfully fight Tenayocan. Having won the favor of the Colhuacan, they formed a marriage alliance by giving a young woman from one of their noble families to marry a prince of Colhuacan. This couple had a son named Coxcoxtli, whose daughter became the mother of the first ruler of Tenochtitlan, the eventual capital city of the Mexica-Aztec.

As mentioned in the last chapter, the Mexica captured the island of Chapultepec on the west side of Lake Texcoco, essentially establishing it as an independent city-state. Their life on this beloved island ended in about twenty years, when several other city-states attacked them, enraged by their audacity to establish an independent city amid their territory. The Tepanec won the war, expelled the Mexica from Chapultepec, and captured the Mexica leader Huehue Huitzilihuitl and his daughter to be human sacrifices to their gods.

The Mexica who survived the battle hid in the marshes around the lake but eventually had to come out to survive. They surrendered to Colhuacan, offering themselves as slaves in return for protection from the Tepanec. As it turns out, the Colhuacan leader was Coxcoxtli, son of the Mexica princess who had married a Colhuacan prince. He gave them permission to settle in Tizapan, an empty, barren land. The Mexica lived there for a few years, assimilating the Colhuacan culture.

Following a grotesque incident in 1303, the Mexica were exiled from Colhuacan. The series of events leading up to the gruesome scene began when the Colhuacan went to war with the Xochimilca, who had built a powerful altepetl to the south of Colhuacan territory. The Xochimilca were Aztec kinsmen of the Mexica from Aztlan; however, the Mexica threw their lot in with the Colhuacan, led by their kinsman Coxcoxtli.

According to the *Codex Aubin*, the Colhuacan were losing, so King Coxcoxtli called on the Mexica: "Go to the Xochimilca who are defeating us and capture 8000 of them to be our slaves," he commanded.

The Mexica requested shields and clubs for this endeavor, but the king refused, so the Mexica set off on their mammoth task. Ever the overachievers, instead of capturing the Xochimilca, they killed them - and not just 8000; they kept on going and killed 32,000! They cut the noses off the warriors, filled their sacks with them, and marched back to King Coxcoxtli.

"O ruler, here are all our captives. We caught 32,000 of them." They dropped the bloody bags full of noses in front of Coxcoxtli.

Horrified, Coxcoxtli called for his advisors. "The Mexica are not human! How did they do this to the Xochimilca? They are a bad omen!"

The Mexica pressed their advantage, "O Ruler, give our earth altar a little something to adorn it."

They wanted Coxcoxtli's daughter; they wanted to worship her as a goddess, they said. Perhaps the Colhuacan king had misgivings, but he gave them his daughter to be worshiped as a goddess. When the king arrived for the ceremony, one of the Mexica priests was strolling around in the skin of his daughter! She had been killed and flayed, and he was wearing her! As can be expected, the Mexica's macabre perspective of how to worship a goddess incited a terrible battle and the Mexica's expulsion from Colhuacan. They then had to wander through the swamps and lake areas as outcasts.

At first, they tried to settle north of Colhuacan, in Mexicaltzingo. But their horrific reputation had preceded them, and the people of that area forced them to keep going. They finally found an island called Nextipac, on the shores of Lake Texcoco, where they settled for a while. But the Colhuacan, their one-time allies turned enemies, attacked them there, burning down their town, leaving no trace that Nextipac had ever existed.

The Mexica fled; using their shields as rafts, they paddled away and hid out among the reeds of the lake edge. The Mexica had lost many of their people, all their belongings, and now they were hiding in the swamp, with the Colhuacan pressing down on them. They were in a desperate situation; what would save them now?

That night, the hummingbird god, Huitzilopochtli, appeared in a dream to one of the tribal leaders: "When morning comes, get up and seek a prickly-pear cactus, standing among the reeds. On it, an eagle will be perched, eating a snake. Here you must build your city, Tenochtitlan. And here you must await your surrounding enemies and conquer them, one by one, all of them."

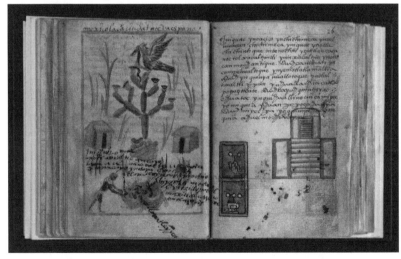

Eagle on cactus eating a snake, from Codex Aubin folio 25[37]

The next morning, the tribal elder called the people together and told him of the prophecy he had received in his dream. The people set off, looking over their shoulders in case the Colhuacan were still following. Their eyes scanned the area, searching among the reeds, an unlikely place for a cactus to grow. And then, on a marshy island on the western shore of Lake Texcoco, they saw an eagle, spreading his wings and perched on a prickly pear cactus growing in the reeds! It was eating a snake it held in its talons.

Eagle on cactus with bird, from the 16th century Tovar Codex.[38]

(Some earlier versions of the story don't include the snake – just the eagle and the cactus. They show the eagle eating the cactus fruit or eating a bird. It's possible the snake might have entered the story after the Spanish arrived, perhaps by mistranslating the Mexica writings.)

---

[38]https://commons.wikimedia.org/wiki/File:The_Eagle,_the_Snake,_and_the_Cactus_in_t he_Founding_of_Tenochtitlan_WDL6749.png

This was the place! After all those years of wandering, of fighting the elements, struggling to survive, longing for a place to call home, here it was! Here was the island where they would build their city Tenochtitlan. It was the year AD 1325. They had left their island home of Aztlan in 1168, and after the long migration had finally come to their new island home.

Building their new city in the middle of a swampy area may have seemed inauspicious beginnings. And yet, this low-lying island on a lake was a strategic location. They would have plenty of food from fish and waterfowl and from farming where there was a constant source of water. Lake Texcoco was connected to other lakes, providing multiple waterways for trade, transportation, and setting out on war expeditions.

Of course, they didn't own the island. It was under the control of the *tlatoani* (king) of the city of Azcapotzalco, the seat of the Tepanec Empire. The Tepanec were the Mexica's kinsmen from Aztlan and one-time allies, but more recently, their enemies. Would the Tepanec king permit them to live there? Yes! In exchange for becoming vassals of Azcapotzalco and mercenary warriors for the Tepanec, they could stay!

All they had to do was fight with the Tepanec against the other altepetls, especially Colhuacan and Texcoco, the city-state of the Acolhua, also kinsmen from Aztlan. Together, the Mexica and the Tepanec defeated Colhuacan and Texcoco, bringing all the territories around Lake Texcoco under the control of the Tepanec Empire. With the area secured, the Mexica could now turn their focus to building their city.

In 1375, Tenoch, their esteemed chieftain of the long migration, died. After their period of mourning, the Mexica gathered to decide who would be the next leader of their fledgling city. It would have to be someone who would command the respect of the surrounding city-states and have ties with the political elite of the region. Nobody in their own group met the criteria, so they started looking further afield, at Colhuacan, of all places.

So, yes, there was that gruesome incident where their priest had dressed himself in the skin of the Colhuacan princess, leading to their exile. And yes, they had allied with the Tepanec to defeat Colhuacan and bring it under Tepanec control. But through their intermarriages with the Colhuacan royals, they had developed important blood ties.

Remember, Coxcoxtli himself was the son of a Mexica princess. Coxcoxtli's daughter, Atotoztli (not the one who was skinned), had married Opochtli Iztahuatzin, a Mexica leader, and given birth to a son named Acamapichtli. This boy was of Mexica lineage but also of Colhuacan royalty – and was related to the Acolhua tribe as well. Through his Colhuacan bloodline, he was a descendent of the Toltecs. The Mexica elders could not think of a better candidate with ties to all the right people to be their next ruler.

Acamapichtli, the first Aztec King (Reigned 1376-1395). From Tovar Codex.[39]

A delegation headed to Texcoco to invite Acamapichtli to be their governor, and he accepted! The young man of twenty came to Tenochtitlan in 1376, greeted with much pageantry. Acamapichtli solidified ties with the Colhuacan by marrying the daughter of the king and then affirmed his standing in his new city by marrying three Mexica women, each from one of the three major houses of Tenochtitlan. The Aztec-Mexica dynasty was now established. Soon, it would grow into multiple city-states and eventually into a great Mesoamerican empire.

[39]https://commons.wikimedia.org/wiki/File:Acamapichtli,_the_First_Aztec_King_(Reigne d_1376%E2%80%9395)_WDL6718.png

Chapter 6: Aztec City-States

For the next fifty years, through canny politics, warfare, and astute alliances, the fierce Mexica rose to prominence, establishing themselves as a political power with dominance over several other city-states. During the reign of their first three kings, they focused on consolidating their own city-state of Tenochtitlan while expanding its size and embarking on massive architectural projects. They also began to take possession of smaller city-states which would pay tribute money, serve as allies against enemy forces, and provide a source of trade. In this chapter, we will explore how they began acquiring these city-states and how the city-states were organized and related to each other.

The Mexica city of Tenochtitlan was developing in a larger Mesoamerican culture that focused on extensive agriculture combined with complex, densely populated urban centers. These large cities served as the religious, political, and economic centers for the surrounding population. Most of these urban areas formed alliances with other cities; the smaller, weaker cities became tributaries to the larger, more powerful cities. The tributaries would provide goods and services, including mercenary soldiers, along with tribute payments to their overlords.

Mexica warriors: Eagle Warrior at the left and Jaguar Warrior at the right brandishing a macuahuitl (a wooden club with sharp obsidian blades). From the Florentine Codex.[40]

In the case of Tenochtitlan, the Mexica were initially allies and tributaries to the Tepanec city of Azcapotzalco. Together, these two cities began to rise in power. Through supplying warriors for successful military campaigns, the Mexica enabled Azcapotzalco to evolve into an empire with major regional power. The Tepanec emperor Tezozomoc greatly appreciated the support from Tenochtitlan and began granting the Mexica part of the tribute as they conquered other city-states together. Eventually, Tenochtitlan became a city-state in its own right.

In the political system of that day, a *tlatoani* was king of a city-state, and a *Huey Tlatoani* was the ruler of a city-state that had other cities as tributaries under it (something like an emperor over an empire). When Acamapichtli was first brought to Tenochtitlan

[40]https://commons.wikimedia.org/wiki/File:Historia_general_de_las_cosas_de_Nueva_Es pa%C3%B1a_vol._1_folio_74v_(cleared_up).png

to rule, his status was that of *cihuacóatl* or governor, as Tenochtitlan was still developing into a proper city. In the next seven years, as Tenochtitlan grew in power and in esteem, it was eventually recognized as a city-state (although still a tributary to the Tepanec). In 1382, Acamapichtli was crowned *Tlatoani* (King) of Tenochtitlan, with great fanfare.

While the Tepanec of Azcapotzalco, with their Tenochtitlan allies, were expanding their power base on the western shores of Lake Texcoco, the Acolhua city of Texcoco was developing into a major contender on the northeastern side of the lake. When war broke out between Azcapotzalco and Texcoco, the Mexica fought with their Tepanec allies, and together they conquered Texcoco.

During Acamapichtli's reign, Mexica warriors continued to fight with the Tepanec against other city-states. Eventually, they were permitted to engage in their own expeditions. In these military campaigns, they conquered the Tlahuaca city of Cuauhnahuac and Xochimilco to the south, making them their first tributary states! The Tlahuaca and Xochimilco were two of the seven tribes from Aztlan, so the Mexica were building the Aztec base of power.

The marshy island on which Tenochtitlan was located was expanded during Acamapichtli's reign by hauling in dirt and rock to build up the original island and by building a causeway to a nearby island. As an island city, Tenochtitlan lacked land to grow enough food for the population. Acamapichtli expanded the chinampas (floating gardens) around the city. After Xochimilco became a tributary city, the Xochimilco shipped fruit and vegetables to Tenochtitlan from their own floating gardens in the south.

Illustration of Tenochtitlan showing causeway and Templo Mayor[41]

The Mexica began replacing their reed houses with houses of stone, wood, and loam. Acamapichtli developed the city into four districts centered around the great temple complex, which included the *Templo Mayor*, a high pyramid with two temples on top. The *Templo Mayor* was rebuilt numerous times over the coming years, becoming taller each time. The temple complex also had a ball court and a skull rack and was surrounded by the palaces of the elite. Canals throughout the city provided transportation. Anthropologists have estimated that the population of Tenochtitlan at its peak was 200,000.

As a political leader, Acamapichtli shrewdly built up the Mexica's strength through forming alliances with other rival clans rather than fighting them. He kept relations steady with the Tepanec emperor Tezozomoc by promptly paying the demanded tribute. Once, when in Tezozomoc's city of Azcapotzalco, Acamapichtli bought a beautiful woman in the slave market. With this slave, he had a son named Itzcoatl, who became Tlatoani of Tenochtitlan in 1427, after Acamapichtli's older son Huitzilihuitl and his grandson Chimalpopoca reigned as kings of Tenochtitlan.

[41] https://commons.wikimedia.org/wiki/File:El_templo_mayor_en_Tenochtitlan.png

Acamapichtli died young in his mid-forties. Before his death, he was eager to settle the matter of his successor. The custom of the Mexica was to elect their leaders. The elders would make this decision, and generally, the next ruler was from the royal family, but not necessarily the oldest son. It could be a nephew or some other relative. From his death bed, Acamapichtli summoned the chiefs of the four districts of Tenochtitlan. He advised them he wanted them to continue the custom of electing their leaders.

The four chiefs held a council and elected Acamapichtli's oldest son Huitzilihuitl, who was only sixteen years old. Acamapichtli approved this choice before he died. A discerning young man, Huitzilihuitl knew his detractors might question his election by only four leaders. He ordered a new election with a larger group of priests, elders, and warrior chiefs to cast their votes and won again, solidifying his right to the throne.

Huitzilihuitl assumed the throne in 1395 and ruled until 1417. The Codex Aubin noted that in the year Huitzilihuitl acceded the throne, a swarm of grasshoppers besieged the area, causing a year of famine. He maintained friendly relations with the Tepanec Emperor Tezozomoc of Azcapotzalco, marrying his daughter Ayauhcihuatl. After this, Tezozomoc lowered Tenochtitlan's tribute payments to a nominal level. Huitzilihuitl and Ayauhcihuatl had a son named Chimalpopoca, who became the next tlatoani. Another wife, Miahuaxihuitl, gave birth to Moctezuma I, who later became the *Huey Tlatoani* of the Aztecs (Huey Tlatoani, not just tlatoani, as by that time Tenochtitlan was an empire).

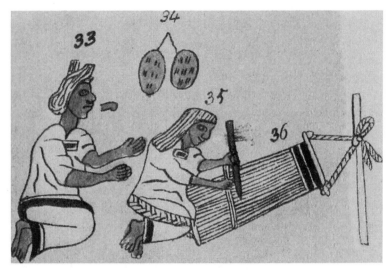

Mother teaching daughter to weave cotton[42]

A wise leader, Huitzilihuitl continued his father's policies of brokering peaceful alliances with neighboring states. During his reign, cotton weaving became an important industry. Previously, the people had worn clothing made from maguey (agave) fiber, which was scratchy, like burlap. Now they could wear soft and cool cotton, which could be dyed in the bright colors the Mexica loved. The cotton industry was so productive that they exported cotton to Azcapotzalco and to Cuauhnahuac, their vassal city in the far south.

When the ruler of the city of Texcoco died in 1409, his son Ixtlixochitl became tlatoani and quickly began challenging the status quo. The Mexica's involvement in this was complicated. Decades earlier, they had allied with the Tepanec in a war against Texcoco and won. At that time, Texcoco had become a tributary city to Azcapotzalco. The new ruler Ixtlixochitl continued paying tribute to the Tepanec city, but when Emperor Tezozomoc of Azcapotzalco offered his daughter in marriage to him, he chose Huitzilihuitl's daughter Matlalcihuatzin instead.

Ixtlixochitl then proclaimed himself "Lord of the Chichimeca," inviting his Mexica father-in-law Huitzilihuitl to become his ally

---

[42] https://commons.wikimedia.org/wiki/File:The_American_Museum_journal_(c1900-(1918))_(18162300141).jpg

against Tezozomoc of Azcapotzalco. That meant Huitzilihuitl had to choose between his father-in-law Tezozomoc and his new son-in-law. Huitzilihuitl chose his long-time ally Tezozomoc.

Angry at the snub to his daughter and Ixtlixochitl's insubordination, Emperor Tezozomoc led his army, along with Mexica warriors, to attack Texcoco. After two years, the joint Tepanec and Mexica forces conquered Texcoco and killed Ixtlixochitl. As a reward for the Mexica's loyalty, Emperor Tezozomoc gave Texcoco to Tenochtitlan as a tributary. Texcoco was a city of the Acolhua tribe, the Mexica's kinsmen from Aztlan. Now the cities of three Aztec tribes – the Acolhua, Tlahuaca, and Xochimilco – were tributaries of the Mexica. Their collection of city-states was growing!

Like his father, Huitzilihuitl died young, at only 38. His son Chimalpopoca, age twenty, assumed the throne in 1417 and ruled until 1427, only ten years. One of his achievements was fulfilling his father's dream of an aqueduct to bring fresh water into Tenochtitlan. Even though they were on an island in a lake, thermal springs around the island made the water saline. The connecting lakes and other parts of Lake Texcoco were fed by freshwater springs, so the Mexica had to get drinking water from there or from the mainland. Chimalpopoca's maternal grandfather, Emperor Tezozomoc of Azcapotzalco, assisted with the project of constructing a wooden aqueduct from Chapultepec to Tenochtitlan. Chimalpopoca also built a causeway to Tlacopan on the mainland, with bridges that could be lifted at night or when threatened by invasion.

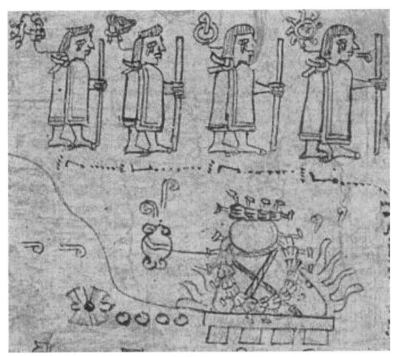

Funeral pyre of Emperor Tezozomoc, from the Codex Xolotl[43]

Intrigue surrounded Chimalpopoca's death when he was only thirty. Was it suicide or an assassination associated with a coup d'état? His grandfather Tezozomoc, the Tepanec Emperor, died in 1427. Tezozomoc's son, Tayatzin, Chimalpopoca's uncle on his mother's side, succeeded his father. Within days, Tayatzin's older brother Maxtla staged a rebellion and stole the throne. Chimalpopoca joined forces with Tayatzin to retake the throne of Azcapotzalco. Tayatzin was killed in the struggle, and warriors from Azcapotzalco invaded Tenochtitlan, captured Chimalpopoca, and took him back to Azcapotzalco, where he was placed in a cage. He either committed suicide by hanging himself with his belt, or he was strangled by his Tepanec captors.

However, some scholars believe his death was at the hands of his Mexica uncle Itzcoatl, who succeeded him as ruler of Tenochtitlan. They say Itzcoatl was the undercover leader of a secret rebel force that had been plotting against their overlords and long-time allies, the Tepanec. As the grandson of Tezozomoc, who

---

[43] https://commons.wikimedia.org/wiki/File:Tezozomoc_funeral.jpg

had generously helped with the aqueduct and in other ways, Chimalpopoca was loyal to the Tepanec. These scholars believed he was secretly assassinated by his uncle Itzcoatl, and his death blamed on the Tepanec.

Regardless of how Chimalpopoca died, the saga between Tenochtitlan and Azcapotzalco continued, ending in the Triple Alliance, which we will cover in the next chapter. For now, let's review more about the city-state culture in the Valley of Mexico to better understand the development of the Aztec Empire.

The Mexica-Aztecs began to grow into an empire through military conquest, trade, and forming valuable alliances. They installed friendly rulers in territories they conquered and intermarried with the ruling dynasties. The *altepetl* or city-states that came under their control were generally able to retain their own leaders and religion, but they had to support the growing Mexica Empire and the tlatoani of Tenochtitlan through tribute payments. They also had to include the Mexica god, Huitzilopochtli, in the worship of their deities. Failure to comply would result in the Mexica military attacking their city and destroying temples and other buildings. Needless to say, this created resentment in some of their tributary cities.

The altepetl (city-states) of the growing Mexica-Aztec empire were organized in a hierarchal system. Each altepetl had its own tlatoani (king) who ruled over the nobles and commoners in his territory. Each city-state had its own capital, which was the trade hub and center for religious activity, around which were spread the agricultural lands and smaller towns and villages.

Most city-states were marked by one specific ethnic identity, although they were all multi-ethnic with several spoken languages. The *lingua-franca* (common language) for all the city-states under Mexica control was Nahuatl, the language group of Aztec tribes as well the Chichimeca tribes and the descendants of the Toltec Empire.

The word *tlatoani* for the ruler of the city-states literally means *one who speaks*, indicating that he was a representative for his people. The tlatoani was not only the political leader but usually also the high priest and commander-in-chief for his city-state. He was considered the owner of all the lands in the altepetl and would receive tribute from these lands and smaller towns and villages. He supervised the markets and temples and served as a judge to resolve disputes brought from the high court. Under the tlatoani was his second-in-command, the *cihuacōātl*, who served as the chief judge of the court system and appointed lower court judges. The cihuacōātl was also the chief financial officer for the tlatoani.

Most tlatoani were of royal blood but usually elected from a pool of four candidates by a council of nobles, warriors, and priests. Once elected, the tlatoani served for life and was permitted to have multiple wives, which generated many children to continue his legacy.

Four Aztec warriors, from the Codex Mendoza[44]

Whenever a city-state was defending its territory or involved in a military campaign against other city-states, the tlatoani, as commander-in-chief, would create war strategies for his military force. He would base this on information he received from scouts, spies, and messengers who assessed the situation at the rival city-state regarding the position of the enemy and points of strength and weakness. He would be informed immediately of the success

[44]

https://commons.wikimedia.org/wiki/File:Four_Aztec_Warriors_in_Drawn_in_Codex_Mendoza.jpg or failure of skirmishes and any deaths or captives. The tlatoani would also rally support from friendly city-states, sending gifts and requesting their help.

The commoners in the smaller towns and villages surrounding the capital city of a city-state were subdivided into smaller units called *calpolli*. Each calpolli would have a *tecutli* (landlord) who would govern that region and distribute the land among the commoners, who usually were kinspeople related through intermarriage. The tecutli or landlord might be of commoner origin but usually rose to nobility status as a representative of his calpolli to the higher authorities.

The farmers did not own their own land; it was more of a feudal land system where farmers would pay tribute to their landlord in the form of a portion of their crops from the land assigned to them, and tradespeople would pay tribute from their manufactured goods like cotton cloth and clothing articles, baskets, pottery, tools, and even paper! Archeologists estimate that a typical altepetl had 10,000 to 15,000 residents in an area of around 30 to 40 square miles.

The Mexica discouraged connections among their tributary city-states, limiting communication and trade between the city-states, preferring them to be dependent on Tenochtitlan as their major trade partner. This made Tenochtitlan more powerful as the major trade center for the Lake Texcoco region. It also helped secure Mexica power. If the city-states started interacting with each other, becoming friendly and trading and intermarrying, this could lead to them forming allies and potentially challenging their Mexica-Aztec overlords.

Each altepetl was its own political unit, separate from the other city-states. Warfare was common between the city-states who were tributaries to the Mexica-Aztec, especially if one was a Nahuatl-speaking tribe and the other was of some other ethnicity.

The Mexica-Aztec continued conquering other Mesoamerican city-states and expanding their empire. In 1430, the Triple Alliance formed between three powerful cities – Tenochtitlan, Texcoco, and Tlacopan (as we will cover in the next chapter). At that point, the lands that had once been part of the Tepanec Empire were divided between the three cities, so each gained more territory.

The Mexica-Aztec Empire ruled most of the city-states around Lake Texcoco, including Azcapotzalco, Colhuacan, Chapultepec, Coyoacan, Chalca, Tenayuca, and Xochimilco.

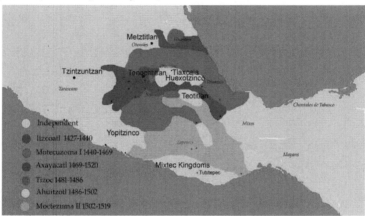

Expansions by various Mexica-Aztec rulers.[45]

Following the formation of the Triple Alliance, the empire continued expansion into areas outside the Valley of Mexico, acquiring Huaxtepec, to the south, in what is now the state of Morelos, and Oaxaca even further south. They conquered Tlaxcala and Cholula in the Pueblo Valley. The empire eventually stretched from the Pacific Ocean to the Gulf of Mexico and as far south as Guatemala. Tenochtitlan ruled over approximately 500 small city-states with up to six million people spanning over 80,000 square miles. When the nomadic Mexica dreamed of ruling an empire, they probably never envisioned how extensive it would one day become.

[45] https://commons.wikimedia.org/wiki/File:Aztecexpansion.png

Chapter 7: The Triple Alliance

His name meant *obsidian snake*, an apt description for the fourth tlatoani of Tenochtitlan. Obsidian was the black volcanic glass the Chichimeca used for arrows, so sharp it penetrated the chainmail armor of the Spaniards. Itzcoatl was like a snake, unnoticed in the grass until the opportunity came for a lethal strike.

His father was Acamapichtli, the first tlatoani of Tenochtitlan. But Itzcoatl was a younger son, and his mother was a slave. While his half-brother Huitzilihuitl reigned, and then when Huitzilihuitl's son Chimalpopoca reigned, Itzcoatl remained in the shadows, quietly forming alliances with other royal sons from nearby cities – the younger sons, born from unimportant wives or concubines. As he secretly plotted his rebellion against the Mexica's Tepanec overlords, Itzcoatl sought out alliances with leading families from Tlacopan and Texcoco, small city-states oppressed by Azcapotzalco.

The chaos following the death of the Tepanec Emperor Tezozomoc gave Itzcoatl the chance to maneuver the situation to his advantage. While Tezozomoc's heirs engaged in a desperate struggle for the Tepanec throne, the mysterious death of Itzcoatl's nephew Chimalpopoca opened the door for Itzcoatl to assume the Mexica throne. Itzcoatl's successful power play eventually resulted in the downfall of Azcapotzalco, the most powerful city in the Valley of Mexico. When Azcapotzalco fell, the Aztec Empire was born.

Events leading up to the great battle of Azcapotzalco began with a coup d'état in the Tepanec city of Azcapotzalco, with Maxtla wresting the throne from his brother. Days after, in Tenochtitlan,

Itzcoatl became tlatoani. The two cities had been strong allies since the founding of Tenochtitlan, with the Mexica aiding Azcapotzalco's rise as the strongest city-state in the Valley of Mexico. Tenochtitlan was technically a tributary city to Azcapotzalco, but the former emperor had reduced the tribute payments to a nominal amount out of gratitude for the Mexica's loyal support.

Now, Maxtla, the new Tepanec *Huey Tlatoani*, blockaded Tenochtitlan, cut off their freshwater supply, and demanded higher tribute payments. The Alcoa city of Texcoco was also victimized by Maxtla's despotic demands. Texcoco's king, Nezahualcoyotl the poet, was half-Alcoa and half-Mexica, the grandson of Huitzilihuitl, second king of Tenochtitlan. Hearing that Maxtla planned to kill him, Nezahualcoyotl fled from Texcoco. While in exile, he had an epiphany, which was recorded later by his great-grandson Juan Bautista Pomar:

"Truly the gods I worship are idols that do not speak nor feel . . . some immensely powerful and unknown god is the creator of the whole universe. He is the only one that can console me in my affliction and help me in such anguish as my heart feels; I want him to be my helper and protection."

Nezahualcoyotl (1402-1472), ruler of Texcoco, from the Codex Ixtlilxochitl.[46]

[46] https://commons.wikimedia.org/wiki/File:Nezahualcoyotl.jpg

Once Nezahualcoyotl regained power in Texcoco, he built a pyramid and wrote hymns to the *unknown God of everywhere, life giver and peerless One.* But that day had not yet come. At the moment, Nezahualcoyotl needed to rally support for his city. He found an ally in the Toltec-Chichimeca city of Huexotzinco, far to the east. Their king agreed to assist Nezahualcoyotl in his struggle against Maxtla.

Meanwhile, Itzcoatl, already friendly with Texcoco and Huexotzinco, was calling in support from another friend, the tlatoani of Tlacopan. Tlacopan was a small Tepanec city that belonged to the city-state of Azcapotzalco, but they had supported the losing side in the civil war for succession in Azcapotzalco. Fearing the wrath of Maxtla, they decided to join forces with Itzcoatl and the Mexica of Tenochtitlan.

Nezahualcoyotl, realizing several city-states were preparing to resist Maxtla and Azcapotzalco, brilliantly envisioned a coalition forming a massive military force to take down the ferocious and mighty Tepanec empire. This alliance consisted of Tenochtitlan, Texcoco, Huexotzinco, Tlacopan, and Tlatelolco (a small Mexica sister-city just next to Tenochtitlan). Over 100,000 warriors formed the coalition army in 1428 to gain ascendency over the Tepanec bastion of Azcapotzalco.

The army formed three divisions which won back three of the Acolhua cities of the kingdom of Texcoco: Otumba and Acolman to the north, and Coatlinchan to the south. Now Nezahualcoyotl marched to his own city of Texcoco and defeated the Tepanec, while another division gained control over Acolhuacan. Once most towns and cities of the kingdom of Texcoco were secured, Nezahualcoyotl reclaimed his crown while the coalition continued to attack isolated Tepanec posts.

Battle of Azcapotzalco, from Tovar Codex, with jaguar warriors and other fighters. To the right, a priest is sacrificing a small child while two other victims lie on the ground.[47]

The coalition warriors then turned to the western shores of Lake Texcoco toward the Tepanec capital of Azcapotzalco. After a siege of 112 days, they overthrew the great city, burning it down and massacring the population. The Tepanec empire, to which they had all been tributary cities, was finally conquered. This turned the three main players, Tenochtitlan, Texcoco, and Tlacopan, into independent city-states. Through seizing power in a coordinated coup d'état, they won freedom for themselves and went on to exert massive power over central Mexico for nearly 100 years. Out of this coalition, the Triple Alliance would be born.

Once the Tepanec Empire was overthrown, the warriors of Huexotzinco returned to their home in the east. The three major powers – the Mexica city of Tenochtitlan, the Acolhua city of Texcoco, and the Tepanec city of Tlacopan – formed a treaty called the Triple Alliance. All three of these tribes were part of the original seven tribes from the caves of Aztlan. These Aztec tribes gave birth to the Aztec Empire, which would soon extend from the Pacific Ocean to the Gulf of Mexico.

---

[47] https://commons.wikimedia.org/wiki/File:The_Battle_of_Azcapotzalco_WDL6746.png

The lands of the Tepanec Empire were divided between the three conquering cities. Part of their agreement was to continue conquering other cities with the coalition army. The new lands they acquired would be jointly held by all three cities. Tribute from conquered cities was to be divided into one-fifth for Tlacopan and two-fifths each for Tenochtitlan and Texcoco. Each of the three kings of the alliance would take turns serving as the *Huey Tlatoani* (emperor) of the consolidated empire, temporarily holding legal power over the other two.

Triple Alliance Territory, with inset showing the location of three major cities: Tenochtitlan, Texcoco, and Tlacopa. The shaded areas indicate the city-states that paid tribute to the Aztec Empire. Notice that not all the lands were connected; Xoconochco, on the border of Guatemala, was hundreds of miles from other Aztec city-states.[48]

Later that year, the alliance forces conquered Colhuacan and Huitzilopochco. Working to gain control of all city-states in the Lake Texcoco region, the coalition army moved swiftly to conquer Xochimilco and Ixtapalapan in 1430, and Mixquic two years later. The only holdouts were the Chalca, eventually defeated in 1465,

[48] Aztec Empire 1519 map-fr.svg: Keepscases & Sémhurderivative work: Rowanwindwhistler, CC BY-SA 4.0 <https://creativecommons.org/licenses/by-sa/4.0>, via Wikimedia Commons
https://commons.wikimedia.org/wiki/File:Aztec_Empire_1519_map-es.svg

and Tlatelolco in 1473.

The primary architect of the Triple Alliance was Itzcoatl's nephew Tlacaelel, a son of King Huitzilihuitl. Tlacaelel was given the title *cihuacōātl*. Now that the city-state of Tenochtitlan had become part of a vast empire, the *Huey Tlatoani* (emperor) served as the executive over external affairs of the empire: war, expansion, tribute, and diplomacy. The *cihuacōātl* managed the internal affairs of the empire and could exercise great influence and power in this position.

Tlacaelel worked diligently to mold the Mexica self-identity as the chosen people called by the god Huitzilopochtli to conquer and rule over other lands. The people of the Aztec Empire worshiped many gods, but Tlacaelel forced the worship of Huitzilopochtli as chief god among all people of the empire. Tlacaelel also endeavored to erase the pre-conquest memories of conquered city-states by burning their historical chronicles. He even burned the chronicles of the Mexica, apparently because they didn't support the narrative of Aztec identity he was seeking to cultivate.

Like other Mesoamerican cultures, human sacrifice had been part of the Mexica culture since they had left Aztlan, but once Tenochtitlan gained dominance in the Triple Alliance, Tlacaelel raised the scale of human sacrifice to horrific numbers to satiate the gods, so the Mexica could maintain power. These daily, large-scale sacrifices demanded victims – lots of victims.

Aztec Warriors, from Florentine Codex[49]

---

[49] https://commons.wikimedia.org/wiki/File:Aztec_warriors.png

In the past, the Mexica had sacrificed prisoners of war, but they were running out of prisoners once they conquered most of the nearby territories. Consequently, Tlacaelel came up with the idea of *Flower Wars*. These were ritual and regulated wars meant for both sides to capture enough warriors to meet their sacrificial needs. The main enemies of the Aztecs were the Tlaxcala, a people the Aztecs never conquered, along with several other groups from the Pueblo area, including the Cholula. Tlacaelel brokered an agreement between Tenochtitlan and Tlaxcala to engage in a type of warfare where the soldiers would capture rather than kill the enemy soldiers. Once each side had captured enough warriors for sacrifices, the battle would end. These battles would be prearranged by the leaders on both sides every twenty days! The Flower Wars were usually with the Tlaxcala but occasionally with Cholula or other cities.

With a united front, the Triple Alliance rapidly expanded its territory as it conquered one city after another. The Empire's rule over these conquered cities was *hegemonic* (indirect). If the ruler of the city agreed to their demands, he could remain tlatoani and enjoy the protection of the Triple Alliance and the accompanying political stability and enhanced economics. He just needed to pay tribute to the Alliance twice a year and supply warriors for their military campaigns. The conquered cities maintained their local autonomy and conducted their local affairs as before, including their own religions, but they had to add in the Mexica god Huitzilopochtli as their chief deity.

Occasionally, the tlatoani of a conquered city refused to submit to the Triple Alliance requirements. One strategy the Aztecs used with this problem was replacing uncooperative leaders with a governor who was not of the royal family. Another was directly taxing the population and leaving the king out of the equation. A third way was to bribe the tlatoani with tributes from another city far away if he continued to be submissive to the empire. If this sort of persuasion didn't work, and a city continued to fight against the empire or kill their delegates, the Aztecs would destroy the city. This happened to the Huastec people to the east. Because they continued fighting fiercely without surrendering, the allied forces killed most of the people in the area, even the elderly, the children, and the women.

The cities of the Triple Alliance presented a daunting military coalition, but they were also surging economically. Wherever trade relations already existed, they would expand these, with the end effect that the three ruling cities on Lake Texcoco were the center of a trade hub that spread out throughout the Valley of Mexico and beyond. They intermarried within the three ruling states to strengthen their ties and cultivated marriage alliances with the royal families of the cities they conquered.

Once peace was finally achieved in the Lake Texcoco region, each of the three ruling cities of the Empire directed their attention inward to reforming and developing their cities. In Tenochtitlan, schools were built in every neighborhood. Commoners had *telpochcalli* schools, which gave basic instruction in religion and provided boys with military training. The *calmecac* schools were for the nobility and for commoners who seemed promising candidates for the priesthood or as artisans. Laws were passed to clearly define the distinction between nobles and commoners and to grant privileges to warriors and priests. A system of courts and judges was established, with levels of punishment for various crimes.

Dams designed by Nezahualcoyotl for Tenochtitlan.
https://commons.wikimedia.org/wiki/File:Dique_Nezahualc%C3%B3yotl_primer_mapa_de_Tenochtitlan.png

In Texcoco, Nezahualcoyotl was transforming his city into a cultural center while gaining fame as an engineer and architect. He consulted with the Mexica on the best plans for constructing a bigger aqueduct into Tenochtitlan, using his engineering genius to devise a dam and dike system to control flooding and separate the brackish water from fresh water around Tenochtitlan. In his own city of Texcoco, he built temples and an exquisite palace on the side of a cliff, with an irrigation system to fill his hot tubs overlooking the city.

Hot tubs overlooking the city designed by Nezahualcoyotl.[50]

Nezahualcoyotl was known for gathering *tlamatini* (*someone who knows something*) to Texcoco. These were scholars, sages, astronomists, wisemen, and philosophers – something like the Magi of Persia. Under his leadership, Texcoco blossomed, influencing a cultural renaissance throughout the Aztec Empire.

Nezahualcoyotl disdained the daily blood sacrifices of Tenochtitlan. In 1467, the year one-reed in the Aztec calendar, the great temple of the god Huitzilopochtli was rebuilt and dedicated in Tenochtitlan. As recorded in the *Codex Ixtlilxochitl* by his descendent Fernando de Alva Cortés Ixtlilxochitl, Nezahualcoyotl prophesied: *"In a year such as this, this temple, now new, will be destroyed . . . then the earth will be diminished; the chiefdoms will end."*

The Aztec calendar was a rotation of 52 reeds or years, so the next year one-reed was 1419. This was the year that Hernán Cortés first entered Tenochtitlan; two years later, the great city fell to the Spaniards.

[50] Misaelos, CC BY-SA 3.0 <https://creativecommons.org/licenses/by-sa/3.0>, via Wikimedia Commons
https://commons.wikimedia.org/wiki/File:Ba%C3%B1os_de_Nezahualcoyotl.JPG

In his own city of Texcoco, Nezahualcoyotl built a great pyramid, on top of which was a temple, nine stories high, dedicated to *Tloque Nahauque, the unknown god, the uncreated and self-existing creator of all things, life-giver.* He permitted no images or idols and no blood sacrifice; only incense and flowers were offered. At dawn, noon, sunset, and midnight, instruments would play, and Nezahualcoyotl would pray.

Nezahualcoyotl wrote the first codification of law for his city-state, covering property rights, crime, and morality. These eighty comprehensive and concise laws seemed strict and the punishments harsh, but his law code was adopted by other city-states of the Aztec Empire. While Tenochtitlan was burning books and rewriting history, Texcoco was preserving the chronicles of the past, with the death penalty for the willful falsification of historical truth.

Nezahualcoyotl implemented a social welfare system to provide food and clothing for widows, wounded soldiers, and the indigent elderly from the royal treasury, along with school fees for orphans. During the great drought, he provided for his citizens from the treasury, perhaps because he guiltily thought the drought was his fault. Like the Hebrew David and Bathsheba, he had fallen madly in love with the young wife of Cuahcuauhtzin, tlatoani of Tepechpan, one of his minor cities. He sent Cuahcuauhtzin to the frontlines to fight the Tlaxcala, where he was killed; Nezahualcoyotl then claimed Azcalxochitzin as his own wife. Immediately, plagues of locusts and severe drought struck, lasting for three years, which Nezahualcoyotl considered as punishment for his sins.

Coronation of Moctezuma I, Fifth Tlatoani of Tenochtitlan, from the Tovar Codex.[51]

Although the three city-states of the Triple Alliance were supposed to be equal partners, Tenochtitlan rose to dominance as its population grew to double that of Texcoco. When Itzcoatl died in 1440, his nephew Moctezuma I assumed the throne of Tenochtitlan, and Nezahualcoyotl traveled to Tenochtitlan to negotiate the continuation of the Triple Alliance. The new terms for the treaty were for Texcoco and Tlacopan to recognize the supremacy of Tenochtitlan.

Nezahualcoyotl arranged a pseudo-battle where his army and the Tenochtitlan warriors met on the battlefield and exchanged insults. Then the Texcoco warriors took off running toward their city with the Mexica warriors in pursuit. At this point, Nezahualcoyotl lit a great fire on top of the primary pyramid of Texcoco, symbolizing his recognition of Tenochtitlan's dominance. Beginning with the reign of Ahuizotl in 1486, the kings of Tenochtitlan were called *Huey Tlatoani* (emperor); the three rulers of the Triple Alliance no longer took turns as the chief leader. The Huey Tlatoani of Tenochtitlan assumed most of the

[51] Juan de Tovar, see page for license, via Wikimedia Commons
https://commons.wikimedia.org/wiki/File:Moctezuma_I,_the_Fifth_Aztec_King.png

duties of running the Aztec Empire.

Nevertheless, the three cities continued to collaborate in military campaigns to conquer and expand their empire even further. The Purépecha (Tarascan) Empire to the northwest was the nemesis of the Aztec Empire. The Purépecha were expanding their own territory, which sometimes involved claiming lands the Aztecs had already conquered.

When Nezahualcoyotl died in 1472, his son Nezahualpilli assumed the throne of Texcoco; like his father, he was a poet and a seeker of wisdom. After Moctezuma II ascended the throne of Tenochtitlan in 15012, Nezahualpilli warned him that his tlamatini (wisemen) had received a prophecy that foreigners would gain dominion over the Valley of Mexico. Moctezuma was dubious and challenged him to a ball game to test the prophecy. When Moctezuma lost, he feared the omen was true. And so it was. Two years after Nezahualpilli died in 1515, explorer Francisco Hernández de Córdoba landed on the Yucatan coast, the beginning of the end for the Aztec Empire.

Chapter 8: War with the Tarascans

While the Mexica were building Tenochtitlan, another empire was evolving in the high volcanic mountains of the present-day state of Michoacán. Soon it would stretch to Jalisco and Guanajuato, reaching the Pacific Ocean. They never called themselves Tarascans. They were the Purépecha. They were always Purépecha. The word Tarascan came centuries later, from a word for brother-in-law; they used it mockingly for the conquistadors who violated their women. But the Spaniards picked it up and used this epithet for the Purépecha.

Islands of Lake Pátzcuaro[52]

The Purépecha culture appeared in the lake basins of Zacapu, Cuitzeo, and Pátzcuaro around 500 BC, where they settled on islands in the large lakes (yet another island people). A Nahuatl-speaking group joined them several centuries later, bringing a culture of ballcourts and *chac mool* figurines. The Purépecha told the Spanish these people were Toltecs, although some archeologists feel they were Teotihuacan. They may have been escaping a series of volcanic eruptions in central Mexico at that time.

Where did the Purépecha come from? Their origins are puzzling, with a language and culture unlike any others in Mesoamerica. Linguistically, their language is unique, unrelated to Nahuatl or any other languages in Mexico. Some linguists find a possible link to the Zuni of New Mexico and Arizona or the Quechua language of the Incas of South America. Their building style and advanced knowledge of complex metallurgy also hints of Incan influence. Were the Purépecha somehow connected to the people of the South American Andes?

Genetic studies say yes. In 2015, Nicolas Brucato and other researchers presented a study on Native American gene flow between Mesoamerica and the Andes; they found a clear Andean component, albeit minuscule, in the genome of the Purépecha-Tarascans (along with the Maya, Mixtec, and Kaqchiken).

Drawing of a balsa raft near Guayaquil, Ecuador[53]

[53] https://en.wikipedia.org/wiki/Pre-Columbian_rafts#/media/File:Andean_raft,_1748.jpg

In 1526, Spanish explorers described ships or large rafts with cotton sails used by the people of Ecuador and Peru along the Pacific coast, large enough to hold twenty men and carry 25 metric tons. It's conceivable that their trade routes could have extended up the Pacific coast as far north as Mexico. Even though the earlier settlements of the Purépecha were inland, they used the river systems flowing to the Pacific as important trade routes. Scholars believe they may have had contact with South American traders from AD 650 onwards.

Aside from archeological and linguistic studies, our primary knowledge of the Purépecha comes from the *Relación de Michoacán*, a history written in 1540 by the Franciscan priest Fray Jeronimo de Acalá. He translated and recorded accounts from Purépecha nobles of their oral history and traditions. Pictograph manuscripts of their history have also survived, including the *Lienzo de Jucutacuto.*

Coyote statuette attributed to Purépecha-Tarascan culture[54]

Around AD 1300, a leader arose among the Purépecha-Tarascans named Tariacuri, from the *Wakúsecha* (*warrior eagle*) clan. Tariacuri had a prophetic dream one night: a vision of gathering all the communities around Lake Pátzcuaro into one state, strong and united. He allied with several nearby friendly cities and began systematically conquering cities around the lake, turning them over to his sons and nephews to rule. After Tariacuri died, his son Hiripan continued military campaigns around nearby Lake Cuitzeo.

Unlike the Aztecs, the Purépecha assimilated the cultures of conquered people into their own. In fact, they were so ethnically diverse that the Purépecha were minorities in their own cities. Similar to the Aztecs, the Purépecha instituted a tributary system from the cities they conquered, with tribute paid in the form of laborers, mercenary soldiers, and goods. More and more territories were incorporated into a highly centralized state as they doubled in size. The new territories brought in significant production and trade of farm produce, minerals, and pottery. Everything was centered around their capital city of Tzintzuntzan, which stood distinct from other ancient Mesoamerican cities.

Round yácata pyramids in Tzintzuntzan[55]

Tzintzuntzan featured astounding and unique monuments and elaborate religious and civic architecture. In the *House of the Wind,* a civic-ceremonial center on a hill overlooking Lake Pátzcuaro, stood five *yácata:* rounded step-pyramids shaped like

[55] Thelmadatter, CC BY-SA 3.0 <https://creativecommons.org/licenses/by-sa/3.0>, via Wikimedia Commons https://commons.wikimedia.org/wiki/File:4thYacatatztztz.JPG

keyholes. They were covered with fitted stone slabs, like the masonry used by the South American Incas.

By AD 1522, Tzintzuntzan had grown to 35,000 people with a total population around the lake region of 80,000 in 90 towns and cities. As the population grew, extensive terracing projects were carried out on the surrounding mountains to provide land for agriculture. As they conquered the Balsas Basin and Jalisco, the Purépecha-Tarascans controlled the mining of silver and gold, with skilled craftsmen to work the precious metals. They were the first people of Mexico to use gold and the only ones who used bronze. Their knowledge and crafting of valuable metals was probably the finest in all ancient Mesoamerica. They were the most important producers and traders of tin, bronze, and copper in Mexico.

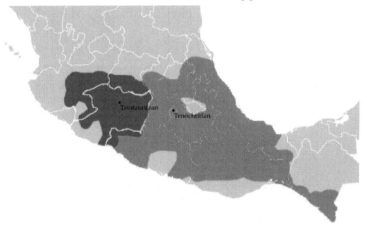

Map showing Purépecha-Tarascan Empire next to Aztec Empire[56]

Eventually, the growing empire of the Purépecha came into direct conflict with the Aztec Empire. The two powers were simultaneously expanding, and both were attempting to conquer and incorporate the same territory that stretched along the northwestern frontier of the Aztec Empire and along the southeastern frontier of the Purépecha. In direct competition for land and resources, they were each blocking the other's expansion projects.

The Purépecha-Tarascans had conquered settlements and territories only to lose them to Aztec expansion, and the same was

---

[56] https://commons.wikimedia.org/wiki/File:Tarascan_aztec_states.png

happening to the Aztecs. From 1440 and into the 1450s, the Purépecha expanded in areas away from Aztec lands and moved east to the Pacific Coast, where they acquired Zacatula. Then they expanded into the Toluca Valley, as well as north to what is now the Mexican state of Guanajuato.

The Purépecha Empire ran their new territories on the frontier differently than how the Aztecs maintained their tributary cities. The Purépecha provided support to these outlying territories from their core – their capital of Tzintzuntzan. They sent resources to their fringe territories and received from them as well, in relatively equal exchange. In the Aztec Empire, it was more a situation of taking but not necessarily giving back. The Purépecha realized they couldn't drain their provinces and endeavored to maintain cordial relations with them.

The Purépecha encouraged the new cultures they conquered to become part of the broader Purépecha culture – to wear their style of clothing and speak their language. If the other people groups assimilated into the mainstream culture, they were considered Purépecha. It wasn't a matter of birth so much as a lifestyle. They did not draw a line between the conquerors and the conquered. Their policy was gentler than the Aztecs, who didn't bother with assimilation and ruled harshly through terror. The Purépecha enjoyed greater harmony with their provinces, while the Aztecs generated animosity and resentment.

The Aztec Empire and the Purépecha Empire fought border skirmishes and jockeyed to grab new territories before the other could get there. Yet, they also experienced periods when the strained relations were relaxed, and in these seasons of détente, they would engage in trade with one another. The trade mostly ended in the mid-1400s when the rivalry intensified.

The simmering relations between the two empires finally exploded into an all-out war from 1469 to 1478. The newly crowned Huey Tlatoani of the Aztecs was Axayacatl, grandson of Moctezuma I. His youthful military skill had won the favor of Viceroy Tlacaelel of Tenochtitlan and King Nezahualcoyotl of Texcoco. When his father died, the council of rulers and elders chose Axayacatl over his two older brothers Ahuitzotl and Tizoc, even though he was only twenty.

As was typical in the region when a new ruler assumed the throne, neighboring kingdoms would take the opportunity to challenge the inexperienced king. In 1469, the year that Axayacatl was crowned king, the Purépecha instigated new border conflicts, which initially did not turn out well for them. Axayacatl was young, but he was a ferocious and shrewd warrior.

In the next few years, Axayacatl launched a bold offensive against the Purépecha. He began to systematically recapture former outlying Aztec lands that the Purépecha had taken in the previous decade. He also started capturing new territory along the edges of the Purépecha frontier, with many bloody and protracted battles between the two empires.

Emboldened by his first nine years of initial success, Axayacatl gathered a force of 32,000 Aztec fighters and marched on the city of Taximaroa (now Hidalgo), the capital city of the Purépecha territory closest to Aztec lands. Taximaroa was prepared. Axayacatl was met by a staggering 50,000 warriors defending Taximaroa – seriously outnumbered! The two armies fought for the entire day; finally, Axayacatl had no choice but to withdraw. The Purépecha had killed at least 20,000 of his men! He'd lost almost two-thirds of his army.

One can imagine Axayacatl and his men plodding home, grieving their comrades and despondent over losing the battle. They were used to winning. What happened this time? In addition to having a much bigger military force and fighting on their own turf, the Purépecha-Tarascans had another major advantage: their knowledge of metallurgy. They had shields of copper that would easily deflect arrows and spears, while the Aztec shields were wood or woven reeds. They had long spears tipped with copper, but the Aztecs used wooden clubs and short spears.

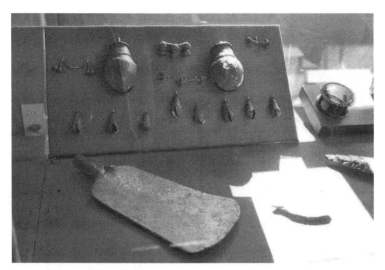

Bronze implements used by Purépecha-Tarascans found in Tzintzuntzan archeological site[57]

Although they won the battle, this experience prompted Tzitzipandáquare, the Purépecha ruler, to build more fortifications and military centers along the Aztec border. He brokered a deal with the Otomies and Matlatzincas, who had been evicted from their homelands by the Aztecs. They were invited to live in Purépecha territory on the border with the Aztecs in return for helping defend the Purépecha lands from the Aztecs. Of course, the Otomies and Matlatzincas were more than happy to fight against the people who had rendered them homeless.

This was the first major defeat the Aztecs had ever suffered since the Triple Alliance had formed. And it happened on Axayacatl's watch. Although he would go on to win several minor triumphs in the next couple of years, this one great loss would forever shadow his reign. Axayacatl died just three years later, barely in his thirties.

Tzitzipandáquare launched a counterattack on the Aztecs later that year, reaching fifty miles out of Tenochtitlan before he was forced back. This prompted the Aztecs to work out a deal with the Purépecha for a demilitarized zone on the frontier between Aztec lands and Purépecha-Tarascan lands. This area between the Balsas

[57] Thelmadatter, CC BY-SA 3.0 <https://creativecommons.org/licenses/by-sa/3.0>, via Wikimedia Commons, https://commons.wikimedia.org/w/index.php?curid=8481277

and Lerma rivers was protected by strategic fortifications overlooking the valleys. Once this cease-fire was settled, the Purépecha turned their attention elsewhere, to other lands they could conquer.

When the Aztec emperor Axayacatl died, he was succeeded by his brother Tizoc in 1481. Tizoc engaged in minor frontier clashes with the Purépecha during his reign; however, the Aztecs considered him to be a weak and inept military ruler. He died after only five years on the throne. Rumors persisted that he was poisoned by Tlacaelel in a desperate plot to end his disastrous reign.

Perhaps the greatest military ruler of the Aztec Empire, Ahuitzotl, was the brother of both Axayacatl and Tizoc - all three from the same mother. He ruled Tenochtitlan from 1486 to 1502. Besides suppressing a rebellion of the Huastec people, doubling the size of the Aztec Empire, and conquering a broad swath of Mexico's Pacific Coast as far south as Guatemala, Ahuitzotl also inflamed the struggle with the Purépecha.

Rather than direct assaults on the Purépecha, Ahuitzotl initially supported and encouraged other people to attack them. He turned to the Chontales, the Cuitlatecs, and other ethnic groups who were allies or tributary cities of the Aztec Empire, enticing them to harass the Purépecha and instigate border skirmishes, in exchange for favors from the Aztecs.

After these other groups softened the defense lines, Ahuitzotl conquered the border city of Otzo in a bloody massacre; none of the population remained - all were killed or fled the area. Ahuitzotl turned the city into an Aztec military outpost. The Purépecha responded by building fortresses close to Otzo to prevent the Aztecs from using it as a foothold. Ahuitzotl then moved further west to the Pacific Coast and conquered Guerrero.

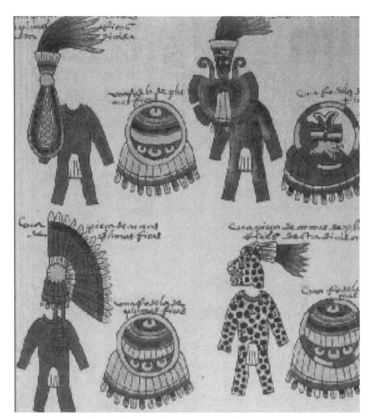

Purépecha-Tarascan traditional religious costumes.[58]

Beginning in 1480, the new Purépecha-Tarascan Emperor Zuangua conquered and occupied regions of what is now the Mexican states of Colima and Jalisco, gaining control of nitratine mines in the area. His reign was resisted by these people, and from 1480 to 1510, the Saltpeter War raged between the Purépecha Empire and the people of Colima, Sayula, Zapotlán, Tapalpa, and Autlán. Ultimately, the Purépecha were expelled from Colima and Jalisco.

Meanwhile, in Tenochtitlan, Ahuitzotl died, and his nephew Moctezuma II was crowned Huey Tlatoani in 1502 – the emperor who was ruling when the Spaniards arrived. Moctezuma spent the first decade of his reign consolidating the immense areas of new territory conquered by Ahuitzotl. Then, in 1515, the Aztec Empire marched against the Purépecha once again, led by the Tlaxcala

---

[58] https://commons.wikimedia.org/wiki/File:Ornamenta_Pur%C3%A9pecha.jpg

general Tlahuicole. Once again, their military campaign ended in failure. Once again, the Aztec warriors withdrew in defeat.

The Purépecha Empire remained unconquered by the Aztec Empire. The Aztecs' failure to gain ascendency over the neighboring empire must have undercut their feelings of invincibility and their self-identity as a chosen people called out by Huitzilopochtli to conquer the lands around them.

The Purépecha and Aztecs soon had a common enemy, the Spanish conquistadors, who initially focused on the Aztec Empire, unaware of a second empire to the northwest. In 1520, while the Spaniards were besieging Tenochtitlan, the Purépecha emperor Zuangua died and was succeeded by Tangaxuan. Almost immediately, Tangaxuan received Aztec emissaries from Tenochtitlan, asking for the Purépecha to ally with them in their desperate struggle against the Spaniards.

Once Tangaxuan extracted crucial information from the Aztecs, he killed the emissaries. He was formulating his own plan. The Aztecs were fighting the Spaniards, and that wasn't going well. Tangaxuan formulated a different tactic, one of diplomacy. He sent a small delegation to the Spaniards to negotiate peace and received a group of the conquistadors into his kingdom, where he plied them with gold and other gifts. His plan backfired.

When Hernán Cortés saw the gold, he suddenly became interested in the Tarascan-Purépecha Empire. Once he conquered Tenochtitlan, he sent one of his captains, Cristóbal de Olid, on a military campaign against the Purépecha in 1522. Amazingly, the Purépecha did not put up a fight. They laid down their weapons. Tangaxuan persisted in his plan of a diplomatic approach rather than suffering the violent end the Aztecs had experienced.

The Tarascans submitted to the Spaniards and accepted the Catholic faith, hoping their empire could continue as a sort of tributary to the Spaniards. For the next eight years, the plan worked. Spanish friars moved in to instruct in Catholicism, while Tangaxuan continued to rule. He continued to collect tribute from his provinces, most of which he kept for himself, sending a portion on to the Spaniards. Hernán Cortés was focusing his attention elsewhere, and the Tarascans weren't causing any trouble.

Nuño de Guzmán's "conquest" of the Tarascans, who had already surrendered years earlier. Note his use of Aztec soldiers (bottom left).[59]

However, the arrangement all came to a sudden and violent end when Nuño de Guzmán was appointed by Spain as the first president of the newly formed *Royal Audiencia of Mexico*. When Guzmán discovered that Tangaxuan had continued as de facto ruler of the Tarascans, he charged him with withholding tribute, heresy, and sodomy, holding a trial by torture. In 1530, Tangaxuan, the last emperor of the Tarascan-Purépecha Empire, was horribly executed.

Fray Jeronimo de Acalá, in *Relación de Michoacán,* documented how Guzmán had the emperor wrapped in a mat tied it to a horse's tail; the mat was set on fire with the horse dragging it around as Tangaxuan burned to death. A crier went with the horse, calling to the people, "Look and pay heed! Look, you lowly people who are all rogues."

This marked the end of the Tarascan-Purépecha Empire. They had coexisted in mutual respect with the Spanish missionaries for

---

[59]

https://en.wikipedia.org/wiki/Michoac%C3%A1n#/media/File:Aztec_Indians_Mexico_Tl axcalan_Cortez.jpg eight years, and now they saw the darker, humiliating, cruel side of their new empire, the side the Aztecs had been experiencing for the past decade.

SECTION THREE: THE SPANISH CONQUEST

Chapter 9: Cortés's Arrival

The year was 1518, and Moctezuma II, Aztec emperor of Tenochtitlan, was troubled. Disturbing omens were disquieting his people: a fire burning in the night sky, the waters of Lake Texcoco suddenly boiling up with high waves flooding the city, a woman wailing in the night – some said it was their mother goddess Coatlicue.

Two years earlier, King Nezahualpilli of Texcoco, his friend and Triple Alliance co-ruler, had died. Nezahualpilli, a seer, had once prophesied that foreigners would overpower the empire. Nezahualpilli's father, Nezahualcoyotl, had prophesied that the great temple would be destroyed in a *one-reed year*. In the Aztec calendar of 52 years, the next year would be a one-reed year. And now, foreigners had arrived in the Mayan region of Yucatan.

Moctezuma was concerned about the unsettled state of the Aztec Empire. After Nezahualpilli died, contention over which son would be Texcoco's next monarch exploded into civil war. Moctezuma had supported Cacamatzin, but the war had ended with the kingdom of Texcoco split three ways between three sons. Cacamatzin ruled the capital city, his brother Ixtlilxochitl – now the sworn enemy of Moctezuma – ruled the northern third of the land, and a third brother ruled the rest. Tenochtitlan and Texcoco had been powerful allies for almost a century. Could Moctezuma depend on the fractured Texcoco in what loomed ahead?

The strange foreigners had first been seen the year earlier in three peculiar and enormous boats that could each carry thirty men or more. The Mayan people had fought and killed over half of them and driven them off. Moctezuma had relaxed momentarily; these aliens were mortal and could be overcome. But this year, four more boats had come. This time they had defeated the Mayan city of Champoton, killing or driving out all the residents. And now their ships were headed north, toward Aztec territory.

Moctezuma II, Huey Tlatoani of Tenochtitlan, 1502-1520[60]

Who were these people? Moctezuma decided to find out. He called a group of his nobles and asked them to take gifts and swiftly travel to the coast. He'd heard these foreigners were interested in gold, so he told his emissaries to include some gold with the gifts. He instructed them to gather information on these men with the shining armor.

What Moctezuma may not have known is that two of these unusual strangers had been living in the Yucatan for the past seven

---

[60] https://commons.wikimedia.org/wiki/File:Moctezuma_Xocoyotzin_Newberry.jpg

years, victims of shipwreck. In 1511, a small Spanish ship was sailing from Panama to Santo Domingo when it wrecked on a sandbar. Sixteen men and two women climbed into the lifeboat and were carried north by a strong current to the Yucatan Peninsula. The dozen or so who were still alive were captured by the Mayans, who immediately sacrificed the captain and four others. The rest were consigned to slavery, and all but two died of disease or being overworked.

The two survivors, a Franciscan priest named Jerónimo de Aguilar and a sailor named Gonzalo Guerrero, managed to escape. But they were later captured by a rival Mayan tribe led by Chief Xamanzana. They lived with Xamanzana's tribe, learning the language and adapting to the new culture. Guerrero proved his worth as a fighter and was rewarded by becoming a war chief; he married a woman from Mayan nobility and began a family.

Six years later, Francisco Hernández de Córdoba petitioned the governor of Cuba for permission to head an expedition to search and explore new lands and resources. At least, that's the story he told Governor Diego Velázquez de Cuéllar. More likely, based on his personal writings, he and his friends needed more indigenous people as slaves for the mines and plantations of Cuba. Permission was granted, and Córdoba set sail from Cuba in 1517 with three ships and 110 men.

They found Mexico by accident after a strong storm blew them to the coast of Yucatan. From their ships, they were amazed to see a large urban area with masonry buildings. The Europeans had not yet encountered a sophisticated culture like this in the New World. On March 4, 1517, the Mayans approached their ships in ten *pirogues* (canoes) with sails and oars. The people smiled and appeared friendly, communicating through sign language that they would come the next day with more boats to help them to land.

They did return the next day, but this time they weren't friendly. Once the Spaniards arrived on shore, the Mayans ambushed them. The Spaniards desperately fought back with their crossbows and firearms and managed to escape back to their ships. They sailed on, but they had run out of water; eventually, thirst drove them to anchor and go ashore to find water. That night, the Mayan chief Mochcouoh attacked them, killing 57 of their men and capturing two more – who were probably sacrificed.

The remainder of the men made it back to the ship, but Córdoba's body was full of arrows, and several other men were mortally wounded. Five died on the voyage back; Córdoba and three more men died just after arriving in Cuba. Sixty-eight of the original 110 perished. Despite the massive casualties, the stories the survivors told of remarkable architecture comparable to European buildings piqued the interest of Governor Velázquez of Cuba. With such an advanced civilization, he strongly suspected this new land had gold and other wealth to be exploited.

Expedition of Juan De Grijalva, 1518[61]

Governor Velázquez wasted no time organizing another expedition. Juan de Grijalva sailed from Cuba in April 1518 with four ships and 170 men. Grijalva's orders were to get all the gold and silver he could acquire and bring it back to Velázquez. Grijalva sailed directly to Champoton, where the indigenous people had so mercilessly slaughtered Córdoba's men. Once again, the Mayans attacked, but Grijalva was prepared. This time the Spaniards won, and the Mayans fled.

Grijalva continued the voyage, sailing westward along the Yucatan peninsula, which the pilot insisted was an island. They arrived in the Tabasco region and were greeted by the local people. The Spaniards gifted them with colored glass beads, and the indigenous people reciprocated with gold necklaces and small gold figurines of lizards and birds. They told the Spaniards much

[61] Jaontiveros, CC BY-SA 4.0 <https://creativecommons.org/licenses/by-sa/4.0>, via Wikimedia Commons
https://en.wikipedia.org/wiki/Juan_de_Grijalva#/media/File:Expedici%C3%B3n_de_Grija lva_1518.svg

gold could be found in the west.

Grijalva continued to sail along the coastline when they saw men on the beach waving white banners, signaling them to come ashore. At this point, they were in the Boca del Rio area, in the Aztec territory – and almost due east from Tenochtitlan. They dropped anchor and went ashore, where they met with the people who had been waving the flags. They were Aztecs, the men Moctezuma had sent to find out more about these strange new people. The Aztec emissaries presented Grijalva with intricately carved gold items, while the conquistadors gave them glass beads. Grijalva took one of the Aztec men with him for a translator, who was baptized and given the name Francisco.

Grijalva claimed the territory for the crown and for Governor Velázquez, giving it the name of *New Spain* (which later came to be used for all the Spanish colonies in the Americas and the Pacific islands). By this point, his navigator had finally realized they had reached another continent –not just an island. When Grijalva arrived back in Cuba and gave Velázquez the gold items and his report, the governor began organizing yet another expedition.

Hernán Cortés[62]

Several months later, on October 23, 1518, Velázquez commissioned Hernán Cortés to lead a third expedition with the objective of exploring, spreading Christianity, and exchanging items with the local people. He did *not* give permission to establish a colony. Cortés set sail to Mexico on February 10, 1519, landing first at Cozumel in the Yucatan peninsula in Mayan territory. He had 11 ships, 109 sailors, 508 soldiers, 16 horses, 13 muskets, ten heavy artillery, four light artillery, and 32 crossbows. Cortés brought two translators: Francisco, the Aztec, and Melchor, a young Mayan man Córdoba had captured earlier. A conquistador on the expedition, Bernal Díaz del Castillo, later chronicled the conquest in *Historia Verdadera de la Conquista de la Nueva España (The True History of the Conquest of New Spain)*.

At Cozumel, Cortés heard about the two Spanish men living in the Yucatan since being shipwrecked eight years earlier. He sent messengers to them with ransom (more glass beads) for the Mayans. Father Jerónimo de Aguilar happily joined the conquistadors, serving as another translator, which worked out well since Melchor managed to slip away back to his own people two days later.

On the other hand, Gonzalo Guerrero had gone native with tattoos and piercings. The Spanish Inquisition was going on, and he could probably imagine being stretched on the rack and burned at the stake for abandoning his faith. When Father Aguilar tried to convince him to come with him, he replied (as recorded by Bernal Díaz del Castillo),

"Brother Aguilar, I am married and have three children, and they look on me as a cacique (lord) here, and captain in time of war. My face is tattooed, and my ears are pierced. What would the Spaniards say about me if they saw me like this? Go, and God's blessing be with you, for you have seen how handsome these children of mine are. Please give me some of those beads you have brought to give to them, and I will tell them that my brothers have sent them from my own country."

Cortés claimed Cozumel for the Spanish crown in March 1519 before setting sail again for the Tabasco region. A year earlier, the Maya-speaking Potoncan people had been cordial with Grijalva, but this time they attacked. Cortés defeated them, captured some of their men as prisoners, and claimed Tabasco for the crown. He was far outnumbered by the Potoncan, but his men fought with guns and cannons, and they terrified the indigenous people by fighting on horseback. They had never seen horses, and they thought the horse and man were all one diabolical creature.

After another failed attack, the Potoncan chiefs approached with gold and other gifts, apologizing for their inhospitable behavior. Cortés forgave them and accepted their gifts but ordered them to stop worshiping idols, which they agreed to do. Cortés asked the Potoncan people where they got their gold, and they told him from Culchua (Cholula) in the interior.

Doña Marina, known as La Malinche[63]

The Potoncan gave 20 women to the Spaniards, and they were baptized as Christians. One woman, Doña Marina, known as La Malinche, became Cortés's mistress and gave birth to his son Martin. She was a Nahuatl-speaking Aztec but had been given or sold to the Maya as a child and was fluent in both Nahuatl and Maya. Her knowledge of both languages made her invaluable as a translator. She didn't know Spanish yet, but Father Aguilar could ask her questions in Mayan, which she could then translate into the Aztecan Nahuatl.

On March 23, Cortés sailed to Veracruz. When he landed on Easter Sunday, he was approached by two Aztec emissaries,

Tendile and Pitalpitoque. Doña Marina and Father Aguilar translated their message: they came to welcome them and learn more about them. The Aztecs built a shelter for the Spaniards, served them a meal, and gave them gifts. They then sat down to paint pictures of Cortés, Father Aguilar, a dog, and a cannon, which they took back to Tenochtitlan to show Moctezuma.

Cortés gave them a demonstration of what his large and small canon, muskets, and crossbows could do. He gave them gifts of glass beads and other items, including a soldier's helmet that he asked them to return to him filled with gold dust. Just as he requested, about a week later, over a hundred men returned, with the helmet full of gold dust along with costly treasures of intricately carved gold and silver items. They also politely relayed Moctezuma's message that Cortés was *not* invited to travel to Tenochtitlan to see the emperor.

Cortés calmly expressed how essential it was that he meet Moctezuma. He gave more gifts for them to take back to the emperor as well as personal gifts for the ambassadors. He asked them to go back to their leader and convince Moctezuma to receive Cortés and his entourage. Shortly after, the emissaries returned, with more gifts of gold but with the emperor's final answer: Cortés was not allowed to see him, and that was the end of the discussion.

For the moment, Cortés turned to other matters. Governor Diego Velázquez of Cuba had only commissioned him to explore new territory, collect treasure, and convert the indigenous people to Catholicism, *not* establish any settlements. Daringly, Cortés colonized anyway, building Villa Rica de la Vera Cruz, which he declared independent of Cuba and subject only to King Charles, the Holy Roman Emperor and monarch of Spain.

Cortés resigned his commission from Velázquez, appointed some of his men for a town council, and then accepted their nomination to be governor-general of the new colony. He immediately sent a ship to Spain with the gold they had collected, accompanied by letters to the king. They described to King Charles all they had discovered and accomplished and their rationale for declaring independence from Cuba and Governor Velázquez.

Once that was all settled, it was time to march to Tenochtitlan! Ignoring Moctezuma's injunction *not* to come, Cortés left 100 men in Veracruz under his trusted captain Juan de Escalante, then marched into the interior in mid-August 1519 with the rest of his soldiers, 15 horsemen, and 15 cannons. Father Aguilar, Doña Marina, and the Aztec Francisco (who had learned Spanish in the past year) also came along; between these three interpreters, they were able to communicate with the various people they encountered.

Cempoala, in relation to Tenochtitlan and other Aztec cities[64]

They reached Cempoala, 25 miles inland, where they resided for two months with the Totonac people. About seventy years earlier, the Totonac people had been conquered by the Aztecs and were now a tributary city. They communicated to Cortés how they loathed their rulers, who demanded tribute payments twice a year, but even worse, they took their children for slave labor and sacrifices to Huitzilopochtli. The Totonac told Cortés they weren't the only disgruntled ones; many conquered city-states in the Aztec frontier were bitter toward Moctezuma.

Just as Cortés was developing friendly relations with the Totonac, he received word of an urgent situation back in the settlement of Villa Rica de la Vera Cruz. Some of the men he left there were loyal to Velázquez; they deplored Cortés' mutiny and how he had gone behind the governor's back to the King of Spain. They were scheming to send one of the ships to Cuba to warn Velázquez. On receiving this news, Cortés rushed back to Vera Cruz, rounded up the conspirators, and hanged the two ringleaders. He cut off the navigator's feet and whipped the rest of the men involved. He also scuttled all the ships, preventing anyone from traveling back to Cuba.

With order restored on the coast, Cortés headed back to Cempoala to resume his mission of diplomacy. With great finesse, he negotiated an alliance with the Totonacs of Cempoala; they agreed to join their warriors with his military force. While he was there, some Aztec emissaries arrived to collect the semi-annual tribute from Cempoala. Cortés cunningly persuaded the Totonac to refuse the tribute and imprison the Aztec delegates. He then freed Moctezuma's officials, feigning innocence in the matter and telling them to inform the emperor that he was willing to assist the Aztecs with the problem of rebellious cities. He skillfully instigated rebellion among the Totonac while assuring Moctezuma that he would ally with the Aztecs against the rebels.

With the Totonac warriors accompanying them, it was now time to resume the march toward Tenochtitlan. Their next challenge would be to subdue the fierce Tlaxcala, the incessant and unconquered enemies of the Aztec, and enlist them in the plan to overcome the mighty Aztec empire.

Chapter 10: The Massacre of Cholula

Tlaxcala lay ahead. What sort of welcome would the conquistadors receive? It was August of 1519, and Cortés and his men, joined by the Totonac warriors, resumed the march toward Tenochtitlan. They were approaching Tlaxcala, a loose confederacy of about 200 towns. Cortés had heard of the fierce reputation of these people but knew they were in constant war with Tenochtitlan. Would they be friendly or hostile?

The Tlaxcala people greeted the Spaniards in full battle array, ferociously fighting Cortés and his allies for three days. Despite their superior weaponry and armor, the Spaniards were succumbing to the brutal assault by the vicious warriors. Conquistador Bernal Díaz del Castillo wrote that the Spaniards were surrounded on every side and probably would have all been killed if the Tlaxcala had not had a sudden change of heart.

Whenever the Tlaxcala fought the frequent battles with the Aztecs, any warriors captured by the other side would be sacrificed to the gods. When they fought Cortés, he amazed them by what he did with the Tlaxcala he captured. The next day, he would return any prisoners-of-war, accompanied by messages of peace and reminders that he too was an enemy of the Aztecs. Eventually, the Tlaxcala realized that the Spaniards would be more useful as allies against the hated Aztecs. The elders convinced their war chief to end the fighting, and with Doña Marina and Father Aguilar translating, they negotiated a truce. Cortés stayed with the Tlaxcala for 20 days, plotting his next move.

Tlaxcala allied with Cortés; painting by unknown Aztec scribes[65]

The great city-state of Cholula lay ahead, with a population of 100,000. The Olmec were believed to have settled the area around 100 BC. Later, a group of Toltecs had migrated there after the fall of Tula. Cholula had become a dominant political force in the region, a center for trade, and a destination for religious pilgrimages. The largest pyramid in all of Mesoamerica stood there, and Cortés estimated 430 temples.

For years, Cholula had existed in an informal alliance with the Tlaxcala, 20 miles to the north. However, the Aztecs exerted great pressure; just two years earlier, Cholula had capitulated and allied with the Aztecs. This meant abandoning their alliance with the Tlaxcala, mortal enemies of the Aztecs; this turned out badly for them as Cortés was now headed their way with 1000 Tlaxcala warriors.

Cortés was still debating his options: whether to start an all-out war with the Aztecs or to continue with a diplomatic approach. Since Cholula was allied with the Aztecs, he had to tread carefully. Back in Tenochtitlan, Moctezuma was fully aware of Cortés's trek toward his kingdom and ordered the Cholula to stop the Spanish. Cortés and his men marched into Cholula with no resistance. However, the city leaders did not come out to greet them, and no one offered them food or water.

Cortés's indigenous friends were uneasy. The Totonac noted fortifications being constructed. Doña Marina took the opportunity to chat with the women of the city in her native Nahuatl language. She learned that the Cholula were planning to murder the Spaniards as they were sleeping. The Tlaxcala were thirsty for revenge against the Cholula for abandoning their alliance, and they kept pushing Cortés to launch an attack.

Finally, Cortés strode into the main temple and confronted the rulers of the city. Yes, they admitted, Moctezuma had ordered them to resist the Spaniards, but they hadn't followed through with his orders. Cortés considered what they were saying, and then he considered the battle preparations his allies had noticed and what Doña Marina had heard. Deciding he could not trust the people of Cholula, he gave the command for a preemptive strike.

The Spaniards and their indigenous allies rounded up the nobility and massacred them, killing 3000 people in three hours. They then set fire to the great, ancient city. This mass killing of a people who had not (yet) been aggressive sent shock waves through the Aztec Empire. Many cities considered it wise to align with the conquistadors rather than risk annihilation. It was at this point that Moctezuma gave in and invited Cortés to visit his city of Tenochtitlan.

The great day arrived. On November 8, 1519, ten months after sailing from Cuba, Cortés and his amassed forces marched unhindered over the causeway that led to Tenochtitlan. He had never seen a city this size. With an estimated population of 200,000, Tenochtitlan probably outnumbered most cities in Europe. An island city in Lake Texcoco, Tenochtitlan had a system of causeways connecting it to points on the mainland and a nearby island.

Moctezuma greets Cortés.[66]

On his litter decorated with feathers, Moctezuma was carried out on the causeway to meet Cortés, with his younger brother Cuitlahuac, his nephew Cacamatzin (co-regent of Texcoco, Tenochtitlan's ally), and his elders and war chiefs. The Aztec rulers were magnificently adorned with feathers, jewels, and gold. The people of the city stood along the causeway and in the high buildings of Tenochtitlan, watching the encounter. Moctezuma formally welcomed Cortés, who introduced himself as the representative of Queen Juana and her son, King Charles of Spain and Holy Roman Emperor.

An awkward moment ensued when Cortés attempted to greet Moctezuma with a customary Castilian embrace, quickly intercepted by Cuitlahuac and Cacamatzin, who made it clear that touching the emperor just wasn't done. Moctezuma eased Cortés's embarrassment by placing a chain of gold around his neck, followed by a garland of flowers. He then led Cortés to the shrine of the goddess Toci, where, according to the *Florentine Codex*, he said:

"My lord . . . you have come to your city; you have come to sit on your place, on your throne. Oh, it has been reserved to you for a small time, it was conserved by those who have gone, your substitutes . . .This is what has been told by our rulers . . .that you would come to ask for your throne, your place, that you would come here. Come to the land, come and rest; take possession of your royal houses, give food to your body."

---

[66]

https://commons.wikimedia.org/wiki/File:Cortez_and_Montezuma_at_Mexican_Temple. jpg

If Moctezuma really said this, he was acknowledging that Cortés was Quetzalcoatl, coming back in the year one reed, as Quetzalcoatl had said he would. If Moctezuma believed this, why did he resist Cortés all those months?

Moctezuma housed Cortés and his chief officers in the royal palace of his deceased father, Axayacatl. According to Bernal Díaz del Castillo, the emperor accepted Cortés as representative of the king of Spain, pledging his loyalty and saying, "As for your great King, I am in his debt and will give him of what I possess." Díaz said that in the palace, the Spaniards found the secret treasure room with golden plates and jewels. "The sight of all that wealth dumbfounded me."

Moctezuma's friendliness deteriorated when Cortés wanted to place a cross and an image of the Virgin Mary in the Templo Major, at the top of the grand pyramid. The emperor and his elders were infuriated, saying they could not offend their gods who gave them health, rain, crops, and victories in battle.

Six days after his arrival in Tenochtitlan, Cortés received the news of an attack on his new town of Villa Rica de la Vera Cruz, 200 miles away on the coast. Qualpopoca, Moctezuma's military commander, had led a force of Aztecs, killing Cortés's dear friend Juan de Escalante, who Cortés had left in charge of the settlement, along with six other Spaniards and many Totonacs.

In response to this treachery, Cortés, accompanied by Doña Marina, Father Aguilar, and five of his captains, accosted Moctezuma, ordering him to come quietly with them to their quarters in Axayacatl's palace. "Don't cry out! Don't raise a commotion! If you do, we will kill you immediately!" From that time on, Moctezuma lived under house arrest with Cortés in Axayacatl's palace.

Moctezuma continues to reign under house arrest.[67]

Despite his imprisonment, Moctezuma continued to oversee affairs of the empire, but under the control of Cortés. Moctezuma assured his people that he had willingly moved into Cortés's palace under the instructions of the gods. The Aztecs were doubtful; they also were growing increasingly perturbed by the presence of the 1000 Tlaxcala warriors in their city, their hated enemies, but allies of Cortés.

With Moctezuma in house arrest, Cortés sent his men to investigate sources of gold in the provinces and forced Moctezuma to pay tribute to the Spanish crown. The Spaniards melted down the gold figurines in the palace and formed gold bars. Cortés also built a Catholic altar in the Templo Major but left the Aztec idols.

The Aztecs were growing increasingly agitated; their priests were saying their gods were angry and would all leave unless the Aztecs killed the Spaniards or forced them back across the sea. Moctezuma warned the Spaniards that they were in mortal danger. With their emperor detained, most of the nobility were turning to his brother Cuitlahuac for leadership. But they hesitated to act without a direct order from Moctezuma. This unsettled state of affairs continued for five months.

67

https://commons.wikimedia.org/wiki/File:Los_informantes_de_moctezuma_Isidro_Mart%C3%ADnez_siglo_XIX.jpg

Then, in April 1520, Moctezuma alerted Cortés that his men had observed a fleet of 19 Spanish ships with 1400 soldiers landing on the coast. Under the command of Pánfilo de Narváez, the troops had been sent by Velázquez, Governor of Cuba, to arrest or kill Cortés for defying the governor's orders. On hearing this news, Cortés left some of his soldiers in Tenochtitlan under the command of Pedro de Alvarado, a seasoned conquistador, giving him strict instructions not to allow Moctezuma to escape.

Cortés and the rest of his troops marched quickly to Cempoala, where Narváez had set up camp. With a surprise night attack, Cortés captured Narváez and convinced the rest of the Spanish soldiers to come over to his side. He told them of the gold they had acquired and promised to make them all rich. With his new recruits, Cortés marched back to Tenochtitlan with 1300 soldiers, 96 horses, and 2000 Tlaxcala warriors.

Cortés was horrified to return to a chaotic situation in Tenochtitlan. In his absence, Alvarado and his fellow conquistadors had killed hundreds of unarmed Aztec nobles in an unprovoked attack, which became known as the *Massacre in the Great Temple*. Cortés interrogated Alvarado and his men and also questioned the Aztecs to try to piece together what had happened on May 22, 1520.

Pedro de Alvarado.[68]

While Cortés was gone, Moctezuma had requested permission to celebrate the important festival of Toxcatl, which honored Tezcatlipoca, a chief Aztec god (you might remember him as the god who tricked Quetzalcoatl, leading to his downfall). Alvarado gave permission, with the stipulation of no human sacrifices and that none of the participants could carry weapons. Normally, a young man who had been impersonating Tezcatlipoca through the past year was sacrificed at this festival, but apparently, the Aztecs decided to follow Alvarado's orders.

About 1000 Aztec noblemen had gathered in the grounds surrounding the great temple, naked but draped in jewels, gold, and silver and wearing elaborate feather headdresses. Drums beat loudly, accompanied by the shrill sound of wind instruments. The men danced in circles, holding hands, singing along with the musicians, praising Tezcatlipoca, and asking him to provide water, grain, good health, and victory. Everyone was enjoying the festival, dancing, and singing, with the music roaring like waves.

Suddenly, Alvarado and the Spanish soldiers appeared, blocking all the exits with ten or twelve men. They then turned on the musicians and dancers, rushing toward the man playing the drums and cutting off both his arms and then his head with such force that it sailed through the air. With no remorse or pity, they brutally slew the celebrants, stripping off their gold and jewels. They sliced off heads and arms, stabbed the men in the gut, so their entrails flowed out, and dashed some to the ground, so their heads were crushed.

The Aztecs ran to the exits but were met and killed by the laughing Spaniards guarding the way out. Some lay down, pretending to be dead, as the blood of the dead ran like water over them, and the stench of entrails filled the air. Others climbed over the walls and screamed to those outside, "Come quickly! Come with spears and shields! Our warriors have been murdered! They have been annihilated!" The Mexica quickly stormed the temple with spears, bows, and javelins. They furiously hurled a barrage of yellow javelins at the Spaniards.

Different explanations were given for the motivation of the massacre. Alvarado told Cortés he had received information that the Aztecs were planning to attack the Spaniards during the festival, so the slaughter was a preemptive strike. Some said they intervened to prevent a human sacrifice, although most of the Spaniards said the Aztecs were only singing and dancing. The Aztecs felt that the Spaniards had attacked the noblemen to steal their gold and jewels.

By the time Cortés got back to Tenochtitlan, the Aztecs had blockaded the palace where the Spaniards were staying and where Moctezuma was still being held. They had elected Cuitlahuac, Moctezuma's brother, as their new tlatoani, renouncing Moctezuma. Somehow, in the confusion and chaos, Moctezuma was killed – a mysterious death.

Moctezuma II struck by stones.[69]

In the Spanish account, Cortés desperately tried to restore order by commanding Moctezuma to come out to the balcony of the palace and speak to the people, asking them to allow the Spaniards to leave the city peacefully and return to the coast. The people scorned his words and threw rocks and darts at him, which

[69] https://commons.wikimedia.org/wiki/File:Stories_of_American_explorers_-_a_historical_reader_(1906)_(14592623230).jpg

the Spaniards tried to deflect with their shields. Diaz reported that three rocks hit Moctezuma, one on the head. He refused treatment and died three days later. The Aztecs said that Moctezuma was strangled by the Spaniards. At this point, the renounced emperor no longer served a purpose for either side.

The Spaniards and their indigenous allies were in a perilous state, running out of water, food, and gunpowder. Cortés requested a one-week ceasefire from the Aztecs, promising that the Spaniards would return all the treasures they had stolen and would leave the city peacefully. Instead of waiting a week, the Spaniards attempted to slip out of the city that night.

Tenochtitlan had multiple causeways running from the island to the mainland or adjoining islands. Each causeway had several gaps covered by bridges that would be removed at night. The Spaniards constructed a portable bridge to take with them, so they could cross those spans. They packed up the gold and other treasures they had accumulated and allowed the Spanish soldiers to take what they wanted. Many of the soldiers filled their pockets and were draped with heavy gold and jewels.

On July 1, 1520, Cortés and his men slipped out of the palace at night, heading for the Tlacopan causeway. A rainstorm aided their escape, blurring visibility and keeping most people indoors. They made it to the causeway and placed their portable bridge over the first gap, but suddenly an alarm went up in the city. A woman drawing water had seen them, as had a priest standing on top of the great pyramid. They hurried across the first span on the portable bridge, but the men had difficulty pulling it back up.

Suddenly, they were attacked from behind and from hundreds of canoes in the water. The Spaniards rushed as fast as possible across the causeway, but they were hindered by the great chests of treasure they were carrying. Some of the soldiers who were weighed down by the heavy gold and jewels in their pockets and belts and around their necks lost their balance and fell into the water, where they drowned.

La Noche Triste, the Night of Weeping.[70]

Cortés and his chief officers were on horseback and had leaped over the open spans of the causeway. But the infantry on foot were desperately fighting the Aztec hordes while attempting to cross the spans. Much of the gold and jewels they had carried out of the city was dropped on the road or fell into the water. Unaware of their plight, Cortés and his horsemen had charged ahead and reached

[70]

https://commons.wikimedia.org/wiki/File:ROHM_D273_Aztecs_continue_their_assault_against_the_conquistadors.jpg the mainland.

When Cortés turned around, he realized the wretched situation his men were in, as he watched wounded and bloodied Spaniards and Tlaxcala limping in. He turned and rode back out on the causeway, weeping as he realized the extent of the slaughter. Cortés himself was wounded, all the artillery was lost. As many as 1000 Spaniards were killed and at least 2000 of their indigenous allies. Some of the Aztec royals who were supportive of the Spaniards also died: Montezuma's son Chimalpopoca, the Tepanec prince Tlaltecatzin, and King Cacamatzin of Texcoco with his three sisters and two brothers. This dark, rainy night of horror was remembered as *La Noche Triste,* the night of weeping.

Chapter 11: The Fall of Tenochtitlan

With the Aztecs in hot pursuit, the Tlaxcala guided the Spaniards around Lake Zumpango, north of Lake Texcoco. Three-quarters of the Spanish conquistadors had perished, and most of the remaining survivors were wounded. Cortés had suffered a head wound but gave orders to press on to a safer place. He later recorded these events in his letters to King Charles, the *Cartas y Relaciones de Hernan Cortés al Emperador Carlos V.*

Guided by their allies, the Spaniards stumbled toward the safety of Tlaxcala lands, carrying their wounded on their backs or on the horses. They constantly fended off skirmishes from bands of Aztecs, who killed one of their horses; starving, they ate the animal, not even leaving his skin. After several days, exhausted and suffering from their wounds, they made it to the town of Otumba, about 50 miles from Tenochtitlan.

The Aztecs swarmed on them in Otumba with such a violent attack that they thought their last day had come. Bernal Díaz del Castillo wrote that the Castilian calvary brought victory in the desperate battle. Time after time, the Spaniards on horseback broke through the Aztec ranks, striking them down right and left. The Aztecs had never experienced a calvary charge. Even so, an estimated horde of 40,000 Aztecs threatened to overwhelm the Spaniards.

Battle of Otumba, by Manuel Rodriguez de Guzman.[71]

Cortés's battle strategy also helped win the day. He instructed the troops to focus on the Aztec leaders and captains. Recognizing an Aztec war chief from his distinctive armor and headdress, Cortés's men separated the warriors from their chief, while a conquistador slew the chief and delivered his battle-standard to Cortés. With their leader dead, the Aztecs faltered, and the Tlaxcala and Spaniards were able to rout them. The war of Otumba was won, but all the 440 surviving conquistadors and countless Tlaxcala were wounded.

The weary victors stood on the hill near Otumba, looking at the mountains in the distance, which their allies told them was Tlaxcala land, where they would find safety and rest. Finally, one week after leaving Tenochtitlan, they reached safety in the town of Gualipan. The people received them with kindness, tending their wounds and providing food and water.

Cortés and his army remained there for three days, meeting with the Tlaxcala nobles from around the region. They promised Cortés they would fight to the death with him against their enemies, as they already had proved they would. In return, they

---

[71] https://commons.wikimedia.org/wiki/File:Manuel_Rodriguez_de_Guzman_-_Battle_of_Otumba_-_1983.591_-_Museum_of_Fine_Arts.jpg

asked for the city of Cholula, an equal share of the plunder, and exemption from future tribute. Once the alliance was renewed, the Tlaxcala told the Spaniards to consider themselves at home and to rest and recover.

For the next few months, the Spaniards rested and recouped, preparing for their next assault. Everything may have seemed bleak for the Spaniards after *La Noche Triste*, but Cortés was determined to defy all odds to reach his goal of conquering the Aztec empire. Reinforcements came from the Villa Rica de la Vera Cruz settlement on the coast, along with the fortuitous arrival of supply ships from Cuba (intended for Narváez) and Spain, bringing more men and horses.

During this time, Cortés formed alliances with the cities of the Acolhua people on the eastern shores of Lake Texcoco. King Ixtlilxochitl, one of the three vice-regents of Texcoco and an enemy of Moctezuma II, sent emissaries to Cortés, offering his troops in the siege of Tenochtitlan. In return, he asked assistance in overcoming the other two vice-regents of Texcoco. These alliances were indispensable for allowing access to Lake Texcoco, not to mention providing more warriors and laborers. One by one, the allied forces worked their way along both sides of the lake and to the east, negotiating treaties with cities, including Huexotzinco, Chalco, Tlamanalco, Xochimilco, Otomi, and Tepanec.

Meanwhile, in September 1520, the Aztecs were struck with smallpox, lasting almost three months. This diminished their population and kept their attention off attacking the Spaniards or defending their city-states around the lake. Among those who died was Cuitlahuac, Moctezuma's brother and the new emperor. He was succeeded by his cousin Cuauhtémoc, the last Aztec emperor. In the spring, the Aztecs rallied enough to launch four attacks on the Spaniards and lost each time.

Since Tenochtitlan was an island city, and the causeways had proved a major complication, Cortés hit on the ingenious idea of building a fleet of 13 small and shallow brigantines for navigating around Lake Texcoco. He set his master carpenter/boat builder Martin Lopez to work, using rigging, hardware, and sails salvaged from the scuttled boats. His master plan was to carry the disassembled brigantines overland and put them together near the lake.

While his men and allies went to work cutting lumber and building the small ships, Cortés set out on a scouting mission around Lake Texcoco and the adjoining lakes. After surveying the land and taking note of how best to invade Tenochtitlan by land and water, Cortés built a 12-foot-deep canal on the eastern side of the lake extending toward where they were building the brigantines. They still had to lug all the pieces of the ships for over a mile. It took 50 days and 8000 people to build the parts of the ships, haul them to the canal, assemble, and then launch them, using labor from the people of Texcoco.

The ships were launched in the canal with sails and oars and cannons on April 28, 1521. Cortés reviewed his Spanish troops, counting 86 horses with riders, 118 archers and musketeers, over 700-foot soldiers with swords and shields, three heavy iron cannons, and fifteen small copper cannons. Each brigantine held 25 men: 12 rowers, 12 crossbow archers and musketeers, and a captain. He rallied the troops by telling them to take fresh courage and renewed spirits since God was leading them to victory, which should inspire them with courage and zeal to conquer or die.

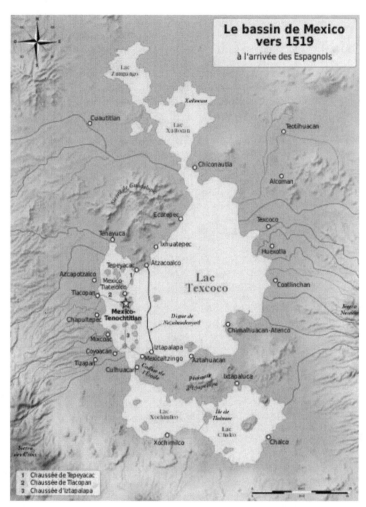

Lake Texcoco with adjoining lakes and nearby territories in as it appeared in 1519. Tenochtitlan is on the western shore connected by causeways to the mainland.[72]

The joint forces of 20,000 indigenous warriors allied with Cortés's men and ships, horses, and cannons sent shock waves across the lake. One division headed to the island of Chapultepec to cut off the aqueduct that provided fresh water to Tenochtitlan. The ships and other two land forces targeted the city of Iztapalapa,

[72] File:Lago de Texcoco-posclásico.png: YavidaxiuFile:Valley of Mexico c.1519-fr.svg: historicair 13:51, 11 September 2007 (UTC)derivative work: Sémhur, CC BY-SA 4.0 <https://creativecommons.org/licenses/by-sa/4.0>, via Wikimedia Commons https://commons.wikimedia.org/wiki/File:Basin_of_Mexico_1519_map-fr.svg

just across the causeway from Tenochtitlan, giving them a chance to try out the brigantines. They were able to surround the city and score what Cortés called "a most brilliant victory."

As the brigantines approached Iztapalapa, some people had run up the mountain next to the city and sent smoke signals, alerting Tenochtitlan. Suddenly, an immense fleet of about 500 canoes charged toward Iztapalapa. When they got close to the ships, they suddenly stopped and floated silently, perhaps wondering how the ships got into the lake and what they were able to do.

In a few minutes, a wind arose, blowing from behind the ships. Cortés instantly gave orders to his commanders to sail toward the canoes, breaking through them and pursuing them. The Aztecs fled as fast as they could paddle, but the wind pushed the brigantines, and they bore down through the midst of the canoes, breaking them and throwing the Aztecs into the water. They followed the canoes for three leagues until those who were left took refuge in the city of Tenochtitlan.

A division of Cortés's army led by Pedro de Alvarado was posted on the hills of Coyoacan, just south of Tenochtitlan, watching and cheering when they saw how well the 13 brigantines performed and how fast they cut through the water. Alvarado's men had just severed the aqueduct carrying fresh water to Tenochtitlan, as thermal springs around the city made the water brackish. Now, this contingent headed for the island city.

A great battle began on the causeway, but this time the Spaniards had the advantage. The brigantines surrounding the city hindered the Aztecs from defending the causeway with their canoes. When Aztecs from other cities around the lake launched a rear attack from the mainland, Cortés ordered some of the calvary to guard the causeway and 10,000 indigenous allies to guard the shore along the lake opposite of Tenochtitlan. At this point, Alvarado's division arrived, fending off the Aztecs who had launched the rear attack and cutting through the causeways to the city. This allowed the brigantines to access the water all around the city and also cut land access to the city, making it difficult for food and reinforcements to get into the city.

Siege of Tenochtitlan, showing battles on the causeways and in the water with the brigantines and Aztec canoes. The city is not to scale; it was far larger than in this painting.[73]

The Spaniards had control of the causeway with their thousands of allies from Tlaxcala and other city-states. They attempted to enter the city, but the Mexica were positioned on the rooftops, shooting arrows at anyone who neared the perimeter. Cortés decided to burn down the houses so that the Mexica wouldn't have the rooftop advantage. Using the brigantines, they burned down many houses and towers around the edge of the city.

Tenochtitlan had a network of canals, like Venice, and the brigantines sailed right into the city through the canals, using their cannons to demolish houses and other buildings. Cortés and his forces fought their way into the middle of the city, setting fire to the temples of the Templo Major religious center. Finally, after a long day of fighting, it began to get dark, so Cortés assembled his forces to return to camp.

As they were retreating, throngs of Mexica pursued them furiously, attacking their rearguard. The cavalry charged the Mexica, impaling them with their lances. Still, with howls and screams, they continued coming, raging in dismay to see their former Aztec allies – the Texcoco, Chalca, and Otomi – burning

<hr />

[73] https://commons.wikimedia.org/wiki/File:The_Conquest_of_Tenochtitlan.jpg

their city and fighting against them, taunting the Mexica by calling out the names of their provinces.

In their counterattack, the Aztecs killed about 40 Spaniards and over 1000 indigenous allies. They captured some of the Spaniards alive and dragged them to the top of the tall towers in the city center, cutting open their chests and pulling out their beating hearts to offer to their gods. The Spaniards watched in horror from the perimeter.

Cortés's initial plan was to retreat to their camp on the mainland at night and make forays into the city during the day, gradually taking ground. This proved problematic, as once they left the city at night, the Aztecs would construct barricades and cover the causeways with rocks and stones to block the horses. Cortés then set up camp on the causeways, ready to fight if the Aztecs ventured out. Each morning, the Spanish forces would invade the city, gradually gaining ground.

Unable to get through the causeways, the Aztecs outside the city began smuggling in food via canoe until Cortés ordered two of the brigantines to stand guard at night. The people inside the city were running out of food and clean water. In desperation, they began drinking the brackish water in the polluted canals, which gave them dysentery. Thousands were dying from hunger, thirst, and illness.

Several more Aztec cities along the lakeshore surrendered, including Iztapalapa, Churubusco, Coluacan, and Mixquic. One month into the siege, over 20,000 of the indigenous allies returned home, frightened by a prophecy from the Aztec shamans that the Spaniards would be dead in ten days. Only about 200 of the Texcoco noblemen remained loyal through this time. Twelve days later, realizing the prophecy was false, the warriors from Tlaxcala, Cholula, Tepanec, and other tribes returned.

Forty-five days had now passed since the Spaniards first launched their brigantines and laid siege to Tenochtitlan. Cortés resolved that they needed to press harder, leveling the city to the ground, neighborhood by neighborhood, until no place was left for the Mexica to hide. On that day, he mustered over 150,000 warriors and accomplished the destruction of much of the city.

Conquistadors and indigenous allies.[74]

Cortés next ordered all three divisions to invade the city from three different points, working their way toward the marketplace in the center. Alvarado's division got there first, stopping to ascend the pyramid, set fire to Huitzilopochtli's temple, and plant the Spanish flags. Four days later, the other two divisions, led by Cortés and Sandoval, fought their way to the center.

Cortés climbed to the top of the highest tower in the Templo Major complex. From there, he realized that about seven-eighths of the city had fallen, and the rest of the population was squeezed into the remaining area. The people were starving, eating the roots

[74]https://commons.wikimedia.org/wiki/File:ROHM_D201_The_conquistadors_enter_ten ochtitlan_to_the_sounds_of_martial_music.jpg

and bark of the trees. Distraught, Cortés ordered his troops to stop fighting, offering terms of peace. But the Aztecs declared they would never surrender and would die fighting.

The next day they reentered the city to find the streets full of women and children, dying of hunger and sickness. Cortés ordered his men not to harm them. The Aztec men remained sequestered in their holdout and did not fight that day.

The following morning, the Spaniards and their allies assembled at daybreak, with the brigantines floating in the water just offshore from the section where the Aztecs were sequestered. When they heard a musket shot, the land troops were to invade that last holdout, driving the Aztecs toward the water and the brigantines. Everyone was told to keep a lookout for Emperor Cuauhtémoc; if they could capture him alive, the war would be over.

At that moment, a multitude of men, women, and children flooded out of the remaining buildings, stumbling and barely alive, surrendering and seeking refuge with the Spaniards. Cortés wrote that he was unable to hold back the Tlaxcala from attacking the defenseless and suffering people. Cortés wrote to King Charles,

"We had more trouble in preventing our allies from killing with such cruelty than we had in fighting the enemy. For no race, however savage, has ever practiced such fierce and unnatural cruelty as the natives of these parts . . . I also charged the captains of our allies to forbid, by all means in their power, the slaughter of these fugitives; yet all my precautions were insufficient to prevent it, and that day more than 15,000 lost their lives."

As the Tlaxcala were brutally massacring the population, hundreds of canoes poured into the lake out of the remaining section of city. The brigantines broke into the midst of the canoes, and the captain of one ship noticed several canoes with people in regal dress. It was Emperor Cuauhtémoc, accompanied by family! He was instantly seized and delivered to Cortés.

The war was over with the capture of the emperor on August 13, 1521 - after a siege of over three months. Cuauhtémoc walked up and laid his hand on Cortés's dagger, telling Cortés to strike him to the heart. Cortés told him, "You have defended your capital like a brave warrior. A Spaniard knows how to respect valor, even in an enemy."

For the next three days, even after the surrender, the Tlaxcala looted the city, raped the women, and slaughtered the civilians, not even sparing the children. The citizens who were able to escape were permitted to settle in Tlatelolco. When the Spaniards did not find the gold and other loot they were expecting, they tortured Cuauhtémoc, broiling the soles of his feet over red-hot coals until he confessed to dumping his gold and jewels into the lake.

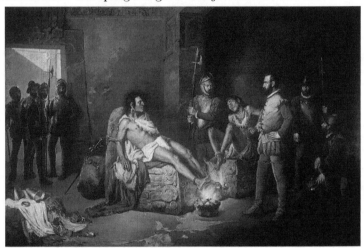

Torture of Cuauhtémoc. By Leandro Izaguirre[75]

Cuauhtémoc, baptized as Fernando Cuauhtémotzín, settled in Tlatelolco for four years, keeping the nominal title of tlatoani, although no longer the sovereign ruler of the empire. Then, in 1525, Cortés took Cuauhtémoc and several of his nobles with him on an expedition to Honduras, fearing that Cuauhtémoc would revolt while he was gone. On the expedition, Cortés executed the last Aztec emperor by hanging, charging his alleged conspiracy to murder Cortés and his crew.

[75] https://commons.wikimedia.org/w/index.php?curid=21809420

Chapter 12: The Founding of New Spain

The Spaniards who conquered the Aztec Empire were primarily interested in three things: God, glory, and gold. Perhaps that order should be reversed. They *said* their chief objective was winning the indigenous people to the Catholic faith, but their actions (like abject cruelty and sexual exploitation of indigenous women) sent mixed messages.

Having just won their country back from Islamic rule, the church in Spain was reasserting itself as the bulwark of Catholicism. The rulers of Spain were adamant that the Catholic faith be spread in their new colonies. Consequently, Catholic friars usually accompanied the conquistadors on military campaigns, ministering to the soldiers and setting up missions for the local people as soon as an area was conquered.

The conquistadors' desire for glory and gold, along with their distance from Spain, engendered an independent and sometimes insubordinate mindset, as when Cortés defied the orders of the governor of Cuba. As New Spain rose from the ashes of the Aztec Empire, the Spanish monarchy realized they needed to rein in the conquistadors and establish a system of checks and balances. This led to the *Council of the Indies*, followed by the *Real Audiencia de México and* the *Viceroyalty of New Spain.*

King Charles of Spain established the *Council of the Indies* in 1524 as a governing body with supreme authority over all of Spain's colonies in the Americas and the Pacific islands. Four years later, he created the first *Audiencia* (high court) of Mexico to bring

Cortés under the oversight and control of the monarchy. It was headed by Nuño Beltrán de Guzmán, who ruthlessly tortured and executed the Tarascan Emperor Tangaxuan, even though he had peacefully surrendered to Spain. Rather than asserting royal authority over the conquistadors, Guzmán abused his position to build his own wealth and power. In 1530 the Audiencia was dissolved, and eventually, Guzmán was arrested for treason and atrocities against the indigenous people and sent to Spain in shackles.

Viceroy don Antonio de Mendoza and Tlaxcala Indians battle with the Caxcanes in the Mixtón war, 1541–42 in Nueva Galicia.[76]

King Charles appointed Don Antonio de Mendoza as the first Viceroy of New Spain (the king's *living image* in Mexico). Mendoza arrived in Mexico in 1537 to exercise authority on behalf of the king, deftly yet diplomatically curbing the power and ambition of Cortés and other conquistadors. He successfully stabilized the flare-ups between the conquistadors and the indigenous people and helped found the first two universities in Mexico: the College at Santa Cruz and the Royal and Pontifical University of Mexico.

For the most part, the leaders of New Spain maintained the preexisting internal structure of the Aztec Empire. Under Spanish rule, these city-states largely continued with either their own indigenous nobility or Spanish governors, paying tribute to the Spanish crown and continuing with their previous landholding and economic structure.

The Spanish crown rewarded the conquistadors with grants of entire indigenous communities in the *Encomienda* system of labor. The indigenous people were not slaves, per se, but working in their community as they previously had in the *calpolli* towns of Mesoamerican civilizations. In this system, each calpolli had a *tecutli* (landlord) governing the region and distributing land to the commoners. The farmers worked their designated land, and farmers and tradespeople would pay tribute to their landlord with a portion of their crops or their manufactured goods. The Encomienda system built on the pre-existing system, except now the tecutli was a Spanish lord. Some of these lords gained notoriety for the horrific abuse of their laborers.

The Aztecs had a system for slavery that included conquered people or captives from war campaigns (those who didn't get sacrificed, enslaving men, women, and children – and branding them on the cheek. Cortés owned a few hundred slaves who worked the gold mines. Slavery of the indigenous people of Mexico ended in the mid-1500s, replaced by black slaves from Africa.

When establishing the new colony of Mexico, Spain didn't send over shiploads of families to colonize the land. It was often just the conquistadors and the missionary friars, especially in the early years. The colonies in Mesoamerica comprised indigenous people with a few Spanish leaders and Catholic friars. The Franciscan (and later Dominican, Augustine, and Jesuit) friars set up missions in existing and new communities of indigenous people.

The Spaniards developed unused land areas into large cattle *ranchos* and plantations (*haciendas*), growing cash crops like banana, cotton, and coffee. These small agricultural communities often grew into towns and cities, such as Veracruz and Guadalajara. The colonists also built new Spanish cities over former great cities of the Aztecs and other indigenous people. For instance, today's sprawling Mexico City sits right on top of what was once Tenochtitlan.

Remains of the Templo Mayor of Tenochtitlan surrounded by modern Mexico City.[77]

When the Aztec Empire was replaced by New Spain, the everyday life of the indigenous people changed significantly in some areas, while other aspects of their culture continued as before. Most continued to speak Nahuatl, which had been the common language of the empire. A few of the indigenous nobility learned Spanish to communicate with the Spaniards. Spanish was mostly used for administrative affairs in the early colonial settlements.

The Spanish friars believed that the people would be more receptive to the Christian faith if it were taught in their own language. To make that happen, the friars first learned Nahuatl (and other languages) and then set about devising written Nahuatl with the Latin alphabet (the same alphabet used in Spanish, English, and most European languages). They then taught some of the indigenous boys and young men to read the Nahuatl language, so they could learn basic Christian teachings and read the parts of the Bible the friars were translating.

Santiago Mission in Jalpan, built in 16ᵗʰ century in Sierra Gorda, Querétaro, Mexico[78]

At first, few people of the former Aztec Empire learned Spanish. For one thing, most of the common people had no schools, so there was no venue for teaching a new language. The Spanish colonies even allowed documents, like wedding and birth certificates and title deeds, to be written in Nahuatl. It wasn't until 1714 that King Philip V of Spain ordered everyone in the Mexican colony to learn Spanish. In 1770, King Charles III mandated Spanish as the only authorized language for education, administration, and documentation (no more birth certificates in Nahuatl).

Franciscan friars learned the indigenous languages and spent much time studying the culture of the people. Through understanding the people's worldview, the friars felt they could contextualize the Gospel, presenting it in a culturally relevant way. They would transcribe their interviews with the indigenous people on their history and culture for hours on end. Some of these accounts have survived, providing us with a wealth of information on the Aztecs and other indigenous cultures in the pre-Columbian period.

---

[78] Tobiascontreras, CC BY-SA 3.0 <https://creativecommons.org/licenses/by-sa/3.0>, via Wikimedia Commons
https://commons.wikimedia.org/wiki/File:Misi%C3%B3n_Santiago_de_Jalpan.jpg

Dominican friars began arriving in 1525 but questioned the efforts of the Franciscans in working within the culture of the local people. The Franciscans tended to believe that all cultures are a mixture of good and evil and that one can retain the good aspects and connect those to the teaching of faith. They didn't try to overturn the people's cultures; they just tried to root out the bad parts (like human sacrifice).

Many Dominicans believed that the pagan cultures were inherently evil – even their languages were evil; their approach was to convert the people and learn Spanish and an entirely new way of life. Priceless pre-Columbian artifacts and native codices (manuscripts) were destroyed in this quest to root out the old culture. When the people hesitated, the Dominicans complained before the Council of the Indies that the indigenous people were incapable of learning, rejected all forms of progress, and were worthy only of slavery.

Franciscan Friar Jacobo de Testera and others in his order rose to the defense of the Aztec tribes, pointing out that if they were incapable of learning, they could not have developed the sophisticated Aztec culture, with huge cities, breath-taking architecture, and exquisite craftsmanship. The first ecclesiastical council of New Spain agreed the indigenous people could understand and embrace the faith and were rational beings capable of self-government.

Most friars working on converting the Mexica and other peoples were initially pleased to see how quickly the people agreed to receive baptism into the Catholic faith. They later discovered that they had simply added Jesus and the Virgin Mary to their pantheon of gods. In the polytheistic Mesoamerican mind, these were nothing more than additional deities. For the past hundred years, the Aztecs permitted the people they conquered to continue worshiping all their other gods if they added Huitzilopochtli as their *primary god.* They didn't perceive the need to discard their gods. Syncretism (blending two or more religions) haunted the church's efforts through the centuries, and to this very day, many people groups in Mexico practice both Catholicism and their ancient religions.

The friars were divided on whether they should baptize the people first and then teach them the faith, or only baptize people who had been taught the faith and understood and received it as their own. Catholic doctrine teaches that the Holy Spirit indwells a person at their baptism (usually as infants) and initiates faith. Many friars believed that without baptizing the people first, they couldn't comprehend the teaching of faith. Thus, mass baptisms (sometimes thousands at a time) were conducted for people who had no clue of anything regarding Christianity.

Franciscan Fray Bernardino de Sahagún.[79]

Regardless of when baptism took place, the friars from all the orders agreed that the people needed to be taught the basics of the Christian faith. Fray Alonso de Molina translated the *Doctrina Christiana* (*Christian Doctrine*) in 1546, compiled a Spanish-

[79] AnonymousUnknown author, CC BY-SA 4.0
<https://creativecommons.org/licenses/by-sa/4.0>, via Wikimedia Commons
https://commons.wikimedia.org/wiki/File:Bernardino_de_Sahag%C3%BAn.jpg

Nahuatl confessional in 1569, and a dictionary in 1571. Franciscan Fray Bernardino de Sahagún translated a catechism, the Psalms, and the Gospels into Nahuatl, and wrote the *Florentine Codex*, which presented the history and culture of the Aztecs.

Missionary-friars went about systematically building missions throughout the country. They would have a church building for worship, an educational section for teaching basics of the faith, and living quarters for the friars. The missions also served as community centers, with shops and wineries selling products the friars produced from their farming and industry. The friars also sometimes served as government officials for their area and often were staunch defenders of basic human rights for the indigenous people, although some were guilty of abuse.

Education took a downward spiral following Spanish colonization. The Aztecs were one of the few ancient civilizations with mandatory education for both boys and girls. At age 14, boys would begin attending a *calmecac* (school for nobility) or a *telpochcalli* (school for common people). The calmecac trained teens to be administrators, priests, teachers, healers, or codex painters; subjects included history, religious rituals, reading and writing, the Aztec ideographic writing, the calendar system, astronomy, statesmanship, and theology. The commoner's school (telpochcalli) taught military fighting, history, and religion – along with a skill or trade like agriculture, craftwork, metalworking, or pottery. Teenage girls learned religious rituals, dancing, singing, household skills, and craftwork. Some girls were trained in midwifery and healing.

At first, nothing was done in the Spanish colonies for educating children, aside from some religious training. In 1536, the Franciscans collaborated with Viceroy Don Antonio de Mendoza to establish the Colegio de Santa Cruz de Tlatelolco to train indigenous young men in the priesthood. This was the first institution of higher education in the Mexico of New Spain. Boys were chosen from the former ruling families of the Aztec empire and taught Spanish, Latin, Nahuatl (reading), music, logic, philosophy, and medicine.

The college failed to produce indigenous priests, partly because the Dominicans pushed through legislation forbidding the native population from ordination to the priesthood. It did, however, produce young men with advanced language skills who provided huge aid to the Franciscans in their evangelization efforts and in recording indigenous history and culture.

The school of San José de los Naturales was founded by the Franciscans in Mexico City to train boys in trades and crafts. The Franciscans also trained scribes in the Nahuatl language to create documents such as wills, petitions to the crown, bills of sale, censuses, and other local legal records. Aside from these efforts, most of the population was unschooled and illiterate. Few girls were educated except a handful in convent schools, training to be nuns. Girls from elite families received private tutoring.

Mexica woman cooking maize, from Florentine Codex.[80]

Those who love Mexican food will be interested to know that it hasn't changed significantly from Aztec days. The Aztec diet was mostly plant-based: maize (corn), beans, tomatoes, guacamole, squash, and chilis. They made tortillas and tamales – just like today – and would occasionally have fish or wild game. Some areas raised domesticated dogs for consumption.

The biggest change the Spaniards brought to the Aztec diet was dairy products and meat from domesticated animals, like cattle, chickens, pigs, ducks, and goats. The Aztecs didn't have farm

---

[80] https://commons.wikimedia.org/wiki/File:Blowing_on_maize.jpg

animals, so this was something new for them. They started making cheese from cow and goat milk, and that's why our tacos have cheese on them today! The Spaniards also brought banana plants, sugar cane, rice, olive oil, garlic, and other spices. The Spanish friars tried to suppress the use of hallucinogenic mushrooms used by the Aztecs in their religious ceremonies, but that quietly persisted into modern times.

The institution of marriage saw changes following Spanish control, especially among the nobility. In Aztec culture, men married in their early twenties, and women married around age 16. Parents arranged marriages, sometimes using a matchmaker. Young people from elite families could only marry other nobles and were often pawns in their families' schemes to create masterful alliances with other important families.

Even though their marriages were arranged, couples had a measure of autonomy in that when their first son was born, they could decide if they wanted to remain in the marriage or go their separate ways. Adultery was punishable by death in the city-state of Texcoco and some other cities. Ordinary Aztec men usually had just one wife, but higher-class men could have multiple wives and concubines. The tlatoani and especially the Huey Tlatoani were known for harems of many wives and concubines.

When the Spaniards converted the Aztecs to Catholicism, they forbade polygamy. They forced the tlatoani of Chalco and other nobility to choose one wife to keep and abandon the rest. Secondary wives and their children had no legal recognition in the new Spanish rule. The children were considered illegitimate and disinherited from property and rank.

The Spaniards didn't practice what they preached when it came to monogamy. Thousands of Spaniards – mostly men – flooded New Spain in the next two centuries. Many were single, and very few of the married men brought their wives and children. The single men often married the indigenous women or lived out-of-wedlock with them. The married men took mistresses from among the Aztec women. A case in point is Cortés himself.

Cortés was married to Catalina Suarez Marcayda when he arrived in Mexico but left her behind in Cuba. Shortly after Cortés arrived in Mexico, he acquired a slave-woman, Doña Marina, as both his translator and mistress, promising Marina he would release her from slavery if she would help him with Moctezuma. Cortés's wife, Catalina, joined him in 1522; three months later, she died suddenly, after an angry outburst regarding Doña Marina, now pregnant with Cortés's son, Martin. Charges of murder were brought against Cortés but dropped. When Marina gave birth, Cortés acknowledged Martin as his son and legitimized him in 1529.

Also, in 1529, he married a Spanish noblewoman Doña Juana de Zúñiga, but shortly before, Cortés helped himself to Doña Isabel, the daughter of Moctezuma II. Isabel had been the exceptionally young bride of two Aztec emperors. After her father's death, she was quickly married to her uncle Cuitlahuac, the new Huey Tlatoani. That marriage lasted 80 days before he died of smallpox. His cousin, Cuauhtémoc, then became emperor – and married Doña Isabel.

Five years later, Cortés executed Isabel's husband, the last Aztec emperor, then gave her in marriage to his friend Alonso de Grado, who died just a few months later. At that point, Cortés took Isabel into his own house. What happened next – either rape or seduction – left Isabel pregnant with Cortés's daughter. To cover his indiscretion and leave himself free to marry Doña Juana, Cortes quickly married Isabel off to another friend, Pedro Gallego de Andrade; Leonor Cortés-Moctezuma was born about five months later. Isabel wanted nothing to do with the baby, suggesting Leonor was the product of rape. Cortés gave her to a distant relative to raise, but provided for her care and included her in his will.

Mestizo child.[81]

What Cortés did to Marina and Isabel (and probably other indigenous women) was repeated thousands of times by other Spanish men. Whether raped, enslaved, wives, or mistresses, thousands of Aztec women gave birth to children with Spanish fathers. These children were called *Mestizos,* a category in the caste system of colonial Mexico. The Spanish government imposed the complex caste system, which determined a person's legal and social status. The priest decided a child's caste at baptism.

Caste depended on two basic factors: where a person was born and who the parents were. The four fundamental tiers (and there were many more) were:

Peninsular: a full-blooded Spaniard born in Spain,

Criollos: a full-blooded Spaniard born in the colonies,

Mestizo: a person of mixed Spanish and indigenous ancestry, and

Indios: an indigenous person of Mexico.

One's caste determined one's vocation, rank, and ability to accumulate wealth. Only Peninsulars could hold the highest administrative and church positions. Mestizos were not permitted to attend university, enter the priesthood, hold government

---

[81] https://commons.wikimedia.org/wiki/File:Mestizo._Mestiza._Mestiza.jpg

positions, or be included in the goldsmith or other artisan guilds. The system generated discontent among the lower castes and eventually led to the Mexican War of Independence in 1810.

SECTION FOUR: ART, CULTURE, & LEGACY

Chapter 13: The Aztec Religion

When the Mexica left their homeland of Aztlan, they were accompanied by their patron Huitzilopochtli, the blood-thirsty hummingbird god. Over the centuries, as they incorporated other deities from the cultures they encountered, they accumulated an immense array of gods and goddesses. Because the Aztecs freely appropriated the gods of other tribes as their own, sometimes their deities would have overlapping identities. For instance, the feathered serpent, Quetzalcoatl, was the god of wind, creation, and rain, but Tlaloc was also the god of the rain, and Ometeotl and Coatlicue were creator deities.

The functions and attributes of the pantheon of Aztec gods were fluid. The Nahuatl word *teotl* is usually translated as *god,* but it can also mean *sacred power.* Some scholars argue that we ought not to categorize these gods as discrete personalities (as with Greek and Roman gods) but as pantheistic forces or powers moving through the cosmos. For example, Tlaloc might be understood as the force or power associated with rain rather than a god.

H. B. Nicholson, a scholar of Aztec culture, classified their gods into three groups. The first group, *Celestial Creators,* included Ometeotl (creator of the universe) and Coatlicue (goddess of Aztlan, creator of the moon and stars, and mother of Huitzilopochtli). The most important god in the second group, *Rain & Agricultural Fertility Gods,* was Tlaloc, god of rain and storms. The third group, *War-Sacrifice/Nourishment of the Sun & Earth Gods,* contained Quetzalcoatl (god of wind, air, and learning), Huitzilopochtli (god of war and the sun), Mictlantecuhtli (god of the underworld), Mixcoatl (god of the hunt, ancestor of the

Toltecs, father of Quetzalcoatl), and Tezcatlipoca (god of the night and sorcery).

Model of the dual temples of Tlaloc and Huitzilopochtli on the Templo Mayor pyramid.[82]

When the Spaniards arrived in the Aztec capital of Tenochtitlan, they observed dual shrines on the top of the largest pyramid (Templo Mayor), where the gods Tlaloc and Huitzilopochtli were worshiped. A temple in the plaza facing the Templo Mayor was devoted to Ehecatl, god of the wind and a manifestation of Quetzalcoatl. These were the three of the four most important Aztec gods.

The fourth of the important gods was Huitzilopochtli's powerful ally, the Toltec god Tezcatlipoca. He was known as the *Adversary* and the *Enemy of Both Sides.* In Toltec mythology, he was the brother of Quetzalcoatl – but also his enemy. Although he could forgive sins, heal sickness, and deliver a man from his ordained fate, he was unlikely to do anything good for anyone due to his arbitrary nature. He was more likely to bring drought and famine. The Aztecs called him *He Whose Slaves We Are.*

Aztec religion pervaded all tiers of society. The Aztec state was a theocracy, with politics and religion intertwined. The kings presided as priests over the monthly festivals and state ceremonies, with the burden of stabilizing both the political and cosmic worlds. All citizens participated in daily rites. Cortés wrote that the people would burn incense in their temples every morning before

[82] https://commons.wikimedia.org/wiki/File:Guide_leaflet_(1901)_(14581791148).jpg

beginning their work for the day. He said sometimes they practiced bloodletting, where they would cut their bodies and let the blood flow over their idols and sprinkle it around the temples.

In a deity impersonation ritual, the priests would choose a young warrior without any defect to be *ixiptla,* becoming a certain god for a season. The Aztecs believed this person actually became that god – and would be clothed as that god – receiving honor and food and female consorts for up to a year. He would be worshiped until the inevitable day came to be sacrificed.

Aztec rituals often reenacted their myths. The Templo Mayor symbolizes one of the greatest myths associated with Huitzilopochtli. When he was in his mother's womb, Coatlicue, his sister, Coyolxauhqui, and her 400 brothers attacked their mother. Just at that moment, Huitzilopochtli emerged from the womb to defend his mother, fully grown and armed for battle. He killed his sister, decapitated her, and threw her down Mount Coatepec. As her body bounced to the bottom of the mountain, it broke into pieces, while her head flew into the sky and became the moon. Huitzilopochtli also ate the hearts of his 400 half-brothers.

Monolithic stone representing the dismembered body of Coyolxauhqui after Huitzilopochtli decapitated her and flung her down the mountain.[83]

In 1978, electrical workers digging at the Templo Mayor pyramid base discovered an enormous monolithic stone representing Coyolxauhqui's dismembered body. This huge round stone was at the foot of the stairs leading up the Huitzilopochtli's temple. The pyramid symbolized the slopes of Mount Coatepec with the body of his sister at the bottom. At the top, the hearts of sacrificial victims were offered to Huitzilopochtli to eat.

The Aztecs followed two calendars. One was the natural 365-day solar calendar, and the other was a religious calendar of 260 days broken into units of 20 days. Each unit had its own gods with accompanying festivals and rituals. For instance, children would be sacrificed during the festival of *Atlcahualo,* honoring Tlaloc, god of rain. The next month would be the festival of *Tlacaxipehualiztli,* where captives would be flayed, and the priests would wear the victim's skin for 20 days.

Every 52 years, the two calendars aligned, and this was celebrated by the extravaganza of the New Fire ceremony. In the months and years leading up to the 52-year ceremony, the pyramid temples would be enlarged and made higher. In preparation, the people would rid their homes of their old clothing, cooking utensils, and other household goods to renew their lives for the new 52-year cycle.

All fires would be quenched at sunset as the priests marched up to the summit of Mount Huizachtecatl, a volcanic mountain on the eastern shore of Lake Texcoco that could be seen by the cities around the lake. The priests sacrificed a victim on the top of the mountain and lit a fire on his chest. That fire lit a nearby bonfire, signifying the new 52-year cycle. Runners lit torches from the bonfire and carried them down the mountain to light fires in the temples and homes.

Aztecs raised dogs, eagles, jaguars, and deer to sacrifice to their gods. Butterflies and hummingbirds were sacrificed to Quetzalcoatl. Self-sacrifice and bloodletting were also common. People would use the thorny tips of the agave plant to pierce their ear lobes, tongues, or genitals, or they would stab themselves with knives. If they caught themselves speaking hurtful words or listening to gossip, they would slit their tongues or ears to rid themselves of the malevolent spirit. For more serious sins, they would strangle themselves or jump off cliffs.

A priest was known as a *giver of things,* and his duty was to give the gods what they were owed through sacrifices, offerings, and ceremonies. The tlatoani of Tenochtitlan was the priest-king of Huitzilopochtli, attending state rituals in the main temples. The Aztec Empire had two high priests who governed the pilgrimage centers of Cholula and Tenochtitlan; they were something like archbishops and even ministered outside the Aztec territory. Under these two men were many levels of priests, priestesses, monks, and nuns who tended the shrines of their deities.

Cortés wrote that temples and shrines were found in every district of Tenochtitlan and the suburbs. He said that living quarters for the priests were next to the shrines. The priests wore black clothing and never cut or combed their hair from the time they entered the priesthood until they left it. The sons of nobles and respected citizens were placed in the temple around age seven or eight, living there as novices and celibate priests until their parents arranged a marriage for them. They were allowed no contact with women and had to abstain from certain foods.

In the *Florentine Codex*, Franciscan friar Sahagún wrote of folk healers or shamans who traveled from place to place, tending to both spiritual and physical ailments and using psychedelic mushrooms and other plants to treat patients. He also mentioned enchanters who dealt with black magic and the occult, grinding the seeds of the morning glory plant to make *Ololiuqui* tea, which brought visions. Sahagún described Ololiuqui intoxication as troubling, making one deranged or possessed, where the person saw terrifying things.

THE GREAT PLAZA—TENOCHTITLAN, MEXICO—A RECONSTRUCTION

The main temple complex in Tenochtitlan.[84]

In front of every major temple was a large courtyard where people gathered to sing, dance, watch the religious rituals, enjoy psychedelic mushrooms, and drink chocolate. Caught up in the tempo of the shrieking flutes and pounding drums, the people would pierce themselves and sprinkle their blood toward the idols.

[84]https://commons.wikimedia.org/wiki/File:General_guide_to_the_exhibition_halls_of_th e_American_Museum_of_Natural_History_(1911)_(14595489267).jpg

The *calli* (temples) were dimly lit by the coals burning incense, filling the darkness with smoke. The floor was covered with flowers and slippery with the blood of sacrifices. In alcoves around the temple's perimeter sat the idols on their pedestals, swathed in jewels, veils, feathers, and bells.

In a letter to the King of Spain, Cortés wrote of one special temple in Tenochtitlan, probably the Templo Mayor:

"Among these temples there is one which far surpasses all the rest, for within its precincts, surrounded by a lofty wall, there is room enough for a town of five hundred families. Around the interior of this enclosure there are handsome edifices, containing large halls and corridors, in which the religious persons attached to the temple reside. There are full forty towers, which are lofty and well built, the largest of which has fifty steps leading to its main body and is higher than the tower of e principal church at Seville. .
.

The interior of the chapels containing the idols consists of curious imagery, wrought in stone with plaster ceilings and woodwork carved in relief and painted with figures of monsters and other objects. Every chapel in them is dedicated to a particular idol, to which they pay their devotions. There are three halls in this grand temple, which contain the principal idols; leading from the halls are chapels with very small doors, to which the light is not admitted, nor are any persons except the priests, and not all of them."

Prisoner led to the top of a pyramid for sacrifice.[85]

Aztecs believed that the human body was a sacred reservoir of divine forces, with the ability to release its energy back into the cosmos. The head and hair contained *tonalli,* an energy responsible for the body's strength and health. The heart contained *teyolia,* tied to human reasoning and perception. It was like a divine fire, especially strong in priests. When a person died, the *teyolia* left the body, and when a warrior died, his teyolia rose to the sun. Aztecs perceived human sacrifice as a means of recycling energy. The energy released from the sacrificial victims nourished the gods, who then nourished humans through rain, food, and other provision. About 20,000 people became the victims of sacrifice each year in different types of ceremonial rituals.

---

[85]

https://commons.wikimedia.org/wiki/File:COM_V2_D273_Prisoners_for_sacrifice_were_decorated.png

Some sacrifices mimicked the dismemberment of Huitzilopochtli's sister ,Coyolxuahqui, cutting off the arms and thighs of the victim. An infamous sacrifice was practiced during the annual festival of Toxcatl, celebrating the *smoking mirror* god Tezcatlipoca. This was a god-impersonating ritual involving a young warrior in perfect condition, who lived for one year as the god *Tezcatlipoca*. Before and during the killing, the people gathered in the vast plaza of the Templo Mayor, piercing themselves until the pavement ran with blood. As the priests carried out the phases of the rituals, the people jumped and twirled to percussive music, led by dancers in striking costumes. After the young man was killed, the priest would add his head to the skull rack. The skull rack represented the divine force of tonalli, which resided in the head.

Beginning in 2015, The National Institute of Anthropology and History collected about 200 skulls from the *tzompantli* (skull rack) in the Templo Mayor area. Analysis of the skulls showed that 75% of the skulls found were young men of warrior age, while 20% were women and 5% were children. The size of the tower that supported the skull rack suggests that thousands of skulls were displayed.

This jaguar-like stone vessel was used to hold the hearts of sacrificial victims.[86]

Huitzilopochtli, the hummingbird god, taught the Mexica about human sacrifice after they left Aztlan. Once they established the Triple Alliance with other Aztec tribes, their god demanded nourishment from a recurring and increasing supply of the blood, hearts, and other body parts of human victims. The priests would push and drag the victim to the god's shrine on top of the Templo Mayor pyramid, where four priests tied the victim and held him in place on a sacrificial table. The high priest (or the tlatoani) would stab the victim in the upper abdomen, quickly reach under the rib cage, rip the heart out of the body, and hold it up – still beating – before the image of Huitzilopochtli. The priest or king then placed the heart in the jaguar vessel, or the basin held by the chac mool figurine. The viscera were fed to the animals in Moctezuma's zoo. Sometimes ritual cannibalism took place, eating the thighs and arms of the victim.

Chac Mool, from Templo Mayor, holding a basin used to receive blood or the heart of a sacrificial victim.[87]

Next to Huitzilopochtli's temple on top of the Templo Mayor pyramid stood the matching temple of the rain god Tlaloc, who demanded the tears of children; small children from noble families were offered by their parents. The *Codex Ixtlilxochitl* estimated that 20% of Aztec children were sacrificed every year; their tears dripping to the ground would cause Tlaloc to drip rain on the soil in the planting season. The *Codex Magliabecchi* records children sacrificed by drowning and mentions two instances of the sacrifice of newborn babies. According to this codex, five of the 18 festivals of the Aztec religious year included child sacrifice.

In 2008, archeologists analyzed the skeletons of 31 children found in the excavation of Temple R in Tlatelolco (just next to Tenochtitlan), dedicated to Ehecatl-Quetzalcoatl, the Toltec-Aztec god of wind and rain. Two-thirds of the children were infants and toddlers, mostly little boys. Archeological evidence indicates they were all killed in a single ceremony, most likely during the great drought of AD 1454–57.

Some vestiges of Aztec religion have endured through the colonial period and until the present day. Aztecs in northern Veracruz still worship a god called Ometotiotsij, who is probably Ometeotl, the creator god. Mexicans celebrate the *Day of the Dead* by incorporating indigenous rites associated with the god of the underworld, Mictlantecuhtli, and his wife, Mictecacihuatl.

The practice of *curanderismo* (traditional folk medicine) goes back to Aztec days and is widespread in Mexico today. Traditional healers are especially important if the illness appears to result from witchcraft. Healers are believed to have spiritual power and use prayers and chanting of incantations, offerings of incense and food, various herbs, and occasionally blood from a sacrificed chicken.

A few Mexicans in the Pueblo region east of Mexico City (former Aztec and Totonac region) still worship the sun god Tonatiuh (a manifestation of Quetzalcoatl), which they call *Jesús* in Spanish. In the early colonial days, the Franciscan friars taught the people about Jesus, with passages like Luke 1:78 about the "rising sun will come to us from heaven." In the Aztec mind, Tonatiuh became Jesus – also known as *the Solar Christ.*

Dancers in the December 12 feast day of Our Lady of Guadalupe, in front of her Basilica.[88]

Tonantzin was an Aztec goddess called *mother earth* and *honored grandmother.* She became associated with the Virgin Mary. The Basilica of Guadalupe was built to honor the Virgin Mary (after several visions of Mary to two men, where she appeared as an Aztec princess). The shrine was built on a site where a temple to Tonantzin had stood and is the most-visited Catholic shrine in the world. Our Lady of Guadalupe is also known as the Queen of Mexico. The Aztecs transmitted their worship of Tonantzin to the Virgin of Guadalupe in the same way that they syncretized the teachings and rituals of Catholicism with their Aztec worldview and religion.

Chapter 14: Crafts, Commerce and Social Life

Everything fell apart when the Spaniards arrived. Until that time, Aztecs lived in a distinctly stratified society, unified by a common quest to expand their empire and spread their religion. The trading class was reaching its zenith when Cortés invaded, and merchants were gaining wealth comparable to the aristocracy. Would the powerful middle-class merchants and traders have eventually broken the strict barriers of the ruling class, generating a more fluid stratification? One can only speculate how the great Aztec Empire might have evolved.

An Aztec baby's destiny mostly depended on his or her parents: their lineage and where they stood in the clearly defined social hierarchy. At the top were the nobility, including political leaders, judges, priests, and military commanders. Next were the artisans, architects, merchants, traders, and lower administrative officials. Under them were construction workers, laborers, and farmers, and finally, there were slaves. Young people had limited opportunity to rise above their parents' social position unless they demonstrated unusual merit.

There were four ways to become a *tlachohtin* (slave*)* in Aztec society. A child or adult could be captured in war or sent as tribute from conquered city-states. The adults were often sacrificed, but children, beautiful women, and some men were kept as slaves. Sometimes criminals were sentenced to slavery. If someone gambled too much and got into deep debt, they could sell themselves. Slavery wasn't always lifelong; one could buy their freedom. Slaves rarely were resold by their masters unless they had the slave's agreement.

Slaves were used for farm labor and construction work and as household servants; beautiful women slaves were purchased to be concubines for the nobility. Slaves who were educated or skilled or who learned quickly could be promoted to higher positions, such as managing their owner's estate or business. They could even own other slaves! Aztec law protected slaves from abuse (other than human sacrifice) and permitted slaves to marry free citizens. Slavery was not inherited; children born to slaves were free.

The largest group in Aztec society were farmers (*macehualtin*). At the lower level were laborers who plowed the fields, planted, watered, weeded, and harvested. Above them were the specialists, who implemented crop rotation, oversaw the construction of the floating gardens and terraced fields, and supervised seeding, transplanting, and harvesting. All farmers were expected to join the military campaigns in the lull between harvesting and planting, and the field laborers assisted with building roads and temples in the off-season.

Irrigation, from Florentine Codex[89]

[89]

https://commons.wikimedia.org/wiki/File:Irrigaci%C3%B3n_con_uictli_C%C3%B3dice_Florentino_libro_XI_f.228.jpg.

Aztecs enjoyed successful agricultural endeavors, even without horses or mules to help with plowing or pulling loads. Some parts of the empire were well-watered, but others needed irrigation, especially in dry seasons or times of drought. The farmers of Mesoamerica had used irrigation systems for centuries, but the Aztecs took it to a higher level with more complex and extensive canals, even diverting rivers to meet their needs. The Aztec city-states around Lake Texcoco were in a mountainous region, so they built terraces up the hills and mountains, where seeds could be planted on level ground.

Chinampas ("floating" gardens) were widely used to cultivate vegetables and flowers. These were constructed by dredging mud up from the lake bottom and alternating that with vegetative matter until they had small rectangular islands where they could grow crops. These island beds had a network of canals running through them for the farmers to access by canoe. The chinampas were so fertile they could grow seven crops a year; seedlings were started on rafts and then transplanted. Tenochtitlan itself had a chinampas system, but its huge population relied on the extensive chinampas of Lake Xochimilco to the south and connected to Lake Texcoco. Farmers in Xochimilco transported produce and flowers by boat to Tenochtitlan and other cities in the lake system.

The Aztecs were exceptionally proud of their artisans, which they called *tolteca* in honor of the highly esteemed Toltec civilization which preceded the Aztecs and became part of their lineage through intermarriage. Skilled Aztec craftsmen were greatly respected and created their amazing carpentry, pottery, metalwork, stone carvings, and other crafts in large workshops. These educated craftworkers executed measurements using geometry and used tools made from copper and obsidian to carve and sculpt stone and wood.

An important craftwork for artisans was building weapons for the warfare that defined the Aztecs. They crafted 6-foot-long blowguns with darts tipped with secretions from poisonous frogs, built war clubs with embedded razor-like obsidian blades and axes with heads of stone or copper, and crafted daggers with beautifully carved hilts from flint or obsidian.

Boatbuilding was an essential craft because Tenochtitlan was an island on a large lake connected to other lakes. Aztecs used the waterways to travel from one city to another and to navigate the canal system interlacing the Tenochtitlan neighborhoods. Flat-bottomed dug-out canoes were used for gardening the chinampas and transportation through the canals, the mainland, and around the lake. The Aztecs also built rafts of planks tied with tight fibers for transporting large objects, such as stone figurines. Engineers and craftsmen were required to design and build canals, dikes, and aqueducts for transportation, managing fluctuating water levels, and delivering fresh drinking water.

Carpenters crafted homes and temples from wood, stone, or adobe bricks with thatched or slate roofs. Aztec stone masons covered the outside of buildings with limestone plaster and carved intricate designs on the front of temples and palaces. Homes held generations of families in rooms built around a central courtyard.

Architects and city planners meticulously devised the plan for the capital city of Tenochtitlan before it was built. With an estimated population of 200,000, the city had four quadrants, each housing around 50,000 people, surrounding the ceremonial center where the main temples were located. Each quadrant was divided into four smaller districts of 10,000 to 15,000 people. These smaller districts were called *calpolli*, like the estates in the countryside, as they each had their own leadership, their own central plaza with a temple and marketplace, and they often specialized in specific craftsmanship – such as pottery or feather work. A canal system served as the major streets through the city, connecting to the surrounding lake.

Mural by Diego Rivera in Palacio Nacional, Mexico City, showing life in Aztec times. In the forefront is the market of Tlatelolco, with the pochteca tlatoque presiding. In the background is the island city of Tenochtitlan with its causeway and canal system.[90]

Merchants and traders accumulated significant wealth and power in the organized and diverse marketplaces of the Aztec Empire. In neighborhood market centers located in each calpolli, *tlacuilo* (merchants) sold precious metals and gems, cotton cloth and clothing, animal hides, vegetables and fruit, wild game, intricate carvings, utensils for the home, and much more. The marketplace drew people together to gossip, share the local news, and learn of important events in the empire.

The *pochteca* (long-distance traders) enjoyed great prestige as they traveled great distances to obtain the coveted goods of the nobility. This was a hereditary position and could bring great wealth. Still, the pochteca were not permitted to display their prosperity by wearing the feathers and rich clothing of nobility. The fine cotton prized by elite Aztecs needed to be grown below an elevation of 5000 feet; it could not be grown in the mountainous regions around Tenochtitlan. Thus, Aztecs had to trade for cotton

[90] Wolfgang Sauber, CC BY-SA 3.0 <https://creativecommons.org/licenses/by-sa/3.0>, via Wikimedia Commons https://commons.wikimedia.org/wiki/File:Murales_Rivera_-_Markt_in_Tlatelolco_1.jpg

grown in distant regions or conquer the area and require them to pay cotton as tribute. The pochteca also acquired cacao beans for chocolate, colorful bird feathers, gems, gold, and animal skins. Because the Aztecs did not use beasts of burden, all these goods had to be transported in boats down the rivers or by porters over land.

The *pochteca tlatoque* served as overseers of the traders. These were the most experienced and accomplished traders who supervised the markets and held court to administer justice to those in the trader class. Another group of long-distance traders called the *naualoztomeca* traveled to hostile territories in disguise; they were spies for the state, picking up information as they interacted with people in the frontier areas.

The *tlaltani* traders specialized in the slave trade, an important source of sacrificial victims. The *tencunenenque* collected tribute in the city-states around the empire. The *Codex Mendoza* details the astounding quantities of goods the tencunenenque collected, such as textiles, grain, feathers, honey, jade, and copper. In a list of tribute from one town, the *Codex Mendoza* recorded they were required to send 1200 bales of cotton each year, and every six months, they would send:

- 800 loads of red and white cloaks with ornamental borders of green, yellow, red, and blue

- 400 loads of lioncloths

- 400 loads of large white cloaks

All this clothing required the women to spend most of their days weaving cloth to meet the tribute demands.

All teenage boys were trained in warfare, and able-bodied adult men had to maintain that training and be prepared to mobilize in the huge military campaigns. However, the Aztecs operated a standing army of the best warriors, who had received advanced training as teens or distinguished themselves on the battlefield. They could come from any class. The warrior class was highly honored and a channel for upward mobility. Social risers in the warrior class were called *eagle nobles.*

The priestly class organized the religious rituals and festivals, ran the mandatory education system, and controlled the artisans.

Some priests specialized in astronomy, medicine, or prophecy. Priests also served as warriors, carrying the effigies of their gods and capturing enemy warriors for sacrifice. Anyone from any class could become a priest, but priests in leadership came from noble families.

Aztec nobility, wearing elaborate feather headdresses, brightly colored capes, earrings, and lip piercings. From folio 65 of the Codex Mendoza.[91]

Tlatoani (kings) and *Huey Tlatoani* (emperors) were elected by the *pipiltin* (nobility). The pipiltin were private landowners, usually of large estates, and formed the ruling councils for the city-states. They were distinguished by their clothing of finest cotton, multiple piercings (nose, ears, tongue, lips), and bright feather capes and headdresses. Teteuhctin served as city and regional governors, lived in grand palaces, and were honored by the *-tzin* suffix at the end of their names.

From the top down, the political structure of the Aztec Empire started with the Huey Tlatoani (emperor). At the beginning of the Triple Alliance, the rulers of Tenochtitlan, Texcoco, and Tlacopan took turns serving as Huey Tlatoani, but eventually, Tenochtitlan provided top leadership. Under him were the tlatoani (kings) of the *altepetls* or city-states (which had smaller cities and towns under their rule). These were broken down into the calpolli, usually kinship units, which were farming villages in the rural areas and neighborhood districts in the big cities.

The altepetls constantly endeavored to gain ascendency over their neighbor city-states through warfare, so they could enrich themselves from tributes they would receive. The altepetls were

[91] https://commons.wikimedia.org/wiki/File:Aztec_high_lords_bottom.png

persistently forming alliances, some short-lived and others long-term, to defend themselves or conquer other regions. This is how the Aztec Triple Alliance was able to overthrow the dominant city of Azcapotzalco and exercise political hegemony (supremacy) over a large portion of Mesoamerica.

The fundamental unit of Aztec society was the family, to whom lineage was paramount. Nobles traced their lineage back to the Toltecs and from there back to Quetzalcoatl. The family tree of both parents was important, although the paternal lineage was foremost. Young men and women could only marry someone in their own social class; brides were expected to be virgins, and the young men were encouraged to be celibate before marriage. The wedding involved a four-day celebration with feasting and speeches; the bride would be covered in gold pyrite dust and adorned with red feathers.

Women were the keepers of the home: cooking, caring for the younger children, teaching their daughters, and weaving (lots of weaving). Aztec women could own their property and maintained control over any inheritance. With proper training before marriage, they could engage as healers, midwives, priestesses, and merchants. Aztec men were the primary wage earners, caregivers, and teachers of their sons once they reached three years old. Married couples lived with the husband's family in multigenerational homes.

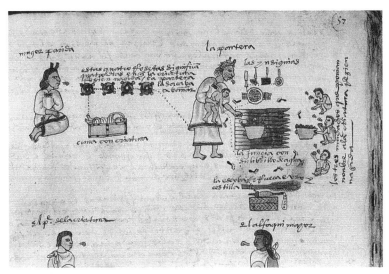

Aztec naming ceremony, from the Codex Mendoza. At the top left, the mother addresses her baby in its cradle. After four days, the midwife takes the baby for ritual bathing and naming (top right). On the right of this scene, three boys call out the name of the infant, and above and below it are symbols of possible future careers for boys and girls.[92]

Four days after a baby was born, the family gathered for a naming ritual, something like a baptism. The midwife would bathe the infant outdoors in the early-morning sun, give the child a name and a gift that symbolized his or her future role in society. A baby girl would often get weaving equipment and a broom, and a boy might get arrows and a shield or utensils representing his father's trade. Babies received a calendar name based on the date of their naming ritual, along with a personal name. To get a more auspicious date for the calendar name, parents might adjust the naming day to the third or fifth day after birth.

The *Codex Mendoza* details the raising of children: their lessons, punishments, and how many tortillas they would eat at each age. Three-year-old boys and girls would get a half tortilla for a meal and eventually work up to two or three in their teens. Beginning at age three, mothers would teach their daughters the first steps in how to weave, and when they were in their early teens, they would learn how to cook. Women spent an inordinate

[92] The Bodleian Library, University of Oxford, CC BY 4.0
<https://creativecommons.org/licenses/by/4.0>, via Wikimedia Commons
https://commons.wikimedia.org/wiki/File:Bodl_Arch.Selden.A.1_roll236.2_frame5.jpg

amount of time weaving to keep up with the tribute demands; thus, much of a girl's training was in that area. Fathers took their sons along to teach them their trade; they taught them other skills such as gathering firewood, cutting reeds for making baskets, and fishing with nets.

Boys and girls received only verbal correction and scolding up to age eight. After that, if children were careless, disobedient, or disrespectful, parents would administer corporal punishment. Sometimes children would be pricked with maguey spines or forced to breathe in the smoke of roasting chili peppers.

Their calpolli leaders supervised the parental education of children. In addition to life skills, the children were expected to learn *huehuetlatolli (sayings of the old)*. These were polite greetings and short speeches for all sorts of occasions, such as saying goodbye to a dying person or celebrating the birth of a child. Occasionally, the children would have to report to their local temples to be tested on their training.

The Mexica were among the first people in the world to mandate compulsory education for both boys and girls of all classes. Around 14 or 15, boys from elite families attended a school for the nobility called *calmecac,* and commoners attended a *telpochcalli* (both described in chapter 12), where they lived in dormitories. Girls attended schools to learn to sing and dance but lived at home. The glorious goal of most boys was to serve their nation as great warriors. At age ten, boys got a short haircut with one lock left long in the back. They wore this hairstyle until they went into battle and captured their first prisoner, and then the lock was cut as a rite of passage.

The Aztecs worked hard, battled even harder, and participated in gruesome religious rituals. But their lives weren't always grim. They did take time to play. They engaged in a ball game – something like basketball – called *Ullamaliztli Tlachtli.* They had to get a rubber ball (courtesy of the Olmec civilization) into a stone hoop but couldn't use their hands (like soccer). Instead, they used their hips, knees, elbows, and heads to keep the ball in the air (which skilled players could do for an hour or more). A lot of gambling was involved. Dancing and singing were sometimes for religious or political events, but also just for fun. Sometimes they would be accompanied by comic sketches.

Aztec board game called Patolli, from Florentine Codex by Bernardino de Sahagún.[93]

And then there were the pillow fights! They had this annual event where the boys would throw grass-filled sacks at the girls, and the girls would chase after them with cactus thorns. Teen boys would challenge rival schools to ballgames and mock battles. Adults and young people enjoyed "board games" on reed mats, using beans for dice.

Let's not forget the zoo! When the conquistadors entered Tenochtitlan, one thing that grabbed their attention was a garden full of plants and strange animals – creatures they had never seen. Many wrote more about the zoo than anything else in the city. They said it was so huge that it took 300 keepers to tend the animals.

The Spaniards didn't know the names of all the animals but listed bears, eagles, wolves, and monkeys, describing what were probably jaguar, ocelot, puma, sloths, armadillos, crocodiles,

[93] https://commons.wikimedia.org/wiki/File:Patolli.jpg

flamingos, and many other birds, and even a bison! The zoo was located on palace grounds, so it was probably reserved for the nobility to enjoy. It wasn't the only zoo either! One conquistador, Bernal Díaz de Castillo, said he saw another one across the lake in Texcoco.

Chapter 15: Aztec Art

Thoughts of Aztec culture often conjure up images of bold and colorful art. Ancient preexisting cultures influenced the flamboyant artistry of the Aztecs – the civilizations they conquered and bordering civilizations with whom they traded. In turn, the Aztecs used their art as a sort of propaganda, exerting their dominance over the city-states of their vast empire. Through military conquest, the Aztecs achieved political dominance and cultural hegemony over their tributary civilizations.

During the 20 years that the migrating Mexica lived in the ruins of Tula, they reverenced the Toltec art and craftsmanship, striving to emulate this spectacular culture, even calling their own artisans *tolteca*. The Mexica also learned from the cultures of the Olmec, Maya, Zapotec, Huastecs, and others. From Oaxaca in the southern reaches of their empire, they imported a community of artists to Tenochtitlan. They combined the diverse artistry of multiple civilizations into their own eclectic style of painting, jewelry, sculptures, ceramics, metalwork, architecture, and more. Grotesque and abstract carvings incongruously existed side-by-side with graceful, naturalistic imagery of humans and animals.

Aztec writing was an art form; however, with no alphabet, it wasn't a fully developed writing system. They combined pictographs with signs that represented sounds. For example, *ma* was the word for *hand*. To write a word with the sound *ma* in it, they would use the picture for hand. If they had a word ending in *tlan* (like Aztlan), they would use the picture for tooth (*tlantli*).

Travel from one place to another was shown by footprints. Travel through time was indicated by dotted lines and number symbols. Speech was shown by *speech scrolls* in front of a person's mouth. Examples of all three are in the previous chapter's picture of the baby's naming ceremony.

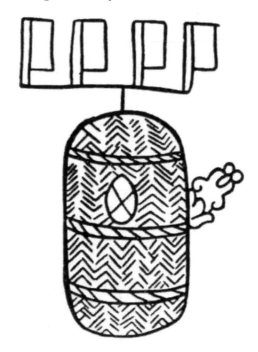

Aztec glyph or pictograph for 80 bales of cacao beans (for chocolate). Each of the four flags at the top represents the number 20. The oval picture on the bale represents cacao beans. (From the Book of Tributes.)[94]

The Aztecs also had a *vigesimal* system (based on the number 20) for writing numerals. One dot (or sometimes a finger) represented 1. Two dots meant 2; 5 was represented by a bar, while 6 was a bar and one dot. Two bars meant 10, and 11 was two bars and a dot, while 20 was a flag, and 21 was a flag and one dot. The hundreds were represented by a feather with a certain number of barbs, each representing 20 units.

Writing and painting require something to write on, so the Aztecs had *amate* paper made from the Amate tree, a type of Ficus. Amate paper was used primarily for codices (manuscripts) and widely used in the Triple Alliance for communication, tribute

---

[94] https://commons.wikimedia.org/wiki/File:Cacao_-
_Fig_1._Aztec_glyph_or_pictograph_for_80_bales_of_cacao.png

records, and rituals. Forty villages (in what is now the state of Morelos) produced about 480,000 sheets of paper annually, which they sent as tribute to the Triple Alliance cities. The paper was made by soaking the bark overnight and then pounding it into sheets with volcanic stones.

Aztecs painted their distinctive art on amate paper, deerskin, cotton canvases, ceramics, wood, and stone. They would sometimes primer the surface with gesso, a mixture of rabbit-skin glue, chalk, and white pigment. The Aztecs commonly used coral, chalk, clay, and stone in paintings and drawings. Many of their paintings were codices; sadly, most of those were destroyed by the Spaniards immediately following the conquest. However, the Spanish government commissioned the *Codex Mendoza,* painted by Aztec artists, and allowed codices dealing with history or tribute payments to be produced.

Aztecs learned the art of painting murals from the remnants of the Teotihuacan culture. The Templo Mayor and other important buildings in Tenochtitlan were adorned with complex murals, depicting people in a similar style as in the codices. An old man and woman pictured in a mural in Tlatelolco (just next to Tenochtitlan) are believed to be Cipactonal and Oxomico, the first man and woman in the first world, something like Adam and Eve – except in Aztec cosmology, the first world didn't survive.

In 2002, archaeologists discovered an ancient cistern in Tlatelolco underneath a colonial church. This was built on the orders of Cuauhtémoc, the last emperor of the Aztecs, who had relocated there with the remnant of Tenochtitlan's citizens after the Spaniards conquered Tenochtitlan. The cistern was 7-feet-deep and 26-feet-wide and was fed from an aqueduct that flowed four miles from Chapultepec Hill. The cistern walls were painted with brightly colored frescos of fishermen casting their nets and people paddling their canoes. They are surrounded by ducks, frogs, herons, and jaguars in the reeds and water lilies of the lake.

"One Flower" ceremony celebrated with two drums, which are called the teponaztli (foreground) and the huehuetl (background). Florentine Codex.

Aztecs loved singing and poetry, and most festivals featured poetry contests, musical presentations, and acrobatic performances. Songs fell into several genres: *Yaocuicatl* was sung to the gods of war, *Teocuicatl* honored the gods of creation and conveyed creation myths, *Xochicuicatl* were songs of flowers used in a metaphorical sense.

Poetry was especially famous among the Acolhua tribe of the Aztecs, who often used parallelism and couplets with concrete concepts to metaphorically describe two perspectives of an abstract idea. For instance, the concept of poetry was expressed as *the flower, the song*. Fortunately, we can read this poetry today, as some of it was preserved by the descendants of the Acolhua royalty of Texcoco and Tepexpan. Here is a hymn by King Nezahualcoyotl of Texcoco:

YOU, AZURE BIRD

You, azure bird, shining parrot, you walk flying. Oh Highest Arbiter, Life Giver: trembling, You extend Yourself here, filling my house, filling my dwelling, here.

Ohuaya, Ohuaya!

With Your piety and grace one can live, oh Author of Life, on earth: trembling,

You extend Yourself here, filling my house, filling my dwelling, here. Ohuaya, Ohuaya!

Aztecs are renowned for their remarkable stone sculpturing, which varied from exquisite miniature figurines to colossal monuments. Aztec sculptures featured realistic carvings of snakes, jaguars, frogs, monkeys, and other animals, as well as massive figures of their deities, encrusted with jewels and layers of gold. Although most carvings preserved through the centuries now appear the color of the stone they were carved from, they were brightly painted and decorated when they were new.

Replica of Aztec Sunstone painted in what scholars believe were the original colors.[95]

A striking example of Aztec sculpture, the enormous *Sunstone* or *Calendarstone* was uncovered in 1790 in the area that once was Templo Mayor in Tenochtitlan. Carved from basalt around 1427, it measures about 12 feet in diameter and 3 feet thick. What is probably the face of the sun-god Tonatiuh grimaces from the middle of the disk, surrounded by four squares representing four of the five suns that consecutively replaced each other through the millennia.

Stone of Moctezuma I, where human gladiators were chained for a battle to the death.[96]

Two unique Aztec sculpture forms are related to the culture of human sacrifice. One is the *cuauhxicalli,* a large stone bowl usually shaped like a jaguar or eagle and used to hold human hearts after sacrifice (see the photo of jaguar cuauhxicalli in chapter 13). The other is the *temalacatl,* a huge stone disk on which two captured warriors stood to fight in one-to-one combat until the death, another form of human sacrifice. Two famous examples of temalacatl stones are the *Stone of Moctezuma I* and the *Stone of Tizoc.*

In 1790, some men building a water canal in central Mexico City discovered a gruesome statue of the goddess Coatlicue. Coatlicue was the earth-mother goddess who lived on Mount Coatepec on Aztlan and the mother of Huitzilopochtli, the hummingbird god. The almost 9-foot-tall statue shows a decapitated woman with two coral snakes representing blood spurting from her neck. (In one version of Huitzilopochtli's birth, her head was cut off by her daughter Coyolxauhqui). Around her neck, she wears a garland of human hands and hearts and a human skull pendant. Her skirt is writhing rattlesnakes, and she has claws for hands and feet to rip into human corpses.

Colossal statue of goddess Coatlicue.[97]

Aztecs believed she would devour the human population if the sun failed to rise, and since that was Huitzilopochtli's job, they were sure to keep him well-fed with sacrifices. After she was dug up, the statue of the goddess was moved to the University of Mexico to be studied. But the professors were worried the locals might start worshiping her again, so that they reburied her, right there on the college campus. In 1803, a visiting scholar dug her up to make drawings and a cast, but he found her so disturbing that he buried her again when he was done. Finally, scholars dug her up for the last time in 1823, and she has managed to stay above ground since, at the National Museum of Anthropology in Mexico City.

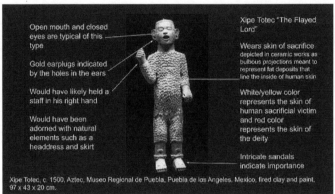

Open mouth and closed eyes are typical of this type

Gold earplugs indicated by the holes in the ears

Would have likely held a staff in his right hand

Would have been adorned with natural elements such as a headdress and skirt

Xipe Totec "The Flayed Lord"

Wears skin of sacrifice depicted in ceramic works as bulbous projections meant to represent fat deposits that line the inside of human skin

White/yellow color represents the skin of human sacrificial victim and red color represents the skin of the deity

Intricate sandals indicate importance

Xipe Totec, c. 1500, Aztec, Museo Regional de Puebla, Puebla de los Angeles, Mexico, fired clay and paint, 97 x 43 x 20 cm.

Small statue of Xipe Totec.[98]

Throughout the Valley of Mexico, smaller stone statues have been discovered in rural areas. These are the gods of agriculture and local deities. A common smaller sculpture is that of Xipe Totec, the maize god, otherwise known as the *Flayed Lord*. Worshiped by the Toltecs and later the Aztecs, he wore the flayed skin of a human sacrifice victim as a symbol of new vegetation.

This pendant carved from jade of Chalchiutlicue (Jade Skirt), a young goddess, is about 2 3/4 x 1 3/8 inches in size.[99]

Artisans also carved tiny sculptures of precious materials, such as amethyst, turquoise, conch shell, rock crystal, and jade. These miniature carvings were usually worn as pendants or earrings.

[99] Cleveland Museum of Art, CC0, via Wikimedia Commons
https://commons.wikimedia.org/wiki/File:Central_Mexico,_Aztec,_13th-16th_century_-_Goddess_Plaque_-_1949.199_-_Cleveland_Museum_of_Art.tif

Double-headed mosaic turquoise serpent.[100]

Aztec artists loved the blue-green color of the turquoise stone and frequently used it in a mosaic form on sculptures and masks. On display in the British Museum is a beautiful double-headed snake carved from a single piece of cedarwood and covered in tiny squares of turquoise. His red mouth and nose are made from the spiny oyster spondylus, and conch shells form his teeth. He was probably worn as a chest ornament in special festivals. Why is he double-headed? In the Nahuatl language, the word *coatl* means *snake,* but it also means *twin,* carrying the idea of cooperation and friendship. X*iuhcoatl* means turquoise snake (or the fire serpent), which represents lightning, linking sky and earth.

Cholula Pottery.[101]

Even without a potter's wheel, Aztec artisans formed beautiful ceramics, including urns for funeral ashes, jugs, cups, eating bowls and plates, cooking pots, mortar vessels for grinding chili peppers, goblets, and vases. Aztec ceramic pieces were usually thin (especially the Cholula pottery) and often featured black geometric designs on an orange background for everyday household pottery. Finer pieces had a cream, red, or black slip (a mixture of clay and water used to decorate ceramics) and might feature flower, leaf, or animal designs.

The artisans of Cholula were famous for their delicate ceramics, known as *Mixteca-Puebla* style, and these were imported to Tenochtitlan for Moctezuma and other nobles. In the early Aztec period, pottery was usually decorated with floral designs and glyphs representing days. Ceramics from the later period featured simple lines, sometimes curved or looped. Aztec pottery was formed in molds or carved from hard clay, then fired in updraft kilns or open-fired in pits at low temperatures.

Featherwork is a dazzling art form that is a classic feature of Aztec culture. Bird feathers in brilliant colors were collected to

---

[101] Sailko, CC BY 3.0 <https://creativecommons.org/licenses/by/3.0>, via Wikimedia Commons
https://commons.wikimedia.org/wiki/File:Mesoamerica,_puebla,_cholula,_mixteca-puebla_(nahua-mixteca),_ciotola_con_piede,_1200-1521_ca._02.jpg

form intricate mosaics, decorate weapons, and weave into headdresses and capes. The most highly prized feathers were from the resplendent quetzal birds, which have long emerald-green tail feathers and scarlet breast feathers. They also used flamingo feathers and other brightly colored feathers, some harvested from the birds in Moctezuma's Zoo. A whole district in the capital city of Tenochtitlan housed the guild of the *Amanteca* feather artisans, who were not required to pay tribute or perform public service.

Moctezuma's headdress of quetzal feathers (reproduction).[102]

The Amanteca artisans would chop feathers into small pieces to use in mosaic art, or feather painting, on shields and cloaks for the idols. The mosaics usually were formed on a base of amate paper, sometimes covered with cotton and paste, and then they would use the precious feathers of the quetzal bird and other birds with striking colors, along with dyed feathers, all chopped up and adhered with glue made from orchid bulbs. Striking headdresses, cloaks, fly whisks, fans, and other decorative objects were made from whole feathers sewn in place with string made from the agave plant.

Metalworking in Mesoamerica had its origins in the Purépecha-Tarascan culture northwest of the Aztec lands, close to the Pacific

[102] Thomas Ledl, CC BY-SA 4.0 <https://creativecommons.org/licenses/by-sa/4.0>, via Wikimedia Commons
https://commons.wikimedia.org/wiki/File:Feather_headdress_Moctezuma_II.JPG

Ocean. From there, elements of technique, form, and style diffused throughout Mesoamerica. The Mixtec civilization of Oaxaca and Pueblo were the dominant goldsmiths. The Mixtec became a tributary region of the Aztecs, and just the Aztecs imported Amanteca featherwork artisans into Tenochtitlan; they probably had a guild of Mixtec goldsmiths plying their trade as well.

Using borrowed technology, imported copper, gold, tin, and lead, and probably imported metallurgists, Aztec artisans manufactured elegant and sophisticated metallurgy. In their Tenochtitlan workshops, they created breath-taking castings of flowers and animals in gold and copper-gold, which were displayed in their pleasure gardens. Their artisans also cast hundreds of tin, arsenic bronze, and copper bells for the Templo Mayor.

The artisans worked the metal in furnaces with extremely high temperatures, where the flames were fanned by blowing air through pipes. They used molds to form metal objects and also hammered the metal into sheets. They implemented a technology called lost-wax casting to make bells and other objects. Aztec artisans were also known for their filigree work. Unfortunately, most of their gold artifacts were melted down by the conquistadors to make gold bricks for currency. Some smaller items survived, such as gold lip rings, earrings, and necklaces.

Just as their Olmec, Toltec, and Teotihuacan predecessors had done, the Aztecs utilized art to fortify their political and cultural supremacy. Their impressive pyramids and temples, their dramatic sculptures, and their exquisite mosaic art represented the central components of their religion. The dazzling and exotic featherwork, bejeweled carvings, and colossal monuments testified to their conquered city-states of the great might and affluence of the Aztec Empire and their right to dominate.

Even their paper imposed their influence on their subject city-states. The Amate paper, which was believed to have special powers, was used to record tribute from dominated cities and villages and became a representation of the transaction between the conquerors and the vanquished. Amate paper was used to register the fine cotton, turquoise, gold, long quetzal feathers, and other luxuries provided as tribute from the far reaches of the empire.

Even the paper itself was produced by conquered people.

When the Aztecs conquered a new region, they permitted the people to continue worshiping their local deities, but they also imposed their own religion - worship of Huitzilopochtli - on the subjugated people. They constructed temples in the main plazas of tributary cities and in the spectacular mountain peaks, imposing the Aztec hummingbird god as supreme through the frescos, sculptures, and metalwork that now covered sites once dedicated to other gods.

They didn't just spread the worship of Huitzilopochtli; they also introduced other deities, such as their agricultural and nature gods. For instance, a relief of the water goddess Chalchiuhtlicue was commissioned to be erected near ancient Tula. Across the empire, artistic structures, carvings, and other Aztec artwork have been found, indicating the cultural influence of the Triple Cities over areas hundreds of miles away.

Aztec jaguar painting next to a mural of Annunciation in the cloister of the Franciscan monastery of Cuautinchan, built in the 1570s.[103]

Even though the Aztec Empire was eventually conquered by the Spanish Empire, their art lived on - to a certain degree. The Amate paper continues to be produced today by Nahua artists

[103] Daniellerandi, CC BY-SA 3.0 <https://creativecommons.org/licenses/by-sa/3.0>, via Wikimedia Commons https://commons.wikimedia.org/wiki/File:Cuautinchan7.JPG

from Guerrero. Franciscan and Austinian friars employed local Aztec artists to decorate their newly constructed churches in the decades following the Spanish conquest. Some Aztec murals have survived until today in churches in Mexico, such as a jaguar and eagle on each side of a mural of the annunciation in the Franciscan monastery of Cuautinchan in Pueblo.

Chapter 16: Aztec Mythology and Cosmology

Cosmology, from an anthropological perspective, is what gives the members of a specific culture a fundamental sense of identity. Cosmology is how a particular civilization perceives the universe: its beginnings and its ultimate destiny. It defines the place of a culture in the complexities of the cosmos, giving meaning to life and driving current actions.

So, what about the Aztecs? What was their cosmology? What did they believe about the origins of the universe? What was their sense of where they came from? How did they self-identify? What did they feel was their role in the cosmos? What did they believe was their ultimate destiny as a civilization?

Because the Aztecs freely borrowed from other cultures to build a cosmological hodgepodge, we will notice some inconsistencies in their myths. For instance, one myth says their hummingbird god, Huitzilopochtli, was the son of the creator god, Ometeotl, while another myth says he was the son of Coatlicue. Myths don't always fit neatly into the historical record.

In Aztec cosmology, the world consisted of three parts: the earth on which humans lived, an underworld called Mictlan (with nine layers), and the upper heavens or planes in the sky (with 13 layers). Humans could inhabit the earth and the underworld but could not penetrate the heavens, except for the lowest layer, and only certain people could do that. The lowest level of the heavens was a place of abundant water called Tlalocan, where the god, Tlaloc, lived.

The Aztecs believed that where a person went after dying depended on what they did in life but, more importantly, on how they died. The soul could go to one of four places: the land of the sun, the land of corn, the lowest heaven (Tlalocan), and the underworld Mictlan.

Mictlantecuhtli, god of the dead.[104]

Mictlan was not a fiery hell or a place of punishment. It was the place most people went after they died – but getting there wasn't easy. They had to go through an arduous journey and pass several trials along the way. When an Aztec person died, his or her loved ones would bury the body with helpful implements to assist them on their journey.

The eastern paradise of the sun was the destination of warriors who died in battle – all warriors, even the enemy warriors. Captured warriors who were sacrificed also went there. A person's soul would remain in the eastern paradise for four years; after that, they would be reincarnated as hummingbirds, eagles, owls, or butterflies, so they could return to earth to see how everything was

---

going and to transmit subtle messages to those who listened.

Childbirth was considered a type of warfare, so if a woman died in the "war," she would go to the western paradise, the house of corn. She could return to the earth in a somewhat malevolent spirit form: the weeping woman of the night and the bringer of bad omens. The Aztecs believed these female spirits haunted crossroads and captured children there, so they would erect temples and leave food at crossroads so weeping women wouldn't kidnap their children.

The paradise of Tlalocan, the lowest level of heaven, was for people who drowned or were killed by lightning. It was also where people who died of leprosy and diseases associated with water went, along with the physically deformed. This afterworld had plenty of food. Interestingly, child sacrifice was often done by drowning; perhaps this was to ensure the babies would go to the paradise of Tlalocan.

In the highest heaven lived Ometecuhtli and Omecihuatl, the dual husband and wife creator gods, known collectively as Ometeotl. They were the dual god: two beings, yet one simultaneously. They were created out of nothing, and for a time, they were the only things that existed; nothing else had been created. Then, Ometeotl gave birth to four children: Xipe Totec (the flayed god), Tezcatlipoca (smoking mirror), Quetzalcoatl (feathered serpent), and Huitzilopochtli (hummingbird).

The *Myth of the Five Suns*, as recorded in the *Codex Chimalpopoca*, tells how the Aztec world came to be. Ometeotl gave the four children the task of creating a sun, a world, people to live in the world, and other gods. Quetzalcoatl and Huitzilopochtli were specifically given this task, but all the brothers were furiously competitive and kept creating drama (except for Xipe Totec, who seemed to stay on the sidelines). Each of the first four ages – earth, wind, fire, and water – ended in catastrophe. It took four attempts to create and sustain a world before they got everything right with the fifth attempt.

In the first creation, the *Age of the First Sun,* Quetzalcoatl and Huitzilopochtli created a sun. But it wasn't bright enough to give adequate light and heat. They then made the first man and first woman: Cipactonal and Oxomico. They were giants who ate acorns and were so strong they could uproot trees with their bare hands. Together, they had many children. The gods looked at their creation and decided it was not good. The sun was too weak.

Tezcatlipoca and Quetzalcoatl[105]

So, Tezcatlipoca changed himself into the sun, which was bright enough and warm enough for the world. After 676 years, Tezcatlipoca's rival Quetzalcoatl was overwhelmed with jealousy that Tezcatlipoca was ruling as the sun. Quetzalcoatl took his club and knocked him out of the sky, and Tezcatlipoca plummeted into the ocean. In his rage at being knocked out of the sky, Tezcatlipoca emerged as a jaguar and ate all the giants, ending the age of the first sun.

In attempt number two, the age of the second sun, Quetzalcoatl took his place as the sun. He created (normal-sized) people who ate pine nuts. After 674 years, Tezcatlipoca took revenge against Quetzalcoatl. He came to the world in a blast of wind, so strong that it blew all the people away and even blew Quetzalcoatl the sun away. The few people who weren't blown away were changed into monkeys, and they ran off to the jungles to live.

In the third attempt, a new age began when Tlaloc, the god of rain, became the sun. This age lasted 364 years, and the people of this world ate the river reeds. In a fit of jealousy, Quetzalcoatl sent a rain of fire and burning stones, killing almost all mankind. Even

---

[105] https://commons.wikimedia.org/wiki/File:Quetzalcoatl_and_Tezcatlipoca.jpg

the sun itself went up in flames. When the flames cooled, the ground was ashen, and the people who survived had become birds – turkeys, to be exact. Quetzalcoatl then gave the world to Tlaloc's wife, Chalchiuhtlicue, the *jade skirt woman.*

When Chalchiuhtlicue, the water goddess, took over the sun's responsibilities, the fourth age began. But she was the goddess of water, so it rained constantly. This age was the shortest, lasting for 312 years. Eventually, the great rain, so long and so hard, covered the earth with a flood that rose above the mountaintops; the people who survived became fish. Even the sun fell out of the sky, and then the sky fell down and covered the earth, so nothing could live on it.

The gods realized that fighting among themselves was counterproductive and that all the worlds they had made had been destroyed by their quarreling. Quetzalcoatl and Tezcatlipoca made peace with each other and went down to rebuild the world. They transformed themselves into great trees that pushed the sky back, dividing it from the earth below.

The gods all gathered around a bonfire in an attempt to create the fifth age – and to finally get it *right.* The gods knew that someone would have to sacrifice themselves to become the next sun for the new age. So, a handsome, strong (yet conceited) god, Tecuciztecatl, prepared himself to jump into the bonfire. Four times, he walked up to the fire, but each time he lost his nerve and walked away in shame.

Tonatiuh, god of the sun.[106]

Finally, Nanahuatl, the smallest and humblest of the gods who was covered in leprosy, jumped into the flames. He became Tonatiuh, the sun; this was the birth of the fifth sun. Humiliated by Nanahuatl's sacrifice, Tecuciztecatl also leaped into the fire and became the moon. However, he was as bright as the sun, which the gods found inappropriate. One of the gods snatched a rabbit and threw it at him. When the rabbit hit the face of the moon, its light was dimmed. That is why the moon has the shape of a rabbit on its face.

Now they had a new problem. The sun was stuck. Tonatiuh, the god of the sun, told the other gods they would have to sacrifice themselves to get him moving. They jumped into the fire and became stars and planets, and finally, Tonatiuh could move across the sky. Because all the gods sacrificed themselves for the people of the earth, now people were expected to sacrifice themselves for the gods.

With the sun moving, Quetzalcoatl took on the task of creating new humans. He went to Mictlan to bring back the bones of the people who had died. Following a tense encounter with the god of the underworld, he took off running with the bag of bones and slipped and fell into a pit, breaking the bones. He eventually made it out and sprinkled his blood on the bones of the dead people, resurrecting them to life. Because they came from bone fragments, the men and women were all different sizes.

As mentioned previously, the Aztecs had two myths about their patron god Huitzilopochtli's birth. The first was probably borrowed from another culture, perhaps the Teotihuacan. The second one seemed to resonate more with the Aztecs, as they reenacted it annually at the Templo Mayor. The Aztecs traced their origins to the birth of Huitzilopochtli on their home island of Aztlan, on Mount Colhuacan (or Coatepec). In this version, Coatlicue (the scary goddess with the snake skirt) is Huitzilopochtli's mother. Coatlicue was sweeping her shrine one day when a ball of hummingbird feathers fell at her feet. She picked up the feathers and tucked them into her waistband, and this made her pregnant. Her other children (400 sons and her daughter, Coyolxauhqui) attacked her because of what they considered a dishonorable pregnancy. At that point, she gave birth to Huitzilopochtli, as mentioned in chapter 13, and he rose to her defense.

The Dominican friar and historian Diego Durán wrote an interesting account about the Aztec's origins in his 1581 book *Historia de las Indias de Nueva Espana* (known as the Durán Codex). Durán had come to Mexico at age seven with his family and became fluent in the Nahuatl language. After he became a priest, he spent much time among the local people, learning their customs and cosmology.

In his book, Durán recorded a story he had translated from an earlier Aztec history about Moctezuma I, the second Aztec Emperor, who ruled from 1440-1469, fifty years before the Spanish showed up. Moctezuma was curious about where their ancestors had lived and what those seven caves were like. He was fascinated by the tales of their ancestral island. Could they ever find it again?

Moctezuma sent for Cuauhcoatl, the royal historian, who told him that Aztlan had been a blissful, happy place whose name meant "whiteness." There was a great hill in the lake called Colhuacan, because it was twisted, and in this hill were caves and grottos of the Aztec ancestors. They lived in leisure, with all sorts of waterfowl – ducks, herons, cranes – at their disposal. They enjoyed the songs of the little birds with red and yellow heads in the groves of trees that grew on the island. Their ancestors got around the lake by canoe and planted floating gardens where they grew maize, chili, tomatoes, amaranth, and beans – which the Aztecs brought with them to the Valley of Mexico.

However, when they abandoned Aztlan and came to the mainland, the world turned against them. They struggled with biting weeds, sharp stones, brambles, and thorns that made it difficult to travel. They found no place to rest – the land was full of snakes, jaguars, and other dangerous creatures. The historian told Moctezuma I that this was what was painted in the ancient books.

Moctezuma organized an expedition to find Aztlan. His brother, Tlacaelel, cautioned him to carefully choose who would go along since this not a war campaign but a knowledge-gathering enterprise. Moctezuma gathered sixty sorcerers for a journey to find their mysterious homeland. They were to search out the place where their deity, Huitzilopochtli, was born and where his mother still lived. They carried with them treasures of gems, gold, vanilla, and cacao beans as gifts for their ancestors and the goddess.

The sorcerers succeeded in locating Aztlan. They arrived at the shores of a great lake, with a hill in the middle, and were delighted to hear the people speaking their own Nahuatl language. The local people carried them in their canoes to the island. At the bottom of the hill, they met an ancient man, the guardian-priest of the sanctuary of Coatlicue, the earth-mother goddess. He asked why they had come, and they told him they had been sent by their Emperor Moctezuma and his advisor Tlacaelel.

The old man frowned; he had never heard of those two men. But he did know the men who had left Aztlan centuries earlier. "Do you know them?" he asked, reciting the names of their ancestral leaders. "No," the sorcerers replied, "Those men all died long ago." The man looked at them, surprised. "But I was here when they left. All of us who saw them go are still alive now!"

The priest led them up the hill to meet the earth-mother goddess, Coatlicue. As they climbed the hill, the sorcerers began to sink into the sand. The priest looked at them quizzically. "What have you been eating?" They told them they had been drinking chocolate and eating the food grown in their new land." "That was your downfall," the priest said. "That's why your people die."

Coatlicue, mother of Huitzilopochtli[107]

Finally, they met the grotesque and filthy goddess, Coatlicue. She told them how she had been weeping ever since her son, Huitzilopochtli, had left. She said that she had not washed or changed her clothes or combed her hair since he had departed. She told them that Huitzilopochtli had left to guide the Aztecs (all seven tribes) on their long pilgrimage from Aztlan to the Valley of Mexico. Coatlicue longed for his promised return.

The goddess shared with them Huitzilopochtli's prophecy of the future he had told her before he left:

"I must make war on all the provinces and cities and towns and places, taking them and subjecting them to my service. But in the same manner that I have conquered them, in this same manner they will be taken from me by conquering strangers, and I will be driven from that land. Then I will return to this place . . . then, mother, my time will be completed, and I will return fleeing to your lap."

The old man, the guardian of Coatlicue's sanctuary, told them the Aztecs had lost their immortality when they consumed rich foods and lusted for gold and other luxuries. He refused to accept the gifts the sorcerers brought but instead gave them gifts of plants and food from the island, where the people lived a simple but idyllic life. They also carried home a cloak made from the hemp of the maguey plant, a gift of the goddess for her sun Huitzilopochtli.

The sorcerers traveled home and related everything that happened to Moctezuma. The emperor broke into tears when he heard of the impending downfall of their empire. He took the maguey-fiber cloak to the temple of Huitzilopochtli. He fearfully consulted with his astrologers and prophets and with the ancient chronicles to identify the strangers who would one day come to conquer them.

In his account of the origins and history of the Aztecs, Friar Diego Durán stated three times that he copied *directly from the Aztec's own written history* as his primary source. The Aztec source document, called *Cronica X,* has been lost, but it served as a resource for other Spanish-language histories.

We can see that the cosmology of the Aztecs affected their beliefs about their role in war and sacrifice. An afterlife of the eastern paradise of the sun for fallen warriors and sacrificed victims would encourage the soldiers as they went to fight battles. It probably made the Aztecs (and their sacrificial victims) feel better about all the human sacrifices they were required to offer. The prophecies of Huitzilopochtli reinforced their mandate as conquerors of the surrounding lands.

But the prophecy also included dismal tidings of their future destiny – one day, they would be defeated by conquering strangers, and their god Huitzilopochtli would fly away from them and back to Aztlan and his mother. A similar prophecy had been given to Moctezuma I by Nezahualcoyotl, king of Texcoco. Moctezuma II had received a prophecy from Nezahualcoyotl's son, Nezahualpilli, that foreigners would overcome the empire. Perhaps this is why Moctezuma II, great-grandson of Moctezuma I, chose not to confront the Spanish conquistadors in an all-out battle, fatalistically submitting to the prophecies.

Conclusion

Before the Aztecs grew into a mighty empire, they lived a simple, unassuming life somewhere northwest of the Valley of Mexico. Whether as fishers and farmers on the idyllic island of Aztlan or simply as Chichimeca hunters and gatherers, they probably had no inkling of the destiny that would one day be theirs.

Without the wheel and without a fully developed alphabet, they emerged from humble beginnings to build a highly organized city of 200,000 people on a swampy island, the largest city in the Americas and one of the largest in the world at the time. They constructed huge temples and pyramids and conquered and ruled an area of 80,000 square miles with up to six million people.

Great civilizations had risen and fallen before these wandering nomads drifted into Central Mexico. These civilizations influenced the Aztecs, masters of assimilation and adaptation, and thus the Aztecs became preservers of these exceptional cultures. The Olmec built the first true cities and the first pyramids of Mesoamerica and carved 11-foot-high colossal heads weighing several tons, which they somehow transported 50 miles to their cities. The transitional culture of the Epi-Olmec developed a sophisticated calendar and writing system at least as early as 32 BC.

Then the mighty Toltec civilization, admired and emulated by the Aztecs, rose to preeminence from their Nahuatl-speaking Chichimeca origins. Fierce Toltec warriors extended their empire from the Pacific to the Gulf, penetrating the Yucatan Peninsula as they spread the Cult of Quetzalcoatl. They built the astonishing 15-foot-high Atlantes of Tula columns to support their massive porticoes, and their famed artisans produced beautiful carvings, artwork, and jewelry.

An unknown force impelled the Mexica and the other Aztec tribes to leave their blissful Aztlan homeland – perhaps a natural disaster, perhaps an internal struggle, or perhaps domination by another culture. For over 100 years, they wandered through a land turned against them – deserts of thorns, sharp rocks, snakes, and poisonous lizards – until they reached the fertile Valley of Mexico. They encountered their kinsmen from Aztlan there, but their fellow Aztecs were unwelcoming, unwilling to compete for the land, resources, and power for which they were striving.

While hiding among the reeds from the Colhuacan army, they received a prophecy from their hummingbird god, Huitzilopochtli: in the morning, they were to search for a prickly-pear cactus among the reeds on which an eagle would be perched. This was where they were to build their city, Tenochtitlan, and then they were to conquer their surrounding enemies, all of them, one by one. After years of wandering, fighting the elements, and struggling to survive, they found the eagle on the cactus, on an island in the lake. They had a place to call home. The next part of the prophecy was an extended military campaign of subjugating provinces and cities.

First, they had to build their city, form important alliances, and grow in strength. Finally, they reached the point where they formed a coalition with other city-states victimized by the despotic demands of their overlords, the Tepanec city-state of Azcapotzalco. After overthrowing Azcapotzalco, the three Aztec tribes – the Mexica of Tenochtitlan, the Acolhua of Texcoco, and the Tepanec of Tlacopan – formed the Triple Alliance. This became the Aztec Empire, with a self-identity as the chosen people called by the god Huitzilopochtli to conquer and rule over other lands.

For almost 200 years, the extraordinary Aztec Empire ruled the Valley of Mexico, expanding to dominate a substantial part of Mesoamerica. They developed a civilization renown for military conquest, extensive market exchange, fascinating culture, and sophisticated agricultural endeavors. They flourished as an intricate religious, political, social, and trade organization of over 500 city-states.

Their downfall came not only because of the Spaniard's superior military technology (calvary, crossbows, cannons) but also the unrest among tributary cultures and the ongoing warfare with non-Aztec civilizations on the outskirts of their civilization. Their tributary provinces were disgruntled regarding high tribute payments with few benefits. Their own city-states and the Aztec's Tlaxcala rivals grieved their children taken as slaves and sacrifices. The Aztecs failed to learn from their own history – the reason they formed an alliance to overthrow the Azcapotzalco Empire was because of the Tepanec cruelty and despotic demands. Now, the Tlaxcala threw in their lot with the Spaniards, and even the Cholula and other allies betrayed them, forming an army of 150,00 indigenous people that marched against the Aztec Empire with the conquistadors.

An ancient proverb says, "Know well the condition of your flocks." The Aztec style of leadership generated animosity and resentment, influencing their flocks to stray. They harshly ruled their provinces through terror rather than in a more harmonious collaboration – as the Purépecha-Tarascan did. Leadership is stewardship; it's actively preparing for the future vitality of one's organization, community, or nation. This is where the Aztecs failed.

The Aztecs constantly attacked and antagonized their undefeated enemies, the Tlaxcala, creating murderous hatred that came back to haunt them. In our society and in our world today, it's better to negotiate a truce with our most intransigent adversaries because one day, we might need them as allies. Antagonism is counterproductive to any endeavor and has doomed many leaders, even in the present day.

How have the Aztecs influenced and inspired the current citizens of Mexico and Central America? Yes. The Aztec economy helped shape the economic structure of modern-day Mexico City. The city of Tenochtitlan had several guilds of skilled craftsmen, but they lacked raw materials. Thus, the Aztecs created an economic exchange of commodities, capital, and assets through tribute, local and long-distance trade, and market transactions, which influenced methods of trade in today's Mexico City.

Ulama.[108]

Much of the everyday culture of the Aztecs pervades the culture of Mexico and Central America, and even the United States. Mexicans still have a diet based on the Aztec core foods: corn, beans, tortillas, tomatoes, guacamole, and chilis, all of which are enjoyed not only in today's Mexico, but also throughout North America. And let's not forget chocolate, loved around the world! Ulama was a favorite ball game of the Aztecs. This game is still played today throughout Mesoamerica. Ulama has some similarities to Mexico's favorite sport of soccer (association football), igniting great passion in communities and as a nation.

Indigenous ladies in Cuetzalan, Puebla, Mexico, wearing huipil clothing. The lady on the left is wearing huarache sandals.[109]

Clothing in Central America and Mexico has origins in Aztec culture. The *cactli* and *huarache* sandals the nobility wore have endured as common footwear and even fashion statements throughout Mexico, Central America, and even around the world. The loose-fitting *huipil* (or *huanengo*) clothing of Aztec ladies is still the favored garment of the indigenous women in Mexico and Central America.

Traditional music, dances, and Aztec artwork are displayed at important festivals. The Nahuatl language has survived, and 1.7 indigenous people in Mexico speak dialects of the ancient language, mostly in the rural areas surrounding Mexico City. One-third of the Nahua people only speak the Nahua language and not Spanish. The Nahua people, ethnically related to the Aztecs and Toltecs, are the largest indigenous people group in Mexico and also live in El Salvador, Honduras, and Nicaragua.

Aztec dance/ritual at Juana de Asbaje Park in Tlalpan, Mexico City.[110]

An interesting vestige of Aztec society was the *pepenilia* - or street scavengers. The people of Tenochtitlan were committed to cleanliness, and the pepenilia were responsible for recovering recyclable items. Today, Mexico City has troops of *pepenadores* who scour the streets for items they can scavenge. The Spanish word *pepenadores* stems from the Nahuatl word, which means to choose or select.

The Aztecs developed (or improved on) numerous achievements in civilization simultaneously but independently of similar achievements in Europe, Africa, and Asia. They used the *chinampas* form of agriculture, a 365-day calendar, and remarkable step pyramids. They implemented advanced city planning and built aqueducts for fresh drinking water in Tenochtitlan. They had a strong sense of order and used a merit system that rewarded hard work and innovation. They had mandatory education for all teens, regardless of class or gender. They had a well-developed justice system, and nobility, who were regarded as role models, were punished more strictly than commoners.

They had a number system, and utilized multiplication, division, and geometry in their trade, in their impressive architecture, and in craftwork. They used algorithms to calculate area. Without knowing the size of the earth, they figured out when eclipses would happen. They kept organized and detailed documents of tribute payments and trade transactions.

When the Spaniards entered Tenochtitlan, they were impressed with its size and its orderliness. They commented on the cleanliness of the people and the pristine streets of the great city. Remember, this was a city of 200,000 people, built over water. They depended on the fish, frogs, ducks, and other water animals for food, so if they polluted the water, they might lose a valuable food source. They relied on a remarkable waste management system to keep Lake Texcoco and their city reasonably clean.

Human excrement and organic waste were recycled as fertilizer for the chinampas. Urine was recycled as a fixative in fabric dying. At night, public areas were lit by burnable trash, which also provided fuel for cooking and warmth in the homes. Dropping litter or dumping human waste on the streets was punishable by law. They understood the importance of trees; cutting one down without permission could generate the death penalty. They recycled whatever they could in a culture that was resource-efficient and minimized waste, serving as a model for cities today.

The Aztecs were culturally and mentally connected to other great Mesoamerican civilizations – such as the Mayas, Toltecs, and Olmecs – through the great significance their religion and their gods played in their lives. They were all polytheistic and shared several of the same deities. They valued hard work, worship, and warfare as their greatest priorities, reflected in their architecture, artwork, sculptures, and paintings.

The legacy of the Aztecs, and specifically the Mexica tribe, lives on in the name of the country and capital city of Mexico and of its people. When the Spaniards arrived, the Mexica city-states of the Triple Alliance were called Mexico-Tenochtitlan. Following the Spanish conquest, they called the city they built over the ruins of Tenochtitlan *La Ciudad de Mexico.* After gaining independence from Spain, the country's official name is the *Estados Unidos Mexicanos* (United Mexican States), but it is more commonly called Mexico.

Flag of Mexico[111]

The flag of Mexico has its coat of arms in the center – the same overall design that has been used since independence from Spain in 1821. The Mexican coat of arms is based on the Aztec pictograph for Tenochtitlan, featuring an eagle with a snake in its claw, perched on a prickly pear cactus on a rock rising out of a lake.

After tracing the rise and fall of the Aztec Empire, what deductions can we make? When gauging the importance of their history in today's contemporary society, we can consider their strengths and their weaknesses. A compelling key to their success was their canny ability to form brilliant alliances. This skill can certainly be put into play in today's organizations, economic endeavors, and politics. The Aztecs were also empowered by vision – a strong sense of who they were and what they were meant to do. A robust self-identity and grasp of a distinct destiny will impel individuals, corporations, and nations to greatness. A third strength was their willingness to learn from other cultures, absorbing their technologies, craftsmanship, and knowledge. When we are willing to learn from other people and other cultures, it opens doors, keeps us relevant, and increases our adaptability and chances of success.

---

[111] https://commons.wikimedia.org/wiki/File:Flag_of_Mexico.jpg

Part 2: The Maya Civilization

An Enthralling Overview of Maya History, Starting from the Olmecs' Domination of Ancient Mexico to the Arrival of Hernan Cortes and the Spanish Conquest

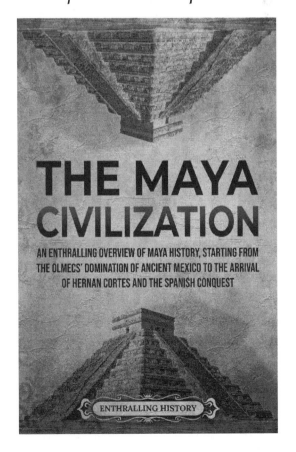

THE MAYA CIVILIZATION

AN ENTHRALLING OVERVIEW OF MAYA HISTORY, STARTING FROM THE OLMECS' DOMINATION OF ANCIENT MEXICO TO THE ARRIVAL OF HERNAN CORTES AND THE SPANISH CONQUEST

ENTHRALLING HISTORY

Introduction

The Maya are one of the most captivating civilizations of Mesoamerican history, with monumental architecture and distinctive artwork is still marveled at today. While popular media has often portrayed the Maya as primitive peoples that revolved around gruesome human sacrifice, they were one of the world's most advanced civilizations during their height of power.

This book aims to inform the reader on the realities of the Maya civilization, from its beginnings on the Gulf Coast to the arrival of the Spanish conquistadors on the Yucatan Peninsula. While no one will ever truly understand the extent of Maya history and culture, this book will use a variety of resources to give a general overview of the timeline of the civilization.

Part one will explore the Olmec, often called the "mother civilization" of the advanced Mesoamerican civilizations that came after it. The breathtaking architectural and artistic achievements, as well as their political and scientific advancements, will be covered. These chapters will largely focus on the Olmec cities of San Lorenzo and La Venta, as well as the Epi-Olmec city of Tres Zapotes. In the concluding chapter of part one, the Preclassic Maya period will be explored: a time period of enormous transformation and growth in the Maya heartland as Olmec society was declining.

Part two will cover the Classic Maya period when the Maya civilization was the dominating force of Central America. First, the Classic urban Maya society will be explored. This will cover their fascinating religious beliefs, their concept of time, and much, much more. These chapters will largely focus on the two largest cities of the Maya lowlands during the classic period, Tikal and Calakmul. The collapse of the Classic Maya city-states and the many theories of why the collapse occurred will then be covered, as well as the rise of cities in the northern Yucatan, namely Chichen Itza.

Part three will revolve around the Postclassic period, as the populations and political and domination of the lowland urban centers dispersed throughout the Yucatan region. The K'iche' Maya of the highlands, the Mayapan league of the northern Yucatan, and the kingdom of Peten Itza of the lowlands will be covered. This will give the reader a great foundation for what Maya society looked like upon the arrival of the Spanish conquistadors.

Part four will explore the decades of Spanish conquest that enveloped the Yucatan region. The numerous conquistadors, their expeditions, and how they affected local Maya populations will be covered.

While this book aims to be comprehensive, many great cities and components of Maya life will surely be left out. However, its text serves as a great starting point for readers that are interested in further learning about one of the world's greatest civilizations.

Kmusser, CC BY-SA 3.0 <http://creativecommons.org/licenses/by-sa/3.0/>, via Wikimedia Commons https://commons.wikimedia.org/wiki/File:Mayamap.png

SECTION ONE: THE OLMECS AND PRECLASSIC MAYA (1400BC-250 AD)

Chapter 1: San Lorenzo Tenochtitlan: The City of the Olmecs

The Olmecs are widely considered the first civilization of Mesoamerica and one of the most prominent "mother cultures" that would eventually become the great Mayan and Aztec civilizations. Up until the 13th century BC, ancient Mesoamerica was largely comprised of small primitive villages scattered throughout Central America. The Olmecs advanced far past the confines of a primitive stone-age civilization and eventually became the dominating people of the Gulf Coast region of southern Mexico.

The Olmecs were exceptional sculptors, and their art would prove highly influential to the Mesoamerican civilizations that emerged in Central America after them. The sculptures and architecture of the Olmecs have proved to be indispensable to understanding their ancient culture, as these stone artifacts have been some of the only traces of the Olmecs that have survived. Not only were they talented sculptors and artisans, but they proved to be excellent administrators, agriculturalists, and diplomats.

The Olmecs expanded on primitive farming villages and created great agricultural city centers, where advanced irrigation and farming methods were used. The first of these city centers was San Lorenzo Tenochtitlan, located around 38 miles away from the Gulf of Mexico in the modern-day state of Veracruz. (This city is not to be confused with the Aztec capital of Tenochtitlan that would emerge many centuries later.)

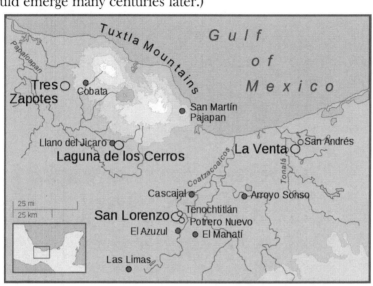

The yellow dots show known Olmec villages and towns. The red dots mark locations
where artifacts or art have been found that are unassociated with habitation

*Madman2001 CC BY-SA 3.0 <http://creativecommons.org/licenses/by-sa/3.0/>, via Wikimedia
Commons https://commons.wikimedia.org/wiki/File:Olmec_Heartland_Overview_4.svg*

San Lorenzo is considered the first advanced Olmec city and
was by far the most prosperous city of the region during
Mesoamerican history's Early Formative period (1800-900 BC).
The city became the dominating power of the Gulf Coastal Plain,
which helped Olmec culture spread widely into other
Mesoamerican societies.

Olmec society was thriving in the region for hundreds of years
before the creation of San Lorenzo. The nearby El Manatí site had
been in use since 1600 BC and prospered as a small coastal town.
The archaeology of the site shows that Olmec settlers began
arriving in the area of San Lorenzo around 1450 BC, and it
increasingly grew into a large village.

However, it was not until the ascension of San Lorenzo as the
dominating power of the region in the 12th century BC that the use
of hunting and gathering practices, agriculture, distinctive Olmec
culture, and administrative skill all came together to form an
advanced Mesoamerican city center.

The city had a socioeconomic political structure that greatly resembled ancient city-states in Europe and Asia, consisting of elite landowners and a peasant working class. The extensive trade networks that connected the city's economy to other Mesoamerican communities throughout the region greatly aided the diffusion of different cultures throughout Central America.

Between 1150 and 900 BC, San Lorenzo enjoyed its peak of dominance in the region until it was eventually replaced as the regional power by the nearby Olmec city of La Venta. By the beginning of the 9th century BC, much of San Lorenzo's population had moved elsewhere. Though there would be later settlements in the city, it would never come close to the prosperity it once possessed. Many scholars speculate that this mass dispersal and exodus of San Lorenzo's population laid the groundwork for the Maya Civilization that would dominate the region years later.

The first excavations of the San Lorenzo site began in 1945 by Mathew Stirling and Philip Drucker, sponsored by the Smithsonian Institute and National Geographic Society. Stirling uncovered many of the first remnants of the Olmec city and greatly surprised the archaeological community by declaring that the city belonged to an ancient civilization that predated the Maya.

However, most of his findings were from 600 to 400 BC, long past the city's golden age. In 1966, Michael Coe led the Yale University Project into the city's ruins, and massive excavation mapping projects were conducted, showing the true timeline of the Olmec city. The San Lorenzo Tenochtitlan Archaeological Project has directed the city's excavation since 1990, and its work has led to the discovery of thousands of artifacts, monuments, and settlement patterns.

City Landscape

The city was located in one of Mesoamerica's largest coastal regions. It was built on elevated ground (160 feet high) surrounded by a plain – including numerous tributaries and water sources. The city's location on elevated ground greatly increased its population density, as people located throughout the wetlands moved to the city to escape flooding. The city's central area covered around 140 acres, and it is estimated that the Olmecs moved between 50,000 and 2,000,000 cubic meters of dirt by basket to build the city.

An estimated 5,500 people could have lived in the immediate city, while 13,000 people could have populated the entire surrounding region. During the city's height, it controlled much of the Coatzacoalcos River basin. However, many areas to the north and east of the city enjoyed considerable autonomy from San Lorenzo's influence, including the city of La Venta.

Fishing, hunting, and gathering throughout the coastal floodplain of the city was the main form of sustenance for the city's population during its initial rise to power. Snook was the primary fish caught by San Lorenzo's fishermen, and aquatic animals made up around 60% of the city's meat consumption. The city also relied on many non-aquatic species for food, such as deer, birds, dogs, and rabbits.

While the city's population initially obtained most of its food from floodplain resources, it increasingly began to rely on agriculture throughout the Early Formative period. An estimated 30 square miles of the region were set aside to cultivate the primary crop of the Olmecs: maize. The city's inhabitants could produce 500 metric tons of maize every year, feeding around 5,500 people. While much of its agricultural sector was devoted to maize production, beans and manioc - a woody shrub also known as yuca - were widely harvested throughout the region.

The city's agricultural land was prosperous because of the region's heavy rainfall and the rich soil nurtured by the Gulf Coast and its numerous water sources. Competition for these fertile soils created competition amongst the city's population, which laid the foundations for San Lorenzo's socioeconomic composition. An elite landowning class was created in the city due to this competition, and the economic system of San Lorenzo increasingly mirrored the systems of many European and Asian kingdoms.

While the ruling elite resided on the elevated plateau of the city, most of the population lived on the plateau's slope. The ruling class lived in large houses built on platforms made of clay, with many of the city's distinctive statues surrounding their houses.

The "Red Palace," which was reserved for the city's most elite, was made of dirt floors and walls that were plastered with sand and stained by hematite. The palace was a complex that included five different structures and a large workshop dedicated to basalt sculptures. Other elite houses were made with basalt, clay, limestone, or mud.

Outside of San Lorenzo, many other nearby settlements and villages were under the direct influence of the city. The nearby settlements of Tenochtitlan and Potrero Nuevo were populated by peasants and farmers that were a central part of the city's agricultural production. These small villages were most likely ruled by elite members of the city's population. These smaller communities were not only used for agricultural production to feed the city's population but also to act as military garrisons for the city's defense.

This shows that San Lorenzo was much more than an agrarian Olmec city. During its peak of power, San Lorenzo became a regional empire that used its surrounding area to further strengthen itself.

The city's engineers also created a sophisticated drainage system. A horseshoe-shaped drainage system comprised of pipes that were made from stone brought water in and out. Some evidence points to water having a ceremonial and religious value in Olmec culture, as many of these water systems were decorated with spiritual inscriptions and objects. The city also built dikes to control flooding around the rivers at Potrero Nuevo and El Azuzul.

Sculptures

The city is famous in the field of archaeology due to the many stone statues and sculptures that have been found throughout the ruins there. The most famous style of these sculptures has been named the "colossal heads."

San Lorenzo Colossal Head 3. This particular head weighs around 9 tons and measures 5.8 feet high and 5.3 feet wide.

The largest of these statues was nine feet tall, with some weighing as much as 28 tons. The heads were usually depicted with headgear that resembles the helmets of early 20th-century American football.

These statues are believed to represent supernatural beings of the Olmec religion, leaders of the city, or revered ancestors of the city's families. Archaeologists have discovered many of these sculptures throughout the San Lorenzo site, and it is believed that there are many more scattered throughout the region. Archaeology has shown that the city was the location for many ceremonies and rituals, and these sculptures were a prominent part of many of the ceremonies.

Even more impressive than the heads themselves is the method in which they were built. Like many other Olmec artifacts, they were built with basaltic rocks. Builders of the statues would travel to the Tuxtla Mountains 40 miles away to retrieve basalt from the Cerro Cinotepeque volcano. It is thought that the stones were dragged to the Coatzacoalcos River, where they were transported by raft to the city. This shows the great sophistication of the

Olmecs, as this would not have been an easy feat.

The sculptors of the city created not only giant head sculptures but also smaller depictions of regional animals. During the early stages of the city's ascension to regional power, animals were frequently used in Olmec artwork, which may indicate that the animal world played an important role in their spirituality. The Olmec sculptors created a distinct style of figurines that depicted a jaguar-human hybrid. Clay ceramic pottery was produced and used throughout San Lorenzo households, and archaeological evidence suggests that ceramics were widely exported out of the city.

An adolescent presenting a were-jaguar baby. It is 22 inches tall and is the largest known greenstone sculpture.

Sculptor and ceramic workshops were run by the elite, and the artwork was largely used to legitimize and maintain the authority of San Lorenzo's highest-class citizens. The sculptures were strategically placed throughout the city at entrances, large plazas, and outside the homes of the elite.

The inhabitants of San Lorenzo were avid traders, frequently trading with neighboring cities and settlements. Obsidian, which was largely used to build weapons and farming equipment, was bought from nine different Mesoamerican sources throughout the highlands of southern Mexico and Guatemala.

Olmec pottery that was created in the city has been found at archaeological sites throughout Central America, especially in the Chiapas state on the modern-day Mexico-Guatemalan border. In fact, more Olmec objects were found at the Canton Corralito site in Chiapas than in the city of San Lorenzo itself. The city mainly exported these objects, as there has been no evidence found at the San Lorenzo site of the city importing pottery or other ceramic objects from outside cultures.

Most of the sculptures were destroyed or damaged around 900 BC, the time period when the city began its steep decline. While experts have not reached a consensus on the exact reason for its decline, the destruction of the sculptures may point to either the conquering of the city by an invading force or a population abandoning it –symbolically destroying all that it stood for.

A ceramic bird-shaped vessel; note the red ochre (a clay pigment). This piece has been dated between the 13th century and the 9th century BC. It can be seen in the Metropolitan Museum of Art, New York, USA.
Metropolitan Museum of Art, CC0, via Wikimedia Commons
https://commons.wikimedia.org/wiki/File:Bird_Vessel_MET_DP23080.jpg

Decline

From 1400 to 900 BC, San Lorenzo enjoyed its peak of power in the region, but from 900 BC to 400 BC, the population began to decline as the population increasingly moved out of the city. From 300 to 50 BC, the population declined even further until it was nearly deserted. The city was eventually repopulated sparsely from 800 to 1000 AD, but it never again reached anywhere close to what it once was.

Experts widely agree that the city declined and was replaced by La Venta as the regional power in the 10th century BC, but the cause of this rapid decline is unknown. The archaeological evidence shows that beginning around 900 BC, no more stone monuments or other large projects were constructed in the city. During this period, the population of the central plateau of the city declined by a staggering 57%.

Some have speculated that it was invaded by a rival city or deteriorated due to environmental changes. The shifting of the nearby ancient rivers away from the city may have severely disrupted the city's vital trade networks, and a drought that occurred during the time of the decline may have led to a decrease in crop yields.

Recent scholarship has shown evidence that throughout the Early Formative period, the city relied mostly on its coastal location for sustenance. Hunting and gathering throughout the floodplain brought many outsiders into the city, contributed to population growth, and created a political system that the elite used to maintain stability in the region. However, as the population increasingly began to rely on agriculture, this system may have begun to unravel.

The decline of San Lorenzo was most likely not caused by a single cataclysmic event but rather changing circumstances that caused its population to move elsewhere. The elite of the city surely relied on its populations' dependency on sustenance from the floodplain to maintain their control over the population, and this system of dependency may have been dismantled by an increased reliance on agriculture as the population increasingly moved into isolated farming villages in the uplands.

Some scholars believe this may indicate that the population of the city may have grown increasingly disillusioned by their government and were more than willing to move out of San Lorenzo when the opportunity presented itself. Others have surmised that the city's population simply saw more opportunity in living in isolated rural farming areas or in other surrounding settlements like La Venta that were increasingly growing more prosperous than San Lorenzo.

While San Lorenzo never again rose as a dominating city in the region after 900 BC, it laid the groundwork for the many Mesoamerican cities that would come after it. The success of the city as a regional power during the Early Formative period showed that the ever-growing developments of Mesoamerican technology, culture, and administration could no longer be confined to primitive Stone Age village society. The death of San Lorenzo as a regional power of the Gulf Coast marked the beginning of advanced Mesoamerican civilization in ancient Central America.

Chapter 2: La Venta: The Olmec Island City

The decline of San Lorenzo around 900 BC marked the neighboring city of La Venta's rise to power in the region. La Venta would enjoy half a millennium of regional dominance during the Middle Formative period (900-400 BC) of Mesoamerican history before it too was deserted by much of its population.

Throughout the Middle Formative period, influences from the city of San Lorenzo spread throughout Central America, as larger settlements and urban centers began to emerge throughout Mesoamerican society. The increased reliance on agriculture meant that Mesoamerican sustenance no longer relied on hunting and gathering, and the ownership of fertile land began to transform the power structures of the region.

As these towns grew, socioeconomic class structures were created, and elite members of cities increasingly demanded luxury items, including everything from stone figurines to blocks of serpentine. This created an explosion of Olmec crafts and artisanship, with many of the cities' elite actively creating workshops to produce these objects in mass. Trade networks throughout the region became used more frequently, as the demand for these items led to cities specializing in some production and importing others.

Not only did settlements grow by increased population density, but distinctive Olmec cultural practices also became more engrained in the region, as these city centers became hotbeds for a variety of Mesoamerican cultural influences. No other city better displayed this explosion of Olmec culture during the Middle Formative period than the city of La Venta.

Many archaeologists believe that La Venta was the largest Olmec city of ancient Mesoamerica, both in population and influence. Compared to the San Lorenzo site, excavations at La Venta indicate that the city ingrained religious ceremony much deeper in its population. City priests had enormous power in La Venta and frequently used rituals and religious doctrine to maintain control of its population. The city was home to Mesoamerica's first pyramid, which attracted people from around the region to participate in its religious ceremonies.

The Great Pyramid at La Venta. It is around 110 feet high and filled with an approximate 3.5 million cubic feet of earth. It is entirely man-made; it has been theorized that the Olmecs built this to represent a mountain, which they considered to be sacred, to use in their religious ceremonies.

It is believed that the city was first settled in 1750 BC and gradually rose in population until the fall of San Lorenzo around 900 BC marked its regional dominance. The city of La Venta was located on Mexico's largest alluvial plane in Mexico, and its territory comprised the area between the Mezcalapa and Coatzacoalcos rivers in the modern-day Mexican state of Tabasco.

The city itself was located on a two-square-mile island in a coastal swamp of the Gulf of Mexico.

The city was located in close proximity to four separate ecosystems: marshes, mangrove swamps, tropical forests, and the ocean. This gave the inhabitants a variety of flora and fauna to hunt and gather throughout the region, though agriculture increasingly began to dominate the city throughout the Middle Formative period. The inhabitants of La Venta made the animals of the floodplain a significant part of their diet and increasingly established maize farms in riparian zones of the region. The city had extensive trade networks throughout the region, as archaeologists have found evidence of small military garrisons in nearby regions that protected the city's trade.

Scholars are unsure of how much of the surrounding area was under the direct control of La Venta. It is believed that the Arroyo Pesquero settlement (20 km to the south) and Arroyo Sonso development (around 35 km to the southeast) may have been controlled by the La Venta government.

Like San Lorenzo, the city had a complex society of different occupations and socioeconomic classes. La Venta had an exceptionally segregated society, as the elite were allowed to attend ceremonies in parts of the city where the rest of the population was not. Most of the city's population lived relatively far away from the central island of the city. Much of the city's population lived in the nearby settlement of San Andres and other neighboring towns and villages.

The city itself was largely built from dirt and clay, as well as the basalt that was transported from the nearby Tuxtla Mountains. Four large basalt "colossal head" sculptures have also been found throughout La Venta; these closely resemble those found at San Lorenzo.

Known as Monument One. It was found about a hundred feet south of the Great Pyramid, and it can be seen today at Villahermosa. This particular head stands at about nine feet high, and it is believed it was created between 800 and 700 BC.

Excavations

Frans Blom and Oliver La Farge first published details about the city in 1925 during an expedition sponsored by Tulane University. They originally thought they discovered a Mayan city until radiocarbon dating showed that it was an older Olmec city. Because of its location in the dense jungle, it took many years for experts to realize the different remnants of the site all belonged to one city.

Mathew Stirling and Philip Drucker led the first excavations of the site throughout the 1940s. These initial excavations were funded by the Smithsonian Institution and the National Geographic Society. Stirling's published works about his findings at La Venta greatly helped scholars understand the Olmec culture.

The National Geographic Society once again funded an expedition led by Philip Drucker, Robert Heizer, and Robert Squier in 1955 that specifically focused on the tombs and plazas of Complex A. Drucker's team discovered a multitude of artifacts, including remnants of Olmec ceramic pottery and jade jewelry. They also made some of the first maps of the city, dividing it into designated zones. The team found a total of 53 different offerings, which ranged from small tombs filled with pottery to massive underground pits filled with large serpentine blocks.

By the early 1960s, most of the city was still largely unexcavated, and many archaeologists believed that the Mexican government was not putting in adequate effort to protect the site. Illegal excavations that were not overseen by professionals, as well as the establishment of a base of operations in the city for an oil company, greatly threatened the future work of archaeologists.

Throughout the 1960s, the National Geographic Society continued funding excavations, and in 1967, it was discovered that the shape of the city mapped out by archaeologists had been completely wrong due to dense jungle foliage covering much of the area. The excavation team also took extensive carbon samples to prove that the inhabitants of the city predated Mayan civilization.

The Instituto Nacional de Antropologia e Historia conducted large excavations throughout the 1980s. These efforts mainly revolved around accurately mapping the city and creating a protective border that would help preserve the site. Since the 1980s, the La Venta site has continually been excavated and has become one of the most studied archaeological sites in the Americas, though it still faces many dangers that could inhibit further accurate excavations.

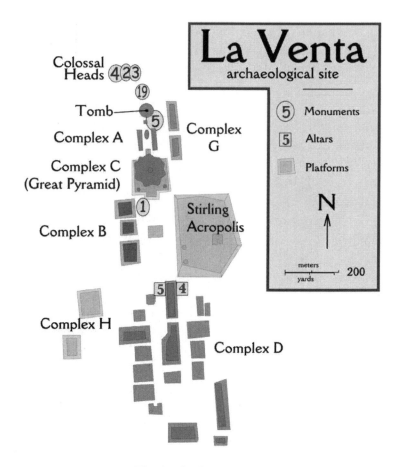

The site plan for La Venta.

In 2009, 23 different sculptures were damaged in the city by members of a Mexican evangelical church who conducted spiritual rituals that involved the pouring of saltwater, grape juice, and oil on these sculptures, including the four colossal head sculptures of the city. Following the incident, the Mexican government was pushed into enacting stricter protection laws by the Mexican population.

The Layout of the City

The central island of the city was reserved for the houses of the elite. The island also included a sacred section restricted to the ruling class, the Great Pyramid, and the plazas in the south of the island.

Numerous altars, mounds, sculptures, and tombs found by excavators at the La Venta site show that the city had a large ceremonial value to the Olmec people of the region. The center of the city served as a massive ceremonial area, with a multitude of mounds, platforms, and tombs all pointed in the same direction, eight degrees west of north. This central area has been divided by archaeologists into four distinct zones.

In the northernmost Complex A, many ceremonial mounds surround two large courts that were only used by the elite of the city. Rows of large basalt columns separated these elite plazas from the rest of the city's population.

There are also numerous tombs built for deceased rulers in this area. Many jade ornaments were found throughout these tombs, as well as mirrors made of iron ore. These items that were left throughout this area have proved to be some of the most valuable offerings of early Mesoamerican history. Unfortunately, due to the humidity of the Gulf Coast climate, only a few bones have survived the centuries. This has made it difficult to understand exactly what kind of people were buried in these tombs.

While compared to other later mounds and plazas of later Mesoamerican society, La Venta's were not especially large; however, they were exceptionally well constructed and finely detailed. The platforms, built mostly from adobe bricks, located throughout the plaza were multi-colored, largely made from dyed sands and clay.

In Complex A, five offerings of large serpentine blocks (imported into the city) were found in the tombs of deceased rulers. Large pavement mosaics were buried in many of these tombs and were decorated with multi-color clays, and some have speculated that they were used to represent spiritual imagery.

One of the unearthed mosaics; it measures around fifteen by twenty feet and consists of nearly five hundred blocks of serpentine.

At the eastern side of the public plaza of Complex B is the Stirling Acropolis, a large platform that was used for public ceremonies and speeches. Three small mounds were also found on the western edge of Complex B.

Complex C is home to what was the tallest structure in Mesoamerica at the time of its construction. The 110 ft tall Great Pyramid located in the very center of the town was built almost entirely out of clay, and numerous tombs and altars have been found on its summit. From that summit, onlookers could survey the entire surrounding area, including the Tuxtla Mountains, where the city obtained most of its basalt from.

It is believed that many rituals and ceremonies were conducted on this summit, as mountains were considered sacred to the Olmec belief system. Today, it more resembles a large hill due to centuries of wind erosion, but it was originally built as a rectangular pyramid that had stepped terraces along its sides.

South of the pyramid was the plaza that was devoted to ceremonies for the larger general population. A large platform stood in the middle of the area, where speeches and rituals were given before large crowds.

Little is known about Complex D, which appears to have been the location for the city's governmental buildings. Twenty mounds have been found throughout this complex, and another large plaza has been found in this complex in the south of the city.

The archaeological evidence of La Venta shows that the artwork styles of the city transformed gradually from full-round sculptures that greatly resembled those in San Lorenzo to relief sculptures that began to take on a uniquely La Ventian style.

The colossal heads found in La Venta were thought to be created around the decline of San Lorenzo, which may indicate that there was considerable cross-pollination of artwork styles during this transitional period. Another sculptural style that became prevalent during this period was the depiction of figures sitting on large thrones, with many appearing to represent the city's leaders.

The sculptural styles of the city greatly reflected the Olmec belief system, as numerous depictions of sacred natural features like mountains and freshwater springs are found throughout the city. Deity figures, often depicted as animal-human hybrids, are also found extensively throughout the city.

Seven altars made of basalt rock were found throughout the city. Altars 4 and 5 were both decorated with figures that may have represented a spiritual deity or a ruler of the city. Altar 4 shows a figure that is inside a cave or the mouth of a fictional creature. Altar 5 shows a figure that is holding a deceased human-jaguar hybrid baby. While some have asserted that this is a sign of Olmec child sacrifice, others believe that it describes a creation story of some kind.

Archaeologist Matthew Stirling and Marion Stirling in Veracruz, Mexico
Alexander Wetmore, CC0, via Wikimedia Commons
https://commons.wikimedia.org/wiki/File:Matthew_and_Marion_Stirling_in_Veracruz,_Mexico.jpg

Much of the details on these altars have been faded due to centuries of erosion, but they all clearly have important spiritual components. Scholars believe that these altars were actually thrones that the leaders of the city would sit on during ceremonies and rituals.

Artifacts

While Mesoamerican scholars are still unsure of the exact religious practices and beliefs of the Olmec, artifacts found throughout La Venta have provided many clues of their spiritual beliefs. Many distinct symbols have been found carved onto stones, objects, or tombs, which could point to symbols used in the Olmec religion. Many depictions of deities, often with hybrid human-animal characteristics, were also carved throughout the city.

A relief from La Venta. This is the earliest known representation of a feathered serpent; it has been dated to 1400 to 400 BC.
Audrey and George Delange, Attribution, via Wikimedia Commons
https://commons.wikimedia.org/wiki/File:La_Venta_Stele_19_(Delange).jpg

Jade was widely considered the most sought-after object for the Mesoamerican elite. Not only was jade extremely difficult to find in the region, but it was also very difficult to shape into jewelry. Making one single jade bead would have required a highly skilled jewelry-maker to spend many hours sawing and shaping the rock. Over 3,000 jade objects were found just in Complex A.

Archaeologists have found many skeletons covered in cinnabar and buried with obsidian mirrors, which were both used to display high status in Mesoamerican culture. The prevalence of these objects throughout tombs and other burial sites throughout the focal points of the city shows the immense wealth that the elite of the city had come to enjoy. It is clear that at La Venta, the socioeconomic gap between the ruling class and the peasant class had widened greatly, and this disparity of wealth played a decisive role in La Venta's cultural and religious practices.

The Legacy of La Venta

San Lorenzo and La Venta shared many characteristics, suggesting that many influences and people may have moved from San Lorenzo to La Venta around the time of the former city's decline. Both cities had very similar styles of sculptures, ceramics, and structures, including the "colossal heads." They also met a similar fate, as the city's population began moving out of the city around 400 BC.

While San Lorenzo was the first capital of advanced Mesoamerican society, La Venta was the first truly urban Mesoamerican society. La Venta showed complexity that dwarfed any other Mesoamerican city of the time period. Perhaps most importantly, La Venta has proven to be one of the most helpful sites to archaeologists who have tried to understand the Olmec culture.

Throughout the Middle Formative period, the city of La Venta acted as much more than a population center; it acted as a cultural hub for the region that solidified its peoples' cultural beliefs and practices. During the golden age of La Venta, massive construction projects carried out throughout the city reflected the rapidly expanding sophistication of Mesoamerican society. The prevalence of sacred and luxury objects among the city's elite, as well as the way that the Olmec belief system was ingrained into the landscape of the city, shows enormous contrast to the small hunter-gatherer villages that comprised the region only a few centuries earlier.

By the end of the Middle Formative period, it was clear that Mesoamerican society was rapidly shifting into an increasingly urban, interconnected civilization that revolved around distinctive cultural practices and beliefs. However, it would soon be clear that the Olmec civilization would not survive the rapidly changing cultural climate of Mesoamerica completely intact.

While archaeologists are still largely conflicted on many parts of the cultural practices, spirituality, and day-to-day life of the Olmecs, La Venta has shed light on many aspects of the changing Mesoamerican landscape throughout the Middle Formative period. Though the city would experience a similar mysterious decline to San Lorenzo, it would forever remain the central archaeological site for Olmec culture and perhaps the final great city of the Olmec people.

Chapter 3: Olmec Decline and the Epi-Olmecs

From 400 to 350 BC, the Olmec population of the Gulf Coast cities decreased drastically. Scholars have not yet reached a consensus on why the Olmec civilization collapsed. Many believe that it was caused by changing environmental factors, which could have destroyed the livelihoods of Olmec communities that were wholly dependent on crop yields.

A change in the flow of the region's river systems may have disrupted both farming operations and trade in the region. The change of river flow may have occurred naturally or from their agricultural practices, which could have silted up the rivers. Other experts believe that the depopulation of the region was caused by volcanic activity.

Around 400 BC, as Olmec society was declining in the region, the Epi-Olmec culture began to grow in the western region of the Olmec heartland. While many distinct Olmec cultural hallmarks were lost in the rise of the Epi-Olmec, most scholars agree that this was a transformation of Olmec culture instead of a direct break from it.

Important Epi-Olmec sites.

The Late Formative period that characterized the rise of the Epi-Olmec saw a large decline in trade and commerce among Mesoamerican societies. The Epi-Olmec art was also vastly inferior to the Olmec art of La Venta and San Lorenzo. The sculptures found in Epi-Olmec settlements like Tres Zapotes had much less detail and depth than traditional Olmec art, suggesting that craftsmanship took on a much less important role in their society.

While much of the great Olmec art of the Epi-Olmec's predecessors focused on depicting their rulers, artists of the Epi-Olmec focused much of their work on capturing historical events. During this period, artwork and inscriptions found throughout Epi-Olmec sites increasingly began to show a date next to it, which was practically unheard of by their predecessors.

These inscriptions largely used the Isthmian Script, the earliest writing system of Mesoamerica, dating back to 500 BC. The script has many characteristics of the Maya script that would be used centuries later. It is believed that the script originated in the Isthmus of Tehuantepec and made its way to Olmec cities through cultural diffusion and Gulf coast trade networks.

Tres Zapotes

The greatest city of the Epi-Olmec, Tres Zapotes, was located on the western portion of the Olmec heartland in modern-day Veracruz on the western part of the Los Tuxtlas Mountain range. The city became populated around 900 BC, around the time of the decline of San Lorenzo, and reached its height of power during the 5th century BC. The city was inhabited well past the 4th century but gradually lost its power in the region.

The location of Tres Zapotes was a prime location for a thriving Olmec city, as it was surrounded by a variety of ecosystems and resources. The nearby upland forests and lowlands swamps proved to be great hunting grounds while also providing the city many natural resources like timber. The nearby mountain range also gave the city access to basalt stone that could be used to erect monuments.

Tres Zapotes also benefited greatly from the Arroyo Hueyapan River running directly through the city. During the golden era of the Olmec, the city was one of the great trading hubs for the Gulf Coast Olmec, and there is evidence that the city traded with other civilizations from northern Guatemala to Central Mexico. However, the proliferation of trade in the region would sharply decline during the Epi-Olmec era.

From 400 BC forward, the city began a transitional period from traditional Olmec to Epi-Olmec culture. While the architectural and artistic achievements of the city dwarfed that of San Lorenzo and La Venta, the Ep-Olmecs made great achievements in the Mesoamerican calendar and writing system that was growing increasingly sophisticated.

Unlike the well-connected trade routes of La Venta and San Lorenzo, Tres Zapotes was not a central hub of Mesoamerican trade networks during the Epi-Olmec era. Some experts believe that the decline in Olmec trade was caused by the cocoa plant, as many trade routes were diverted to Maya cocoa traders. The epi-Olmec also traded much less luxury elite items like jade and obsidian, indicating that the cities' elite's material wealth greatly declined, or the epi-Olmec were forced to shift their focus from the region's trade to sustenance and survival.

Structures

Over 150 structures have been found throughout the Tres Zapotes archaeological site, with most being built sometime between 400 BC and 200 AD. While Olmec cities tended to have a main central plaza or courtyard in the center of the city, the layout of Tres Zapotes was much more dispersed and spread out. Many of the site's most famous structures were found well outside the center of the city.

The dwellings of the ruling elite were also decentralized, with several royal areas spread out through the site. This may indicate that the system was ruled by several different families or factions instead of one governing body.

Two colossal giant heads have been found in the vicinity of the city's ruins, though they are much smaller than those found at San Lorenzo and La Venta. The sculptures found at the city's archaeological site highlight this transformation, as traditional religious depictions gradually turned into more secular historical depictions.

Monument A from Tres Zapotes. It stands around five feet tall and five feet wide. It weighs close to eight tons.

Stela C, one of Tres Zapotes' most famous structures, included an inscription of one of the city's powerful rulers depicted as a jaguar-like figure. But more importantly, the stela includes a date from the Long Count calendar. While the calendar had been gradually developing throughout the Olmec heartland, Tres Zapotes was one of the first cities where a date was inscribed on architecture. This calendar would soon become a central part of Mesoamerican life and one of the defining features of the Maya civilization.

By the mid-3rd century AD, the surrounding settlements of Cerro de las Mesas and Remojadas replaced Tres Zapotes as the dominating cities of the region. Unlike the two preceding cities, Tres Zapotes did not see a sudden depopulation of its inhabitants. The city would remain populated up to 900 AD but would gradually leave its Olmec influences behind in its transition to Classical Veracruz culture.

The Legacy of the Olmec

While trade was already an integral part of Mesoamerican society before the rise of the Olmecs, they were the first merchants of the region to travel regularly travel across long distances to trade with other cities and civilizations. These trade routes brought great economic prosperity to the Gulf Coast cities like San Lorenzo and La Venta, but more importantly, they spread Olmec cultural influences far and wide throughout Central America. These merchants also brought back cultural ideas from other civilizations and populations to the Olmec cities. The prevalence of Olmec trade in the region caused Mesoamerica to be more closely connected and contributed to great cultural diffusion between populations.

Many of the religious beliefs of later civilizations like the Aztecs and Maya stem from the Olmec pantheon, with many worshiping the same gods as the Olmec did centuries before them. The human-jaguar figures that were found throughout Olmec cities would later become a central part of later Mesoamerican religion. The tombs and structures of many Classic Maya cities depicted their divine rulers as jaguar figures that greatly resemble the Olmec depictions.

The Olmec artists, artisans, and architects made perhaps the most impressive achievements of early Mesoamerican society. The colossal, intricately constructed structures that were found throughout the Olmec cities dwarfed anything that had been constructed in Central America before. Though some designs, such as the colossal heads, would be left in the past, the civilizations that came after the Olmec used cities like San Lorenzo as a shining example of what a powerful urban center should be.

The Olmec are credited with creating the first solidified writing system of Mesoamerica. They also made great progress in creating an accurate calendrical system and mapping the solar system. All three of these Olmec innovations would be gradually perfected and expanded upon by the Maya.

At the beginning of the 5th century BC, the Epi-Olmec emerged as a transitional civilization, expanding on the innovations and foundations of their predecessors while leaving other antiquated cultural ideas in the past. The Zapotec civilization to the south on the Pacific coast, the great city of Teotihuacan in the Valley of Mexico, and the Maya civilization of the Yucatan to the east would soon emerge as the dominating peoples of Mesoamerica.

While the Olmec would gradually fade into the distant background of the region's political order, these civilizations would continually build upon what Mesoamerica's first advanced civilization created.

Chapter 4: The Preclassic Maya Era

As Olmec society on the Gulf Coast was gradually transforming into the Classical Veracruz culture, to the east, the small settlements of the Yucatan Peninsula were increasingly growing larger. Though these small towns had many characteristics of the Olmec, they began to develop many distinct cultural characteristics of their own. As the Olmec cities of the Gulf were gradually declining, the Maya of the Yucatan were slowly becoming the greatest civilization of Central America.

The Preclassic Maya period includes the establishment of permanent settlements around the beginning of the first millennium BC up to the Classic period around 250 AD. The Preclassic period is divided into the Early Preclassic (before 1000 BC), Middle Preclassic (1000-400 BC), and Late Preclassic (400 BC-250 AD). The largest cities of the Preclassic were El Mirador, Cival, San Bartolo, Seibal, Nakbe, and Uaxactun.

In the decades leading up to the beginning of the Classic period in 250 AD, there was a "Preclassic Collapse," when many of the cities that flourished during the Preclassic period were rapidly depopulated. This would create a mass dispersal of their populations, who moved to other cities that would become the great urban centers of the Classic period.

The Yucatán Peninsula

During the Olmec golden age, Maya settlements were increasingly growing more complex throughout the Yucatan Peninsula, which would eventually become the Maya heartland. The peninsula is largely comprised of lowland plains of dense rainforest that have very few hilly or mountainous regions.

The most northern regions of the peninsula receive much less rainfall than the other regions, making the northern cities especially susceptible to drought. The ground of the northern and northwest regions in the coastal plain is largely made of limestone, and this region of the peninsula has a plethora of natural limestone cave systems created by erosion from rainfall. The region is also known for its massive sinkholes, which are created when these cave systems collapse.

The northeastern region is largely known for its vast swamplands, which served as a great defensive boundary between other regions of the peninsula. The northern coastal plain had very few river systems, with most of the peninsula's rivers being located in the southern lowlands and highlands.

The Petén Basin, located in the central lowlands, is characterized by a diverse array of topographic features, including dense rainforests, swamps, and lakes. The annual rainfall for the entire peninsula is 43 inches, with the wet season running from June to September and the dry season running from October to May. The Petén region receives the most rainfall in the peninsula, which contributed to it becoming the dominant region for the great cities of the Classic period.

Early Preclassic

Evidence has shown that agriculture existed in the Maya lowlands dating back to 3000 BC.These were most likely nomadic or sparsely populated populations that gradually created permanent villages. Hunting and gathering was the primary source of sustenance for the Preclassic Mayas, though the cultivation of maize increasingly became the dominant food source.

Ceramic pottery began to be created during this period, with many styles borrowed from the Olmecs and other neighboring Mesoamerican cultures. The Early Preclassic Mayas had a close trading relationship with the Olmecs, and immense cultural diffusion occurred between the two cultures.

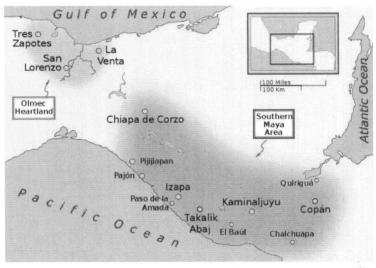

A map of the major southern Mayan cities.

Middle Preclassic

By the beginning of the first millennium BC, the city of Aguada Fénix was a prosperous urban center in Tabasco. The construction of Aguada Fénix marked the beginning of the permanent agrarian settlements of the Maya people. Up until the city's construction, the Maya people of the region were largely nomadic and didn't produce a significant amount of pottery.

The archaeological record points to this point in Maya history as a time when distinctive Maya ceramics were produced more frequently, and settlements became larger and more populated. This period of transformation marked the beginning of the Maya city-states that would soon dominate the region.

Trade between different regions and settlements became more frequent, and the exchange of luxury items such as jade and obsidian artifacts increased greatly. Infrastructure projects, such as canals and irrigation systems, became larger and more complex as well.

The small settlements of the Preclassic increasingly took on the organizational characteristics of large cities, such as having large plazas in their center and a vast array of ceremonial monuments and structures. Many of the architectural projects of this period borrowed heavily from the nearby Olmec cities like La Venta and San Lorenzo.

Evidence has also pointed to a rise in warfare during this period, as Maya weapons greatly improved, and kings were increasingly depicted as warriorlike figures. There have also been discoveries of mass graves that are dated to this period that show evidence of the execution of prisoners of war.

Late Preclassic

By the Late Preclassic, the city of Kaminaljuyu controlled much of the Maya highlands, while the city of El Mirador controlled the lowlands. There is evidence that the Maya of the highlands began to expand north into the southern and central lowlands during this period, where the great cities of the Classic period would soon emerge.

Many Olmec cultural practices and beliefs inspired the Maya, as their own distinctive cultural practices became increasingly complex. Throughout the Preclassic and into the Classic, the Maya people began to create a civilization that increasingly had its own characteristics that broke away from the Gulf Olmec traditions and began to create a distinctive Maya culture. By the Late Preclassic, the iconic Mayan stepped pyramids were being built in some cities, indicating that spirituality and religion increasingly became an integral part of city life.

Late Preclassic Maya sculpture found in Kaminaljuyu.

Preclassic Agriculture

Many scholars have been puzzled by the population size of the Maya cities of the Preclassic and Classic periods throughout the Yucatan Peninsula. The cities of the lowlands were located in one of the most unlikely places in the world for an advanced agricultural civilization. The Yucatan Peninsula and its surrounding area were filled with dense rainforests, infertile soils, impenetrable swamplands, and severe seasonal droughts.

Just like the early Olmecs, the Maya gradually transformed from small settlements of hunter-gatherers to large settlements of agriculturalists centered around the cultivation of maize. While maize was the primary crop of the Maya people, beans, squash, and many other crops were also grown by Maya farmers.

Despite not having the advantage of metal tools and domesticated animals that the contemporary farmers of Europe had, the Maya were some of the most advanced agriculturalists of their time. The Maya largely used slash and burn agricultural techniques. This method involved cutting down a given forested area and then burning it. Crops would then be planted in the nutrient-rich ashy dirt of the burnt area. After using this burnt area several times, they would move to new land to allow the area to regenerate. This proved to be a highly effective method for the Maya, though as the Classic cities grew, it would also contribute to heavy deforestation of the lowlands.

The Maya also used complex irrigation and terracing techniques by taking advantage of the many swamps dispersed throughout the Yucatan region. Maya engineers used ingenious methods to divert water sources throughout the wetlands into canals to create more fertile arable land. In the mountainous highlands, terraces were frequently cut into the sides of mountains to grow maize.

Gender also played a major role in agricultural Maya society. While men tended the fields, hunted, and fought in battles, women were put in charge of running the home and carrying out domestic duties.

By the Classic period, Maya agriculture and water management had become extremely efficient and could support large urban populations. The surplus of crops and a large growing population that could craft luxury items like ceramics led to increased trade throughout Maya society.

El Mirador used a water collection system; above, you can see the stucco friezes that adorned it.

El Mirador

There is no better example of the ingenious methods used in Preclassic agriculture than El Mirador. The city of El Mirador was the great city of the Maya lowlands during the Late Preclassic. It blossomed as the central trading hub of the region from around 300 BC to the 1st century AD.

El Mirador was surrounded by a multitude of wet swamplands, which turned the city into one of the most efficient agricultural centers in the region. The farmers brought hundreds of tons of mud from the swampy areas and used it to create terraces throughout the city's farms. The pH of the soil was increased by adding lime to it, which allowed the nutrient-deplete soil of the region to grow a variety of crops.

Around the beginning of the Common Era, El Mirador and many other neighboring cities saw a massive exodus of its population as part of the "Preclassic collapse." Environmental studies have shown that the region surrounding El Mirador was heavily deforested by the time of the collapse. A large proportion of the surrounding forest was cut down to produce lime and for other architectural projects.

With the absence of trees in the region, much of the nutrient-deplete soil was no longer held down by natural vegetation and was swept into the swamplands by heavy rainfall. The nutrient-rich mud of the swamps that once served as the secret ingredient for the city's agricultural boom was gradually covered by layers of soil from the surrounding areas.

Preclassic Architecture

The timeline of Maya architecture shows the great progression of their civilization. From their roots in stone age village communities, by the Late Preclassic period, the Maya were constructing some of Mesoamerica's largest and most complex structures. The many impressive monuments and buildings of the lowland Classic cities were predominately built with limestone, while the highland cities mostly used sandstone and igneous rocks.

A photo of La Danta, a temple located in El Mirador. It stands at around 236 feet tall and is considered to be one of the largest pyramids in the world.

While initially, the Maya built structures out of necessity to support their growing populations, the architecture of the lowlands increasingly began to be characterized by elements that promoted the city's political and religious order. The architecture was increasingly decorated with hieroglyphs and inscriptions of Maya gods, historical events, and powerful rulers. The ruling class used the architecture of the city to solidify their divine power by making religion an integral part of their cities.

Throughout the Classic period, the rulers of the Maya became inexorably linked with their architecture. The religious element of these structures echoed the belief that these great cities were constructed by divine rulers who were put on the throne by the gods. Sculptures, monuments, inscriptions, and sacred temples were all built depicting past rulers, stressing the divinity and historical significance of the ruling dynasty. In examples where scholars believe the population of the cities overthrew their rulers in revolution or revolt, many of these sacred structures and monuments were defaced and purposefully damaged.

Aside from the political and practical utility of these structures, they also possessed great astronomical and religious significance. Many of the great structures of the Maya urban centers were built oriented towards a cardinal direction. The north and south represented the heavens and the underworld, while the east and west were associated with the sun's rising and setting.

Great plazas were located in the center of nearly every Classic Maya city, usually surrounded by the city's pyramids and other large structures. These plazas served as places for the population to congregate and observe large ceremonies. Different parts of the cities were connected by causeways, which were wide streets that were made out of stone or wood. These streets all led to the central plaza and connected the city to outside settlements with which it had a trading or political relationship.

The Classic Maya architects borrowed many different architectural styles from throughout Mesoamerica. The style that was chosen often reflected an alliance system, trading relationship, or cultural background with another city. For example, the great Maya city of Tikal had many architectural designs that mirrored styles seen in the city of Teotihuacan in Central Mexico. The similarity of architecture reflects the close relationship between the two cities, as Teotihuacan conquered Tikal in the Early Classic period and maintained a strong cultural connection with the city throughout Tikal's political apogee.

Many cities in the Maya lowlands also had architectural styles that mirrored the Toltec city of Tullan in Central Mexico. Some evidence has shown that the Toltecs invaded some regions of the Maya heartland during the Terminal Classic and Postclassic periods. The Puuc style of architecture seen in cities like Chichen Itza had its roots in the center of the Maya Yucatan heartland. It used a repetitive geometric style that often included masked figures of the Maya gods.

An example of the Puuc style. This particular building is in Uxmal.
Diego Delso, CC BY-SA 4.0 <https://creativecommons.org/licenses/by-sa/4.0>, via Wikimedia Commons https://commons.wikimedia.org/wiki/File:Cuadrangulo_de_las_monjas-Uxmal-Yucatan-Mexico0265.JPG

Most of the Maya population lived in thatched-roof hamlets with one or two rooms, while the royal elite lived in palace complexes comprised of several rooms. The elite complexes grew extensively throughout the Classic period, and by the 9th century, many of them had their own courtyards and water supplies.

An example of a traditional Mayan house.

While the everyday Maya population buried their deceased relatives in small tombs near their homes, the royalty was buried in elaborate tombs and temples. The burial practices of an elite figure depended on how powerful the ruler was. Most rulers were buried with valuable, sacred items like jade in decorated tombs located in a part of the city dedicated to the commemoration of the deceased elite. More powerful rulers had entire temples and pyramids dedicated to them, with many including a visual depiction of the ruler and their name and time of death.

The great step pyramids are often viewed today as the iconic symbol of the Classic Maya. These pyramids were largely dedicated to deceased rulers, and many rituals would be carried out at the top of the staircases in honor of the gods.

Many large structures built by the Maya, including the step pyramids, were continually built and rebuilt. As one structure began to grow obsolete, a new structure would be constructed on the outside of it. This allowed Maya rulers to construct buildings that were ostensibly completely new and possessed the former structure's solid foundation.

The Classic Maya also constructed some of the world's first advanced water management systems with massive reservoirs that collected rainwater for their cities. As the region was constantly under the threat of seasonal droughts and had very few riparian sources, the Classic Maya populations came to depend heavily on these urban reservoirs.

The urban Maya erected thousands of "stelae," slabs of rock often inscribed with historical events, religious depictions, or portraits of rulers. Many of the stelae included dates from the Maya calendars, which have greatly aided archaeologists in creating a timeline for Maya history.

Preclassic Collapse

A Preclassic collapse occurred around 100 AD, and scholars have yet to reach a consensus on the causes of the rapid depopulation of the Preclassic cities. Scientific evidence points to a series of droughts that enveloped the region during this period, which may have led to inadequate water supplies for the growing urban population. There is also evidence that many of the Preclassical cities had been heavily deforested by the first millennium AD, and their water supplies had been heavily contaminated by urban runoff.

Whatever the causes were, this collapse of the Preclassic cities paved the way for the population boom in the southern and central lowlands that would characterize the Classic period.

As the populations of Preclassic cities like El Mirador collapsed, ideas and culture dispersed throughout the Yucatan Peninsula. This dispersal of the Maya across the Yucatan created immense cultural diffusion, as the Maya began to settle into the towns that would soon become the greatest cities of Mesoamerica.

SECTION TWO:
THE CLASSIC MAYA ERA
(250-900 AD)

Chapter 5: Classic Maya Society

The Classic period of the Maya civilization was the apogee of Maya cultural, scientific, and political achievements. The cities of Tikal, Calakmul, Palenque, and Copan became the great cities of the Maya civilization. During this period, the greatest monuments and temples that define the civilization today were constructed by divine rulers who ruled over great regional political empires. The rulers of the classic period took on secular leadership and a spiritual role that proclaimed them as divine figures ordained by the gods.

The Classic period is divided into three distinct periods: During the Early Classic (250-550), the urban centers of the southern and central lowlands became the dominating cities of the Maya civilization. The Late Classic (550-830) saw these cities at their peak of population, architecture, and political power. This period saw constant warfare throughout the lowlands, as a power struggle ensued between the great cities and their alliances. The Terminal Classic (830-950) was the time of the "Classic Maya Collapse," when these cities were rapidly abandoned by their inhabitants, never to be densely populated again.

Classic Maya Political System

Unlike the Aztec civilization, which had a centralized government in its capital of Teotochtitcal, the cities of the Maya civilization acted as independent states that acted autonomously. Vast alliance systems were formed throughout the Maya heartland that linked these cities with cultural ties, military alliances, or trading partners.

More powerful cities also brought smaller vassal cities under their control, which usually paid tribute to the larger city in exchange for military protection and access to trade networks. Within the cities of the Classic period, the urban Mayan political systems revolved around hereditary rulers who believed that the gods chose them to rule their populations.

The Classic Maya had four socioeconomic levels. The kings and high royalty of the largest cities like Tikal and Calakmul were considered the highest class of Maya society. Next were the smaller vassal states' leaders, who were considered close military allies and trading partners with the larger city. Next were the village settlements that were ruled by regional nobility. Last were the hamlets located in the periphery of urban Maya society, which were solely dedicated to farming or some other small-scale production of goods.

Powerful kings in Maya cities did not become common until around the 4th century AD, when large stelae began being erected throughout urban areas that commemorated the city's royalty. The royalty considered themselves halfway between humans and gods and believed they had a sacred duty to act as an intermediary between the two.

There are examples of queens ruling cities, but this usually only happened when there was not a suitable male heir for the throne. Young men of royal families that were destined for the throne were often military leaders and led campaigns against enemy city-states.

Kings were expected to be on the battlefield and personally lead their troops into battle. The capturing of enemy royalty was one of the most important parts of Maya warfare. Captured kings or nobles were not always executed, but many were sacrificed in large ritualistic ceremonies.

Enormous, lavish palaces where the royal families resided were an inescapable part of Classic Maya urban centers. These palaces would usually be constructed in the city's central plaza near the great temples and other large structures.

Throughout the Classic period, the royalty of the Maya cities increasingly lived lavishly. The small, modest palaces of the Early Classic eventually turned into elaborate complexes by the

Terminal Classic. Many scholars have pointed to revolution or an overthrow of the royal class due to rising income inequality as a possible reason for the collapse of the Classic cities. It would make sense that a population that increasingly found itself in dire circumstances would grow resentment towards a divine ruling class that lived so extravagantly right before their eyes in the center of their city.

<u>Religion</u>

It is impossible to visit the ruins of the Classic Maya cities today without noticing the evidence of a complex spiritual belief system. The gods of the Maya played an integral role throughout their society, from agriculture to the divine rulership of kings. The spirituality of the Maya revolved around the belief that the entire world was enveloped by "k'uh," which translates to "sacred."

Maya priests were tasked with overseeing the religious order of their society. This entailed conducting ceremonies and observing the sky to decipher the "will of the gods."

Some Maya gave the sun and moon distinct characters, with the sun being a masculine figure and the moon being feminine. They believed the gods placed the sun and moon on earth but were brought into the heavens as punishment due to the feminine moon's infidelity.

Death was an important part of the Maya religion, especially for rulers. Entire sections of cities were solely dedicated to the burials and commemoration of deceased rulers. The Maya believed that the soul traveled to the underworlds after death, which is often depicted as a dark place ruled by jaguar-like gods.

The Maya believed that time worked cyclically instead of linearly. They believed that different worlds had existed before them, and many others would exist after them. They believed that their world would come to an abrupt ending one day, and the gods would create a new world.

While the practice of human sacrifice is certainly overblown in popular media depicting the Maya, it was practiced widely in the Classic cities. The shedding of human blood was considered a divine and necessary offering to the gods. Prisoners of war and rulers of rival cities were the most commonly sacrificed peoples.

The creation of the universe is one of the most important components of the Maya religion. In the beginning, the sky and earth were attached to each other, and there was no room for any life to exist on the planet. The gods planted a large tree on the earth to lift up the sky and create room for the existence of life. While the tree grew, its roots stretched down to the depths of the underworld, and its branches reached up into the upper world. Animals and vegetation began to inhabit the Earth, but the gods were displeased because there were no advanced beings that could use verbal communication to praise them, so they created humans.

The Maya Creation Story

The Maya believed that they were living in the third cyclical creation of the universe and that the two previous ones had been destroyed. They believed that theirs too would eventually be destroyed by the gods.

In the first creation of the universe, the people were made entirely of mud, meaning they could not move or think critically. The gods were displeased with the mud beings and destroyed the world with floods of boiling water. The gods then made humans out of wood. While they were much more productive and advanced than the mud people, they were soulless and did not praise their gods. Like the population before them, the gods destroyed them with water. The beings that were somehow able to survive these two universes were believed to be monkeys.

Modern humans were created in the third creation when the gods decided to make the beings out of dough made from maize and the blood of gods. The gods considered the four beings they created too intelligent, and they were afraid they would overthrow them and take control of the universe. The gods decided to blur their minds so they would be less divine and intelligent.

The destruction of the universe occurred when the beings no longer worshiped their gods. This made it imperative for the Maya to continually and emphatically make religious worship a central component of society.

Pantheon and Mythology

The Maya pantheon is comprised of a long list of divine deities that cover nearly every component of life for the Maya people. While many of the deities were a universal part of the religious beliefs of all the Maya people, the pantheon could change significantly based on the region. As seen below, many of these gods had similar characteristics. The dependence of the Maya on rain and agriculture for their survival made the sun, rain, and weather symbols like the lightning bolt reoccurring themes in the pantheon.

Itzamná is considered the main creator of the universe and is often portrayed as an iguana or an elderly figure. He was also the god of wisdom, writing, and knowledge. He was also considered one of the most important sun gods. His wife, Chebel Yax, is also often portrayed as an iguana-like figure. Both figures are considered as two of the highest-ranking deities of the Maya pantheon.

A depiction of Itzamna.
https://commons.wikimedia.org/wiki/File:God_D_Itzamna.jpg

Huracán, the deity of the wind and sky, is also credited with being one of the universe's creators to the highland Maya. He is depicted as a one-legged god who is often holding a lightning bolt.

K'inich Ajaw was one of the most powerful sun gods of the religion. The sun gods were considered some of the most powerful and sacred gods because of the Maya's reliance on agriculture and freshwater: too little sun and their crops wouldn't grow, and too much son would bring severe droughts that would devastate the region. Every day, he was born in the east as the sun rose and aged throughout the day until the sun set in the west. After the sun disappeared beyond the horizon, he would turn into a jaguar-like figure and become a warrior in the underworld

Hun H'unahpu is considered the most important of the deities, as he was the god of maize, the central food of Mesoamerica. He was most often depicted as a young man with long hair. The second most important god was Chak, the rain god. Chak is often depicted as a man-reptile hybrid. The Maya believed that both Chak and Hun H'unahpu required human blood.

K'awiil is most often described as the god of royalty and lightning and is depicted with a lightning bolt in his hand. Ah Puch, also called Kisim, is the god of death and is most often portrayed as a rotting skeleton figure. He is often depicted holding an owl, which was considered an intermediary messenger between Earth and the underworld.

Akan is another death god that is specifically associated with drinking and disease. Akan is often depicted vomiting and holding wine, and in some depictions, he is cutting off his own head. Ix Chel is the god of rainbows, often depicted wearing a headdress made of snakes. She represents femininity, along with childbirth and fertility, and is often depicted with images of the moon.

The Ceiba tree, a tropical tree species native to Central America, was sacred to the Maya people. The Ceiba is often cited in Maya inscriptions as the tree in the creation story that the gods planted to separate Earth from the skies. Its essential role in the creation story made it the symbol of the universe for the Maya. Inscriptions of the tree describe its roots flowing down into the underworld, while its large trunk represented the Earth's existence in the middle world, and its branches reach up to the upper world. Depictions of the tree exist in the codices and many inscriptions and murals found throughout Classic Maya cities.

An example of a Ceiba tree; this picture was taken in Chiapas, Mexico.
AlejandroLinaresGarcia, CC BY-SA 3.0 <https://creativecommons.org/licenses/by-sa/3.0>, via Wikimedia Commons https://commons.wikimedia.org/wiki/File:LaPochotaChiapa1.jpg

The cardinal directions were important to the Maya, especially east and west, because of the sun's rising and setting. Each direction was given a different color, with north being white, east being red, south being yellow, and west being black. Particular gods were assigned these directions, and many temples, tombs, and shrines were built perfectly facing a cardinal direction because of their spiritual significance.

The Maya believe that the universe existed in three levels. The middle world is Earth, while the gods inhabit the upper world and underworld. The upper world contained thirteen levels, while the underworld was comprised of nine levels.

The underworld, called "Xibalba" by the highland K'iche and "Mitnal" by the Yucatec, was important to the Maya belief system. The underworld was ruled by an array of terrifying, bloodthirsty gods who would periodically ascend to earth to bring death and destruction to mankind. Souls entered the underworld either through a water-filled underground cavern or through the sky and would be confronted by a hellscape of ghastly scenes and creatures.

Astronomy

It is impossible to discuss the religious beliefs of the Maya without mentioning their connection with astronomy. The Maya were some of the most advanced astronomers in the world and were able to accurately count the exact solar year of the region.

The Maya used towering observatories and temples to theorize about the solar system, which they used for secular scheduling of agricultural production and water storage. However, the study of astronomy went far beyond pragmatic scheduling and timekeeping. Astronomy played a major role in the spiritual and religious beliefs of the Maya as well.

The observatory at Chichen Itza; it is known as Caracol.
User:R.123 Attribution-ShareAlike 2.5 Generic (CC BY-SA 2.5)
https://creativecommons.org/licenses/by-sa/2.5/ via Wikimedia Commons,
https://commons.wikimedia.org/wiki/File:El_Caracol_observatory.jpg

They believed that when observing the night sky, they were being shown messages and revelations by their gods. The Maya believed that the Earth was located in the center of the universe and that the planets and stars above were gods that were moving throughout the spiritual realm.

The sun was one of the most important aspects of Maya astronomy, and the sun god, Kinich Ahau, was one of the most important deities of their religion. The Maya believed that Kinich Ahau would travel to the underworld at night after staying in the sky throughout the daytime.

The moon also played an important role in the Maya belief system. The Maya believed that the moon goddess, Ix Chel, fought the sun god every day, forcing him to make his journey down to the underworld.

Astronomy also played a role in ruling dynasties, as many murals of the Maya displayed rulers wearing clothing that symbolize the stars and planets. The astronomer-priests of Maya cities also had tremendous power. A war could be delayed until a certain planet or star was in the right place, or a new ruler could be put in place only during certain celestial cycles.

The planet Venus played an especially significant role in the Maya belief system. Venus symbolized warfare to the Maya, and attacks and conquest would be timed with the positioning of the planet.

While the planets played a significant role in the Maya belief system, the stars had a more practical place in the Maya civilization. The positions of stars were largely used to plan and schedule agricultural production.

Many monuments throughout the Maya cities have clear connections to astrology, and many buildings throughout the cities are nearly perfectly aligned with cardinal directions. The city of Chichen Itza has one of the most famous examples of this astronomical architecture. During the equinox, the sun lights up the stairs to one of the city's largest pyramids, giving the onlooker the illusion of a snake climbing up the staircase.

A picture taken during the spring equinox of 2009. It is thought the appearance of the snake represents Kukulkan, the feathered serpent deity.

Rituals and Ceremonies

Though human sacrifice has been a defining characteristic of the Maya civilization in popular media, it was most likely less common than these depictions. The most commonly sacrificed people were prisoners of war and captured rival leaders. The most common method of sacrifice was decapitation, though heart extraction, largely influenced by the Aztecs of Central Mexico, had become a common method by the end of the Classic period.

Bloodletting was practiced much more frequently than lethal human sacrifice. It was usually practiced by the nobility, as their blood was considered sacred. The practice was important to the Maya people because the gods spilled their blood in creating the universe. The spilling of their own blood showed gratitude and proved their allegiance to the gods for the creation of the Maya people. Bloodletting was usually practiced by the nobility, usually making incisions on the tongue or genitals with stingray spines.

Topographic features of the Maya heartland were a sacred part of the Maya belief system. Elaborate ceremonies were conducted on mountaintops, in cave systems that were believed to lead to the underworld, or at sinkholes that served as places of ritual sacrifice.

The Maya believed that the gods gave them their land, and these features served as sacred locations to connect with the spiritual realm. Many of these landmarks, most notably a large sinkhole in the city of Chichen Itza, would regularly be used as a pilgrimage site. Maya populations also had a number of regional shrines devoted to local saints that were journeyed to regularly.

Priests were the leaders of spiritual life in Maya society, overseeing ceremonies, sacrifices, and probably the construction of sacred temples and other religious architecture. The priests also had tremendous knowledge of other subjects, such as astronomy, timekeeping, and mathematics. The synthesis of these subjects and the traditional religious beliefs gave priests enormous power in the Maya political system. Priests would often decide the ascension of rulers to the throne or the right time to go to war based on the cycle of the planets or the religious significance of dates on the calendar.

Body Modification

Body modification was a widespread part of Maya culture. Piercings, tattoos, and the sharpening of teeth were often used for individualistic expression that displayed a person's cultural ties or their political status. These often excruciatingly painful modifications would often serve as a rite of passage for young men who aspired to be warriors or were in line to become rulers.

One of the most painful of these was cranium modification, which was a cultural practice probably handed down from the Olmec. This entailed shaping the head into a variety of shapes using an array of different devices, including special cradles that were used to compress the skull while laying down and a device made of paddles that the child could wear throughout the day. The most common shape was a tall skull with a flattened forehead, which was usually created by clamping two paddles on each side of the child's head.

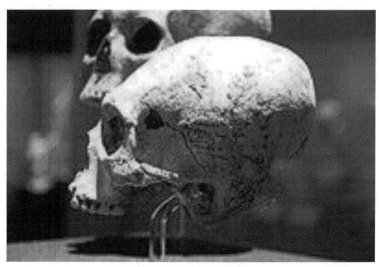
A deformed female Olmec skull.
Gary Todd, CC0, via Wikimedia Commons
https://commons.wikimedia.org/wiki/File:Gulf_Coast_Classic_Period_Elongated_Skull_Deformed_for_Beauty.jpg

By the time of the 10th century, this practice had become widespread throughout the population of Maya cities, though citizens belonging to the lower classes normally had less obvious modifications. In many cities, the members of elite families were forced to go through some form of cranium modification. This process usually began when the children were toddlers, a time when the skull is still in the growing process and more malleable than a fully formed adult skull.

Dental modification was also widely practiced throughout Maya society. Many Maya warriors sharpened their teeth to intimidate enemies, while many noblewomen had precious stones like jade drilled into their teeth.

Body paint was an important Maya cultural practice and would be specially used during ceremonies. Priests would often color themselves red using cinnabar during religious occasions, and sacrificial victims were often painted before their blood was spilled for the gods. Tattoos were a sign of great bravery for Maya men, as it was an extremely painful process. Most tattoos were simply cut into the body with obsidian weapons. Piercings were common among Maya populations, as jewelry made from precious stones was a marker of high status or beauty.

Writing System

Many components of the Maya hieroglyphic system were passed down from their Olmec predecessors. Maya hieroglyphs and inscriptions became common throughout Yucatan settlements by 300 BC, and by the beginning of the Classic period, the Maya writing system was an integral part of the architecture of the region's urban centers. Stelae, temples, and tombs were covered in inscriptions giving descriptions of historical events, mythology, or the names of rulers.

The script used by the Maya combined symbols and images that denote certain objects or actions with symbols that represented pronunciations of the spoken language. While it is not fully known how much of the urban Maya populations were literate, the full comprehension of the writing system was most likely only taught to the elite, as reading and writing were considered sacred abilities given by the gods.

The Codices

The Maya took scrupulous notes on their history, astronomical observations, and their belief system, but nearly all of these records were destroyed by the Spanish missionaries of the 16th century. These missionaries destroyed these records to erase both the native religion of the Maya and their pre-Colombian history. Four of these extensive historical records, called the "codices," survived the evangelization efforts of the missionaries and have been a tremendously helpful tool for understanding the Maya civilization.

The most important of these codices is the Dresden Codex. It is considered one of the oldest and best-preserved books written by Mesoamericans, despite heavy water damage inflicted on it by the allied bombing of Dresden during World War II. The discovery of the Dresden Codex showed historians and archaeologists the great extent of Maya astronomical knowledge. The Madrid Codex explains many of the religious beliefs of the Maya and many parts of everyday Mesoamerican life. The Paris Codex solely covers the rituals and ceremonies of the Maya. The Grolier Codex, located today in Mexico City, is the only codex whose authenticity is under question.

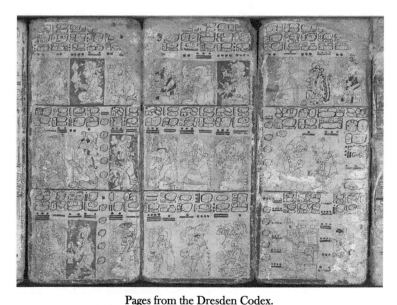

Pages from the Dresden Codex.
https://commons.wikimedia.org/wiki/File:CodexPages6_8.jpg

Popol Vuh and Chilam Balam

The Popol Vuh, which translates to "The Book of the People" in the Mayan language, is one of the most sacred books of the Maya people. It was written by the K'iche' Maya of the Guatemalan Highlands, mainly focusing on the highland Maya religion. It also goes into detail about the settlement of the highlands by the K'iche' people. The book is considered so sacred because Spanish priests destroyed most Maya texts during the 16th and 17th centuries.

A Maya scribe wrote the Popol Vuh during the 16th century, and it became a cherished text of the highland K'iche' people. When the Spanish conquered the region, the Maya were able to keep it hidden until a trusted Spanish priest that was beloved by the local population was allowed to see it. Knowing that it was an important historical and cultural artifact of the local Maya, the priest translated it into Spanish.

Along with the religion's creation story, which greatly resembles the creation story of the lowland Maya, the Popol Vuh includes one of the most important chronicles of the Maya religion: the story of the Hero Twins.

The Chilam Balam is also one of the sacred texts of the Maya. The series of texts date back to the 18th century and display the breadth of lowland Maya culture, religion, and daily life. The writer of the texts created a great historical timeline, describing the migration patterns and ruling dynasties of the lowland Maya. Many riddles and poems were written in the texts and a collection of prophecies made by Maya priests.

Dance and Music

Music was a central part of Classic Maya society. Though there is no evidence of stringed instruments being used by the Maya, wind and percussion instruments were widely used during both secular and religious occasions. Primitive trumpet-like instruments were made of clay and wood, and many flutes were found in Maya cites. Drums and rattles were the main percussion instruments of Maya music and were a common household item in many regions.

Music was used by Maya populations while preparing for battle, performing rituals, or during celebrations, such as weddings. Many musical and dance traditions have survived and are performed by many modern Maya peoples throughout Central America today.

Cacao

Cacao was an integral part of the Olmec diet and their trade, but the Maya truly made the crop an essential part of their culture. Along with maize, the cacao plant was considered one of the most divine crops of the Maya heartland. According to the Maya religion, the plant was given to the people of the religion on a mountaintop by the gods.

The plant was largely drunken by the royal elite, who most often consumed it in its liquid form, which probably greatly resembled modern "hot cocoa." Cacao beans were also used widely as currency throughout the Mesoamerican trade systems. The plant was used as a medicine for many illnesses, and cacao beans would often be buried with loved ones to be used during their voyage through the underworld.

Mathematics

The Maya mathematicians were some of the most advanced in all of the Americas. Three symbols were used to count: number one was represented by a small dot, number five was represented by a bar, and a shell was used to represent zero. The use of zero is especially impressive, as very few civilizations in the world used it in their numerical system.

These numbers were used for a variety of reasons. Basic math was needed for commerce and the exchange of goods. Symbols were used because it was so easy for Maya populations to use them in their everyday lives. It was also used for more important reasons, such as making predictions based on the calendrical system.

Calendars

The Maya were fascinated with time, and timekeeping was inexorable with both their studies of astronomy and their religious beliefs.

Scholars believe that the first calendar of Mesoamerica dates back to 1500 BC, and the Maya increasingly perfected it throughout the Preclassic and Classic periods. The Maya had several calendars that were widely used throughout the Classic period, with the Calendar Round and Long Count being the most prominent.

The Calendar Round was largely used to document the holy days for religious rituals and ceremonies. This calendar used a 260-day cycle that included twenty thirteen-day periods. The Haab used a 365-day solar year that is divided into eighteen months with twenty days and one extra five-day month. The Maya inscribed pictures to each month, as they believed every month in the calendar possessed its own distinct "personality."

The Long Count Calendar, also called the "universal cycle," was used for longer periods. This calendar had strong ties to the Maya religion and the belief that the world was constantly destroyed and rebuilt by the gods. Each Long Count cycle was 2,880,000 days long, with each new cycle bringing a complete rebirth of the universe. These calendrical cycles would match every 52 years, which would mark the beginning of a new Maya century.

The calendrical system that the Maya created was an essential part of their urban society. The calendar was used to calculate when to plant crops, when to anticipate the wet or dry season, and the best time to conduct warfare. The calendar was calculated by the positioning of the stars and planets, which they believed were signs from the gods. Priests used the calendar to document both holy days for celebrations and "unlucky days," when sacrifices would have to be made to appease the gods.

These calendars have also been an indispensable tool for historians and archaeologists, as many central events were painted and encrypted with dates from the Maya calendars.

The Maya calendar gained international attention in the year 2012, as the Long Count calendar reached the end of its cycle on December 21st. While popular media increasingly speculated that this was an apocalyptic doomsday prophesy, the date was simply the end of the Maya calendar year.

Classic Maya Warfare

For many years, Mesoamerican scholars believed that the Maya were an exceptionally peaceful civilization. They proposed that the Classic period was a period of great peace throughout the Maya lowlands, as the city's prospered as their culture and art flourished.

However, modern knowledge of the Maya has completely flipped this view of the civilization on its head. The fractured state of the Maya heartland meant that cities were constantly competing for resources and political control of the region.

The seasonal droughts of the lowlands, the small number of freshwater sources, and the general infertility of the Yucatan soil made land and water the most sought-after resources for the Classic Maya. As the population of the urban cities grew, these resources became both more in-demand and scarce, leading to a massive spike in regional rivalries and warfare.

Larger cities had well-trained armies that proved to be some of Mesoamerica's most formidable military forces. These armies often made long, perilous journeys that spanned for hundreds of miles through the dense rainforest. The main weapons of the Maya were swords, spears, and bow-and-arrows, with most of these weapons being made of obsidian. The taking of prisoners was a central component of Maya warfare, especially the capture of royalty. These prisoners would often be the prime victims when human sacrifices were performed.

By the end of the Classic period, many war-torn central and southern lowlands leaders had built massive defensive fortifications around their cities. There is also evidence that the rural populations that once lived carefree on the periphery of the urban cities gradually moved inwards closer to the city. This shows that destructive warfare had become a real existential threat for many Maya populations by this time. Over the next three chapters, we will explore how warfare and many other factors led to the downfall of the Classic Maya urban centers.

Chapter 6: Tikal: The Maya Jaguar God City

Tikal was one of the Maya civilization's largest cities of the Classic period. It was located in modern-day northern Guatemala in the Petén Basin, 40 miles southwest of the modern towns of Flores and Santa Elena and 188 miles north of Guatemala City.

Tikal is located in the middle of the highlighted area.

The city has been one of the most studied Mesoamerican sites due to its expansive documentation of rulers and its many temples, tombs, and monuments. The archaeological site became part of the Tikal National Park in 1955, making it the first federally protected area in the country. It was officially classified as a UNESCO World Heritage Site in 1979.

The city's total area was over 6.2 square miles, with around 3,000 structures being found throughout the site. Some of Tikal's oldest architecture dates back to the 4th century BC, and evidence of agricultural production in the city dates back to 1000 BC.

A collection of Maya ceramics that dated back to 700-400 BC were discovered throughout the archaeological site, indicating the presence of a permanent, urbanized population characterized by distinctive Maya cultural influences. Many of the initial major construction projects for the city took place from 400 to 300 BC, a period when Tikal was much smaller than the nearby northern cities of El Mirador and Nakbe. The dynasty of rulers of the city began in the 1st century AD and included more than 33 rulers throughout 800 years of dynastic rule.

The city enjoyed its height of regional dominance from 200 to 900 AD. Tikal dominated the Maya lowlands throughout its peak of power. Scholars have not reached a consensus on the population figures for the city, with estimates ranging from 10,000 to 90,000. From 700 to 830 AD, the city saw a massive increase in its population, but this rapidly decreased during the 9th century. The city was nearly completely abandoned by the beginning of the 11th century.

The city was located on some of the region's most fertile soils and had expansive trade networks extending throughout Mesoamerica. However, the city had no freshwater sources located in its immediate proximity, which made it very vulnerable to droughts that were brought on with the unpredictable rainfall of the region.

The city used ten large reservoirs that were used to collect rainwater in an intricate water management system that helped the city survive through dry seasons. The city's engineers built large, sloped surfaces with canals surrounding these reservoirs that were designed to catch as much rainwater as possible.

Structures

The city's most famous area is the Great Plaza, which includes an array of palaces, altars, and two of the Maya's largest pyramids facing each other on either side of the plaza. Several causeways made of limestone were built to connect the different sections of the city, acting as streets for the population and could also serve as dams during the wet season.

A recent picture of Tikal's plaza.
chensiyuan, CC BY-SA 4.0 <https://creativecommons.org/licenses/by-sa/4.0>, via Wikimedia Commons https://commons.wikimedia.org/wiki/File:Tikal_mayan_ruins_2009.jpg

The 154-feet-tall Temple I, also known as the "Temple of the Great Jaguar," was built in the 730s to commemorate the death of the ruler Jasaw Chan K'awil, who led the city in its victory against the rival city of Calakmul. Temple II, the "Temple of the Mask," towers at 125 feet tall and is believed to have been constructed by Kasaw Chan K'awil in honor of his deceased wife.

On the periphery of the Great Plaza is Tikal's tallest pyramid, the Temple of the Double Serpent, towering at 230 feet tall. It is believed that the temple was built in honor of the son of Jasaw Chan K'awiil in 740. Along with these three pyramids located in the very center of the city, five other pyramids have been found throughout the archaeological site that were built for a deceased ruler.

The North Acropolis is to the north of the Great Plaza, which includes two and a half acres of sacred tombs and temples. The Acropolis has been one of the most studied archaeological sites of Mesoamerica. Construction of the North Acropolis began during the mid-4th century BC and became the central location for the burial of deceased rulers.

A view of the North Acropolis from the plaza.

To the south of the plaza is the Central Acropolis, which was home to the main royal place for the ruling elite. During the early years of the Classic period, the palace was a modest ceremonial building, but as Tikal gradually became a powerful Maya city, the palace was improved to reflect the city's growing political power in the lowlands.

The Mundo Perdido is a large 650,000 square foot plaza home to the Lost World Pyramid, one of the city's premier attractions. The plaza has a special significance for the city's history, as it was the first large plaza to be constructed during the Preclassic period and ultimately the last plaza to be abandoned after the city's decline.

The restored western side of the Lost World Pyramid. It was rebuilt many times by the Maya; the first phase dates to the end of the Middle Preclassic, and the last phase dates to around 300 AD.

By the time of the city's decline, the palace had become a massive complex with multiple buildings, courtyards, and even its own water reservoir. The city also had seven ball courts, used for a Mesoamerican ball game that was played by the population.

Early Classic Tikal

The Classic period brought a period of divine rulership to the Maya cities. Rulers were increasingly seen as divine figures that were put on the throne by the gods' will. Monuments and temples were increasingly constructed in their honor, which has helped archaeologists map out the timeline of the city's rulers.

The Tikal dynasty was created by Yax Ehb Xook in the 1st century AD, and there would be 33 rulers of the city by the 10th century. There is evidence that in 317 AD, a queen named Lady Unen Bahlam ruled the city, ending centuries of an exclusively male dynasty.

Throughout the Early Classic period, the cities of Tikal and Calakmul became the dominating powers of the Maya heartland. As Tikal grew, it increasingly facilitated trade with its neighbors, which helped other cities in the region grow as well. However, this new power dynamic in the Maya heartland also made Takal many enemies. The Maya states of Uaxactun, Caracol, Naranjo, and Calakmul would all engage in conflict with Tikal throughout the Classic period.

During the Early Classic period, Tikal actively fought against the city of Uaxactun in numerous battles. The rival state of Caracol defeated Tikal during the Early Classic period, and Caracol took Tikal's place as the dominating power of the Maya lowlands for some time until Tikal remerged as the most powerful city in the region.

Relationship with Teotihuacan

Teotihuacan, a large city tucked into the Valley of Mexico, had a close relationship with Tikal. By the beginning of the 3rd century AD, the city of Teotihuacan had multiple embassies built in Tikal, despite being over 800 miles away. Many of Tikal's monuments and buildings built during this period had direct influences from Teotihuacan, the greatest city of Mesoamerica at the time. There is also evidence that the two populations even practiced the same religion and worshiped many of the same gods.

Tikal's fourteenth king, Chak Tok Ich'aak, constructed a grand palace that would serve as one of the city's most important structures for centuries. Evidence points to an overthrow of Chak Tok Ich'aak by the king of Teotihuacan, Siyah K'ak, in the late 4th century AD. It is also believed that this invasion was conducted with the help of some political factions within Tikal.

Upon capturing the city, Chak Tok Ich'aak was executed, and Siyah K'ak's son, Yax Nuun Ayiin I, was named ruler of the city and ruled for 47 years. Tikal would soon gain complete autonomy from the city's political power, as Teotihuacan began to decline in the 6th century. However, as Tikal rose to prominence, the cities would remain both military allies and great trading partners.

Rivalry with Calakmul

During the 6th century, the cities of Tikal and Calakmul became rival regional powers, with both forming alliances with nearby cities. Over the next centuries leading up to the Terminal period, a Maya "cold war" ensued between the two cities as each vied for political influence in the lowlands.

Calakmul quickly shifted the scale of power in its favor by establishing an alliance system with many cities throughout the lowlands, including El Zotz, El Peru, and Caracol. The alliance successfully defeated Tikal in 562 AD. While the battle did not completely destroy Tikal, its regional dominance rapidly declined for several decades. This defeat sparked a period that has been called the "Tikal hiatus," a period when no large construction projects or writing took place in the city. In the late 6th century, many of the city's monuments and structures were defaced.

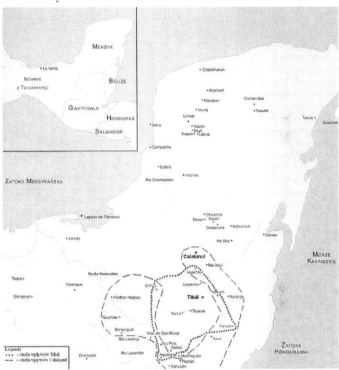

A map of Tikal's and Calakmul's allies and zone of influence.
https://commons.wikimedia.org/wiki/File:Map_Kaan_%26_Mutal.jpg

Caracol and Calakmul rose to prominence as the two most prosperous cities of the region during the Tikal hiatus. Tikal's defeat marked the end of the Early Classic and the beginning of the Late Classic Maya period.

However, Tikal slowly began to regain its strength and once again emerged as the main rival of Calakmul and its allies. Tikal created the settlement of Dos Pilas 68 miles southwest of the city in 629. Dos Pilas served as a defensive military outpost that protected the city's trade interests near the Pasion River.

In 655, Calakmul successfully invaded Dos Pilas, and the king of the city was forced to become a vassal ruler to Calakmul. With significant aid and guidance from Calakmul, Dos Pilas soon declared war on its former ruling city. Dos Pilas successfully attacked Tikal in 657, forcing Tikal's royalty to escape the city. In 672, Tikal attacked Dos Pilas in retaliation, forcing the city's rulers to flee into exile.

In 738, Tikal won a decisive victory in a head-on battle with its rival and executed the king of Calakmul. This defeat destroyed both the military and political strength of Calakmul, and the city rapidly declined. Though Tikal ultimately won the war against Calakmul, it would soon meet the same fate as its rival during the Terminal Classic period.

Settlements and Colonies

Tikal conquered a small settlement northeast of the city named Rio Azul during the late 4th century. An inscription dated to 385 found in Rio Azul depicts the city's ruling elite being executed by warriors of Tikal.

Rio Azul became closely linked to Tikal, both as a defensive garrison to protect from northern invasions and also served as a trading outpost to Caribbean trade routes. The small city also aided Tikal in its war with Calakmul due to its location on the Hondo River, which connected Calakmul to the Atlantic.

The city of Uaxactun and many other smaller Maya settlements like Bejucal and Motul de San José in the region were eventually brought under the control of Tikal. By the mid-5th century, the city controlled sixteen square miles.

Aside from these settlements that were used as military garrisons and strongholds, Tikal had many natural defensive barriers, including swamps both to the east and west of the city. During the 5th century, a massive 46 square defensive fortification system was constructed to protect the city, which indicates that warfare was growing increasingly common throughout the southern and central lowlands.

Relationship with Copan

By the 5th century, the southern city of Copan became under the control of Tikal, as the city began to spread its influence throughout southeastern Maya territory. There is evidence that the founder of the dynasty of Copan, K'inich Yax K'uk Mo', grew up in Tikal and may have been put in charge of the city by Tikal's intervention. After that, the city became one of Tikal's closest allies, both as a trading partner and a military ally.

A vassal state of Copan, Quiriguá, rebelled against its ruler in 738 and won its independence. Some experts believe that this move towards independence was aided by Calakmul, as diminishing Copan's political power would have greatly weakened Tikal's alliance system.

Terminal Classic Period

The 9th century marked a steep period of decline for the city and much of the rest of the Maya cities in the lowlands. As warfare increasingly engulfed the region, Tikal's inhabitants increasingly moved closer inwards to be protected by the city's defenses. Trade routes that connected the city with the rest of Mesoamerica were severely disrupted, and the costs of warfare drained both the city's economy and its population's morale.

Many experts believe that the fall of Tikal was caused partially by overcrowded land that caused immense environmental degradation for the area, leading to a collapse of agricultural production. The agricultural practices of the city caused massive environmental degradation in the area, as the land became over-farmed and overpopulated. The surrounding area was heavily deforested, and the soil had been depleted of its nutrients, making cultivating crops during a severe drought impossible. As a severe seasonal drought enveloped the area, these environmental problems were greatly exacerbated.

High amounts of toxic chemicals like mercury and phosphate also contaminated much of the city's water sources. Recent scholarship has indicated that the complex water management system created by the city's engineers may have contributed to the city's downfall.

The widespread use of cinnabar dye, which contains high amounts of mercury, would have resulted in a high runoff of the toxic substance into the water sources during heavy rains. Cinnabar was an escapable part of Classic Maya cities, as it was used to paint the exterior of buildings and as a dye for clothing. Also, large amounts of phosphate were found in these reservoirs, causing a blooming of toxic algae. The reservoir that was the most polluted was found near the royal palace of the city, meaning that the rulers may have been the most affected by the toxic water supplies.

By the 9th century, the reservoirs that the city's population relied on for centuries were heavily polluted. This proved to be horrific timing, as the region would experience a series of severe droughts throughout the final years of the Classic period. With no water supplies left in the city and no rainwater to collect, the population had no choice but to leave the city.

Water is an integral part of any civilization, but it was especially important in the spiritual beliefs of the Classic Maya. The pollution of their only water sources and the lack of natural rainfall may have also brought a divine spiritual element to the decline of Tikal, as much of the city's population may have believed that the city had been cursed or punished by the gods.

Between 830 and 950, Tikal's government rapidly collapsed, and much of its population left the city. Throughout the 9th-century, neighboring vassal settlements began to erect monuments that celebrated their own local rulers and customs, indicating that they used Tikal's decline as an opportunity for their independence.

Some monuments were erected in the late 9th century in an attempt to rejuvenate the city but to no avail. By the beginning of the 11th century, the city had become almost completely abandoned, with the remaining inhabitants living spread out among the city's ruins.

During the early 16th century, Spanish conquistador Hernan Cortes and his expeditionary force unknowingly passed right by Tikal and the abandoned ruins of what was only centuries before one of the greatest cities of the Maya civilization. Tikal's collapse marked a definitive moment for the Maya people. One of the region's largest cities that showcased the pinnacle of Maya art, architecture, and culture was swallowed up by the forest, never to be populated again.

Chapter 7: Calakmul: The Lost Maya Empire

Calakmul was one of the most prominent cities of the lowlands during the Classic period and proved to be the greatest rival of Tikal. The site is today located in the state of Campeche in Mexico, 22 miles from the Mexican-Guatemalan border.

Calakmul was the leading city of the "Snake Kingdom," which ruled over much of the central lowlands for the majority of the Classic period. At its height, the city was inhabited by an estimated 50,000 people, and the total area of the city spanned 7.7 square miles. Calakmul rises 115 feet above sea level with a large swampy area located to its immediate west. Its location gave the city's population access to the especially fertile soils of the swampy regions, making it one of the most productive agricultural regions of the central lowlands.

At its peak of regional dominance, the kingdom controlled 5,000 square miles of territory. The city controlled 20 settlements throughout its territory, with the combined population of these settlements being 200,000. Combining these settlements, rural areas, and the city itself, the total population of the city's kingdom was an estimated 1.5 million people during the Classic period.

However, just like Tikal, during the 9th century, the city's population plummeted rapidly to 10% of what it was only a few decades before.

There have been 6,750 structures discovered throughout the city's archaeological site, and despite its remote location away from any modern settlements, it has been one of the most excavated sites of the Yucatan Peninsula.

The Layout of the City

The primary material used to construct the many stone structures of the city was soft limestone, which is especially susceptible to erosion. The use of this material and the city's especially remote location in the dense central lowland rainforest has presented many challenges for archaeology teams in their studies of the city.

The site is a shining example of the complexity of the Maya water management systems, as large canals and reservoirs are dispersed throughout the city. The city is home to the largest reservoir of the entire Classic Maya civilization, with a surface area of 540,000 square feet. The water in this colossal reservoir was collected from a small stream that flowed into it during the wet seasons. The Calakmul region receives much less rainfall than the rest of the central and southern lowlands, so this water management system was crucial to the survival and prosperity of the city.

The 13 different reservoirs found throughout the city could hold a combined 44,000,000 gallons of water, which could potentially support a population of 100,000 people. These reservoir systems were probably solely used for consumption by the city's population, as there is no evidence of them being used in an agricultural capacity.

The city had eight different large causeways that ran through it. These causeways connected the city's periphery to its center and connected the city to its neighboring allied cities, such as El Mirador and Nakbe. The longest of these causeways, which linked the city to its close ally (El Mirador), stretched 24 miles.

Structures 1 and 2 are the main pyramids of Calakmul, located in the very center of the city. Structure 1 is 160 feet tall and has a group of small stelae erected at its base. Structure 2 is one of the largest structures of the Maya civilization, towering at 148 feet tall. Like many other Classic pyramids, Structure 2 has multiple other temples inside of it, with each structure built on top of the other.

A photo of Structure 2. Like other Mayan pyramids, Structure 2 reached its massive size over years of building upon the original foundation.

A tomb found in Structure 2 was one of the wealthiest tombs found in the Maya world, filled with many valuable artifacts made of jade, obsidian, and many ceramic crafts. It is believed that the tomb belonged to a powerful king who rose to power during the 7th century.

Structure 7 is a 79-foot-high pyramid located on the northern section of the plaza. At the very top of the pyramid is a small three-room temple that was found with a patolli game board in it. Patolli was one of the most common board games of the Maya and was played both by the city's population and their rulers. The game was often played with heavy gambling and largely revolved around luck.

One hundred and seventeen stelae have been found throughout the city's ruins, the largest number of any Classic Maya city. Most of these depicted rulers of the royal Calakmul dynasty and their wives. Like many other structures throughout Calakmul, the inscriptions have been heavily eroded due to the soft limestone composition.

The Classic Maya Marketplace

Many expansive murals were painted throughout Calakmul that depicted ordinary life in the city. Large scenes of a busy marketplace depict the bustling, populous metropolis and the everyday interactions of the Classic Maya citizenry. This is different from many other Classic cities, whose murals focus on their divine rulers, the Maya deities, or epic battle scenes.

Throughout the Classic period, urban centers like Calakmul had large, lively marketplaces that served as the economic powerhouses of the cities. These markets were usually located in the central plaza of the cities and served as a place of congregation for the city's population as they conducted their daily errands and activities. Merchants traveled throughout the Maya area and beyond, selling regional luxury items made in the city and buying exotic items from cities throughout Mesoamerica.

Most merchants of the urban centers sold their goods within the confines of the city, most likely traveling to the rural outskirts of the region to buy goods from agriculturalists and other producers. While those who traveled outside the city for trade were most likely exclusively male, both men and women could be sellers in the marketplace.

At Calakmul, the long-stretching causeways that led to other neighboring cities were most likely used by both sellers and buyers daily. It is well documented that Calakmul maintained a great trading relationship throughout the entirety of the Classic period.

The traveling merchants, called the "polom," traveled long distances to trade with other cities, with some even making frequent journeys to Central Mexico. These merchants were most often from the lower socioeconomic classes of the city, as merchants didn't have the high-class status like the long-distance traders of other Mesoamerican societies like the Aztecs.

Workshops were an essential part of Maya cities, as they made ceramics, jewelry, and other artisanal goods that were unique to the city. These cultural objects and their distinctive styles became hallmarks of the city and were sold across Mesoamerica. Cities that had close alliances, such as El Mirador and Calakmul, tended to have a considerable cross-diffusion of artisanal cultural goods.

A ceramic plate found in Calakmul, dated to 600–800 AD.

In the rural areas in the periphery of the cities, farmers often traded crops and goods with neighbors. When farmers had a surplus of crops during a good season, they often brought them into the marketplace to sell to the urban population. It appears that everyday sellers had great power within the cities' economies, though it is likely that the ruling class placed a tax on transactions within the city.

Early History

The cities of Calakmul and El Mirador were both prominent cities during the Preclassic period, and evidence indicates that they had a very close trading relationship. Calakmul eventually far surpassed El Mirador during the Classic period, and it is believed that many of the inhabitants of El Mirador relocated to Calakmul during the Late Preclassic. The cities of Calakmul, El Mirador, Nakbe, and El Tintal were all connected by a network of causeways, suggesting that the population could freely travel between cities.

Rivalry with Tikal

During the mid-6th century, the city began creating an alliance with many cities throughout the lowlands, and a war broke out with Tikal. The two cities became the "superpowers" of the lowlands, as each city created alliance systems and fought proxy wars to diminish the other's political power. Most scholars agree that this rivalry was most likely over control of the resources and trade routes of the region rather than an ideological war.

While Tikal had a much larger population, the leaders of Camakal proved to be shrewd diplomats that formed an alliance with the majority of the cities and settlements throughout the region. Throughout the 6th and 7th century Tikal was completely surrounded by the alliance system of Calakmul. Tikal found itself completely cut off from the rest of the lowlands, and most of its allies had either been defeated or sided with Calakmul.

During this period, Calakmul had nearly undisputed political control of the entire region, and its vast alliance system formed many new trade networks that brought the city great wealth. Many of the conquered cities throughout the region were classified as vassal states that were forced to pay tribute to Cara Kamal.

After Calakmul defeated Tikal in battle during the early 7th century, Tikal went into a rapid decline, making Calakmul the region's dominating city and ushered in the Late Classic period.

However, Tikal soon bounced back and defeated Calakmul in a great battle in 695. The king of Calakmul was killed in battle, and the city's political power sharply declined into the Terminal Classic period.

War with Palenque and Naranjo

In 599, Calakmul and the small town of Santa Elena attacked Palenque and sacked the city. After the defeat, Palenque was forced to become a vassal city and pay tribute to Calakmul. However, after only a decade after the battle, the city began to make moves towards independence, which angered the ruler of Calakmul.

In 611, Calakmul attacked Palenque, and many of the city's nobles were killed. The city was sacked by the Calakmul forces and went into a rapid decline from which it never recovered during the Classic period. It is believed that the rulers of Calakmul had a great political interest in taking the region of Palenque. They were afraid that the city would eventually ally with Tikal, and it could serve as an outpost for some of the greatest trade routes of the lowlands.

Sometime during the 620s, the nearby city of Naranjo, which had become a vassal state, rebelled against Calakmul. After some failed attempts, the city was eventually retaken in 631. The king of Naranjo was taken as a prisoner by the Calakmul warriors, and inscriptions indicate that he was tortured and executed. Inscriptions from Calakmul suggest that not only was the king executed after the battle but the entire royal family was killed. Calakmul then instated a new royal family that was firmly loyal to its political authority.

Relationship with Dos Pilas

Dos Pilas was a small settlement established by Tikal in 629 that was used to protect its trade routes on the Pasión River. The brother of the king of Tikal was named king of Dos Pilas in 635 and would fight with Tikal against Calakmul for many years.

In 648, Dos Pilas was attacked by Calakmul, resulting in the capture of the king of the city and the death of a noble elite from Tikal. Instead of executing the king of Dos Pilas, Calakmul decided instead to put him on his former throne as a vassal king to fight against his former ally, Tikal.

In 657, Dos Pilas, now with the aid and guidance of Calakmul, attacked Tikal and forced much of the ruling class to flee the city. Despite the two formerly allied cities now being enemies, Dos Pilas still used many symbols and emblems of Tikal throughout their conflict. Many scholars believe that the rulers of Dos Pilas had ambitions of taking the throne of Tikal.

In 672, Tikal attacked Dos Pilas, taking over the city and forcing many of its rulers into exile. Calakmul intervened and began to consolidate its alliance system with the hope that it could fully encircle Tikal and its territory.

In 677, Calakmul attacked Dos Pilas, taking over the city and reinstating the former king on the throne. Two years later, an allied force of Dos Pilas and Calakmul defeated Tikal in a major battle, though this victory did not seem to have a large impact on the Tikal-Calakmul conflict.

Decline

The city constructed five different stelae in the early 740s. By this time, the political power of Calakmul was a fraction of what it once was. Throughout the lowlands, many of Calakmul's most loyal allies were defeated by Tikal. Calakmul's rulers' political power was wholly dependent on this strong alliance system, and as it began to crumble, the city began to decline too.

One of the stela found in Calakmul; this one is dated to the 730s.
Gary Todd, CC0, via Wikimedia Commons
https://commons.wikimedia.org/wiki/File:Classic_Maya_Stele_51,_Calakmul,_Campeche.jpg

Throughout the Terminal Classic period, Calakmul began to focus on trade from its surrounding area in the central lowlands to the northern Yucatan. This may indicate that the Calakmul government foresaw the region's decline and hoped to stay afloat by establishing relationships with growing cities in the north like Chichen Itza.

The last structures of any kind that were built in Classic Calakmul were three stelae constructed in 810, which is around the time historians believe the city's government completely collapsed. During this period, cities that Calakmul once ruled increasingly began to erect their own cultural monuments and break away from the distinctive cultural practices of their former overlords.

There is evidence that a small population, maybe even part of the ruling class, stayed in the city after it was heavily depopulated throughout the 9th century. Some monuments were built, but they were very crudely constructed compared to the Classic period monuments. This may have been an attempt to reinvigorate the city and bring it back to what it once was.

After centuries of political domination in the central and southern lowlands, by the Terminal Classic period, the great cities of Calakmul and Tikal were abandoned ruins hidden amongst the vast Central American rainforest.

Out of all of the great cities of the Classic period, it has puzzled historians why the two greatest cities collapsed so quickly and were never populated again. A large part was certainly the centuries of warfare, as constant fighting surely drained the cities economically.

Historians are still unsure of what exactly led to the abrupt deterioration of Calakmul and the other Classic cities, but a growing body of evidence points to a few likely causes. The following chapter will discuss the numerous theories and evidence that point to why the two giants of the lowlands collapsed.

Chapter 8: The Collapse of the Classic Era

Between the 8th and 9th centuries, the Maya cities of the southern lowlands were rapidly depopulated. This period has been called the "Classic Maya Collapse," as the Classic Maya period was replaced by the Postclassic Maya period. The 9th century is often classified as the Terminal Classic period.

While many theories have been made about the collapse, experts are unsure of what exactly led to the disintegration of urban Maya society in the lowlands. There is evidence that the region's great cities, including Tikal, Calakmul, and Palenque, deteriorated throughout the 8th and 9th centuries and then were soon completely abandoned.

During this period of decline, there were no writings made on monuments and no large construction projects that were conducted within the cities. However, this collapse did not bring an end to the Maya civilization.

In fact, as the great cities of the southern lowlands began to fail, the cities of the northern Yucatan filled the power vacuum and began to prosper as the new dominating cities of the Maya world. Many of these new cities in the north carried over many cultural traditions and characteristics of the Classic Maya, though many artistic styles were left in the past.

The city of Chichen Itza became the dominant power of the peninsula during the collapse, and many other cities both in both the northern Yucatan and the highlands to the south prospered up until the Spanish conquests. While this period is often referred to as the "Maya Collapse," many Mesoamerican experts reject this terminology. They believe instead that the power that culminated in the cities of the southern lowlands shifted and dispersed out throughout the region.

Theories of the Collapse

Mesoamerican scholars have suggested almost one hundred different theories, and they have not been able to reach a consensus on a unified explanation. However, a number of themes seem to be accepted by the academic community as contributing factors to the collapse.

A collapse of the Maya's urban centers due to environmental factors tends to be one of the leading theories. Many scholars believe that a severe drought or series of droughts in the region caused the sudden decline. Another theory that scholars have explored is an invasion by the Toltecs of Central Mexico or another outsider cultural group. However, most scholars do not believe that there is enough evidence that a military invasion collapsed Maya society by itself.

Mesoamerican scholars have continually proposed a theory that the overland trade routes that dominated the lowlands, which made cities like Tikal and Calakmul economic hubs of trade, were replaced by overseas trade routes that traveled around the peninsula. The abandonment of the lowland trade routes may have been caused by the constant warfare of the region, as many merchants surely would have chosen to travel by sea than trek through the war-torn lowlands. This would have shifted the power dynamic of the Yucatan Maya away from the southern and central lowlands to the coastal region. The dissolution of trade routes that connected the Maya people for centuries would have surely led to the deterioration of the cities in the region.

A large, widespread drought that enveloped the region is the most commonly accepted theory among Mesoamerican scholars. Modern research has shown that the region saw a 40% decrease in annual rainfall during the Terminal period. A drought would have inhibited the population from cultivating agriculture, which the cities had become wholly reliant on, and damaged many of the fertile soils throughout the lowlands. While the central cities would have begun to collapse quickly during a prolonged drought, the cities near the coast like Chichen Itza would have been much less affected by the drought, as they have relatively more freshwater sources.

While many people think of the Maya heartland as a tropical rainforest with an abundance of annual abundance, the region was especially prone to prolonged drought and had very few freshwater sources. Many environmentalists today are amazed that the Maya people thrived in such an inhospitable region of the world.

The Maya combatted their lack of permanent freshwater sources by many ingenious methods of collecting rainwater. However, a severe prolonged drought may have made these water storage practices untenable for the large populations of the cities. Also, there is clear evidence that these water supplies were heavily polluted by the time of the collapse.

The Maya were some of the most advanced agriculturalists in the world, as they used a variety of techniques and innovations to cultivate the land to feed the large populations of the urban cities. However, the use of slash-and-burn agricultural practices would have led to immense deforestation throughout the Maya heartland. This immense, widespread environmental degradation would have taken the forests decades to recover.

There is also some evidence of revolution or rebellion by the populations of the cities against their rulers. Many sacred monuments and structures were defaced and damaged around the time of the collapse, which may point to the population symbolically destroying the sacred structures of the ruling class before abandoning the cities.

The cities that came to power after the Classic collapse show a much less "divine worship" of their rulers, and it seems that the Postclassic populations sought more pragmatic, secular governments than those of the Classic. As drought, deforestation, and warfare enveloped the region, it would make sense that the Classic populations would quickly turn on their rulers, who preached that they were divinely put on the throne by the gods to protect their people.

While Mesoamerican scholars have been searching for a primary theory on the Classic Maya collapse, the collapse of the classic cities of the lowlands was most likely caused by a combination of environmental, economic, and political factors that may never be fully understood.

Despite the popular belief that the collapse brought an end to the Maya civilization, many regions of the Maya heartland prospered after the 10th century, especially on the peninsula's northern coast.

What has puzzled many scholars is why the central and southern lowlands weren't repopulated after the collapse. The Classic Maya urban centers were characterized by a constant cycle of development, collapse, and disbursement. After many examples of "collapses," most notably during the Preclassic period, the Maya people disbursed elsewhere in the region, and soon new urban centers emerged.

However, the southern and central lowlands would never be densely populated again after the collapse, making historians wonder where these people went. The populations that left these cities most likely moved north through the Yucatan towards the Atlantic coast, while others traveled east and west, joining other Mesoamerican societies.

Water storage methods, along with many other administrative innovations, had become extremely complex by the Classic period. The repopulation of the region would have entailed a complete reconstruction of these water storage systems, a massive labor-intensive project that may not have seemed worthwhile. There may have also been a religious or spiritual element, as many may have chosen not to return because they believed the gods condemned the cities.

As the great cities like Tikal collapsed in the south, the northern cities like Chichen Itza filled the power vacuum and carried forward the torch of the Classic Maya. However, the Classic Maya collapse undoubtedly brought an end to the centuries-long progression from primitive agrarian villages to the great temples of Tikal and Cakamral. The collapse of the Classic Maya cities of the lowlands did not mean the collapse of the Maya civilization, but it would never be the same.

The artistic and cultural achievements of the Classic Maya were swallowed up by the jungle and left behind as the population dispersed elsewhere. During the Postclassic period, the Maya people would undergo a series of enormous transformations as they tried to fill the void that the collapse created.

Chapter 9: Chichen Itza: The Wonder City

The city of Chichen Itza was located in the modern-day Tinúm Municipality of the Yucatán State of Mexico, located in the northern Yucatan Peninsula. Chichen Itza was considered one of the largest pre-Colombian Maya cities and came to be one of the most prosperous cities of the Yucatan during the Terminal Classic period.

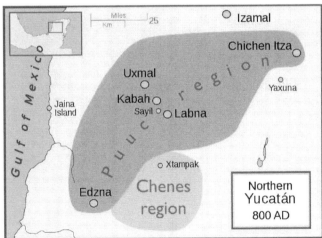

A map of the upper Yucatan Peninsula.

No machine-readable author provided. Madman2001 assumed (based on copyright claims)., CC BY-SA 3.0 <http://creativecommons.org/licenses/by-sa/3.0/>, via Wikimedia Commons https://commons.wikimedia.org/wiki/File:Maya_site_northern_Yucatan_800_AD.svg

Some experts believe that the city had an especially diverse population, which would reflect the city's diversity of artistic and architectural styles. This was mostly caused by an influx of Maya migrants from cities like Tikal that traveled north towards the coast after the collapse of the Classic period.

Four different sinkholes, or "cenotes," served as the main freshwater sources for the city's population. There has also been evidence that the cenotes were used for human sacrifice to the rain god Chaac, as found in the most famous of the cenotes, the Cenote Sagrado. Many sacred objects that are commonplace in Maya burials, such as jade, were found in these sinkholes, along with human remains. Most of the human remains found were of children.

The Cenote Sagrado ("Sacred Cenote"). It has been suggested that many of the human sacrifices were killed prior to being thrown in the cenote. Since only some cenotes held human remains, it is possible the Maya believed certain cenotes led to the underworld.
Salhedine, CC BY-SA 4.0 <https://creativecommons.org/licenses/by-sa/4.0>, via Wikimedia Commons
https://commons.wikimedia.org/wiki/File:Cenote_Xtoloc_en_Chich%C3%A9n_Itz%C3%A1.jpg

The name Chichen Itza translates to "at the mouth of the well of the Itza," which probably refers to the large cenotes and the heavy influence of Itza culture in the city. While Itza-Puuc styles characterize the architecture of the northern part of the city, the southern part of the city is heavily influenced by Toltec styles. Some scholars have hypothesized that this was caused by a large migration or possible invasion by the Toltecs. However, most believe that it simply reflects interaction with the great Toltec city of Tula.

From the early 10th to the mid-11th century, Chichen Itza rose to prominence as the most prosperous city of the Yucatan Peninsula, boasting a population of 35,000. During its height of power, the city took advantage of its prime location on the coast of the northern Yucatan Peninsula and became an important economic power of the Maya lowland trade routes.

The city created Isla Cerritos as one of the most important Central American ports. As the southern and central lowlands erupted into constant warfare throughout the Classic period, many trade routes were disrupted. Overseas trade routes around the peninsula instead of across it became more common, giving cities near the coast like Chichen Itza a great economic advantage. With its close proximity to the sea, merchants of Chichen Itza were able to sail throughout the Gulf of Mexico, obtaining items that were rare to the Yucatan region, such as gold and obsidian from Central Mexico.

The Layout of the City

The most prominent structures of the city center covered an area of around two square miles, making it one of the largest urban centers in the northern Yucatan. The engineers of the city leveled out the ground in the center of the city in order to construct many of the city's greatest structures.

The city had many causeways, or streets, which connected the various sections of the city to the central plaza. The city was full of stone buildings that formed different functions, ranging from residential homes to administrative buildings used by the government. The structures of the southern part of the city, called "Old Chichen," had many characteristics of the Puuc style of architecture that originated in the central Yucatan lowlands.

El Castillo, a 98-foot pyramid located in the center of the city, is the most prominent architectural project of Chichen Itza. Not only was the construction of the structure an impressive architectural feat, but it also highlights the sophistication of their knowledge of astronomy and timekeeping.

A picture of El Castillo, also known as the Pyramid of Kukulkan.
Daniel Schwen, CC BY-SA 4.0 <https://creativecommons.org/licenses/by-sa/4.0>, via Wikimedia Commons https://commons.wikimedia.org/wiki/File:Chichen_Itza_3.jpg

The pyramid was constructed with four sides that each had 91 stairs and faced every cardinal direction. The four sides and their staircases add up to 365, the total number of days in the year. During the equinoxes of autumn and spring, a large shadow taking a snake's shape is cast down the stairs. A large inscription of a snake is located at the top of the pyramid, representing one of the Maya's gods. El Castillo was built on top of another older temple dedicated to the jaguar god of the underworld. By the Classic period, this was a common practice in Maya cities.

The detail and thought put into the construction of El Castillo show the great breadth of knowledge and beliefs that permeated Maya society and how it intertwined with their great architectural feats.

Excavations have shown that a great marketplace existed below the pyramids, suggesting that the large plaza was used for large crowds to watch rituals take place at the top of the pyramid and congregate with fellow citizens and shop.

The Caracol, a large structure used as an observatory for the city's astronomers, was constructed sometime before the 9th century. Many scholars believe that this building was used to view Venus and may have been dedicated to Kukulkan, the Maya wind god.

The Temple of the Warriors is a complex that was built sometime between the 9th and 11th centuries. The temple walls were decorated with large depictions of Maya warriors and battle and has many inscriptions of feathered serpents. The temple closely resembles a similar found in the Toltec capital city of Tula, which has led many historians to suggest that there was considerable cultural diffusion between the two cities.

The Temple of the Warriors. Many of the murals inside the complex depict battles and warriors.

Chichen Itza is also home to the largest ball court of Mesoamerica, at 545 feet long and 223 feet wide. There are many inscriptions on the walls of the court showing victorious players displaying the decapitated heads of their opponents.

There are numerous theories on how the ballgame was played. Most believe that the game's goal was to keep the ball from hitting the ground by hitting it against the walls, most likely with the players' hips. The ball used was made of rubber and could weigh up to nine pounds. While the game was most likely played often recreationally by the city's population, the inscriptions at the ball court of Chichen Itza indicate that there may have been a ritualistic element to the game.

The ball court at Chichen Itza.

Overlooking the ball court, the Temple of the Jaguar is a large temple complex with many inscriptions of the Maya feathered serpent deities and a large depiction of a battle. In the lower temple of the complex, there is a throne decorated with an inscription of a jaguar figure, similar to the throne in El Castillo.

Adjacent to the Great Ball Court was the Temple of the Bearded Man, a small temple that has an inscription of a large, bearded man. Right across from the Temple of the Bearded Man is a larger structure, but it was destroyed beyond recognition.

Maya Blue and Sacrifice

During the heyday of the city, these buildings would have been painted in an array of festive colors. The Chichen Itza metropolis would have looked much different from the drab stone ruins found at the modern site.

One of the most popular colors used throughout Maya cities like Chichen Itza was "Maya Blue." The pigment was used throughout cities on sculptures, pottery, and murals. The turquoise color comes from the combination of indigo plant material and palygorskite ore. These ingredients were combined in small kilns at high temperatures of up to 200 degrees Celsius. The pigment is extremely resilient and long-lasting, as many murals and objects still have visible traces of the color despite centuries of erosion.

An example of Maya artwork that uses Maya Blue.
https://commons.wikimedia.org/wiki/File:Azulm6.jpg

Maya artists began using the color to paint murals during the latter part of the Preclassic era, and the use of the pigment soon began to spread to monuments, stelae, and pottery throughout the cities. It was the main color of Chaak, the rain deity, who also happened to be the central figure in Maya human sacrifices.

When the city priests anticipated a drought, they would often choose a victim for either nonlethal bloodletting or, in more dire cases of drought, human sacrifice. To appease Chaak, a victim would be fully painted with the pigment and sacrificed in the city's central plaza.

The extent of human sacrifice in the Maya is unknown to scholars, as inscriptions and depictions of the sacrifices left by the Maya have kept the topic a mystery in terms of its methods and frequency. Prisoners of war were certainly used most frequently for sacrifices. The victims could have been either beheaded or disemboweled, most likely in a ritualistic ceremony conducted by the city priests. More extreme examples, like being thrown into the Chichen Itza cenotes, were most likely very rare occurrences.

The capturing of kings and other royalty of a rival city often led to public executions and sacrifices. These killings celebrated the political victory of defeating a rival leader and spiritually gave the gods royal blood.

Most sacrifices were likely not lethal, as ceremonial objects and artifacts were symbolically given to the gods as material sacrifices. The practice of "bloodletting" was also frequently practiced when citizens of the city made small, non-lethal cuts on their bodies as a blood sacrifice.

Early History

The city was first populated and constructed between the 6th and 8th centuries and was further developed throughout the 10th and 11th centuries as it grew into a prosperous trading hub for the Yucatan.

Despite its location near the Gulf Coast, the northern Yucatan is considered one of the driest and arid regions of the Maya heartland. Chichen Itza probably became an ideal location for settlers due to the many water supplies located in its natural cave systems and sinkholes.

Rise to power

The city had already risen to prominence by the beginning of the 7th century, as it became a vital regional trade city in the northern lowlands. With the decline of many of the large cities in the south (like Tikal), Chichen Itza became the dominant political, cultural, and economic power of the Maya lowlands during the late 9th century.

Leading up to Chichen Itza's rise to regional dominance, the two neighboring cities of Yaxuna and Coba, who were close allies, both began to decline. Some experts believe that Chichen Itza may have played a direct role in these cities' decline, either by direct intervention or simply out-competing them economically.

After enjoying a period of regional prosperity, the city began to decline around the year 900. During this time, an influx of migrants of the Itza culture from the south arrived in the city and began to revitalize the city's northern half. Throughout the 10th century, the neighboring city of Uxmal, a close ally of Chichen Itza, rapidly declined and paved the way for Chichen Itza to ascend to power once again.

Decline

Evidence shows that by the beginning of the 12th century, the city had declined as a weaker city in the region, marking the rise of the neighboring city of Mayapan. During this period, Chichen Itza allied with both Mayapan and Uxmal, called the League of Mayapan, which will be covered in Part 4.

When the Spanish conquistadors arrived in Chichen Itza, they noted a large population was still living in the city. However, some experts believe that this population may have been living in the outskirts of the city's ruins. The Spanish also noted that the Cenote Sagrado continued to serve as a sacred place for the Maya people.

Chichen Itza today is one of the most visited sites of Mesoamerica due to its many great structures and monuments like El Castillo. While it only maintained its regional dominance of the northern Yucatan for a short time after the Classic Maya collapse, the city proved itself worthy of carrying the torch of the Classic cities to the south.

The breathtaking achievements of the city's population, its blend of Itza and Toltec influences, and its economic prosperity near overseas trade routes showed that despite the collapse of the great Classic cities, the Maya civilization was more alive than ever. The decline of Chichen Itza marked the beginning of a new era in northern Yucatan when the city of Mayapan became the most powerful city in the region.

SECTION THREE:
THE POSTCLASSIC MAYA
ERA (900-1511 AD)

Chapter 10: The K'iche' Kingdom of Q'umarkaj

Q'umarkaj

The Kingdom of Q'umarkaj (also called Utatlán in the Maya language) was located in Guatemala's highlands. The city was created by King Q'uq'umatz, which translates to "Feathered Serpent" in the K'iche' language at the beginning of the 15th century.

Q'umarkaj was situated on a large plateau in the Guatemalan highlands, 1.6 miles west of the modern city of Santa Cruz del Quiche. The archaeological site covers an area of 1,300,000 square feet, making it one of the largest sites of the Maya highlands. At its height, the city of Q'umarkaj and its immediate surrounding area had a population of 15,000 people.

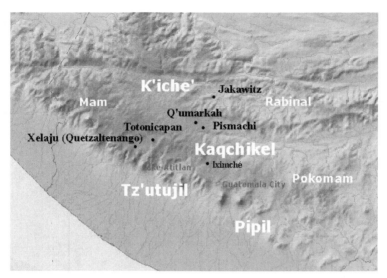

This map shows the important centers of K'iche', which is located in southern Guatemala.

https://commons.wikimedia.org/wiki/File:Postclassicguatemalahighlands.png

There was a deeply rooted socioeconomic order in the city, as the K'iche' comprised three different lineages: The Nima were elite ruling class, the Tamub were merchants, and the Ilok'ab were the primary warriors of the K'iche'.

Founding of the City

The exact origin of the K'iche speaking peoples is still up for debate among scholars. Still, most agree that they most likely originated from the Tabasco region of the Gulf Coast of Mexico. These peoples traveled along the Gulf Coast and through the southern lowlands to reach the city, though some scholars believe they may have traveled along the Pacific coast to reach the Guatemalan highlands. Most of these people probably made the journey around Chichen Itza's decline in the northern Yucatan, sometime in the 12th century.

The Layout of the City

The city contained eleven plazas surrounded by an array of temples and complexes, all elevated on a series of terraces. These structures all tend to be around the same size, though the structures surrounding the central plaza are the city's largest structures.

A large series of ditches separated the elite administrative area of the city from the majority of the residential living areas, reflecting the deep socioeconomic divisions in the city. Many of these houses seem to have cultural markers that differ greatly from the elite structures of the city. This has caused many scholars to hypothesize that the city's citizenry was possibly conquered by a population that made themselves the elite ruling class after the conquest and allowed their citizens to retain their cultural identity.

Early History

The K'iche' were a Maya people that had settled in the highlands sometime around 600 BC. There is archaeological evidence that the region was populated to some degree as far back as the Preclassic period, but most of the city's artifacts are dated to the Postclassic. During the Late Postclassic, the area of the city probably had around 15,000 people living in it.

The capitals of the K'iche' kingdom were originally at Jakawitz and then Pismachi, but at the beginning of the 15th-century, King Q'uq'umatz chose the area for its great natural defensive position on the tall plateau. King Q'uq'umatz would maintain a spiritual legacy among the K'iche' people after his death, as he was described as a mythical figure who could transform himself into various animals.

Political Order

The socioeconomic factions within K'iche' society run deep, as the nobles, or "ajaw," claimed to be descendants of foreign invaders from the Gulf Coast that conquered the region during the beginning of the 13th century. The invaders took over the region's political power and abandoned many of their Gulf cultural traditions, fully integrating into the K'iche' culture of their conquered subjects.

The vassals of the K'iche', or "al k'ajol," served as the lower classes of highland society. They served as workers, farmers, and soldiers and usually did not have any opportunities for upward mobility in the political system. The vassals, however, could earn high titles in the military for showing bravery and skill on the battlefield. Merchants were slightly higher on the socioeconomic ladder than the vassals but were forced to pay tributes to the noble class.

The kingdom was ruled by a government comprised of four power powerful figures: the king, king-elect, and two captains. Each of these rulers belonged to the most celebrated lineages of the city.

Expansion

Throughout the 15th century, the K'iche' gradually began expanding their territory throughout the region and created a powerful alliance with the Kaqchikel, a powerful Maya people of the midwestern highlands.

During this period, Q'uq'umatz offered the ruler of the K'oja, a nearby Maya culture of the Cuchumatan mountains, his daughter for marriage. However, instead, the K'oja killed Q'uq'umatz's daughter when she arrived in their territory. This sparked a bloody war between the two cities.

King Q'uq'umatz ultimately died in battle while fighting against the K'oja and was succeeded by his son, K'iq'ab, who vowed to defeat the K'oja. He entered the city of K'oja with a large military force, killed the king, and sacked the city. He also recovered his father's remains and brought a large number of prisoners, as well as many valuable jade artifacts. The K'iche' military also brought many areas near K'oja under their control after the victory.

K'iq'ab continued to bring great prosperity to the kingdom as he went on greatly military conquests that expanded K'iche' territory to the Okos River in the west and the Motagua River to the east.

Decline

As K'iq'ab's territory expanded, civil war broke out at Q'umarkaj as the vassals attempted to overthrow the royal class. Two of K'iq'ab's sons joined in with the vassals, killing many high-ranking nobles of the city. High-ranking members of the allied Kaqchikel warriors were forced to flee back to their territory.

K'iq'ab was nearly killed during the uprising but fled to the city's periphery with some troops that remained loyal to him. The king agreed to make some concessions to the rebels, which created a new noble class of lords. K'iq'ab died soon after in 1475. Despite the great territorial expansion that characterized his reign, the city was much weaker than it was when he ascended the throne, largely due to the internal unrest of the city's political structure and the dissolution of its alliance with Kaqchikel.

Following the death of K'iq'ab, the city became entangled in bloody warfare with its neighbors, including the Tz'tutjil people and its former ally, the Kaqchikel. The K'iche' attempted to conquer the capital city of the Kaqhickel but were defeated. This sparked a sharp decline in the K'iche' military and political power in the region.

By the time Spanish conquistadors arrived in the Guatemalan highlands in 1524, the city of Q'umarkaj was a shadow of what it was during the 15th century. Q'umarka completely drained itself of its former glory due to its dysfunctional internal political system and its hunger for territorial expansion.

Chapter 11: The League of Mayapan

The Mayapan league was formed in 987 AD by Maya ruler Ah Mekat Tutul Xiu. The league was a political alliance between the northern Yucatan cities of Chichen Itza, Mayapan, and Uxmal. The league was centered around the city of Chichen Itza, which was the most powerful city in the region during the Early Postclassic. The league was also comprised of many smaller cities and villages throughout the region, but it is unclear how much power these smaller polities had when it came to governance.

This league was most likely created due to the crumbling of the great Classic cities to the south, as the Maya of the northern Yucatan feared that the increasing warfare could spread to the north or that an influx of desperate migrants would take over the region. The league's creation was also undoubtedly caused by the heavy droughts and disruption of trade routes that characterized the time. The northern Yucatec Maya may have tried to carry forward and implement the most important takeaway of the Classic Maya collapse: that lack of peace, stability, and cooperation caused the decline of the greatest cities of the lowlands. The alliance was created to maintain some semblance of a centralized government in the region, promoting peace and trade among the northern Yucatec Maya.

However, throughout the Postclassic period, the league quickly began to crumble due to internal struggles between the three cities. Mayapan gradually replaced Chichen Itza as the most powerful city of the northern Yucatan.

Mayapan

Mayapan was located 100 kilometers west of Chichen Itza and became the most powerful city of the northern Yucatan from the early 13th to the mid-15th century. Over 4,000 structures have been found throughout its archaeological site, and experts believe up to 17,000 people could have lived in the city during its height.

Mayapan, which translates to "banner of the Maya," served as the last great capital of the Maya in the northern Yucatan and is considered one of the most densely populated cities to ever exist. The city was formed during the 11th century by the Cocom, an elite family from Chichen Itza that fled due to political rivalry.

The Temple of Kukulkan. It is similar to the one at Chichen Itza, although archaeologists consider the latter to be far superior in terms of craftsmanship.

Pavel Vorobiev, CC BY-SA 3.0 <https://creativecommons.org/licenses/by-sa/3.0>, via Wikimedia Commons https://commons.wikimedia.org/wiki/File:Mayapan_%272010_-_31.JPG

The city was abandoned abruptly during the mid-15th century, and there is evidence that part of the city may have been burned to the ground. Archaeological evidence points to increased warfare in the northern Yucatan throughout the 14th and 15th centuries, and by Mayapan's decline, large defensive fortifications had been constructed around the city.

Uxmal

Uxmal was a powerful city in the northern Yucatan region from around 850 to 900 AD during the Terminal Classic period. Beginning around the year 1000, the city's population began to leave the city, possibly migrating to the nearby cities of Chichen Itza and Mayapan. By 1200 the city was nearly abandoned.

The city was founded by the Tutal Xiues, a Maya people that traveled eastward from the Gulf Coast to the northern Yucatan sometime during the Late Classic. The city most likely joined the League of Mayapan during its decline, making it the weakest city in the alliance.

Toltec Influence and Possible Invasion

The architectural layout of Chichen Itza has long been a hot topic for debate among Maya scholars, with some believing that the presence of Toltec influences in the city may point to a Toltec invasion of the northern Yucatan urban centers. Both the cities of Mayapan and Uxmal also had many Toltec architectural/cultural characteristics, which many point to the League of Mayapan forming partly due to a shared Toltec cultural heritage.

Many scholars who worked in the Carnegie Institution of Washington research programs of the mid-20th century concluded that before the possible Postclassic invasion, Chichen Itza was populated by a different Maya cultural group, meaning that the Itzas would eventually take over the city during the Postclassic were the Toltecs from Tulla.

However, recent scholarship has largely disproved this theory. Most academic scholars now maintain that the Itza of Chichen Itza simply had great trading and diplomatic relations with the Toltec of Tulla, which shaped their cultural and architectural styles.

Dissolution of the League

By 1175 the league began to unravel. While archaeology has not yet proven the following narrative of the league's dissolution, it is cited in multiple Maya sources and is accepted by many Mesoamerican scholars.

Ceel Cauich Ah was thrown into the sacred cenote of Chichen Itza and somehow managed to survive. Due to the sacred nature of the cenote to the Maya people, Ceel Cauich Ah proclaimed himself the divine ruler of the region. Most of Chichen Itza's population did not accept him as ruler, while much of Mayapan's population did.

Upon the league's dissolution, Chichen Itza was replaced by Mayapan as the greatest city of the northern peninsula. The city of Uxmal declared war on the Cocom people of Mayapan in 1441, officially bringing an end to the league.

Chapter 12: Peten Itza: The Last Maya Kingdom

The last great Maya kingdom was the kingdom of Peten Itza, revolving around the city of Nojpetén. Twenty-one sacred temples have been throughout the city's archaeological site. The city was considered one of the central centers of the Itza during the Postclassic period.

The city was isolated on an island in Lake Petén, and it appears that no bridges or other structures connected the city to the rest of the lowlands. The city remained relatively politically and diplomatically isolated, as it only had relationships with the Itza cities of Chakok'at, Ch'ich, and Chakan. By the time of the Spanish conquests, an estimated 60,000 people lived in the city.

The location of Peten Itza

Lake Peten is the largest body of water in the Maya heartland and was the home for the Itza Maya people for centuries. The Peten lakes region comprised a group of eight large lakes linked together that stretched 80 kilometers from east to west. The freshwater sources of the river are a small number of seasonal streams that flow throughout the area. By far, the largest lake in the region is Lake Peten Itza, which covers an area of around 100 kilometers.

The Itza People

The Itza were not a single unified cultural people but were instead made up of many different powerful family clans that ruled the area. The Itza also had great influence in the cities of Chichen Itza and Mayapan in the northern Yucatan during the Postclassic. A great proportion of the Itza population from these northern regions most likely migrated southwards to the lake during the decline of Chichen Itza and Mayapan leading up to the arrival of the Spanish.

Both the northern and southern Itza were known as some of Mesoamerica's greatest merchants, overseeing long-distance trade routes from Central Mexico to southern regions of Central America.

The Itza people most likely originated in the Peten Basin of the southern lowlands, with a large proportion of their population migrating up to the northern Yucatan during the collapse of the lowlands, and then a large wave of Itza migrants moving back down to Peten following the collapse of the League of Mayapan.

The academic community has yet to reach a consensus on the origins of the Itza as a unified kingdom and when they began to gain political influence in the Peten lakes. Multiple inscriptions found in Maya cities in modern-day Belize, as well as northern cities like Chichen Itza, seem to mention interactions with an Itza leader during the Late Classic period.

The Peten Itza Government

By the time of the arrival of the Spanish during the 16th century, the Peten region had become a well-organized, hierarchical political region that was ruled by a series of elite Itza families, greatly resembling the governmental structures of the northern Itza cities like Chichen Itza.

Many historians believe that the widespread influence of the Itzas in both the northern and southern lowlands hints at a great military force that integrated their conquered people into Itza society. After conquering a population, they most likely encouraged them to marry into elite families, which would allow some of the conquered peoples to become high-ranking royalty in Itza society. This not only gave the Itza conqueror large, already well-established cities and populations to expand on but also diminished the likelihood of rebellion or political unrest within their governmental structures. By making their conquered peoples a powerful part of the Itza government, the Itza were able to spread their influence throughout the Maya heartland without alienating or decimating populations of fellow Mayas.

The ruler of the Peten Itza people throughout the 16th and 17th centuries was always given the title of "Ajaw Kan Ek" in Spanish records. He lived in the capital island city of Nojpetén and held the highest governmental position of the entire Peten region.

The governments of the Itza provinces were generally comprised of eight people. These eight officials were divided into junior-senior pairs based on the cardinal directions. For example, the governing council of one of the western provinces would consist of a senior official who oversaw the affairs of the province, while a junior official oversaw the largest town in that province.

The larger Itza confederacy, which acted as a unified kingdom of the Peten region, was comprised of a governing council made up of the four senior provincial officials, along with thirteen "ach kats" that ruled the small settlements throughout the periphery of the confederacy.

The full territory controlled by the Itzas during their height of power is not yet fully known, though it is clear that they were some of the region's greatest agriculturalists, with fields stretching throughout the central-southern lowlands.

Spanish Contact

After conquering the Aztec Empire of Central Mexico, Spanish conquistador Hernan Cortes traveled through the Peten Itza region. In March 1525, the expeditionary force arrived on the shore of Lake Peten Itza, where ruler Aj Kan Ek received him'. After witnessing Catholic mass, Aj Kan Ek' immediately converted to Christianity and invited the men into the city of Nojpeten.

After the encounter, no other Spanish forces attempted to enter the Peten Basin for nearly a century, mostly due to its impenetrable jungle cover. In 1618 two Spanish missionaries departed the settlement of Merida to convert the Itza of the Peten. The ruler of Peten Itza welcomed the missionaries but refused to abandon the native Maya religion. After one of the missionaries attempted to destroy a statue of a deity, the native population began to grow agitated at the visitors. Only after one of the missionaries conducted a peaceful sermon did the natives calm down. The Spaniards left soon after and established a friendly relationship with the ruler of the Peten Itza.

The next year the missionaries returned to Lake Peten and were again well-received by the ruler. However, the city's priests increasingly saw the Spanish as a threat to their religion and persuaded the ruler to banish them from the kingdom. A Maya military force suddenly surrounded the living quarters of the missionaries, and the Spaniards were forced to leave downriver on a canoe.

After the failed attempts at evangelization, Spanish Captain Francisco de Mirones set out to conquer Peten Itza in 1622. A missionary named Diego Delgado also traveled with the force but became increasingly disillusioned by the treatment of the indigenous peoples by the conquistadors. Delgado split off from Mirones with his own expeditionary force, largely made up of evangelized Mayas from the eastern lowlands. Upon entering the city of Nojpeten, which had not encountered Christian missionaries since 1618, they were immediately taken as prisoners and then sacrificed to the gods. Upon the arrival of Mirones, he and his men were found unarmed in a nearby church by the Peten Itza warriors and were slaughtered. These two failed missions in Peten Itza halted all Spanish attempts to conquer or evangelize the region until 1695.

In 1695 Martín de Ursúa y Arizmendi, the governor of the Yucatan province, began to construct a road from the western Yucatan to Lake Peten. Missionary Andrés de Avendaño traveled on the road and arrived on the shore of Lake Peten to a welcoming group of Itza. The ruler of the Peten Itza arrived the next day, inviting the missionary group into Nojpeten. While in the city, Avendaño baptized many of the city's children and made several attempts to convert the Peten Itza ruler. The ruler said that the time was not right for their conversion and that Avendaño should return in a few months to successfully evangelize the population. The ruler discovered a plot devised by a faction within the city to kill Avendaño and quickly advised them to leave the city.

In December of that year, the Itza ruler sent messengers to Merida to surrender to the Spanish crown. Conquistador Pedro de Zubiaur traveled to Peten with a small military force but was ambushed by a large Maya force. Many of the Spaniards were killed or taken prisoner, and when a relief force arrived the next day, they were too beaten by the Maya warriors. After this failed conquest, Martín de Ursúa began to plan for a massive attack on the Peten Itza region.

Ursúa led his army to Lake Peten in 1697, and the Peten ruler immediately sent a group of envoys that surrendered to the Spaniards. Ursúa accepted the surrender and invited the ruler to visit his camp on the lakeshore the next day. However, the next day, instead of the scheduled arrival of the ruler, a massive force of Maya warriors began to surround the Spanish camp. Now knowing that the only way to conquer the region was with military force, Ursúa led his men on an assault of Nojpeten. Many of the city's defenders died in the ensuing battle for the island, and the Spanish took very few casualties. Ursúa renamed the city "Our Lady of Remedy and Saint Paul, Lake of the Itza."

SECTION FOUR:
SPANISH CONTACT AND CONQUEST (1511-1697 AD)

Chapter 13: First Encounters and Yucatan Exploration

During the Late Postclassic period, Spanish forces reached the Yucatan Peninsula. They began a strategy of herding the local Maya into small colonial settlements that probably resembled modern concentration or internment camps. Many of the Maya either fled into remote areas of the rainforest or joined in with other cities that the Spanish had not yet conquered.

The diverse, ruptured political order of the Maya Yucatan presented a challenge to the Spanish conquistadors, as there was not a central city, state, or authority that could be overthrown, as seen with the Aztecs of Central Mexico. Instead, the Spanish were forced to conquer the region city by city, village by village. The Spanish tackled this problem by taking advantage of political rivalries between Maya populations, making alliances that pit the cities against each other.

The Maya who chose to resist fought a guerilla war against the Spanish invaders and their allies, largely using hit-and-run ambush tactics. While the Spanish had vastly superior weaponry, including small artillery, steel swords, and cavalry, the Maya warriors proved to be fierce fighters who used the terrain of the region to their advantage. The Spanish cavalry became the largest determining factor in battles throughout the conquests. Spanish cavalry charges were extremely effective against fellow European armies, but against the Maya (who had never seen horses before), these charges often caused an immediate, frenzied retreat.

Even more deadly than the Spanish invaders themselves was the plethora of diseases they brought to the region. Diseases like smallpox, measles, and eventually malaria ravaged the local populations throughout the Americas, and both the Maya highlands and lowlands saw enormous mortality rates from these diseases throughout the 16th century.

Biases

The following chapters will explore the Spanish conquests of the Maya heartland: a time period when the Maya people got their first bitter taste of European colonialism as the Spanish attempted to conquer an indigenous population that fought ferociously for the survival of both its culture and people.

It should be noted that most of what is known about these conquests comes from Spanish sources, which tended to have a Euro-centric bias towards depicting the Maya as savages who needed to be civilized by high European culture. (Just as the Maya made biased historical records that depict the Spanish as murderous brutes.) We will never know the full extent of Spanish atrocities against the Maya people, nor the full accuracy of the Spanish depictions of Maya "savagery," such as human sacrifice.

However biased these sources may be, they are unfortunately the only way to begin to understand the conquests of the Americas. How accurate these details, stories, and depictions are may never be fully known. However, by giving a detailed, objective narrative from both Spanish and Maya sources, a general overview of this period of enormous transformation and change in the Maya civilization can begin to be uncovered.

First Encounters

It is believed that the first time the Spanish encountered the Maya of the Yucatan was in 1502 when an expedition led by famed Spanish explorer Christopher Columbus encountered Maya traders off the coast of the peninsula.

Columbus landed on the island of Guanaja off the coast of Honduras during his fourth expedition to the Americas. He then sent his younger brother, Bartholomew Columbus, to explore the island and its waters. While scouting out the region, Bartholomew encountered a large canoe that was being driven by a Maya crew from the Yucatan Peninsula. Many luxury goods were on board, making it very likely it was a trading canoe that was traveling south to trade with other Mesoamerican societies.

Instead of trying to exchange information with the Maya crew or establish a cordial relationship, the Spanish crew instead looted the canoe and took the captain as a prisoner, with hopes that he could serve as an interpreter for future conquest. This first encounter between the Spaniards and Maya would set the grim tone for decades of conquest and exploitation throughout the Yucatan.

The remaining crew traveled back to the peninsula and began to spread the word of their encounter with the Spanish. The news began to spread through coastal Maya cities of the white invaders, and many began to believe they were sent by the feathered serpent god Kukulkan, a powerful deity of the northern lowlands.

In 1511, the "Santa Maria de la Barca" was shipwrecked off the coast of Jamaica in the Caribbean Sea. Captain Pedro de Valdivia and his crew decided to float westward on one of the ship's small boats. Over the course of two weeks, half of the crew died from dehydration and heat exposure. The survivors landed on the eastern coast of the Yucatan, where a not-so-welcoming reception awaited them.

According to Spanish sources, the local Maya lord, Halach Uinik, took the surviving crew as prisoners. The captain and four other crew members were immediately killed in a ritualistic sacrifice, and the local population ate their bodies.

Aguilar and Guerrero

Two of the survivors, Geronimo de Aguilar and Gonzalo Guerrero, escaped from their Maya captors but were captured by another Maya lord. The two men served as slaves in the Maya town of Chetumal for eight years, eventually becoming fluent in the Maya language. Aguilar was eventually rescued by a Spanish expeditionary force led by Hernan Cortes, whom he served as a translator for during his campaigns in Central Mexico.

Guerrero followed a much different path towards freedom. By the time Aguilar was rescued, Guerrero had been partially assimilated into the local Maya culture. He had become a high-ranking member of the Maya town's military force and had taken on many cultural practices of the local population, including traditional Maya piercings and tattoos. He had married a local Maya woman and may have been the first father of mestizo mixed children in the Americas.

Guerrero's fellow Spaniards made several attempts to retrieve him, but he refused to leave the Maya village. There is evidence that Guerrero may have even led campaigns of the local Maya in their fight against his former comrades.

A statue of Guerrero in Akumal, Mexico.
https://commons.wikimedia.org/wiki/File:EstatuaAkumal.jpg

Francisco Hernández de Córdoba

The first Spanish expeditionary force to land on the peninsula was under the command of Francisco Hernández de Córdoba. The fleet departed from Cuba in 1517 and arrived near the northern coast of the peninsula. Córdoba chose not to land due to the dangerous coastal shallows but spotted a small indigenous settlement on the coast. Several Maya canoes rowed out to the ship the next day and had a friendly exchange with the Spanish crew after boarding the vessel.

Deciding that the local population would welcome his forces peacefully, Córdoba decided to land on the shore. The small expeditionary force began to journey to the local city when local Maya warriors attacked them. Some of the crew were wounded by arrows from the ambush, but they were able to successfully push back the Maya attackers. The Maya often used flint arrowheads, meaning they would often shatter inside wounds and cause horrible infections, which would later cause the deaths of two of the wounded men.

After successfully fighting off the attackers, the Spanish forces moved on to the fringes of the nearby city, where they sacked some of the Maya temples and other buildings. The Spaniards found many gold items, which filled the men with great excitement for the riches that could be found in the region. After taking two prisoners to serve as interpreters, Córdoba and his men returned to their ship to continue their expedition.

As the fleet sailed southward down the western coastline of the peninsula, the crew grew dangerously low on their freshwater supplies. The crew arrived at the coastal Maya city of Campeche in February 1517 and immediately sent a party into the city to retrieve water. The city's population allowed them to enter the city and take some water in their casks, but the situation soon soured as the leaders of the city ordered them to return to their ship.

The ship continued sailing southwards for over a week, eventually landing near the Maya city of Champotón. Upon landing on the coast, the crew quickly found a freshwater source but were soon met by a group of warriors from the city. The ship was able to replenish its water supply, but the expeditionary force found itself completely surrounded by a significant Maya force by the next day.

During the hour-long battle that ensued, over half of the Spanish force was killed, and every surviving Spaniard was wounded. At the end of the battle, the surviving men made a frantic scramble to their ships and set sail for the Caribbean.

The story of the expedition was documented by Captain Córdoba, who succumbed to his wounds shortly after the battle at Champotón. More importantly, he also wrote in detail about the gold and other wealthy artifacts found in the Maya region. While the narrative of this expedition did not have a happy ending for the first Spaniards to explore the Maya heartland, it did not deter further expeditions. The prospects of potential untouched wealth in the Maya territory only further heightened the growing fervor of Spanish conquest in the Americas.

Juan de Grijalva

In 1518, Juan de Grijalva was sent by his uncle, Cuban Governor Diego Velázquez, on the second expedition to the Yucatan. Velázquez was highly optimistic about the reports of gold on the coastal areas of the peninsula and gave his nephew four ships for the expedition.

In April 1518, the fleet arrived on the island of Cozumel off the eastern Yucatan coast. Grijalva and his men made several attempts to interact with the island's population, but then they fled from the coast upon the arrival of the ships. After cruising down the peninsula's east coast, Grijalva decided to turn back and sail down the western coast.

The force reached the city of Campeche and attempted to negotiate a trade for drinking water, but the city's population declined. The angered captain then opened fire on the city with a mounted cannon, which caused much of the population to abandon the city and flee into the forest. While the fleet was approaching Champotón, a band of Maya warriors in canoes appeared, but they quickly fled to shore when Grijalva began firing his cannons.

The fleet then sailed to the Tabasco region of the Gulf Coast, where a group of Maya warriors stared at them from the coastline but did not show any signs of attack. Grijalva used his translators to conduct a small trade transaction with the group, who told him about the great wealth of the Aztecs in Central Mexico. The fleet then sailed west to the Central Mexican coastline and saw many signs of the great Aztec Empire.

On their voyage back to the Caribbean to report on the great Aztec Empire, the fleet stopped at Champotón to avenge the Spaniards killed at the city during the previous expedition. The ensuing battle had similar results as the first, and a large number of the expeditionary force was wounded and forced to flee back to their ships.

While these two expeditions only resulted in brief encounters with coastal Maya populations, they sowed the seeds for the ensuing conquests that would ravage Maya society. The immense untouched wealth of Mesoamerica was confirmed by these perilous voyages, and now it was only a matter of time before the great conquistadors of the 15th century arrived to take it.

Chapter 14: Hernan Cortes and Pedro de Alvarado

As rumors spread throughout Spain and the Spanish-controlled Caribbean about the potential riches of Mesoamerica, the greatest of the Spanish explorers emerged as the captain of the most ambitious expedition of the Americas yet. Hernan Cortes was captivated by stories of the great wealth of the Aztec Empire in Central Mexico. He saw the Yucatan Peninsula as not only a place of great potential wealth itself but also a prime landing location and base of operations for the eventual push to the Aztec heartland.

Cortes was put in charge of an 11-ship fleet and 500 men for the expedition. Many crew members like Pedro de Alvarado would become some of the most famous (or infamous) conquistadors of the Spanish conquests.

An engraving of Cortes by the 19th-century artist William Holl.
https://commons.wikimedia.org/wiki/File:Cortes-Hernan-LOC.jpg

Cortes' Expedition

Just like the expedition before them, the fleet first arrived at the island of Cozumel. However, Cortes knew that his expedition had to bring a much more permanent element to the Spanish influence of the Americas. Sacred Maya temples were defaced upon arriving on the island, and a Christian cross was raised on their roofs. As mentioned in the previous chapter, Cortes also sent a search party to the peninsula that rescued Geronimo de Aguilar, who would serve as his translator.

The fleet then traveled west around the peninsula, eventually reaching the Tabasco region of the Gulf Coast. The Spanish forces landed at the mouth of what Cortes named the Grijalva River, near the Maya town of Potonchan. Maya warriors emerged from the town, and a great battle ensued, ending with a decisive Spanish victory after immense Maya casualties.

The Fall of the Aztecs

After the battle, Cortes was approached by the defeated Maya nobles, who offered him various goods, including gold items and young Maya women. One of these women, named Marina, would play a critical role in conquering Mexico and the Aztecs.

Marina's father was an Aztec chief, and after his death, she was sold into slavery by her mother. She eventually ended up in the Tabasco region after being sold to the Maya of the Gulf Coast. The combination of her great educational background growing up in a noble Aztec family and her fluency in both the Maya and Aztec languages made her a great asset to Cortes.

The young slave proved to be much more than a translator. She proved to be a tremendous asset to the conquest of Mexico, as she taught the Spaniards about the intricacies of Mesoamerican culture and the geography of the region. She would also become a mistress of Cortes during the voyage, and the couple would have a son together.

After the victory in Tabasco, Cortes led his fleet northwest along the coast into the heart of the Aztec Empire. After defeating the Tlaxcalans and Cholula, Cortes formed a powerful alliance with many Central Mexican peoples that were more than willing to help overthrow their Aztec overlords. Cortes eventually captured the capital city of Tenochtitlan in 1521, renaming it Mexico City.

The new city would serve as the capital for New Spain and became the center of Spanish colonialism in the Americas.

Interactions with the Maya in Soconusco

After hearing that the Aztec Empire had fallen so quickly to the Spanish, the Kaqchikel and K'iche' Maya of the highlands both sent their diplomats to proclaim their allegiance to the Spanish rule of Mexico. The following year Cortes sent a scouting party to Soconusco in the southwest of the Chiapas region in the Serra Madre de Chiapas Mountain Range. Despite the allegiance of the K'iche' and Kaqchickel to Spain, the scouts reported that both Maya kingdoms were attacking peoples in Soconusco that were loyal allies to Spain.

With these two Maya kingdoms potentially disrupting Spanish control of the region, Cortes sent Pedro de Alvarado with a massive military force made up of both Spanish troops and Mesoamerican allies to quell the unrest and fully conquer modern-day Guatemala.

Alvarado had completely conquered the Soconusco region by early 1524. While in most Spanish-controlled regions, the indigenous populations were rounded up into the colonial settlements, the Maya of the highlands were largely allowed to stay in their territory due to their cacao orchards, which were considered one of the most valuable crops of New Spain.

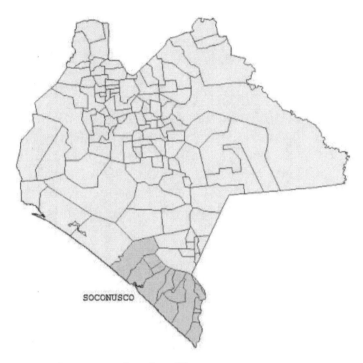

Location of Soconusco.
https://commons.wikimedia.org/wiki/File:Soconusco.png

Encomienda

The encomienda system was a hallmark of the brutality and exploitation of the conquests. It was the Spanish crown's answer to not being able to establish a centralized colonial government amongst the hostile indigenous populations of the Americas. The encomienda system permitted Spanish colonists to live in any unconquered land they wished. Of course, this land was usually occupied by local populations that were not keen on having new Spanish rulers.

By settling the territory, they effectively owned it in the eyes of the Spanish crown. They had the responsibility of acting as administrators for the land and its local population, which largely meant protecting them from outside invaders, converting them to Christianity, and establishing other institutions, such as an educational system. However, this system almost always turned exploitative. Colonists usually settled on the land with the aid of a military force, conquering the locals and looting much of their wealth. Local Mayas were taken and sold as slaves or worked in fields with little to no pay. The locals were also forced to give up many of their supplies and provisions, causing widespread famine throughout the local villages.

All of this went unpunished by the colonial authorities, as the encomienda system became a blank check signed by the Spanish crown for unchecked exploitation and atrocity throughout the Americas. Under the guise of "civilizing" the native populations, the Spanish authorities allowed the conquistadors and colonists to freely decimate and exploit the Maya people.

Cortes' Conquest of the Lowlands

With the Soconusco region firmly in Spanish control, Cortes set his sight on modern-day Honduras. Cortes had sent one of his most trusted captains, Cristóbal de Olid, to conquer the region, but Olid went rogue and declared himself ruler of the region independent from New Spain.

Cortes departed from the Aztec heartland in October 1524 with a military force largely made up of indigenous Mexican troops. After passing through the Gulf Tabasco region, Cortes led his men into the dense rainforest of the southern Maya lowlands, passing right by the abandoned ruins of Tikal. In March 1525, the force arrived at Lake Peten Itza and was received by the local Mayas. The Maya king who met Cortes was so impressed with the Catholic priests after they held a small ceremony to celebrate mass that he declared that he and his people would immediately convert to Christianity.

After visiting Nojpeten, Cortes embarked on his most arduous part of the expedition yet. His forces crossed into modern-day Belize in the Maya Mountains, and many men and horses died when they found themselves lost in modern-day eastern Guatemala. The men nearly starved to death before they found a young Maya child that led them to a nearby village. Within a few weeks, Cortes finally reached his destination in Honduras with a fraction of the men he departed Central Mexico with. To his surprise, he found that the territory had been reclaimed for New Spain, as his own men killed the rogue captain.

Conquest of the Highlands

In early 1524, Pedro de Alvarado led Spanish forces through the Pacific coastal plain, eventually reaching the K'iche Maya of the

Guatemalan highlands. A K'iche military force desperately tried to stop Alvarado from crossing the Samala River but was ultimately unsuccessful. After crossing the river and sending the Maya into retreat, the Spanish sacked the region's villages.

Alvarado clashed with a formidable defensive force at the city of Xetulul on February 8th, and after defeating the Maya, he raided the city and set up his camp in their central plaza. The Spanish force then moved on to the Sierra Madre mountains, where another Maya force ambushed him. After causing the local warriors to flee, he moved on to the city of Xelaju, whose entire population had fled after hearing about the Spanish entrance into the Sierra Madres.

On February 18th, a massive army of 30,000 K'iche' warriors led an attack on Alvarado, but he successfully repulsed the attack, inflicting heavy casualties on the K'iche' army. After their disastrous defeat, the K'iche' lords sued for peace and asked Alvarado to visit Q'umarkaj. At the local city of Tzakaha, Easter Mass was performed, a church was built, and many of the natives were baptized and converted.

Throughout March, Alvarado and his men resided in a small encampment on the outskirts of Q'umarkaj. Alvarado eventually invited two of the city's most powerful leaders to meet with him at the encampment, and as soon as they arrived, he took them as prisoners. Upon hearing the news of their leaders' capture, the K'iche' launched an assault on the camp but were repulsed. After the successful defense of the camp, Alvarado burned the two leaders alive, attacked the city, and razed it to the ground.

After destroying the city, Alvarado reached out to the nearby Kaqchikel people and proposed an alliance to fight the surviving K'iche' warriors that fled the city. After hearing of Q'umarkaj's destruction, numerous other Maya people throughout the highlands surrendered to Alvarado.

In April, Alvarado and his men entered the city of Iximche and established friendly relations with its Kaqchikel rulers. The kings gave the Spanish force many native Maya troops to help defeat the K'iche' and the Tz'utujil. In July, Alvarado decided to make Iximche the capital of colonial Guatemala, renaming it "St. James of the Knights of Guatemala."

Alvarado then sent two envoys to the Tz'utujil to persuade them to surrender, but both the Spaniards were killed. The Spanish immediately met the Tz'utujil for battle at a local lake with a massive force, including many Kaqchikel soldiers. After a devastating cavalry charge, the Tz'utujil retreated in a frenzy to an island in the lake. The Spanish then attacked the survivors that fled onto the island, though many Tz'utujil were able to escape by swimming to shore.

After the battle, the Spanish and Kaqchikel marched into the Tz'utujils' capital of Tecpan to find it completely abandoned. The Maya rulers of the city soon sent envoys to Alvarado's camp about their desire to surrender.

The scenery one could see from Tecpan.

Prelude to the Chiapas Conquest

Conquistador Luis Marín was sent into the Chiapas in 1524 to conduct reconnaissance for the upcoming conquest of the region. He departed from Coatzacoalcos on the Gulf Coast with a small expeditionary force, eventually clashing in battle with a force of Chiapanecos warriors on the Grijalva River. After defeating the Maya force, Marín traveled through a settlement populated by Zinacantecos, who would prove to be some of the most loyal Spanish allies in the Chiapas region.

As Marín neared the city of Chamula, he was approached by a group of Tzotzil Mayas, who welcomed him peacefully. However, when he got closer to the city, he began meeting hostile resistance from local warriors and found that the population had fled with their food supplies. Marín was ambushed by the Chamula warriors, who were placed on the top of a cliff, throwing spears down at the Spanish forces. When Marín and his men finally reached Chamula, they found that it was completely abandoned. The Spaniards rode on to Huixtan, an allied city of the Tzotzil, where the population also deserted the city. After defeating the small defensive force there, the Spanish decided to return to Coatzacoalcos.

Kaqchikel Revolt

Despite the strong alliance between the Kaqchikel rulers and Alvarado, the Kaqhickel increasingly grew disillusioned by the exorbitant tributes of gold demanded by the Spanish. After the Kaqchikel refused to pay, the population quickly abandoned the capital city, anticipating a Spanish attack. The Kaqchikel that now lived in the remote forests of the region began to conduct a guerilla war against the conquistadors.

Marín established a new colonial settlement in the region, but it was soon moved eastward to the Almolonga Valley due to constant attacks by Kaqchikel rebels. The Kaqchikel continued their guerilla war against the Spanish until 1530, when two Kaqchikel rulers finally surrendered to Marín.

Zaculeu

The brother of Pedro de Alvarado, Gonzalo de Alvarado y Contreras, conquered the city of Xinabahul in 1525 with a large military force largely made up of native allied troops. He then moved on to the city of Momostenango, which was swiftly taken by the Spanish forces. After taking Momostenango, his forces trekked to Huehuetenango, where a large Mam Maya army met him. The Spanish forces led a cavalry charge on the warriors, who quickly broke into a frenzied retreat and ran for the forest. After reaching the city, the Spaniards founds it completely abandoned.

The ruler of the Mam heard of the Spanish victory and established a strong defense at the city of Zaculeu as the Spaniards approached. He used his large alliance system of the neighboring

Maya peoples to defend the city. Still, Alvarado was able to break through many of the defenses during the initial stages of the battle. The Mam warriors withdrew inside the walled defenses of the city as a large Maya reinforcement force attacked the Spaniards from the north. Alvarado's men quickly decimated the reinforcements, and the Spanish launched a siege on Zaculeu that would last for months. By the time the siege was lifted, most of the population of the city was dead, with many of the starving survivors resorting to cannibalism. After the brutal siege, a large garrison was built in Huehuetenango.

Chapter 15: Conquest of the Chiapas

Pedro de Portocarrero was put in charge of a new conquest into the Chiapas region. In early 1528, his forces created a base of operations at San Cristóbal de Los Llanos, which the Tojolabal Maya people controlled. After creating a garrison there, the force gradually pushed on towards the Ocosingo Valley. Portocarrero's expedition into Chiapas was extraordinarily successful, and by the end of the year, the Spanish controlled nearly all of the highlands of Chiapas.

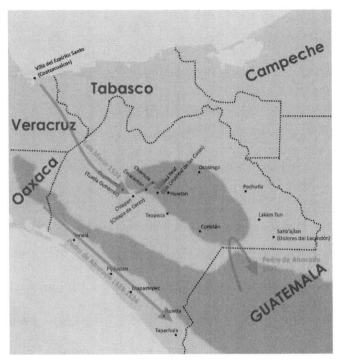

Early entry routes to Chiapas, 1523-1525.
Simon Burchell, CC BY-SA 4.0 <https://creativecommons.org/licenses/by-sa/4.0>, via Wikimedia Commons
https://commons.wikimedia.org/wiki/File:Chiapas_conquest_routes_1523_to_1525.png

Diego Mazariegos

That same year, Diego Mazariegos brought a force into the Chiapas region, where much of the population had been killed due to both widespread famine and disease. The local city of Zinacantan, who was complaining about revolts against the new Spanish government, asked for assistance in quelling the rebels, and Mazariegos sent a small force that quickly put down the rebellion.

Mazariegos had been given the orders to turn the highlands of Chiapas into a province for the Spanish crown. After securing Zinacantan, he then led his force to Chiapas, where they created a small garrison called "Villa Real" that would serve as a temporary base of operations for the Chiapas conquest.

Many of the Spaniards who were already in the Chiapas highlands greeted Mazariegos and his men with bitterness, as the region was considered one of the most prized areas of the highlands. Mazariegos ordered Portocarrero and his men to leave the area, and the two men met in the city of Coatzacoalcos to negotiate. It was agreed that the Spanish colonists living in San Cristóbal de Los Llanos would migrate to Villa Real, which was now in the Jovel Valley.

After the negotiations, Portocarrero left the region, returning to Guatemala, and Mazariegos began to encourage local Spaniards to venture into untouched Maya territory. The expansion into these territories was made easier because a large percentage of the local Maya population had been killed.

Rebellion

The main Spanish settlement of Villa Real in the Jovel valley found itself surrounded by an increasingly hostile local Maya population that was constantly fighting for survival. The Spanish forces brought disease to the local Maya and forced them to regularly give up their resources, such as food and water. As famine began to devastate already deteriorating Maya populations, they began to plan a rebellion against the Spaniards. Seeing that Villa Real was now isolated from Spanish reinforcements and supplies, the Maya rose up against their new masters. The only local Maya population that didn't rebel was the city of Zinacantan.

When the local Maya refused to hand over supplies to the colonists of Villa Real, the Spanish led a series of cavalry assaults on the local villages. The Maya withdrew with their families into the remote mountains and caves of the region that served as defensive strongholds. The Spanish and Central Mexican indigenous troops engaged in a head-on battle with the local Maya at Quetzatlepeque, resulting in a Spanish victory despite several casualties. Despite the victory, the rest of the Chiapas population remained hostile to the Spanish.

Mazariegos was soon forced to leave the region due to falling severely ill and was replaced by Juan Enriquez de Guzman as the leader of Villa Real. Guzman attempted to spread Spanish influence throughout the region, but the local population remained noncompliant with the colonial authority.

Ciudad Real

Pedro de Alvarado took over as governor of the Chiapas province in 1531 and immediately renamed Villa Real as San

Cristóbal de Los Llanos. A Spanish force attacked the local Maya city of Puyumatlan, and while they were not able to fully take the city, they took many Maya slaves that could be sold in New Spain's growing slave market.

The taking of local slaves became one of the essential parts of the Spanish conquests, as the raiding of small villages usually resulted in few casualties, and slaves could be sold for high prices in the slave market. The capturing of slaves by the conquistadors aided them greatly in their aspirations of conquest, as it created a continuous cycle that made the conquests largely self-funding. Slaves were captured and sold for high prices on the market, and then that money would then be used to buy more horses and weapons, which would be used to capture more slaves and territory. In fact, throughout some periods of the conquest, many conquistadors focused more on conducting small slave-capturing raids on local populations than expanding their territory. However, this obviously contributed to the growing hostility of the local populations.

In 1535, the San Cristóbal de Los Llanos was renamed Ciudad Real, and the colony began to grow into the 1540s as new colonists arrived from throughout New Spain.

Bartolome de Las Casas and the Evangelization of the Chiapas

As the conquests lingered on, many Catholics throughout the Caribbean colonies and Spain began to voice humanitarian concerns about the treatment of the indigenous people of the Americas. Bartolome de Las Casas became the most prominent critic of the humanitarian disaster unfolding throughout the New World.

Las Casas included this image of the Spanish committing atrocities during the conquest of Cuba in his book.
https://commons.wikimedia.org/wiki/File:Bartolom%C3%A9_de_las_Casas_Regionum_355385740_MG_8829_A3-f1.tif

Las Casas was a Spanish priest that helped evangelize indigenous populations during the conquest of the Caribbean. After seeing the horrors of the conquests firsthand, he returned to Europe in 1515 and began campaigning for an investigation that would bring to light the atrocities of the conquistadors. While Las Casas was in favor of colonization and the assimilation of the indigenous people into Spanish Catholic culture, he hoped that he could transform the unchecked genocidal expansion of the Americas into peaceful colonization. One strategy was to send Catholic farmers to the Americas, as they were much more prone to be peaceful colonists than the violent, militant conquistadors.

Las Casas put this strategy to practice in modern-day Venezuela in 1520. He departed Spain with a group of farmers, proclaiming that he would set up a city where the natives and farmers would live peacefully together in an equal, free society. Les Casas hoped to create an alternative to the genocide and exploitation of the conquerors. He hoped to convert the indigenous peoples to Catholicism and at least partially assimilate them into European culture while also giving them the same status as the Spaniards.

However, the plan was doomed from the start. Not only was he only able to recruit a very small number of farmers and laborers to travel to the Americas, but he also met great opposition from local Spanish landlords once they arrived. The town was abandoned in 1522 when it was attacked by nearby indigenous peoples.

After his disastrous experiment in the Americas, Las Casas began writing the Historia de las Indias, which chronicled his experiences during the conquests. The book gave a grim chronicle of the events of the conquests but with a prophetic, religious flavor. The book's main theme prophesized that – one day – Spain would be divinely punished for the horror it brought to the people of the Americas. La Casas made arrangements to make sure that the book would not be published until after his death. Subsequent writings would increasingly have a more secular tone, as he accused the Spaniards of decimating the native population because of their greed for gold and riches.

The Spanish monarchy passed the "New Laws" in 1542, which focused on setting up more officiated administrative systems throughout the conquered regions that would help diminish violence, raiding, and looting against the local populations. This was an immense victory for Las Casas, who King Charles chose to act as the colonial bishop for the Chiapas region.

Las Casas sailed to the Americas in 1544 with a group of followers, arriving in Ciudad Real in March 1545. The arrival of Las Casas and the Dominicans brought sweeping changes to the region's administration, and many local colonists voiced opposition to the new religious interference. The colonists eventually drove the clergy out of Ciudad Real with threats of violence, and they were forced to operate out of nearby rural villages. As the group began evangelizing the region, they eventually moved back into Ciudad Real after tensions with the colonists cooled. However, Las Casas' power as bishop would soon be dismantled by influential colonists who used their power to lobby the Spanish crown.

The New Laws did not succeed in their mission, and King Charles was forced to throw out many of the laws' central provisions. Powerful colonists throughout New Spain threatened rebellion if the laws were enforced, and Charles grew afraid of losing the new American territories he had invested so much in. Despite this, the New Laws served as a monumental moment in the Spanish conquest, as the Spanish Catholic Church, one of the most powerful institutions in the country, began to condemn the brutality of the conquistadors.

After the dissolution of the New Laws, the local colonists increasingly grew hostile to Las Casas, and he was eventually forced to flee the region entirely. After returning to Spain in 1547, he spent the rest of his life writing and preaching about the plight of the indigenous people of the Americas and the devastation caused by the conquests. In the eyes of many indigenous groups, Las Casas would certainly not be a perfect historical figure, as he did advocate for colonization and the conversion of indigenous peoples to Catholicism. However, Las Casas has been celebrated by many Latin American leaders who acknowledge the extraordinary risks he took by speaking out against the powerful conquistadors and the colonial aspirations of the Spanish crown.

Las Casas saw firsthand the moral degradation of the conquests from within and used his power in the Catholic Church to educate the European governments and their populations about the brutal realities of exploration in the New World. Las Casas was one of the first figures to advocate for the native people of the Americas, who were increasingly losing their land, population, and culture to the ever-tightening grip of Spanish colonialism.

Despite the great humanitarian efforts of Las Casas and his fellow Dominican evangelists, these missionaries also went to great lengths to destroy the sacred religious beliefs of the Chiapas Maya. The Dominicans destroyed many sacred Maya temples and monuments throughout the Chiapas region, replacing them with Christian churches.

The missionaries used manipulative tactics to persuade the native population to convert, such as using the biblical book of revelations to convince them that they would be divinely punished if they didn't abandon their own religious beliefs. With the rapid, complete destruction of their lives and livelihoods occurring all around them, it's not hard to understand why so much of the native Maya population began to believe the apocalyptic warnings of the missionaries and convert to Christianity.

Chapter 16: Conquest of the Yucatan Peninsula

As the conquests of the Aztec Empire in Central Mexico were bringing the conquistadors and Spanish crown a massive amount of wealth, the northern Yucatan Peninsula largely stayed on the periphery of colonial ambitions. The fragmented state of the cities and the seemingly impenetrable dense rainforest made the Maya heartland a far less desirable territory to plunder.

Francisco de Montejo

However, in 1526 Francisco de Montejo, a veteran conquistador who helped Cortes conquer the Aztecs, officially received permission from the Spanish crown to conquer the Yucatan. He landed near the village of Xelha in the northeast of the peninsula with 400 men and immediately renamed it "Salamanca de Xelha." The men soon began to run out of food and provisions and increasingly began making raids on local Maya villagers. After the Mayas fled with their food supplies into the rainforest, the men showed signs of declining morale, and Montejo grew concerned that they may hijack a ship and desert. To curb this threat, he burned down all four ships that were docked near the settlement.

The force gradually became accustomed to the harsh conditions of the peninsula and began to spread Spanish influence throughout the northeast Yucatan. In 1528, Montejo and his men arrived in the Maya city of Chaucaca, only to find it completely empty. In the early hours of the morning the following day, the men were ambushed by a force of the city's Maya warriors who had fled to the forest before Montejo's arrival. The Spaniards were able to successfully repulse the attack and immediately departed for the city of Ake. Upon their arrival, a large battle ensued that led to a decisive Spanish victory that left over a thousand Maya warriors dead. After this massive Maya defeat, the local rulers surrendered to Montejo.

After visiting a few other Maya settlements Montejo and his men returned to their base of operations in Xelha, only to find that local Maya killed more than half of the men stationed there. An entire force of Spaniards that were stationed near the village of Pole was also found dead.

After escaping to the Caribbean with his men, in 1529, Montejo became mayor of Tabasco on the Gulf Coast. However, he was not yet finished with his ultimate goal of taking the Yucatan. After several failed attempts to create settlements that would serve as launching points for the conquest of the peninsula, Montejo established a garrison at the city of Campeche. Alonso d' Avila traveled overland throughout the east of the peninsula to form a settlement but was forced to eventually flee to modern-day Honduras due to hostile locals.

A large local Maya military force led an assault on the Spanish troops in Campeche, but Montejo was able to repulse the attack. The local Maya lord, Aj Canul, immediately met with Montejo after the defeat and surrendered. Montejo's son, a high-ranking conquistador by this point, was able to establish the new Spanish colony at the city of Chichen Itza, called Ciudad Real. Some months later, the local Maya ruler was killed during an alleged attempt to assassinate Montejo's son. The death of the Maya ruler further heightened the hostilities between the locals and the Spaniards, and the garrison at Chichen Itza was attacked in the summer of 1533. The Spanish forces were forced to abandon Ciudad Real and flee west to friendlier Maya territories.

The Xiu Maya population in the northwest of the peninsula became the greatest ally of the Spanish during their conquests. Their territory became a safe haven for the conquistadors as they continued attempts to conquer hostile regions. Montejo made a return to Campeche to establish friendlier relations with the Maya there, but rumors of conquistador Francisco Pizarro's expeditions in the Inca heartland in South America began breaking the morale of Montejo's men. While both the conquests of the Aztecs in Central Mexico and the Incas in Peru found enormous wealth, the only thing the Yucatan had brought to the conquistadors were hostile local Maya populations. While the gold uncovered by the initial expeditions was promising, it seemed to many of the Spaniards that they were trying to conquer a civilization that had no wealth or riches worth conquering.

Montejo's men began to desert him for other opportunities in the Americas, and Montejo and his son returned to the Gulf Veracruz region. Montejo and Alvarado engaged in a bitter rivalry over the governorship of Honduras, with Alvarado eventually emerging as the victor.

A Franciscan friar named Jacobo de Testera sailed to the western Yucatan to attempt evangelization and bring the locals into the Spanish Empire peacefully. A loyal friend of fellow evangelist Bartolome de las Casas, Testera had also witnessed firsthand the cruelty of the conquistadors and hoped to bring peaceful colonization to the Yucatan. However, this mission soon fell apart. After arriving in Champoton in 1535, the friar and the conquistadors stationed there became increasingly hostile towards each other, and Testera was forced to abandon his efforts to evangelize the western Yucatan.

After the friar's departure, the Spanish military force in Champoton persuaded the local Maya lords to submit. However, this proved to be a very small victory, as the Spanish garrison was left isolated, surrounded by local populations that had only grown more hostile since their arrival. The bitter reality of the Yucatan conquest disheartened many conquistadors, who increasingly abandoned the prospects of capturing the Maya heartland.

The ruins of a church that had been built with stones from Mayan temples.

The Effects of Conquest on the Maya

After almost twenty years of conquest in the peninsula, the Spaniards now only occupied one isolated outpost on the western coast. While unfathomable amounts of gold and riches were being uncovered throughout the Americas, the Yucatan seemed to be not only one of the most unconquerable regions but also did not have enough wealth to make the conquests worthwhile in the first place. The Maya heartland, which only a few centuries before had been home to the greatest civilization of the Americas, was increasingly seen as a waste of Spanish resources, lives, and time.

While the Spanish strategized on what to do with the Yucatan, the Maya civilization struggled to survive. Since the Spanish arrived, disease from the Old Word had ravaged their populations. The Spanish's attempts to pit Maya populations against each other worked, and now Maya cities and villages that for centuries considered each other friends, allies, neighbors, and kin increasingly saw each other as potential enemies. While the Maya heartland was never a fully peaceful one, the entrance of the Spanish conquistadors into the fragile, fragmented political ecosystem of the Yucatan created a paranoid environment that inhibited any attempts of unification among the Maya to defend their homeland.

Disease, famine, and political manipulation had permanently ruptured any semblance of Maya unification, as each city and village began fighting for its survival in the new destructive landscape created by the Spanish conquests. All the Maya could do now was hold on to their cultural systems that were still firmly in place and anticipate the next arrival of the conquistadors in the northern Yucatan.

The Colonization of the Northern Yucatan

Montejo's son, Montejo the Younger, took over the colonization of the northern Yucatan from his father in 1540. The next year, he brought his troops first to Champoton and then to Campeche, where he created the Yucatan's first local colonial town council. Montejo the Younger knew that to avoid the mistakes of the earlier conquests of the peninsula, he had to create stable local administrative power structures that would attract colonists and create a permanent Spanish colonial presence in the region. After creating the council, he approached the local Maya settlements and ordered them to surrender, which many local lords agreed to.

However, the local Canul Maya ruler remained hostile, and Montejo the Younger sent his cousin to their city. The second colonial town council, Merida, was created near the Canul city, and the Spanish troops garrisoned there were approached by the Canul lord. He hoped to establish peace with the Spaniards. The ruler, Tutul Xiu, was awestruck by the priests when they Catholic mass and immediately converted to Christianity.

The submission of Tutul Xiu to the Spanish at Merida was one of the most important moments of the Yucatan conquest. Tutul Xiu was one of the most influential rulers of the Maya world, and his surrender created a domino effect, as Maya rulers throughout the west Yucatan began to submit to Spanish colonial authority. While the rulers of the eastern Yucatan remained hostile to the Spanish, the increasing influence in the west gave the Spaniards the breathing-room and native allies they needed to fully conquer the entirety of the Maya heartland.

Spanish forces were sent eastward, where many rulers accepted the Spaniards peacefully, and those that didn't were swiftly defeated. As these forces reached the far-east Yucatan Maya, many remained hostile and were able to stay independent from Spanish authority. However, by 1546 the Spanish had much of the western and central parts of the northern Yucatan firmly under their control.

In November 1546, the most powerful Maya lords of the independent eastern regions conducted a massive, well-organized rebellion against the Spanish colonial authorities. Garrisons and colonial settlements throughout the west were attacked by Maya warriors, leading to heavy casualties on both sides. The Maya were eventually defeated in a final climactic battle, and much of the population of the western provinces fled southwards to the central and southern lowlands. After 30 years of conquest, the Spanish had finally captured the northern Yucatan.

Chapter 17: The Final Conquests

With the northern Yucatan and most of the highlands now firmly under Spanish control, the central and southern lowlands, namely the Peten Basin, became the last surviving independent Maya region. Thousands of Maya from throughout the region continually poured into the region to escape famine, disease, slavery, and the colonial system. The Spanish saw this as a massive threat, as their encomienda system was heavily reliant on the labor of indigenous locals.

This region would be – by far – the most unconquerable territory of all of Central America. Aside from the dense rainforests, there were very freshwater sources to sustain a military force during campaigns, and settlements tended to be somewhat isolated. The people of the region, especially the Itza Maya, were the fiercest warriors the Spanish had yet encountered in the Americas.

By the mid-16th century, the Itza had learned many of the tactics of the Spanish from the migrants who fled the northern Yucatan and the highlands and began to use their terrain to their advantage by using hit-and-run tactics on the conquistadors. Due to the region's dense forest, the Spanish were robbed of their greatest military advantage: the use of cavalry. However, the decline of trade in the region and the increased isolation of Itza communities meant that it was only a matter of time before they too fell to the Spanish.

As covered in Chapter 12, the conquest of the Peten Basin began with the arrival of the missionaries during the mid-16th century. The city of Nojpeten was the final major Maya city to fall to the Spanish, finally being conquered in March 1697. The region held out for over 150 years after the initial Yucatan conquests.

After centuries of progression from the Olmec cities on the Gulf Coast to the city centers of the lowlands, the great Maya civilization now found itself fully at the mercy of the Spanish colonial government.

Conclusion

The complete conquest of the Maya heartland would not be the end of the hardship for the Maya people. In fact, it was only the beginning. From the Spanish crown to the modern Guatemalan government, the Maya people would experience many years of exploitation and oppression.

So, what can be learned about the Maya civilization, and how can those lessons be used in a modern context? How do the stone step pyramids have anything to do with the modern skyscrapers of our great cities like New York City or Dubai? How could an ancient belief system comprised of mythical gods have anything to do with 21st-century life? While the Maya civilization of the Yucatan Peninsula may seem too distant in the past to draw modern lessons from, the 21st-century international landscape serves as a direct reflection of the ancient Maya political system.

The Maya had long-distance trade routes throughout the Yucatan that created a complex economy within Central America, greatly mirroring the international trade systems of today. How could one study the conflict between Tikal and Calakmul and not think about the U.S.-Soviet Cold War, where each side fought proxy wars and created alliance systems to gain political dominance? While modern international studies dwarf that of the Maya, nearly every theme of the 21st-century international order can be seen within the Maya civilization within a relatively small area on the Yucatan Peninsula.

Many of the international problems society faces today, from war to income inequality, to environmental degradation, are often looked at as modern problems. The threats that the Maya civilization faced show that many of these problems are not solely born out of the 21ˢᵗ century. Instead, they are human problems that have been a part of our history since the beginning of time. Thus, instead of condemning the lessons of ancient civilizations of the past as "too old to be relevant," we should study the problems they faced and how they combatted them.

Inherent in the Maya belief system was time. The Maya were not only fascinated with it; they were obsessed with it. Time was studied largely through astronomical observation and record-keeping to keep track of agricultural seasons, conduct religious ceremonies, and many other time-reliant necessities.

The central idea revolving around time for the Maya was their belief that their universe would eventually be destroyed by the gods and replaced anew by another. Out of all their astoundingly astronomical and mathematical theories, their breathtaking architecture that is still marveled at today, their lively cultural practices and art that could compete with anything that was being produced in contemporary Europe, perhaps their concept of the "destruction of the universe" was the one thing that the Maya got wrong.

The survival and thriving of the Maya people of today show that universes, worlds, and civilizations are never truly destroyed. Instead, history goes through a cyclical pattern of destruction, dispersal, and creation that combines the remnants of the old with the inventions of the new.

Though the decline of Tikal and Calakmul meant the destruction of a peninsula-wide political system and the great urban centers of the era, their populations brought the remnants of what made these cities great to other regions. There, the Maya populations learned from the errors of the great lowland urban centers and expanded upon them. Though the Spanish conquistadors ravaged the Yucatan with their aspirations of conquest and evangelization, the Maya people firmly held on to their culture and history. Though the nearby cities and towns may have Spanish names and spoken language, the Maya have found their place in modern Central American life while also keeping a firm hold on to their cultural heritage.

The Maya civilization never collapsed, nor did it die out due to the brutal conquests of the conquistadors; the Maya civilization has survived to the present day despite the apocalyptic collapse of the Terminal Classic and the conquests of the 16th century. The survival of the Maya has shown that no matter how apocalyptic a threat may be, a strong, resilient cultural foundation will stay strong in its people.

It is hard not to point out the bitter irony that as Catholicism is declining amongst the population of Spain today, the traditional culture of the rural Maya peoples has remained an inherent, inexorable part of their lives. Though the immense brutality of the Spanish conquests and collapse of the Maya city-states may not show it, it is clear that the gods of the Maya are still watching over their people of the Yucatan today.

Part 3: The Olmec Civilization

An Enthralling Overview of the History of the Olmecs, Starting from Agriculture in Mesoamerica to the Fall of La Venta

THE OLMEC CIVILIZATION

AN ENTHRALLING OVERVIEW OF THE HISTORY OF THE OLMECS, STARTING FROM AGRICULTURE IN MESOAMERICA TO THE FALL OF LA VENTA

ENTHRALLING HISTORY

Introduction

Several civilizations have been described as shrouded in mystery due to inaccurate detailed information available to history lovers. The Olmecs civilization happens to be one of such civilizations with many unanswered questions.

The Olmecs arrived on the Gulf of Mexico around 1500 BCE and came with new engineering, religion, and agricultural ideas. Within a short while, they rose to the limelight and became the envy of the region due to their rapid development. There are questions like where they came from, their origin, and ultimately, what led to their fall?

Scholars are divided in their opinion about the Olmec civilization and the stories around them. Some historians opine that the Olmecs have origins from the region itself and are not migrants - as they have often been portrayed. In contrast, others believe that the Olmecs were travelers who settled in Mesoamerican and improved civilization.

In this book, we will be telling it all, and what better way is there to approach the topic than to begin with the Pre-Olmec Mesoamerican period where it all started? We have left no stone unturned on covering this topic. Also covered in this book are the Archaic periods and the different phases within the Mesoamerican region.

This book presents the Olmecs' amazing history and contributions to the modern-day regions in the most comprehensive and easy-to-understand way - more so than anything similar you might find. The author has consciously considered the concerns of beginners and those who struggle with history. Furthermore, the book will transit to covering everything you need to know about the Olmecs, from the origin to the fall. So, even if you struggled to understand history before now, you will have fun reading this one and recommending it to your friends and family.

Let's get right into it.

Chapter 1: The First Settlements

The Archaic Period, which is the era that preceded the invention of pottery, is also known as the *preceramic period*. It is a period in Mesoamerican history that started sometime around 8,000 BCE (Before the Common Era) to 2000 BCE. This period was mostly known for the transition from reliance on mostly hunting for feeding to a more settled way of living which led to the rise of agriculture for feeding the fast-growing population. Mesoamerica is made up of modern-day:

- Costa Rica
- Central Mexico
- El Salvador
- Nicaragua
- Guatemala
- Belize

This Archaic Period is traditionally categorized into Early, 2000 to 1000 BCE; Middle, which was between 1000 to 400 BCE; and Late/Terminal Period, which was between 100 to 250 BCE. This period was before the Lithic (or Paleoindian) Period and followed by the Pre-Classic Period. It is still unclear when exactly the Lithic Period ended and when the Archaic Period started; however, many believe it was related to climate change – the metamorphosis from the ice age to the present – and the fact that remains from extinct animals from the ice age were never found.

The Archaic Period

This period was a notable time in the Mesoamerican regions because it marked the beginning of a change in lifestyle from people who moved about hunting for wild animals to more settled arrangements. With this emerging lifestyle, the people stayed longer in some of these places and, in the process, developed agricultural skills because they relied more on the produce than hunting. The first permanent settlements discovered were in the Gulf of Mexico, the Caribbean, and the Pacific Seacoast. These settlements are, for the most part as a result of the abundance of marine life and food resources.

Archaeologists discovered the use of various locations for different durations of time. For example, several sites on the Chiapas coast, like the Cerro de las Conchas, showed evidence of all-year settlements. Others can be found in modern-day Belize along the Caribbean coast, some inland settlements towards Cobweb Swamp and Colha.

Although the exact origin of Mesoamerican agriculture remains unclear, historians and scholars believe that several generations of people into major regions localized many species of wild plants during the Archaic era; these later served as the agricultural foundation of the Pre-Classic and Classic Mesoamerican civilization. These plants include beans, chili peppers, and maize, often grown together in a maize field.

While the origin of maize remains inconclusive and the debates continue, the regions that did well in agriculture – especially the domestication of wild plants – were the highlands of Oaxaca and Tehuacan, that is modern-day southeast of the Valley of Mexico, the coastal lowlands of the Gulf of Mexico and Pacific.

The more the people chose to stay longer in a particular place, the faster their populations increased due to the reliance on agriculture and other types of food found on the seashore. This population expansion soon led to the birth of a more sophisticated society differentiated mainly by their craft, trades, and emerging social class. These early Olmecs traded obsidian, chert, flint, textiles, and feathers.

Let's look at the categories that emerged during the Archaic Period, the difference in economic, cultural, and political developments. Also, we will be looking at the similarities and regional variations. Four primary Mesoamerican cultures emerged in the Pre-classic Period: The Valley of Oaxaca, the Olmecs, the Gulf of Mexico Littoral, the Valley of Mexico, and the Maya Zone.

Early Pre-Classic Period - 2000 to 1000 BCE

The central feature of the early Pre-Classic Period was the expansion in population and further complexity of the settlement. Some of the most notable advances found in archeological records include the creation of specialized crafts, unique figurines, and pottery. Also, during this period, there was more extensive trading between the regional networks, more social complexities, and the emergence of warfare.

Evidence of war within the region was discovered dating to 1800 BCE, especially on the Oaxacan valley among the Zapotec and other surrounding areas. These battles grew increasingly complex as the Pre-Classic period faded away and birthed the dominance of the Monte Albans over Oaxaca.

During this time, signs of widening social differences prevailed, including acquiring status goods, variation in the houses built, and funerary rituals. This period was also known for discovering the first form of ceramics in Mesoamerica around the Chiapas coast, extending to what is now known as El Salvador.

This early Pre-Classic Period also saw the emergence of the Olmec, the "mother culture" of Mesoamerican polities and states that followed.

Middle Pre-Classic - 1000 to 400 BCE

The middle Pre-Classic Period saw further development and expansion of these complex societies from the Early Pre-Classic. For example, unity and hierarchical government systems became widespread in the region like the Maya lowlands and highlands, Chalcatzingo, the Mexican Valley, and the Valley of Oaxaca. Some of these societies changed from traditional chiefdom systems to *states*. This was also a time when kings and other royals were treated as the mouthpiece of the gods; hence they could not be questioned or opposed. This change in the approach to rulers was noted among the Monte Alban I of c. 500 - 200 BCE in the Valley of Oaxaca. During this period, the kings/rulers were *divinely selected*, so they answered to no one. All their words and actions were believed to have come from the gods.

The Middle Pre-Classic Period also experienced growth and population density, which made social differentiation more pronounced. The gap between the elite and the commoners widened further. The ruling and religious elites acquired spiritual powers to stamp their authority.

As for culture, this was a time of crystallization of the pan-Mesoamerican culture zone. There was massive and ongoing buying and selling of goods and exchanging ideas across the regions; this included religious beliefs and sacred items. Other high valued items and precious stones like pearl oyster shells, pyrite, jade, quetzal feathers, and magnetite were also exchanged. An immense jump in buying and selling was also notably ongoing during this period, and architecture took a front seat to it all with the construction of unique architectural carved monuments; one of them was found on the Oaxaca valley, dating back to 1000 BCE.

Furthermore, the introduction of idol worship started in 500 BCE. Among the Monte Alban 1 rulers, more than 300 idols were erected, carved with various inscriptions like dates and events. Many of these inscriptions included writings describing wars and the sacrifice of prisoners of war. Scholars are still studying some of these symbols.

The Maya, too, experienced some of these developments in symbols and monuments with massively carved stones or wooden slabs that displayed the ruler's power, authority, and legitimacy. The Maya monuments of the Pre-Classic period were carved from Chiapas to far as East and South El Salvador.

The need to take over and rule over other smaller areas increased considerably in the region. The population explosion helped intensify agricultural processes, and we see the development of more complex water control technologies. The increased complexity of the society was also felt and seen in the pottery designs as production soared and became available in more sophisticated and elaborate forms.

Later/Terminal Pre-Classic Period - 100 to 250 BCE

This period was defined by the veritable urban transformation, which laid the foundation for the flourishing presence of states and polities of the Classic period. For example, in the North and

Western parts of the region specifically, Nayarit, Colima, and Jalisco, there was gradual urbanization, state-building construction, and significant architectural edifices but not on the scale seen in the other parts of the region. In the southern region, the Monte Alban II of c. 250 BCE to 1CE, the rulers held tight to power and control over the area while expanding the construction of residential and ceremonial centers. Construction of the colossal city of Teotihuacan began during this period. Located in central Mexico, this civilization would later dominate most of the Mesoamerican region.

The North and West, which is modern-day Nayarit, Jalisco, and Colima, experienced urbanization, state-building, and monumental architectural development but on a lower scale when compared to other regions. The style of pottery, artistic designs from these regions, and funeral rituals and practices further reflected the apparent regional variations among the territories.

In the Eastern part of Mesoamerica, there were massive developments of all kinds, notably in the Tres Zapotec of the Olmecs along the Gulf Coast. On the other hand, neighboring locations like La Venta and San Lorenzo declined in power and influence.

The Mayans stood out among the societies in the region that experienced rapid developments in the terminal Pre-Classic period. The people developed and advanced their writings, astrology, and mathematics. Their architectural skills were notable in their structural designs and urban planning. They also won and dominated more territories within the region, giving them more power and control. Other advancements in this civilization eventually made them unique in the Classic period.

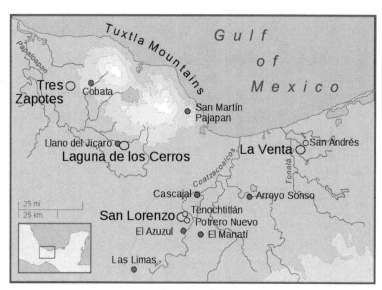

Olmec heartland

Early Settlements

The Archaic period was an era of transition for the Mesoamerican people who gradually transformed from being wondering hunter-gatherers to partly settled or sedentary rummagers and farmers. Based on a study's outcome on remains at the Mexican Gulf Coast, humans started co-existing and built permanent houses close to each other between around 3000 and 1800 BCE. They began with items that could get burnt easily and later to more durable material and structures. The people participated actively in trading activities, especially obsidian trade.

Examples of these early changes are temporary, seasonal shelters, like the Gulia Naquitz, a rock shelter in the Valley of Oaxaca. A band of nomads was discovered to have used this shelter as a settlement between 8000 and 6500 BCE at least six times. The speed of this development was not at the same rate in all the regions.

Also, travelers and temporary settlers took shelter in the El Gigante rock shelter located in the Southern Highlands of modern-day Honduras. Evidence that the rock shelter was only occupied during the wet season was supported by the presence of a unique type of plants, which could only have gotten there by settlers who

---

used the place mainly during the wet season from July to September. Also, during the Archaic period of 4,700 BCE, from May to October. Several settlements that merged into a village-like arrangement were identified around the Chiapas sea coast and the Caribbean.

It was clear that the Sea and Lagoon nearby provided resources that made the settlers stay longer and, in most cases, all year-round. Shell mounds found at these sites were examples of evidence that proved this extended stay, and some of these shells have been dated back to between 5500 and 3500 BCE.

Additionally, the non-existence of Archaic animal remains, and the short supply of artifacts further revealed that Cerro de las Conchas was used more as a collection and processing point for sea and lagoon resources. While this site might have been temporally inhabited, the situation was different at the inland camps with signs of all-year-round settlements.

"More permanent sites are identified in the archaeological record with greater frequency dating to 3000 BCE and later. The site of Zohapilco *on* Lake Chalco *in the Basin of Mexico has evidence of year-round settlement before a volcanic eruption around 3000 BCE. The site of* Colha *and nearby swamps, such as Cobweb Swamp and* Pulltrouser Swamp*, show evidence of permanent settlement by 3000 BCE. Actun Halal, a rock shelter in* Belize*, was occupied as early as 2400 to 2130 BCE. Permanent villages are seen even later in the Valley of Oaxaca by 2000 BCE and in the* Valley of Tehuacan *by 1500 BCE. Based on these findings, it appears that people settled in resource-rich areas, such as along the coasts or by lakes, earlier than in semi-arid and arid environments like the Valleys of Oaxaca and Tehuacan. As agriculture developed, the population increased and settlements expanded into more marginal, less resource-rich areas. "Extracted* from Wikipedia - Mesoamerican Archaic Period.

Based on these discoveries, it appears that the resource-rich areas like the coasts by the lakes were first used as settlements and more heavily populated than the semi-arid and drylands, such as in the Valley of Oaxaca and Tehuacan. The more agriculture developed, the more populations expanded and more settlements we required; that led to the expansion into more minor resources-rich marginal areas.

The El Gigante Rock Shelter

At 1300 meters above sea levels and above the Estanzuela River Valley, the El Gigante rock shelter gives you a comprehensive view of the Southern part of today's Central Honduras. Only authorized personnel are allowed; the site is completely enclosed due to the lower rim being 3 to 4 meters above the slope leading to it. Over thousands of years, the presence of accumulated sediment at the entrance tells a story of how the vault shields settlers in the rock shelter from rain and wind.

These same conditions have made it possible for the settlers to survive through different seasons and remain consistent in the advancement of their vocations. Evidence of preserved vocations has been found among the artifacts recovered from the area, including leather and woven fibers remnants. Another significant find at the El Gigante is the region's most prominent and probably the most preserved basketry collection, dating to 11,000 years. That makes it one of the oldest artifacts found in Mesoamerica.

Also found in the El Gigante are human remains, showing that giant humans once took shelter in the rock. Additionally, there are many bones from sea species like crab, as well as deer, armadillos, and rabbits. Also discovered are plant remains like avocado, hog plums, wild beans, soursop, and most recently, cobs of early domesticated maize.

Mesoamerican has been described as one of the first places in the world where wild plant domestication occurred. The massive collection of well-preserved farm plants further buttresses the accuracy of the timing and trajectory of domestication in Central America and the Mesoamerican territories. Beans, maize, and squash were some of the plants well-preserved and discovered at this site. We also had a further understanding of how the settlers managed their prized trees through the presence of an extensive collection of partly-domesticated resources like coyol palms, ciruela, acorns, and several species of sapote. An even more profound understanding of this domestication was seen in the samples of avocado pits and rinds.

Based on the archeological test performed on botanical remains found in the rock shelter, the early human settlement at El Gigante dates back to about 11,000 years ago to the Archaic period. Between 5,700 and 2000 BCE saw the transition from a larger scale to more aggressive cultivation of maize – mainly because the original tropical forest retrogressed in the valleys nearby due to massive fires. These fires made the people move from their previously favored pine-oak lands, massively migrating from the original highland villages to lands where they could farm more around the valley floors.

El Gigante is not the only rock shelter in Honduras, but none of the others that come close to it are *deposits.* El Gigante is indeed massive and majestic, with its cubicle measured at 42 mm wide, 17 mm deep, and 12 mm high. Again, unlike what is obtainable at the other rock shelters around Honduras, only a few negative paintings of hands are left of the rock-art collection from El Gigante. Based on all discoveries to date, no other rock shelter comes close to El Gigante in size, dimension, and setting in all of Central and Mesoamerica.

Chapter 2: Domesticated Agriculture

Adaptation of Agriculture

The domestication of agriculture refers to adapting or evolving wild plants into types that can be cultivated for or raised for human consumption - and this was the predominant type of farming in the Archaic period. However, it took the people of Mesoamerica thousands of years to adapt agriculture as a means of livelihood due to many reasons, but primarily due to rainfall, soil types, and the terrains. The increased dependence on the domesticated plant was a much slower process for the people of the region.

It appears that climate change impacted the resources available to roaming hunter-gatherers and led them to adopt new ways of getting food. No doubt climate change played a massive role in the emergence of plant domestication, but there are other complex reasons why people started depending on agriculture as their means of livelihood. While the Archaic people boosted their reliance on domesticated plants, they never stopped moving from one place to another in search of wild plants and hunting animals, which was their predominant means of feeding.

The first forms of cultivation (and the early stages of domestication) possibly involved some variation of dooryard horticulture. The Archaic people used some of the lands in their settlements or shelters to plant and nurture different plant species. Gradually, agriculture started booming along with the demand for domesticated crops. The Archaic people resorted to farming methods like the slash-and-burn due to the increased demand for more land for agriculture. With this method, they were able to recover more lands away from their settlements and villages.

Farm tools like the chipped stones adzes (a tool similar to an ax) give us a deeper insight into how digging took place and how trees were cut down to gain more ground for farming during the Archaic period. We also understand the people from this period better – and most significantly, how they interacted with the environment.

The people of this era preferred the farming method of slash-and-burn cultivation style. As the name suggested, it involved cutting forest trees to make room for more farmlands, as evidenced by the high level of charcoal found at the sites. The burnt layer of ash provided the freshly cleared land with rich nutrients to fertilize the crops. Other evidence that supported the use of slash-and-burn included the presence of low levels of pollen and the several corn pollens found at the site. This style of farming was used for farming several crops, especially maize dating 7300 BCE in the Caribbean and Balsas regions.

Between 5200 BCE and 3,500 BCE, we confirmed wide forest clearing in the Maya lowland on the Gulf coast. Additionally, charcoal levels at the Chiapas coast remained high after 3500 BCE, suggesting more people's attempts to recover more farmlands. The farmland recovery and high charcoal levels continued into 2500 BCE when the people started moving closer to sea and lagoon resources. This migration has been linked to forest clearing using the burning method. Paleoecologically, evidence across the north of Belize showed that people started cultivating manioc and maize before 3000 BCE. However, massive forest clearance and increased maize farming only began after 2000 BCE.

Towards the end of the Archaic period and into the Pre-Classic, the Mesoamericans started improvising on different types of farming, as discussed below.

Terracing

The terrace farming method is a set of sloped structured earth on the plane ground cut into consecutive declining flat platforms or surfaces. This farming method is labor-intensive and one of the earliest types of farming dating back to the Archaic period. The heap of earth looks like long stretches of steps, and they make farming more effective.

Graduated terraces are commonly used to cultivate on hilly surfaces or mountainous terrains. Also, they serve as a means of regulating erosion and surface runoff, and they are also used for growing crops that need irrigation.

Raised Fields

This type of farming is done on a large and elevated piece of land, bounded mainly by ditches filled with water to control environmental factors like frost damage, moisture level, and flooding. Raised field agriculture was primarily common among the pre-Hispanics in Latin America, like people from Budi Lake Mapuche and tropical lowlands.

These Pre-Hispanic raised fields are quite familiar from the regions near Santa Cruz de Mompox in the northern part of Colombia and the Llanos de Moxos region of lowland modern-day Bolivia. In the highlands of Bolivia, the Tiwanaku tribe close to

Lake Titicaca also used this farming method, called "waru" or *camellones*. There are also ancient raised fields that have been traced back to Central America at Pulltrouser Swamp in Belize, where the Maya civilization practiced this type of farming. Other Ancient people who practiced raised fields were the people of Toltec and Aztec on the shore of Lake Texcoco, where it was called *chinampas*.

Crop Rotation

Crop rotation was another system of farming observed to have started in the Archaic period and become common among the Mesoamericans. The adaptation to these farming systems helps increase farming activities and reduces the over-reliance on the slash-and-burn farming system.

Domestication Agriculture

As the people of Mesoamerica became more settlers than foragers, they became more reliant on agriculture and some particular type of plants, making Mesoamerica one of the largest independent plant domestication areas in the world. The requirement for surviving the settlement arrangement included unique and intensive domestication processes, like selectively collecting bigger seeds to cultivate and preserve.

Several sites have been uncovered to help us understand how and when agriculture started in Mesoamerica, but many details were tampered with, impairing our ability to piece together an exact picture. For instance, the Guila Naquitz site in southern Mexico possesses rich evidence of the transition from hunting to farming and food production by the Mesoamericans. Strong evidence of the use of edible plants like wild beans and seeds from other grass that provided nutrients was found. Others include:

- Acorn (Quercus species)
- Prickly pear (Opuntia species)
- Pinon pine nut (Pinus edulis)
- mesquite seeds (Prosopis species)

We also have plants like:

- Squash (Cucurbita pepo)
- Maize (Zea mays)

- Beans (in the Phaseolus genus)

- Chili peppers (Capsicum genus)

The Mesoamerican Archaic people chose plants they could conveniently preserve with a genetic makeup that can be tampered with easily. Some of these plants include chili peppers (Capsicum genus), squash (Cucurbita pepo), beans (in the Phaseolus genus), and maize (Zea mays). The successful farming of these domesticated plants led to a boost in a more dependable food supply for the Archaic peoples, making room for more settlements and population expansion.

Domestication of Maize

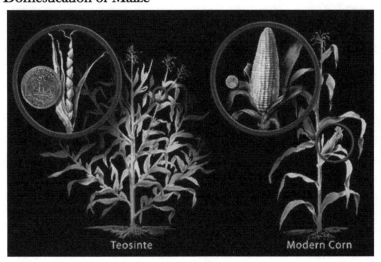

Maize was probably one of the most important crops to be domesticated during the Archaic period. It also played a critical role for the Mesoamericans because it was valuable, nutritional, and easy to preserve. Despite its popularity and use among the regions and in archaeological records of the Mesoamericans, the actual origin of corn is still shrouded in misery. While the oldest maize cob was discovered in cob form in Gulia Naquitz dating back to between 6,300 and 6000 BCE, it is most likely not domesticated there (because it showed up suddenly in a domesticated form).

One series showed that multiple mutations had been claimed to be responsible for the domestication of the maize cob; however, there are no records for these mutations. Instead of relying on conspiracy or guesswork, the researcher decided it was better to conduct genetic analysis. This approach eventually paid off because it showed a different wild plant, gamma (Tripsacum acetylides), was a wild plant crossed-bred with teosinte to produce the structure of the modern-day maize. Unlike teosinte, Tripsacum was entirely edible. The Mesoamericans possibly identified teosinte-Tripsacum in the wild and decided to cross them for trials. There's also the possibility of tests of the teosinte with other plants with sugary leaves and stalks.

Mesoamerican chewed leaves and stalks of early maize for the sweet flavor it provided. At the same time, starch and sugar were also valuable ingredients for producing alcohol, which was a vital consumable for social gatherings.

Archaeological evidence revealed that the Balsa region was one of the first sites where the corn was domesticated before spreading to the neighboring areas. Also, teosinte has been genetically traced to the wild plant domesticated as maize. Highland Mexico is one of the known locations where the earliest maize was sighted. After going through the process of radio carbonation, the two maize types (Zea diploperennis and Zea mays parviglumis) found at the Gulia rock dated back to 4300 BCE.

The maize found on the Chiapas coast around 3000 BCE could only have been a trade product because of the form in which it was found. So, it was not a surprise to find maize in neighboring Colha about the same 3000 BCE, which would have spread to Northern Belize within the same timeline. It was no longer new to find maize by 2600 BCE in Guatemala, Mirador, Nakbe, and Central Belize, specifically in Actun Halal by 2210 BCE.

Notwithstanding its origin and where it was first domesticated, maize became a staple crop in the Mesoamerican regions and various settlements. It was prepared and consumed in different forms: maizemeal paste, flat cake, tortillas, gruel, or even ground or boiled in limewater.

Domestication of Squash

The dates of remains found at the Gulia Naquitz sites suggest that the region's people carried out multiple squash domestications. A good example is a squash (Cucurbita pepo) which appears to have also been domesticated around 8000 BCE. Like the maze, squash was another widely domesticated plant and spread across the regions through trade. Various squash seeds bigger than the ones from the wild were also discovered at the Gulia Naquitz site, further proving that domestication was taking place. One of the biggest of these squash seeds has been dated to 10,000 BCE, one of the oldest validations of domestication by the Mesoamericans.

Unsuccessful Domestication

It was clear not all the domestication attempts by the Mesoamericans were successful. They had several failed and abandoned attempts, like that of the wild plant *foxtail*. Additionally, the San Andres site is filled with evidence of abandoned domestication like the pollen from domesticated cords dating to 7000 to 6000 BCE.

Cotton seeds and pollen dating to 4000 BCE were also found at the site; researchers believe they came from domesticated wild sunflowers, but the people seem to have encountered some difficulties with the Mexican sunflower. It appears the wild plant which was found in eastern North America belonged to another species. The other reason for the problem could have been due to the mobile nature of the low-density population. The bottled gourd (Lagenaria siceraria) was the other domesticated non-edible plant domesticated around the same 8000 BCE found at the Gulia Naquitz site. However, the bottled gourd was non-consumable farm produce; instead, it was used for water and other liquids.

Leftovers of wild plants like a different version of squash, corn, manioc, chili pepper, and beans were discovered on tools dating to the Archaic period sites around northern Belize, which further clarifies that these plants were already domesticated since that period. About the same time, other essential crops were found in the region and included Cacao, cotton, quinoa (Chenopodium quinoa), common beans, lima beans, and tomatoes. In terms of domesticated animals, this period was found to have dogs,

Muscovy duck, and turkey.

Villagers and Agriculture in Mesoamerica

The village settlements were still uncommon in Mesoamerica until the Early Formative Period, which started around 3800 BCE, after the domestication of maize. The village setting was formed by the parents and their children's family, the extended family. This extended family provided the workforce required to care for the farms. Steadily, small unit settlements became villages, and later – based on nearby flat-topped pyramids – larger local units flourished.

Eventually, societies believed to be more advanced, like the Olmecs, constructed large towns notable for molding colossal stone heads. By 2000 BCE, more refined and developed societies had emerged and dominated smaller formative groups like the Toltec, Maya, and Aztec. Technology was developed to supply water to all-year-round farming across all the smaller towns and empires. Food channels were also created to meet the need of urban centers.

Chapter 3: Tools and Trade

The more Mesoamerican's moved away from roaming hunting as their primary feeding source, the more they embraced agriculture. As we have seen, the conversion of wild plants into edible ones spread across the regions, and more members of the population depended on agriculture. This dependence means more land will be needed for farming, which automatically means tools will be required to farm effectively.

The Northern Belize Chart-Bearing Zone (NBCBZ) seemed to be the hub of manufacturing stone tools in the archaic period. There was massive evidence of stone tool materials, technologies, and uses during this period. There was also much adaptation and diversification in using these tools around archaeological sites like the Colha. One of the most effective tools was the NBCNZ chert or the Colha chert, which was higher quality and different from the cherts made from other regions. By early 3000 BCE, the Colha chert had emerged as a primary material for forming stone tools. This evolution of stone tools did not stop, as it was also observed in the Pre-classic and Classic periods.

Another special-purpose production workshop was discovered within Colha, where constricted adzes (were manufactured in large quantities. This discovery suggests the origin of the commercialization of stone tools, especially as Constricted Adzes of the same style and shape were found in all the Mesoamerican regions. The tools manufactured were mostly bifacially constructed from local chert. For example, Constricted adzes were almost general-purpose tools used chiefly for digging, cutting woods, and clearing the forest for more farmlands.

Quite a number of stone flaked tools were found across the region, but the notable ones were the bifacially Lowe and Sawmill points. These tools were mainly used as fishing tools and weapons for hunting or even as knives. The people applied different methods in the filling of these tools to keep them sharp and effective. Practically all stone tool production methods practiced in subsequent periods were present and prevalent in the Archaic periods. Evidence of stone tools used in processing farm produce like cutting and grinding was found on chipped and ground stones.

More about these tools later; first, let us talk about trade.

Trading

Not much is known about trading in the Archaic period. There is evidence here and there showing that trading and long-distance buying and selling occurred during this period. On the other hand, stone tools were used to confirm the possibility of trading activities and networks in all the Mesoamerican regions. Some archaeologist has pointed to the fact that the coastal people of Chantuto in Southern Mexico bought and sold obsidian. For example, 57 high-value obsidians belonging to the highlands of Guatemala ended up at the Tlacuachero shell dump in Chiapas.

Their presence there could only have been through trading and also to be possibly used for trading. It was also discovered that settlements around the Basin of Mexico traded to buy foreign green obsidian instead of traveling to harvest it from the source. Furthermore, Colha Chert from the region has been discovered outside Mesoamerica, indicating that the Colha chert might have been involved in trade exchanges.

Tools

Now let's take a critical look at some of these tools that played vital roles in the transition from a foraging way of life to a more sedentary arrangement that involved farming. As we have seen earlier, some of these tools were also used as a product of exchange in trade, but were they also used as currency? We shall see.

Obsidian

Environmental examination of the origins of the obsidian was part of the research carried out in the region, which revealed how the precious rocky object was used in long-distance trades. It further provided details on the relevance of the obsidian in the daily life of the region's people, particularly in the performance of rituals, trade, and socio-cultural lives.

According to Wikipedia, "It is obtained by either quarrying source sites or in nodule form from riverbeds or fractured outcrops.

Following the removal of the cortex (when applicable), bifacial, unifacial, and expedient flake stone tools could be produced through lithic reduction. The use of pecking, grinding, and carving techniques may also be employed to produce figurines, jewelry, eccentrics, or other types of objects. Prismatic blade production, a technique employing a pressure flaking-like technique that removed blades from a polyhedral core, was ubiquitous throughout Mesoamerica. "

Production Methods

The glassy internal structure of the obsidian makes it easier to structure into different edges. It tends to break in predictable and straightforward ways through the fracture in the rock. This contributed to its abundant use in the Mesoamerican regions. Obsidian is obtained in nodule form or through quarrying from fractured outcrops or riverbeds. Once the cortex is removed, where necessary, unifacial, bifacial, and proper flake stone tools can be made through lithic reduction. Other purposes of the obsidian include grinding, pecking, and carving techniques to produce eccentrics, jewelry, figurines, and other objects. Widely common among Mesoamerican people was Prismatic blade production, a method of applying pressure flaking that detaches blades from the polyhedral core.

Many regions in Mesoamerica did not have direct access to the obsidian source, which made distribution quite limited. This scarcity led to a different method of managing the tool to rejuvenate it—some of these methods involved re-sharpening the edges for grass cutting and other purposes. As the tool becomes blunt, the function is charged from cutting to other uses like scratching and scraping. Other forms of sharpening the precious rocky stone and extending it involve shaping it to look like other tools such as drills. They were also made to serve as projectile points.

Locations in Mesoamerica with Obsidian

As mentioned earlier, obsidian was not available in large deposits across the regions irrespective of its uses and popularity. Here are locations where archaeologists have confirmed the availability in great quantity.

In the South-central lowlands Gulf of Mexico

- Altontonga and Zaragoza
- Las Derrumbadas
- Pico de Orizaba
- Guadalupe

Central Lowlands of Mexico

- Partodo
- Cranzido

On the Highlands of Mexico

- Santa Elena
- Paredon

In Central Highlands of Mexico

- Malpais
- Otumba
- Tapalcingo
- Tulancingo
- Zacaultipan
- Multiple quarries in Pachuca

In West Mexico

- Zinapecuaro
- Ucareo

San Martin Jilotepeque, Tajumulo, Ixtepeque, Tajumulco and El Chaval are known sources and location where Pre-Colombians Mesoamericans exploited. It is also confirmed that nearly all the obsidian found in Maya and Olmec sites came from these locations.

Value or Worth

The relevance of obsidian in Mesoamerica can be compared to that of modern-day steel now. The rocky glass was massively distributed across the regions via trade activities. However, there is evidence of different values placed on obsidian by different regions within Mesoamerica. A good example is during the Pre-Classic period, obsidian was quite rare and only found mainly in the lowland regions with high status and ritual value.

Also, among the Mayans, evidence revealed the obsidian was primarily found among the privileged. The lower-class Mayans only started having access to more obsidian towards the end of the Classic period. Even then, the upper-class Maya people continued to access the limited supply of prestigious Teotihuacan green obsidian.

The value of the obsidian is slightly different among the Teotihuacan people, where the obsidian was traded as a waste of human effort in movements across long distances. The obsidian was exchanged or traded for high-status prestigious items. Teotihuacan is a rare type of obsidian that played an essential role in its rise to power and served as a trade element that boosted the growing economy.

Valuable items like ear-spools contained elements of obsidian. However, this item was also found among the lower-class people. So, the value placed on the obsidian varied. Obsidian was a vital trade item with different values, but there is no evidence that it played the role of a currency in Mesoamerica.

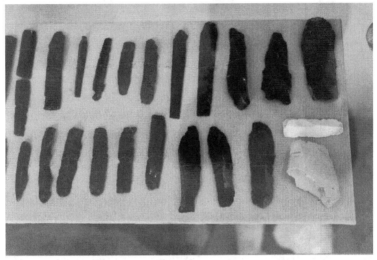

Colha Chert

Population expansion and the need for more arable lands are responsible for stone tool workshops at the Colha site. The high level of Cenozoic limestone present in Colha indicated how the site and the workshops made the most of the sources and location of the site. The people also developed a niche for themselves by using a well-traveled route to boost trade for their type of chert in the Maya trade market, which might have expanded to the Greater Antilles.

Colha was the primary supplier of chert within the region during the Pre-Classic and Classic periods. There were 36 workshops found at the Colha site. They were estimated to have produced well over four million cherts and obsidian tools and eccentrics distributed primarily through trades within the Mesoamerican regions during the Maya reign. This placed the chert on the same higher level of relevance as the obsidian.

Flaked Stones

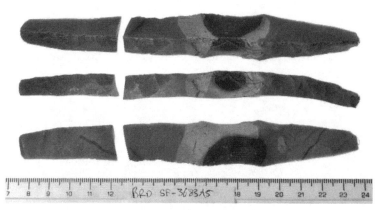

Flaked stone tools were essential in pre-Hispanic Mesoamerica and served many purposes, including ceremonial, militaristic, and domestic uses. The multicolored stone tool was found in what is known as present-day El Salvador, some parts of Honduras, Belize, Guatemala, and Mexico. Flaked stone is another product made from obsidian used for multiple activities. Flake tools are made in bifacial or unifacial forms to have projectile points like knives.

However, this equipment was not as standard as other blade tools aside during the early Mesoamerican prehistory or at a site like Colha where cherts were manufactured, and obsidian was in short supply.

Constricted Adzes

The constricted uniface, bifacial or chipped stone adze is a diagnostic tool discovered in the Preceramic period and northern Belize of Mesoamerica. Special-purpose workshops were also found in the Colha site, where constricted adzes were manufactured. This tool was primarily used for clearing the forest to create more land for farming. Additionally, it was known to be effective for digging and cutting wet and dry woods.

Lowe and Sawmill

Also discovered at the Colha site in Belize (and dated to the Archaic period between 8000 to 900 BCE) are 54 Lowe Points, 21 sawmill points, 4 Allspice, and 2 Ya'axche points. These bifacial stone tools are often diagonal on alternate-opposite edges and indicate various levels of reworking and re-sharpening, which impacts the size and shape of the blade and the size of the tool. The Lowe and sawmill served different purposes to the region's people; they have been used as spear points, harpoons, knives, and dart points.

The Lowe points, in particular, were affixed to thrusting or throwing spears. They have also been used as knives. On the other hand, Sawmill points were used as spear throwers, dart points, and knives.

Spears and Harpoons

In addition to farming, hunting and fishing were other vital means of livelihood for the people of Mesoamerica. The predominant tool used for hunting and fishing is spears and harpoons. Historically, Mesoamerica was the only Archaic civilization in the world that thrived without the successful domestication of animals like cattle, horses, sheep, and pigs. So, gathering, hunting, and fishing provided all the nutrients required by the growing population, which means the farmlands and the aquatic environment were the most productive landscape in Mesoamerica.

Spears and harpoons played vital roles in successful hunting and fishing in Mesoamerica. The harpoon is a long spear-like weapon used in fishing. The head is made up of carved stone, and in some cases obsidian, the edges are rough such that when it pierces the animal, the rough part of the weapon will pull it out of the water. The process involved thrusting the spear into the water quick enough to spear the fish and get it out of water. The harpoon was also used for hunting fast-moving marine mammals and large fishes.

Metallurgy in Mesoamerica

Metallurgy is extracting, purifying, and modifying metals and metal fashioning by people of the Americas before the Europeans arrived at the region in the late 15th century. A recent discovery showed that gold artifacts were found in the Andean region as far back as 2155 - 1936 BCE. In North America, copper dated to about 5000 BCE, which means the indigenous Americans have been familiar with and using metals from the Archaic period.

Also, these metals would have been discovered and used in their natural form without the need for smelting and shaping into desirable forms using hot and cold pounding and without the use of chemicals for modification and blending. There has not been any evidence showing this metal's melting, smelting, and casting in prehistoric Northern America. However, the story was different in the southern part of America. The people of the region did a lot of smelting and casting and deliberately mixed other metals.

For Mesoamerica, and Western Mexico in particular, Metallurgy noticeably developed after the contact with South Americans through marine traders from Ecuador and Colombia. Like in other parts of the Americas where the metals first appeared, they became material for the elite in the Mesoamerican region. The peculiar color, reflection, and quality appealed to the elite and led to several technological advancements within the region. Lookalike metal artifacts were found in Western Mexico and used in the same way the Ecuadorians used theirs. There were archaeological discoveries of items like needles, copper rings, and bells, which were cast using lost wax casting similar to those in Colombia.

Several other tools were discovered within the region during this period, but these are the most prominent ones. The process and method of making these tools include striking these stones directly against each other and hard and soft hammer flaking.

Chapter 4: Important Sites and Artifacts

We now focus our attention on critical Archaic remains discovered as a result of extensive research. Several sites like the Valley of Oaxaca, home of the Zapotecs, the Tehuacan Valley, the location of the Cuscatlán Cave, Colha, Gulia Naquitz, and the Chiapas coast were explored, and many artifacts were discovered, which we will also be discussing – in no particular order.

Valley of Oaxaca

"Valles Centralles" or Central Valleys is the name it is fondly called today, but in the Mesoamerican era, it's mostly called Valley of Oaxaca, and it is a rich site for many people in the region. Today, it's a state in southern Mexico and consists of districts like Ejutla, Tlacolula, Ocotlan, Zimatlan, Zachila, Centro, and Elta. The "Y" shaped valley is located within the Sierra Madre Mountains. The shape looks like a right side up alphabet "Y," with each point of the alphabet having specific names; the northwestern Elta arm, the central-southern Valle Grande, and the Tlacolula to the east.

This valley was also home to one of the most advanced societies in the region, the Zapotecs, and later the Mixtec culture, who dominated several smaller territories for a long time but later got run over by the Spanish. Like the Tehuacan Valley, Oaxaca has been inhabited for more than 10,000 years.

Several archaeological findings were made at the different sites in the Oaxacan valley, including findings at Geo-shin, Gulia Naquiltz, Monte Alban, Mitla, and San Jose Yagul. Oaxaca City, located at the heart of the valley, is currently the state capital.

Archaeologists discovered many historical sites in the Oaxaca Valley, including San Jose, Yagul, Monte Alban, Mitla, Gulia Naquitz, and Geo-shin. Currently, Oaxaca City, the state's capital, is located in the valley's heart.

Zapotec Civilization

The Zapotec people, also known as the "Cloud People," lived in the Southern highlands of central Mesoamerica in the Valley of Oaxaca. They occupied the land from 500 BCE to 900 CE, the latter Pre-Classic period to the end of the Classic. The initial capital was at Monte Alban and later Milta. Although they were notable for their advanced societies, had good dealings with others, and shared similar cultures with advanced civilizations like the Olmecs, Teotihuacan, and Mayan, the Zapotecs also oppressed the southern highlands with their advanced army and weapons. They were known for being good "businessmen" and even adopted their version of the Oto-Zapotecan language.

Origin and Advancement

The Zapotecs, like several societies in the region, emerged from the population that relied heavily on agriculture and expanded in the Oaxacan valley. They developed advanced methods of agriculture and stood toe to toe with similar civilizations in business dealings. For example, they had a grand alliance with the Olmecs on the Gulf Coast that furthered the construction of an impressive capital site at Monte Alban and stretched their oppression for the region during the Classic period. From the city's look, you could tell it was deliberately and strategically constructed to overlook three important valleys that developed between 500 BCE and 900 CE.

Zapotec consists of other vital settlements different from the capital, and more than 15 elite palaces were identified in the city's valleys. There are shreds of evidence that the Zapotecs might have been divided into three separate groups:

- The Valley Zapotecs, based in the Valley of Oaxaca
- The Sierra Zapotecs, in the northern part
- The Southern Zapotecs, based in the south and east around the Isthmus of Tehuantepec

The well-known Zapotec sites can be found spread across the "Y" shaped Valley of Oaxaca. They are Milta, Tlacolula, Abasolo, Ocotlan, Zimatlan, Zachila, San Jose Mogote, Etla, Huitzo, Oaxaca, and Monte Alban. Mitla would later place a significant role in the history of the Zapotecs. The city is notable from 900 CE for its unique buildings strategically arranged around plazas, richly decorated ornamented with reliefs and symmetrical designs.

As we draw a curtain on the Pre-Classic era, there were notable advancements in the unique type of art of the Zapotecs. They further improved in their writings and pushed further in architecture with unique designs and construction of centers for different gods and purposes. In engineering projects, they developed improvised irrigation systems among several cities within their control. For example, at Hierve el Agua, artificial terraced hillsides were constructed to transfer water from the canal of natural springs to several farmlands across the city.

The Zapotecs did not advance in isolation; they had contacts with other people within the region for different purposes. For instance, evidence at sites like Dainzu tells the story better. A large stoned-faced raised stage with reliefs reveals players playing a particular Mesoamerican ball game while wearing protective gear. It gets even more interesting because, in the basin of Mexico, the Teotihuacan's had an admirable relationship with the Zapotecs that they reserved a quarter of their cities for any Zapotecs willing to settle there.

Zapotec Writing

The Zapotec people developed a unique writing system known as one of the first in the Mesoamerican regions. Those that followed, like the Maya, Aztec, and Mixtec civilization, improved on it. They used a logo-syllabic system of writing that uses different symbols to represent each syllable of their language.

The Many Phases of Monte Alban

The story of Zapotec is incomplete without talking about the Monte Alban phases because that was where the formation took place. As mentioned earlier, some of the Monte Albans' noticeable advancements were unification and divine kingship. The unification of Monte Alban and Zapotec led to external domination and political expansion towards the end of Monte Alban 1 (400 BCE to 100 BCE) all through Monte Alban 2 (100 BCE to 200 CE).

Powered by a better and improvised military and weapons, Zapotec rulers from Monte Alban conquered and plundered kingdoms beyond the Valleys of Oaxaca. Their dominance was so compelling and pronounced that by the end of the second monte Alban, the Zapotecs' military and political dominance had spread from Quiotepec in Northern to Ocelotepec and Chiltepec in the South.

Monte Alban cities became famous and admired for their political, religious, and cultural influence in the region and retained this status until 700 CE.

Religions, Deities, and Artifacts

Like what we have in modern-day, the Zapotec religion was rich and confusing, just like several Mesoamerican religions. There were deities for things or events that appeared regular like Sun, Rain, Wind, Earth, and even War. Among the most important ones was the

- Bat-god, the deity of fertility and corn
- Beyda, the deity of wind and seed
- Casino, the deity of rain and lightning
- Patio Cozobi, a deity of corn
- Copijcha, the deity of sun and war
- Coquebila, the god of the center of the earth
- Huechaara, a female mother goddess of hunting and fishing,
- Kedo, god of justice,
- Ndan, androgynous god of the oceans,
- Pixee Pacala, the god of love

- Coqui Xee, the god of infinity.

Also, individual cities and villages were known to have their guardian deities. For example;

- Coquenexo (Lord of Multiplication), guardian of Zoquiapa,
- Coqui Bezelo, and Xonaxi Quecuva (gods of the underworld and death), guardian of Milta and Teocuicuilco
- Cozicha Cozee, guardian of Ocelotepec.

The people offered prayers, offerings, and sacrifices to these deities in the hope of bringing good fortunes and intervening in their affairs. For instance, they prayed for crops to grow well, for rainfall to end a drought, or for the gods to bring fertility to the land and the populace. It was commonplace in the Mesoamerican region for the societies to use symbols to represent different days of the months; the Zapotecs adopted this. For example, Pija was represented by drought, Xoo, earthquake, while A crocodile represented chilla.

There are indications that the Zapotec carried out human sacrifices, especially to the fertility gods, and performed elaborate ritual ball games in the Monte Alban court. Also common were cleansing and dedication rituals for new religious sites and temples when completed. Also found were evidence of rare pieces of pearls, obsidian, and jade found in a stockpile in Oaxaca to support this claim.

The Fall of the Zapotecs

Although they tried to avoid confronting the Spanish invaders, the Zapotecs were eventually overrun and destroyed by the Spaniards after losing a war to the Aztecs from 1497 to 1502. The invaders took advantage of the weak military and peace-seeking of the Zapotecs and defeated them after five years of trying, which ended in 1527.

All attempts at revolting by the population were quelled by the arrival of steel weapons and new diseases. Later again, there were uprisings here and there against the new government and ruler, but they were all checked. However, hundreds of Zapotec dialects and seven languages survived and are spread all over Mexico and Los

Angeles, California.

Tehuacan (tewa'kan) Valley

The Tehuacan Valley is located in the southeastern part of the Valley of Mexico and has been inhabited for more than 10,000 years. In 1960, the site was surveyed and excavated by archaeologist Robert MacNeish, and his team and the discoveries made have been very beneficial and key to understanding the people of Mesoamerica in the Archaic period. However, there have been controversies about some of the artifacts and other items found at the site, leading to multiple new analyses and examinations. In a particular site on the valley was the Coxcatlan Cave, which contained 15 to 33 components from the archaic period. Items found include;

- Small maize cobs,

- Remains from squash beans,

- Chili peppers and bottle gourd.

Modern-day Tehuacan, nicknamed "The Place of Gods," is the second-largest city in the Puebla, Mexico, in the southeast of the Valley of Tehuacan and surrounded by states like Veracruz and Oaxaca.

Maize Domestication

Historically, the Valley of Tehuacan was the first place archaeologists found the oldest farmed maize. From the exploration and findings on the site, archeologists believed the Valley of Tehuacan was the origin of the first maize cultivated by man. The discovery of more than 10,000 cobs of teosinte in the Coxcatlan Cave further buttresses their conclusion. Among the original findings in the cave were maize (only the size of a cigarette!) with not as many corn seeds as what we have today, wild and inedible maize, and teosinte.

Further re-evaluation was carried out on the findings at the site, and it involved testing samples from neighboring sites like Cueva Coxcatlan and Cueva San Marcos. The earliest dates were 4700 BP or 3600 BCE. Newer sites with evidence of early maize have been recently discovered in the Balsas River valley that continued downstream into the Guerrero state. More evidence has emerged that further confirms Balsas River Valley as one of the first sites in the world where teosinte was initially being cross-bred with other edible plants – more than 9,000 years ago – to produce the type of maize we have today. The peculiar teosinte from Balsas, which has now been confirmed as one of the first sources of domesticated maize, was mainly found at the valley's heart and was believed to have grown in other parts of the valley.

Coxcatlan Cave

Richard MacNeish and his team, while on an inspection tour of the Tehuacan Valley, discovered the Coxcatlan Cave in the Tehuacan Valley of Puebla Valley, Mexico. It is now a Mesoamerican archaeological site where more than 75% of stone tools were excavated.

There are several zones in the Coxcatlan Cave. To understand it better, archeologists have divided the zone occupied by humans into four cultural phases; the Ajuereado, El Reego, Abejas, and Coxcatlan phases. These phases were separated based on changes in stone technology, basketry, woven matting, and the pattern of settlements.

The zones inhabited by settlers who did not get involved in pottery, also known as the Preceramic zones, are the first levels of the rock shelter. The principal evidence of humans in the Tehuacan Valley happened during the Ajuereado phase.

The Coxcatlan phase dating between 5000 and 3000 BCE was when the settlers and inhabitants carried out a lot of cross-breeding between wild plants and edible ones. Discoveries also revealed that humans and animals shared time at the cave due to the non-permanent nature of the humans. These people were predominantly hunters, temporary settlers who constructed make-shift villages.

Artifacts

Some relevant artifacts found in the Coxcatlan cave dated to 5000 BCE. For example, the maize cobs, beans, and squash were some of the oldest versions in the region. Ink pen with vessels was another artifact found at the cave and discovered to use material traced to the Preceramic era.

Further analysis of the excavated items at the site revealed more information about 42 types of occupation by the people, 28 dwelling places, and seven cultural phases. Other archaeological zones in the Coxcatlan Cave uncovered signs of the ceramic period type of occupation. At the same time, evidence supports the presence of archaeological remains in the top layers of the cave.

Colha

The Colha archaeological site is another critical location that unveils a lot and plays a crucial role in the Mesoamerican period. It holds a rich history of workshops, stone tools, and the equipment used to transition from hunting to farming by people of the region. Located in the northern part of the country, Colha, Belize, is a Maya archaeological site. It is one of the earlier sites in the Maya region of Mesoamerica. It continues to hold relevant archaeological records of the Maya people and culture deep into the Pre-Classic period.

Excavation from the archaeological site in Colha made it easier to describe the occupation of the people from Early Preceramic 3400 - 1900 BCE to the Middle Postclassic period of 1150 - 1300. Its population expansion peaked in the Late Pre-Classic 400 BCE-CE 100) and in the Late Classic CE 600 - 850. These peaks in population expansion had a lot to do with stone tool workshops at the Colha site.

Colha was reputed as the access to top quality chart due to its strategic location around well-traveled routes in the region. It was also located around a principal source of Cenozoic limestone. The Mayans took advantage of these and created a niche for themselves as the source of the best chert in the region. This market later extended to the Greater Anthills. Colha eventually became the leading supplier of stone tools for the whole Mesoamerica from the Pre-Classic and Classic periods.

Figures obtained from Wikimili suggest that *"an estimated 4 million obsidian, chert tools and other important tools were produced and distributed in the Maya era and they all came from the 36 workshops located at the site."* So, when it comes to the trade and distribution of tools and rare items in Mesoamerica, the story is not complete without the mention of Colha and the Mayans.

The Presence of Obsidian at the Colha Site

In addition to the numerous workshops for constructing and carving stone tools used for hunting and farming, there was evidence of the high presence of top-quality obsidian at the Colha archaeological site.

According to a 2017 Cambridge University Publication,

"This study explores the early use of obsidian at the Maya site of Colha in northern Belize and the implications that variations in source distribution have for the site and its regional connections. Energy dispersive x-ray fluorescence (EDXRF) analysis of 104 specimens of obsidian from Preclassic contexts at the site identified El Chayal obsidian as the most common overall followed closely by that from San Martin Jilotepeque. Ixtepeque obsidian, not common in many Preclassic assemblages, was also strongly represented. The results revealed a Middle Preclassic dependence on San Martin obsidian gradually diminishing through the Preclassic to the Classic period, when San Martin all but disappears from the site. A corresponding increase in El Chayal obsidian use through time at Colha coincides with the rise of Kaminaljuyu in the Guatemalan highlands. Analysis of the obsidian by context indicated that El Chayal obsidian dominated in architectural and ritual deposits while Ixtepeque obsidian was the most common in workshops. San Martin accounted for a slightly greater percentage than El Chayal obsidian in middens, with Ixtepeque materials notably less common. The data indicate that Colha was connected to a broad distribution network from the Middle Preclassic onward, and that obsidian source variability was greater during the Preclassic than the subsequent Classic period."

(Brown, D., Dreiss, M., & Hughes, R. (2004). Preclassic Obsidian Procurement and Utilization at the Maya Site of Colha, Belize. Latin American Antiquity, 15(2), 222-240. doi:10.2307/4141555)

Gulia Naquitz

The Gulia Naquitz Cave in Oaxaca, Mexico, is an archaeological site notable for the early domestication of several crops like squash from Cucurbita, bottled gourds (Lagenaria siceraria) teosinte, the wild ancestors of maize. As far as the continent was concerned, Gulia Naquitz was the site of the earliest known domestication of squash. Although there was evidence backing the presence of maize in its early wild form, a closer reexamination of the pollen and the location of the find proved that the maize could not have been domesticated there. It is likely a product of trade or some form of exchange.

Way of Life

Although evidence revealed the earliest human presence dates to about 10,750 BCE, settlements did not continue all year round. For example, humans stopped inhabiting the rock shelter about 500 BCE. Evidence revealed how the rock shelters inhabitants were not permanent settlers; instead, they were preceramic hunter-gatherers who inhabited the rock shelter on six different occasions, mainly around August to December.

Domestication

The earliest indication of squash domestication dates back to 8,000 – 10,750, which was 4000 years before the domestication of other crops like beans and maize in the region. Evidence to support this was found during the 1960 excavation of the cave and four other Mexican caves.

Further exploration was carried out at the Gulia Naquitz site in 1970 by a team from the University of Michigan, which provided more accurate dates to support evidence of domesticated C. Pepo (field pumpkin) in the form of increased skin thickness and larger trunks in the newer level layers of the cave. By approximately 8000 BP (Before Present Years—the term is mainly used in the field of geology and archaeology with 1950 as the starting year), the field pumpkin trunks found were more than 0.39 in (10 mm) thick. Wild Cucurbita stems were below the 0.33 In (10 mm) limit. These changes in fruits' size and shape are signs of intentional cross-breeding of C. pepo, which occurred not later than 8000 years BP. About the same time, the average skin thickness increased from 0.033 in (0.84 mm) to 0.045 in (1.15 mm).

The agricultural technique of domesticating wild forest crops occurred more than 5000 to 6,400 years in Mesoamerica, starting with squash, then followed closely with the maize and then the beans, making them a part of the three sisters agricultural system of companion planting. Other edible plants recovered at the Gulia Naquitz site include pinyon, acorns, hackberries, cactus fruits, chili pepper, Amaranth, Chenopodium, agave, and mesquite pods.

Chiapas Coast

Chiapas de Corzo, is home to the Pre-Columbian Mesoamerican archaeological site in Chiapas. The site has been occupied since the Early Formative period of ca. 1200 BCE. It became famous as the regional center around 700 to 500 BCE during the Middle Formative period. By this time, its public territory had reached 18 to 20 hectares in size and settlements close to 70 hectares. Chiapas controlled the routes due to its proximity to the Grijalva River, located in the Central Depression of Chiapas. The hills and courts at the site date back to 700 BCE, with palaces and temples built towards the end of the Formative or Pre-Classic period between 100 BCE and 200 CE.

Artifacts and Important Findings

Archaeologists' fundamental discoveries include the 2008 finds of a considerable Middle Formative period Olmec ax deposit at the lower part of Chiapas de Corzo's Hill eleven pyramid. This Olmec ax deposit date back to 700 BCE and is the second of this type of findings in Chiapas after the neighboring San Isidro.

The oldest pyramidal tomb in Mesoamerica was discovered in 2010 when archaeologists found a 2,700 years-old tomb of a dignitary inside Hill 11. According to Bruce Backhand, the tomb looked more like an Olmec dignitary than a Mayan.

Also found at the Chiapas site is the oldest long count calendar discovered in Mesoamerica, December 36 BCE, found on Stela 2. All that is left of the ruins is the day-name and digits "7.16.3.2.13.).

Chiapas is also known for its broken pieces of ceramic materials containing Epi-Olmec script dating to as early as 300 BCE. These pieces are the oldest examples of writing yet to be found.

This unique archaeological site contains possibly the first examples of a palace complex built on hills in Mesoamerica. The royal tower, which was ceremoniously taken down some centuries later, was elegantly constructed in the first century CE.

Mesoamerica was rich in clay products, but none comes close to what was found in Chiapas, especially in the formative periods where clay artifacts like cylinder seals and flat clay stamps were found. Also, in terms of burial arrangements and cemetery organization, Chiapas showcased the most comprehensive and probably the best ordered and subdivided in the whole region as far as the formative period was concerned. More than 250 burial places have been dug up at the famous Chiapas de Corzo site, dating to the formative period. Quite a number of these cemeteries were located below hill 1 plaza.

In the whole Mesoamerican region, there's no site where more ceramic artifacts in the form of flat stamps and cylinder seals were found like those found in Chiapas. For example, Tlatilco Hieroglyphs were discovered at the site suspected to have been carved around 100 BCE.

Gheo-Shih

This area is nearly two hectares of open land located on the Milta River delta below the Gulia Naquitz site. This site was mainly occupied during the Middle Archaic period of 5000 to 4000 BCE and was famous for some unique artifacts found there like:

- Ground-stone tools
- Butchering tools
- Projectile points
- Drilled stone pendants

Other exciting discoveries at this site were rocky structures that were possibly used as shelters, an arrangement of stones that formed what looked like a court, a dance arena, and a road.

Santa Marta Cave

This archaeological site is located in highland Chiapas, Mexico, and was temporarily inhabited by hunter-gatherers till 3500 BCE and later dumped until 1300 BCE when farmers occupied it again. Items found on the site are teosinte cocoa pollen and ground-stone tools.

Zohalpico

This site is at the edge of Chalco Lake in the Valley of Mexico. The people were year-round inhabitants who depended on farming and agriculture for sustainability. There was evidence that they might have domesticated Amaranth and corn during this time.

The site was later covered and taken over by ashes from a volcanic eruption which made it inhabitable for a long time. However, it was once again occupied within the next century. After the eruption, there was multiplication in maize pollen, pumpkin, and gourds.

Actun Halal

It was strategically sited in Macal River Valley in Western Belize. The rock shelter was occupied around 2,400 to 1210 BCE, and some of the artifacts found there include signs of production of cotton, Constricted adzes, and Maize.

Xihuatoxtla Rock Shelter

This site is located at the creek of the central Balsas River and dates between 6990 and 6610. Hand and milling stones and 251 chipped stones were among the items discovered at the site.

Tlacuachero Shell Mound

This archaeological site was one of those that settlers in the regions used seasonally. The primary activities at this site are processing marine resources like clams, fish, and sea turtles. The discovery of 57 obsidian flakes suggests they were products of trades or exchanges with other societies within the region. Also excavated at the site were two tombs.

Cerro de las Conchas

We have talked about several shell mounds; the list is incomplete without the one found at Cerro de las Conchas dating between 5500 and 3500 BCE and measuring close to 4 meters high and 100 meters wide. This was another seasonal site used primarily for marine transactions. The site is located at the edge of El Hueyate Mangrove harbor.

Chapter 5: The Origin of the Olmecs

The Olmec – General Overview

The Olmec are fascinating people with a great culture. The whole Mesoamerican region had a unique civilization and advancement that raised questions about who they were, if they were initially from Mesoamerica or if they were travelers. We are going to unpack all of that and more in this chapter.

Archeologists and explorers believed the Olmec culture and civilization existed long before the Mayan or Monte Albans, and they go way back to 1800 BCE. There is even evidence to support their existence long before that time in places like modern-day Guatemala. The Olmecs have been appropriately identified as the first temple builders in all of Mesoamerican and what is known as Mexico and environs today, and it's definitely not the Mayans.

Several advancements that were previously credited to the Mayans have since been traced to the Olmecs. For example, the famous long-count Mayan Calendar (and others found in the Maya era) originated and was developed by the Olmecs. Some of the reasons why the origin of the Olmecs is shrouded in a lot of controversies include the clues of some epic Olmec scripts that suggest the emergence or combination of multiple cultures that form the civilization.

Some theories support the fact that the script was from Africa; others have argued that they may be Chinese, and another group concluded they might be Polynesians. All the arguments are familiar: the Olmecs did not look like native Mexicans or even Native Americans. A little more on these controversies later.

All the attributes ascribed to the Olmecs, like the level of their civilization, the uniqueness of their cultures, and how different they were from the other people in the region, are known as "archaeological civilizations." That means, based on a collection of artifacts that archaeologists thought to belong to a particular society. In essence, archaeological cultures are based on the generic appellation of the objects discovered in that areas and not on text.

In this instance, scholars concluded that all the artifacts excavated in the area covering the northern Isthmus of Tehuantepec dating from 1200 – 500 CE could only have belonged to one culture and civilization known as the Olmecs. For example, the name *Olmec* (which means "rubber people" or "rubber producers") was not particularly the name of the people, but a scholar put it together. He derived the name from a combination of Aztec (Nahuatl) words "Olmecatl." The words "people who dwell in the rubber nation." So, people just simplified it to rubber people. This is mainly because Olmec references the place where most of the artifacts were found and the production of rubber that went on there.

The Olmec site is a major center of activities, with several cities emerging and known for different historical purposes. Still, none is as crucial to the story of the Olmec civilization as La Venta and San Lorenzo. Modern-day Veracruz is about 35 miles on the southern part of the Gulf of Mexico and stood tall and popular around 1150 – 900 CE. Similarly, La Venta, which is Modern-day Tabasco, was located about 9 miles on the eastern part of San Lorenzo around the Mexican Gulf Coast. On its part, La Venta reached its peak around 900 to 500 CE.

Discoveries at the locations where the Olmecs dwelled revealed further information about the people and the type of diet they relied on. For example, food items like maize and other crops were not originally from the people. Instead, they were added because they predominantly relied on fishing and hunting for their diet and livelihood.

The Olmec people were credited for being skilled at creating massive structures like the many colossal stones heads found at the sites. Some of the other creations on that list include massive stone thrones used by rulers to depict power and divinity and different type of slaps that serve multiple purposes. They undoubtedly created the popular ball game, which was quite common in all the civilizations within the region. Part of the evidence that supports this is that the object of the game, the ball, is made of rubber, and the Olmecs were the people close to the source of rubber, and they were pretty good with creating items from the raw material.

The Olmecs were good with their production of rubber items and creating structures out of the soil. They built sand structures like pyramids, ceramics, and mounds of different sizes and shapes until they were predominantly known for their unique significant size creation. Their unique structures also influenced several civilizations in the region.

The Olmec civilization was one of the most robust and advanced cultures that influenced the early Americas. Although in the last century we started to see their strong influence dissipate, especially with the arrival of the Common Era, the Olmec civilization is still referred to as the mother culture of other societies that showed up in the regions many years down the line.

There were well-known cultures like the Teotihuacan, Totonac, Maya, and Zapotec civilizations famous for their unique arts, outstanding architectures, and advanced cultures that put them ahead of the other cultures in the Mesoamerican region. However, all these civilizations still have their origin traced back to what they shared with the Olmecs at some point in time through contacts.

The Origin of the Olmecs

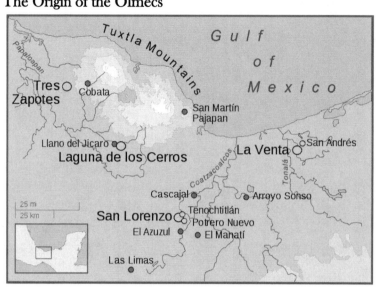

As mentioned earlier, the people of the rubber nation, also known as the Olmecs, were the most influential and stood out during the Mesoamerican era. All other known civilizations can trace their advancement to the Olmecs. As a result of the rapid developments the people experienced in Soconnusco, they settled in today's Veracruz and Tabasco, or what is known as the hot and humid valleys of Mexico.

The origin of the Olmecs is shrouded in deep controversy, and we will look at some of these controversies later and what led to the conclusion by these scholars involved. One account believed that the Olmecs possibly came from neighboring Mixe Zoque or Mokaya civilization.

The formative period primarily belonged to the Olmecs because they thrived and expanded extensively in the Mesoamerican region around 1500 to 400 BCE. The Olmec era is divided into two; the Pre-Olmec cultures mainly existed from 2500 BCE, but by 1600 to 1500 BCE, the Early-Olmec culture had commenced and was located in San Lorenzo Tenochtitlan on the southeastern coast of Veracruz.

From their various practices and ways of life, it was accessible to how they laid a solid foundation for other emerging civilizations in the region to copy, adapt and make improvements. It was also clear that the Olmecs practice blood-shedding rituals; whether it was a human sacrifice or animal sacrifices, the controversy is still on.

Some scholars have put the commencement of the Olmec civilization at 1400 and 1200 BCE; however, some later excavations and discoveries have since adjusted the origin to 1600 - 1500 BCE. These discoveries were at the shrine in El Manati, San Lorenzo. Eventually, the Olmecs adopted the diets available in the region, like farming maize and other food crops. There were signs of farming being a major source of livelihood from some of the remains discovered at Tabasco and further suggested that they likely started around 5100 and 4600 BCE. These diets and food items were also adopted by later Olmec civilizations just as they did the technologies.

The development of the Olmec people and their culture was made easy by the ecosystem, consisting of well-watered alluvial soil. In addition to that, the Coatzacoalcos river basin provided the people with a great transport network. There has been a strong comparison of the Olmec environment and climate with other advanced civilizations like the Nile, Indus, and Mesopotamia.

The productive nature of the environment ushered in a good and bad experience for the people because the dense population started giving rise to classes. Eventually, the elite class emerged and pushed for the production of unique items to differentiate the Olmec culture. This would lead to producing some of the known luxury artifacts, symbols, and sophisticated items.

Several of these luxury items made from magnetite, jade, and obsidian were out of the reach of the lower class of the population. They were items for the rich, and the fact that they came from outside the Olmec society does buttress the point that the people had extensive trading activities within the region. There are three likely sources named as the origin for the high valued obsidian found among the Olmec elites. For example, the most luxurious jade found among the Olmec elites has been traced and found to have originated from the eastern part of Guatemala, known as the

Montague River valley. It could have come from El Chayal, which is closer to the Olmec society in the highlands of Guatemala. Other likely sources are Puebla and San Martin Jilotepeque. These locations were only some kilometers away from the Olmecs.

A few sites shed more light on the Olmec culture due to some Olmec artifacts found there. One such site is the Mezcala culture which is in modern-day Guerrero. There was more Olmecs type of artifacts found there than those found in the Veracruz – Tabasco sites. A city known as Teopantecuanitlan in Guerrero is one of such cities relevant to the Olmec culture. One other relevant object from the Amuco-Abelimo site, an apparent Olmec creation that dates back to 1530 BCE, was found in Guerrero.

The Colossal Heads and The First Excavation

The colossal heads have turned out to be synonymous with the Olmec civilization. They molded human heads from massive stones or large pieces of movable rocks. They are of different heights from 3.8 to 11.2 ft. some of these heads have been found to date back to 900 BCE. The question has been asked what these heads genuinely represent or if they were worshiped as gods or if they were a representation of some royalties. It would seem more like the latter dues to the different features on the faces.

Most of the heads were that of matured adults with the following features:

- Fleshy cheeks
- Slightly-crossed eyes
- Flat noses
- headdresses
- Frowning or smiling faces
- The back of the stones is often flat with no unique designs since they are not meant to be seen as much as the front.

To further bolster this point, these features are still found among the locals of modern-day Veracruz and Tabasco. From the remains found at the sites, it appears the carvings took place at the Sierra de Los Tuxtlas mountains in Veracruz and then moved to other locations within the civilization.

The massive size of the stone heads and the carving location revealed that the final products might have been transported either through a chain of humans or some means of transportation. The distance covered in moving these stones is sometimes up to 250 km. All these efforts put into the sculpting and movements of the stones further suggest their relevance to the people. The heads either represent some powerful leaders or some influential elites in the societies.

The efforts that go into each head almost made them uniquely different and evidenced that they were carved after particular individuals and not just a general production. Some of the heads were even carved wearing headgears, suggesting a representation of royalty or warriors. In the whole region, the Olmec colossal heads stand out and are unique to that civilization.

Jose Maria Melgar Serrano discovered the first colossal stone head officially in 1862. However, due to poor data collection and management, the discovery was not recognized or reported outside the shores of Mexico. Fast forward to 1938; the same site was excavated by Matthew Stirling, which led to the Olmec civilization's archaeological study.

Within the Olmec region on the Gulf Coast of Mexico, there were 17 stones heads found from four sites. Generally, most heads were carved from slightly rounded rocks or stones; however, two unique designs were found in San Lorenzo Tenochtitlan carved from giant stone thrones. Another structure was found in a nearby site in Guatemala, specifically at Takalik Abaj. It was a stone throne that looked like it was carved out of a colossal head. Also, it was the only structure that was found outside the Olmec society.

Arriving at an actual date for each of the monuments remains a major challenge for researchers and archaeologists because many of them were tampered with before the commencement of archaeological investigations. However, several of these Colossal Heads have been dated back to the Early Pre-Classic period of 1500 - 100- BCE, while a few others to the Middle Pre-Classics of 1000 - 400 BCE. The least colossal head weighs around 6 tons, while the bigger ones vary between 40 and 50 tons. It is important to note that the enormous, colossal head found seemed to be uncompleted and abandoned close to where the stone originated.

The reasons remain unclear.

Fringe Theories of Alternative Origins

As mentioned earlier, the origin of the Olmecs seems to still generate quite a controversy among scholars, researchers, and archaeologists. Some suggestions contradict the generally known and accepted origins of the Olmec civilization and attribute it to have originated from other cultures, with Africa at the top of that list. Those who push these theories claim that contact with another world outside the Mesoamerican region might have led to the origin of the Olmecs.

While these ideas of other origins have been famous, they are still not accepted as the official position of mainstream researchers who are well versed in the region's history. Although these theories are considered fringe, the history of the Olmec civilization will not be incomplete without talking about them.

African Origins

Several scholars have been pushing the idea that the Olmecs originated from or were related to people from some part of Africa. These experts have based their theories on their personal opinion about the interpretations of some of the features of the Olmec artifacts. They further believed that the manner of speaking, way of life, genetics, general mannerism, and the structure of the bones found at the sites looked like those from some part of Africa.

The first person to push the idea of the African connection of the Olmec is the scholar who discovered the first colossal head in 1862 at Tres Zapotes (formerly Hueyapan), Jose Melgar. In the published paper, he likened the colossal head to that of a "Negro race." The opening in the publication was later proved in the early part of the 20th century by Leo Wiener and a couple of other scholars. Some modern-era supporters of this idea, like Clyde Admad Winters and Ivan Van Sertima, have further narrowed down the origin of the Olmec to the Mende people in the western part of Africa.

Suggestions of Epigraphic Proofs

These researchers and scholars mentioned earlier, along with other modern-day proponents of the idea that the Olmecs' origin came from Africa, claimed that the writing systems found in

Mesoamerica, which we have traced to the Olmec civilization, look very much like the African scripts. Here's how some pushed their claims;

- Early in the 19th century, French Polymath Constantine Samuel Rafinesque opined that the popular Maya writing style and inscriptions could only have come from the Libyco-Berber style, which has its roots in West Africa.

- A linguist and an American historian, Leo Wiener (and a few others) thought that Epi-Olmec and Olmec symbols and Vai script share close similarities. The Vai script is from Liberia in West Africa. Other close similarities include:
  - ➢ Inscriptions on the Tuxtla Statuette,
  - ➢ Cascajal Block
  - ➢ Teo Mask
  - ➢ The Celts in offering at La Venta

Mesoamerican scholars and researchers have continuously debunked these claims of African origin or relation with the Olmecs. Great work is ongoing to translate the Maya scripts found at the sites, but the same cannot be said of the Olmec glyphs.

Chinese Origins

Similar to theories like African origin, some writers believe that Chinese refugees immensely impacted the Olmec civilization. They linked this influence to the ending part of the Chang dynasty. Here are some of those views and how they arrived at their conclusions:

- Betty Meggers projected that the Chinese Shang empire played an essential role in the emergence of the Olmec civilization around 1200 BCE. She was of the Smithsonian Institution and an archeologist who was famous for her work in South America.

- In collaboration with Chen Hanping, Mike Xu suggested in his book, published in 1996, that the La Venta celts thought to bear African marks originated from the Chinese.

Again, like the African claims, the Mesoamerican researchers have knocked down Betty and Mike's claims. According to them, Mike Xu's evidence could only have been coincidental markings and more look-alike than actual Chinese markings. They further pointed out that the Olmecs ceramics bore similar marking with the Chinese oracle bone inscriptions, but they are not related. In a 1997 article, Claire Liu extensively discussed the existence of jade in both culture and shared knowledge of the North.

Jaredite Origins

"*In the* Book of Mormon *(1830), a text regarded as* scripture *by churches and members of the* Latter Day Saint *movement, the* Jaredites *are described in the* Book of Ether *as a people who left the Old World in ancient times and founded a civilization in the Americas. Mainstream American history and literature specialists place the academic setting for the Book of Mormon among the 'mound-builders" of North America. The work is therefore classified in the American "mound-builder" genre of the 19th century.*

However, Mormon *scholars and authors seek to demonstrate that events described in the Book of Mormon have a literal foundation. A famous* Book of Mormon geography model *places the scene of the Jaredite arrival and subsequent development in lands around the* Isthmus of Tehuantepec *in Mesoamerica. However, the tradition leading to this Mesoamerican model does not originate with the Book of Mormon, but with an enthusiastic interest in* John Lloyd Stephens*'s 1841 bestseller, Incidents of travel in Central America Chiapas, and Yucatan. Mormon founder* Joseph Smith *placed the arrival of the Jaredites in "the lake country of America" (region of* Lake Ontario*), allowing for the eventual migration of Book of Mormon peoples to Mexico and Central America."*

Therefore, some Mormon scholars identify the Olmec civilization with the Jaredites, citing similarities and noting that the period the Olmecs flourished and later declined corresponds roughly with the Jaredite civilization timeline." —extracted from Wikipedia.

Nordic Origins

On his part, Michael Coe wrote,

"The presence of Uncle Sam inspired Thor Heyerdahl, the Norwegian explorer and author of Kon Tiki, among others to claim a Nordic ancestry for at least some of the Olmec leadership... [However], it is extremely misleading to use the testimony of artistic representations to prove ethnic theories. The Olmec were American Indians, not Negroes (as Melgar had thought) or Nordic supermen."

Michael Coe was an explorer and a cultural diffusionist.

The major takeaway from all the theories and counter-theory is that the Olmecs were a unique set of people who were possibly from more than one place. They were probably travelers who eventually settled in Mesoamerica because they showcased a peculiar civilization that originated from their society and later rubbed off on the whole Mesoamerican region.

While scholars have argued back and forth about the origin of the Olmecs, there has not been any form of an argument about the influence of the Olmecs on the region. Every known civilization in writing, technology, structures, monument, sports, and others in the region have been successfully traced back to the Olmecs.

Chapter 6: San Lorenzo Tenochtitlan

General Overview

San Lorenzo is not merely another archaeological site in Mesoamerica. It has been confirmed as the oldest Olmec city established. Based on excavations at the city, there is evidence that the city had taken the form of an Olmec site as far back as 1150 BCE and was possibly invaded and destroyed around 900 BCE.

At a time when most Mesoamerican cities were outdated and without a form, San Lorenzo was already known for great advancement and achieving incredible feats, especially in the Early Formative period. Experts have attributed these exceptional developments and achievements to the peculiar location of the city and the ecosystem.

Not only did the city enjoy almost all year-round rainfall, but it also enjoyed rich seaside soil positioned along the broad. That is not all; it had rich artificial mounds that held water around the southern Gulf coast, which was great for their agriculture. This condition was perfect for maize farming, and it gave the Olmecs a significant edge over the rest of the regions. It was eventually known as the fertile crescent of the area.

However, as the population expanded, it became evident that the levee lands were not enough, leading to competition among the people for who would control what portion. The competition eventually led to rivalry and conflicts. Soon classes emerged and possibly led to the emergence and dominance of a powerful farming class who were possibly well-armed than the other members of the society. This incident would later lead to creating the elite class in San Lorenzo within the Olmec civilization.

In describing the physical appearance of the city,

"In appearance, the San Lorenzo site is a compact plateau rising about 160 feet (about 49 meters) above the surrounding plains. Cutting into it are deep ravines that were once thought to be natural but are now known to be artificial, formed by the construction of long ridges that jut out from the plateau on the northwest, west, and south sides. Excavations have proved that at least the top 25 to 35 feet (about 8 to 11 meters) of the site was built by human labor. There are about 200 small mounds on the site's surface, each of which once supported a dwelling house of pole and thatch, which indicates that it was both a ceremonial center with political and religious functions and a minuscule town."
Description extracted from Britannica.com

The Olmecs are fondly known for their advanced civilization and the numerous stone heads that littered their society and environs, but no other place compared to San Lorenzo in the carving, molding, and construction of stone heads. The site had unique stone monuments that were believed to have been images of powerful characters within the society. However, it was observed that several of these stone monuments were intentionally damaged at around 900 BCE. Many were buried in ridges and other locations. There were attempts to cart away some of these monuments, but the size and weight might have made it impossible to move, but smaller ones would have been taken away possibly by invaders.

Some of these monuments mainly were made from basalt and weighed as much as 44 tons. The basalt source was at the Tuxtla Mountains in Cerro Cintepec, where there was a volcanic flow. One mystery that still surrounds these stones is how they were moved to several locations with this community. Some theory talks about how the stones must have been pulled or rolled to the nearest stream and then mounted on rafts up the Coatzacoalcos River.

Another theory opined about how moving these stones to their desired location would have taken many days. One thing is evident in all of these theories, the number of humans that would have been needed to move these stone monuments would have been enormous, and the people responsible for moving the stones must have belonged to a lower class.

The stone heads are attention-grabbing due to the almost flawless look they have natural human faces. You can easily interpret the emotions expressed by each stone head from pain to power, control, and smiles. Most of these stone heads came from San Lorenzo. More about the stone heads later...

In addition to their advanced civilization and stone heads, the Olmecs were also known for their temples and deities, often combined with animals and humans. For instance, there's a popular deity of a partly jaguar and a human infant. Some of these deities were sculpted, entangled, or crying. Also, scholars have concluded that the "jaguar" is a central part of the Olmec art because it is often fused humans to form a deity. It also shed more light on the most recent nature of the Olmec society.

Olmec monuments and artifacts were primarily spherical, with a showcase of great technicality and skills. The striking resemblances would make you assume modern tools were used for these carvings, but in fact, stone tools were the main instruments used to achieve these remarkable feats. The methods used were pounding and pecking. Also noticeable is a unique design seen in the pottery and ceramic figurines that mainly were nude and without sex and had traits of the jaguar.

The presence of some exotic raw material in San Lorenzo showed the distinction in classes, and the taste for luxury items and further suggested the Olmecs were involved in massive trade networks within the region. Top on the list of the commodities traded was Obsidian which served as flakes, blades, and darts. These were mainly imported from Guatemala and the highlands of Mexico. Other luxury items traded for and found in San Lorenzo include:

- Iron ores, used as mirrors and other purposes

- Serpentine, used by goldsmiths

However, the jade was conspicuously absent in the region during this period and would not show up until after 900 BCE during the city's fall.

Further evidence of trading with the region's people was seen in the early Formative period when the Olmec sent out a small group from the Gulf coast into the highland of Mesoamerica in what seems like a negotiation for the safe passage of goods bound for San Lorenzo. Also, there have been discoveries of San Lorenzo type of ceramics in the form of figurines at various burial sites in the Valley of Mexico like the Tlapacoya and Morelos. The Olmecs continued to be actively involved in the region even into the Middle Formative period – and possibly at its peak.

San Lorenzo-type Olmec ceramics and figurines have been found in burials at several sites in the Valley of Mexico, such as Tlapacoya, and in the state of Morelos. There is evidence that the Olmec sent groups from their Gulf coast "heartland" into the Mesoamerican highlands toward the end of the Early Formative, in all likelihood to guarantee that goods bound for San Lorenzo would reach their destination. The Olmec involvement with the rest of Mesoamerica continued into the Middle Formative and probably reached its peak at that time.

Suffice to say; other known Olmec cities came to light in the Early Formative period:

- Laguna de Los Cerro in Veracruz, specifically the southern part of Cerro Cintepec, seems to have been another Olmec site because of their large number of unique sculptures found at the site.

- On the eastern part of the Tabasco border, La Venta was another known site that seemed to have only emerged after the peak and fall of San Lorenzo.

Now, let's get into details and specifics.

Why is San Lorenzo Relevant to the Olmec Civilization?

San Lorenzo is the name adopted by archaeologists to describe the location of three archeological sites, namely:

- The San Lorenzo site

- The Tenochtitlan site

- The Potrero Nuevo site

All three sites are located in Veracruz, Mexico. These sites alongside Tres Zapotes and La Venta were quite prominent and played pivotal roles in the cultural development and civilization of the Olmecs. By 900 BCE, San Lorenzo had established itself as the center of the Olmecs. These days San Lorenzo is known chiefly for the Olmec stone heads found there –especially one that weighs 28 metric tons and is about 9.8 ft high.

The San Lorenzo Tenochtitlan site can easily be mixed up with the Aztec site in Mexico, but they are not the same. The similarity is only in names, which was also due to some administrative translation of the Aztec words.

The Description of San Lorenzo

Artifacts dating to 1600 BCE found at El Manati were some of the earlier signs of the Olmec cultures. It tells how the previous settlers had taken to agriculture and lived in the site for hundreds of years before development came and eventually emerged into a regional center for the Olmec civilization.

The emergence of a complex state was first noticed among the Olmecs before other parts of the region eventually copied it. San Lorenzo was the first city to demonstrate such complexity. The site is responsible for dominating the gulf coast lowlands and imposing the Olmec way of life on other territories. One of the colossal heads found at San Lorenzo stands at about 9.3 feet tall and 6.9 feet wide!

Mesoamerican researchers and scholars are unified in the division of the Olmec history to be broken down into four stages:

- The Formative - 1700 to 1300 BCE
- The Integration - 1300 to 00 BCE
- Expansion - 900 to 300 BCE, and
- Disintegration - 300 to 200 BCE

Another phrase commonly used by archeologists to describe the Olmecs time is the "Formative Period." This was the critical time when the state-like complexities started rising and gaining fruition.

Before its fall and the eventual emergence of the La Venta, by 1200 BCE, San Lorenzo was already the largest city in Mesoamerica, and it had that status up until 900 BCE. However, by 800 BCE, the human population at San Lorenzo had reduced to almost zero. Furthermore, there were attempts to annex the site's plateau around 600 to 400 BCE and from circa 800 to 1000 CE.

Unlike what was obtainable at La Venta, which was located and surrounded by a swampy environment, San Lorenzo was strategically situated in an ecosystem that was friendly for farming. The site enjoyed all-year rainfall, and the land was excellent for agriculture. Furthermore, it appears as though the place was more of a ceremonial city; even today, people from the Olmec society gather for rituals and events.

The city had no walls, and the people were, for the most part, medium to large scale farmers. It has been estimated that the San Lorenzo structures and ceremonial centers could accommodate 5,500 people and that the whole area along with the hinterlands could reach 13,000 people. These numbers are by far lower than the population that existed in the city back in its heyday.

There was evidence to support the conquering and dominance of neighboring territories. For example, San Lorenzo controlled a large portion of the Coatzacoalcos and its lands – even to the east, where La Venta eventually emerged and became popular. Other areas like the Tuxtla Mountains had societies that were not under the control of san Lorenzo.

"Built on some 700 hectares (1,700 acres) of high ground between then-active tributaries, the core of San Lorenzo covers 55 hectares (140 acres) that were further modified through extensive filling and leveling; by one estimate 500,000 to 2,000,000 cubic meters (18,000,000 to 71,000,000 cu ft) of earthen fill were needed, moved by the basket load. The rulers of San Lorenzo played a crucial role in integrating a population that changed the natural environment into sacred and secular landscapes for the glorification of the San Lorenzo polity."

"Archaeologists Michael Coe and Richard Diehl calculated that the 77 square kilometers (30 sq mi) area of San Lorenzo that they studied could produce approximately 500 metric tons (490 long tons; 550 short tons) of maize annually, enough to feed 5,556 people, more than the estimated population at the time. Residents of San Lorenzo also consumed domestic dog, snook, tarpon, mojarra, catfish, and turtles. Although some claim that manioc was

cultivated here, no evidence for this has been found." Excerpts from Wikipedia on San Lorenzo Tenochtitlan.

San Lorenzo was also known for its extensive and elaborate drainage system, which had been discovered to serve other purposes beyond providing water for the people. Scholars have linked the water supply system as worship to a supernatural water deity.

The drainages were uniquely designed and constructed using buried stones to form pipes that channeled water around. However, while fresh spring water was present at the elevated lands, the lowlands cannot be said. Again, this may be due to the existence of classes in the city among the people. For example, "U" shaped stones were arranged to control water to the edges of the high grounds, which is a clear sign of the ruling class displaying their control of the resources meant for the whole populace.

Initial Excavation and Archaeological History

Many research and archeological works have been carried out at the San Lorenzo site; it's also essential to add that there has been quite a bit of controversy. However, Matthew Stirling is recognized as the first person to start excavation in 1938 after several visits. Four other archaeological works were carried out on the site between 1940 and 1979, one of which was led by Michael Coe and Richard Diehl of Yale University between 1966 and 1968 (before taking a break and resuming in 1990.) Coe's work focused more on emphasizing the formation of patterns within the community and at regional levels among the Olmecs.

The name "San Lorenzo Tenochtitlan" was the brainchild of Matthew Stirling, who named the area based on the three nearby villages and settlements. All three locations were found around the west of Coatzacoalcos. The original name for the area remains unknown. On the other hand, Tenochtitlan's archeological site still bears the same name and falls within a village with the same name on the northern side of the Island, while Potrero Nuevo can be found on the hilly eastern part of the plateau.

Stone Sculptures of San Lorenzo

The San Lorenzo archaeological site is also peculiar for the types, quantity, and variations of sculptures it showcased. The expertise that went into some carvings is close to what we have in the modern era, but the sculptors mainly relied on stone tools to charge those astonishing results. Some carvings were for humans but of higher classes, while others represented the deities the people worshiped. As of the last count, more than 124 stone sculptures have been discovered, and it is believed that there are still a lot more buried and yet to be unearthed.

These stone images vary in size, from the massive Colossal Heads that weigh about 28 tons (because they were made from basalts which are bi-products of volcanic eruption and mostly found at the Cerro Cintepec) to smaller images the size of pots. The level of work on these stones only shows the power of a powerful character and a deity that the people worshipped.

The Eight Major Phases of Occupation

In their 1960 excavation exercise at the San Lorenzo site, Michael Coe and his colleague Richard Diehl listed the eight phases of occupation as follows

- The Orochi Phase, ca 1750 to 1150 BCE

- The Bajio Phase, ca 1550 to 1450 BCE. These two were the pre-Olmec Formative successions.

- The Chicharras Phase, ca 1450 to 1400 BCE. This was the period when more artifacts showed up at the site. It also falls under the Early Formative period.

- The San Lorenzo Phase, ca 1400 to 1000 BCE. The city reached its peak but later suffered a decline as we entered the Middle Formative period.

- The Namaste Phase, ca 1000 to 800 BCE.

- The Palangana Phase, ca 300 to 50 BCE. These phases saw a decline in population as we slid into the Late Formative period.

- The Remplas Phase, ca 300 to 50 BCE. There was no occupation record during this period like we had in the Early and Middle Classic periods.

- The Villa Alta Phase, 800 to 1000 BCE. Again, we saw signs of reoccupation of the site.

Architecture

Remains found at the San Lorenzo site suggest that the city might have been a hub for carving several sculptures found in the Olmec civilization. In addition to the sizeable colossal stone heads, giant thrones, felines, figurines, birds, images of more miniature humans, among others, were also discovered. Some of these images were symbols of the supernatural powers of the rulers and deities, while others represented some monsters. A significant percentage of these images were carved out of basalt brought into San Lorenzo.

One can quickly identify the classes in San Lorenzo based on their taste and the type of structures they lived in, even in the part of the city they chose to reside in. For example, the elites built for themselves large structures lifted on low soil platforms and showed their powers and authorities through some of the monuments found on the site. A particular elite structure named the "Red Palace" was constructed using compressed soil for the floors and walls and then plastered with sand mixed with hematite.

"Massive columns that were 4 meters (13 ft) tall and carved out of basalt supported the structure's roof, and L-shaped basalt benches are thought to have been used as step coverings. Blocks of bentonite clay and limestone have been found in the debris and may have been used in the walls. Several structures had walls that were made of thick mud and 40 centimeters (16 in) thick and lacked post-molds. They were evidently constructed using a rammed earth technique." "Other structures employed bentonite masonry fixed with mud mortar. Floors were made of gravel or packed earth or paved with bentonite blocks." Description was extracted from Wikipedia.

The lower-class people lived literarily on the lower part of the plateau, which goes down 40 meters below the higher lands. Their house was built with inexpensive materials like thatched wattle-and-daub.

The Olmecs displayed their technical skills in construction with the building of the San Lorenzo terraces. You could tell the amount of labor that had gone into creating such masterpieces. For example, one of the terraces hung from a 7-meter-high wall. It remains unclear if this was contracted at the order of their rulers or if it was an act of ingenuity by the lower-class people.

Carl Wendt, an Olmec Household archeologist, carried out further archaeological work in some areas in San Lorenzo to determine how the people lived and the type of structure they built. His study focused more on particular areas and not the entire site. For example, he studied the El Bajio part of Remilino and other central parts of San Lorenzo. Additionally, he paid special attention to the refuse and waste left behind to arrive at his conclusions.

Part of Wendt's findings included the fact that the architectural patterns and organization of the San Lorenzo lowlands were similar to that found in the Maya highlands houses and huts. The structures were replete in spaces and built to have different areas for separate activities like resting, cooking, storage and others. They further explained that although detached, they were structured to be a part of a central patio.

Exchange from San Lorenzo to the Rest of the Region

San Lorenzo was indeed the center of the Olmec civilization while it existed. Many artifacts like figurines and pottery designs were found all over the region. A good example was at the Canton Corralito archeological site in Chiapas, where more than 5,000 figurines, pottery works, and other objects that originated from San Lorenzo were found.

As a matter of fact, there were even more Initial Olmec objects (dating to 1250 - 1150 BCE) and Early Olmec objects (from 1150 - 1000 BCE) found at the same site - even more than found in San Lorenzo when they originated from. During the early Olmec period:

- 15% of the carved pottery is known as Calzadas Carved. They are believed to contain possible supernatural elements.

- 9% of the Incised pottery, known as Limon Incised, is primarily used for decorations in homes and temples.

All originated from San Lorenzo. Interestingly, no items found and examined in San Lorenzo originated from other parts of the region.

Chapter 7: Cultural Achievements and San Lorenzo's Decline

Jose Maria Melgar was the first archeologist to discover the first Olmec stone head back in 1862 and wrote this about his findings,

"In 1862, I was in the region of San Andres Tuxtla, a town in the state of Veracruz, Mexico. During my excursions, I learned that a Colossal Head had been unearthed a few years before, in the following manner. Some one-and-a-half leagues from a sugar-cane hacienda, on the western slopes of the Sierra of San Martín, a laborer of the hacienda, while cutting the forest for his field, discovered on the surface of the ground what looked like the bottom of a great iron kettle turned upside down. He notified the owner of the hacienda, who ordered its excavation. And in the place of the kettle was discovered the abovementioned head. It was left in the excavation as one would not think to move it, being of granite and measuring two yards in height with corresponding proportions... On my arrival at the hacienda, I asked the owner of the property where the head was discovered, to take me to look at it. We went, and I was struck with surprise: as a work of art, it is without exaggeration a magnificent sculpture...what astonished me was the Ethiopic type represented. I reflected that there had undoubtedly been Negroes in this country, and that this had been in the first epoch of the world."

Since that time, more than 17 confirmed colossal stone heads had been found within the Olmec archeological civilization, and ten of those were discovered in San Lorenzo. We will focus more on the stone heads in this part since we have already discussed how the carvings were created, the likely means of movement, and the magnificent work in them.

The Ten Colossal Stone Heads of San Lorenzo

The colossal heads found in San Lorenzo seemed to have been arranged or placed side by side along almost equal distances from the north to the southern part of the site. A few stone heads were also found in ditches close to the sources but buried by erosion. This is contrary to some suggestions that they were hidden away from human sight.

It would seem as these heads formed some route that led to the central part of the city and possibly a showcase of power and authority of the traditional rulers at the time. Some stone heads have clearly gone through recarving, converting them from old thrones to serve other purposes. Here's a list of all ten stones and the information available about them. The colossal stone heads have been labeled numerically for easy identification.

San Lorenzo Monument 1 - Colossal Head 1

- Discovery: This particular colossal stone head was found facing up like someone asleep facing upwards. Erosion had created a path through the top of the head, which made it visible to the archeologist, who noticed the eyes and later other parts of the head. It was discovered in 1945 by Stirling and his colleagues.

- Size: it weighs about 25.3 tons, measures 2.11m/6.9 ft, wide and 2.84m/9.3ft high.

- Materials: Large quantity of broken ceramic were found around the stone alongside figurines

- Dating: Some of these materials have been tested and found to date back to 800 - 400 BCE and others as far back as the Villa Alta Phase of 800 - 1000 CE.

- Description: This stone was uniquely carved, showing a headdress tied by a headband to the back, probably to keep the hair from being rough from the wind. The upper part of the headdress is designed with decorations in repeated patterns to form a U-shape. The expression on the face is that of a wrinkled, aged character, with lips slightly open but still covering the teeth. His cheeks are puffy, and the ears were perfectly designed to reflect a unique deformation on that part of the character's face – or it could be a mistake by the sculptor!

- Current Location: Colossal Stone Head 1 is currently sitting in Museo de Antropologia de Xalapa.

San Lorenzo Monument 2 – Colossal Head 2

rosemania, CC BY 2.0 <https://creativecommons.org/licenses/by/2.0>, via Wikimedia Commons
https://commons.wikimedia.org/wiki/File:San_Lorenzo_Colossal_Head_2,_from_Veracruz.jpg

- Discovery: Discovered by Stirling in 1945, like the stone head 1, it was found face up facing the sky. However, this one was not an original because it was clearly undergoing a recarving process from a stone throne to a colossal head. You can tell from the apparent damage or incomplete nature of the alteration.

- Size: This stone weighs about 20 tons, stands at 2.69m/8.8ft high, and measures 1.83m/6ft wide by 1.05m/3.4ft deep.

- Material/Dating: The material found around this head has been dated to the Early Pre-Classic and Later Classic periods.

- Description: This monument was carved wearing a complicated headdress with a headband tied to the back of the head and three birds in the form of the character's forehead. Stone Head 2 was severely damaged from multiple holes appearing on the face and indicating abandonment, maybe because the reworking was not going well. However, from what we can see, the image seems to represent an elderly male character wearing a frown face with his lips slightly open to reveal part of his teeth.

- Current Location: Colossal Stone Head 2 is currently in the Museo Nacional de Antropologia as part of the exhibitions that tell the story of the Olmecs.

San Lorenzo Monument 3 – Colossal Head 3

- Discovery: this stone head was discovered in 1946 by Stirling. Unlike stone heads 1 and 2, stone head 3 was found in a gully, face-down, and the wet ground made it particularly difficult to turn over and move. The actual origin of this stone head remains unknown, but it was found southwest of San Lorenzo.

- Size: This stone weighs 9.4 tons, measuring 1.78 meters/5.8ft high, 1.63 meters/5.3ft wide, and 0.95 meters/3.1ft deep.

- Description: This particular stone head has a frowning eyebrow with defined eyelids, thick, slightly parted lips, with a broken lower lip.

- Current Location: The stone head 3 is currently at the Museo Antropologia de Xalapa.

San Lorenzo Monument 4 – Colossal Head 4

- Discovery: Again, this stone head was discovered by Matthew Stirling in 1946. Stone head 4 seems to have been well-preserved when excavated, and it was found lying sideways. The head was found around the northwest of the central hill, towards the brink of the gully.

- Size: Stone heads 4 weigh only 6 tons, 1.78meters/5.8ft

high, 1.17 meters/3.8meters wide, 0.95 meters/3.1ft deep.

- Material: The ceramics material found at the location of stone head 4 was consistent with that found at the site of stone head 5, making it difficult to arrive at an accurate date.

- Description: The face is nicely structured to look like an elderly male with lower cheekbones, a creased forehead, and a slightly opened mouth.

- Current Location: Museo de Antropologia de Xalapa.

San Lorenzo Monument 5 - Colossal Head 5

- Discovery: Yet another 1946 discovery by Stirling, found face-down on the southern section of the San Lorenzo mound. This was another masterpiece by the sculptors and was well preserved too, but the back of the head was slightly damaged. The point where it was found seems to be the original location based on the ceramic material found there.

- Size: the stone weighs 11.6 tons, 1.86 meters/6.1ft high, measuring 1.47 meters/4.8ft wide and 1.15 meters/3.8ft deep.

- Material/Dating: Based on the materials found at the particular site of Headstone 5, it was dated to San Lorenzo and Villa Alta phases of 1,400 - 1000 and 800 - 1000 AD

- Description: The head represents the face of an older adult with evident sleep bags below his eyes and an aging line that runs across the nose. The forehead shows an unmistakable frown. The parted lips did not reveal the teeth.

- Current Location: Colossal stone head 5 has been moved to the Museo de Antropologia de Xalapa in Mexico for display and other Olmec collections.

San Lorenzo Monument 17 - Colossal Head 6

- Discovery: This stone head is one of the smaller ones and was discovered by a local farmer before it was later excavated in 1965 by Roman Pina Chan and Luis Aveleyra. It was found looking downward.

- Size: it weighs about 8 to 10 tons, 1.67 meters/5.5ft high, 1.41 meters/4.6ft wide, and 1.26 meters/4.1ft deep.

- Description: The face shows some incongruity in shape, which could have only been due to an error by the sculptor or damage in transit. The character is an older male, with aging lines under the eyes and across the face; extra skin can be seen beneath the eyes, indicating old age.

- Current Location: it was first moved to the Metropolitan Museum of Art in New York but was returned to Mexico in 1970 to be the Museo Nacional Antropologia.

San Lorenzo Monument 53 – Colossal Head 7

Cdennis, CC0, via Wikimedia Commons
https://commons.wikimedia.org/wiki/File:San_Lorenzo_Colossal_Head_7.jpg

- Discovery: It was discovered by a team of archaeologists from Yale University and Instituto Nacional de Antropologia de Historica. It is evident that it was a reworked job from the original form of a monumental stone throne. The stone was found face-up and slightly buried by erosion; also, not only was it poorly preserved, it had suffered obvious and deliberate damages.

- Size: Weighs 18 tons, 2.7meters/8.9ft high, 1.85meters/6.1ft wide, and 1.35meters/4.4ft deep.

- Description: It seems the mouth was carved to be open, but the lips are badly destroyed. The entire face is covered with wrinkles, indicating the character of a much older male with sagging cheeks and deep-set eyes.

- Current Location: Stone head 7 is currently sitting at the Museo de Antropologia de Xalapa, Mexico.

San Lorenzo Monument 61 - Colossal Head 8

- Discovery: This particular stone head has been described by many as one of the best works of art by the Olmecs. It was discovered on the southern part of the monumental throne lying on its side. The actual discovery occurred while a magnetometer survey of the site was being conducted in 1968, and it looked like it was reburied after the initial unrecorded discovery. Also, it is one of the well-preserved stone heads that didn't suffer any physical damage.

- Size: This stone head weighs 13 tons, standing at 2.2 meters/7.2ft high, measuring 1.65meters/5.4ft wide by 1.6 meters/5.2ft deep.

- Dating: it has been dated back to the Pre-Classic period.

- Description: Again, like the other stones, it's the face of a matured adult character with its forehead revealing an unmistakable frown, mouth slightly open to reveal the dental setting. While the face seems to have been carved out of natural material, the ears were represented by a single question mark shape.

- Current Location: The stone head was moved to the Museo de Antropologia de Xalapa in 1986. It still sits today, along with other discovered Colossal Head stones from the Olmec era.

San Lorenzo Monument 66 – Colossal Head 9

- Discovery: Stone head 9 was one of the most accessible finds because it seemed like it was exposed by erosion of the gully around the location of the head, but the date of discovery was put at 1982. It was found leaning on the right side and upwards with signs of erosion on the face.

- Size: it weighs about 10 tons, standing at 1.65 meters/5.4ft high, 1.36 meters/4.5ft wide, and 1.17 meters/3.8ft deep.

- Description: This head stone was carved, revealing this character as one who wears a piece of nose jewelry with a wrinkled face – but smiling, unlike most previous heads. It also has wide eyes and sagging cheeks. The only noticeable damage was to the upper lip. It was also mutilated with nine strange dents to the headdress.

- Current Location: Stone head 9 was left at the point of discovery for a while before it was eventually moved to Museo de Antropologia de Xalapa

San Lorenzo Monument 89 – Colossal Head 10

- Discovery: This stone head was discovered in a canyon in 1994 with the help of a magnetometer and eventually excavated by Ann Cyphers. The way it was found looked like it was buried lying face up.

- Size: it weighs about 8 tons, stands at 1.8 meter/5.9ft high, 1.43 meters/4.7ft by 0.92 meters/3ft deep.

- Description: This stone head has three unique tiny lines (like a bird's foot) on the forehead, with large ears extending further than the headdress. The face is a fully-grown adult, with sagging cheeks, a closed mouth, and revealing some lines under the eyes. Extra care seems to have gone into carving the lips, as they are very pronounced.

- Current Location: Stone Head 10 has since been moved to the Museo Comunitario se San Lorenzo Tenochtitlan around Texistepec.

The Famous Ball Game

Kåre Thor Olsen, CC BY-SA 2.5 <https://creativecommons.org/licenses/by-sa/2.5>, via Wikimedia Commons
https://commons.wikimedia.org/wiki/File:Chich%C3%A9n_Itz%C3%A1_Goal.jpg

So much has been said about the famous Mesoamerican ball game. The sport has cut across all classes in the region. This ball game has been traced back to 1400 BCE and is possibly the first team sport in history. The Olmecs have been identified as the first society to play this game from 1200 – 400 BCE. It was from them the game spread to the rest of the Mesoamerican region. However, it remains unclear if they were responsible for creating the game or copied it from other cultures outside of the region.

The Mayans were also known to have played the famous ball game in the Classical Maya, but they named theirs "pitz." The Aztec would later play the same ball game and called it "ollamalitli," a traditional Aztec name. The fact that the ball is made of rubber is the more reason why many believed it must have originated from the Olmecs, who have been tagged the "rubber people" or "people of the rubber name."

Interestingly the same ball game is still being played today in many parts of Mexico but with some modification and a new name called "ulama." Historically, this sport has been in existence for more than 3,400 years, making it the oldest sport because it has survived many generations – and still counting. It's also important to mention that it's the first ball game to use rubber in its ball.

The Rules of the Game and Gambling

As we have noticed, different civilizations have a separate name for the ball, but the general name back in the Mesoamerican era was "ulli." The game's rules seem pretty simple but achieving the goal – now, that's the challenging part!

The target of the players is to shoot the rubber ball through a vertical hoop (about 35" wide), such hoop being elevated. Although the ball was made from rubber, it still weighed about 4.1 kilos or 9 pounds. The field where the sporting action takes place is called "tlachtili," and covered an area of 100 to 300 feet long with erected walls on both sides where the stone rings hung.

The standard court had the shape of an "I" with a long line that runs through the middle of the tlachtili, and from that long line, there are sloping floors that meet the walls.

Players would be penalized for using any part other than their head, legs, elbows, or hips when passing the ball, and the ball was not allowed to touch the ground. Any team that got the ball through the brick rings won! Due to the height of the hoop, which was about 20 feet off the ground, the game proved difficult, but there were other ways teams could score points. Any team that hit one of the six markers on the edges of the tlachtili would score points.

Though money had not yet emerged – and just like today – sports and betting were hard to separate. Gambling was a major aspect of the ball game, and it was recorded that the people gambled with anything and everything possible to entertain themselves. For example, some ancient folks used precious objects like Obsidian, feathers, and fine ceramics, while others gambled their wives, children, or even their lives! To put it simply, many winners took charge of the loser – his property and any other "asset."

Rewards for Winning and Losing

Sports served different purposes in each society. For some, it was mere entertainment or a means of unifying the people, while for others, the ball game had more religious relevance with severe consequences.

Some civilizations presented the winners with trophies that have been carved into the shape of a human head, called "hacha." There is speculation that earlier hachas might have been actual human heads. Palma was likely the costume that the players might have worn or used as ceremonial attire. The game gear worn was often protective because of the high risk involved. For example, the size and weight of the ball have been known to break the bones of players.

There are other types of trophies presented to winners in the form of stone yokes tied around the waist, on the arm, and in the form of rings. Most of these trophies often ended up in the grave with the individuals that won them. Some believe they were used to buy safe passage to the "other side."

Some of the religious and ritual aspects of the game involve sacrificing the team leader or, in some cases, the entire losing team to some form of deity. These sacrificial rituals were seen on courts at El Tajib and Chichen Itza, where losing teams were found having lost their limbs. Another fate of the losing team is evidenced by the presence of *tzompantli* (a large tray where skulls of the dead were showcased); in this way, players were made aware of their possible fate should they lose!

The Fall of San Lorenzo

After what seems like a glorious start and achieving the status of being the center of the Olmec civilization, San Lorenzo eventually fell and lost its glory. The situation is so bad that no one can accurately say what was responsible for the city's demise.

For example, Coe and Diehl initially submitted that the city's fall might have been as a result of internal fighting and possible invasion by neighboring cities, but Diehl has since backed away from that conclusion. In explaining his new position, Diehl believes that the state of the stone heads that were being recurved and reused before being dumped could not have been a result of warfare. Another renowned archaeologist and Professor of Anthropology at the University of Florida, Dr. David C. Grove, said,

"...almost nothing is known of their 'demise,' but because Olmec is an archaeological culture defined by certain artifacts, the 'end' of the Olmec is merely the disappearance of that artifact complex. There is no data to indicate whether the decline of the major Olmec centers and the disappearance of the defining artifacts complex was rapid or gradual. The late Pre-Classic monuments at Tres Zapotec strongly suggest that over time, the Olmec simply evolved out of the traits by which they were originally defined. Whatever the case, their legacy is most clearly found in the rulership monuments of the Classic period Maya."

Other theories include the drastic climate change, which was a common occurrence around that time. Maybe the people abandoned the city when the condition became unbearable. Others opine that the likelihood of an epidemic was responsible for the decline of San Lorenzo – but there's no evidence to support that either.

Research is ongoing. Perhaps we'll learn why San Lorenzo fell to its knees after rising to such height and attaining the center's status to one of the world's most advanced civilizations of that time.

Chapter 8: The Rise of La Venta

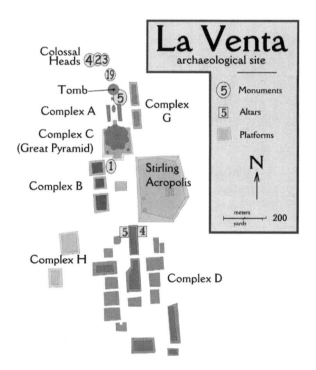

Archaeological Site Plan of La Venta

La Venta is a significant historical site in Mesoamerica between 800 and 400 BCE, part of the Middle Pre-classic period. This ancient Olmec settlement came as a replacement for San Lorenzo after its fall in the 10th century BCE. The site was occupied for 500 years before its abandonment at the beginning of the 4th century BCE.

La Venta was discovered in 1925 by archaeologists Frans Blom and Olivier La Farge. It was initially thought to be a Mayan site until radiocarbon techniques advanced. The archaeological site is now known for its planned layout, massive stone monuments, and the Great Pyramid. In addition, it has provided the most important archaeological finds from ancient Mesoamerica.

Geographical Location of La Venta

La Venta is located in present-day Tabasco, Mexico, close to its Gulf Coast. It was built on an island surrounded by the Tonalá River. The river currently divides the Mexican states of Veracruz and Tabasco.

La Venta spans about 16 kilometers inland and is less than 10 meters above sea level. It contains a little above 5.2 square kilometers of dry land, surrounded by vegetation and water bodies.

The Structure of La Venta

Most of the structures from La Venta were built from earth and clay. Only a few used basalt, andesite, and limestone in the foundations. One beautiful thing about the site is its well-planned layout. The main structures are oriented $8°$ west of north and are believed to be aligned with some star or constellation. The structures located on the east and west sides are similarly set.

Only a few of the residential structures in La Venta have survived.

The Great Pyramid of La Venta

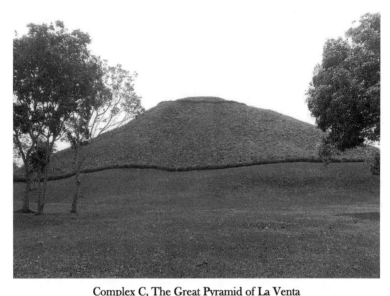

Complex C, The Great Pyramid of La Venta

The Great Pyramid is the major La Venta structure and is found at the site's center. It is shaped like a fluted cone. Also referred to as Complex C, it is one of the oldest pyramids known in Mesoamerica. The structure is a high clay mound with a length of 110 feet and an estimated 100,000 cubic meters. It was once thought to be created after the shape of a volcano or mountain. However, recent research shows that it was previously a rectangular pyramid, and the present shape is attributed to the 2500 years of erosion.

On the southern side of the pyramid is a deviation from the standard shape. It is believed to be an area of burned clay, a stock of buried offerings, or a tomb. The date of the Great Pyramid was determined through radiocarbon dating to be between 364-424 BCE.

Complex A

Complex A, La Venta
https://commons.wikimedia.org/wiki/File:La_Venta_Complejo_A.jpg

Complex A is located north of the Great Pyramid and comprises about three acres. It consists of mounds (heap of earth or rock) and plazas (open areas), surrounded by basalt columns which probably denotes limited access. The mounds were burial and ceremonial structures.

Underneath the mounds and plazas in Complex A are a variety of offerings and buried objects, including jade ornaments and polished mirrors. Five huge offerings made of serpentine blocks were also buried, one of which consisted of 50 tons of serpentine blocks covered in 4000 tons of clay.

Also excavated from complex A are three rectangular mosaic pavements representing jaguar masks. Each of the pavements measured 15 by 20 feet and consisted of 485 blocks of serpentine. After their completion, these structures were buried intentionally by covering them with clay and earth.

Located north of the Great Pyramid is also a ceremonial enclosure containing several tombs where deceased Olmec rulers were buried. The site consisted of five formal tombs, each with unique details while still maintaining the sites' structure.

Complex B

Complex B is located south of the Great Pyramid. Its plaza appears to be specially built for public gatherings. The plaza is about 400 meters long and over 100 meters wide and located in the southern part of what is known as the "great pyramid," and from the Stirling Acropolis, it is toward the west; but from the Complex B Platform, it is situated toward the east. The Stirling Acropolis was given the name as a mark of honor to the great work done by Stirling and his team as the first archaeologist to work on La Venta as far back as the 1940s.

Based on the details that went into the layout, Mesoamerican historians believed the platforms around the plaza were used as some sort of stages where religious and rituals are carried out. Complex B contained numerous monuments and a large plaza, and it is believed to have served as the primary site where La Venta rulers carry out ritual performances. The rituals carried out were possibly related to the Altars, Stelae (sculpted stone slabs with figures or inscriptions), and Monuments found in the area. The sculptures were placed in such a way that they could easily convey their messages to the audience.

Complex E

While there are currently no buildings in this area, analysis of the soil revealed the possibility that it had been a residential zone.

In total, seventy-seven carved stone monuments have been found in La Venta. They include four colossal heads, four multi-ton greenstone offerings, three mosaic pavements of serpentine blocks, a tomb of basalt columns, and numerous small jade figures and ornaments. The location of La Venta made it impossible to have natural stones and basalts like in San Lorenzo, the previous Olmec center. Therefore, there was a limitation of stone monuments; the ones found at the site mostly came from the Tuxtla Mountains in Cerro Cintepec.

Colossal Heads

Colossal heads, made from basalt, are the most popular of the La Venta monuments. Four colossal heads were found on the site and were officially called, Monuments 1-4. Monument 1 was located south of the Great Pyramid. And monuments 2 to 4 were located north of Complex A. The heads weighed about 18 tons, with a maximum height of 9 feet 4 inches. It is unsure how the Olmecs moved such huge stones. They were believed to be carved as early as 850 BCE.

The colossal heads were sculpted from basalt boulders. The facial features such as eyes, mouth, nostrils, cheeks, lips – and sometimes dimples – were drilled into the stone. These heads are striking because the Olmecs did not have any metal tools and used hard hand-held stones for sculpting.

Most Colossal Heads are taller than an average human being and consist only of a head and face. The back of the heads is flat, denoting that the sculptures were created to be viewed only from the front and sides. The sculptures also include a helmet similar to the American football helmet of the 1920s. Each sculpture is unique, with distinct features indicating that they were humans that existed. Most archaeologists today think that the heads represent highly esteemed Olmec rulers with great power.

Some theories suggest that the heads signified rulership and were placed in specific sites to show political dominance. The four heads of La Venta were initially positioned facing outwards as if they were guarding the vicinity.

The colossal heads are of great importance to both researchers and modern Mexicans, revealing more about the Olmec culture. They are also an intriguing attraction to many visitors and are currently found in museums close to the La Venta site.

Altars

Altar 4, La Venta

They are also referred to as *thrones* and were carved from basalt stones. Seven basalt altars were found in La Venta, and they depict the rulers during important rituals or ceremonies. The common ones are altars 4 and 5.

Altar 4 shows a figure sitting at the mouth of a cave and holding a rope with his hands – a rope that winds around the bottom of the altar to another figure. It is believed that the sculpture suggests a ruler taking hostages to sacrifice them to the gods. On the other hand, some believe that the figures attached to the rope are ancestors aiding the ruler.

Altar 5 has a very close resemblance to Altar 4 in design and construction, but the carved figure is holding what looks like a baby were-jaguar.

Other Artifacts

Jade Ornaments

Offering #4 from La Venta is a group of small stone figures also known as jade ornaments. The celts are thin, smooth structures ground from stone and tapered at one or both ends. The group consisted of 17 images arranged straight facing upwards right in front of the jade celts. While one of the figures was made of eroded granite, others were made of greenstone. Greenstone was highly valued among Olmecs and consisted of green and bluish-green rocks.

The head of the figures appears elongated. The face contains eyes that look swollen and have an almond shape. Additionally, the nostrils and ears were drilled for appropriate representation. The knees and elbows are slightly bent with a hand on each side of the figure. The figures look similar but are unique in features like height, color, and facial features.

The figures and the celts were used to create scenes. Most scholars believe that Offering #4 represents a mythological or historical scene – a ritual to honor a dignitary, a meeting to carry out a human sacrifice, or a marriage ceremony. It was also confirmed that the celts are backdrops and represent Stelae, showing that the site is of great importance to the people.

Polished Iron Ore Mirrors

These mirrors were fashioned from iron ore, mainly hematite, ilmenite, and magnetite. They were polished to give a reflective surface. The mirrors also had holes close to their edges, indicating that they had been worn as chest ornaments. These mirrors were majorly excavated from offerings; seven were unearthed from Complex A at La Venta. Mirrors were a significant part of the Olmecs and were used in rituals and daily lives.

Religion

Specific patterns in the Olmec culture were symbolic with probable ritual meaning. A symbol showing an 'X' in a rectangular box has been seen in La Venta stones and was passed on to cultures inspired by Olmecs.

Also, some Olmec arts show a relationship between animals and spirituality, as evidenced in elites wearing headdresses having feathers and other animal forms. Additionally, shark teeth and stingray remains were found at feasting sites at San Andrés.

Artifacts found at La Venta formed a part of their religion. Celts and jade ornaments were offered to deities during ceremonies. Iron ore mirrors were also used during rituals. In addition, the Olmecs believed in supernatural beings, as seen in some of their artifacts.

La Venta as a Ceremonial and Civic Center

La Venta was mainly dominated by Complex A, the Great Pyramid, and the large plaza to their south. The site's unique design shows the relevance of the ruler's role in mediating between the water and earth realm.

The site had various agricultural and marine resources, and a large number of the La Venta occupants were fishermen and agriculturalists. As a result, they made their homes close to the creeks and rivers that surrounded La Venta. So, based on the location of their settlement, they naturally depended on marine life like fish, shellfish, and others, but they later shifted to maize, palm, kinds of cotton, bears, and other farm produce grown primarily on gardens and small ridges.

The Great Pyramid divides La Venta into northern and southern sectors. It is believed that access to the northern ceremonial sector of Complex A was limited to the elite. As for commoners, they habited distant sites such as San Andrés. Unlike what we found in another part of the region where there were dedicated places for burial, La Venta had tombs and monuments strategically arranged and located in the mounds and platform, and many buried offerings were found in these platforms.

Worthy of note is that La Venta had skilled craftsmen who created the unique monuments that La Venta is known for today. A cylinder seal and other forms of writing were also found on the site showing that a writing system existed in La Venta.

Excavations and Current La Venta Site

Excavators of the La Venta site were members of the Smithsonian Institution and included Matthew Stirling, Philip Drucker, Waldo Wedel, and Robert Heizer. The excavations were mainly carried out between 1942 and 1955, after which the site was extensively damaged by looting and civic development. Furthermore, a three-dimensional map of Complex A was designed by Gillespie and Volk and published in 2014.

Most of the archaeological sites were destroyed due to the construction of a nearby petroleum refinery and the removal of significant monuments without any markers to signify their original locations. As a result, excavations are now challenging to carry out. Several artifacts have been moved from their original location and other places like the Parque Museo La Venta, also known as the La Venta Museum. The museum's location is in Villa Hermosa (in modern-day Tabasco), and the site is now protected as an archaeological park.

Chapter 9: Custom and Society

Olmec, Long-count Calendar

Adrian Hernandez, CC BY-SA 4.0 <https://creativecommons.org/licenses/by-sa/4.0>, via Wikimedia Commons https://commons.wikimedia.org/wiki/File:La_Mojarra_Estela_1_(Escritura_superior).jpg

The status of the Olmecs as the first society to develop in the Americas make it essential for us to dive into the customs and type of society that the people had. The progressive advancement of the

Olmec has been divided into:

1. Early Formative 1800 to 900 BCE
2. Middle Formative 900 to 400 BCE
3. Late/Terminal Formative 400 BCE to 200 CE.

Scholars often used the phrase "mother culture" to describe the Olmec because their culture and civilization were not only the first to stand out, but it spread all through the Mesoamerican region, and the influence was evident in several societies. This influence was so profound that, at some point, some scholars attributed the civilization seen in the region to the Mayans and Aztecs. That error has since been corrected.

Coming from a society that was mostly known to rely on agriculture on the Gulf Lowlands from as far back as 1600 BCE, during the Early Formative periods, the culture had massive influence and control in the Olmec heartlands, which was located on the southern Gulf of Mexico and the shores in Tabasco and Veracruz. The first known Olmec center was San Lorenzo which falls into modern-day Veracruz.

While San Lorenzo reigned as the major Olmec center around 1200 BCE, La Venta began to grow. While the Olmec culture was notably practiced there, it never reached nor came close to the level of development seen in San Lorenzo until around 900 BCE. Then like San Lorenzo, after 500 years of occupation, La Venta too was abandoned around the early part of the 4th century.

From its coastal location on an island in a swamp looking over Rio Palma, evidence found at the site revealed that La Venta did more than influence the cultures of surrounding cities but had political control over some part of the region between Mezcalapa and Coatzacoalcos Rivers.

It is not surprising that the La Venta Olmecs transitioned from relying on seafood to agriculture. Much has been said about the strategic location of the city. For Example, the La Venta is located among different types of ecosystems like a tropical forest (where they could clear lands for farming), marshes, swamps, and the Gulf of Mexico. The humid climate with an annual temperature of 26 Degrees Celsius and nearly 2,000 millimeters of annual rainfall made the ground perfect for farming.

The archaeological site at La Venta had many residential buildings, which could only have indicated the population expansion the cities experienced. At the same time, it was regarded as the new Olmec center. Some of these residential buildings have survived through many centuries and still exist at the site today. It was observed that there were no structures dedicated to food production, religious, economic, and military operations. The main La Venta site is a complex made from clay and constructed stretching 20Km towards the north-south, while the site is designed from west to north.

As mentioned earlier, there was a limited supply of stones and rocks in La Venta, so the people relied more on clay for their residential buildings and other structures. That is much different from what was obtainable at the Maya and among the Aztecs. The large basalt stones found at the site were not used to build residential apartments but used strictly for carving monuments like Colossal Heads, altars, several stelae, and stone thrones. That is the extent of the scarcity of stone and rock at the site. The little that was available was brought in and used wisely. A good example was the basalts columns deposited at Complex A; they did not originate from within the city but could have come from nearby places like Punta Roca Partida, in San Andres.

How the mounds, residential buildings, complexes, and monuments at La Venta were arranged provides insight into the unique ceremonial nature of the city. In the words of Rebecca Gonzalez-Lauck, "one of the earliest examples of large-scale ideological communications through the interaction of architecture and sculpture." Rebecca is an Award-Winning Mexican Archaeologist.

Social Structure at La Venta

The social structure of La Venta had power concentration; likewise, the level architecture, type of artifacts, and luxury items found at the site speak volumes. Among the cities that represented the culture and civilization of the Olmecs, La Venta was the largest of them all and adopted a complex royal system based on hierarchy made up of the ruler, the elites, and the ruled. In the midst of all these was the priest, who was believed to be the mouthpiece of the gods and had power over life and death and, in some instances, *political influence.* The actual political structure the Olmecs adopted is still unclear, but new findings and dating would probably shed more light on this elusive, most advanced civilization.

"The nature of the political organization and social integration of Olmec centers remains a point of scholarly contention. General consensus advocates the notion of a theocratic chiefdom. Such a sociopolitical system involves governance of each center by a single, elite individual, or chief, who exercises authority over all things religious and monetary. With respect to the former, artistic representations' iconographic symbols and motifs suggest that the Olmecs practiced a religion distinguished by shamanism. Shamans, or shamanic chiefs, mediated between the natural, earthly realm and the supernatural realm of the ancestors and deities. As first pointed out by Peter Furst in 1968, Olmec sculpture also depicts shamans' supernatural power and ability to transform from human to animal spirits. Use of psychotropic drugs may have facilitated shamanic transformations. Aside from religious activities, the chief's monetary responsibilities were related to food production and collection of tribute. An elite minority, presumably related to the chief, would have also exercised economic control over food tribute and trade networks. Trade with Mesoamerican groups distant from the Olmec is evidenced by materials such as blue-green jade from the Motagua Valley in Guatemala, fine white kaolin clay from Chalcatzingo, magnetite from the Valley of Oaxaca, and obsidian from central Mexico and the Maya highlands. Interactions via trade would have afforded the opportunity for communication of religious, social, and political ideas as well.

Much of this dialogue between the Olmecs and their distant Mesoamerican neighbors is supported by the appearance of Olmec art, or local expressions with characteristic features, in widely dispersed locales. Olmec art possesses distinctive stylistic traits that first appeared in the Olmec heartland between 1250-1150 B.C. Rulership and shamanism are the dominant themes. Most notable for their size and early dates are the three-dimensional human figures carved from stone. These include colossal basalt stone heads, seated and kneeling individuals, throne-like altars, and stelae. The effort that would have been required to procure enormous basalt boulders from their source, the Tuxtlas Mountains, cannot be overstated. First reported in 1862 at the site of Hueyapan in Veracruz, colossal stone heads were, in fact, investigators' earliest exposure to Olmec culture. Scholars have convincingly argued that carved heads portray individual Olmec leaders. Often these monuments were found defaced or intentionally broken, which possibly signified the cessation of a leader's rule or life. Olmec-style art is also found on a considerably smaller scale, as exemplified by portable artifacts." Extracted from Anthropology – Olmecs.

Some artifacts and signs found on them were an indication of classes that existed. For example, the feathered headdresses, type of jewelry, and the specific body part where the jewelry was worn are good indicators. Wearing a mirror was very common among some elite, and you could tell it had a special place in the people's culture. Luxury and other objects with high value attached to them were a sign of economic, political, royal, and religious power in the La Venta polity. The rulers and elite used all these to command power and demanded respect from the lower class in the city.

Several scholars and archaeologists agree that at the peak of the reigns of La Venta, the population would have been up to 18,000 people. In addition to the mysteries of La Venta, the sand at the site did not preserve the remains of people buried, which made it nearly impossible to identify the differences in burial arrangement and locations at the site. However, the Colossal Heads found at various site locations support evidence that the elite had a firm grip over the lower class. Furthermore, constructing a residential abode for the elite would have involved massive labor with many people from the lower class.

Recent excavations have also revealed how the city must have been divided into some parts, especially the best part of the city, reserved for the elites and the less productive part for the lower class. All these were indications that social classes existed; therefore, social inequality must have been the order of the day – and part of the complexity of the La Venta Olmecs.

Burials Sites and Rituals

Buried Mosaics or Pavements from La Venta, consisting of nearly 500 blocks of serpentine

Among the many discoveries at the La Venta site are burial places, especially in locations like Mound A, but the environment made it impossible to support to preserve any form of remains because organic material doesn't do well with the type of acidic soil found in La Venta. The only signs of remains the site had to offer were found in a basalt tomb and contained:

- A burnt skullcap
- Shark tooth
- Stingray spines
- Some milk teeth

There was a high concentration of some items like jade celts at these burials places, and it would look like they were a form of requirement for ritual purposes for a particular class of people, but no human remains were found so, it was difficult to confirm this. Other artifacts include beads, plaques, jewelry, obsidian, earspools, spangles, and rare items. Whether they fell off the bodies of decomposed people buried there or were placed there as ritual rites remain to be seen, but one thing was sure, it was a common find at several burial sites.

Structure A-2 – Mound A

The platform is made of clay and looks very much like a burial site. Within the platform were decomposed bones of human remains that were poorly preserved, and items found there include cinnabar, a red paint-like substance commonly used in the region to indicate status. Also found on the platform were jade, masks, and figurines, along with mirrors and obsidian, which have long been established as class items among the elites.

For example, the mirror carried a special significance meaning it mainly was worn or used by the royals, priests, and the elite. It was not particularly common among the lower class of the Olmecs. The stelae and other relevant carvings and monuments showed several Olmec leaders wearing them on their chest, forehead, and arms. The nature of the burials found inside the platform shows that the corpses might have been wrapped before being buried.

Urn Burials

The urn burial was discovered in Complex E, which was more of a residential area in the city. Also found were pieces of bones and teeth, all buried in ceramic pots. According to Rust, *"The fill immediately around this large urn was clean, yellow sand, and the urn was covered with an inverted fine-paste orange bowl with flaring walls; the bowl's interior was painted red and incised with the double-line-break pattern on the inside rim."*

Like many things from the Olmecs, this system of managing a complex society by breaking it into classes was replicated in several civilizations in Mesoamerica. Classes were noticed all over the region, and the priest and royals were treated and semi-gods. They, in turn, ruled and controlled the people using fear and manipulation. From places of abode to final resting places, the gap among the class kept widening. It all started with the Olmecs and was then passed down to other cultures that followed.

Chapter 10: Economy and Religion

The Olmecs laid the foundation for artistic innovation in Mesoamerica. The artifacts discovered there still help in understanding what they believed and how they lived. The Olmecs built their economy by exporting some of these products while importing those they did not have.

The Economy of La Venta

Basalt rocks used in the creation of stone monuments were brought in from the Tuxtla mountains. It's been suggested that the rocks were traded with another culture, but it is still uncertain.

From the well-sculpted stone monuments seen in La Venta, the site used many highly skilled artisans. The Olmecs also created elegant vessels and ceramic figures out of clay. There is a possibility that more goods were exported than imported. And this could have led to the Olmecs building their relationships with other cultures. These resulted in the elites possessing significant power with luxury goods and feasting foods like cocoa and maize beer.

Agriculture in La Venta

La Venta had a wide variety of plants and animals. The animals were mostly sea animals, deer, and other small animals. La Venta and its surrounding sites mainly depended on hunting wild animals. Dogs were the only animals domesticated by the Olmec.

Due to the rich, alluvial soil located along the river banks, La Venta had a bountiful harvest every year. Maize was the primary plant they cultivated.

Religion and Rituals

Monument 19, a feathered serpent
Audrey and George Delange, Attribution, via Wikimedia Commons
https://commons.wikimedia.org/wiki/File:La_Venta_Stele_19_(Delange).jpg

Some patterns seen in La Venta have been thought to have a ritual meaning. An example is the crossed band symbol which appears as an 'X' in a rectangular box. Many stones in La Venta and other Olmec sites have been found to possess this symbol.

The religious activities of the Olmec were performed by rulers, priests, and shamans. The rulers appear to be the most important religious figures because of their connection to Olmec deities. It is believed that the Olmecs had different supernatural beings, as evidenced in Olmec artifacts.

Olmec Dragon (Earth Monster)

It is portrayed as a crocodile-like being with flaming eyebrows around the nose and its tongue split in two. The Earth Monster also has prominent fangs (long, pointed teeth). His mouth, sometimes open, is seen as a cave. In the Olmec culture, it is one of the supernatural beings most commonly depicted, thought to represent agriculture, fertility, and fire.

Maize Deity

Maize was an essential and common crop to the Olmecs, so it is not surprising that they assigned a god to it. The Maize Deity is identified by maize growing from his cleft head. It is usually seen in the figures of rulers. A carved celt (originally found in Veracruz) shows a depiction of the Maize Deity.

Rain Spirit and Were-Jaguar

In 1955, Matthew Stirling proposed that Were-Jaguar resulted from a mating between a jaguar and a woman. From that time, any figure showing almond-shaped eyes, downturned mouth, and a cleft head were described as a "Were-Jaguar."

Some researchers believe that the rain spirit and Were-Jaguar are the same. Others believe that they are two separate supernatural beings. It is suggested that the Olmec rain spirit had Were-Jaguar features and had other attributes, including a headband, headdress, pleated ear bars, and a "crossed bar'" icon on the chest/or navel.

Banded-Eye God

The banded-eye god has a cleft head and a downturned mouth. The eyes are almond-shaped with a narrow band or stripe that runs along the side of its face. The banded-eye god appears more human than other Olmec gods. It is represented on the famous Olmec Statue, Las Limas Monument 1.

Feathered Serpent

Feathered or plumed serpent, now known throughout Mesoamerica, first appeared in Olmec culture. It is seen as a rattlesnake with feathers on its head. It is represented in Monument 19 from La Venta. Though not very common in Olmec arts, later equivalents such as the Aztec deity, Quetzalcoatl, and the Maya deity, Kukulkan, had a more important place in Mesoamerican religion.

Fish or Shark Monster

Monument 58 is one of the artifacts used to depict the Fish Monster. It has also appeared in stone carvings, pottery, and celts and represents the underworld. Its shark tooth and monster-like head identify the Fish Monster. It also possesses "crossed bands," a dorsal fin, and a split tail. Shark teeth uncovered from some Olmec sites show that the Fish Monster was honored in some rituals.

Bird Monster

The Bird Monster is portrayed as a frightening bird, sometimes with features of a reptile. It is usually found in the carved figures of rulers, especially in their dresses. The bird monster image also appears on many other artifacts, including on a crucial altar.

Animals and Spirituality

The Olmecs paid special significance to jaguars, eagles, caimans, snakes, and sharks. Numerous artifacts from Olmecs show animal characteristics combined with human features, and there seems to be a connection between animals and spirituality among the Olmecs. For example, Olmec elites wore headdresses with feathers and other animal forms.

Some sea creatures were also sacred to the Olmec. Shark teeth and stingrays have been found at feasting sites in San Andres, a nearby elite center. It is also clear that those in La Venta shared the same ideology.

Olmec Artifacts

The different artifacts found in La Venta have been of great importance in understanding the Olmec religion. There is no ideal strategy for fully understanding the Olmec artifacts due to the lack of written documents – most of what is known as a result of repeated patterns that are symbolic.

Many of the pieces initially located at La Venta have been moved to the La Venta Park in Villahermosa, Mexico. Tabasco poet, Carlos Pellicer, championed the movement, designing, organizing, and assembling the park in 1957. Pellicer began to rescue many archaeological pieces from La Venta when he discovered that the site was being destroyed by the petroleum refinery built near it. He also placed them in a natural environment as they were supposed to be when they were found.

More than 50 Olmec artifacts are present in La Venta Park. The park presents a jungle-like environment similar to the original La Venta site.

Jade ornaments

Offering #4 from La Venta is a group of small stone figures also known as jade ornaments. This group consisted of seventeen figures placed upright arranged in front of six jade celts. While one of the figures was made of eroded granite, others were made of greenstone. Greenstone was highly valued among Olmecs and consisted of green and bluish-green stones. The celts are thin, smooth structures ground from stone and tapered at one or both ends.

The head of the figures appears elongated. The face contains eyes that look swollen and have an almond shape. Additionally, the nostrils and ears are drilled for appropriate representation. The knees and elbows are slightly bent with a hand on each side of the figure. The figures look similar but are unique in features like height, color, and facial features.

The figures and the celts were used to create scenes. Most scholars believe that Offering #4 represents a mythological or historical scene – a ritual to honor a dignitary, a meeting to carry out a human sacrifice, or a marriage ceremony. It was also confirmed that the celts are backdrops and represent Stelae, showing that the site is of great importance.

Polished Iron Ore Mirrors

These mirrors were fashioned from iron ore, mainly hematite, ilmenite, and magnetite. They were polished to give a reflective surface. The mirrors also had holes close to their edges, indicating that they had been worn as chest ornaments. Fragments of this mirror have been discovered in abundance in La Venta. They were majorly excavated from offerings; seven were unearthed from Complex A at La Venta. Mirrors seemed to have been very significant in the Olmec culture and were used in rituals and daily life.

Celts or "Pseudo axes"

They are made of jade. Most are smooth, but a few are decorated with what are thought to be religious symbols.

They were very common in both burials and offerings. Together with jade offerings, celts were offered to deities during ceremonies at La Venta.

Stelae

Stelae are stone monuments that have sculpted elements on them. In stela's, the sculpted elements are raised, and the background appears lower.

Stela 2 shows the figure of a King with multiple figures (supposedly bodyguards) protecting the King. The King is seen holding a staff of power and wearing a headdress. There are also representations of spikes or thunders on the sculpture.

Stela 3 shows two figures. One is a bearded, long nose man, known famously as the 'Uncle Sam' figure. It is believed that the sculpture represents the meeting of two dignitaries – the Olmec and another culture. The two figures are both standing on a sacred rock, sharing information. Some figures are seen floating or flying while the two are having their meeting.

Stela 19, found in the La Venta site, has been found to have a very unusual carving. The figure in the middle appears to hold something that looks like a bag, handle, or lever. The figure is also seen seated within the body of a plumed serpent. The serpent's head has a helmet with 'crossed bars,' typical of numerous Olmec monuments. The plumed serpent continues round the stela and ends in a rattlesnake tail.

Stela 19 is thought to be one of the first representations of Quetzalcoatl (Aztec deity), who first arrived on Mexico's Gulf coast and left the Serpent sanctuary many years later. The carving is assumed to be revering where Quetzalcoatl first arrived and where he left. It is vital in the Quetzalcoatl story; his link with the Olmec eventually spread onto the Aztec and Mayan world.

Basalt columns

Complex A, an area restricted to the elites, was surrounded by basalt columns. Basalt columns served as fences and were primarily used to delineate sacred precincts from public spaces.

They were about 25 feet long and had strange cut marks on them.

Other Monuments

Monument 13

This monument was found close to the sacred precinct of La Venta. It is also known as 'The traveler.' The sculpture shows a figure wearing a turban and sandal, carrying something like a flag. It has been thought to represent a meeting with a different culture – someone who arrived in the Olmec world.

Monument 20

Monument 20 looks like a large piece of shark. It was made out of serpentine and is thought to represent marine life.

Monument 59

Monument 59 is a Were-Jaguar or Human-like Jaguar. Its limbs appear stretched out, holding a spherical object or a type of slab. The sculpture also has multiple marks and carvings.

Monument 63

Monument 63 shows a figure with a banner. The figure wears a headdress and has a beard. Above the individual is a great fish with massive jaws, dorsal fins, and teeth that suggest it could be a shark. The sculpture represents the great god Quetzalcoatl, or one of the many travelers in the Olmec world. At the back of the sculpture are several cut marks and indentations, probably representing several language systems.

Monument 64

Monument 64 appears to be ahead with a vast cleft in the middle of the skull. The aperture could also be a part of the helmet. The sculpture also had long thin eyes and an abnormal mouth. It is believed to represent a Were-Jaguar.

Monument 77

Monument 77 is also called "The Governor." It was seen at the entrance to the sacred precinct of La Venta and appeared to be guarding the Pyramid and sacred area. It looks like a classic kind of Egyptian-looking statue with a cloak at its back representing a jaguar. It also wears a headdress similar to those of the Egyptians.

Human figures or Deities?

Numerous important figures have been found in many stone monuments in La Venta. Scholars are still unsure which of them are human rulers or gods since there seems to be a slight difference between the deities and the Olmec rulers in their ideology.

Writing System in La Venta

The Olmec had a form of a writing system that used symbols. And this is seen in the cylinder seal and other forms of writing found at San Andreas.

Chapter 11: Decline and the Epi-Olmecs

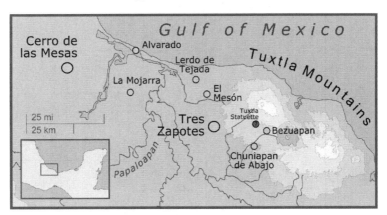

Important Epi-Olmec sites

We have earlier established that the Olmec culture was the first complex civilization that later spread throughout the Mesoamerican region. Along with their ways of life, the people thrived along the Gulf of Mexico from around 1200 to 400 BCE. Several scholars have described them as the forebearers of modern civilization and later societies, like the Mayan and Aztecs. The writing systems and calendar styles that we later saw in other emerging societies and improved by other cultures originated from the Olmecs.

However, at about 400 BCE, just like San Lorenzo, the Olmec city of La Venta declined after replacing San Lorenzo – which had served the people for 2000 years. The decline of the city took the Olmec Classic Era along with it. The reason for the decline of La Venta, like the previous Olmec center, is still unclear, mainly because the city fell long before the arrival of the Europeans to the region.

As we now know, the two great Olmec cities of San Lorenzo and La Venta were named based on the location of archaeologist findings. Their original names have been lost in time and are still to be discovered. San Lorenzo enjoyed a great run as the epic center of the Olmec culture and was located on an island around 1200 to 900 BCE; then went into decline and was replaced by La Venta.

La Venta went into decline around 400 BCE and was abandoned entirely. The fall of the great city of La Venta also signified the end of the Classic Olmec culture. There are still remnants of La Venta scattered all over the region, but their culture is long lost and extinct. The Olmecs built and managed an extensive trade network while the cities were thriving, but all that fell apart as the city declined. All the unique items known with the culture, like pottery styles, sculptures, jades, which all had peculiar Olmec motifs, were no longer made.

Historians, researchers, and archaeologists specializing in Mesoamerican artifacts have not reached a consensus on precisely what happened to the Olmec civilizations or what caused them to decline. However, some think that it could be a combination of several things. For example, the society relied heavily on farming and some crops like maize, potatoes, and squash for their livelihood; this could have made them vulnerable to climate change. Some scholars are even of the opinion that a volcanic eruption could have covered the whole area in ash or even distorted the flow of water that comes from the river, thereby disrupting their irrigation system and eventually leading to famine.

There were also stories of an outbreak of an epidemic that could have wiped out the population. Artificial human actions were not left out of the theories because some believed that was war between La Venta and neighboring societies, and this could have led to the fall of the cities, but there is no evidence to support these stories, not even the signs of an internal war between the cities. The likely conclusion that most scholars are leaning towards in agreement is over farming, destruction of the forest for farming, and eventually climate change.

The Emergence of Epi-Olmec Culture

When La Venta, the last Olmec center, fell, the Olmec culture did not go into extinction; instead, it transitioned into what we now know as the Epi-Olmec culture. This was a connection between the original culture from the Classic era mixed with the culture of the people of Veracruz, and this is because the remnants of La Venta fled or moved to neighboring cities, especially Veracruz.

The remnants could not establish control of the Olmec culture in their newfound homes but coexisted with the people as they practiced a lighter version of what they used to have. The migrated Olmec and the Veracruz culture thrived along with the northern Olmec lands for another 500 years.

So, the Epi-Olmec culture emerged around the Formative Period and became successful in present-day Veracruz. They lived mainly along the Papaloapan River from around 300BCE to 250 CE. The Epi-Olmec culture never reached the height and achievement of the original culture, especially in the artifacts (like the Colossal Heads and other monuments), neither was it close in complexity. However, it did better than the original Olmec culture in the improvement of writing and calendar systems.

The cities that benefited from the influx of the original Olmec as La Venta fell include:

- Tres Zapotes
- Cerro de les Mesas
- El Tajin
- El Meson,
- Chunipan de Abajo
- Lerdo de Tejada

Among these cities, Tres Zapotes and Cerro de Mesas were the two cities with the lost glory of San Lorenzo and La Venta, the original Olmec centers. However, it was only a *look-alike;* they never came close to matching any of the fallen cities, but important artifacts found at the site, like improved writing system, calendrics, and astronomy, made them worthy of being studied.

Tres Zapotes

In January 1939, American and archaeologist Mathew Stirling and his wife, Marion Stirling (an authority like her husband), and a team of other archaeologists led another expedition to Veracruz, Mexico. The was just one of Stirling's 14 expeditions; he was already a known and respected name in different parts of the Americas. This particular venture was sponsored by a joint effort of the National Geographic Society and the Smithsonian Institution.

While exploring several mounds around the Arroyo Hueyapan in Tres Zapotes, right in front of the tallest mounds at that time, the team discovered carved rocked like a pillar, but it was a monument next to an ancient altar. The carved monolith, named Stela C, turned out to be one of the best discoveries of Stirling's work in the Americas. Stela C had a peculiar carving of a were-jaguar sculptured on it to the side, which looked closely like some of the discoveries at the major Olmec centers.

Also, the Mayan center was only a hundred miles away from the site of the discoveries. After a careful study of Stela C, archaeologists concluded that it had to be the symbol of authority for a powerful ruler that reigned in the city. In one part of the carving, Stirling saw what looked like a date from his experience with Maya inscriptions; it had bars and dots. He wrote out the numbers and took them to their camp to show his wife Marion, the expert at ancient American writing styles.

While attempting to translate the writing, Marion noticed that the top half of Stela C was missing, and it was the part that indicated that the period was called a Baktun. However, based on her experience, he guessed what it could mean and arrived at a date that reads: "3rd September, 32 BC." Three decades after her educated guess, Marion was validated when the top half was discovered; her date was accurate.

At the time of Stirling's finding, the Stela C was the earliest known Mesoamerican long-count calendar that existed, but several decades later, Stela 2, which was found at a small site named

Chiapas de Corzo in Mexico, would later surpass Stirling's finding. Stela 2 was translated to have a confirmed date of 6th December 36 BCE. Additionally, when Stirling and his team discovered Stela C, they concluded that it was a Mayan-style long-count calendar dating system, hence an invention of the Mayans. However, the findings in Veracruz have debunked Stirling's conclusion and pushed the date further back in time. In essence, history has been re-written.

The expedition to Tres Zapotes was a rich find for Sterling and his team. It had a wealth of archaeological artifacts like several pieces of jades, thousands of fragments from the pottery system, and a few Colossal Heads similar to what had been found in San Lorenzo and other Olmec centers. Scholars believe that the wealth of discovery at the Tres Zapotec site further confirms that the city was occupied for more than 2000 years and probably the longest-occupied of all the Olmec Centers. That leads us to wonder: Who were these people are and how could they coexist for that long?

The Tres Zapotes archaeological site is currently located between the Papaloapan River basin and the Tuxtla Mountains and has access to the Veracruz lowlands swamps and the forested uplands. The mountains were primary sources of stone structures and sculptures, and the was a fairly regular supply of water running through Arroyo Hueyapan. The Tres Zapotes site has a daily temperature of 78 degrees which gives it a classification, "tropical monsoon," and farming was carried on all year round. The site was also a perfect location for trade networks, and evidence found at the site revealed that Tres Zapotes had trade dealings with other neighboring societies for the extended period it was occupied.

The gradual emergence of the Tres Zapotes site started when San Lorenzo (and later, La Venta) was experiencing a decline. Based on the archaeological findings at the Tres Zapotes, scholars put the date of founding the site at 1500 BCE, but it did not gain the status and authority of being the Olmec center until about 900 BCE – or what is known as the Middle Formative Period. The first architectural monumental building appeared around the same time – 500 BCE.

It remains unclear how Tres Zapotes became an Epi-Olmec center while previously great cities like San Lorenzo and La Venta fell. Some scholars believe that the city likely took in refugees from the fallen cities. Or perhaps the people just continued practicing the Olmec way of life even after the fall of the former Olmec centers. Whichever position you choose, one thing is clear, Tres Zapotes had remnants of the Olmecs, and they carried on the Olmec tradition while other centers suffered a decline.

Artifacts found at the site further proved that Tres Zapotes attained the status of being an Olmec center even though the complexity of the society tilted more towards that of the Mayans than the Aztecs *in the way the cities functioned.* Rather than have a central ruler, the cities were allowed to function as separate political entities. Additionally, evidence revealed that the political arrangement at Tres Zapotes was further broken down to ruling royal families and other smaller factions. Experts of Mesoamerican history believe this political setting in Tres Zapotes became more evident during the Epi-Olmec period in the cities.

By 400 BCE, the glory of La Venta was eventually lost. At the same time, Tres Zapotes became the undisputed center of the Olmecs. The city started going through cultural changes and what we now know as the Epi-Olmec period. Tres Zapotes and many neighboring cities experienced cultural changes and advancement in a civilization like they had never experienced before, and it's all because of the influx and influence of the Olmec in their societies.

Compared to the advancement seen in the previous Olmec centers, the Epi-Olmec experienced a much cruder advancement in art and architectural requirements. However, it was the time when the calendar system advanced a great deal within the region. When compared to later development in ancient Mexico, it seems unrefined. For example, the Tres Zapotes area was known as the base for the script called *Isthmian.* This type of writing was found all over several monuments and artifacts, and it became even more evident that it was the basis of the Mayan writing system some centuries down the line.

Excavations at the Tres Zapotes site uncovered more than 160 mounds and platforms, and they were dated back to the epi-Olmec period of 400 BCE to 200 CE. These mounds were grouped and labeled into four:

- Group 1
- Group 2

- Group 3
- Nestle Group

Each mound was made up of ruling political setups, royalties, and temples. For example, Group 2, which happens to be the most massive of the four, is strategically located at the middle of the site, while others were about a mile away from the four Groups.

Mesoamerican historians have concluded that the setting could only mean that Epi-Olmec Tres Zapotes was broken down into four political arrangements: royalties and ruling families. These four royal families ruled over the other parts of the cities in a decentralized system of governing.

It was also noted that the Epi-Olmec period was when there was little to zero flow of artifacts into the city, which was a sign that trade networks previously enjoyed at San Lorenzo and La Venta had collapsed. This was evident in the lack of finesse seen in the monuments, arts, pottery, and other architectural structures like what was obtainable during the original Olmecs. A further example can be seen in the type of basalt used by the Epi-Olmecs; it was more of inferior quality and must have made carving difficult. It could also be that the people lacked experienced craftsmen like the Olmecs had because many artifacts reflected the lack of detail.

Archaeologists noticed that by the dawn of the Classical era, the Tres Zapotes were not wholly abandoned yet, but there had been a significant shift in the people's way of life and culture. By 100 to 200 CE, it was evident that the Mesoamerican region was experiencing yet another type of change. Tres Zapotes, which had initially been influenced by the Olmec culture and civilization and had been on the western part of the homeland that made Epi-Olmec transition easier, once again changed alliance. The once Epi-Olmec center had now become a part of a different culture from the southern edge known as the *Classic Veracruz Culture*, or what some called the Gulf Coast Classic Culture. There were a few cities that came up at this time, but Tres Zapotes stood tall.

Some of these changes that came with the cultural shift at Tres Zapotes included the resumption of long-distance trading with other region members. The closed economy was finally opening up again – as it had been in San Lorenzo and La Venta. Also worthy of note was that the Classic Veracruz Culture experienced a further widened gap between the elites and the lower class. The social hierarchy experience during the Epi-Olmec was narrowed down, and wealth was now more in the hands of fewer people than it was previously. Just like what it was under the Olmecs for 2000 years, power became a lot more centralized.

The demand for unique crafts also increased; importation of luxury items from distant trade partners also rose to a new height. Lastly, religion grew in intensity, with a more formal structure now taking shape. The need for the elites to establish power and control among the people led to religious and ritual activities reaching new heights in Tres Zapotes, and the Classic Veracruz had several ceremonies to show off this power and control. These involved human sacrifices.

Once again, the Mesoamerican ball game was quite popular during this period, and it served as bridging the gap between the elites and other categories in the culture.

Gradually, art was taking shape and becoming more refined and unique in Tres Zapotes. A good example was the discovery of strange-looking carved figurines and statues with wheels and smiling faces. The findings revealed that they could have only been made in the earlier ADs, at a time known as the *Totonac civilization*. Some of the unique patterns noticed by archaeologists are still being studied in order to be translated.

The Classic Maya and the city of Teotihuacan in the Mexican highlands were the other civilizations that existed simultaneously with the Classic Veracruz culture. Archaeological findings at the Tres Zapotes site revealed the role of these nearby cultures on Tres Zapotes, which could only have been through trade networks.

Interestingly, some centuries after the fall of Teotihuacan, the Classic Mayan civilization also experienced a decline. As if the same thing plagued it, Tres Zapotes followed suit by losing its shine and went into decline. By 900 CE, Tres Zapotes was abandoned entirely, and only a few settlers were left to survive through the century. And so, it was that the 2,000 plus years run of Tres Zapotes as the Epi-Olmec center came to an end. No cities in ancient Mexican history had ever been inhabited for that long.

To date, discoveries are still being made concerning the city of Tres Zapotes.

Conclusion

The Olmec civilization is not getting the attention it should – despite its role in Mesoamerica and possibly in the world. We have carefully taken you on a journey from the first settlement in the region to what we have in modern-day Central America.

We began our journey by tracing it from as far back as 8000 BCE, a period known as the Archaic period before the emergence of pottery. This was when humans relied more on wild animals for sustenance; a period when hunting was the main occupation of the people. This was also the time where the people were always on the move. They had no particular place they could call home. Their movement depended on several factors like climate change, the availability of wild animals, the status of their settlements, and many others.

For better understanding, we broke down the Archaic period into the following categories:

- Early Pre-Classic Period - 2000 to 1000 BCE
- Middle Pre-Classic - 1000 to 400 BCE
- Later/Terminal Pre-Classic Period - 100 to 250 BCE

Each of these periods is unique to the region because further developments took place in the people's lives and cultures. We started noticing some form of complexity in societies as the people started moving around within the region.

The early settlements show that people started transiting from hunting to farming, from travelers to temporary settlers, and eventually seasonal and permanent settlers. This period was unique in Mesoamerica because the people began showing more interest in farming, and the population started to expand and become even more complex.

We noticed how the people took shelter in various rock shelters across the region. An example of one of them is the El Gigante rock shelter. Other settlements took shape around coastal resources, which is again based on the resources available; remember, there and a move away from hunting into another form of feeding the population.

The more extended settlement later led to the need for more farmlands, which led to clearing the forest using various crude tools and farming methods. Notably, domestication started, and maize became the most valued farm produce in the region.

Artifacts found at several archaeological sites across the region revealed how the people managed themselves without metal resources. Stone tools were the predominant method used to achieve farming, hunting, and sculpturing.

Obsidian proved to be another invaluable resource for the Olmecs, playing a particular part in the people's lives by being used as a tool, objects in religious rituals, and later in trade.

We also took you on a ride around some important archaeological sites within the region while talking about their uniqueness, the artifacts found there, and what made them stand out. We discussed religion, the various gods they worshipped, and the relevance of some of their rituals.

Then we talked about the Olmec, how they were called the "people of the rubber nation," "the rubber people" – all because they were located at a primary source of rubber raw material. We dove into the controversy surrounding the Olmecs' origin, the different views expressed by several scholars, and the reasons behind their position. Some even later changed their original position to a newer version – thanks to new archeological discoveries!

However, one thing was clear and agreeable to all the scholars: the Olmecs were more advanced in civilization and general way of life than considered at first. We can thank them for many advances and contributions to our modern society, like writing and long-count calendars.

The Olmecs were predominantly farmers who relied on specific farm products like maize. They also developed a unique irrigation system that supplied water across the cities and made it possible for all-year-round farming. As seen in other parts of the region, the Obsidian played a unique role among the people alongside other luxury items from other parts of the region.

The Olmecs enjoyed trading with other parts of the region and beyond. Scholars have argued that these trade networks and relationships with other parts of the region were responsible for their peculiar advancement and the complex nature of their society.

The history of the Olmecs is incomplete without talking about the Colossal Heads. These were massive stones with human faces that had striking resemblances carved on them using only stone tools. Some of these stone heads weigh as much as 40 tons and stand taller than most humans when upright. You have to admire the expertise in carving these faces because it was not one face for all, but each stone head had different features. This master-crafting was also seen in other artifacts like pottery, idols, and other architectural monuments.

The Olmecs were the first to create a class among the people in lifestyles and living arrangements. The elites had separate quarters distinct from the lower classes. The elites controlled the lower classes with religion and created fear among them with human sacrifices. The royals were treated as gods, and their words were laws because it was assumed that the gods were speaking through them.

We also noticed how various Olmec centers started from San Lorenzo to La Venta and eventually Tres Zapotes. These cities attained great prominence with unique developments before they eventually fell, one after the other. Several reasons have been attributed to the fall of these great centers, but they are all mere suggestions; no concrete conclusion has been arrived at. This is also because the Olmec civilization itself is based on archaeological findings and not on texts.

La Venta was the other Olmec center that came to the limelight after the fall of San Lorenzo and was occupied for about 500-years; it was a much more complex society, with class separation into royals, elites, and the low class. The inequality in wealth and other social standing widened further. Some luxury items were meant only for the elite. The priests were treated as having control over life and death and even wielded some political powers. We also noticed how the economy of La Venta thrived based on its strategic location and the ecosystems nearby. While San Lorenzo was known for its Colossal Heads and other monuments, La Venta was known for its complexes, plazas, and platforms.

The Olmecs had good trading relationships with neighboring civilizations like the Mayans and the Aztecs; they also dominated a few cities. This was evident in Epi-Olmec Tres Zapotes, where the cities were not wholly an Olmec center. Still, some versions of Olmec civilization and culture were practiced among the people for many years. Some scholars had even said that the presence of the Olmecs in Tres Zapotes (and everything they brought along when they abandoned La Venta) was the reason why Tres Zapotes became the regions where cities were most inhabited – lasting more than 2000 years!

Tres Zapotec, as Epi-Olmec center, initially closed its borders and did not transact business with other parts of the region until it underwent another transition that changed everything, and business resumed again with neighbors and faraway partners.

We cannot forget the role the Mesoamerican ball game played among the Olmecs. During the high of San Lorenzo as the Olmec center, we saw how the ball game was used among different political entities to serve different purposes. For some, it was mere entertainment that fostered unity, especially among the elites and the lower classes. For others, the sport had far-reaching consequences like losing your limps and even being sacrificed! This ball game is still in existence today and is the oldest ball game in the world.

The writing system found at the Olmec sites is the oldest in the region and possibly globally; it is still being translated. The Mayans' writing system and long-count calendars – initially thought to be the oldest and most advanced – have been correctly traced to the

Olmecs.

You might call the Olmecs the oldest civilization in the Americas, and some might call them the *forgotten civilization.* However, history will not forget the role the Olmecs played in the history of the human race in general - and in the Americas specifically.

Part 4: The Toltec Civilization

An Enthralling Overview of the History of the Toltecs, Starting from the Classic Maya Period in Mesoamerica to the Rise of the Aztec Empire

Introduction

The Toltec Empire was a pre-Columbian Mesoamerican civilization that flourished in the 10th and 11th centuries in central Mexico. The Toltecs arrived in central Mexico from the northern deserts and dominated the region because of their artisanship and tactile warfare. The Toltecs were so fierce and respectable that the Aztecs claimed to have descended from them. Whether or not this claim is true is a contested topic among historians. The Aztecs admired the Toltecs for their art, architecture, and culture, most of which the Aztecs adopted in their cities and towns. The Aztecs also adopted the Toltec language, Nahuatl, and in the Aztec society, the word for Toltec came to mean "artisan."

Most of what we know about the Toltecs today has been passed down to us through the Aztecs. These accounts are shrouded in myth and regard the Toltec empire as the apex of culture, sophistication, and civilization. Historicists believe the Aztec accounts of the Toltecs, drawing parallels to the corresponding archaeological evidence to support their claims. On the other hand, anti-historicists claim Aztec stories about the Toltecs cannot be taken at face value since they hinder actual research into the origin and culture of the Toltec civilization.

In the 6th century, the religious city of Teotihuacán was ravaged, and most of its major monuments were burned to the ground. Teotihuacán was the grandest and most distinguished city of Mesoamerica in the Classic Era. At its peak, Teotihuacán was a striking wonder of architecture and design with a soaring population of around 200,000. Historians today believe that the Toltecs either burned and destroyed the revered ancient city or, at least, had a hand in its destruction. The fact that the Toltecs rose from the ashes of Teotihuacán makes this proposition even more appealing. Today, we do not remember the Toltecs as great innovators like their neighbors, the Zapotecs, neither do we remember them as scientific and mathematical prodigies like the classic-age Mayans. We remember them as fearsome warriors who waged war in the name of religion. They established a permanent standing army with different warrior castes. Disciplined, skillful, and highly trained, the Toltec army used forts, garrisons, supply depots, and reserve units. They extended their power throughout the region, conquering several kingdoms, states, towns, villages, and settlements.

The Aztecs also revered the Toltecs for their capital city of Tula. The city was an urban center for the community with prominent pyramids and a large square. The largest pyramid in the city was known as *the Pyramid of Quetzalcoatl.* Quetzalcoatl, or *"the serpent of precious feathers,"* is a mythic figure worshipped by the Aztecs and other Mesoamerican cultures. Historians believe that one of the plazas in Tula could host around 100,000 people. They think it was probably used for festivals and big events. The city also had two ball courts where people would play a form of a ball game that was ubiquitous throughout the Mesoamerican region.

Central America

At the beginning of the 10th century, the Toltecs started encroaching on Mayan territory. Mayans had their share of big cities like Tikal and Chichen Itza, whose respective populations far exceeded that of Tula in its heyday. The semi-mythical king, Kukulcan, conquered the Mayan-controlled Yucatán Peninsula. There is a large temple in the city of Chichen Itza in the Yucatán Peninsula that was built in honor of Kukulcan. In addition to the Kukulcan temple, El Castillo, historians and archaeologists have noticed striking similarities between the Pyramid of Quetzalcoatl and the Temple of Warriors at Chichen Itza. Considering how the Mayans were already under the influence of Teotihuacán for a long time, it stands to reason that the Toltecs likely inherited that position from the Teotihuacán. With their vast-reaching empire, the Toltecs controlled one of the largest Mesoamerican empires in history for a little less than a century. From 1018 to 1025, a great famine took over the land resulting in the demise of the Toltecs. Over the next century, the Toltec authority diminished as civil wars, religious disputes, uprisings, and famines ravaged the land. In 1122, Tula burned to the ground.

Experts have been debating the role of the Toltecs for a long time. Some argue that the Aztecs exaggerated the myth of the Toltec civilization. Others claim that despite mythical events, the accounts of the Aztecs have the ring of truth to them. Unfortunately, the Aztec emperor Itzcoatl burned down historical codices and paintings, and later, the Spanish looted, plundered, and destroyed most relics and works of art. Today, we have a very narrow understanding of the Toltecs as compared to the Aztecs, the Maya, and other Mesoamerican civilizations.

In this book, we will delve into the history of the Toltecs, including the civilizations that preceded and followed them. To grasp the influence of the Toltecs on Mesoamerican life, one must understand what was happening before the Toltecs arrived, what changes they brought about, and how it affected life after them. We will dissect the relationship between the Maya and the Toltecs and try to understand how the Toltecs shaped the Aztec way of life. We will also discuss the arts, weaponry, social life, and mythical rulers of this glorious civilization. Moreover, we will discuss the different theories regarding their emergence in the early 10th century and their eventual demise in the 11th century.

SECTION ONE:
THE CLASSIC MAYAN ERA
(250 BCE – 900 CE)

Chapter 1: The Great Mayan Cities

The Mayan civilization started developing in modern-day Guatemala, Belize, southeastern Mexico, west Honduras, and west El Salvador around 2000 BCE. This era is referred to as the Preclassic Period of the Maya – it continues up to 250. The Maya were not a common people but a collection of disparate settlements with similar cultures that developed in tandem with each other. The word "Maya" is used today largely as an umbrella term. These settlements did not call themselves Maya, nor did they identify themselves as a cohesive unit.

The first true civilization to appear in the Preclassic period was the Olmec. The Olmecs appeared around 1200 BCE in the modern-day tropical lowlands of the Gulf of Mexico. The major Mayan cities of Tikal, Calakmul, and Copán would develop to its southeast and carry the notable influence of the Olmec culture. The Olmecs were discovered by large sculptures of carved stone depicting their heads. Seventeen of these helmet-wearing heads have survived down the centuries. Four of those seventeen were found in the capital city La Venta, which was the cultural hub of the Olmec. The complex and developed architecture implies that it served as a center for the Olmec state. Nevertheless, the earliest known Olmec center was San Lorenzo. It was not until the decline of San Lorenzo that La Venta became the major center of Olmec activity.

In the Middle Preclassic Period – from 1000 BCE to 400 BCE – small villages grew and formed cities. In the Late Preclassic Period – ranging from 400 BCE-250 CE – large cities started appearing on the map. Several cities sprouted up in Petén Basin, a region located in southeastern Mexico and northern Guatemala. The city of El Mirador in Petén is widely regarded as one of the first capital cities of the Mayan civilization. Although the city had been around since the 6th century BCE, it reached its zenith in the 3rd century BCE. Another site that dominated through the Middle Preclassic Era was Nakbe that was closely connected to El Mirador. The Guatemalan Highlands, located in the south of Guatemala, was also home to different cities. One of the major cities of this region was Kaminaljuyu. After studying the remains, archaeologists think the Mayans created it before the end of the Preclassic Era in 250. Urban developments in nearby areas have hindered the ability of experts to estimate the size, scale, and political and economic significance of the city.

The Mayan civilization extended from 7000 BCE to 1524 CE, but it started to unlock its true potential in the 3rd century. The exponential evolution of the Mayan civilization started around 250, marking the beginning of the Classic Period of the Mayas. In the Classic Period, the Mayans developed a penchant for artistic and intellectual pursuits. They started to engage in large-level construction and started establishing large cities. Full of monumental architecture, sculpture, and art, these cities often contained 5,000 to 50,000 inhabitants. The greatest of these Mayan cities was Tikal, also known by its older name, *"Yax Mutal."* The city had been around since 300 BCE, but it truly came into its own after the collapse of the Preclassic period in which major cities like El Mirador and Kaminaljuyu were deserted and severely depopulated. The population of Tikal began to grow in the Preclassic Period and continued to grow rapidly through the Classic Period.

Tikal
https://unsplash.com/photos/dqtz7uLc2F4

While Tikal was finding its footing in the Early Classic Period, another city appeared in the Valley of Mexico known as Teotihuacán. The initial settlements in the area date as far back as the 6th century BCE. The settlements did not evolve into an urban phenomenon until the 2nd century BCE, when farmers working on the hillside started to migrate into the valley. In the 1st century BCE, Teotihuacán was turnings into a metropolitan unlike any other in Mesoamerica. From the 1st century to the 4th century, the city underwent a period of massive expansion and progress. From 350 to 650, the city witnessed its peak era, also known as the classical period of the Teotihuacán. During this time, the city's population skyrocketed to around 125,000, making it one of the biggest cities of the ancient world. Historians assume that the most imposing factor of the city's attraction was the religious sentiments attached to it. With great power comes great influence, and Teotihuacán was no exception to this rule. As the might of the city increased, it started influencing neighborly states and regions, including Tikal. Its influence might have extended to the city of Chichen Itza in the north.

The Maya capitals were usually surrounded by smaller cities that contributed to the wealth and prosperity of the entire kingdom. The kings preferred to work from and live in these capitals because of their proximity to other cities and their vast strategic relevance. Tikal was surrounded by many Maya cities and settlements, and Tikal's relationship with these states often varied.

Inscriptions detail relations with Uaxactun, Caracol, Naranjo, and especially Calakmul, with whom Tikal would go on to develop a fierce rivalry. But Tikal was a big city, and even though it had its share of squabbles with nearby states, it had also developed relations with faraway cities like Teotihuacán. Records show that Teotihuacán had embassies in Tikal in the 1ˢᵗ century, but it was not until the 4ᵗʰ century that the dealings between the two cities intensified.

In 378, Tikal came into direct contact with Teotihuacán – we do not know whether it was in the form of a direct invasion or intervention via puppet rulers, but from this point onward, we find that the foreigners exert a substantial impact on the arts, culture, rituals, and other social practices in Tikal. Under the hegemony of Teotihuacán, Tikal began to expand. In the 4ᵗʰ century BCE, Tikal conquered Uaxactun and allied with Kaminaljuyu, increasing its access to the major trade routes in the region. In 426, Tikal's ever-expansive regime also enveloped Copán, an agricultural site that had become a city of obvious geographical importance. In the same year, the Tikal-Copán alliance founded the site of Quiriguá near Copán. Tikal sponsored the dynastic rise of Copán, and the remains of the site imply characteristics of Teotihuacán.

Around this time, another city named Calakmul was at the forefront of Mayan glory. Calakmul was a major state in the north of the Petén region that had access to trade networks with cities like El Mirador, Nakbe, and El Tintal. The city dates to the Preclassic Period, but it turned into a major Maya power in the Classic Era. Tikal and Calakmul were superpowers in their own right – and as is the case with superpowers, only one could come out on top. Hence began an immense competition and rivalry between the two city-states. Both cities established their networks of allied cities and engaged in a series of wars known as the Tikal-Calakmul Wars.

550 marks the beginning of the Late Classic Era of the Mayan civilization. Researchers estimate Calakmul's peak population in this era reached 50,000, and its authority over land extended as far as 150 km; it covered an area of roughly 70 square km. Much like Tikal, Calakmul had secondary cities around it that contributed to its growth and population. The cities of Naachtun, Oxpemul, Uxul, Sasilha, and La Muñeca had a combined population of

around 200,000. Despite all this, Calakmul was the inferior city since the grandiose Tikal was home to around half a million people at the time. The first war ran its course from 537 to 572. Calakmul conquered a major city called Yaxchilan and continued to ally itself with states that were against the rule of Tikal. In 562, Tikal won a short-lived victory in the city-state of Caracol, an ally of Calakmul. But it was not to be as Caracol and Calakmul soon turned the tables and defeated Tikal. This initiated a long hibernation period for Tikal, also known as the "Tikal hiatus," during which the city went through a major lapse in urban and commercial progression.

Tikal's influence in the region plummeted, and the opposing forces may have forcibly removed most of its population. In the following years, Calakmul gained the upper hand in the region, but not for long. Tikal's influence had lessened, but it had not diminished. Over the next 100 years, Tikal and Calakmul engaged in a cold war. Tikal continued to defeat its local rivals, some of whom had helped Calakmul in the first war.

In 629, Tikal founded a military outpost, Dos Pilas, to control trade routes along the Pasión River located in the northern lowlands of Guatemala. In 648, Dos Pilas aligned with Calakmul, started a proxy-war against Tikal, and consequently gave rise to the Second War between the two Mayan superpowers. In 672, Tikal attacked and captured Dos Pilas. The exiled leader of Dos Pilas retaliated and captured a Tikal lord in 679, giving Calakmul a temporary foothold in the region. From 692 to 695, Calakmul dominated Tikal when by a twist of fate, Tikal turned the tables by winning a major battle against Calakmul. The war continued until 705, when Tikal was defeated once again and Dos Pilas started to come into its own.

In the meantime, the city of Teotihuacán witnessed a major decline. Initially, archaeologists thought that invaders razed and burnt it to the ground. However, historians in recent times have pointed out that the burning was restricted to elite structures, hypothesizing that the city might have gone through a class conflict that resulted in a violent uprising. This theory carries a lot of weight as the timeframe coincides with the extreme climate change in the Northern Hemisphere in 535 and 536. Several other Mayan cities will undergo the same fate in the Classic Maya Collapse of the 8th and 9th centuries. From the ashes of Teotihuacán rose the Toltec empire, but we will get to that in due time.

Even after the fall of Teotihuacán, Tikal continued its tradition of impressive architecture and culture, but things were not looking well on other fronts. Quiriguá, which existed as an extension and a vassal of Copán, declared independence and shifted its allegiance to Calakmul in 738. This era marks the Third War between the two city-states. Copán wanted to retaliate against the smaller state but was probably afraid of Calakmul's military intervention. In one fell swoop, Calakmul managed to weaken an ally of Tikal and gained a small vassal state in return. The terms favored Quiriguá as well because it was quite far away from Calakmul and did not have to fear a complete usurpation. Tikal took over two major allies of Calakmul, El Peru, and Naranjo, in 743 and 744, respectively. Calakmul's influence in the region waned significantly as it lost control of its extensive trade network, vassals, and allies. Despite having emerged victorious, Tikal was in bad shape as well.

In the mid-8th century, we arrive at the Classic Maya collapse, also known as the Terminal Classic Era of the Mayans. In this period, populations started to decrease throughout the land, and major cities were deserted. Cities like Copán, Tikal, and Calakmul went into decline, both economically and politically. Archaeologists notice a decrease in large-scale architectural construction during this period and a cessation of inscriptions detailing crucial events. This sudden collapse is a strange archaeological mystery that is yet to be solved. The last record of a reign in Copán refers to 763. Similarly, monuments were raised in Calakmul in 790, 800, and 810, but little activity is recorded after that. From this point onward, the state's vassals started to erect their monuments, signaling a relocation of population and authority. Several theories exist to explain the collapse of the Mayan civilization, including epidemics, droughts, foreign invasions, internal religious and political squabbles, uprisings, and ecological collapse. All these theories try to understand how the collapse came about, but it is important to note that the Maya continued to exist and even flourish after their Classic Era. However, the civilization returned to numerous highs over the years, the glory of the Classic Era never returned.

After reading about a "lost city" in the writings of John Lloyd

Stephens and his illustrator Frederick Catherwood, the commissioner and the governor of Petén visited the site of Tikal in the mid-19th century. It soon became a center of interest for archaeologists around the world. Nevertheless, it was not a discovery for the locals residing alongside the ancient city for centuries. Today, the Tikal site consists of approximately 3000 structures, including tall temples, nine plazas and courts, palaces, a market complex, ten reservoirs, and a unique ball court, all connected by causeways. Looking at Tikal and other Maya cities of the ancient world, we realize that the cities span outward – haphazardly and without a grid structure. By studying their location, it is clear that major cities were positioned to aid trade and provide benefits of a tactile nature. Cities with favorable food production and trade routes would naturally expand into capital states.

Chapter 2: Mayan Social Life and Economy

As discussed before, historians categorize ancient Mayan life into three major epochs: the Preclassic Period, the Classic Period, and the Postclassic Period. The Preclassic Period extends from 2000 BCE to 250 CE and charts the rise of the Mayan empire from humble settlements to magnanimous metropolitans. It is unclear how long the Mayans had inhabited the Mesoamerican land, but we do know that before 2000 BCE, the Mayans were purely hunters. Somewhere around the 2000 BCE mark, they introduced an agrarian element to their hunter-gatherer lifestyle. One of the first crops they learned to grow was corn, which soon became the staple crop of the region. They also learned to farm beans, chilies, tomatoes, squash, and cocoa during the Preclassic Period. Evidence suggests that cocoa may have been used as an alcoholic beverage since the 15th century BCE. Despite cultivating food, their diet mainly consisted of gathered edibles and meat from fish and land animals.

The Olmecs were the first to develop a system of writing, although it was not as legible or complete as the later scripts and hieroglyphics in Mayan chronology. They also developed urban environments with different rituals and practices like ballgames, chocolate drinking, and jaguar worship. They envied jade and developed trade routes across the land to obtain it. This trade network connected different regions and states and would keep expanding through the Classic Period. Trade routes also help spread the cultural features of the Olmecs throughout Mesoamerica.

From the 10th century BCE to the 4th century BCE, agricultural life became increasingly complex. Canals and irrigation systems that required coordinated human effort started appearing. The Olmecs erected statues and monuments, constructed causeways, and adopted corn as a crucial diet component. At the end of the Preclassic Period, the states of Kaminaljuyu and El Mirador emerged, and the Mayan way of life started to take form.

In the Classic Period, the Maya established an agricultural base for their economy. In Mesoamerica, agriculture used to be and still is a challenging endeavor. The condition of the soil is unsavory, and there is an apparent lack of usable land. In any case, agriculture is a risky venture anywhere in the world, and throughout history, various civilizations have applied different techniques to alleviate the risks. For instance, in medieval times, European farmers used scattered strips of land to alleviate risks and make up for potential losses. Most Mesoamerican civilizations countered this issue by switching between different strips of land during various seasons, allowing them to adapt to the low-nutrient soil. The Maya, like the Olmecs before them and the Aztecs after them, cultivated corn, beans, and squash in conjunction. The corn sucks nitrogen out of the soil, and the beans help rejuvenate it. Some historians hint at soil erosion as one of the major causes for the collapse of Teotihuacán. To avoid falling prey to this catastrophe, the Maya grew most of their food products in forest gardens known as "pet kot." The Maya created raised fields and terraces – large sections of receding flatlands on a sloped plane. The Maya connected raised fields by canals, giving birth to a sophisticated irrigation system on farming lands. Terracing with proper irrigation prevents the depletion of nutrients. The Mayan diet consisted primarily of corn, fish, honey, beans, turkey, vegetables, and chocolate drinks. In addition to agriculture, they obtained food from foraging and hunting.

Despite having grown with squash and beans, maize was the signature crop. The Mayan story of human creation talks about gods who created humans from yellow and white corn. These ideas were in keeping with the pantheon of animal gods that the Olmecs worshipped. The ceremonial centers, temples, pyramids, and plazas emphasize the rigorous religious sentiment in Mayan communities. The construction of stone structures, mostly religious ones, was a source of attraction and often contributed to the appeal of a metropolitan. The city of Teotihuacán started as a religious center and then turned into one of the biggest cities in Mesoamerican history.

The advent of urban centers allowed the Mayans to make serious headway in the fields of mathematics and astronomy. They invented the concept of zero: a representation of a non-entity that helped them solve difficult problems. They created a complex calendar that facilitated agricultural produce over multiple cycles. The Mayans also developed a sophisticated writing system that was far more comprehensive than the Olmec one. They used the inner bark of fig trees to make paper and wrote hieroglyphs in extensive codices. They had inherited their love of sculpture from the Olmecs and fondly inscribed on stone and reliefs. Most of what we know about the Mayans comes from these hieroglyphic accounts on pottery, stone slabs, and structures. These accounts reveal that while Mayans were mostly farmers, they had their fair share of violence and conflict as well. Uprisings were quite common, and city-states often engaged in battles to usurp control of the region.

As far back as the Preclassic Era, the Mayan society had a radical divide between the elite and commoners. With time, the Mayan society became more complex and sophisticated by specialization and division of labor. These distinctions also streamlined the political and social hegemony. As small rural communities turned into small cities and small cities turned into staples of dazzling architecture and culture, the interaction of political and prestigious classes blossomed into a unique nexus. The wealthy factions turned into clans and nobilities. The Maya aristocracy resided in the cultural hub. One would find the most profound and extraordinary artistic statements in this area: glamorous buildings, divine inscriptions, and beautiful sculptures.

The highest authority belonged to the king and court. The king used to be the ultimate supreme leader – a semi-divine figure worthy of mythical lore. The king acted as the middle ground between the realm of the mortals and the realm of the gods, and the masses often identified him with the maize god. The idea gains more credibility when one looks at the semi-mythical emperor Kukulcan who eventually became the feathered serpent god in the religion and mythology of the Yucatec Maya. Kukulcan is sometimes associated with the Aztec god Quetzalcoatl, and some historians believe that the two are the same deity.

The Maya civilization was a patrilineal society, meaning that the power passed from a king to his son. Typically, the eldest son would take over the king's duties, but this was not always the case. The successor had to meet certain criteria to ascend to the throne. The potential king must have possessed great military and tactical skills since the unstable Mayan terrain often called for kings to engage in battles. The coronation of the new king usually calls for a highly sophisticated ceremony – in this respect, the Maya were not different. The kings inaugurated their reign by sitting on a jaguar-skin cushion, holding a scepter, and wearing a jade headband and a headdress made of quetzal feathers. A king would bypass his son in favor of his queen if the sanctity of the nation were at stake. Quite similar to modern times, the transition of power needed to be peaceful, and the king and the nobility would elaborate before making a decision.

Not based on a bureaucratic or even a democratic model, the Mayan political structure was purely hierarchical. Different polities formed different royal courts, each catering to its own needs. Noble titles were restricted to these royal courts and the aristocracy. The aristocrats usually sponsored the court officials, and while all these nobles had a considerable say in the matters of state, the most notable authority was that of the "divine lord." Nevertheless, the sociological and political impact of the aristocracy increased as the Maya population witnessed significant growth from the Early and Middle Classic Periods to the Late Classic Period. With expansion and diversification, especially during the Classic Era, other factions like the priesthood and warrior classes also rose to prominence. Differences between these various classes often led to compromises – dynamic political institutions were formed to alleviate the situation, and disagreements were resolved in public settings where the Maya performed their usual rituals of dance and human sacrifice.

By the Late Classic Era, the title of the divine lord had lost some of its prestige. The Maya referred to the members of the ruling class as "ajaw" and the divine lord as the "k'uhul ajaw." The hieroglyphic inscriptions associate ajaw and other royal titleholders with certain city structures. Another title for the royal bloodline was "kalomte," but that was given only to the most formidable and commanding emperors. The kalomte would command the ajaw who, in turn, commanded "sajal," an official in charge of a small site of military importance. A sajal could be a regional governor or a war captain in charge of prisoners of war.

Like any society, the largest sector of the population comprised of commoners who made up around ninety percent of the entire Mayan population. The commoners formed the backbone of the Mayan economy. They cultivated various edible foods, engaged in trade and commerce across different cities, interacted with each other in marketplaces in big cities, and created some of the most unique luxury items and jewelry. Yet, very little is known about them. There are little to no remains of civilian houses – time, natural catastrophes, and ecological damage have had their way to them. The king, nobility, and aristocracy bankrolled artists and other individuals of cultural importance. Anyone who was not of noble birth was considered a commoner, so it is unsurprising that they do not feature in the inscriptions, hieroglyphs, or artwork.

The major source of Mayan economic activity was agriculture, raw goods, and trade. They used to extract raw materials like jade, wood, gold, and copper from the terrain. They used these and other raw materials to manufacture clothing, weapons, paper, furniture, codices, and luxury items. The artisans and workers made up a strong middle class that produced commodities and exotic goods. The most valued commodities were salt as it helped in the preservation of food, cocoa since the Maya were fond of drinking it and valued it immensely, and metals like jade and obsidian for their obvious economic value. The most skilled mathematicians, artists, and artisans would bypass this chain of command and sell their services separately. The Maya relied on the knowledge of astronomers, architects, scribes, sculptors, artists, mathematicians, and farming experts. They even had a service sector where experts in specialized fields would sell their services.

An educated merchant governor used to direct regional trade by assessing the production and supply of the goods. Atop the middle-class structure sat advisors of varying knowledge and skill. The advisory board was responsible for maintaining trade and, consequently, stable relations between different states. By ensuring supervision across all strands of the middle and lower classes, the Maya had developed a highly urbanized society with varying modes of integration.

The small towns kept to themselves, rarely engaging in long-distance trade – if ever –, relying heavily on the local exchange. Even the most efficient and capable households depended on local exchange for essential items. With time, smaller settlements began to specialize in specific goods and services. In the Classic Period, the cities grew tenfold, and trade between different cities and realms became quite common, providing a boost to the smaller villages and towns. Smaller villages became a part of the trade routes, and as such, started to witness more activity. Traders needed to stop and rest, and small villages provided a welcome change from the harshness of the routes. This helped invigorate the economy of small towns, and the Mayan society soon turned into a highly integrated trading empire.

The Maya used a basic barter system for the exchange of goods. During the Postclassic Era, cocoa beans were widely used in everyday deals. Since most Mesoamerican civilizations valued jade, gold, and copper highly, they were utilized for expensive purchases and large orders. As the Maya lifestyle based on local and foreign exchange gained traction, the trading network extended beyond Mayan territory and throughout all of Mesoamerica.

Chapter 3: Great Monuments of the Maya

A mere glance at Tikal serves as a gentle reminder of how architecturally advanced the Mayans were. After defeating the neighboring state of Calakmul, the people of Tikal ushered into a prolific period of planning and building gigantic structures and astonishing monuments. During this time, the city's inhabitants erected Temples I and II. Like most Mayan cities, the inhabitants of Tikal abandoned their ascending pyramids and statuesque structures after the decline. Over the years, the forests hid the foundations of these structures underneath their quiet shelter, away from prying eyes. In 1839, John Lloyd Stephens, accompanied by Frederick Catherwood, arrived in Central America. Passing through a harsh landscape – thanks to civil war, political instability, and strife – they finally arrived at a marvelous carved stone slab. As they proceeded with their expedition in and around the area, they stumbled upon more stairways, agricultural terraces, and stone walls. It caught the interest of various scholars, and several researchers and travelers started traveling to Central America.

The remains of Tikal boast more than 3000 structures, including enormous palaces and soaring temples connected by causeways. The structures were erected with the extensive use of limestone, and their design depicts the influence of Teotihuacán. The city also housed ball courts for playing Mesoamerican ballgame, smaller pyramids, platforms, stone monuments, administrative buildings, a market complex, reservoirs, and residences. The large structures portray the trademark features of Maya art and architecture: stepped pyramids, raised platforms, and long staircases accompanied by vaulted chambers and images of gods. The Great Plaza lies in the middle of the city, shielded by a temple on the east and another on the west. The North and Central Acropolis feature on the other two sides of the plaza. Built approximately in the 4th century, the Great Plaza and the North Acropolis have captured the imagination of researchers for quite a long time. A major reason for the scholarly interest is the navigational complexity of the two structures. Both the Great Plaza and the North Acropolis were built along a north-south axis, serving as evidence of the Maya's acclaimed knowledge of astronomy. Contrary to these two structures, Temples I and II, built in the Late Classic Era, stand across an east-west axis. The temples stood at impressive heights of 47 and 38 meters, respectively.

Temples I and II are just two temples in a group of six prominent pyramids with temples. The pyramids, titled Temples I-VI, all feature at least one large stairway and contain temples on their respective summits. These six temples were erected in the 8th and 9th centuries. The roof comb of Temple I was adorned with a giant sculpture of a Maya king. The temple contained a large collection of inscribed objects such as bone tubes and strips depicting humans as well as the ancient Mayan deities. The site also had jade ornaments and ceramic vessels. The doorways of Temples I and II are spanned by partially carved wooden lintels. The Temple III, known as the "Temple of the Jaguar Priest," has a height of 55 meters and boasts drawings of deities and rituals. Temple IV is the tallest structure of the family and stands at a whopping height of 70 meters. Although a couple of other structures may have been taller in their heyday, it is the largest existing Mayan structure and the second-largest existing pre-Columbian structure in the New World. Fifty-seven meters tall, Temple V is the second largest structure of Tikal. Finally, Temple VI stands at a modest 12 meters and is known as the "Temple of the Inscriptions" on account of having a lengthy hieroglyphic text on the back and sides of its roof comb. The hieroglyphics narrate the history of Tikal, starting from Preclassic Times in 1139 BCE.

All the great Mayan rulers dwelled in the five-story royal palace in the Great Plaza. It has enclosed courtyards for bloodletting and sacrificial ceremonies as well as spacious galleries. The North Acropolis contains temples built on two flat surfaces. It served as a funerary complex and as a burial ground for the nobility. The structure was vertically extended, and additional temples were added on top of the old structure for every subsequent royal burial. Just like the North Acropolis, there is also a South Acropolis to the southwest of the Great Plaza. To the west of the South Acropolis lie the architectural group of "Mundo Perdido," or the "lost world." The Mundo Perdido is situated alongside the Plaza of the Seven Temples and is home to the largest ceremonial complex in the entire city. Embellished with stucco masks of the Sun god, the Lost World Pyramid is the largest in Mundo Perdido and was probably built in the Late Preclassic times. The complex dates to the Preclassic Era and has been reconstructed many times.

As much as the glorious structures of the ancient Maya seduce us today, the tale of the ancient Maya was much more alluring before John Lloyd Stephens stumbled upon the ancient ruins in the 19th century. The Mayan legend fascinated scientists, archaeologists, and historians for centuries. The daring individuals who ventured into Central America in search of Mayan relics and lost cities had to rely on, more than anything else, sheer luck. It was difficult to approach the area with adequate preparation and knowledge because the Western world had just heard myths and stories. Although the Mayan civilization was merely a curiosity for the North Americans and Europeans, it was an absolute material reality for the local populations of Central and South America. Various populations in Guatemala, Belize, Peru, and Mexico had been living alongside these ruins for centuries. For them, the tall structures sticking out of canopies and forests were not the remnants of a lost civilization but the sign and heritage of their ancestors. The enchanting lore of the great Mayan empire implies that they were a lost civilization when in fact, the Maya continue to live to this day. Almost six million Mayans exist today in Mexico, Peru, and other parts of the continent.

For decades following the watershed expedition, researchers used the old-fashioned way of discovering ancient structures, both in the Yucatán Peninsula and in the south. They traversed by foot, kept an eye out for ruins, and if luck was on their side, they would stumble upon a majestic structure. In recent times, this approach has become obsolete with the advent of LIDAR technology. LIDAR, which stands for "Light and Distance Ranging," is a mapping technology that measures and maps different ranges on a terrain. The LIDAR-equipped aircraft fly over the forests and map the land, revealing the hidden secrets beneath. It has helped researchers find the largest Preclassic Mayan ruin located in Tabasco, known as "Aguada Fénix." It is the oldest and largest ceremonial Maya site known to modern man.

Another example is the Maya village of Kiuic, situated in the Yucatán region. The site of Kiuic reveals a large royal palace built atop the remains of a smaller pyramid. Intellectuals think that building on top of a pre-existing structure was a way of legitimizing power. Near the site of Kiuic, archaeologists have found multiple structures, implying that a bigger population traveled to and settled in the region during the Classic Era. The region under discussion has no natural water sources, so the Maya built underground cisterns, called chultuns, for capturing and storing rainwater over long periods. The Maya would form underground chambers and cover them with stucco. Interestingly, the rooftops and plazas of the large pyramid structures were used to capture the rainwater. Made mostly from stone, the magnificent pyramid structures mirror the religious hegemony of the Mayan religion. Some historians associate the pyramids' design – starting with a broad surface and becoming more and more exclusive as it goes up – as a subconscious response to the religious, political, and economic class divide. There is a consensus among archaeologists that the pyramidal structure was a reflection of the sacred caves where the Maya went for worship and other religious purposes. If one looks at the Temple of the Inscriptions in Palenque, the largest pyramid at the site of Palenque – not to be confused with Temple VI of Tikal that is also referred by that name – one finds that its staircase is built beside a nine-chambered platform. The nine chambers represent the nine levels of Xibalba, the Mayan underworld. Nevertheless, it is apparent that the Maya also knew how to adapt the urban design to serve their religious and practical needs.

Researchers denote some Mayan structures as e-groups. An e-group is a stepped pyramid structure built on a west-facing platform. A raised and elongated structure usually exists on the eastern side with a staircase. The staircases were decorated with stucco and exhibit panels of great art. These structures and their parent platform usually stand with the pinpoint precision of astronomical proportions, leading scholars to believe that astronomers used them as observatories. The e-groups gave rise to another prominent architectural group known as the triadic pyramids. Inspired by e-groups, the triadic pyramids would have an elevated platform with a staircase and two structures facing inwards on both sides of the surface. These complexes are mostly oriented towards the west, but in rare cases, they utilize the north-south axis as well. Triadic pyramids are common in the Petén region, especially in Nakbe, where there are more than a dozen of them.

Situated near Kiuic is a prominent city of the ancient Maya: Uxmal. Uxmal is one of the most majestic architectural statements of the Yucatán region. Here, the four extraneous structures of the Nunnery Quadrangle, with surrounding courtyards and small walls, depict several religious events and entities, including the feathered serpent known as Quetzalcoatl. The structure was constructed as a temple with thirteen doorways in the north building and nine in the south building. The thirteen doorways in the north building represent the levels of the Maya heaven, whereas the nine doorways in the south building mirror the nine levels of the Maya underworld. These four buildings are a perfect representation of the Puuc style of architecture. The Puuc style emanated from the Late Classic era but reached its pinnacle after it, during the Terminal Classic Era. Uxmal also has the House of the Pigeons for ritual and ceremonial purposes and a 24-room House of the Governor that was built in the 10th century.

Another important city of the Yucatán region was Chichen Itza, where archaeologists have found a building believed to be an astronomical observatory. As mentioned before, the Mayans had developed a calendar. In Chichen Itza, one can find an obvious example of how they incorporated their astronomical findings into structural design. An astounding 25-meter pyramid in the city, which the Spanish called "El Castillo," has 365 steps. Another indicator of their mathematical and astronomical prowess is that the shadow falls on the steps of El Castillo on the spring and autumn equinoxes.

The Maya were disciplined in how the city developed its communes over time. They designated different districts to maintain some semblance of the status quo. The Maya integrated their local landscape's topography into their city planning schemes. Some cities were built on top of limestone plains, allowing them to expand towards the horizon, while others were built in the hills, making it easier to construct tall temples and palaces. As cities would grow, the astronomers would decide on an axis based on the region's topography. Then, they would build monumental plazas and palaces according to the predetermined alignment. These religious and governmental structures constituted the heart of the ancient Maya cities. Large causeways connected these monuments across the city. Alongside the larger structures, they established platforms for hosting secondary structures. Outside the vibrant cultural hubs, there were smaller temples and shrines. However, like any civilization, they had their share of oversights. For instance, experts find no signs of advanced city planning in the Yucatán. There is no apparent grid structure, and cities appear to have expanded haphazardly. This is in stark contrast to other Mesoamerican cities like Teotihuacán that rigidly followed grid plans.

Chapter 4: Mayan Sciences, Religion, and Language

The most fascinating aspect of pre-Columbian New World civilizations is that they evolved right beside the Old World without any contact. Therefore, their alternative timeline presents an interesting challenge to our understanding of how human cultures have progressed over the centuries. Just as there is some resemblance between ancient cultures of the New World and the Old World, there are also vast differences between them. For example, for quite some time, humans have looked back at the invention of the wheel as a landmark achievement in ancient history. Yet, the Maya were completely oblivious to the practical uses of the wheel. They understood the concept, as many artifacts show, but did not put it to good use. Excavated toys and other small devices contain wheels, but no evidence points to the everyday use of wheels. Metal was another inessential tool for the Maya, and they managed to pull off feats of technology and construction without it. Similarly, if one were to invert perspectives, many inventions that were central to the Mesoamerican way of life were absent from Europe, Africa, and Asia.

The Maya used mica for creating a rainbow of glittery paints and developed complex looms for weaving cloth – the former has tons of technological uses today, and the latter is a common item. Research reveals that the Maya were building vulcanized rubber products as well. Comparing the progression of the New World and the Old World might seem like comparing apples and oranges, but the acute observer will find a horde of similarities between the two. The spread and establishment of religious ideas follow parallel trajectories. On both sides of the Pacific, religion has worked as an effective sociological instrument. It has been a productive ideology for bringing communities together and giving a common purpose to the masses. On both sides, superstition and tradition prevailed over logic and reason. Comprehensive languages and scripts were devised to counter this deficiency and to improve effective communication.

How much mathematical and scientific knowledge did the Maya have? How did interpret the world in a religious and spiritual framework? What languages did they speak? Are there any comparisons to be drawn with other cultures?

The Mayan understanding of science and mathematics was closely linked with astronomy since they believed the cosmos had a direct impact on their daily life. The activity of stargazing had such a strong social presence that it found its way into their religion. As mentioned before, the Maya had a strong grasp of the subject, exemplified by the different calendars that were in common use. They could calculate equinoxes and solstices and incorporated this data into their monuments. They also used the astronomical cycles to keep track of planting and harvesting cycles. This remarkable feat is rendered even more impressive when one realizes that they did so without the use of any complex equipment like telescopes. They used to sit in their observatories and stare at the sky.

The Maya used two overlapping calendars in conjunction with each other, collectively known as the "Calendar Round." Many communities across the Guatemalan Highlands used the Calendar Round and continue to do so. The first calendar, Tzolk'in, translated as "division of days," was a 260-day sacred cycle that dictated religious and ritualistic ceremonies. Today, different tribes use different names for the calendar, including "the sense of the day" and "the organization of time," but nobody knows the ancient name. The second calendar, Haab', was a secular calendar of 365 days, representing the solar year. The Mayan calculations were more precise than the Spanish who arrived in the New World. The Calendar Round completes one iteration after 52 cycles of

Haab'.

The tzolk'in calendar developed a significant presence throughout Mesoamerica and can be traced back to the Olmecs and the Zapotecs. Different theories have tried to explain the calendar's origins. One theory draws the reader's attention towards the Mayan numeral system, which has a base of 20, and the Mayan heavens or the upper world, which contains 13 levels. Another theory postulates that the system is closely linked to the middle world or Earth and is in keeping with the period of human gestation. So, the calendar was devised to help midwives keep track of birth cycles. Others maintain that the calendar is highly attuned to the Guatemalan climate and was probably created to track agricultural cycles.

Tzolk'in contains two cycles: the name of the day and a number. There are twenty individual days, and each repetition of the day is numbered from one to thirteen. Each day has an association with events and omens. One day symbolizes death, another is associated with maize and symbolizes abundance, and so on. Tzolk'in was an eminent part of the day-to-day routine of the Maya, and as such, it frequently appears in different codices and inscriptions. They used tzolk'in for various purposes like maize cultivation, setting wedding dates, and associating personality traits according to birthdays.

On the other hand, Haab' consists of eighteen months of twenty days with a final stretch of five days. A date on the calendar consists of the numbered day of the month followed by the name of the month. The last five days of the year, called Wayeb', mark a dangerous and unlucky time for the Maya people. During this time, the portals between the Mayan underworld and the middle world open up, inviting a host of evil spirits and energies. To fight against these misfortunes, the Maya held special rituals and often stay inside and wash their hair until the year is over.

To know the date on the Calendar Round, one needs to know four factors: the day and number in tzolk'in and the numbered day and month in Haab'. The Calendar Round measured time in a loop that would repeat every 52 years. Every date would recur in 52 years, making it impossible to create an absolute chronology of events. To get rid of this issue, a Mayan priest devised another system called the "Long Count" in the 3rd century BCE. The Long Count identified each day against a fixed date in the past. Scholars think the base date is August 11th, 3114 BCE. This date holds tremendous religious value for the Mayan people since it is the presumed date of the Mayan creation. The Long Count groups different sets to tell the date: *baktun* means 144,000 days, *k'atun* means 7,200 days, *tun* means 360 days, *winal* means 20 days, and *kin* means one day. Whenever the Mayans needed to recall an event that did not occur in the same Calendar Round cycle, they would refer to the Long Count. In addition to being inclusive of earlier dates, it was also more legible and concise, making it the format of choice for monuments. The Mayans also used an abbreviated form of Long Count called the "Short Count." The Long Count worked quite similarly to the Calendar Round, but its largest interval, the "Grand Cycle," was much longer – 13 baktuns or 5,139 solar years, to be precise.

The Maya had a penchant for tradition and stories, as epitomized by the religious hierarchy and the disciplined social conduct based on their calendars. While the Maya religion is a belief system, it is, in turn, a part of the larger Maya custom and heritage. These traditions accumulated over multiple centuries, and the belief system accommodated them accordingly. One of these practices is the association of landmarks with religious sentiments. Some communities assigned specific days and dates with certain shrines and mountains, indicating the best time for worshipping there. Most of the rituals would take place near, on, or inside the sacred landmarks. The calendars, cosmology, and geography were used to determine the spiritual importance of each landmark.

The oral transition of rituals from one generation to another depended on the propagation of adventurous tales, which required storytellers. To ensure a fluid flow, a doctrine was established. Individuals could enter the priesthood and other religious orders after rigorous training and evaluation. At the temple of Uxmal, one image of the feathered serpent swallows an individual, and another spits it out. Scholars believe this represents an initiation ritual of the Uxmal Maya where an individual would undergo the most humiliating and meticulous test. The priests would sequester the individual and impose exercises of self-mortification and bloodletting. The corresponding artwork shows individuals piercing their genitals and other body parts. Elsewhere, the Maya usually conducted their priestly initiations inside caves or at other landmarks.

Offerings and other contractual rituals followed strict guidelines, as they were believed to be a connection to the other worlds. The offerings to deities could range from crops like maize, cacao drinks, and honey liquor to pottery, jewelry, animals, and even humans. They also buried sacrificial artifacts and items under floors and altars, but these were not "offerings" in the theological sense of the word. Some Maya buried the bones of their ancestors under their house as a way of showing gratitude and warding off evil spirits. The sacrifices either marked a yearly offering or served as a specific prayer – the Maya often prayed for rain or the end of a drought.

The religious functionaries were tasked with the duties of praying and carrying out sacrifices on behalf of royalty, pure lineages, and the community as a whole. The Maya considered their caves to be the most enlightening and sacred landmarks. The study of these caves reveals some of the earliest Maya art and gives insight into many of their religious habits. Archaeologists have found several signs of shamanism in these caves, implying that the priests made contact with the other world by consuming hallucinogenic substances as part of a cult-like ritual.

Most of what we know about the Maya priesthood today comes from the accounts of Spanish missionaries and the codices that survived the Spanish invasion. Coupled with a large number of inscriptions, these codices have allowed researchers to discern a lot of information about the languages and writing scripts of the ancient Maya. The Maya writing system was a remarkable achievement of pre-Columbian Mesoamerica. There had been several writing systems in Mesoamerica, but none of them were as efficient and complete as the Mayan system. The Olmecs and the Zapotecs were the earliest civilization to develop their scripts, beating the other cultures by a few centuries.

The Mayan writing system was probably preceded by proto-Mayan, a combination of different local languages, including the Olmec language. The earliest examples of the Mayan writing system and its variants date back to the 3rd century BCE. During the Classic period, the Mayan language branched out into two major variants or dialects based on location: the Yucatán Peninsula in the north and Petén Basin in the south. In the 3rd century, the Mayan script started to come into its own and assumed a formal and consistent form. Despite the regional shift, both variants are referred to as the "Classic Maya language" since most Mayan inscriptions, whether in the north or the south, were written in this era and had similarities and overlapping modes and styles.

The Maya script remained in use until the arrival of the Europeans. The Maya used to write on stone monuments, lintels, ceramics, stelae, and most importantly, paper produced from tree bark – the paper was used to assemble codices. Three Mayan codices have been preserved in their original form; others have been partially damaged or lost. These include the Dresden Codex, the Madrid Codex, and the Paris Codex. A fourth codex, the Grolier Codex, belongs to Toltec-Maya rather than the Maya. Including the inscribed monuments, pottery, and codices, archaeologists have recovered more than 10,000 individual texts to date.

The Mayan writing system has a logosyllabic script composed of individual glyphs connected in succession to form a glyph block. The glyph blocks usually consist of the main signs and corresponding affixes. The main signs can be abstract or material: it can be the image of the described noun or a signal for something a little complex. On the other hand, the affixes hint at the speech elements. The Maya commoners were largely illiterate, and cities and communities had scribes who were responsible for writing during working hours. They charged hefty fees for their services and usually belonged to elite families. Excavations have revealed some writing supplements. In particular, a sculpture in Copán shows scribes with inkpots. Other representations depict women scribes, implying that women participated in art and calligraphy.

The confusing aspect of the term "Maya" is that it does not correspond to any single culture; rather, it combines multiple Mesoamerican cultures with overarching similarities. The northern Maya evolved quite differently from the southern ones, language and all, despite stemming from the same metaphorical well. Ascertaining how much the dialects varied might be a tad too difficult, but as far as written language is concerned, the Maya had a relatively consistent style with subtle variations that stretched all over the region.

SECTION TWO: THE TOLTECS (674 CE – 1122 CE)

Chapter 5: Chichen Itza and the Toltec Connection

The southern Maya had a different route to regional ascendancy than their northern contemporaries. In the Late Classic Period, Chichen Itza became the primary state of the northern Maya. Located in the east of the Yucatán Peninsula, the site is home to one of the new Seven Wonders of the World: El Castillo. El Castillo is a testament to the Maya's command of cosmology, but the historical significance of El Castillo and Chichen Itza far surpasses their remarkable astronomical proportions. The name Chichen Itza translates to "at the mouth of the well of Itza," Itza being a Maya ethnic group native to Petén Basin in northern Guatemala and some parts of Belize. The Itza probably originated near Lake Petén Itza in Guatemala and formed the Classic Period city of Motul de San José. At the end of the Middle Classic Period and the beginning of the Late Classic Period, they settled at Chichen Itza. However, the word "Itza" could have also simply meant "enchantment of the water" without being a specific reference to the demographic.

The rise of Chichen Itza was not an isolated phenomenon. Chichen Itza turned into a prominent site around the 7th century, but the core site matured during the 8th, 9th, and 10th centuries. This timeline coincides with the fall of two major neighboring cities: Coba to the east and Yaxuna to the south. Chichen Itza might have directly contributed to their downfall – or the unrelated downfall of the cities might have brought more people and more power to Chichen Itza – the exact details are blurry. The Toltecs also rose to power during this time, concluding historians to draw parallels between the growth of both cultures. Some accounts imply a migration from Tula, the Toltec center. At this time, Chichen Itza ascended to a rare stature, exerted influence over the local trade and politics of the region, and led the way in terms of religious ideology. The city could obtain locally unavailable goods by traveling long distances: they acquired gold from Southern America and obsidian from Central Mexico.

Chichen Itza became famous among archaeologists and tourists around the world when John Lloyd Stephens published his book, "Incidents of Travel in Yucatán," in 1843. In 1894, the United States' consul to Yucatán, Edward Herbert Thompson, conducted a detailed examination of the city and took the excavated artifacts back home. In 1926, the Mexican government seized Thompson's plantation, accused him of stealing the artifacts, and proceeded to take control of the ancient site. In 1944, the Mexican Supreme Court decided in favor of Thompson, who was no longer alive. The property was given to his heirs, who sold it to Fernando Barbachano Peon, a tourism pioneer. The land was privately owned until 2010 when the state of Yucatán bought it and handed the reigns of site administration over to Instituto Nacional de Antropología e Historia, Mexico's national institute of anthropology and history.

The remains of Chichen Itza today only hint at the metropolitan's former glory. In its heyday, the city covered at least 5 square kilometers or 1.9 square miles. The population might have risen as high as 50,000, a substantial number for any city in the world at the time. Divided into multiple districts by low walls, it contained around a hundred small pathways that linked sites throughout the city. While the landscape appears flat and concise, archaeologists believe it to be a deception. They think that in a mountainous region like the Yucatán, it would be hard to find such a large and flat piece of land. They are almost certain that the entire area was flattened by the Mayans to develop the city, an act that would have taken quite a long time considering the technology and tools of the time.

Chichen Itza
https://unsplash.com/photos/eCySkpvdFhE

Let us start with the elephant in the room: El Castillo. Also known as "The Temple of Kukulkan," the giant pyramid is one of the most visited sites on the planet. When the sun sets on the equinoxes, the shadow of a snake writhes down the steps and connects with the sculpted head at the base. Resting on the "Northern Platform," El Castillo was built over a smaller pyramid. The smaller pyramid may not be visible from the outside, but it continues to exist. The structure stands at the height of 30 meters (or 98 feet), while the small temple at the summit is 6 meters (or 20 feet) high. Consisting of nine terraces that recede in size as one moves up, the Temple of Kukulkan is incredibly well proportioned. Studies reveal that El Castillo sits atop a cenote; the city of Chichen Itza has several cenotes – large water bodies used for drinking and sacrificial rites. So far, four cenotes or natural sinkholes have been discovered near Chichen Itza; researchers suspect there may be more. Expeditions have revealed jade, pottery, gold, and human remains at the bottom of some cenotes. The most sacred cenote is located to the north of the core city and was probably used for sacrificial offerings to the rain god Chaac – crops, items of daily use, or human beings. The Maya may have believed that the cenotes were portals to the Maya underworld. So, the location of El Castillo also poses a major question: did the Maya consider the cenote underneath the temple as the most sacred of all? The structure's nine terraces also mirror the nine levels of the underworld. It might just be a coincidence, but that proposition seems rather unlikely.

The Northern Platform also contains the largest Mesoamerican ballcourt. The court has parallel walls with scoring rings at the top. The players would have had to hit a rubber ball through them to win the game. Chichen Itza may have had up to thirteen ballcourts. The sculptures on the courts' parallel walls shine a light on the rules and traditions of the game. The Platform of Eagles and the Jaguars, located adjacent to the ballcourt, depicts Toltec influence. Heading south from the Northern Platform, one ends up at the "Osario Group." It was home to many important buildings of the city like the Osario Temple and the nunnery, Las Monjas. The oldest part of the city is Chichen Viejo.

Various districts of the city have different architectural styles. This either shows the natural progression of the city – the Mayans were not acute city planners – or it shows the prevalence of a heterogeneous, cosmopolitan culture. The blend of migrating factions may have contributed to pluralism in the society. Excavations and subsequent studies regarding the city show increasing signs of Toltec-Maya, rather than just Maya. Consider the Temple of the Warriors, a large complex that is home to a stepped pyramid and a horde of cultural artifacts. A temple in the city of Tula, known as Temple B, is eerily similar to the Temple of the Warriors except in size. Scholars consider the Toltec-Maya connection a unique and unprecedented episode in Mesoamerica.

The architectural similarities between Chichen Itza and the capital city of the Toltecs, Tula, have been a controversial subject over the years. Early scholars noted that Tula has a pyramid that is similar to El Castillo. They theorized that the Toltecs took over Chichen Itza around the 9th and 10th centuries. This helped explain the change in architectural style in the Terminal Classic Era. Some speculated that the original inhabitants of Chichen Itza abandoned the site, and the Toltecs gained control of it. Others believed that the Toltec king, Kukulkan, and his successors invaded Chichen Itza on multiple occasions.

Some of these beliefs have since been refuted, and others are under scrutiny. Today, scholars usually believe that historical accounts from the era imply a migration from Tula to Chichen Itza – the extent of the migration is under debate. One Tula account, in particular, implies that a Tula king traveled towards Chichen Itza. Similarly, an account from Chichen Itza records the arrival of a king from the west. Recent research has shown that most structures of either style were built before the assumed invasion, interference, or arrival of the Toltecs. Radiocarbon dating has revealed that almost all of the structures in question were erected around the same time. The new research also reveals that the Toltec-Maya structures in Chichen Itza are older than the corresponding structures in Tula. Considering this new information, most older theories fail to explain the situation adequately.

Despite these new revelations, scientists lack any real information that will help them understand the introduction of these cultural influences. Modern historians are still working on explaining this phenomenon. Some theorists argue that the trade between the two cities might be the missing link in the story. The people of Chichen Itza were using commodities that can be found in New Mexico and Arizona, leading experts to conclude that they were engaged in long-distance trade. We know that the Maya had established extensive trade routes throughout the region, so they were most likely trading with the Toltecs as well. It is possible that the inhabitants of Chichen Itza, impressed by the Toltec culture, decided to integrate those values into their culture. Another theory postulates that the city's origins hold the key to the mystery. Chichen Itza was a cosmopolitan city in every sense of the word. The destruction of Coba and Yaxuna would have added to the city's population. The prevalence of various cultures would have certainly contributed to the diversity of the style. Moreover, since the prevalent style is Toltec-Maya, Chichen Itza was probably a city of two major ethnicities: the Toltecs and the Maya, leading to a duality of style.

As of yet, there is no definite evidence that shows that the Toltecs controlled Chichen Itza. And, since carbon dating procedures inform us that the structures of Chichen Itza are older than the Toltec structures of the same style, some historians think that we need to invert our perspective. Instead of assuming that the Toltecs influenced the Maya, we must wonder if Chichen Itza influenced Tula. This theory is not widely accepted. Scholars point out that there were Toltec-style buildings in Chichen Itza. Therefore, even if Chichen Itza was the senior city and held sway over the culture of Tula, the Toltec structures in the Mayan city still pose a question mark.

The existence of a connection is not under dispute. While the connection between the two peoples is generally accepted, the lack of information looms large over the historical accounts. As much as theorists have speculated over the nature of their relationship, no concrete knowledge is available. The issue comes down to the lack of evidence; little to no texts survived the Spanish conquest. Scholarly speculations are based entirely on the art and architecture of the cities. Take note that the Maya painted colorful inscriptions and sculptures – a far cry from the monotonous color of the artifacts we see today. Time and climate may have waned the monuments' vibrant look, but archaeologists believe that the Maya were quite fond of colors.

The Mayan city continued to soar until the 13th century, when the neighboring city of Mayapan assumed control. Some Mayan sources explain how this came about. As discussed earlier, the Mayans considered cenotes sacred landmarks. According to the accounts, the ruler of Mayapan jumped into the cenote, made it out alive, and prophesied his rise to power. Research shows that Chichen Itza was looted and plundered at least once. Mayapan may or may not have had something to do with it. By the end of the 11th century, the city was witnessing a decline. Sometime around the 13th century, Mayapan rose to become a major force of the Yucatán. In the 15th century, Mayapan fell into ruins and was abandoned in the 16th century. When the Spanish arrived in the 16th century, they found people residing at Chichen Itza. Whether this population was located in the original city or a settlement close to it remains a matter of some ambiguity.

Chapter 6: The Question about the Toltecs

The Aztecs, comprised of different ethnic groups from all over central Mexico, came to dominate the region in the 14th century. The term "Aztec," like Maya, is an umbrella term - it does not refer to an individual people but to many different tribes and cultures of a similar vein. The Aztec Empire was based on the alliance of three city-states, including the illustrious city of Teotihuacán. Looking at the chronology of the Mayan collapse and the Aztec ascent, one realizes that there is a major gap in the modern understanding of Mesoamerican history. After all, the Classic Maya collapse occurred during the 8th and 9th centuries, and the Aztecs rose to power in the 14th century. The phenomenal gap between these two epochs calls for critical examination. Therefore, the Toltecs are of tremendous interest to modern archaeology.

The Toltecs feature heavily in Aztec texts where their presence conveys a grandiose ideal - a mythical stream of cultural, economic, and political achievement. The Aztecs thought that monarchs were an extension of divine entities, so they claimed that as descendants of the Toltecs - a royal bloodline - they had a divine right to rule. The oral tradition of the Aztecs regales tales of a great people who rose from the ashes of the Classic Maya and commenced a new era in the story of Mesoamerica. The Toltecs probably emanated from eastern and central Mexico and founded the esteemed city of Tula, known in the native Nahuatl language as "Tōllān." In this city, the people lived in buildings made of jade and gold. The Aztecs attributed almost all the artistic and scientific contributions of Mesoamerica to the Toltecs. The origins of Toltecs are shrouded in mystery.

The Aztecs describe the Toltec Empire as a society of warriors that worshipped a storm god – either the Aztec god Tlaloc or the Maya god Chaac. A wise king called Quetzalcoatl ruled the vast kingdom. The Aztec accounts refer to Cē Ācatl Topiltzin Quetzalcoatl as a humble and courageous king who prioritized education amongst the vassals, teaching them to read, write, and measure time. He taught them to work with luxurious metals like gold, jade, and feathers. He trained them in agricultural skills, telling them how to grow cotton and use it to create objects of artistic and practical value. He taught them to raise maize and cacao. The Aztec inscriptions say that Quetzalcoatl was born in 843 and died in 895. You might be noticing minor discrepancies and some exaggeration because we know that maize and cacao were used in Mayan societies long before the 9th century.

The Aztecs further credit Quetzalcoatl with the construction of four prayer houses and a temple for promoting spiritual enlightenment. The temple had majestic columns with meticulous carvings of serpents. After some sorcerers in the city tricked Quetzalcoatl, he fled to the east in shame. When he reached the shore, he burned himself and rose to the sky, metamorphosing into a morning star. In Uxmal, there are clear signs of the cult of Quetzalcoatl. Despite the connection, we are not aware whether an actual individual had anything to do with it or if Quetzalcoatl was a story that reached the area. Most Aztec accounts say that Quetzalcoatl left for the east, but there is a text that serves as an outlier. It says that after burying important artifacts, Quetzalcoatl burned Tollan down to the ground. Our understanding of the feathered serpent god of the Toltecs and the Aztecs is still quite blurry and offers no clear answers. After all, most of what we know about the Toltecs today has been passed down to us by the Aztecs. Opinions differ on the veracity of different accounts: some call the historical precision of the Aztec accounts into question; others declare them to be semi-mythical accounts.

So, did the Toltec Empire exist, or was it merely a fable told by the Aztecs?

If one were to draw a comparison with other ancient civilizations, one is inclined to notice similarities between the Aztec accounts of the Toltecs and the stories of the Old Testament. Studies have verified the narrative of the sacred Jewish texts to quite an extent. However, historians are still divided on an issue. There is no way to establish the validity of the texts' fantastic elements. Our understanding of ancient texts relies heavily on means that lie beyond the premises of elementary approaches like the Socratic Method. One simply cannot acquire hard-boiled evidence about every little detail, so supposition and intelligent guessing are common techniques in archaeology. Due to the lack of evidence, disagreements are a natural part of scientific and historical discourse regarding Mesoamerican cultures as well. The opinions of modern intellectuals on the Toltec Empire are categorized as historicist perspectives and non-historicist perspectives.

Historicists acknowledge that a large part of the Aztec narrative is mythological, and it would be misleading to take it at face value. However, they think that comparative analysis and critical attention to detail can yield some historical knowledge of genuine value. As such, the Aztec accounts should not be dismissed as unreliable sources. In the late 1850s, a Frenchman, Désiré Charnay, arrived in Yucatán. Inspired by John Lloyd Stephens' books, he started to explore Mesoamerican sites and extensively photographed the architecture, inscriptions, and artifacts. He continued his expeditions for the better part of the mid-to-late 19th century. He raised enough money to follow the journey of Quetzacoatl from Tula towards the Yucatán Peninsula, becoming the first archaeologist to do so. When he arrived at Chichen Itza, a ball court and some serpent columns immediately struck him. Noticing the similarities between Tula and Chichen Itza, he concluded that Tula was the capital city of the Toltecs. His historicist perspective posits that the Toltecs violently took over Chichen Itza. As discussed in the previous chapter, there is no direct evidence that backs up this theory. If anything, recent studies have rendered this perspective quite problematic and rather unsavory.

After the initial excursion, many scholars weighed in on the matter. In the next few years, intellectuals started to see the term "Toltec" in a very different light. They started associating the word "Toltec" with certain cultural traits that appeared in the Guatemalan Highlands, Chichen Itza, and Mayapan during the Postclassic period. These traits are also known as the "Mexican" influences of the Maya. The historicist perspective was the prevalent school of thought for most of the 20th century. Some of these historicist scholars believed that the Toltecs were a distinct ethnic group that either emanated from Tula or settled there eventually. They theorized that the Toltec Empire either dominated or decisively influenced the landscape of central Mexico from the 10th century to the 12th century. According to them, the Aztec myth of Tollan was a reference to the site of Tula. The Aztec term "Tollan" has always been a matter of debate. The Aztecs used it frequently, often referring to the Mexican city-states. Some historians, like Enrique Florescano, posited that it might originally have been a reference to the mighty Teotihuacán, and as time went by, the Mayan texts started to refer to Chichen Itza as Tollan. Other historicists like H.B Nicholson and Nigel Davies were a little skeptical of the prevalent historicist arguments. They felt that they needed to apply critical methods and untangle the mythical elements from the factual accounts.

During the 19th century, Daniel Garrison Brinton – an American historian and ethnologist – argued against the belief that an empire was based on the site of Tula. Subsequent anti-historicists dismiss Aztec texts and inscriptions as religious texts with minor historical value. Some anti-historicists are completely dismissive of the Aztec stories, arguing that the Toltec Empire is the fourth of the five ages of the Aztecs' religious framework. Most anti-historicists claim that, outside of a few emperors and their battles, any value ascribed to the Aztec tales is a misguided attempt to find answers in places where there are none. They also call attention to the idea that the states of Teotihuacán and Tenochtitlan were the most substantial contributors to the culture of Mesoamerica. Relatively, the Toltec influence falls quite short.

Recent studies have negated historicist views, and comparative analyses of the situation have favored anti-historicist perspectives. The term "comparative analysis" simply refers to the inference of conclusions based on the comparison between two things – documents, processes, objects, or something else. Modern historical research often opts for a comparative approach. In comparative historical research, one examines the relevant historical events by theory building, referencing the current epoch, and comparing the events with other historical events. The approach gains a lot of its momentum by understanding the broader sociological traits and their consequent manifestations. The study of the Toltecs presents the same issues that one usually encounters in comparative historical research. The historical data is incomplete, the scale and complexity of the social systems are unknown, and personal records like memoirs or letters that we have could be and probably are biased.

These days, scholars have started to favor the original approach of Brinton based on a critical evaluation of the accounts. Modern research frames the word "Toltec" quite differently. According to them, the Aztecs reminisced about the sophistication, vigor, and ferocity of Classic and Postclassic Mesoamerican civilizations by granting them a fabled status. Considering that they treated kings as semi-divine figures, this proposition does not appear baseless.

Some modern historians maintain that the task of understanding Toltecs, with our current data, is unsurmountable. The Aztec accounts are incredibly hard to decipher because of their ambiguity. As we know, the Aztecs had a cyclical understanding of time, which further hinders our search for answers. Quetzalcoatl is the biggest example of this misunderstanding because two figures are associated with the name. The first one was the founding father of the Toltecs and a great ruler who exercised his valiance and might on his enemies. The second one was the last ruler of the Toltecs who foresaw the decline of the Toltecs as their power across Mesoamerica withered and whimpered. The Toltec priests forced Quetzalcoatl into a life of shame and humiliation, and he had to leave his homeland. This confusion makes it impossible to differentiate between Quetzalcoatl, the deity, and Topiltzin Cē Ācatl, a historical figure.

The Aztecs were of Nahua ethnicity, and in the Nahuatl language, *Toltec* meant artist, artisan, or wise man. This was in stark contrast to the word, Chichimecayotl, which is a reference to the Chichimecas. Some considered them to be barbarians or uncivilized people who were yet to be urbanized. If we apply this model to the Postclassic and Terminal Classic Periods, the Aztecs could have used the word "Tollan" to refer to any urban center with a respectable reputation and "Toltecs" to refer to its inhabitants. The titles of several places throughout Mesoamerica referenced Tollan. It is also possible that individuals asserted themselves to be Toltecs - descendants of urban nobility - because the Mesoamericans cherished and admired pure bloodlines. This interpretation seems even more plausible when one notices that different settlements of the Itza Mayas, the Aztecs, and the K'iche claim to have been founded by Quetzalcoatl.

In the Postclassic Era, increasing signs of "Mexican" traits started appearing in a large part of Mesoamerica. The usual Toltec traits include the chacmool sculptures found in Tula and Chichen Itza - relief sculptures depicting the feathered serpent - and large galleries with adorned columns. When the Toltec characteristics started to show up in the region, their inclusion into other cultures was selective. The cultures welcomed the Toltec attributes into their way of life - instead of an external force shoving it down their throats. Skeptics do not deny this; however, they ascribe this phenomenon to different events. Teotihuacán may have been destroyed in the Classic Era, but its inhabitants did not suffer the same fate. They lost their homes, were displaced, migrated, and probably took their culture to other parts of the region. The Mexican traits could simply have been the evolution of those cultural ideas in conjunction with the various civilizations of Mesoamerica. In recent years, scholars have refrained from calling Tula the breeding grounds of a great empire. They use the word "Toltecs" to describe the inhabitants of Tula.

These various interpretations serve as different versions of the truth. The objective truth of the Toltecs still eludes us. Some interpretations have fared better than others over time, but that does not speak to their validity. Without any substantial evidence, we cannot claim to know who the Toltecs were, whether the Toltec Empire existed, or what Tula stood for - which brings us to the most intriguing part of the mystery: Tula.

Chapter 7: Tula: City of the Toltecs

Tula is a Mesoamerican archaeological site located in the Mexican state of Hidalgo. Many historians and archaeologists believe it to be the regional center of the Toltec Empire. It exists 75 kilometers north of Mexico City, in the modern city of Tula de Allende. Like Chichen Itza, it is almost a two-hour drive from Mexico City, albeit in a completely different direction. The site lies within alluvial bottoms and houses the Rosas and the Tula rivers. The remains of the ancient city are located on two sides of a low ridge. Tula is a Nahuatl language name that roughly translates to "near the cattails."

The city reached its zenith around 850. and fell into decline around 1150. It was the eminent metropolitan of its era, bridging the gap between the fall of Teotihuacán and the rise of the Aztec center, Tenochtitlan. Like much of the information regarding the Toltecs, modern research provides one with varied interpretations and conflicting viewpoints about the site of Tula.

One must wonder: *When the Aztecs mentioned "Tollan," were they referring to the site of Tula in Hidalgo?*

Tula

Extensive research conducted on the sites and relevant anthropological studies estimate Tula as the likely capital of the Toltecs, and historians have continued to favor this narrative over the years. Before we establish the significance of the site of Tula, we have to demonstrate, as a prerequisite, that Tula was indeed Tollan. Whenever we try to restrict Tollan to any set of archaeological ruins, we tend to encounter a few problems. In the case of Tula, one notices that Tula was considerably large, but it could not possibly have had much influence over the entire region. It participated in trade but did not exert much control beyond its neighboring states. Therefore, it is quite unlikely that it spawned an entire empire of mighty warriors and wise, upstanding civilians. All of this hints at the possibility of semantic overlap. We know that the Aztecs used the word in different contexts, so it is quite possible that Tula was the original Tollan, and afterward, the phrase caught on.

On the other hand, should one venture a little further and arrive at Teotihuacán, one cannot overlook the fact that it had perished centuries before the Toltecs' appearance. Therefore, Teotihuacán seems unlikely to have been the original Tollan.

However, some intellectuals postulate that Teotihuacán could have been ravaged and looted by the Toltecs.

If Tollan was a reference to a single, distinct city, it probably referenced the site of Tula, Hidalgo. Furthermore, the site of Tula displays many sculptures depicting the cosmology and mythology of Quetzalcoatl. The discovery of a glyph that shows the birthday and birth name of the great Toltec leader, Topiltzin Cē Ācatl, further solidifies Tula's position as the center of Toltec activity.

The earliest known settlements at the site of Tula date back to around 400 BCE, with various indigenous tribes inhabiting it over the years. During the Middle and Late Classic Era, the site probably fell under the control of Teotihuacán, as shown by the pottery designs on the site. In the Late Classic Era, the southern Maya lowlands were growing feeble and declining in population. During the 10th, 11th, and 12th centuries, the diaspora of Teotihuacán and the southern Maya was dissolving into the region, leading to new settlements, political alliances, and the development of trade routes. The power vacuum brought more power to the smaller states. During this period, we notice new trade routes and innovative art styles appearing on the sites of Xochicalco, Cholula, Cacaxtla, and, most importantly, Chichen Itza. Observing the Tula ceramics, one finds that they change significantly during this time. Not only that, but the settlements also witnessed their share of dynamism as people started to settle on hilltops. The consequent architecture shows clear signs of pluralism and implies that the new societies were probably multi-ethnic. It is quite feasible that an ethnic group – like the Toltecs – absorbed the dislocated masses and expanded their city.

Tula was established as a small town around 750. If you visit Tula today, you will notice two clusters of structures on the site. One of these is called Tula Chico (small Tula), while the other is called Tula Grande (big Tula). During the Early Classic Period, the city populace was concentrated at Tula Chico. Compared to other sites of the era, Tula Chico has visibly smaller structures. It probably contributed to regional trade and politics in a minor fashion. At the beginning of the Late Classic Period, Tula expanded and turned into an urban populace covering around 1.5 square kilometers. Tula Chico continued to prosper during the Late Classic Era and, at its height, might have spanned five or six square kilometers with a population of 19,000 to 27,000. In the second half of the century, Tula Chico was abandoned, and Tula Grande began to form. Today, some original parts of Tula Chico might be buried under Tula Grande. In the Terminal Classic Era, Tula Grande continued to expand. At its height, the city spanned almost 14 square kilometers and boasted a population of around 60,000. Another 20,000 to 25,000 people populated the city's outer limits.

Like the architects of Teotihuacán, the Toltecs aligned most city structures at 17 degrees east of true north. However, they aligned the first village to the true north. The ceremonial structure of Tula was built on a limestone base that was surrounded in three directions by steep banks. The civic-ceremonial district at the heart of the ancient city is known as the Sacred Precinct. It is a large, quadrangular plaza, surrounded by a couple of L-shaped structures, Pyramid B, Pyramid C, and the Quemado Palace. The city also consists of two Mesoamerican ballcourts and several other large buildings. This entire area hints at many architectural innovations, signifying crucial changes in the city's social life. There is a perceivable expansion of ritual space, and considerable emphasis is placed upon the spiritual guidance of the masses. The Toltecs started to engage in ritual practices in an extravagant, public fashion. With three narrow meeting halls surrounding its three sides, the central plaza can hold up to 100,000 people at a time. The columns of the meeting halls face towards the plaza, and the plaza has almost 1,000 meters of benches embellished with depictions of ceremonies.

The most exotic, fantastic, and appealing structure of the site is, unquestionably, Pyramid B. The pyramid, commonly known as "the Pyramid of Quetzalcoatl" or "the Pyramid of the Morning Star," is a five-stepped pyramid that mirrors the design of the Temple of the Warriors at Chichen Itza. The morning star is a reference to the planet Venus, which holds enormous astrological importance to Mesoamerican civilizations; it disappears at night and reappears in the morning. The evening star symbolizes Quetzalcoatl's time on earth as a human entity, and the Toltecs believed that just like the morning star, he would appear once again. Sometimes, the temple is also referred to as the "Temple of Tlahuizcalpantecuhtli," which roughly translates to the Temple of the Lord of the Dawn.

At the top of the pyramid, one finds four majestic, colossal warrior statues standing at the height of 4.6 meters or 15 feet, called the "Atlantean warriors." Originally, these figures functioned as large columns that supported the temple's roof. The "Atlantean" connotation comes from 19th century North American and European scholars. No feature of the figures implies any kind of Atlantean influence or similarity. Dating procedures approximate that the statues were erected around 750 or shortly afterward.

The Toltecs used basalt stone to build the statues, which is not locally available. Each statue is divided into four sections that are stacked on top of each other. When archaeologists initially discovered them, some sections had fallen to the ground. The statues are probably based on the likeness of four Toltec warriors. The menacing statues tower way above the average human being and instill a spine-tingling aura. Their steadfast eyes convey a stoic calm and a sense of duty towards their fellow brethren. Each figure can be seen wearing a butterfly breastplate and headdresses made of feathers and serpent scales. They carry sun-shaped shields on their backs, spear throwers in one hand, and spears in the other. Their presence at the center of Tula may have been a demonstration of power. These statues reinforce the image of Toltecs as skillful artists and mighty warriors.

The Temple of Quetzalcoatl serves a function of the Tula school of art and architecture. When compared with similar structures in Teotihuacán and Tenochtitlan, the buildings are smaller. This decrease in size mimics another phenomenon: the city of Tula was much smaller in size than the metropolitans mentioned above. The Toltecs may have opted for a reduction in size and scale, but they decorated their structures most affectionately. The five terraces of the main temple portray various natural and supernatural entities like marching felines, birds eating human hearts, and human bodies appearing from the mouth of the feathered serpent. The motif of the feathered serpent eating and expelling humans from the mouth also appears at Uxmal.

The other temple of the city, Temple Mayor or the "Temple of the Sun," is no longer intact, but it used to serve as the city's main temple. In its original form, it would have been the larger of the two main temples. Beside the main temple and across a narrow alley, one looks upon the burnt remains of the Palace Quemado, the probable residence of the Tula ruler. In front of the Palace, one stumbles upon a few headless chacmools - reclining sculptures. Out of the seven chacmools, just one has survived in its complete form. The friezes in the area illustrate the story of Mixcoatl and Tlahuizcalpantecuhtli via colorful depictions of eagles, jaguars, coyotes, birdmen, and other creatures. Mixcoatl is presumed to be the father of Quetzalcoatl, whereas Tlahuizcalpantecuhtli is the form of the feathered serpent upon his inevitable return.

The most impressive artistic statement, Coatepantli, or the Wall of Snakes, sits opposite to these friezes. The best-known artwork at Tula was made from local sedimentary stone and contains brightly colored reliefs. It shows serpents devouring human beings, per the motif of Quetzalcoat's worship and human sacrifice rituals. Another important artwork is the frieze of the Caciques that lies in a hall connecting the main pyramid with the main plaza. Art historians interpret the nineteen men shown in it as either local chiefs or merchants. Modern Tula has an on-site museum and an orientation center that displays stone sculptures and other archaeological discoveries. In general, the subjects of the Toltec art are quite similar to that of Teotihuacán and reinforce the same religious believes and ideologies.

Most Mesoamerican experts believe that the establishment of inter-regional trade routes brought a lot of traffic from Teotihuacán. Trade networks were engaged in the exchange of obsidian and salt by the 4th century. The steady flow of traffic increased exponentially after the fall of the Teotihuacán. In the 8th century, the markets of Tula started to reach their maximum potential. Aristocrats, artisans, and rich merchants were elite figures in the central city, whereas farmers lived in the city's outer vicinity. Researchers have proposed that the area received more rainfall during the Classic Era, accounting for the lack of natural irrigation. Excavations have revealed proof of the cultivation of chili peppers, corn, beans, squash, amaranth, and maguey. Like the Maya and many other Mesoamerican civilizations, corn was the major source of food. At the time, Tula was very rich in obsidian, and, thus, it was part of an important trade route. The city had an agricultural base, but many people were involved in mining and crafting obsidian.

Tula witnessed a sudden demise during the 11th and 12th centuries when a significant portion of the population abandoned their houses and migrated to other areas. Not much is known about the collapse of the Toltecs. According to some, natural disasters made it impossible to sustain life in the region; others theorize that internal strife ruined the city. The internal strife theory ties in with the story of Quetzalcoatl, who was betrayed by local chiefs. Despite the fall, Tula continued to exist until the Spanish invasion of the Americas.

Tula has been overlooked compared to other great cities of Mesoamerica like Teotihuacán, Monte Alban, and Tenochtitlan. It has not been the target of extensive research like the other cities. Nevertheless, the lack of research constitutes a fraction of the issues one faces when confronted with the puzzle of Tula. The overwhelming lack of evidence makes it difficult to make a consistent hypothesis. Whatever theory you might lean toward, the fact remains that the Toltecs' impact on the region cannot be underestimated. Some have proposed that it was a small site with relatively little effect on the broader landscape of Mesoamerica. Recent excavations have revealed large residential complexes just outside the ceremonial center, subsequently negating the "uninfluential" premise. The impact of Toltec art spread throughout the land. When the Spanish arrived in the New World, Quetzalcoatl was already a cult figure, widely worshipped all over Central America. It had even seeped its way into Aztec ideology.

Chapter 8: Cē Ācatl Topiltzin: The Mythic Toltec King

In 1504, Hernan Cortes, a Spanish teenager, arrived in the New World. After aiding Diego Velázquez in the conquest of Cuba, he was elevated to a higher designation and was due for inland Mexico. However, his superiors changed their minds and ordered him to stay. In 1519, the Spanish conquistador ignored his superior's orders and headed inland to secure Mexico for colonization in an act of mutiny. After stopping briefly in Trinidad to stock up on resources and hire extra help, he reached the Yucatán Peninsula. In the name of the Spanish crown, he defeated foe after foe. Throughout his journey, he took full advantage of the tribal dispositions of the indigenous people. By turning one tribe against the other, he would side with some tribes and vanquish others. When the Spanish reached the Aztec capital of Tenochtitlan, they had a massive army. The Aztec king, Montezuma, allowed Cortes and his army to enter the city to learn about their weaknesses. He awarded gifts of gold, jade, and obsidian to the Spanish army. In a letter to King Charles, Cortes claims that the Aztecs believed him to be Quetzalcoatl or an embassy of Quetzalcoatl. The belief of Quetzalcoatl was so widespread throughout the Mesoamerican land that it even rendered kings vulnerable to invaders.

Hernan Cortes took Montezuma captive and sacked the grand city of Tenochtitlan, essentially bringing an end to Aztec glory. The Aztecs associated Montezuma's hesitation towards conflict with his belief in the return of the feathered deity. Nevertheless, one must realize that this story came out after the Spanish had taken over the city, which makes many historians wonder if the Aztecs fabricated the story to save face. While Montezuma was providing treats to the Spaniards, his army had started a war with the Spanish army outside the city. Montezuma may have simply treated the Spanish as potential allies who could have helped him enlarge his kingdom. Whether the tale of the Aztec king's belief in Quetzalcoatl is true or not, it serves as a delightful distraction to rationalize defeat. The distraction worked only because of the prevalent faith in the feathered serpent of Tollan. In modern literature, some scholars take issue with the phrase "the cult of Quetzalcoatl" because it was much less a cult than a reverent religious and political ideology that engulfed the entire region.

Was Quetzalcoatl a single individual – a Toltec emperor of profound insight and raw, potent vigor? Alternatively, was he an idea that extended beyond an individual figure and encompassed something broader?

Quetzalcoatl translates literally to "serpent of precious feathers" and loosely to "Quetzal-feathered serpent." A quetzal – to be precise, a resplendent quetzal – is a bird that can be found in different parts of Mexico. The Guatemalan flag has an image of the bird, and it happens to be the national bird of the nation as well. Quetzalcoatl belonged in the most esteemed company of Aztec gods, along with Tlaloc, Huitzilopochtli, and Tezcatlipoca. Most people believed him to be the god of sun, wind, and learning, among other things. Different interpretations of Quetzalcoatl existed in different regions, and it would be naïve to look for consistencies among these different narratives. In certain eras, some regions thought of him as the god of vegetation while others associated him with the planet Venus, arts, craft, and knowledge. For instance, the Huastec people of central Mexico associated him with Ehécatl, the wind god, whose attire was quite like their own. The Temple of Quetzalcoatl, located in the Aztec city of Tenochtitlan, is a circular structure because it is believed that the round shape of the architecture was symbolic of wind. Sharp edges are obstacles to the wind, whereas circular shapes seem to aid its dynamism. Similarly, in the states of Veracruz and San Luis Potosi in east-central Mexico – which were home to the Huastec people – one registers the same observation.

Detailed drawings of Quetzalcoatl show him adorned with quetzal feathers and wearing an ornate talisman around his neck. Such stones and jewelry represented different elemental forces of the cosmos. The earliest known act of the feathered serpent's worship dates to around the first century BCE or the first century CE, whereas the earliest iconographic depiction of the deity dates back to around 900 BCE on an Olmec site. In the Olmec depiction, a serpent ascends behind a person engaged in a ritual. This artwork may prove that a divine feathered serpent existed in the Mesoamerican religious pantheon for quite some time; however, historians emphasize that the specific deity of Quetzalcoatl appeared in the Classic Era. There are also a few representations of feathered serpents in Teotihuacán during the Preclassic Era, but in these images, the feathered serpent was drawn as a primal entity with no human features. The human features started to appear during the Classic Era. After the fall of Teotihuacán, the cult of the feathered serpent started to gain prominence. Historians attribute this to the iconography and inscriptions found at different sites across central Mexico like Cholula and Cacaxtla. In particular, Cholula might have been the most prominent center of Quetzalcoatl worship over the following years.

Quetzalcoatl is often conflated with the Toltec king, Cē Ācatl Topiltzin, who ruled a sophisticated and vicious empire during the 10th century. The title, Cē Ācatl Topiltzin Quetzalcoatl, roughly translates to "Our Prince One-Reed Precious Serpent." Several tales recall the life and genius of the Toltec emperor. He was born in Tepoztlan on "1 Acatl," which corresponds to May 13, 895. Accounts differ when it comes to his parents.

There are many different tales of how Quetzalcoatl came to be. According to one story, he was born to the Aztec deity Chimalman, meaning "shield-hand," who was a virgin. According to another story, she swallowed an emerald and conceived Quetzalcoatl. The most popular belief is that his father was

Mixcoatl, another Toltec deity and presumably an earlier Toltec king. The story goes that Mixcoatl shot an arrow at Chimalman, who got pregnant and gave birth nine months later. Mixcoatl, which means "Cloud Serpent," was the god of war, fire, and hunting. In drawings and sculptures, he can be seen wearing red-striped clothing and a black mask over his eyes. The god of the morning star, Tlahuizcalpantecuhtli, who is the second rendition of Quetzalcoatl - as the morning star -, also has the same features. Moreover, Mixcoatl carries hunting gear, a bow, and arrows, the likes of which can be seen on the Atlantean statues at Tula. The Aztecs revered Mixcoatl but not as much as they revered some of their other deities. Many indigenous groups like the Otomi and the Chichimecs highly appreciated Mixcoatl. At the ancient sites of Tlaxcala and Huejotzingo, people worshipped him as the central deity.

In his early childhood, Topiltzin proved his mettle as a fierce warrior. Tales credit him for leading his people to the city of Tollan, where he served as a Toltec priest. Most Mesoamerican cultures, including the Maya, Toltecs, and Aztecs, emphasized tribal conflict, war, and human sacrifice. Both themes feature heavily throughout Mesoamerican history. Even some European invaders noted that the indigenous people belonged to a strict tribal culture and were often at war with each other over simple disputes. After all, the invaders exploited this weakness to a great extent, working on the policy of divide and conquer. All this serves to illuminate the statue of Topiltzin among the Mesoamerican civilizations and his humanist reputation among his vassals. The Toltecs saw him as the single most eminent leader in terms of spiritual and sociological resolve. His preference for peace and restrain led him to preach sophisticated and cultured ideals and abolish all human sacrifice. Myths describe that Quetzalcoatl avoided offering humans as sacrificial offerings. Instead, he opted for birds, snakes, butterflies, and other animals. He also swore priests to celibacy and refrained them from using intoxicating substances. We know that the Maya had ritualistic ceremonies in underground caves where they used hallucinogenic substances.

According to the tales, Topiltzin traveled across the land, conquering some settlements and preaching his values to others. He even established new societies and communities using his spiritual faculties. At this point, accounts differ as to what happened with Topiltzin. Some believe that after spreading his word across the land, he set off to the east, convinced that he would find his holy resting place there. Others believe he traveled to Tlapallan, a region on the Gulf Coast of Mexico, where he used a pyre to offer the ultimate sacrifice. By burning and shedding his skin, he was transformed into the Morning Star. Another version states that he embarked on a raft of snakes and disappeared over the horizon to the east.

After Tollan, Cholula is the most important city in regard to Quetzalcoatl. In its heyday, Cholula was the second most populated city in all of Mexico, with a population of around 100,000. The city's population started to decrease in the 8th century, but it remained a hub of religious activities for the next few centuries. Today, Cholula is a tourist attraction for its Great Pyramid, the largest archaeological site of a pyramid in the New World. It is the largest monument ever constructed anywhere throughout history and was built in honor of the feathered serpent. Mythology dictates that after escaping a flood, a giant named Xelhua built the pyramid. In truth, it was probably built in four exhausting stages from the 3rd century BCE to the 9th century CE. By the time construction had finished, the pyramid was six times the size of its original proportions. A Mesoamerican school of thought believed that Topiltzin would return to reclaim Cholula.

Chronology has been a persistent issue with Quetzalcoatl. Cholula's apex was already behind it in the 8th century, and Topiltzin came to power in the 10th century. There is a massive gap between the two events. Since Mesoamerican cultures thought of their kings as semi-divine figures and their understanding of time was cyclical, Topiltzin possibly built upon the conquests of his predecessors. According to Fernando de Alva Cortés Ixtlilxóchitl, a historian of partial Aztec descent, Topiltzin ruled during the 10th century. According to another document, Codex Ramirez, Topiltzin ruled during the 12th century.

The Aztec rulers used religious leverage to gain power, empowering the myth of the Toltec emperor whenever it suited them. As heirs of the Quetzalcoatl bloodline - real or claimed - they asserted that they were the rightful successors to the throne. The diffusion of religious sentiment allowed them to earn the throne and keep it. They could always fall back on the running excuse that they were merely keeping it warm for the feathered serpent. Concocting a religious ideology allowed them to tap into the collective subconscious of the vassals. They were able to convince people of ideas and rituals that were in complete contradiction to Topiltzin's teachings. For instance, they began performing large ceremonial human sacrifices that had been abolished in the Toltec's prime epoch. The Aztecs continued this cycle of lies and deception well into the Postclassic and Colonial times.

Excluding minor and circumstantial evidence, all these tales have been relayed to us via five major sources. The first source, *Historia de los Mexicanos por sus pinturas,* was written by an unknown Spaniard in an attempt to capture the story of the Toltecs. This version is quite brief and possibly inaccurate, probably due to a lack of understanding of the indigenous languages. According to this version, the unnamed mother dies after giving birth to Topiltzin. As he grows up, Topiltzin spends seven years in the quiet sanctity of mountains. At this time, he performs bloodletting rituals and prays with resolve. The gods bestow his wish to become a great warrior, and he starts to wage war and becomes popular among the masses, elevating him to the position of emperor. For 42 years, he maintains peace and harmony in his kingdom but is asked to leave the city of Tollan at the end. He passes through towns, establishes villages, and arrives at Tlapallan only to die the very next day.

In a translation by Catholic friars, called the "Libro de oro y tesoro indico," Topiltzin is recorded as the son of a leader of Teotihuacán. He erects a monument in the memory of his murdered father, takes revenge on his killer, and sets off for Tollan. A translation by Frenchman André Thevet places him as the son of Mixcoatl and Chimalman. The mother dies at birth, and the father is killed by Topiltzin's brothers. He avenges his father's killers and migrates to the city of Tollan. In this version, he serves as an emperor for 160 years. In the end, he flees to Tlapallan once again. A fourth translation was written by a native, the "Leyenda de los soles," or the "Legend of the Suns," which elaborates on the parents of Quetzalcoatl. The fifth source, known as "Florentine Codex," is a collection of texts gathered from native informants.

In all these versions, the Aztec god, Tezcatlipoca, translated as "smoking mirror," is responsible for ousting Topiltzin from Tollan. After Quetzalcoatl struck Tezcatlipoca down and transformed him into a jaguar, he retaliated by striking down Quetzalcoatl. He is often described as the arch-nemesis of the serpent god Quetzalcoatl.

Chapter 9: Tula's Collapse and the Toltec Diaspora

What goes up must come down.

The statement has been valid since before an apple landed on Isaac Newton's head. Its scientific implications may be relatively modern, but in the subject of history, plenty of precedents could serve as our guiding principle. We can see the idea repeatedly manifested throughout history. Mesopotamia was home to the glory and might of impenetrable empires, but all of them had to fall. When the time came, even the Western Roman Empire, the greatest superpower of its era, could not escape the clutches of inevitable demise. With the fall of Constantinople, the Eastern Roman Empire fell as well. The fall of the Western Roman Empire and the Eastern Roman Empire are separated by almost ten centuries. For some empires, it takes centuries to crumble, each conquest a mere tally in the larger scheme of things. For others, the fall is often quick and callous. It comes like a bolt of lightning, felling everything in its path like dominoes. Even in individuals and stories, in arts and literature, the rule holds immeasurable value. The most fascinating aspect of Adam's story is the fall. In music, a crescendo means nothing without the rumbles that precede it.

In the case of the Toltecs, the fall was quick and unforgiving. It all started with the death of Cē Ācatl Topiltzin or Quetzalcoatl.

Understanding the fall of Toltecs requires a brief detour. To appreciate the depth of events, it is important to gain an understanding of the Toltecs' rise to power.

Codex Chimalpopoca, an Aztec manuscript, reveals the stories of Quetzalcoatl in three stages. According to the first part of the codex, Anales de Cuauhtitlan – meaning the "Annals of Cuauhtitlan" – during their initial migrations, the Toltecs reached Manenhi. They renamed this land to Tollan and established a theocratic system, which they quickly abandoned in favor of a monarchy. Some migrants settled in the city, whereas others traversed further west in search of new territories and villages. The scholarly disputes regarding chronology are prevalent in this document as well. Different people interpret the dates of the document differently. Some think that the date of the Toltecs' arrival in Tollan belongs to the 7th century, while others translate it to the 8th century. The second part of the codex deals with deities and religion, and the third part contains the Leyenda de los soles. According to some sources, when they arrived at Tollan, the leader of the Toltecs was a man name Huemac. Some intellectuals believe that the Toltecs migrated from the deserts in the northwest, arrived at Culhuacan first, and then proceeded to Tollan. Others say it was Chalchiutlanetzin, and some maintain that it was Cē Ācatl Topiltzin Quetzalcoatl. Some researchers think that Quetzalcoatl was merely a rank the Toltecs associated with not just Topiltzin, but all of their leaders.

The Toltec demographic belonged to different tribes, including Nonoalcas and Chichimecas. According to the Florentine Codex, the Nonoalcas were an important ethnic group at Tollan. On the other hand, Chichimecas were the "inhabitants of Chichiman," and Chichiman means an "area of milk." They were part of a nomadic tribe that was usually on the move. During the Late Classic and Postclassic Era, they wore minimal clothing that only obscured their genitalia, used and ate berries, roots, and hunted animals. This was a function of their minimal lifestyle. They could not afford luxuries, nor did they have time for innovation, so instead of wearing clothes that covered them completely, they preferred to paint their bodies. Because of their pluralist roots, the Toltecs were able to establish contact and trade with other tribes.

Hidalgo is bordered by San Luis Potosi in the north, Puebla in the east, Tlaxcala in the southeast, Queretaro in the west, and Veracruz in the northeast. As the Toltec influence started to grow in the region, it reached La Huasteca in the north. La Huasteca includes parts of Veracruz, Hidalgo, Queretaro, Puebla, San Luis Potosi, and other modern states. Here they encountered two major tribes: the Otomi people and the Huastec people. The existence of people in this region dates to the 10th century BCE, making them one of the earliest civilizations of Mesoamerica. The Otomi tribe were probably the original inhabitants of the site, predating the Nahuatl speakers by several centuries. The Otomi were nomads as well and even contributed to the population of Teotihuacán. All this information ties into the fall of the Toltecs.

According to some fables, Tezcatlipoca appeared before the king, Quetzalcoatl, in the form of an older man and offered him an elixir that would make him younger. This was a deceitful offering as the drink was nothing more than an alcoholic beverage. Topiltzin called for his sister, the princess, and they both indulged in the hazy delights of alcohol. In their drunken stupor, they engaged in scandalous behavior, which left Topiltzin shamed and embarrassed to the core. You might remember that in another tale, the priests were responsible for betraying Topiltzin, but here it is Tezcatlipoca in the form of an older man. Parallels exist between the two narratives as most priests in the city could very well have been old males.

Disgraced and humiliated, Quetzalcoatl left Tollan and headed for Tlillan-Tlapallan. The death or exile of Quetzalcoatl left a hole in the once-prosperous region. The event sowed the seed of discontent and internal strife in the community, which brought about intense political and civil instability. Civil war broke out in Tollan between the supporters of Tezcatlipoca and the supporters of Quetzalcoatl. Most Nonoalca people were adherents of Quetzalcoatl and preferred his humanist ideals, including his contempt for human sacrifices. On the other hand, the followers of Tezcatlipoca's ideology, mostly descendants of the Chichimeca tribe, believed in the supreme power of mass processions and public sacrifices. This can also be seen in the design and architecture at Tula, where the ceremonial structures get larger as the people switch from Tula Chico to the new district.

Around 1000, Tula started to witness agricultural issues. The climate began to dry up, and a shortage of rainfall followed. The agricultural sector did not produce enough corn, their staple crop, to feed the whole city, and with more problems rearing their heads, it failed to reach its minimum target. With the famine, the internal ethnical discord between the Nonoalca and the Chichimeca intensified. Eventually, Tezcatlipoca's worshippers proved too much for the cult of Quetzalcoatl. The devotees of the feathered serpent finally tasted defeat at the hands of their adversaries.

Some authors mention that after the death of Topiltzin, the Toltecs started to migrate from Tollan to other cities at an unprecedented pace. The civil war in Tollan and the consequent defeat probably prompted this migration. Most of them left for the Yucatán Peninsula, where they finally ended up at Uxmal. The most powerful site in western Yucatán, Uxmal, was taken over by Toltec invaders around 1000. After 1100, construction in the city slowed down dramatically, and by 1200, it seems to have ceased altogether. Quetzalcoatl was probably introduced in the Itza region in the late 10th century. The Itza were descendants of the Putun Maya, famous for their Puuc architectural style, and the Toltec Maya. It is probable that the Itzans, of partly Toltec descent, welcomed the Toltec migrants to the Yucatán Peninsula. Around this time, the introduction of Mexican traits increased significantly in the Yucatán region. It is important to notice that the pyramids at Chichen Itza predate similar structures in Tula, so the migrations could have been taking place for some time.

When things took a turn for the worse, even the local Chichimeca started leaving the city, which encouraged even more civil disorder. The natural disasters – climate change and soil leeching – added fire to the fuel. Around 1150, a lot of Tula inhabitants had abandoned their living quarters. Just like in Teotihuacán, most structures were burned and destroyed. The ceremonial center in the heart of the city was burned during the 12th century.

Many exiled groups ended up going to the modern state of Puebla, specifically the city of Cholula. Cholula dates to the 2nd century BCE and was an important trading post for the region during the Postclassic Era. Around Tula, there were no natural water bodies to help the city with irrigation or to fulfill the public's drinking needs. This was not the case in Cholula, where rainfalls were abundant in the summer, and the city was surrounded by snowy mountains. In the summer, the snow from the mountains melted and flowed down. These favorable conditions might have beguiled the famine-ridden exiles. Furthermore, the city was no stranger to an influx of foreigners. During the Late Classic Era and the Early Postclassic Era, the Olmec-Xicallanca, a group from the Gulf Coast, had taken over the city and made it their capital. Around 1200, the Toltecs – most of them from the Chichimeca background – took over the city.

Briefly, after the Spanish conquest of the Aztecs, a Dominican friar by the name of Diego Durán wrote a few seminal texts about the Aztec culture. In his work, "The History of the Indies of New Spain," also known as the "Duran Codex," he weaves together the story of the Aztec creation as well as the history of the region leading up to the Spanish conquest. Duran writes that around 1115, the northern tribes, including but not restricted to Chichimecas, Otomi, and Huastecs, started to launch attacks against different domains of Tollan. After some vicious and violent battles, the Toltecs were on the back foot. Both sides were taking heavy losses. War makes people appeal to their gods, and so, human sacrifice prevailed as the common form of prayer. According to Duran, Huemac, who is referred to in some texts as the first ruler of Tollan, left the city with his proletariat and migrated to the city of Xaltocan, an Otomi city. Huemac had lost the trust of the people. They split up into different groups, abandoned him, and went their separate ways. In 1122, Huemac, faced with degradation and humiliation, hanged himself in the city of Chapultepec. The people of Teotihuacán controlled Chapultepec during the Classic Era. The Toltecs referred to Chapultepec, Hidalgo as the "Grasshopper Hill." Archeologists have found remains of a Toltec altar on the hill's summit.

Tollan had been abandoned, and the Toltecs had spread not just in the Valley of Mexico – but all across Mesoamerica. A small population still existed at the ruins of Tollan. Tula fell under the reign of a nearby city-state called Culhuacan, which served as a haven for the aristocrats of the Toltec capital. Culhuacan was under the control of Teotihuacán for most of the Middle Classic Period. Traditional stories dictate that it was the first Toltec city and was founded by Mixcoatl, the father of Quetzalcoatl, probably sometime around the 8ᵗʰ century. Culhuacan, which survived until the 14ᵗʰ century, was a predominantly Toltec city with Chichimeca influence.

City-states like Culhuacan were known as "altepetl," which translates to "the water, the mountain," in Nahuatl. The Toltecs diffused into the region, and several city-states – or altepetl – took over the dominions formerly ruled by the Toltecs. Most Toltecs started using the term *Quetzalcoatl,* willy-nilly to align themselves with the royal bloodline. This enabled them to land high designations in different cities across the region. This overuse of the term *Quetzalcoatl* is one of the main reasons researchers find it so hard to distinguish between different rulers of the Toltecs.

The Toltecs had finally dispersed into various fractions. The fall of the Toltecs brought about a power vacuum in Mesoamerica. The incessant conflict was a pragmatic reality in pre-Columbian Mesoamerica, and during this time, different tribes started egregiously going against one another in a bid to come out on top. From the ashes of the Toltecs rose a culture that would go on to become the hallmark of Mesoamerican civilization, the Aztecs. With Toltec heritage now the standard of nobility across Mesoamerica, it is not surprising that the Aztecs hitched their wagon to the idea of being Toltecs' descendants.

Chapter 10: The Rise of the Aztecs

The Aztec Empire was the biggest empire of Mesoamerica. At its apex, it controlled most of northern Mesoamerica and imposed its will and ideals on neighboring states. When the word "Aztec" is used, modern terminology tends to treat it as a reference to the alliance of three Nahuatl-speaking city-states in central Mexico. In broader terms, they were Nahua people who developed city-states in central Mexico after arriving from the north. Their rise was certainly not an isolated phenomenon and came about as a result of Toltec dispersion. Just like the Toltecs benefited from the Classic Maya Collapse of the 8th and 9th centuries, the Aztecs gained from the collapse of a concentrated Toltec rule.

We know the Aztecs rose to prominence in the Postclassic Period of Mesoamerican chronology. But where did they come from?

As we have witnessed with the Maya and the Toltecs, the accounts of the Aztecs are largely supernatural and mythical. They contain supernatural beings, individuals, sites, and phenomena that physically manifest themselves on Earth. Ethnohistorians have extracted tons of information from studying these tales and other pieces of archaeological evidence. The lineage of the Nahuatl-speaking people, or the Nahua, goes back to the Chichimec people. As discussed before, Chichimec were nomadic people who migrated from the north to the Valley of Mexico. In the north, they used to reside in San Luis Potosi, Zacatecas, and Guanajuato. San Luis Potosi was home to Otomi and Chichimec people. Zacatecas, roughly translated from Nahuatl as "where there is abundant grass," was the home of different ethnic groups that were often at war with each other. Guanajuato had inhabitants since the 8th century BCE approximately. Their influence continued to spread throughout the region and reached Zacatecas, Hidalgo, Queretaro, and other regions. They are often associated with the Toltecs because the decline of their cities happened alongside the decline of the Toltecs.

The Nahua legends speak of seven tribes that lived in the place of seven caves. Each cave was associated with a Nahua tribe: Xochimilca, Tlahuica, Acolhua, Tlaxcalteca, Tepaneca, Chalca, or Mexica. For most of these tribes, the story of migration is quite similar. They claim their place of origin to be Aztlan, "the Place of Herons." The word Aztec derives from the word "Aztlan" and translates to the "people from Aztlan." Whether Aztlan is a mythical place or a historical one is a matter of debate. Those who believe it to be real place it somewhere in northwestern Mexico or the southwest US. Diego Duran details a series of events in which the Aztec emperor, Montezuma I, sent an expedition to find the true location of Aztlan. At the time, the continent was not aptly mapped, making it hard to pinpoint a precise location. In the latter half of the 20th century, Mexican scholars started to speculate that an island called the Mexcaltitán de Uribe may have been the original birthing place of the Aztecs. Nobody knows if there is some truth to this proposition, but the site has recently started gaining tourists' attention.

According to the records, a drought took over the lands of northern Mexico and the southwestern US, forcing the Chichimeca tribes to migrate and arrive in central Mexico. After the earlier tribes arrived in the valley, they started to settle down and create small city-states or altepetl. The ruler of each state, called the Tlatoani, received tribute from all over the land and oversaw trade, religion, litigation, and military. In the beginning, the city-states kept meddling in each other's affairs and igniting needless disputes. With the incessant routine of conflict, none of the states gained much ground.

After two centuries of migrations, Mexica, the last tribe to arrive after the fall of the Toltecs, reached the Valley of Mexico. In the Aztec codices, the Mexica people can be seen carrying idols of their patron deity, Huitzilopochtli. Legend has it that the Mexica were eager to find a sign relayed to them by the Huitzilopochtli. In particular, they were looking for "an eagle with a snake in its beak, perched on a prickly pear cactus."

Around 1250, the Mexica reached the Valley but could not find any good agricultural land. They became vassals of Culhuacan, the city-state of choice for the displaced aristocrats of Tollan. The city gave them Chapultepec, the place the Toltecs called the grasshopper hill. Chapultepec was relatively infertile, so Mexica could not farm there. In the end, the Mexica ended up serving as mercenaries for the state of Culhuacan. At one point, Culhuacan called upon the services of Mexica on the battlefield, and they obliged. As a reward, the grateful emperor sent one of his daughters to govern over the Mexica. On the orders of one of their gods, the tribe killed the daughter by skinning her alive. In a fit of fury, the emperor initiated an offensive against the Mexica. The Mexica were driven from the land.

The nomads roamed free until they reached Lake Texcoco, where they saw the sign of Huitzilopochtli. The piece of land was right in the middle of a marsh, and there was no solid ground to stand. They established a settlement there in 1325 and named it Tenochtitlan. The city's unhospitable location served as a blessing in disguise. There was no easy access to the city; it was only reachable by boats. The city was defensibly sound, and the unusual landscape was great for fending off attackers. Thanks to the impenetrable defense, trade witnessed a boom, and the city started to grow exponentially. The Mexica started to build residential complexes. Aqueducts were set up to provide fresh water to the city. In the heart of the city, they designed a sacred precinct where they built Mesoamerican ballcourts, schools, and quarters for the priests. The Mexica had been awestruck by the magnificence and grandeur of Teotihuacán and Tula. They aspired to reach the level of sophistication and prestige of the great Toltec cities. They believed Teotihuacán was a sacred and holy site and carried ornaments and objects from the city to use in Tenochtitlan. They started erecting palaces and constructed the breathtaking Templo

Mayor, also known as Huey Teocalli. The great temple was devoted to Huitzilopochtli and Ehecatl.

Huitzilopochtli was the ultimate god of war, and the Aztecs offered him sacrifices to attain his blessing on the battlefield. The origin mythologies talk about Huitzilopochtli as the youngest of four sons. One of his brothers was Quetzalcoatl. Their parents, two gods, had created the universe. They instructed them to bring peace, harmony, and order to the world. So, they created the male and female forms, and the Earth and the Sun. Initially, Huitzilopochtli may not have been the chief deity of the Mexica and may have been elevated to the stature of Quetzalcoatl, Tezcatlipoca, and other gods after the Aztecs found his sign in the valley.

The Mexica had shown their valor and fortitude time and time again. They quickly developed a reputation as mighty warriors. This was especially important in the Postclassic Era because all the tribes were consumed in the habitual back-and-forth. When the Mexica rose as a force to be dreaded and feared, they quickly gained the respect of neighboring tribes. The Mexica had allied with the state of Azcopotzalco – the capital city of the Tepanec people ruled by the emperor Tezozomoc – and paid tribute to them. The Tepanecs spoke the Nahuatl language and shared the same religious pantheon as the Aztecs. The Mexica aided the growth of Azcopotzalco, and it started to expand as a tributary empire. The only real problem Mexica faced at the time was a lack of legitimacy. The emperor of Mexica was not considered a real king. To alleviate this, they sent a proposal to a ruler of Culhuacan, asking for the hand of his daughter. The request was granted. In 1372, the son from the wedding, Acamapichtli, became the first emperor, or tlatoani, of Tenochtitlan.

Texcoco, the city of the Acolhua people, was growing in the east of the basin. It had originally been founded by the Chichimecs, but the Acolhua people purged them from the city and took over. Tensions were running high between the Acolhua and the Tepanecs. Matters escalated, and war broke out between the two. The Mexica sided with their allies, the Tepanecs, and defeated the Acolhua. As a result, Azcapotzalco received Texcoco as a tributary. At the beginning of the 15th century, the Tepanec king died. The city fell into civil war with the emergence of two potential rulers.

The Mexica preferred Tayahauh, who had been initially enthroned, but his son, Maxtla, usurped power from under him. Maxtla was angered by the fact that the Mexica had not supported him, so he turned on them. He then declared war against the Acolhua as well. The Texcoco king fled and started to look for reinforcements. He received help from the city of Huexotzinco in Puebla and the city of Tlacopan on the western shore of Lake Texcoco. Tenochtitlan joined hands with Texcoco, Tlacopan, and Huexotzinco and engaged in the war against Azcapotzalco. Warfare in Mexico had a somewhat eccentric approach in that they focused on capturing enemies alive for rituals and sacrifices. In 1428, the union of the four cities emerged victoriously.

After the war, Tenochtitlan, Texcoco, and Tlacopan formed an alliance that would commemorate the beginning of the Aztec empire – known today as the Triple Alliance. The spoils of war were distributed among the three cities, with two-fifth of the land going to Tenochtitlan, another two-fifth going to Texcoco, and one-fifth going to Tlacopan. The son of Tezozomoc assumed the position of the ruler in Tlacopan. Tlacopan remained a minor player in the alliance. On the other hand, Texcoco was a dazzling city that fully profited from the tributes. At the time, it was famous for its huge libraries with numerous texts from older Mesoamerican cultures. At its peak, it probably had a population of more than 24,000. Today, it is located in the greater metropolitan area of the Mexican capital, Mexico City. For a brief period in the late 1820s, Texcoco served as the capital of Mexico.

Tenochtitlan became the capital of the Aztec Empire. After allying, the three cities comprising the Aztec Empire became the collective superpower of the region and took control of central Mexico. They continued to exert their power over the Mesoamerican landscape until the arrival of the Spanish. The most significant reason for the Aztecs' loss to the Europeans was the diseases of the Old World. The Mesoamericans succumbed to the oncoming illnesses because their immune systems had evolved differently from the immune system of the invaders.

And, just like that, the Aztec Empire was no more.

The average Joe is liable to mix up different Mesoamerican civilizations. Most of them share major similarities, so it is easy to mistake one for the other. They were mostly tribal cultures with polytheistic beliefs. They were often nomadic and did not mind packing up and leaving a site once it had started to decline. They were often at war with one another, they practiced bloodletting, human sacrifices, and often held public processions and ceremonies. Almost all major Mesoamerican civilizations took an interest in cosmology and the movement of celestial bodies, using a calendar to keep track of their movement. Almost all of them had a writing system, either rudimentary or advanced. Often people get confused by the different cultures. One must ask the question: Aside from their timelines, what is the difference between the Maya, the Aztecs, and other Mesoamerican cultures?

The Maya was a combination of tribes that had settled in southern Mexico and northern Central America and spoke different languages that are termed collectively as Mayan languages. On the other hand, the Aztecs lived in Central Mexico and, for the most part, spoke the Nahuatl language across the board. In between these two civilizations are the mysterious Toltecs, who act as a connecting paragraph in the annals of history.

SECTION THREE: THE TOLTEC LEGACY: SOCIETY, ARTS, AND CULTURE

Chapter 11: Social Structure

When the Spanish conquest of the Aztecs happened, Nahuatl-speaking groups were widespread all over Mesoamerica. These groups had arrived from the north and had settled in the Valley of Mexico. Most of these groups were unique and diverse, and their languages were variants of each other. Despite the minor linguistic differences, these tribes had the same cultural blueprint. One can notice the similarities in Mesoamerican civilizations throughout history, but these similarities were intensified in the Late Classic and Postclassic Periods, courtesy of the Nahua people who started to arrive in central Mexico. As these people started to work together to form large urban communities, a way of life started to appear that would continue up until the Colonial Period and, to some extent, continues to this day.

Some historians think that the Toltecs arrived in central Mexico as a distinct ethnic group from the deserts in the northwest, stopped at Culhuacan – their first urban city –, and then settled in Tollan. Others believe they were simply urbanized folk as opposed to the ubiquitous barbarians, i.e., the Chichimecs. The beginning of urbanized living, first in Teotihuacán and then in Tula, changed the landscape of the entire region. Large communes started to form that helped each other grow. The trend towards socialization did have its share of issues. Having no prior experience, most Mesoamerican civilizations, including the Toltecs, fell prey to quite similar troubles.

The biggest issue was the establishment of a class structure that relegated a select few to the comforts and luxuries that were unavailable to the rest. This discrepancy in resource availability is apparent in the Toltec Empire. The Toltec civilization was largely a military aristocracy – the respected military force was full of fearsome and menacing warriors of unmatched resilience. The soldiers were responsible for maintaining the peace and upholding the covenants of law and order. The higher echelons of society consisted of military leaders, priests, and sometimes even merchants and artisans.

During their initial nomadic days, the Toltecs maintained their lifestyle by roaming around the land and locating settlements from whom they would demand tributes after taking over. They would take over one village or city, convert its inhabitants into loyal tributaries, and head over to the next settlement. Despite the back-and-forth skirmishes between different groups, this warriors-taking-tribute approach was novel for its time. The constant clashes had shaped their image as warriors, but there was one major problem: Teotihuacán. The power and influence of Teotihuacán across Mesoamerica were unprecedented for its time, and the city often threw a wrench in the Toltecs' plans. As long as the capital city lasted, it was hard to go against it or its allies. Once Teotihuacán fell, and its commercial networks fell into disarray, the Toltecs picked the villages apart one by one. Some believe that even the burning of Teotihuacán happened at the hands of the Toltecs. Some sources cite that Mixcoatl led the most significant military campaigns towards the Valley of Mexico.

When they discovered Tula and settled there, the population was already brimming with warriors. Most of the military was used to exert power over the small towns, states, and dominions around central Mexico. This was necessary to continue with their habit of collecting tributes from other states. The tributes that arrived from other groups usually found their way into the treasury or the purses of the aristocracy, but sometimes, the aristocrats would distribute their wealth among the lower classes of their group. The Triple Alliance of the Aztecs adopted the same model. The aristocrats also collected tributes from their local vassals.

Mesoamerican tribes were almost exclusively devout and staunch in their religious beliefs. The Toltecs were no exception.

Religion played a crucial role in the normal functioning of society. It had evolved beyond faith and had embedded itself into the social fabric. It was so endemic among the tribes of Mexico that it almost seemed like a universal law. Political and military decisions were taken based on religious ideologies. Sacrificial rituals were performed to appease the gods so that they would grant victory to their followers. This deep-seated belief in their pantheon of gods allowed the Toltecs to persevere over the centuries. Even in their early days, there were extremely cautious of which way their gods were leaning to avoid vexing them. The Toltec religion was shamanic, and people often conducted religious practices without strict adherence to a specific place or building. They had pantheistic beliefs, so they thought that the natural forces of the world were manifestations of a higher power. They worshipped water, earth, and sun, and as such, the location was not of paramount importance. With the advent of urbanization, they got more comfortable with processions and social rituals. The Mesoamerican ball game was the biggest example of their religious beliefs. Some historians think that the winners were sacrificed as a way of spiritual vindication and exaltation. Others believe that the losers were sacrificed to the gods, essentially killing two birds with one stone.

Eventually, the first king was crowned who, as discussed earlier, could have been one of many potential figures. The king was the leader of the physical as well as spiritual realms. He would often keep the military class very close since the commerce of the Empire depended on it. The priests were important for conducting religious ceremonies and advising the public in spiritual and social situations. The nobles and religious leaders wore jewelry and donned bright attires. The military had a uniform, but the prestigious heroes would wear lavish clothes with lots of jewelry. Some people think that the Toltec nobility might have kept slaves as well, but the evidence for this is quite circumstantial. Proponents of this theory say that the Toltecs can be seen dragging weeping individuals from the Huastec tribe in some drawings. However, these people could easily have been on their way to a sacrificial ceremony.

Under the upper class of the military and priests, there was probably a middle class of artists, merchants, astronomers, sculptors, and other skilled workers. This demographic may not have enjoyed the liberties of the elites, but they were, by and large, sophisticated people who spent a healthy life and received social benefits. The commoners were builders involved in the construction of monuments or farmers who worked in the outskirts of the cities. They did not possess the honor or stature of the nobles. As opposed to the vibrant attires of the aristocrats, the commoners wore a simple loincloth and a Tilma, known in Nahuatl as "tilmàtli." The commoners did not belong to the Toltec bloodline – or in many cases, the fabricated royal bloodline – and would probably have come from other groups or vassal states. The elites held almost all major designations in government. They enforced restrictions so that no commoner could reach a major rank in the army or priesthood. The most exceptional commoners who had displayed feats of strength and wisdom were welcomed into the government, albeit in offices of lesser value.

Agriculture may have been central to the Toltec economy, but there are major issues in ascertaining whether their agricultural produce was cultivated locally or imported from other places as a form of tribute. Should the latter be true, the probability of slavery in the Postclassic Era increases. According to most estimates, maize, beans, and chili peppers were cultivated around Tula, whereas cacao and mushrooms were imported. Most of the cultivation was done using the technique of hill terracing. Their irrigation systems, although not exemplary, were better than most Mesoamerican civilizations. The Toltecs extracted different parts of corn vegetation for medicinal and ornamental purposes, used cotton for weaving clothes, and used the maguey plant for fermenting alcoholic drinks. The land of Tula was probably fertile in the Postclassic Period, but during the occasional famine or drought, the Toltecs harvested and consumed amaranth. As far as trade is concerned, we know that textiles and ceramics were exported from Tula, and jade, turquoise, obsidian, exotic bird, and animal skins made their way into the city. The Toltecs were adept at establishing monopolies and forbade the bartering of rare goods to other cultures. They also knew when to increase and decrease prices according to the supply and demand of an item.

The Maya used to conduct extensive trade throughout the region, and with the emergence of Teotihuacán, more routes started to pop up. This vast existing network helped the Toltecs launch their trade. Archaeologists have uncovered pottery from Nicaragua, Costa Rica, and Guatemala in Tula, proving that the Toltecs conducted trade over long distances. Some ceramic material from Veracruz has also been found at Tula. Moreover, Tula was involved in the production of pottery, bowls, and items made from obsidian. It is not known whether Tula was directly involved in the production of these goods or a nearby area produced them under the directions of Tula.

The expansion of trade and territory using staunch religious ideology might have proved costly for the Toltecs in the long run. Some people credit their strict adherence to war-like ways for their eventual demise. The Toltecs expanded at an exponential pace throughout Mesoamerica based on violence. This makes historians wonder if they were sharp enough to take full advantage of their political and economic circumstances. Some theorists think that the Gulf Coast might have been at the forefront of trade in Mesoamerica instead of Tollan.

The rapid expansion of the empire did not allow the multiple ethnicities of the empire to integrate peacefully. There is plenty of room for error when a multi-ethnic empire has numerous vassal states of a diverse ethnic makeup under its rule. These issues might have been integral in igniting the constant civil wars between the cults of Quetzalcoatl and Tezcatlipoca. The battles with the Otomi and the Huastec people may have also been the result of rapid expansion and lack of cohesion between the different factions of society.

A lot of literature discusses the possibility of the Toltecs being several groups of Nahuatl-speaking people that did not constitute an "empire." The people who prefer this position think that these groups had overlapping similarities and formed cultural hybrids with other groups and cultures. Consequently, the Toltecs of Tula were somewhat different from the Toltecs of Chichen Itza, who, in turn, were quite different from the Toltec Maya, and so on. They point out that the terms Toltec and Tollan could have referred to more than four particular groups and four different states, respectively. The variations of the Toltecs include the group at Tula de Allende, the Toltec-Maya who inhabited Chichen Itza, the inhabitants of Teotihuacán and its surroundings, and the ethnic group Tolteca Chichimeca. These various possible versions of the Toltecs had differences in their social conduct, but if one were to paint with a broad stroke, it would be hard to discern the differences. Because of the similarities in social conduct, religion, and origins of all these groups, it is hard to distinguish between them unless someone stumbles upon major discoveries in the future. Not only that, but the evolution of all groups also followed similar trajectories when they shifted from agrarian communes to urban states.

Normally, we associate rural life with a free and uninhibited lifestyle with little to no social contact. Its appreciation depends on one's sensitivity towards nature. However, in the case of ancient civilization, this was often not the case. Agricultural lifestyles endorsed tribalism and served as a breeding ground for false notions of tribal superiority and ethnic dominance. Loyalty to the tribe would often become a source of egotism and eventually give rise to greed and lust for power. Most Mesoamerican tribes were nomadic, which means that they were almost always on the move. They rarely had time to settle down and make time for civilized progression. Every activity was geared towards short-term survival. This behavior is quite common in the animal kingdom. Fortunately, man learns to socialize. Gradually, he starts to understand that inter-community and intra-community relations are not always a zero-sum game. Many occasions call for communication, and acting on these opportunities often leads to a rewarding outcome for all parties involved. Tribalism had always prevailed in Mesoamerica, which is why the development of Teotihuacán and the ensuing Toltec Empire were life-altering revelations for the locals.

Chapter 12: Arts, Sculpture, and Architecture

The Toltecs were master artisans, sculptures, and architects. They were revered throughout the land for their decorations of pottery, ornaments, jewelry, stonemasonry, and buildings. It is no wonder that the word, Toltec, became synonymous with the word, artist, in Mesoamerican lands. These praises were certainly warranted, as anyone can gather from the remains of Tula. One must remember that Tula was destroyed and burned, so what we see on the site today might be a very small area within the larger premises of the original city.

Tula and other Toltec territories were raided and looted after the demise of their empire. Aztecs, who held them in high regard, would often take relics, valuables, and stone carvings while passing through lands of the former empire. Archaeological research dictates that the Aztecs took relics from Teotihuacán as well. The Spanish invasions took care of the rest. As far as we know, the Spanish burnt written codices of the Toltecs without exception – pending discovery. The Spanish did the same to the Maya and Aztec codices, too, but somehow, some documents have survived. Some post-conquest codices were also compiled to transcribe the history of the Aztecs and the Maya. In the Colonial Era, priceless artwork was looted and sold on the black market. Unfortunately, for these reasons, most Toltec art has been lost to the annals of history, unlike most Mayan and Aztec artifacts that have survived to date. Even the sculptures of ancient Olmec have survived the brunt of time. In the case of the Toltecs, the most significant pieces of their legacy include the collective site of Tula Chico and Tula Grande and an obsidian workshop near Tula. However, enough of it has survived to serve as a testament to their majestic prowess in the arts. Their emergence had such a distinct impact on areas in the north of Mexico and central Mexico that civilizations in those areas witnessed a rejuvenation of spirit. The Huastec in the north and the Tarascos in the west are witnesses to this adventurous fervor. From this period onwards, these cultures started to develop lasting architectural and sculptural statements.

The Classic Period in Mesoamerica saw the apex of Mayan creativity. Some even believe that it was as relevant for the region as Renaissance was for Europe. Most of these Maya contributions show Mexican values, hinting at a Toltec-Maya collaboration. We know that these Mexican values infiltrated not just central Mexico but southern Mexico and northern parts of Central America as well. In Chichen Itza, we see the themes of Toltec art develop in tandem with Tula. Eagles and jaguars devour human hearts, and gathered skulls are placed on altars called "tzompantli." Tzompantli had a scaffold-like construction of poles and was found in several Mesoamerican civilizations, including the Maya and the Aztec cities. The skulls normally belonged to sacrificial victims and war captives. The tzompantli at Tula has rows of stone carvings on the sides of a broad platform that depict the skulls of the sacrificial victims. The real skulls of the victims were displayed on these platforms. In Chichen Itza, the tzompantli appears on the sidewalls of the ballcourt. Other Maya cities like Uxmal also have some examples of the ancient device. This practice probably appeared in Tula in the late stages, shortly before its fall. The Aztecs continued the tradition, and a tzompantli still exists in Tenochtitlan. There were at least five more tzompantli in the Aztec capital city when the Spanish arrived. In different Aztec codices, we can see the tzompantli depicted in the context of ballgames.

Looking at Toltec art, one instantly reaches the same conclusion that one reaches when looking at works from the High Renaissance: It was a cultural phenomenon that pervaded multiple cities, a mode of conversation – not just between different minds but also between different lifestyles and social values. The one thing that unites almost all Toltec art is the consistent use of religious motifs. This religious current permeated every aspect of their lives.

These people were not privy to the Greek revolution of reason and logic, so they regaled themselves with myths and fables that seeped into the sociological framework. One watches in awe as the warriors and priests perform their duties, and the gods go about their divine work in the images. The events exaggerated, the figures elevated to heroes, these works of art are, first and foremost, dramatic works. For instance, the relief at Building 4 in Tula shows a procession heading towards a man dressed as a feathered serpent. Some believe that the Atlantean statues at the heart of the city were not depictions of the average Toltec warrior but a representation of Tlahuizcalpantecuhtli - the god of the morning star who was one of the many forms of Quetzalcoatl - or his followers.

The Atlantean sculptures are among the finest examples of Toltec art. Carrying a curved weapon, darts, and knives, these figures are renowned for their solemn devotion and grand scale. This sentiment extends itself to the smaller ceramic and stone figurines as well as relief and stone carvings. Most of what we know about Toltec art comes from these figures since the stone at the site of Tula has persevered against the hardships of climate and time. The signature sculpture of perhaps the entire Toltec civilization is the reclining figure of a man. Known as "chacmool," these figures represent male warriors facing 90 degrees from the front, supporting themselves on their elbows and knees and carrying a bowl or a disc in their lap. For the most part, the chacmools portrayed slain soldiers who were carrying offerings to the gods. The receptacle in the middle of the sculpture carries alcoholic drink, tortilla, tamale, turkey, feathers, tobacco, or incense. The 12 chacmools in Tula have standardized features and are quite similar except for some minor changes. It is quite probable that the ones in Tula represent war captives. As the influence of the Toltecs grew, chacmools started to appear all over Mesoamerica. They started appearing in the Yucatán and even as far away as Costa Rica. The chacmools at Chichen Itza are not all similar and vary somewhat in their features. The Aztec chacmools have an association with water and are often linked with the god of rain.

Toltec art is also credited with the introduction of plumbate – a distinct style of glazed pottery that uses metals like copper, silver, and gold. Usually associated with the use of a special type of clay, it was one of the most unique artistic statements of its time, evolving because of Toltec ingenuity. The Toltecs were known for their orange-colored and dark-colored plumbate pottery with a glossy exterior full of incised decoration, portraying a variety of styles. The Toltecs also perfected the inlays in turquoise and other materials. Around this time, archaeologists notice the appearance of metals throughout Mesoamerica. Metals like gold and silver started being used for creating different items, probably popularized by their use as metallic gleams in plumbate.

The motifs from sculpture appear in different structures throughout the city architecture as well. The architecture of the Toltecs is exemplary for its time. The Toltecs derived most of their architectural influences from Teotihuacán but added freshness, character, and nuance to them. The city square of Tula is largely reminiscent of the one at Teotihuacán, both in design and pattern. The Pyramid C at Tula has the same astronomical orientation as the Aztec city. Despite the influence, Toltec art evolves heavily from the basic premise. At the time, no civilization was designing cities based on grid plans - Teotihuacán first popularized the idea – but most of Tula was designed according to a grid plan. At its peak, it had a population of 85,000 that was creatively spread out throughout the city's central districts and outskirts. At least 60,000 people lived inside the city and 25,000 right outside of it. Granted, the peak population of Tula was much smaller than other Mesoamerican metropolitans, but it was the biggest Mesoamerican city of its era. The structures were made from stone, and then an adobe finish was applied to them. The pyramids, palaces, and other royal buildings had relief sculptures and friezes on the fringes. Tula has a ton of relief sculptures and friezes, including the Wall of Serpents that has elaborate carvings of snakes devouring human beings as well as geometric designs. The wall separated the sacred precinct from the rest of the city.

The people who lived in the city lived in large apartment complexes. Most of them would have been aristocrats or belonged to the middle class. The city also had palaces and group homes. The city was divided into districts: people from different backgrounds and socio-economic standing would have lived in different neighborhoods. The smaller classes outside the city would probably have lived in houses made of lower-grade materials, making them susceptible to environmental damage. They have probably perished after years of perpetual damage.

Several houses may have perished, and great monuments may have been burned, but fortunately, archaeologists have found thousands of pieces of pottery at Tula. Some of these items were locally produced, while others were brought there from far away; some of them are in great shape, while others are partially damaged. Experts think that Tula's brand of plumbate pottery was unique and original. The Aztecs were adamant that the Toltecs had refined the art of clay. Excavations have revealed that the Toltecs made Mazapan-style ceramics for themselves and brought other styles of pottery from foreign lands as tribute or imports. The local potters were also adept at creating pottery pieces with faces. Not only that, but the Toltecs also made nose rings, earplugs, and other forms of jewelry using jade, turquoise, and gold.

Near the end of the 10th century, the western region of Mexico saw an uptick in creative zeal and vigor. Up until that point, they had carried minor influences from the Olmecs and the artisans of Teotihuacán. Incorporating the Toltec influence, they started creating exquisite items of gold and silver, as well as polychrome vessels. This rebirth was not restricted to small-scale arts but extended to architecture as well. During this period, the Tarascan region began erecting buildings using stone. Tzintzuntzan, meaning "place of hummingbirds," the ceremonial center at the Tarascan state capital is the prime example of this change. Here we find the Yacatas, five rounded pyramids that stand atop a large platform. At the summit of the pyramids, there were wooden temples for performing sacred rites. Just like the western areas of Mexico, the northern areas were highly influenced by the artistic endeavors in central Mexico - exemplified by the case of La Quemada. The tribes that constituted the Aztec Empire originated from the north, and that region was home to nomadic people. The people there became more and more interested in small-scale arts like sculpture and pottery. For instance, in Casas Grandes, people produced intricate pottery designs based on geometric patterns.

The Toltecs may have made their name because of their military prowess, but they were just as talented in the artistic department. With great experiences comes the need for expression. What we see with the evolution of arts in Toltec society is not unusual. It is a perfectly sound response to the whims of the time. The ancient world was nowhere as fixated on the global perspective as the modern world. They did not have the luxury to travel distances as tourists and engage with other cultures. The Toltecs were nomadic, so they would often encounter other groups and had a militaristic approach to politics, which kept them in contact with those groups. For the ancient Mesoamerican world, this kind of exposure was extremely exciting. With the tributes pouring in to Tula and the newfound activity on trade routes, people were coming in touch with different perspectives and novel ideas. The most common example of this is the mysterious connection between Tula and Chichen Itza.

The Toltec influence of arts took over the entire Mesoamerican land, and even their fall from grace could not hamper the pace of this expansion. In times like these, art becomes a sort of conversation, a back-and-forth between different artists living in the same landscape and somewhat similar conditions. The artistic genius of the Toltecs and its impact in Mesoamerica is undeniable. Coming into power in the Late Classic Era and taking over the collective subconscious of the entire region in the Postclassic Era, the Toltecs have certainly left their mark in the pre-Columbian history of the New World. We may not fully understand them, but we know how they felt.

Chapter 13: Warfare and Weaponry

Finally, we arrive at the central pillar of Toltec life, the tenet that helped them build their empire and prosper as a people: *Warfare.*

Mesoamerican cultures upheld priests as the highest authority. The Toltecs were the first Mesoamerican society where the military was showered with the same prestige and status as priests. They elevated warfare from the needless clashes and skirmishes based on hate and fearmongering – and turned it into a viable source of income. When they left the northwestern deserts and arrived in central Mexico, they battered and bullied other groups into submission, quickly carving out their space in the harsh landscape. They opposed the idea of bloodshed and useless killing and would often take war captives to serve the needs of the group at large. These needs fluctuated between economic and spiritual. They would often need other groups to send them tribute, and when they took prisoners, they would put them to work or offer them to the gods.

Historical data regarding their vassal states is limited, but we know that the Toltecs held some states in central Mexico as vassals and demanded the tribute of food, goods, weapons, and soldiers. Historians are divided regarding the scope of this exercise. Some believe that it may have reached the Gulf Coast. Whether it was to and from trade with the Gulf Coast or a one-way journey of tribute is unknown. As far as solid, conclusive evidence is concerned, we rarely come across it when dealing with the Toltecs. There is no definitive evidence that the Toltecs held sway over any state more than 1000 kilometers away from Tula. We notice the socio-political influence of Toltec art all over the region, but that does not speak to the extent of the Toltec empire. Historians mostly believe that while the Toltecs probably held military influence over their neighboring areas, their influences in far-off regions can be attributed to trade or exile groups.

The Toltecs developed a military mindset from a young age. Those who wished to master Toltec knowledge would often study in telpochcalli and then in calmécaca – these were centers for education, and here, they would gain their basic understanding of the spiritual war. The intense religious perspective of the world helped them realize the transient and ephemeral nature of life. Such an understanding was crucial to weed out resistance, cowardice, and fear from the minds and hearts of the disciples. The men and women who partook in the activities at these institutions were known as warriors. They would learn to deceive their ego, control their impulses, stonewall the material inertia of the world, and allow harmony and peace into their inner sanctum. In some ways, the Toltec understanding of the world paralleled the teachings of Buddhism, but that is a discussion for another time.

The warriors were taught to look for their one true aim: their purpose in life. The object of the training was to help them reveal their personalities to themselves. The rest was not of any consequence – his iron will and determination would see to it that his mission was achieved. The possibilities of the spirit were endless, and so, worldly achievements were never beyond the realm of possibility. The idea was that the few basic forces that control the world manifested themselves in different physical manners, so if one could harness the spiritual force of the self, he could fulfill his purpose in the vast cosmology of events.

To enforce this understanding, the Toltecs had military orders, including but not restricted to the eagle, the coyote, and the jaguar. Some people like to refer to these religious warrior orders as cults. Excavations have revealed a small statue of a Tlaloc warrior cult in a ballcourt in Tula. Such statues have also been found at Teotihuacán. As discussed briefly in an earlier chapter, some people thought that the Atlantean statues might have been divine or semi-divine figures. They are adorned with the symbols of Quetzalcoatl that depict them as servants of the god. This may be in part due to the Toltec warrior's allegiance to a particular warrior cult. Think back to the cults of Tezcatlipoca and Quetzalcoatl, who went head-to-head against each other in a battle for supremacy. After Topiltzin left Tollan, the Toltecs chose Huitzilopochtli as their patron. If you don't recall, Huitzilopochtli was the Nahua god of war. He was worshipped by the Mexica and was the patron deity of Tenochtitlan.

The language of ancient Mesoamerica was often quite poetic. Things were not elaborated by pale descriptions. The concepts of the spirit were relayed with the power of abstraction. Metaphors were used to engage with the reader on an intuitive level. The great philosophers were not master of reason; they were masters of language. For explaining the concept of the warrior, their metaphoric language uses the words "flower" and "song." The Toltecs believed that wisdom was full of inherent beauty, and the embodiment of this beauty could only be achieved by the expression of the spirit. So, beauty was the proverbial garden where the songs, the flowers of wisdom, grew. As mentioned earlier, students of higher education were known as warriors, and most of them would serve as members of the military force. With the beautiful use of language, the Toltecs emphasized that a great warrior was the one who was sensitive to the order of things, responsible to his purpose, and disciplined in his execution.

The warrior's sensitivity kept him for killing for the sake of killing. He or she would refrain from conflict unless it was called for. By becoming conscious of the world and its inhabitants, he realized that they are self-aware beings as well. Some may delve into the conscious abstractions of the world more than others, but everyone exhibits awareness of other beings and the world around them. To avail them of their lives for the cultivation of one's ego would be an egregious sin and a loss for one's soul. Responsibility defers one, once again, to the order of things. A single human being does not inhabit the world. People live, they die, others take their place, everyone is equally helpless before nature. Therefore, the warrior was called upon to realize his responsibility – not just to himself but also to the natural world at large. He could not give in to pride or greed, he could not be fixated on the follies of the world, and he should only have been loyal to his ultimate aim in the world - the ambition of his spirit. This sense of responsibility distinguished the warrior from the average Joe in the street. The warrior had the responsibility to manifest his wisdom and knowledge by the power of action. The third tenet, discipline, was the willpower to execute said action. The Toltec warriors had a completely different understanding of discipline than the one often preached in the modern world. For the Toltecs, discipline was a personal regime and did not belong to a group or a political cause. Although it could have only belonged to the warrior, it needed to be cultivated. His will and resolve were tested to see whether he was up to the task. If the spirit were pure, it would get the body to fulfill its spiritual responsibility. To achieve discipline, he had to be sensitive towards the inner and outer workings of the world and had to know his responsibility to both. Only then, it was believed, could he master the art of discipline. This mindset was quite humbling for the warrior. Its goal was to turn warriors into solemn beings, very much like the priests who governed high society.

The Quetzalcoatl was the ultimate expression of this ideal. The feathered serpent slithered on the earth, touched it, and learned its secrets. When it was time, the quetzal - the sacred bird - spread its wings and left the earth in search of a new path among the clouds. Quetzalcoatl symbolized the importance of the other planes of existence and removed emphasis from the one the warriors saw, heard, and breathed in. All these ideas can be found in the Cantares Mexicanos, a Nahuatl manuscript from the 16th century that contains poems and songs. Historical data indicates that the realization of all these ideals was not always possible. Things would often spiral out of control, descending the city of Tula into turmoil and chaos. The warrior cults would go against each other, as demonstrated by the cults of Quetzalcoatl and Tezcatlipoca.

Skilled, terrifying, and highly trained, the Toltecs had a standing army in their states and garrisons in other states as well. The standing army would defend against foes, whereas the foreign legions would keep the vassal states in check and protect them from outside interference. They also had reserve units in the cities that they could call upon in times of need. The neighboring states were not in awe of the Toltecs because of their skills on the battlefield. They respected them for building a system that incorporated military values so aptly into the everyday life of an urban environment. For instance, Tula did not have any heavy defenses incorporated into the city design. Bear in mind that Tula had a grid plan, so they must have had time to work out the needs of the city. The Toltecs were confident in their ability to protect the city from outsiders, no matter what.

The Toltec warriors can be seen in different statues, friezes, stelae, and other works of art found at Tula and other sites. For protection, they wore decorative chest plates and cotton armors that were heavily padded to deflect oncoming arrows and spears. The breastplate would often have an image of a jaguar, a coyote, or an eagle to distinguish the warrior's cult. A short kilt was worn to protect the lower half of the torso. Their helmets were adorned with feathers, and they used sandals and straps to obscure legs and ankles, but these would have provided little in the way of protection. They preferred small, round shields because they wrapped one arm from the shoulder down in padding. An armored tunic was uncovered in the Burned Palace of Tula. Made of seashells, this elegant and well-crafted armor probably belonged to a high-level officer or a member of the nobility. Their choice of weapons was rather interesting. They liked to use swords, maces, knives, and curved clubs with blades for close-range combat, fastening them with a belt. For ranged combat, they employed atlatls, which launches spears or javelins. They would use it to shoot long darts with remarkable precision.

The true genius of the Toltecs lay not in teaching their warriors to effectively yield a sword but in managing the psychological and sociological aspects associated with military service. Their unshaken trust in their abilities and the depth of their tactical and strategic ventures were more than enough to strike fear in the hearts of their enemies. By extracting students of higher education, they were able to bring the cream of the crop to the military. However, this practice also proved to be their downfall. No matter how well-educated and well-disciplined a military force is, it will always succumb to greed, lust, and agendas of power. Such is the nature of the work – engaging in battles, thriving in tough situations, and priding yourself on the toughness of competition are all actions that induce adrenaline. It is quite easy to succumb to it, which is why military regimes throughout history have had a hard time keeping up with the needs of the state.

It is possible that natural disasters, instead of the unusual social structure, wiped the Toltec empire from the face of the Earth – just as they believed: everything is ephemeral, and change is the only constant. Civilizations rise, and civilizations fall. Sometimes, it takes centuries; sometimes, it takes years. But the demise is inevitable. After all, whatever goes up must come down. Unfortunately, for the Toltecs, the fall came like a bolt of lightning.

Conclusion

In the Classic Period of Mesoamerican civilization, the Maya entered their golden age. During this time, the Maya erected monuments based on the calculations of their Long Count calendar. As they opted for large-scale construction, they ushered in a new era in the history of the region. The innovation and the ambitious outlook of the lowland Maya inspired their neighbors. The Maya wrote inscriptions, integrated calendars into their daily lives, and emphasized artistic and intellectual development. A wave of urbanism followed. Art historians have likened the Classic Maya's influence to that of the Renaissance in Europe. As the Maya shifted from a purely agrarian culture to an urban lifestyle, they started to form small city-states. These states quickly began interacting with each other, forming alliances, forging trade routes, and navigating a competitive environment.

At the same time, a religious center emerged in the Mexican Highlands, known as "Teotihuacán." What began as a ceremonial site soon started to attract migrants from all over the region. The city witnessed an influx of the Zapotec, the Mixtec, and the Maya people, turning it into a multi-ethnic state. In a short time, the city developed its reputation as the most extravagant city of Mesoamerica and started to exert its influence on its neighbors, including the Maya. In the Late Classic Period, famine and drought took over the land, and the unforgiving climate made it difficult to survive in the city. The city was eventually burnt and looted - probably due to internal strife -, and a hefty majority of the population migrated to the surrounding areas. After the fall of Teotihuacán, the Maya started to witness some internal issues as well. The states of Tikal and Calakmul went to war. After a long back-and-forth, the Maya were weakened. Teotihuacán was proof that a metropolitan city could be established in the region.

In the Late and Terminal Classic Periods, some nomadic groups started arriving in Central Mexico from the north. Some of these tribes settled on the site of Tula and gave birth to the Toltec Empire. Some people think that the Toltecs had been living there for a few centuries and were even involved in the destruction of Teotihuacán. Others believe that they arrived shortly after the fall of Teotihuacán and imbued the land with an aura of wisdom and fear.

So, who were the Toltecs? Where did they come from? Where did they go?

Nobody knows. All we have is the art of speculation. Presumably, they migrated from the north, settled at Culhuacan, and finally arrived at Tula. In Tula, the Toltecs were ruled by the mesmerizing figure of Cē Ācatl Topiltzin, also known as "Quetzalcoatl." The feathered serpent educated them, teaching them how to grow crops, read a calendar, and engage with the spiritual essence of the self. Like most Mesoamerican cultures, the Toltecs were religious people who practiced human sacrifice and bloodletting.

The Toltecs had a military-based society where warriors were groomed from a young age. They were the first civilization in Mesoamerica that turned its combat skills into a viable source of income. Their military conquests were backed by their religious foundations. They took over the city-states of the region and demanded tributes from them. Units were sent to vassal states to maintain peace and receive regular tributes. The Toltecs had a fondness for warrior cults, and excavations reveal that warriors belonged to orders of jaguars, coyotes, and eagles. These cults had specific religious ideologies and were responsible for the biggest divide in Toltec society. Some supported the cult of Quetzalcoatl, whereas others supported the cult of Tezcatlipoca. In some ways, the religious ambitions of the two cults were opposite to each other.

Cē Ācatl Topiltzin Quetzalcoatl was renowned for his humanist ideals. He abolished the Mesoamerican tradition of human sacrifice and only offered foods and animals to the gods. The insight of Topiltzin helped Tula thrive and prosper for years. One day, Tezcatlipoca appeared before him as an old man and tricked him. After being humiliated, Quetzalcoatl left the city and headed east. When he reached the shore, he burnt himself on a pyre and turned into a star – to return in the future. This, of course, is the mythological version of the story as told by the Aztecs. After the self-imposed exile of Topiltzin, Tula was razed and burnt to the ground. Many people believe that the cults probably went to war against one another, and Tezcatlipoca emerged victoriously. Some refute that statement and claim that natural disasters caused famine, hunger, and disease, forcing people to flee. Theorists like to speculate, but the fact of the matter is that *nobody knows what happened.*

The cult of Quetzalcoatl did spread throughout the region. For instance, it is known that there was some mysterious connection between the city of Tula and the Maya city, Chichen Itza. The Temple of Quetzalcoatl in Chichen Iza, also known as "El Castillo," depicts the shadow of a serpent on the equinoxes. Moreover, one finds many drawings and inscriptions of the feathered serpent in Uxmal. Even though the image of the feathered serpent existed in the Preclassic Era, Quetzalcoatl did not appear until the Late Classic Era.

The cult of Quetzalcoatl permeated the land of central Mexico. The Aztecs added him to the pantheon of their gods and held him in high esteem. They revered the Toltecs so much that they claimed to have descended from them. It was common practice to claim Toltec descent to get recognized as nobles, making it extremely difficult for historians to differentiate between the historical figure, Topiltzin, and the god, Quetzalcoatl. The cult of Quetzalcoatl was a widely held belief among the Aztecs. It is said that when Hernan Cortes invaded Mesoamerica, the Aztec king, Montezuma, mistook him for the reincarnation of Quetzalcoatl.

In addition to being great warriors, the Toltecs were also great artists. The Aztecs were in awe of their scientific and artistic achievements. The Toltecs developed their style of pottery called plumbate pottery. They were responsible for popularizing metalwork in Mesoamerica. They used jade, silver, obsidian, gold, and copper to create pottery, jewelry, and other items. They also made major contributions to the fields of sculpture and architecture. The Atlantean statues standing in the middle of Tula are fine examples of their talent and skill. The Toltecs were also responsible for introducing large-scale terraced agriculture and high-quality ceramics.

The Toltecs introduced a new political system in Mesoamerica: militarism. It became the norm for various empires in the Terminal Classic and Postclassic Periods, including the Aztecs. The Aztec Empire, an alliance of three states, sustained itself by collecting tributes from its vassals. The Toltecs are the missing part of the story – the invisible link that joins the Maya and Teotihuacán to the Aztec Empire. We may not know who they were, where they came from, or how they disappeared, but their contributions to world heritage stand as proof of their undeniable genius.

Part 5: Teotihuacan

An Enthralling Overview of the First Large City in Mesoamerica and Its Influence on Mesoamerican Civilizations Such as the Maya Civilization and Aztecs

Introduction

The Mexica-Aztecs wandered into the ancient ruins, gazing around in awe. They had left their home of Aztlán over a century earlier, roaming as nomads through the harsh terrain of northwestern Mexico. Now, in the late 13ᵗʰ century CE, the Mexica-Aztecs had reached an extraordinary city that had been, for the most part, abandoned five centuries earlier. They gazed at the pyramids in wonder; the highest towered 216 feet over the city center. They inspected the vivid murals and fascinating carvings.

Overcome by reverence and excitement, the Aztecs whispered, "This must be where the gods were born!"

And so, they named it Teotihuacan, which in their Nahuatl language meant "the place where the gods emerged." Its original name remains a mystery. The ancient ruins lay in a fertile basin with rivers and a mild climate. Yet, curiously, the Aztecs left the city and its ghosts behind, pressing southwest another fifty miles, circling the shores of Lake Texcoco. Following their hummingbird god, Huitzilopochtli, they established their city of Tenochtitlan on an island in a swamp. And yet, that famous city never came close to approaching the scale and grandeur of Teotihuacan. The Aztecs' entire temple complex at Tenochtitlan was only about one-sixth the size of Teotihuacan's Avenue of the Dead, with its monumental pyramids and impressive temples.

Mesoamerica is a region extending from Mexico to Costa Rica that has similar cultural features. As one of the earliest cradles of

Mesoamerican urban civilization, Teotihuacan rivaled the Maya cities in sophistication. At its zenith, it was the largest city in the Americas and among the six largest cities worldwide. Rather than being monocultural, Teotihuacan was a cosmopolitan city, welcoming immigrants from cultures hundreds of miles away.

Settled by 200 BCE, perhaps as early as 400 BCE, its inhabitants built the city's most prominent structures from around 100 to 350 CE. From that point until 650 CE, the city was in its golden age, with an estimated population between 125,000 to 200,000 living in apartment complexes in the urban core. Monumental city structures lined a north-south axis, with the Pyramid of the Sun in the center and the Pyramid of the Moon at the north end. To the south, fifteen smaller pyramids surrounded a sunken plaza with the Temple of the Plumed Serpent. Stone-sided canals rerouted the San Juan River to intersect the Avenue of the Dead, which linked the pyramids. They built all of this without the wheel and beasts of burden.

Pyramid of the Moon

Polimerek, CC BY-SA 3.0 <https://creativecommons.org/licenses/by-sa/3.0>, via Wikimedia Commons: https://commons.wikimedia.org/wiki/File:Teotihuacan_Pyramid_of_the_moon_3.jpg

Teotihuacan was a prosperous trade center. One of its chief exports was the razor-sharp volcanic obsidian glass used as arrowheads, spearheads, and knife blades. Craftsmen in numerous workshops west of the Pyramid of the Moon worked on the glass, which was formed from molten magma and mined from the nearby Sierra de las Navajas and Otumba Mountains. Green obsidian objects manufactured at Teotihuacan have been found in the Maya citadel of Tikal in Guatemala, almost eight hundred miles away.

Teotihuacan's origins, culture, and history continue to mystify archaeologists. Who built the incredible city? The ancient Toltecs? But their culture emerged toward the end of Teotihuacan's collapse. Maybe the Totonacs from the east? They had a population living within the city; however, their culture didn't arise until around 300 CE. They probably contributed to Teotihuacan's apex but not its origins. Did a massive volcano drive the Zapotec, Mixtec, and Maya into the valley? Since its original settlers are unknown, this book follows anthropologist George L. Cowgill's example of referring to the city's inhabitants as "Teotihuacanos."[112]

Teotihuacan's collapse began around 550 CE with a series of fires and intentional destruction. What happened? Was the city rocked by internal revolts or by an outside invasion? Teotihuacan had no defensive walls or military fortifications, suggesting it did not fear external threats. By 750 CE, the city was nearly empty. Did a massive volcanic eruption trigger climate change that led to famine?

This overview of Teotihuacan will explore these questions and other captivating mysteries of this vast city and its intriguing population. We will unpack the possible origins of the city's builders and the theories surrounding its development into a major Mesoamerican center. We will discover how the city was organized and review the remarkable pottery, paintings, and murals produced by its citizens. Teotihuacan was a religious epicenter, and we will investigate its people's core beliefs, philosophies, and the deities they worshiped. We will also explore the latest findings regarding the great pyramids and what they tell us about the city's culture.

Teotihuacan was not an island unto itself. Part of its supremacy was its status as a top Mesoamerican trade center. This book will examine its relations with the Maya and the Zapotecs and how these civilizations exchanged ideas and technologies. The city lay nearly abandoned when the Aztecs came on the scene, but it markedly influenced the Nahuatl-speaking tribes. Discover how the Aztecs made religious pilgrimages to Teotihuacan's pyramids and colonized the region.

---

[112] George L. Cowgill, *Ancient Teotihuacan: Early Urbanism in Central Mexico (Case Studies in Early Societies)* (Cambridge: Cambridge University Press, 2015), 5.

Scholars write many histories for other scholars in academic language that most people find challenging to follow. This book provides a comprehensive, carefully researched overview of Teotihuacan in an engaging narrative. Despite being only a few miles north of Mexico City, Teotihuacan's archaeological studies are still rudimentary and ongoing. Researchers are currently cataloging and analyzing discoveries, and this book explores the more recently published studies.

Learning about history has multiple benefits. Teotihuacan's history helps us comprehend how migrations, weather events, cultural blending, innovative breakthroughs, and other circumstances can shape local and world events. Teotihuacan provides an intriguing example of how a megacity can successfully blend migrants of multiple ethnicities and provide comfortable housing for its entire population. As we dive into history, we gain essential perspectives of the past and how it impacts our present-day challenges. Let's step back in time to twenty-four centuries ago to explore the rise of the stunning city of Teotihuacan and discover its catalysts for transformation.

SECTION ONE: A HISTORY OF TEOTIHUACAN (300 BCE–650 CE)

Chapter 1: Possible Origins and First Settlements

Did you know that camels and mammoths once roamed the valley where Teotihuacan would eventually be built? The late Pleistocene-era camels were about the size of today's camels but somewhat resembled modern-day llamas. In 2019, workers digging a new garbage dump discovered mammoth traps in Tultepec, about twenty miles west of Teotihuacan. Archaeologists rushed to the area and found fourteen mammoth skeletons and some camel vertebrae after ten months of excavation. The level of technology used by the early humans astonished the researchers.[113]

Thousands of years later, Teotihuacan grew into a city in the northeastern Basin of Mexico. The 3,700-square-mile Basin (or Valley) of Mexico includes today's Mexico City (about twenty-five miles southwest of Teotihuacan) and extends east to the Gulf of Mexico. Although called a "valley," it is a highlands plateau at least 7,000 feet above sea level; Teotihuacan's altitude is 7,500 feet. High mountains surround the Basin of Mexico, many of which are volcanoes, and the region is prone to earthquakes.

What settlements were in the Valley of Mexico in the Preclassic

---

[113] "Mammoth Traps near Mexico City Are First Ever Found," *Mexico News Daily,* November 8, 2019. https://mexiconewsdaily.com/news/mammoth-traps-near-mexico-city-are-first-ever-found/

or Formative period (1500 BCE–300 CE) before the Teotihuacanos arrived? One of the earliest chiefdom centers was Tlatilco, about twenty-five miles west of where Teotihuacan would be built. Tlatilco emerged as a population center about 1450 BCE, covering an area of about 160 acres. Its culture faded around 800 BCE, at least four hundred years before Teotihuacan emerged.

The Tlatilco people fashioned rather bizarre terracotta figurines, usually depicting women with large hips and thighs, slanting eyes, and elaborate hairstyles. Most of the figurines are only around six inches long; some are pregnant or holding children. One embraces a small dog, indicating dogs were pets, not just food or guards. One lady is quite the contortionist, as she sits in a yoga or acrobatic pose with her feet resting on the back of her head. A few figurines have two faces or two heads. Some of the Tlatilco pottery reflected Olmec influences, but others were unique to Tlatilco.

The Acrobat of Tlatilco, circa 1300 to 800 BCE

The Olmec culture, Mesoamerica's first major civilization, emerged around 1600 BCE. They were southeast of the Valley of Mexico but influenced Preclassic cultures like Tlatilco in central Mexico. Their three major cities were in the coastal regions along the Gulf of Mexico, about 350 miles southeast of Teotihuacan. The Olmecs developed a basalt aqueduct with water-storage cisterns, which piped fresh water to their cities. Their vast trading system stretched from the Valley of Mexico to Guatemala.

The Olmecs harvested sap from rubber trees and made the world's first rubber balls, which they used in ballgames; hence, the Aztecs named them "Olmec" or "rubber people." The Olmecs' La Venta Pyramid, built shortly before the Olmec collapse around 400 BCE, might be Mesoamerica's first pyramid. And let's not forget chocolate! The Olmecs figured out how to make a chocolate drink from cacao beans. They also developed a primitive writing system with glyphs or elemental symbols.

The Olmec civilization collapsed at about the same time as Tlatilco, probably due to volcanic eruptions, earthquakes, and disruptions to the river system. The Olmec culture would not have directly impacted the Teotihuacanos unless the remnants of the population migrated to the Valley of Mexico, which is a distinct possibility. However, archaeologists believe the Olmecs developed archetypal traits that laid the groundwork for later Mesoamerican cultures. They cite examples such as pyramids, ball courts, and ceremonial centers, all of which researchers have found in Teotihuacan.[114]

The Olmec culture faded before Teotihuacan's construction. However, the "Epi-Olmec" cities of Tres Zapotes and Cerro de la Mesas emerged on the western borders of the former Olmec territory around 300 BCE and endured until 250 CE. These cities coexisted with Teotihuacan and appeared to be offshoots of Olmec culture. They were less organized and lacked refined art, yet they had a sophisticated hieroglyphic writing system.

The Cuicuilco culture emerged around 1200 BCE and flourished with several cities from 800 BCE to 150 CE. It lay on Lake Texcoco's southern shore, about forty-five miles south of Teotihuacan in today's southwestern outskirts of Mexico City. It preceded Teotihuacan and coexisted as a hostile rival through its

---

[114] Ronald A. Grennes-Ravitz and G. H. Coleman, "The Quintessential Role of Olmec in the Central Highlands of Mexico: A Refutation," *American Antiquity* 41, no. 2 (1976): 196. https://doi.org/10.2307/279172.

Preclassic period. Cuicuilco was probably the first organized hierarchal city-state and religious center in the Basin of Mexico.

Like the Olmec civilization, Cuicuilco had a hydraulic system bringing water into the city. It grew from an agricultural center into a city of twenty thousand people. The city was home to pyramids, irrigation canals, and a stratified social system. It began to decline in the 1st century BCE, possibly due to minor volcanic activity. Between 245 and 315 CE, the nearby Xitle volcano erupted, covering Cuicuilco with lava and ash and killing most of the remaining residents.

The Maya civilization did not extend to the Valley of Mexico, but it had a significant impact on central Mexico's culture. The Maya are notable for the continuous occupation of the Yucatán Peninsula, southern Mexico, Guatemala, Belize, El Salvador, and Honduras. One excavated village in Belize dates to 2600 BCE. Some of their agricultural villages eventually grew into cities as the centuries passed, and the Maya began building large ceremonial structures by 750 BCE.

By the time Teotihuacan was built in central Mexico, the Maya had a sophisticated writing system and several large cities, such as El Mirador in Guatemala, which had a population of 100,000 at its peak. Once the Teotihuacanos rose to power, they actively interacted with the Maya, despite the distance between the civilizations. They had a strong trade connection, but at their peak, the Teotihuacanos inserted themselves into Maya politics. They even toppled Maya rulers in Guatemala and Honduras, enthroning Teotihuacan princes in their place.[115]

A Franciscan friar named Sahagún compiled ethnographic research in the 16th century based on interviews with the Aztecs and other Nahuatl-speaking tribes. In his *Florentine Codex*, written in Nahuatl and Spanish, he wrote the Aztec creation narrative. After the gods failed in their first four attempts at creation, they gathered around a bonfire at Teotihuacan, moaning, "Oh gods, who will have the burden of lighting the world?"

---

[115] Arthur Demarest, *Ancient Maya: The Rise and Fall of a Forest Civilization* (Cambridge: Cambridge University Press, 2004), 218. ISBN 978-0-521-53390-4. OCLC 51438896.

One of the gods would have to sacrifice himself to make a new sun, and the handsome god Tecuciztecatl volunteered. However, he couldn't work up the nerve to throw himself into the fire. So, the smallest and humblest god, Nanahuatl, jumped into the fire. Embarrassed by his cowardice, Tecuciztecatl threw himself in after Nanahuatl. The gods looked up to see two suns shining in the sky. How inappropriate! Disgusted, one god flung a rabbit into Tecuciztecatl's face, dimming his light. He became the moon. The myth explains the shape of the rabbit on the moon's face but also indicates the Aztec concept that Teotihuacan existed before the world's fifth and final creation.

The Aztecs thought Teotihuacan was the city of the gods, but who were the human Teotihuacanos who initially settled the region? What were their origins? One theory is that the Totonac people, who now populate the areas of Veracruz and Puebla to the south, built Teotihuacan. Their oral tradition says they originally lived in the northeastern section of the Valley of Mexico and built Teotihuacan. After the city's fall, the Totonacs say they migrated to the regions they currently occupy, especially El Tajin.

Archaeological evidence in Teotihuacan and El Tajin shows a strong connection between the cities. For instance, El Tajin-style decorative scrollwork appears in Teotihuacan, and the city imported Totonac ceramics from the Gulf Coast. Teotihuacan established a base for obsidian in southern Veracruz's Tuxtla Mountains in the 4th century CE. However, whether the connection between the cities was mainly through trade or whether the Teotihuacanos were actually Totonac is unproven.

Totonac chief figurine, circa 300–600 CE.

Anthropologists George Cowgill and Tatsuya Murakami speculated that the Teotihuacanos may not have been one single tribe but embraced synoecism: several societies coming together. They believed this group of multiple peoples shared administrative equality. What would be the point of merging? Cowgill suggested it may have been for mutual defense against the Cuicuilco, the Valley of Mexico's most powerful civilization at Teotihuacan's inception.[116]

Who were the original tribes in the theoretical merger? Archaeological finds indicate at least one hundred small settlements existed in the valley before Teotihuacan was settled, with populations of the largest cities reaching four thousand. But besides Cuicuilco, these settlements did not appear to have a clear center; they seemed to all be independent of each other. It is possible remnants of the Olmec or Epi-Olmec civilizations made their way into the northeastern Valley of Mexico and merged with other cultures. Teotihuacan ceramics include Olmec motifs, and

---

[116] Matthew Robb, ed, *Teotihuacan: City of Water, City of Fire* (Berkeley: University of California Press, 2017), 21.

its art reflects similar cosmological concepts. Olmec-style stone channels, apparently used for piping water, are under the Pyramid of the Sun.

Cowgill, who systematically mapped Teotihuacan, believes that from 150 to 1 BCE, the Teotihuacan settlement grew to hold a population of up to forty thousand people and covered three square miles.[117] Anthropologists call this period Teotihuacan's Early Formative Phase or Patlachique Phase, based on the type of ceramics from this period. Most of its monumental pyramids and other massive structures had yet to be built, except for several complexes with a group of three small pyramids and perhaps the first stage of the Pyramid of the Moon. Yet this was an extraordinary size for a Mesoamerican city in that era. It was undoubtedly the largest in the Valley of Mexico at that time. Cuicuilco was the only other sizeable city in central Mexico during that era, and it had twenty thousand residents at its peak and was already in decline due to volcanic activity.

Anthropologists Claudia García-Des Lauriers and Tatsuya Murakami believe that Teotihuacan was probably a cluster of independent communities at that point in time. They concur with Cowgill that several cultures may have come together for mutual benefit without a central government or one ruler dominating the whole city. However, they collaborated on projects, such as building canals from the San Juan River.[118]

Teotihuacan's Late Formative Phase, or Tzacualli Ceramic Phase, stretched from 1 to 150 CE. By 100 CE, Teotihuacan had doubled in population, with around eighty thousand people living in the city, and construction began on some of the city's monumental structures. The Teotihuacanos built the original Pyramid of the Moon around 100 CE and continued enlarging it until around 400 to 450 CE.

[117] George L. Cowgill, "State and Society at Teotihuacan, Mexico," *Annual Review of Anthropology* 26 (1997): 133. http://www.jstor.org/stable/2952518.

[118] Claudia García-Des Lauriers, ed. and Tatsuya Murakami, ed, *Teotihuacan and Early Classic Mesoamerica: Multiscalar Perspectives on Power, Identity, and Interregional Relations* (Louisville: University Press of Colorado, 2021).

A feathered-serpent carving from Teotihuacan's Feathered Serpent Temple.

Jami Dwyer, CC BY-SA 2.0 <https://creativecommons.org/licenses/by-sa/2.0>, via Wikimedia

Commons;

https://commons.wikimedia.org/wiki/File:Teotihuacan_Feathered_Serpent_(Jami_Dwyer).jpg

Cowgill speculated that a powerful and charismatic dictator ruled the city in the late 2nd century, instigating its ambitious projects in the Early Classic or Miccaotli Phase from 150 to 200 CE.[119] The Teotihuacanos launched an energetic building program in the city center, which included the construction of the Feathered Serpent Temple on the southern end of the three-mile Avenue of the Dead.

They also built the Ciudadela (Citadel), the expansive thirty-eight-acre sunken courtyard surrounding it. The discovery of over two hundred skeletons of people sacrificed at the Feathered Serpent Temple suggests a potential transition in the government. Human sacrifice had been a religious rite in Mesoamerica for over a millennium but not on this scale. The sacrifice of this many people points to a harsh, despotic government at this point. The construction of the Pyramid of the Sun may have begun around 200 CE or perhaps later; the pyramid served as the city's epicenter. A building connected to the pyramid may have been the ruler's

---

[119] Robb, *Teotihuacan: City of Water*, 22.

palace.

With about eighty thousand people around 100 CE, Teotihuacan grew rapidly for nearly a century. The city's population leveled off around 200 CE. Estimates for its ultimate size vary between 125,000 to 200,000, but the area could not agriculturally support a population larger than 200,000. Not only did the city grow, but the immediate region in a twenty-mile radius around the city also more than tripled in population. Meanwhile, the number of people in the rest of the Valley of Mexico declined.

Anthropologist Cowgill said that most of the Basin of Mexico's population moved into Teotihuacan between 100 to 200 CE.[120] What caused this massive migration and explosive growth? Who else was living in the Valley of Mexico or nearby in this period? Scholars speculate that volcanic eruptions at Cuicuilco, the Puebla-Tlaxcala Valley, and elsewhere in the south led to refugees flooding the city. Other migrants probably came to Teotihuacan with hopes of securing a better standard of living. They were drawn to Teotihuacan as a sacred destination, economic hub, and robust regional capital.

Nahua (or Nahuatl) speakers (the Toltecs, Aztecs, and Chichimeca) had not yet arrived in the Basin of Mexico, at least not enough to be influential.[121] Some archaeologists initially believed the Toltecs or other Nahuatl speakers built Teotihuacan or migrated to the city, influencing its later periods. They point to similarities in architecture and images. However, it is more likely that the Toltecs, Aztecs, and other groups borrowed from the Teotihuacanos rather than vice versa. For one thing, many of Teotihuacan's images were unique and had no counterparts in later Nahuatl cultures.[122] Secondly, there was a time issue. The Nahuatl speakers began migrating into the area as the great city declined.

With the Nahuatl speakers not yet in the picture, the migrants into Teotihuacan most likely came from the south. Refugees almost certainly came from Cuicuilco, where the population

[120] Cowgill, "State and Society," 129.

[121] Cowgill, "State and Society," 131.

[122] Cowgill, "State and Society," 133.

markedly declined in the same period, even before the final devastating volcanic eruption covered the city with lava. Maya migrants likely arrived in Teotihuacan, as their civilization experienced a temporary collapse in this era for unknown reasons. The smaller Teotihuacan pyramids are remarkably similar to some Maya pyramids.

Other migrants included the Mixtec and Zapotec tribes of the Oaxaca region of southwestern Mexico, forming middle-class sub-societies in Teotihuacan. The Zapotec had been a dominant force in southwestern Mexico since 500 BCE. The Mixtec alternated between being rivals and allies of the Zapotec. As their populations grew, the Zapotec and Mixtec began migrating to Teotihuacan as early as 200 BCE.

They formed distinct neighborhoods or *barrios* in Teotihuacan after 100 CE, with temples and apartment complexes. Teotihuacan's ethnic barrios often featured specialty craft production. The city had over six hundred craft workshops that produced pottery, ceramic figurines, obsidian weaponry, jade objects, baskets, leatherwork, and featherwork apparel or art. Although they integrated into the Teotihuacan culture, the Oaxacan tribes maintained some ethnic customs, such as funeral urn burials. The decorative urns were placed in groups of five over the tomb, above the door's lintel, or somewhere near but not in the tomb. What the urns held is a mystery, as nothing remains in them.

A Zapotec funerary urn.
Cleveland Museum of Art, CC0, via Wikimedia Commons;
https://commons.wikimedia.org/wiki/File:Mexico,_Oaxaca,_Zapotec_Culture_-
Funerary_Urn_-_1944.78_-_Cleveland_Museum_of_Art.tif

The influx of migrants into Teotihuacan in the first two centuries of the Common Era markedly changed the city's demographics into a cosmopolitan population. Architecture and art began to reflect diverse cultures and religions. Yet Teotihuacan art continued to be distinctive from typical Mesoamerican art; for instance, it rarely portrayed individuals, like the Tlatilco figurines or the Olmec colossal heads. Its overall architectural style reflected its precursor civilizations in the Valley of Mexico and Puebla-Tlaxcala Valley but with a new twist. Examples setting Teotihuacan apart from neighboring cultures include apartment complexes and locating its pyramids on a north-south axis along a processional way.[123]

Migration into Teotihuacan also changed its triad of functions as a spiritual, trade, and manufacturing center. It previously served as a ceremonial religious center, but it became a worship nucleus for the multiple religions of its diverse ethnicities. Teotihuacan did not seem to elevate one particular deity over others. Its religious art and artifacts display the shared goals of all its people: rain, productive harvests, economic prosperity, fertility, an effective military, and sustaining the celestial balance.

By absorbing most of the Valley of Mexico's population, Teotihuacan became the de facto capital of the valley's remaining settlements. It had always been a manufacturing center and unrivaled trade hub, and that continued, with trade routes extending throughout Mesoamerica. The various ethnicities brought exciting technologies to blend with the Teotihuacanos' expertise in producing obsidian weaponry, pottery, and other crafts.

---

[123] Robb, *Teotihuacan: City of Water*, 15.

Chapter 2: Teotihuacan's Glory Days

"Teotihuacan? Are you sure? That's nine hundred miles northwest!"

"Yes! Look at this pyramid's steep slope and this right-angle panel. It's like a table. That's talud-tablero. That's classic Teotihuacan!"

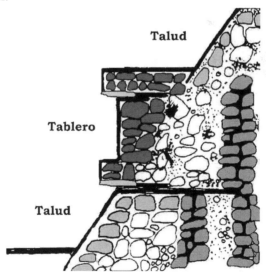

An example of the Teotihuacan talud-tablero architectural feature.

HJPD, CC BY-SA 3.0 <https://creativecommons.org/licenses/by-sa/3.0>, via Wikimedia Commons; https://commons.wikimedia.org/wiki/File:TableroTalud.jpg

Teotihuacan architecture and other finds in the western suburbs of Guatemala City showcased the long arm of Teotihuacan influence. Teotihuacan reveled in its glory days from about 350 to 600 CE. It developed into a super city-state, rising as the leading power throughout a large swathe of Mesoamerica during the Classic period (150–600 CE). Archaeologists have found obsidian, pottery, and other objects from Teotihuacan at sites throughout central Mexico and stretching south to the Maya region in Guatemala, Belize, and Honduras.

Teotihuacan controlled most of the Valley of Mexico in its zenith. Outside of the Valley of Mexico, it regulated outlying settlements that were important trade destinations and controlled the routes between them and Teotihuacan. The city had complex relationships with civilizations throughout Mesoamerica. Some of these interactions occurred between the migrant populations living in Teotihuacan and their kinsmen in Maya and Zapotec territories.

In their glory days, the Teotihuacanos had several secondary centers in central Mexico. They had a settlement called Chingdu, near what became the Toltec city of Tollan (Tula), about sixty miles northwest of Teotihuacan. This smaller city modeled Teotihuacan's layout and architecture. It was a key source of lime, which was needed in construction projects, and artifacts showed it had a mixed population of Teotihuacanos and Zapotecs. Holt Mehta was a town south of Chingdu that also left a blend of Teotihuacan and Zapotec artifacts. Eighty miles northwest of Tollan lay El Rosario in Querétaro, a far-flung colony of Teotihuacan.[124]

About twenty-one miles northeast, the Teotihuacanos established Tepeapulco, close to where they mined obsidian. It may have served as a craft center for manufacturing obsidian knives, arrowheads, and other weapons. Calpulalpan lay to the east, a gateway to trade with the Teotihuacan corridor to Veracruz, Oaxaca, and the Puebla region. Two smaller centers lay on Lake Texcoco's shores: Azcapotzalco on the western shore and Cerro Portezuelo on the lake's southeastern side.

---

[124] Cowgill, "State and Society," 134.

In Teotihuacan's Early Classic and Mid-Classic Phases, leading up to its zenith, the city experienced shifts in leadership that sparked a flurry of construction for several centuries. Archaeologists believe that Teotihuacan's ruling class exercised an intense power grab in its Early Classic Phase from around 150 to 200 CE. What may have previously been a loose coalition of semi-independent communities now came under a central government with decisive leadership.

The city embarked on a staggering urban renewal project in Teotihuacan's Mid-Classic Phase, or Tlamimilolpa Ceramic Phase, stretching from 200 to 350 CE. The metropolis erected about 2,300 housing complexes for the expanding population. Each compound housed about sixty to one hundred people in single-story homes surrounded by shared courtyards. Between 250 to 350 CE, some scholars believe that Teotihuacan's government shifted from a strong centralized monarchy to a decentralized administration, perhaps led by a council.

The Teotihuacanos upgraded the Pyramid of the Moon three times from 250 to 350 CE, enlarging it significantly with each renovation. Although archaeologists found no human sacrifices in its earliest three layers, the layers built from 250 to 350 all contained human sacrifices. The Pyramid of the Sun was once thought to have been constructed by 200 CE, but recent radiocarbon dating points closer to the mid-200s. The Teotihuacanos sacrificed multiple babies and children when they built this pyramid. The children's skeletal remains have been found under the pyramid and at the four corners of each layer of the pyramid. This has led some scholars to theorize the pyramid was dedicated to the god of storms, known as Tlaloc to the Aztecs, as he was associated with child sacrifice.

This stone mask from Teotihuacan's Xolalpan era was a grave offering.

The city's Late Classic phases were the Xolalpan Ceramic era from 350 to 550 CE and the Metepec Ceramic era from 550 to 600 CE. The Xolalpan era was Teotihuacan's height of power, with the city's great pyramids, temples, and housing projects mostly completed. Teotihuacan now focused outward, expanding its vast trade empire and even conquering Maya cities about eight hundred miles southeast in Guatemala and Honduras.

The city's Maya residents experienced violent turmoil around 350 CE. Scholars believe that elite Maya, who served as diplomats and trade facilitators, lived near the west side of the Avenue of the Dead, between the Sun and Moon pyramids. Recent excavations at the Plaza of Columns in that part of the city have uncovered Maya murals, ceramics, and other artifacts. However, the murals appear to have been destroyed and buried. A pit of charred bones, believed to be Maya, points to a massacre around 350 CE.[125] Three elderly Maya men, wearing the regalia of nobility, were sacrificed at the top of the Pyramid of the Moon around this time.[126]

Although two more rebuilding phases took place in the Mid-Classic era, they replaced older structures rather than expanded the city. The population appears to have stabilized in the Early Classic period. The city may have changed religious ideology in the Xolalpan era, around 350 CE. This was when the Adosada platform was erected directly in front of the Feathered Serpent Temple, partially blocking its view.[127] This transition would have been close to the time King Spearthrower Owl came to the throne of Teotihuacan, ruling from 374 to 439 CE, according to Maya inscriptions.

Scholars debate the nature of Teotihuacan's control over the rest of the Valley of Mexico and even the rest of Mesoamerica during its glory days. Did it exert sovereign power? Were the outlying cities colonies that paid tribute and answered to Teotihuacan mandates? Was Teotihuacan ultimately the center of an empire? Earlier archaeologists and anthropologists believed Teotihuacan exercised hegemony or superior influence over other cities and civilizations. They pointed to Teotihuacan's mammoth size and city planning, its incredible scale of workshops producing wares, and its international population.

Some scholars argued that Teotihuacan ran an empire similar to the Aztec Empire, which appeared a thousand years later, where city-states under its control paid tribute, usually in the form of goods. If so, tribute could be grain, dried fish, or other food for Teotihuacan's massive population. Tribute could be paid in gems, precious metals, or limestone rock, which was used to make mortar for construction. It could also be textiles. Mesoamericans had already developed weaving technology long before the Classic

---

[125] Lizzie Wade, "The Arrival of Strangers: New Evidence Points to a Clash Between Two Ancient Mesoamerican Cultures, Teotihuacan and the Maya," *Science* (February 27, 2020) https://www.science.org/content/article/astounding-new-finds-suggest-ancient-empire-may-be-hiding-plain-sight

[126] Arizona State University, "Ceremonial Burial At Moon Pyramid Shows Teotihuacan Rulers Had Mayan Connection," *Science Daily*, October 29, 2002.

[127] Lauriers and Murakami, *Teotihuacan and Early Classic Mesoamerica.*

period. For instance, some Tlatilco female figurines wore short, ballerina-type skirts. Interestingly, weaving implements were found more often in men's graves. Teotihuacan figurines and murals feature men with loincloths, short skirts, and sometimes ponchos. Cotton cloth began to appear in Mesoamerica by 900 BCE.

About one hundred miles south of Teotihuacan lies today's state of Morelos, which was the closest source of cotton. As Teotihuacan rose in population and power, it markedly influenced Morelos's architecture, city organization, and art styles. Teotihuacan's artifacts show little evidence of cotton spindle whorls, so in all likelihood, Morelos exported cotton fabric rather than raw cotton to Teotihuacan.

Other scholars reject the notion that Teotihuacan was the capital of a political empire. Instead, they theorize that Teotihuacan was a commercial empire. The Teotihuacanos had a near monopoly on green obsidian, which they could trade for other goods like food or textiles. The finds at Kaminaljuyu led some to believe it might have been a Teotihuacan enclave that controlled local resources like the cacao bean and developed social complexity in the Maya civilization. From its core in central Mexico, Teotihuacan's trade relationships influenced other cultures at its periphery.

Interestingly, our information regarding Teotihuacan royalty, such as the only names that we have, comes from the Maya, not the Teotihuacanos. The Maya erected stone pillars (stelae) with inscriptions documenting their accomplishments and events, and the Maya kings lauded their achievements in writing and art. Although the Teotihuacanos had a limited writing system of glyphs, as yet undeciphered, they seem to have been used for labels rather than lengthy texts.

The Teotihuacan kings also seemed more modest. One of the rare instances of a portrait of a Teotihuacan king was that of First Crocodile, who ruled over the Maya city of Tikal. The only reason we have his portrayal is that the Maya carved his images into rock, something the Teotihuacanos did not do. Annabeth Headrick, professor of ancient American art history at the University of Denver, labels the Teotihuacan royalty as the "invisible kings." "The Teotihuacan rulers simply do not announce their presence with the straightforwardness that Mesoamerican scholars have come to expect."[128]

With multiple ethnicities, Teotihuacan was a cosmopolitan city with social and cultural diversity. Archaeological evidence demonstrates that Oaxacan, Maya, and Gulf Coast immigrants to Teotihuacan maintained their cultural identity and homeland links. These connections led to complex interregional exchanges and intricate political and social systems. The residents of Tlailotlacan, the Oaxaca Barrio in Teotihuacan, maintained a strong relationship with their homeland. Teotihuacan may have been the overlord of Monte Albán, the Oaxacan capital. Archaeological digs in Oaxaca territory on the Pacific Coast Rio Verde Valley show evidence of upheaval of Oaxaca towns and social organization, suggesting a Teotihuacan invasion.

How was the city of Teotihuacan governed? Did it have a king? Or a ruling council? Scholars hotly debate the nature of Teotihuacan's administration. Its politics most likely shifted over the years as the city grew, faced new challenges, and became increasingly multi-ethnic. Anthropologist René Millon, who collaborated with George Cowgill in mapping Teotihuacan, proposed that the city was an oligarchic republic. An oligarchy is a small group of people ruling a city-state. They are usually of elite status and sometimes from one family. Millon suggested that Teotihuacan may have had a small group of elected people running the government for at least the latter part of its history.

Some scholars believe Teotihuacan may have been modeled after the Epi-Olmec culture, which had something approaching a republic or oligarchy (or maybe both) rather than a king. The Epi-Olmec was a continuation of the Olmec civilization, albeit on a diminished scale. Although Olmec cities had palaces and colossal heads that probably represented kings, some Epi-Olmec cities show no evidence of a palace or grand central plaza. The Olmec city of Tres Zapotes had colossal heads in its earlier history, but its later history reveals four almost-identical plazas located about a half-mile apart. Radiocarbon dating showed they were all occupied

---

[128] Annabeth Headrick, *The Teotihuacan Trinity: The Sociopolitical Structure of an Ancient Mesoamerican City* (Austin: University of Texas Press, 2017).

from around 400 BCE to 1 CE, indicating the city had a decentralized government. Tres Zapotes also did not show a clear distinction in wealth between its families in the Epi-Olmec era.

What do Teotihuacan's remains tell us about its government? Intriguingly, its art shows the people giving honor and deference to their deities but not to other people.[129] Could their government and social system have been egalitarian? The mapping project revealed other clues. René Millon used low-altitude aerial surveying to produce a city base map. Then archaeologists took sections of the city and recorded things like temple mounds and any artifacts discovered in each section. Once they completed mapping and recording, which took years, the archaeologists began interpreting their findings.

The mapping project discovered that around 200 CE, Teotihuacan transitioned from small (usually one-room) houses to two thousand compounds of one-story apartment buildings. The compounds represented kinship, ethnicity, and occupation. Something was conspicuously missing; the researchers did not find images, statues, or stelae that could clearly represent a king. They did not find opulent burial sites, although some believed the Teotihuacanos may have buried important kings under the pyramids, which were later looted. Archaeologist and art historian Esther Pasztory proposed that Teotihuacan could have been a collective and corporate society.

Cowgill thought it unlikely that Teotihuacan ever had hereditary kings, although he did believe that in its earlier glory days, single rulers may have administered the city. Cowgill was reasonably sure that Teotihuacan's initial surge in population and building of monuments happened during the rule of strong monarchs who ruled alone. He didn't think it possible that a committee could have accomplished the audacious feats that took place in that era. But later, after the pyramids were completed, he thought an oligarchy was possible instead of a single autocratic ruler.

Cowgill also conceded the possibility of a collective society from around 250 to 650 CE that placed the needs of the whole over the individual. He pointed out that in the 200s, the massive building

---

[129] Cowgill, "State and Society," 136.

project of apartment buildings for almost the entire population took place. He said they could have been building more pyramids but instead gave attention to the population's needs, with a single plan encompassing all segments of society.

Cowgill pointed to evidence that this paradigm shift had violent beginnings. The Teotihuacanos built the Feathered Serpent Temple around 200 CE and buried over two hundred sacrificed humans under it. About a century later, the Feathered Serpent Temple burned in what was apparently civil unrest. Builders used clay fragments from the temple to erect the Adosada platform in front of the temple. Instead of building a new temple on top of the burned Feather Serpent Temple, they simply left its burnt ruins standing there, blocked from view by the Adosada platform.

Cowgill thought perhaps the violent burning of the temple represented a people's revolt against a brutal regime. Even though a time gap existed between the temple's construction and the uprising, Cowgill speculated that a weaker ruler replaced a succession of strong kings. During this more ineffectual king's rule, the disgruntled population finally took the chance to stage a revolution, perhaps protesting the brutal ritual of massive human sacrifice. He theorized that Teotihuacan might have been a collective government in its earliest days, interrupted by several powerful autocratic kings. Then the city finally returned to its original collective rule after the revolt.[130]

The dates of human sacrifices at the three pyramids and the Plaza of Columns may support Cowgill's theory of a revolt against the government ritual of human sacrifice. The first known instance of human sacrifice as a state ritual was at the Feathered Serpent Pyramid between 150 to 200 CE. The Teotihuacanos sacrificed humans during their Moon Pyramid renovations between 250 to 350 and during their construction of the Sun Pyramid at roughly the same time.

A massacre, potentially human sacrifice, happened at the Plaza of Columns around 350 CE. Archaeologists haven't unearthed evidence of human sacrifice after around 350 CE at the central Avenue of the Dead monuments. Human sacrifice may have

---

[130] Cowgill, *State and Society*, 154-6.

continued at the local level around the city but didn't appear to be a state ritual during Teotihuacan's glory days.

In Teotihuacan's golden age, its massive population was at its height. The city grew wealthy through its vast trade network and ruled some Maya urban centers. The pyramids and urban housing were completed, except for periodic renovations. Teotihuacan's zenith, which lasted for three centuries, strongly influenced the rest of Mesoamerica. It was probably the first multi-ethnic city in the Americas and certainly the largest of its day.

Chapter 3: Decline and Ruin

What happened to the resplendent city of Teotihuacan? What was the cause of its mysterious decline? How was it ultimately brought to ruin around 650 CE? And why was this thriving metropolis abandoned?

Many leading Mesoamerican cities fell to invading forces, such as the Aztec Tenochtitlan's fall to the Spaniards and their tribal allies. Others fell to the forces of nature; volcanic eruptions, earthquakes, or changes in the river systems were devastating at times. But none of these appeared to have happened in Teotihuacan. What did happen? Why did the largest city in the Americas become a ghost town?

Cowgill noted that Teotihuacan's political organization began gradually declining as early as 450 to 500 CE, decades before an abrupt and violent outbreak against its religious and administrative center. He pointed to the slowdown in the import of luxury goods. The city began shrinking in size to perhaps half the population it had at its zenith. The upper middle class, who served as intermediaries between the ruling class and the city's workers, became wealthier. Perhaps their increased power threatened the top elites.

Teotihuacan appeared to experience a breakdown in city services, such as garbage pickup. Archaeologists found garbage piled six feet high on some residential streets. They also found signs of the swift evacuation of some neighborhoods. Artisans left their tools and the crafts they'd been working on in the middle of their workshop floors, pointing to an abrupt and destructive event.[131]

Did internal strife lead to Teotihuacan's final collapse? Linda Manzanilla, professor at the Institute of Anthropological Research of the National Autonomous University of Mexico, thinks so. She notes that part of what made Teotihuacan great was its blend of ethnicities, which had been displaced from other parts of Mexico by volcanic eruptions. These immigrants arrived in two major waves in the 1st and 4th centuries CE and employed their expertise in crafts and other trades, building the city's economy.[132]

Volcanic gases flow from Popocatepetl's crater.
Luis Alvaz, CC BY-SA 4.0 <https://creativecommons.org/licenses/by-sa/4.0>, via Wikimedia Commons;
https://commons.wikimedia.org/wiki/File:Popocat%C3%A9petl_desde_el_este_(Puebla)_03.jpg

The first wave was escapees from the Popocatepetl volcanic eruption of the 1st century CE. Popocatepetl is about sixty miles south of Teotihuacan and forty-three miles southeast of today's Mexico City in the Pueblo region. Although still an active volcano today, it also had glaciers until 2001, when they melted due to

[131] Robb, *Teotihuacan: City of Water*, 25.

[132] Linda R. Manzanilla, "Cooperation and Tensions in Multiethnic Corporate Societies Using Teotihuacan, Central Mexico, as a Case Study," *Proceedings of the National Academy of Sciences*. 112, no. 30 (March 2015): 9210-11. https://doi.org/10.1073/pnas.141988111.

volcanic activity. In the late 1ˢᵗ century CE, Popocatepetl exploded with a VEI-6 eruption. It was as powerful as the 1883 Krakatoa eruption in Indonesia, sending ash and pumice seventeen miles into the air.

Some of the survivors of Popocatepetl's detonation probably found a home in Teotihuacan, which, at that point, was already a bustling city of more than forty thousand people. It grew to about eighty thousand people by the end of the 1ˢᵗ century, partially due to refugees filtering in from Pueblo who had been displaced by the volcano. Between 245 and 315 CE, the Xitle volcano in today's southwestern Mexico City erupted, putting the Cuicuilco population to flight and bringing more refugees to Teotihuacan.

These two mass immigrations significantly changed Teotihuacan's demographics. The Pueblo group fleeing Popocatepetl arrived before Teotihuacan built its apartment complexes and may have spawned that project. The influx of refugees from Cuicuilco may have precipitated the apparent shift in leadership or religion in the mid-4ᵗʰ century when the Feathered Serpent Temple burned. This migrant inflow could have spawned a foreign dynasty of kings, such as Spearthrower Owl, who invaded the Maya cities to the south.

Initially, the immigrants to Teotihuacan must have found it a pleasant haven as they settled in the city's suburbs. Perhaps they were even invited by the city leaders who needed specialized workers in specific fields. The newcomers could put their skills to work in construction, clothing manufacturing, cutting gemstones, or military service. Manzanilla believes the competition was fierce between the ethnic neighborhoods. Who could produce the most sought-after luxury goods, the finest artwork, or the most accomplished musicians? The barrios featured distinct specialties based on their skillsets acquired in their lands of origin. For instance, many of the residents of Teopancazco, a neighborhood excavated by Manzanilla, came from the Gulf Coast region. They were skilled in weaving cotton and sewing garments.

Dr. Manzanilla believes that Teotihuacan's ruling elite controlled the imported raw materials, which likely led to tension between the government and the neighborhoods. The native Teotihuacanos weren't necessarily the elite. Isotropic analysis of skeletal remains and artifacts shows Teotihuacanos in lower-status compounds in the city's outskirts. Its upper-middle-class craftsmen and neighborhood chiefs often came from different regions. But foreigners were also sacrificial victims at the Moon Pyramid and Feathered Serpent Pyramid. The city likely experienced shifts in leadership throughout its history, where immigrants may have revolted and taken control.

Dr. Manzanilla spent eight years excavating and analyzing one multi-ethnic neighborhood center, Teopancazco, in the city's south. Her team examined human remains for disease, injuries, and nutritional status. DNA analysis revealed that the neighborhood had a mixture of native Teotihuacanos who lived alongside migrants from Chiapas, Hidalgo, Oaxaca, Puebla, Tlaxcala, and the Gulf Coast. Many of the immigrants had suffered from insufficient nutrition as infants, and Teotihuacan may have seemed like the land of plenty. Manzanilla even suggests the city may have had a food distribution program.[133]

But the city was also a land of horror for the migrants. Almost one-third of the buried skeletons in the Teopancazco neighborhood, primarily young migrant men, showed a violent death, with their heads chopped off. Twenty-nine victims were decapitated at one time in a ceremonial event around 350 CE. The severed heads were set in a crater with a plate or bowl over each one. This human sacrifice happened not long after refugees probably arrived from the Xitle volcanic eruption. It was also approximately when the Feathered Serpent Temple was burned and shortly before or during the reign of King Spearthrower Owl.

Only 15 percent of all adult burials in the Teopancazco district were women, although other neighborhoods in the city had a nearly equal number of buried men and women. Why were there fewer women? Were they buried elsewhere? So far, these questions remain unanswered. The corpses of many newborn babies, with an equal number of boys and girls, were buried in one area in the northeastern section of the neighborhood. Were these newborns sacrificial victims?

[133] Linda R. Manzanilla, "Cooperation and Tensions," 9212-15.

Skeletons found at Teotihuacan.
Carlos Alonso Caballero Vallejo, CC BY-SA 4.0
<https://creativecommons.org/licenses/by-sa/4.0>, via Wikimedia Commons;
https://commons.wikimedia.org/wiki/File:Osamentas_en_Teotihuac%C3%A1n.jpg

Three human remains, including a girl, showed auditory exostosis: bony growth in the ear canal caused by frequent swimming in chilly water. They probably were divers for shells and other items. Over 15 percent of the skeletons, including five infants, had an overgrowth of the skull's spongy marrow space, probably caused by parasites or anemia. Twenty-nine percent of the adult human remains showed signs of malnutrition in infancy. Yet they overcame it, perhaps by emigrating to Teotihuacan and enjoying a higher standard of living. The diet of some of the people in the neighborhood included seafood. Although Teotihuacan was about 150 miles from the Gulf, traders from Veracruz imported dried fish. Corn was their dietary staple; their main protein were dogs and domestic turkeys fed on corn.

Marks on the workers' bodies and artifacts left behind indicate the neighborhood's employment focused on manufacturing fishing nets. They also produced headdresses and clothing for the upper middle class and painted pottery and murals. One specialty clothing intrinsic to the neighborhood was seashells sewn on cotton cloth. The district appeared somewhat affluent, with many imported luxury items, like semi-precious stones and delicate ceramics from Puebla and Tlaxcala.

The migrants brought their craftsmanship experience with them and probably engaged in fierce competition with other city neighborhoods for economic power and status. Manzanilla believes the districts had local organization and leadership, with intermediate elites negotiating access to the natural resources under the control of the ruling elites. These local elites also organized sales and export of manufactured items. Tensions between the levels of society set the stage for collapse.

Manzanilla theorizes that clashes between ethnic groups, wealthy businessmen, and the government led to a chaotic scene. As tensions boiled over, the people revolted against the elite and mobbed the sites representing the government. Manzanilla dates this revolt to about 550 CE, although Cowgill thought it was closer to 650 CE. The rioters burned the temples and administrative buildings lining the Avenue of the Dead and vandalized sculptures. Manzanilla believes this was an internal revolt against the leading powers, not a foreign invasion.[134] No severe damage occurred in the neighborhoods surrounding the administrative center. The city limped along with a much-reduced population for another century, apparently under the same administrative organization. But it would no longer be the shining star of Mesoamerica.

Anthropologist Ross Hassig theorized that economic decline led to Teotihuacan's fall. About one-third of the city's population worked as craftspeople, producing garments, elaborate feathered headdresses, exquisite ceramics, obsidian objects, and more. Teotihuacan was like a gigantic manufacturing plant, producing goods that flowed through Mesoamerica. However, Teotihuacan depended on reliable trade to obtain the raw materials for its production of goods. It also needed to channel the finished goods to markets hundreds of miles away.

Teotihuacan established trading centers in opportune areas and also negotiated with Maya cities and other cultures for the exchange of goods through their territories. Teotihuacan even conquered several Maya cities in southern Mexico, Guatemala, and Honduras that became essential outposts in the trade channels

---

[134] Linda R. Manzanilla, "Cooperation and Tensions," 9214-15.

to Central America. But the trade centers were so far-flung that it was difficult for Teotihuacan to maintain control of its vast trade network.

Hassig described a scenario where some of Teotihuacan's allies began diverting their trade to other civilizations that were rising in power. The conquered Maya cities threw off Teotihuacan's dominance, becoming autonomous. Rival cities impeded the Teotihuacanos' travels through their territories. As trade broke down, Teotihuacan could not get the raw materials it needed for its artisans, nor could it sell its products to such a large market. Hassig believed this breakdown in trade led to an economic downturn and unrest among its population.[135]

Another theory for Teotihuacan's collapse is famine caused by lengthy droughts due to the worst period of global cooling in the past two millennia. Climate change in the Northern Hemisphere began in 536 CE, and its acute phase lasted two or three years. However, prolonged cooler temperatures enveloped the globe for a century or longer. Interestingly, this happened shortly before rioting broke out in Teotihuacan. Were the two interrelated?

Scientists initially thought that the Ilopango volcanic eruption in El Salvador caused global climate change. The explosion was fifty times stronger than Mount St. Helens in 1980 and left ash deposits covering seventy-seven thousand square miles. It would have killed all life in the immediate region. However, a recent analysis of tree rings in the area and ice cores in Greenland pushed the date of the Ilopango eruption back to 431 CE. Scientists still believe that a volcanic eruption *somewhere* caused the global cooling event, although meteorites or comet fragments might have been responsible.

Mesoamerica did not suffer from the pandemics that decimated the European and Asian populations in this era. However, archaeological evidence points to a high rate of stillborn births, newborn deaths, and child mortality among Teotihuacan's lower classes from around 500 to 650 CE. Of the 166 skeletons exhumed from graves in an apartment compound in a poorer

---

[135] Ross Hassig, *War and Society in Ancient Mesoamerica* (Berkeley: University of California Press, 1992), 82-89.

neighborhood of craftspeople, 52 were babies who were stillborn or died immediately after birth. Analysis showed the fetuses stopped growing in the last month of pregnancy. The mothers were probably not eating enough to sustain a healthy late-term pregnancy.[136] Only 38 percent of infants born in this era survived into their teen years, and few adults lived past the age of forty-five.[137]

Global cooling affected the harvest, which could have plunged Teotihuacan into famine. The region is semi-arid, and feeding a city with a population between 125,000 and 200,000 was a mammoth undertaking. Even a minuscule rainfall reduction would have reduced agricultural output, dramatically reducing the available food. An actual drought and the resulting crop failure would have thrust the city into starvation.

Geoscientists Michael Lachniet and Juan Pablo Bernal-Uruchurtu analyzed rainfall in the Basin of Mexico going back two millennia, using a stalagmite from southwestern Mexico. Variations in oxygen isotopes have a strong relationship with precipitation, and the researchers found significant variations in the strength of monsoons in Mesoamerica. They compared their rainfall reconstruction to societal changes in Teotihuacan. The researchers discovered severe drought conditions due to a weakening monsoon in Mesoamerica around 750 CE. However, leading up to that point, there was a drying trend that lasted centuries.[138]

Teotihuacan is 7,500 feet above sea level in the chilly, semi-arid highlands of the Basin of Mexico. The Rio San Juan flowed directly through the city (via canals engineered by the Teotihuacanos), and the Rio San Lorenzo was nearby. Both rivers flowed south and emptied into Lake Texcoco. The city depended

---

[136] Rebecca Storey, "Perinatal Mortality at Pre-Columbian Teotihuacan," *American Journal of Biological Anthropology*. 69, no. 4 (April 1986): 541-548.

[137] Rebecca Storey, "An Estimate of Mortality in a Pre-Columbian Urban Population," *American Anthropologist* 87, no. 3 (1985): 519–35. http://www.jstor.org/stable/678874.

[138] Matthew S. Lachniet and Juan Pablo Bernal-Uruchurtu, "AD 550–600 Collapse at Teotihuacan: Testing Climatic Forcing from a 2400-Year Mesoamerican Rainfall Reconstruction," in Harvey Weiss (ed.), *Megadrought and Collapse: From Early Agriculture to Angkor* (New York, Oxford Academic, 2017), 183. https://doi.org/10.1093/oso/9780199329199.003.0006, accessed 17 Nov. 2022.

heavily on rainfall collection and the river system, which fed their irrigation canals, providing drinking water and irrigation for their maize fields. If the rainfall was low, the aquifer that sustained the rivers would not be replenished.

A southern oscillation of El Niño, influenced by warming ocean temperatures in the Southern Hemisphere, caused this period of decreased rainfall. Teotihuacan had no nearby lake for a water source; it depended entirely on the spring-fed rivers and rain. If the farmers could not grow enough corn, the people would go hungry. The food shortage due to decades of decreased rainfall could have precipitated the internal revolt around 550 CE.

Government destabilization would have affected the maintenance of the canals and food distribution, magnifying the food shortage issue. Like a row of dominos knocking each other down, the city would have rapidly gone downhill as one factor influenced another. Lack of adequate nutrition would have led to more stillbirths and high child mortality. The population would have been unable to maintain its numbers. Without a doubt, many of the Teotihuacanos left the city, migrating to more promising regions, such as south to Lake Texcoco, where new settlements were springing up.

Teotihuacan stumbled through its last century with a dwindling population and an unraveling government. As it grew weaker, several other cities rose to power to the south: Cholula and Cacaxtla in the Pueblo region and Xochicalco in the Morelos area. These cities may have allied to gain a monopoly on Mesoamerican trade, weakening Teotihuacan even further. Northeast of Teotihuacan, the small town of Tollan (Tula), a Teotihuacan colony, began to grow, perhaps because of migrants from Teotihuacan. The Toltec people entered the region shortly after, making Tollan their capital.

Most likely, a combination of interconnected factors led to the derailment of Teotihuacan's society and administrative system, paving the way for its ultimate collapse. It's improbable that a single phenomenon thrust the mighty metropolis into near oblivion. Drought, food shortages, rising competition from other cities, and economic and social tensions leading to a class revolt probably all played interrelated roles in the city's demise.

SECTION TWO: SOCIAL LIFE AND POPULATION

Chapter 4: City Structure

Kunhejw stood on the mountain ridge with his brother, Bllinh Yixe, his mouth open in awe as he gazed at the massive city of Teotihuacan. An astonishingly high pyramid rose in the city's center, with two smaller pyramids at the north and south ends of a wide boulevard. Several years earlier, Bllinh Yixe had left the Zapotec city of Dani Baán. He traveled north to Teotihuacan to find employment for his expertise in Gray Ware pottery-making. He had recently returned to Oaxaca and recruited his brother to join him.

"There, to the west! That's the Oaxaca Barrio. That's where we'll live. But first, let me show you the main avenue!"

The men descended into the city's outskirts from the south, approaching the three-mile main avenue that ran north, dividing the city. Overwhelmed by the majesty of its massive monuments, Kunhejw felt the broad street pulling him forward to explore new wonders. The avenue drew his eye to the imposing long-extinct volcano to the north. He turned toward the exquisite temples on each side of the boulevard, feeling like a ridiculously small rabbit in their shadow.

"This main avenue is the city's core, where most of the trade with other cities takes place." Bllinh Yixe waved at the temples and their altars, with smoke wafting up. "It's also where you'll find most of the large temples. The Teotihuacanos worship some of the same gods we do, although they use different names. They also have some of their own. See all those palaces? That's where business and government take place."

Kunhejw and Bllinh Yixe walked up the avenue alongside a group of traders entering the city with huge packs on their backs. They approached the Ciudadela compound's formidable walls ringed with temples on their right. Bllinh Yixe guided Kunhejw off the main boulevard to a grand staircase leading up to the Ciudadela. At the top of the wall, they looked down on an enormous plaza.

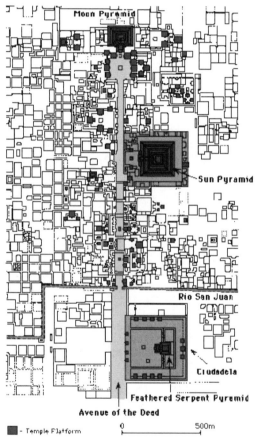

Teotihuacan: Reconstruction of Cetral Zone

Drawing by Mike Ritchie and Kumiko Sugiyama
after Millon 1973, Millon, Drewitt, and Cowgill 1973

Teotihucan layout

"They say the entire city can fit into this plaza!" Bllinh Yixe breathed. He pointed to a stunning pyramid with elaborate stone carvings of grimacing serpent heads adorning each level. "Look! That's the Feathered Serpent Pyramid. The major temples are along this main avenue, but the neighborhood barrios also have temples."

After taking in the breathtaking sight, the men prepared to descend the steps back to the avenue. On the opposite side of the street was another enclosed compound where vendors were selling their wares. From their vantage point at the top of the steps, they could see a prominent avenue extending west from the compound.

"That's West Avenue. We'll take that later to get to Tlailotlacan, the Oaxaca Barrio, where we live. The East Avenue is behind us, on the other side of this temple."

The men descended the steps and continued on their northward path up the boulevard, crossing a bridge over a sizeable stone-sided canal.

"That's the river. They diverted it with canals that go right through the city!"

They continued walking north toward the highest pyramid looming above the avenue to their right. Architectural structures built into the street occasionally interrupted their path. They climbed a flight of stairs to a broad platform, then descended into an expansive courtyard. Some of these courtyards featured a temple or some other structure. The avenue on the northern end of each courtyard was higher than the southern end, leading the men on a gradual uphill climb.[139]

The men continued along the avenue, hemmed in by high walls on each side. Intermittently, staircases led up the walls on both sides to palaces and temples. They finally came abreast of the great Sun Pyramid, surrounded by walls with another grand staircase. "People travel for weeks just to see this pyramid!" Bllinh Yixe bragged. "They worship the god of the storm, something like our Cocijo."

---

[139] Headrick, *The Teotihuacan Trinity.*

Their final stop was the focal point at the far northern end of the avenue, where the Moon Pyramid stood in front of the towering volcano, which it mirrored. As they drew closer, they could see numerous temples surrounding it and steep steps leading up the pyramid's slope. Smoke rose from an enormous altar in front of the pyramid.

This Avenue of the Dead model shows the Sun Pyramid on the right and the Moon Pyramid at the end of the boulevard (top of photo).

"They worship the goddess here. This is her temple."

"Which goddess?" Kunhejw asked.

"The Great Goddess," his brother answered. "The goddess of creation, the earth, fertility, and water."

"What do they sacrifice to her?" Kunhejw asked.

"Oh, incense, obsidian figurines, jaguars, snakes, birds, that sort of thing."

"People? Do they sacrifice people?" Kunhejw inquired apprehensively.

"Well, yes, doesn't everybody? But that's nothing for you to worry about."

"And why not? I'm guessing migrants like us would be likely sacrificial victims."

"Well, with our fine craftsmanship, we're too valuable to sacrifice! Enough of that sort of talk. Let's explore the neighborhoods! I'll show you where we live. We need to head back down to the southern end of the avenue."

A mural in the Tetitla neighborhood believed to be the Great Goddess.
Adrian Hernandez, CC BY-SA 4.0 <https://creativecommons.org/licenses/by-sa/4.0>, via Wikimedia Commons; https://commons.wikimedia.org/wiki/File:Tetitla_Diosa_de_Jade.jpg

After retracing their steps, Bllinh Yixe led Kunhejw off the main avenue to West Avenue, past the grand palaces and temples. After about a mile, the street split into two smaller lanes meandering through the neighborhoods. Bllinh Yixe guided Kunhejw to the left.

"This is the Teopancazco district. Many people from the eastern sea live here. They make nets and clothing and have a lot of trade with the coast. You can always find seafood here! Our Oaxaca neighborhood is just to the west of this one. We're right on the city outskirts."

Kunhejw inspected the buildings they were passing. The walls were built of rubble and concrete and plastered with lime.[140] The compound walls bordering the street each appeared to be about two hundred feet long. "These look like palaces!"

---

[140] Cowgill, *State and Society*, 137.

Bllinh Yixe laughed. "We have palaces for the nobility, but those are near the main avenue. In the rest of the city, these large buildings house several families. At least twenty people live in each apartment compound, usually sixty or more. The biggest ones have about one hundred people. Ours has ten families. Sixty people altogether. Well, sixty-one, now that you're here. We're all Zapotec. I married a girl from my own compound."

"I look forward to meeting her! How many of these apartment compounds are there?"

"Two thousand! Can you imagine? They built all these after they built the pyramids. We have fifteen Zapotec compounds.[141] And here we are now, in Tlailotlacan, the Oaxaca Barrio."

Bllinh Yixe pointed down a street heading west. "Those are the workshops for our district, way down there at the edge of the city. We mainly produce ceramics, mostly Gray Ware pottery. Also, some craftsmen carve statues, funerary urns, and cult images of the gods. The workshops are on the city's outskirts, so the smoke from firing the pottery is away from the residential area."

They continued strolling down a grid of narrow streets, winding through one-story apartment complexes surrounded by high walls. Vendors displayed vegetables, fruit, corn cakes, fresh river fish, and dried shrimp on blankets. The pungent odor of dried seafood mingled with incense wafting up from altars and smells of cooking inside the compounds.

"How do you not get lost in this city?" Kunhejw asked. "These buildings all look the same!"

"You'll figure it out after a while. In the city center, the streets run north and south, east and west. Out here, they curve around a bit."

Finally, they arrived at a wooden gate, which Bllinh Yixe swung open. "This is our compound. Let's go in!"

Stepping from the maze of masonry walls into the central courtyard, Kunhejw looked about him with delight. Three houses

---

[141] Maria Teresa Palomares Rodriguez, *The Oaxaca Barrio in Teotihuacan: Mortuary Customs and Ethnicity in Mesoamerica's Greatest Metropolis* (Carbondale: Southern Illinois University, 2013), 24.

with front porches facing the large patio were a riot of color. They were built of cobblestone, but brightly painted murals covered the lower sections. The courtyard was open to the sky, and there was a large basin to catch the rainwater.

This restored home in Teotihuacan's Tetitla neighborhood features a stone masonry wall with brilliant red, green, and gold murals on the plastered lower half.
YoelResidente, CC BY-SA 4.0 <https://creativecommons.org/licenses/by-sa/4.0>, via Wikimedia Commons; https://commons.wikimedia.org/wiki/File:Mural_Tetitla.jpg

Bllinh Yixe pointed to the basin. "This basin has pipes that run underground and into a sewer system that runs along the street. We empty the chamber pots into the sewer, and the rain coming through the pipes washes it away. It works great as long as we have rain. During the dry season, it's smelly."

Pots of tomatoes, squash vines, and brilliant flowers soaked up the sun. Small children ran about gleefully as several women gossiped while pounding corn. An altar stood in the middle of the patio. Kunhejw stepped forward to inspect the deity.

"Is that Cocijo?" he asked.

"Yes, our Zapotec god of rain and lightning."

Kunhejw noticed a stone platform behind the altar, rising about two feet above the courtyard's cobblestones. "What is that?"

"That's a tomb. There are others here, but they're underground—under the cobblestones. This one has a special honor; she was the wife of our compound's leader. She was the mother of five children but also the mother to us all. Most of us have left our families behind."

Bllinh Yixe wrapped his arm around his brother's shoulders. "I'm so glad you're here! It's good to have family nearby!"

He pointed to the tomb. "When her husband or children die, they'll be buried with her. They'll remove her skeleton, paint the bones with red ochre, and bury those with her family member."[142]

"Like we do at home!" Kunhejw remarked as his brother nodded.

Two smaller houses and one large one bordered the central courtyard. "There's three more houses behind these and several smaller courtyards," Bllinh Yixe explained. "One of the houses has several rooms; it's for a bigger family. Most of the houses have two or three rooms. Then there are several one-room buildings around the compound; they're for the single men or storage."

Bllinh Yixe led his brother to the right side of the courtyard and down a path along the compound's outer wall. They came out onto a smaller patio. Bright red paint bordered the walls of these houses. They walked up to a smaller house in the corner with pots of chilis and tomatoes in front. A young woman squatted on the porch, chopping peppers as her baby swung in a hammock by her side. She rose with a smile when she saw the men.

"This is my wife, my little bird, Pxise." Bllinh Yixe cradled his wife's face with his hands. "And here is my eagle!" He reached into the hammock and swung his son high in the air as the baby squealed with glee. "This is Bsia!"

"What a handsome boy!" Kunhejw laughed.

He turned to his sister-in-law, and they bowed to each other. Pxise quickly scooped water from a large urn into pottery cups and handed them to the men, who drank gratefully.

"Have a rest! You must be starving! I'll have a meal ready soon."

---

[142] Rodriguez, *The Oaxaca Barrio*, 47.

Pxise bustled about a fire in a brazier, stirring a clay cazuela pot of beans with the peppers she'd just chopped. She quickly patted corn dough into tortillas and flipped them on a griddle. In a few minutes, she guided the men inside. Kunhejw looked around at the large room that opened into a smaller room. There were no windows; the sun coming through the door lit the room.

Kunhejw looked down at the stone slab floor covered with plaster. A large mat lay in the middle of the room. "A plaster floor! At home, we just have pounded dirt. This is so much nicer!"

Pxise placed a pot of beans and chilis next to a plate of tortillas in the middle of the mat. Everyone sat cross-legged around the food, hungrily scooping the beans with their tortillas.

While Kunhejw, Pxise, and Bllinh Yixe consumed their modest meal in a typical apartment compound, other residents of Teotihuacan sat down to more elaborate dishes. Life was different in the multiple palaces where the elites lived and in the temples along the main avenue. The Aztecs called this primary boulevard the Avenue of the Dead, assuming that the pyramids were tombs of great kings. They might have been, although no evidence has been found of grand royal tombs. But the temple compounds were homes for the living, with residential quarters for those who tended the shrines and performed priesthood duties.

The city also had palaces with civic functions and housing for elite leaders. The Xalla complex was the seat of power located west of the Avenue of the Dead, between the Sun Pyramid and the Moon Pyramid. Covering about 600,000 square feet, its ten-foot-wide double walls surrounded the palace's twenty-nine buildings. In addition to living quarters for royalty, the palace also had administrative areas, religious shrines, a treasury, a craftsmen sector, and housing for domestic staff.

The Xalla compound had a central religious plaza divided into four sections, each with a small pyramid surrounding the plaza's main temple. Manzanilla speculated that the four sections may have represented four co-rulers, each ruling one of Teotihuacan's four quarters, which would have been divided by the Avenue of the Dead and the East and West Avenues. Many of the walls and stairs were painted red or had red borders. The temple in the center of the central religious plaza was like layers of an onion, with five phases of reconstruction, each encompassing the original structure. Black, blue, green, orange, and red paint adorned the interior.

The northern pyramid was dedicated to the fire god, the east pyramid to the god of the storm, the south to the mountain god, and the east to the water goddess. The eastern pyramid featured red-painted talud-tablero architecture and a stone mosaic of jaguars, flowers, and vines. A series of courtyards, porticoes, and rooms extended from the eastern platform with distinct architecture, suggesting the priesthood or royalty connected to the storm god might have been a different ethnicity than the mainstream Teotihuacanos.

The Xalla complex suffered the fate of other administrative and religious buildings along the Avenue of the Dead during what apparently was a revolt of the common people against their rulers. According to radiocarbon and archaeomagnetic dating, Manzanilla reports that a great fire destroyed the buildings around 550 CE. Her team found fragments of a shattered fire god cult image, suggesting not only a political riot but also a religious revolt.[143]

The partially restored Quetzalpapálotl Palace.
Armineaghayan, CC BY-SA 4.0 <https://creativecommons.org/licenses/by-sa/4.0>, via Wikimedia Commons;
https://commons.wikimedia.org/wiki/File:Wiki_Loves_Pyramids,_Wikimania15,_ArmA g_(16).JPG

---

[143] Robb, *Teotihuacan: City of Water*, 118.

The Ciudadela compound, which held the Feathered Serpent Temple, had temple housing to the north and south of the pyramid. These walled compounds also appeared at the Moon Pyramid's Palace of the Jaguars, the Quetzalpapálotl Palace, and the Sun Pyramid. Rows of single rooms with dazzling murals opened into a central courtyard. Porticoes connected residential spaces to the main plaza.

The Quetzalpapálotl Palace, south of the Moon Pyramid, is also called the "butterfly palace" because it has numerous reliefs on its walls in the shape of butterfly wings. Murals on the walls show jaguars blowing on conch shells and water dripping from the beaks of green birds. There are actually two palaces; the first was built around 250 CE and then covered over by a new palace built around 450 CE.

Teotihuacan covered eight square miles on an exact grid oriented 15.5 degrees east of true north. It was centuries ahead of its time with its precise urban planning and relatively egalitarian housing compounds, where about 90 percent of the population lived. In 2021, Nawa Sugiyama and her team used lidar laser mapping technology to analyze the parts of the great city that still lie underground.

They were astounded to find that Teotihuacan's builders dug down to the bedrock and sometimes even further, using the bedrock to level out areas and for building materials. Many modern buildings and agricultural fields follow the same patterns as the ancient city over which they lie.[144] The remains of Teotihuacan's central monuments are awe-inspiring, but even more so when one realizes apartment compounds for at least 125,000 people surrounded them. The city's relatively high quality of life, demonstrated by the housing and imported luxury goods, was unparalleled in Mesoamerica.

---

[144] University of California – Riverside, "Modern Activities Follow the Contours of Ancient Teotihuacan: Lidar Mapping Study Reveals Vast Landscape Modifications That Still Influence Construction and Farming," *ScienceDaily*, September 20, 2021. www.sciencedaily.com/releases/2021/09/210920173156.htm.

Chapter 5: Arts and Crafts

Generally speaking, artwork provokes an emotional response in the viewer. It might elicit feelings such as fear, awe, tenderness, sadness, humor, anger, or serenity. Artwork also gives us some insight into the artists: their personalities, moods, and outlook on life. The curious thing about Teotihuacan art is that most of it neither triggers emotions nor tells us much about the artists.

Art historian Esther Pasztory described the city's art as "remote and impersonal" and noted that specific individuals, such as kings, were not glorified in its artwork. She speculated that a Teotihuacan core value was an integrated, egalitarian community, and thus, their art featured nature and deities, such as the Great Goddess, not specific people.[145] Archaeologist George Cowgill agreed that Teotihuacan art revealed aspects of its society:

"Human beings are shown subordinate only to deities, not to other human beings. This has implications about the political system, or about how the system was represented, but it also suggests something about socialization of children and about preferred character traits." [146]

The Teotihuacan artists represented humans as inconsequential. Their actions and participation in ceremonies

---

[145] Esther Pasztory, *Teotihuacan: An Experiment in Living* (Norman: University of Oklahoma Press, 1997), xv-xvi.

[146] Cowgill, "State and Society," 136.

were more significant. Teotihuacan artwork used images of the same person, animal, or scenes over and over again, like designs on wallpaper. For example, the repeated sculpture of a serpent head encircled by feathers appears in rows on every level going up the Feathered Serpent Pyramid. Although they are repetitive, the fierce serpent heads are rare examples of Teotihuacan art that evoke the sensations of unbridled dominance and danger. Pasztory noted that the repetitive nature of Teotihuacan's art pervaded the barrios; the people may have been required to follow a particular pattern to reflect their shared identity.[147]

The coyote warriors in this mural in the Atetelco Palace all look identical. Notice the hooked-shaped symbols near their mouths; these are speech scrolls.

Wolfgang Sauber, CC BY-SA 3.0 <https://creativecommons.org/licenses/by-sa/3.0>, via Wikimedia Commons; https://commons.wikimedia.org/wiki/File:Teotihuac%C3%A1n_-_Palacio_de_Atetelco_Wandmalerei_3.jpg

In most Teotihuacan art, the people look stiff and emotionless, with faces and bodies obscured by masks, elaborate costumes, and rich ornaments. The Maya, Olmecs, and other Mesoamericans usually portrayed humans realistically. But many Teotihuacan images were peculiar, representing humans in a cartoonish fashion, all head and stocky torso, supported by short, knee-less legs,

---

[147] Pasztory, *Teotihuacan: An Experiment in Living*, xv.

almost like ducks.

This Teotihuacan mural portrayed a priest wearing an elaborate crocodile-head mask and feathered headdress. The two paisley-shaped designs coming from his hand are speech scrolls. The shells and other designs on the scrolls may represent sounds, words, or the type of sound, like blowing on a conch shell. He holds an incense burner in his right hand, and an offering of flower petals flows from his left hand.

UNESCO / Dominique Roger, CC BY-SA 3.0 IGO
<https://creativecommons.org/licenses/by-sa/3.0/igo/deed.en>, via Wikimedia Commons;
https://commons.wikimedia.org/wiki/File:Painting,_Mexico_-_UNESCO_-
PHOTO0000001337_0001.tiff

Perhaps the Aztec thought creation began at Teotihuacan because the city seemed to have no history; it never recorded its history in its monuments, artwork, or writing. Pasztory pointed out that its architecture and art focused on primordial creation myths. The neighborhood compounds, city planning, murals, and sculptures indicate impersonal organization. Teotihuacan is unique from other Mesoamerican civilizations in that its art celebrated the people's shared identity, even though they were ethnically diverse. It focused on the collective population rather than individual kings or ethnicities.

Ceramics in Teotihuacan were both practical and ornamental. Potters made everyday clay cooking pots, water vessels, and dinnerware, but they also formed exquisite ceramics for use in the temples and graves and to decorate the palaces. Potters formed vessels by rolling clay and by using molds. They would roll the clay into long strips and then press the ends together to form a circle. They placed one on top of the other to build up a vessel. Teotihuacan potters tended to use molds more often than rolling clay, thus producing multiple identical pieces. Clay could be pressed into or over a mold. Sometimes, several molds formed parts of a whole, which the potters then pressed together.

Intriguingly, the Teotihuacanos never developed a potter's wheel or any utilitarian wheel at all, such as wheeled carts. But they did have ceramic toys with wheels! Although archaeologists have found no evidence of carts with wheels to haul all the stone needed to build the mammoth pyramids, they have discovered two miniature wheeled figurines. The craftsmen passed an axle through holes or loops on the ceramic animal's front and back legs and attached wheels to each axle. Whether these were actually children's toys or had some ceremonial use, one wonders why they didn't apply the same technology to ease their back-breaking labor.

Archaeologists found wheeled ceramic figurines like this one in Teotihuacan.
Madman, CC BY-SA 3.0 <http://creativecommons.org/licenses/by-sa/3.0/>, via Wikimedia Commons;
https://commons.wikimedia.org/wiki/File:Remojadas_Wheeled_Figurine.jpg

As archaeologists worked through layers of over a millennium of human habitation, they discovered changes in Teotihuacan's pottery. Form, manufacturing techniques, raw materials, and styles of ceramics transformed as time passed, partially due to new ethnic groups moving into the city. Thus, anthropologists refer to Teotihuacan's various phases of history by the type of ceramics prevalent in that era.

The Oaxaca Barrio made Gray Ware using quartz sand. The pottery was gray and had an unpolished surface, usually unpainted but sometimes with a reddish or pinkish wash. These bowls, jars, pitchers, and dippers were mostly for everyday use. Another type of ceramic was the delicate, lightweight, brightly colored Thin Orange Ware. It was mass-produced in Pueblo to the south, then imported to Teotihuacan's Tlajinga district, where highly specialized artists painted them. The Thin Orange Ware was a fine china often reserved for burials. Despite the inherent difficulty of transporting delicate ceramics without beasts of burden, the Teotihuacanos traded the painted Thin Orange Ware throughout Mesoamerica.

The southern Tlajinga district was also famous for San Martin Orange Utility Ware, which were mostly large everyday vessels for cooking and storage. Other distinctive ceramics were ornate hourglass-shaped incense burners made with molds and mass-produced for the city's use and for trade abroad. They featured images of deities and were used in ceremonies and burials. Sometimes, they were broken, and the shards were scattered around the body in a grave.

Another well-known Teotihuacan pottery type was the tripod vessel. Craftsmen formed these pots of coiled clay. Although these vessels are found in other locations in Mexico and Guatemala, this eye-catching style originated in Teotihuacan. They reached other places via trade or perhaps were imitations of potters in other regions. The tripod vessels came in assorted sizes and colors and are primarily found in the graves of aristocratic people.

This tripod vessel features a fresco of the goggle-eyed Storm God.
*https://commons.wikimedia.org/wiki/File:Tripod_Vessel_with_Image_of_Tlaloc_LACM
A_AC1993.217.16.jpg*

Brilliantly painted murals are everywhere in Teotihuacan. Pasztory described the fascinating wall paintings she observed on her first visit to the mammoth city:

"Everywhere I went on that first visit, I saw the remains of painted walls ... consisting of enigmatic faces, hands scattering jade ornaments, animals such as birds and turtles, flowers, plants, drops of water, and mysterious signs. The colors were a resonant combination of reds, greens, blues, and yellows. The surfaces were hard, like a glaze, due perhaps to polishing, and shimmered with tiny mica pieces embedded in paint—red specular hematite. As far as I could tell, no one knew anything much about them."[148]

In the 1960s, an architect and art collector named Harold Wagner became enthralled with Teotihuacan artwork; he even bought a house in Mexico. Through questionable means, he

---

[148] Pasztory, *Teotihuacan: An Experiment in Living,* 8.

obtained over seventy pieces of murals from the ancient city, which he bequeathed to the de Young Museum in San Francisco at his death. Dating from 400 to 700 CE, most of the murals came from one large compound or palace called Techinantitla, a few yards away from the Pyramid of the Moon. At about seventy-seven thousand square feet, Techinantitla was one of the largest compounds in the city; its large temple suggests it may have been a barrio center. The rest of the mural pieces came from a compound south of Techinantitla called Tlacuilapaxco.

The mural pieces were up to five inches thick, with a base of volcanic ash mixed with clay and crushed pottery. A smooth, thin coat of lime covered the base, and then frescos of deities, feathered serpents, birds, animals, and trees were painted on the surface. The murals have retained their red, green, and gold colors surprisingly well for almost two millennia and display precise detail. Some murals depict bloodletting and gruesome heart sacrifices, and the green feathered serpent is a prominent figure.

The murals tend to have a two-dimensional nature with no illusion of depth. The people, animals, and foliage seem to float in space, like objects cut out from a picture and pasted on a wall. The Teotihuacanos appeared disinterested in achieving realism in their artwork, and the abstract nature of their paintings seemed purposeful. Pasztory believed that the Teotihuacanos had the ability to portray realistic images, and they occasionally did, as with the Mountain of Abundance mural. But they preferred using more abstract art, most likely to project a message.

Pasztory theorized that the repetitive, depersonalized images may have visually elevated a cohesive whole over distinctive individualism. Teotihuacan was a cosmopolitan city, with numerous ethnicities represented in its population. Instead of focusing on their differences, the city artwork represented a collective ideology by portraying nearly identical images.[149]

Glorifying the collective whole over individualism reminds one of Mao-era China when everyone wore the same grey or dull-blue

---

[149] Esther Pasztory, "Still Invisible: The Problem of the Aesthetics of Abstraction for Pre-Columbian Art and Its Implications for Other Cultures," *Anthropology and Aesthetics* 104 (1990-1991): 19-20. https://doi.org/10.1086/RESvn1ms20166829

Mao jacket and trousers. Pasztory, whose own family fled Hungary after anti-communist revolutions, felt that Teotihuacan was a social experiment where being part of the group brought shared benefits. Farmers held equal status to warriors and rulers. Everyone lived in similar housing with a view of the Pyramid of the Sun, worked for the state, and prospered as the state thrived. The artwork reflected the city's sociopolitical ideals.

The extraordinary Mountain Stream mural in the Tepantitla district deviates from the usual abstract, repetitive, and impersonal depiction of humans. In this brilliant crimson mural, also known as the Mountain of Abundance, the humans are distinctive from each other and are realistic in form (although not in skin color). The people are painted in three skin colors: yellow, blue, and red. Perhaps this color variation signifies social ranking or ethnicity, but they comingle as if they are relatively equal. One person has a red body and a blue face. They wear loincloths or skirts and seem to be actively engaged in play and everyday activities. A yellow man gives a smaller blue person a piggyback ride while four individuals are linked together in a chain. While the children frolic, other people talk, point at each other, and pick flowers by a stream.

The intricate Mountain of Abundance mural.

Scholars are at odds with what the mountain scene represents, especially what is happening inside the mountain. The mountain flows with water and fish, both of which empty into a river. But at the top of the peak, a human appears to be falling into the mountain's bowels. Some historians interpret this to mean the mountain is eating the humans, whose blood feeds the stream that gushes out below. They believe it represents a common Mesoamerican theme: human sacrifice brings life and abundance. Perhaps the four individuals linked together are not playful children but chained prisoners on their way to becoming sacrificial victims.

Since the Mountain of Abundance mural is located directly below another mural and both have a crimson background, many scholars assume they are related. The top mural depicts either a ruler or a deity, most likely a god, as it is almost double the size of the other two figures. The central figure's face (or what some consider part of its headdress) is believed to be the quetzal bird, which did not live in Teotihuacan but in the southern rainforests. The central figure could be the first human ancestor, but most believe it's either the storm god or the Great Goddess (Spider Woman).

This mural is located directly above the Mountain of Abundance mural. Some scholars think the deity in the center is the Great Goddess (Spider Woman).

An attendant, probably a priest, is at each side, facing the central deity. Each wears an elaborate headdress almost as high as their body. All three figures are draped in jewelry and feathers. Above the deity's head grows a tree from which a spider hangs by a thread directly over the god's headdress. Under the god is a cave-like opening filled with seeds and maize, and to the right and left of the cave are waves, with starfish and shells swirling along the bottom of the mural. Water drips from the god's hands into the waves.

Anthropologists once thought that Teotihuacan had no writing system, which seems odd, given the complexity of the city's vast neighborhood compounds and elaborate monuments. How did the builders determine the geometrics involved in the city's precise astronomical alignment? How did they calculate the dimensions of the pyramids and communicate that to the builders? How did they manage a metropolis with at least 125,000 people without written communication?

In recent decades, researchers have realized that recurring images on pottery and murals were actually hieroglyphs: pictures representing words, symbols, or sounds. Unlike Maya hieroglyphs, which can be read in sentences and provide copious information, the Teotihuacan hieroglyph symbols usually appear as individual symbols. These hieroglyphs still haven't been deciphered, but they seem to represent single nouns—perhaps the names of people or dates. The Maya carved hieroglyphs into stone stelae (pillars) and painted them on ceramics. They recorded details about their kings, such as the dates of their births and deaths and what they accomplished in their reigns. But the Teotihuacanos seemed to have left only single words.

However, speech scrolls emerging from people's mouths or objects they hold (like conch shells) in Teotihuacan art may point to more sophisticated writing. In Mesoamerica, the paisley-shaped speech scrolls represented sounds a person made, such as speech or song. They may have also represented the sound of a conch blowing. Speech scrolls sometimes appear to describe the type of words spoken; knives might express angry or insulting comments, and feathers might denote soft words. On rare occasions, especially with the Aztecs, symbols are found elsewhere in the art piece to indicate the content of the speech.

All the people in this section of the Tepantitla mural have speech scrolls. Do the symbols close to the scrolls represent words in a more sophisticated writing system than previously thought?

https://commons.wikimedia.org/wiki/File:Tepantitla-Mountain-of-Abundance_mural.jpg

The Mountain of Abundance mural in the Tepantitla compound has over twenty speech scrolls. In the smaller section of the mural, you can see multiple symbols close to the speech scrolls: butterflies, a snake-like symbol, and an object that looks like a shell with two worms coming out. These symbols might represent words or concepts.

The repetitive themes of water, mountains, flowering trees, and butterflies in Teotihuacan art reflect the worldview of its people. Some of these themes are repeated in the art of later Mesoamerican cultures, and some remain distinctive to Teotihuacan. Teotihuacan's art is displayed in its large and vivid murals, ceramics, and tiny figurines. The city's art seemed to be a way to integrate a diverse population and portray common religious and sociopolitical themes.

Chapter 6: Commercial Life

If you visited Teotihuacan today, the Avenue of the Dead and the three main pyramids still reign supreme. Thousands of tourists doggedly trek through the ruins, clambering up the Pyramid of the Sun and posing for selfies at the top. What they may not realize is that the adjacent town and rural landscape extending out around them cover the ancient city's suburbs. Buried under the fire-ant mounds and prickly pear cacti lie the residential compounds and once-bustling workshops that drove Teotihuacan's lucrative commercial life.

An ongoing flood of migrants into Teotihuacan came to take advantage of its robust economic system and access to diverse resources throughout Mesoamerica. Even the lower tiers of society enjoyed a relatively good living with standardized, comfortable housing featuring courtyards and drains. Innovation exploded as various ethnic groups came together, sharing ideas, developing new craft techniques, and spurring a bustling economy.

Teotihuacan's economic system focused on five essential endeavors: skilled craftsmen workshops, trade imports and exports, mineral mining, agriculture, and taxes. The craftsmen needed raw materials for their work, so they mined obsidian and imported other items like gems, shells, cloth, and feathers. The finished products from the workshops were sold in the city and exported to distant regions. A population of 125,000 or more needed to eat, so agriculture in the rural area surrounding

Teotihuacan provided most of the maize, vegetables, and meat consumed by the citizens. The government collected taxes, sometimes in the form of labor or goods, to support the city's infrastructure and ruling class.

Much of Teotihuacan's commercial life revolved around its workshops, which produced obsidian, ceramics, clothing, jewelry, and other goods. Some anthropologists estimate that the city had as many as four hundred workshops for obsidian alone. Ancient Mesoamericans used knife blades, spearheads, beads, and other goods crafted from obsidian glass. The people of central Mexico in the Classic period did not use metals, so volcanic obsidian was a precious resource for producing sharp implements.

The source for most of the obsidian used in Teotihuacan to craft spearheads, knives, and other implements was the Otumba mountain range about ten miles northeast. However, the tools and weapons made from Otumba obsidian were mostly meant for local use, not trade. A higher grade of obsidian came from Pachuca, about twenty miles north. There, the green obsidian, a hallmark of Teotihuacan craftsmanship, was mined.

A Teotihuacan workshop produced this obsidian spearhead or knife blade.
Sigvald Linné, CC0, via Wikimedia Commons;

The city used copious amounts of the Pachuca green obsidian implements, but they also traded this coveted resource throughout Mesoamerica. Although Teotihuacan was central Mexico's leading obsidian source, it wasn't the only player in the obsidian manufacturing and trading industry. Archaeological evidence shows the city had rivals in the obsidian business that continued trading the valuable resource after Teotihuacan's fall. Obsidian craftsmen in Tlajinga and other parts of the city worked with a core chunk of obsidian glass. In a "knapping" process, they peeled layers off to form razor-sharp blades. Tiny shards and fragments fell away, and today's archaeologists analyze this obsidian debris to learn about Teotihuacan's economy at the local level.

The 1960s Mapping Project collected 230,000 pieces of volcanic obsidian glass in Teotihuacan. Boston University archaeologist David Carballo and his colleagues have systematically unearthed several apartment complexes in Tlajinga, a district covering about one square kilometer. As they sorted through and analyzed thousands of pottery shards and bone remnants, they collected about one million obsidian pieces, totaling over nine hundred pounds.

As Carballo and his associates analyzed the obsidian production in the Tlajinga district, they realized that not all the workshops were large-scale, government-managed institutions. They found evidence of multiple small-scale workshops in independent households. The varying skill levels pointed to apprentice training for the next generation of young people in the compounds. The robustly commercialized neighborhoods enjoyed ample opportunity for market exchange.[150]

Archaeologist David Walton noted, "The more we excavate households in Mesoamerica, the more we realize that domestic economies are the engine that's driving the whole economic system. It's coming from the ground up."[151]

---

[150] David M. Carballo, "The Social Organization of Craft Production and Interregional Exchange at Teotihuacan," in *Merchants, Markets, and Exchange in the Pre-Columbian World*, ed. Kenneth D. Hirth, 113 (Dumbarton Oaks Pre-Columbian Symposia and Colloquia, 2013). https://sites.bu.edu/patt-es/files/2014/10/Carballo2013_Merchants.pdf

[151] Barbara Moran, "Lessons from Teo," *The Brink*, Boston University, 2015. https://www.bu.edu/articles/2015/archaeology-teotihuacan-mexico/.

This "ground-up" economic system centered on the apartment compounds, where sixty or more people, related by kinship or at least ethnicity, lived in a communal setting. In these small-scale economies, the compound dwellers likely divided tasks among themselves for efficiency, which required trust and cooperation. The city leadership also promoted a theme of commonality rather than individuality, creating a sense of cohesion among the various ethnic groups producing an assortment of goods.[152]

Teotihuacan was a key trade center for imports like cotton and feathers while exporting goods like obsidian objects and ceramics throughout Mexico and into Central America. David Carballo has identified four primary trade commodities circulating throughout Mesoamerica: ceramics, cotton, lime (the mineral), and obsidian. He has evaluated possible trade routes and merchant activities of these goods as they relate to Teotihuacan. With no horses or mules, the traders carried their wares on their backs. Only about ten miles from Lake Xaltocan in the Texcoco lake system, they could take advantage of canoe travel around the connecting lakes.

---

[152] Carballo, "Craft Production and Interregional Exchange," 116.

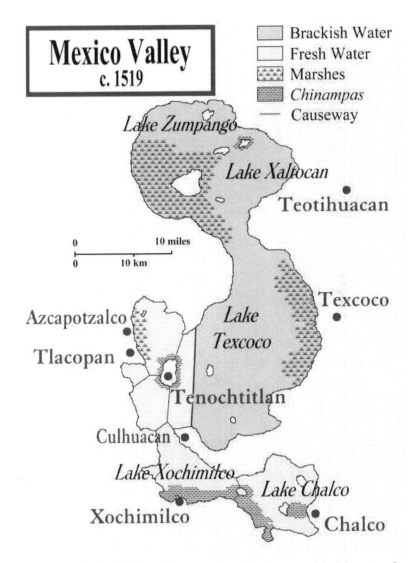

Mexico Valley
c. 1519

Brackish Water
Fresh Water
Marshes
Chinampas
— Causeway

Lake Zumpango

Lake Xaltocan

Teotihuacan

0   10 miles

0   10 km

Azcapotzalco

Tlacopan

Lake Texcoco

Texcoco

Tenochtitlan

Culhuacan

Lake Xochimilco

Lake Chalco

Xochimilco

Chalco

Teotihuacan (to the right) was close enough to take advantage of the lake system for trade, although several cities on this map did not yet exist.

Madman2001, CC BY-SA 3.0 <http://creativecommons.org/licenses/by-sa/3.0/>, via Wikimedia Commons; https://commons.wikimedia.org/wiki/File:Lake_Texcoco_c_1519.png

They could exit the Valley of Mexico through a mountain pass leading southeast into the Puebla-Tlaxcala region. Carballo calls this route the Tlaxcala Corridor. From there, merchants had access to Veracruz's Gulf shores, the Yucatán Peninsula, Guatemala, Belize, and Honduras. Carballo also notes that the eastern Valley of Mexico had easy access to resources in northern

639

Mexico.[153]

The Tlajinga district produced the San Martin Orange Utility Ware pottery, which was used locally and became a popular export. Other areas of the city made pottery ollas: clay jars with fat bases and short necks. Women used these for cooking and storing water, grain, and dried foods. They also used unglazed ollas to cool water. The water seeped into the unglazed pottery; as it evaporated on the outside of the jar, it cooled the water inside. The ollas that the Teotihuacanos sold for trade were usually burnished to a high sheen, which helped make them waterproof without a glaze. They burnished the pottery by rubbing it with a smooth object like a polished stone.

Another favorite ceramic used locally and also traded was cazuela dishes. These were shallow, unglazed cooking pots manufactured in large workshops and small shops scattered throughout the city. The early forms of cazuelas were mostly burnished and locally made in decentralized workshops. Later, San Martin Orange Ware, which was often crafted in large, clustered workshops, dominated the Teotihuacan cazuela trade. The San Martin Orange Ware was generally produced with molds and fired at hot temperatures.

Construction workers used limestone to make mortar for building projects. Mural artists would plaster the sides of buildings with lime before painting murals. Lime was also used in the "nixtamalization" process of preparing corn by soaking it in limewater. This made it easier to hull and grind the kernels and enabled dough to form. Teotihuacanos used a lot of lime, but it wasn't readily available. Limestone had to be imported from the Lake Zumpango region and Hidalgo in the north or Pueblo and Morelos in the south.

Thousands of tons of lime were needed to stucco the pyramids, temples, palaces, and dwellings. The limestone was reduced into powdered quicklime by burning it in kilns, probably at the quarry where it was mined. Engineers Luis Alberto Barba Pingarrón and José Luis Córdova Frunz estimated that transporting the needed amount of lime required 140 porters hauling the lime into the city

---

[153] Carballo, "Craft Production and Interregional Exchange," 115.

each day, especially at the height of the building projects. Analysis of the lime used at Teotihuacan points to the Chingú region of southern Hidalgo as the primary source of limestone.[154]

Cotton was grown and woven into cloth in other regions of Mexico, then transported to Teotihuacan to be made into clothing, especially elaborately decorated apparel for the elite. Teotihuacan did not grow cotton since the plant requires a more humid environment; furthermore, Teotihuacan's available agricultural space was designated for food production. Morelos, to the south, provided Teotihuacan's major cotton imports. Morelos was also an essential source of avocado and other fruit requiring a warmer environment.

Workers from the Veracruz area on the Gulf Coast populated the Merchants' Barrio in Teotihuacan and tailored everyday clothing for the population from imported cotton cloth. The women probably sewed the clothing while their menfolk engaged in long-distance trade between Teotihuacan and Veracruz, which was about a ten-day journey. The Teopancazco Barrio produced the more elaborate clothing worn by priests and the elite.

Lapidary workshops that cut and polished gems produced breathtaking works of art that adorned temples and graves and also made their way through Mesoamerican trade routes. As with other workshops, the gem cutters received most of their uncut gems from other places. Archaeologists have found a barrio of lapidary workers on Teotihuacan's eastern outskirts and numerous small household workshops. In addition to working with precious stones, they also carved seashells. Cowgill believes the state or temples sponsored most lapidary work.

In the 2010s, archaeologist Sergio Gómez began excavating a recently discovered tunnel under the Feathered Serpent Pyramid. One of his exciting finds was an amber sphere the size of a tennis ball, which may have held tobacco.[155] Mexico's primary source of amber is the Simojovel region of Chiapas in southern Mexico, about five hundred miles from Teotihuacan. Teotihuacan lapidary

---

[154] Carballo, "Craft Production and Interregional Exchange," 125-6.

[155] Reuters, "Riches of Artifacts under Pyramid Reveals Ancient Mexican Culture," *Daily Sabah*

workshops did not work with amber, so trade must have brought this treasure to the city. The tunnel walls under the Feathered Serpent Temple glittered with iron pyrite or fool's gold. Gómez and his team have unearthed thousands of beads, disks, and other iron pyrite pieces, which he believes traders may have imported from Honduras.

This tiny Teotihuacan figurine is jadeite, a rare, hard form of jade.
Wikipedia Loves Art participant "artifacts," CC BY 2.5
<https://creativecommons.org/licenses/by/2.5>, via Wikimedia Commons;
https://commons.wikimedia.org/wiki/File:WLA_lacma_Teotihuacan_jadeite_male.jpg

The Teotihuacan Mapping Project, led by the University of Rochester's René Millon, collected over eight thousand pieces of precious stones, including serpentine and jadeite. Craftsmen sewed clothing and decorative items with shell specimens from the Pacific Ocean and the Gulf of Mexico. These shells and fine stones formed beads, figurines, pendants, and other ornaments. The researchers concluded that much of the lapidary work was produced for the middle-class Teotihuacanos. Other workshops abutted the temples and pyramids, suggesting they were under temple or palace control.

All of the shells and precious stones were imported from elsewhere. Traders hauled the shells from the Gulf region of Veracruz, about two hundred miles away, and from the Pacific, about four hundred miles away. A fascinating green serpentine mask found under the Pyramid of the Sun may have been carved in Teotihuacan out of precious stones imported from northeastern Mexico. The jadeite articles found in Teotihuacan probably came from eastern Guatemala, nine hundred miles south.

To feed its massive population, one of Teotihuacan's primary economic activities was agriculture. Teotihuacan sat on a highland plateau watered by two small rivers draining into the Texcoco lake system. Although it did not receive copious rainfall, the springs in the valley gushed up to 1,500 liters of water a second, enabling the irrigation of about 7,500 acres of farmland. Teotihuacan's leadership would have organized coordinated labor to dig canals and maintain them.[156]

Tens of thousands of farmers cultivated the land to feed 125,000 people or more. The primary grains were maize (corn) and amaranth. The farmers also grew vegetables and fruit, including chili peppers, prickly pear cacti, pumpkin, and tomatoes. Pinto beans and other beans provided a vital protein source, and some barrios consumed a remarkable amount of seafood. The seafood included fish, mussels, and crawfish harvested from the rivers; thus, fishermen were part of Teotihuacan's workforce. Dried seafood from the Veracruz region was a significant import.

When Carballo's archaeological team analyzed animal bones in the Tlajinga district, they were surprised that even the non-elite sections of society consumed a remarkable amount of meat. This included turkeys and dogs raised for food, probably within the residential compounds. However, large-scale animal management was lucrative in some parts of the city.

Archaeologist Andrew Somerville and his team used isotope

---

[156] Carballo, "Craft Production and Interregional Exchange," 115.

analysis to study whether the Teotihuacanos raised and bred rabbits for food. They discovered that the Oztoyahualco residential complex raised cottontail rabbits and jackrabbits that were fed maize. Rabbit bones were found throughout the city, and analysis indicates that some were wild rabbits that would have been hunted or trapped. However, domestic grain-fed rabbits from Oztoyahualco and elsewhere would have provided a steady meat source for the city.[157]

As the largest city in the Americas for its day and among the largest in the world, Teotihuacan housed its population in its meticulously planned apartment complexes. The city's grid layout and careful planning of the monuments along the Avenue of the Dead all speak to the diligent organization and mapping of the entire city. Building all these structures required massive resources in terms of construction materials and the skilled workforce needed to erect and decorate them. Where did the money come from to do all this?

The "money" didn't come from anywhere, as Mesoamericans did not have coins or other money in that time period. They sometimes used cacao beans, which were used to make chocolate, as currency. But cacao bean trees didn't grow in the Mexican Plateau. These trees grew in the southern rainforests, so most of Teotihuacan's population wouldn't have had access to cacao. Teotihuacanos used a barter system, trading the goods they made in their barrios for food and other necessities.

A barter system would meet the economic need at its lowest level. But how did the city maintain its infrastructures, such as its streets, canals, and drains? How was garbage pickup organized? How did the city purchase the construction materials for building pyramids and apartments? Who paid for the upkeep of the priests and administrators and the necessary sacrifices to keep the gods happy?

---

[157] Somerville, A. D., et al, "Animal Management at the Ancient Metropolis of Teotihuacan, Mexico: Stable Isotope Analysis of Leporid (Cottontail and Jackrabbit) Bone Mineral," *PLoS One*. (2016 Aug 17);11(8):e0159982. doi: 10.1371/journal.pone.0159982. PMID: 27532515; PMCID: PMC4988673.

Carballo theorizes that the city had a labor tax. All residents would work a certain number of days for their barrio, the city as a whole, and the maintenance of the temples and palaces. Individuals and neighborhood districts probably also paid taxes in the form of the goods they produced. The government and temples may have owned the larger workshops, especially the ones close to the city center. Many temples and palace complexes had workshops within them, producing specialty items for religious rituals.

Teotihuacan was a bustling trade metropolis with a network covering thousands of miles of territory in Mesoamerica. It grew into a megacity through its widespread, dynamic, and intricate economy, which probably operated on both a private, individual level and a city-wide collective endeavor.

Chapter 7: Religion and Ritual

So much of Teotihuacan is a question mark. We don't even know the city's actual name, only the one the Aztecs gave it a thousand years later, meaning "the place where the gods emerged." The Aztecs couldn't understand how ordinary humans could build the massive Pyramid of the Sun and the other stunning pyramids and palaces. It must have been gods or giants who constructed the city, or perhaps it arose from the primordial mist, as symbolized by the city's artwork and architectural symbolism.

The Aztecs who first walked into Teotihuacan's crumbling ruins may not have understood much more about the city's religion than we do. They were from northwestern Mexico, where the Chichimeca (the Aztecs' ancestors) didn't build temples or worship images of their gods. But the Aztecs had sojourned for twenty years in the ruins of the Toltec city of Tollan. Tollan had once been a Teotihuacan colony, and the remnant of the Teotihuacanos still living in the region influenced the Toltecs.

Likewise, the Aztecs absorbed the culture of the few Toltecs left in Tollan. Thus, the Aztecs may have recognized some gods or understood what the semi-abstract murals represented. We don't even know the names of the Teotihuacanos' gods. If they look similar to other Mesoamerican gods or seem to have comparable functions, they're often called by the names of the Aztec gods and deities from other cultures.

Most of what we know about the Teotihuacan religion is what its people left behind: the pyramids, the other temples, the brilliant murals, the sculptures, and the sacrifices. But five anthropologists can look at the same mural and present five different interpretations. They can make educated guesses if they observe similar themes from other Mesoamerican cultures. Since the Teotihuacanos interacted so freely with the Maya, Zapotecs, and other Mesoamerican cultures, it's reasonable to assume they shared religious beliefs. But some of Teotihuacan's art is so abstract and unique that it has no parallel.

We do know that Teotihuacan was a religious epicenter for the Basin of Mexico and perhaps even for all of Mesoamerica. It had more temples than any other city in Mexico. The Teotihuacanos meticulously designed their city, with its ceremonial avenue aligned precisely 15.5 degrees east of north, oriented to the sun's movement. The Avenue of the Dead led gradually uphill to its culmination at the Moon Pyramid, framed by the sacred Cerro Gordo volcano in the distance.

The creation myths of ancient Mesoamericans often begin with a world in complete darkness covered by water. A Maya scripture speaks of only the water and sky existing and no other created things. Only the green Feathered Serpent stirred through the waters as the Creator. When the Feathered Serpent said, "Let it be," the land arose out of the water, and thus, the earth formed.[158]

Some archaeologists, such as the late Michael Coe at Yale, believed that Teotihuacan's entire city was a metaphor for life rising out of a vast sea. He noted that shells, waves, and other marine motifs covered the Temple of the Feathered Serpent, which he believed pointed to the universe's creation from a watery void. Another Mesoamerican concept was humans emerging from a dark cave, often within a mountain. Teotihuacan art seems to reflect this thematic element.[159]

---

[158] Clemency Chase Coggins, "Creation Religion and the Numbers at Teotihuacan and Izapa." *RES: Anthropology and Aesthetics*, no. 29/30 (1996): 19. http://www.jstor.org/stable/20166942.

[159] Matthew Shaer, "A Secret Tunnel Found in Mexico May Finally Solve the Mysteries of Teotihuacán." *Smithsonian Magazine* (June 2016). https://www.smithsonianmag.com/history/discovery-secret-tunnel-mexico-solve-mysteries-

A concept about creation that pervaded Mesoamerica was that the gods created the earth in four divisional directions, as related in a Quiche scripture:

"The Maker, Modeler, Mother-Father of life proceeded to complete the emergence of all the sky-earth: the four-fold siding, four-fold cornering, measuring, four-fold staking, halving the cord, stretching the cord, in the sky, on the earth, the four sides, the four corners."[160]

Teotihuacan was a model of this four corners concept. The Avenue of the Dead ran north and south through the city's center and was bisected by the East-West Avenue, creating four quadrants of the city. At that intersection, the Great Compound lay to the west and the Ciudadela to the east. The Great Compound was probably the city's central marketplace, and the Ciudadela held the Feathered Serpent Temple.

Archaeological evidence points to Teotihuacan having a religious system resembling the Maya cities of Tikal and El Mirador in Guatemala. The Maya worshiped the celestial bodies of the sun, moon, and earth, the Feathered Serpent, and a jaguar deity that protected men. Tikal and El Mirador preceded Teotihuacan and were also contemporaries and trade partners. Teotihuacan ruled Tikal for about a century, beginning in 378 CE.

Esther Pasztory believed that the migrants who flooded into Teotihuacan brought their "village-level" rituals with them. These household rituals were separate from the state religion and its practices. They involved family issues and domestic matters that weren't related to the city as a whole. It wasn't a matter of resisting the state religion but of continuing a personal belief system based on ancestral ways and individual needs.

Some household rituals seemed universal, permeating the city, yet unrelated to the state religion or politics. One example is Huehueteotl, an Aztec word meaning "Old God." These ceramic figurines depicted an elderly, wrinkled man sitting cross-legged and balancing a brazier on his head. George Cowgill thought they might have represented a cult of the hearth. The Aztecs later copied this

teotihuacan-180959070/.

[160] Coggins, "Creation Religion," 20.

image and worshiped it as a fire deity, but whether it held the same meaning in Teotihuacan is questionable.[161]

The Old Man, possibly a fire god or god of earthquakes and rain.
روسا Y, CC BY-SA 4.0 <https://creativecommons.org/licenses/by-sa/4.0>, via Wikimedia Commons; https://commons.wikimedia.org/wiki/File:Huehueteotl,_Teotihuac%C3%A1n.JPG

The Yucatán Peninsula, Veracruz, and the Guatemalan Highlands have similar images. The Old Man may have been a Maya import of the deity they called "Mam" ("Grandfather"), a mountain spirit that brought earthquakes and downpours. Or the reverse might be the case, and Teotihuacan exported the Old Man to the Maya on the Gulf Coast.

Archaeologist Hasso von Winning proposed a different theory. The city of Cuicuilco, forty-five miles south, predated Teotihuacan by centuries and then coexisted until a volcanic lava flow covered it in the 3rd century CE. In all likelihood, the survivors began migrating to Teotihuacan around 150 CE when the city's decline began, caused by earlier volcanic eruptions. According to von Winning, Cuicuilco had the oldest images of the Old Man deity in the Basin of Mexico; Teotihuacan's images were virtually identical

---

[161] Cowgill, "State and Society," 141.

to Cuicuilco's.

The Cuicuilco Old Man deity was associated with the Xitle volcano that ultimately destroyed the city. But Teotihuacan had no rumbling volcano looming over the city. The Old Man may have morphed from a terrifying fire god into a grandfatherly god of the hearth and the father of the rest of the gods and of humans. Small, double-chambered incense burners were used in household rituals that may have represented the larger stone carvings of the Old Man with the brazier on his head. The use of these double-chambered incense burners died out when Teotihuacan collapsed.[162]

Another potential ritual related to household religion is the burial of babies and stillborn children close to or under the altars in the courtyards of apartment compounds. Were these infants sacrificial offerings? We know that the Teotihuacanos sacrificed babies and children at the Pyramid of the Sun. But Teotihuacan also had a high infant mortality rate, especially in the last couple of centuries before its demise. Almost one-third of the burials in one compound's patio were newborns. Anthropologist Rebecca Storey's research indicated that in the last century before Teotihuacan's final collapse, many fetuses stopped growing in the third trimester. Sadly, the mothers were not eating enough. So, why were these babies buried close to the altar? Mesoamericans considered babies to have a closer connection to the gods because infants had not lived long in the physical world.[163]

A ritual that appears to be more at the personal level than part of the state religion was the habit of carving geometric designs like rectangles, circles, and crosses. A common theme was a circle within a circle bisected by a cross, a symbol also found in the Zapotec and Maya regions. At first, scholars thought the symbols had astronomical significance or were used in city planning, which may be the case. However, many have been found in neighborhoods, sometimes even on the floor of an ordinary home. They might represent a sacred calendar, divination, or even a

---

[162] Hasso von Winning, "The Old Fire God and His Symbolism at Teotihuacan," *Indiana*, Vol. 4 (1977). https://doi.org/10.18441/ind.v4i0. 10-11.

[163] Cowgill, "State and Society," 142.

game.

Although grand temples, especially the majestic pyramids, lined the city's main avenue, the individual apartment compounds usually had their own small shrines. The central courtyard generally had three platforms on the north, east, and south with the altar in the center. The platforms often had a room with a porch at the top of the platforms. These mini-temples imply that the residents of each apartment complex engaged in joint worship and sacrifices.

The state religion only included a handful of gods. A prominent deity was the Feathered Serpent, which the Toltecs and Aztecs later worshiped as Quetzalcoatl, one of their primary gods. The Olmecs were the first to worship this god, which was depicted as a rattlesnake with a crest, feathers, and sometimes legs. The Maya called him Waxaklahun Ubah Kan, the War Serpent. In Teotihuacan, he represented the state's authority and was associated with the military. The Toltecs, who entered central Mexico close to the time of Teotihuacan's collapse, considered the serpent as the Teotihuacan Lord of Creation.

The green Feathered Serpent looms over four sacrificed human hearts on this tripod ceramic pot.
Cleveland Museum of Art, CC0, via Wikimedia Commons;
https://commons.wikimedia.org/wiki/File:Clevelandart_1965.20_(cropped).jpg

Teotihuacan art shows the serpent with the sacrifice of human hearts. When the Teotihuacanos built the Feathered Serpent Temple, they sacrificed over two hundred people, who were buried around the pyramid. Most sacrificial victims were warriors wearing military attire and buried with spearheads and dart points. Young women of unknown status and high-status males were also sacrificed at the temple's dedication.

Another deity, sometimes called Tlaloc after the Aztec rain god, was Teotihuacan's god of the storm and war. This god is goggled-eyed with fangs and a missing or diminutive lower jaw. He is sometimes portrayed with a lightning bolt or with seaweed in his mouth. Other times, he is pictured with weapons, suggesting a relationship with the military. This god had a dual nature as the provider of fertility and rain but also a lethal god of lightning and hail.

Some scholars have questioned whether murals supposedly depicting the male storm god might actually portray the Great Goddess or Spider Woman. Anthropologist Peter Furst and art historian Esther Pasztory pointed out "feminine" elements in at least two murals, including a green bird and a spider in the deity's headdress. They believed the deity was a maternal goddess of fertility and agriculture. Archaeologist Karl Taube named her Spider Woman because of her fanged nose pendants and the spiders found in her murals. Pasztory theorized that the Great Goddess was Teotihuacan's principal deity, especially after 200 CE when murals depicting her emerged.

In and around the Pyramid of the Sun are carvings of skulls and jaguars. These may portray death and the underworld. The great pyramid may have represented both day and night, life and death. Just west of the Moon Pyramid is the Palace of the Jaguars, so named because of a dazzling mural of a jaguar blowing a conch shell from which blood drips. He may be a war god, and the blood might represent the heart of a conquered victim. This mural and one in Tetitla show the jaguar wearing a headdress of feathers, perhaps connecting him to the Feathered Serpent.

The jaguar is blowing a conch shell that drips blood.
Dennis Jarvis from Halifax, Canada, CC BY-SA 2.0
<*https://creativecommons.org/licenses/by-sa/2.0*>, *via Wikimedia Commons;*
https://commons.wikimedia.org/wiki/File:Mexico-3401 (2213945451).jpg

Typical Mesoamerican religious rituals were not tranquil affairs. Blood rituals were common and involved the practice of voluntary bloodletting, animal sacrifice, and human sacrifice. In bloodletting, a person cuts or pierces themselves enough for blood to flow using an obsidian blade, stingray spine, or shark teeth. The bloodletter usually cuts his tongue, but he could cut other parts of his body, such as his cheek or lips. He might even cut his genitals, especially if he were praying for fertility. Ordinary citizens usually only observed this gory practice; the people who pierced themselves were rulers or priests standing in a central courtyard or on a pyramid for all to see. The bloodletters were usually men, although a carving shows one Maya queen pulling a rope through her tongue.

This Teotihuacan mural appears to show a bloodletting ritual.
Cleveland Museum of Art, CC0, via Wikimedia Commons;
https://commons.wikimedia.org/wiki/File:Clevelandart 1963.252 (cropped).jpg

One mural fragment from Teotihuacan apparently depicts bloodletting. Although most Teotihuacan murals feature a crimson color along with green and gold, this mural's dominant color is blood red. It shows a priest who appears to be praying for rain and a good harvest, based on the speech scroll picturing plants and shells. In front of him is a bundle of reeds, which in Mesoamerica represented years. Four maguey cactus spines pierce the reeds, and another bundle behind him shows two more cactus spines. The priest has likely impaled himself with the thorns to make a blood offering to the deity. One of his hands is flowing with an offering of flowers and red drops of blood.

The Teotihuacanos also offered animal sacrifices. In 2004, anthropologists Saburo Sugiyama and Rubén Cabrera were exploring the Moon Pyramid when they discovered a vault in the pyramid's core. It dated to its third reconstruction and had an incredible sacrificial cache:

"This dedicatory chamber included the remains of over fifty animals, the majority representing the most dangerous carnivores on the landscape, such as eagles, felines (jaguars and pumas), canines (wolves, coyotes, and hybrids between wolves and dogs) and rattlesnake. Faced with this extraordinary faunal assemblage, we investigate the dynamic ritual processes which took place during the dedication ceremony."[164]

Archaeologists found at least 194 wild animal skeletons in and under the Sun and Moon Pyramids. Analysis of the predatory animals' remains indicates that many were probably kept captive for some time before their sacrifice. The predators ate animals whose primary diet was corn. Some speculate that the wild cats and wolves might have eaten humans or killed them as part of the sacrificial ritual before they were killed themselves. Paintings in Teotihuacan show these carnivores eating human hearts and in a procession carrying large knives.

Wild animals weren't the only sacrifices that anthropologists found under the pyramids. As they explored the bowels of the Moon Pyramid, Sugiyama and Cabrera found the skeletons of twelve humans, ten of which were headless. Anthropologists once thought the city didn't engage in the bloodthirsty human sacrifices that pervaded most Mesoamerican cultures. The grisly bones quickly put that notion to rest. The more the archaeologists explored all three pyramids, the more they found stark evidence of human sacrifices, some on a massive scale.

When the Teotihuacanos dedicated their pyramids, they ritually sacrificed human victims and buried them under or inside the temples or around their perimeter. In the case of the Feathered Serpent Pyramid, archaeologists have unearthed over two hundred human remains. They also found human skin in a tunnel leading under the Feathered Serpent Pyramid, suggesting the flaying of sacrificial victims. The Teotihuacanos decapitated many of the victims and removed the hearts from some as a separate offering. Some died from head trauma, and some humans and animals were buried alive.

Human sacrifice didn't just happen at the pyramids; it pervaded the city. As archaeologists excavated the Teopancazco Barrio, primarily populated with people from the Gulf Coast, they found that almost one-third of the skeletons had been decapitated. Analysis of the bones showed they were young men from outside

---

[164]Sugiyama, Nawa, et al, "Animal Management, Preparation and Sacrifice: Reconstructing Burial 6 at the Moon Pyramid, Teotihuacan, México," *Anthropozoologica*, 48(2), 467-485, (1 December 2013).

of Teotihuacan, possibly migrants or war captives. In one ritual around 350 CE, the heads were cut off twenty-nine victims.[165]

Analysis showed these beheaded skeletons were primarily young men from the corridor between the Gulf Coast and Teotihuacan. Perhaps they were from rival tribes that interfered with the bustling trade between Teopancazco and the coast. But why give them a ceremonial burial with the heads placed in a crater with a bowl over each head? Did they believe this gave them power over their enemies' spirits?

When migrants from multiple cultures arrived in Teotihuacan, did they keep their former religious customs? Maria Rodriguez explored that question in her study of the mortuary traditions in the Oaxaca Barrio of Teotihuacan. She found that the Zapotec migrants kept some aspects of their homeland's culture but eventually formed a new cultural identity. Rodriguez discovered that typical graves were almost six feet long, about two and a half feet wide, and about one foot deep. The Zapotecs in Teotihuacan buried grave offerings with their loved ones, including miniature ceramic dishes, dogs, figurines, beads, and obsidian objects. They usually buried their dead under the floors of their homes or in the courtyard of their apartment compound. This differed from the homeland, where tombs were typically located in public places, such as under a temple.

A peculiar custom was occasionally keeping an individual's skull, with its first three vertebrae attached, in the courtyard next to a staircase. Whether these people died a natural death or were sacrificial victims is unknown. One mortuary custom the Zapotecs brought with them from the homeland was reusing a grave, presumably one of a deceased relative. The first person was usually buried in an extended position, but when the second person died, the first person's bones would be moved to a corner of the grave and often covered with red ochre. This allowed the new corpse to be buried in a full-length position. Rodriguez believed the red ochre was a sign of respect and reverence for ancestors.

Burying dogs with people was another custom the Zapotecs brought with them to Teotihuacan. Birds were also sometimes

---

[165] Manzanilla, "Cooperation and Tensions," 9212-15.

buried with individuals of high status. A third Zapotec burial offering was urns carved to represent Cocijo, a Zapotec version of the storm god or Tlaloc. They also buried figurines that were the Zapotec Old God, similar to the Teotihuacan Old God but with an elaborate headdress.[166]

Much of Teotihuacan remains a mystery. Yet anthropologists have gleaned much from burials, murals, sculptures, and other evidence, arriving at the conclusion that religion and rituals in Teotihuacan were similar to other Mesoamerican cultures. No doubt, as a multi-ethnic city, the migrants brought their religions with them. These various belief systems may have melded to form the Teotihuacanos' understanding of the cosmos and their place in it.

---

[166] Rodriguez, *The Oaxaca Barrio*, 32-73.

Chapter 8: The Great Pyramids

Unlike Egypt's pyramids, which were massive tombs for dead pharaohs, Teotihuacan's three great pyramids were temples. The Aztecs called Teotihuacan's main boulevard the Avenue of the Dead, assuming mighty kings lay buried in the towering pyramids, but no royal tombs have been found. Instead, the three pyramids collectively served as the central anchor of state worship for the city that sprawled east and west.

Each temple was unique. The size, shape, and construction differed, with each carrying a symbolic meaning. The entire city arose from a master plan that started with the pyramids as the city's central focus and used highly sophisticated architectural and engineering techniques. Although each pyramid was individually distinctive, they formed a harmoniously balanced and complementary whole. The city architects determined the placement of the pyramids along the Avenue of the Dead in a northerly direction based on the setting sun's path on April 29th and August 12th.

Why these two dates? The Mesoamericans followed a 260-day ritual calendar from August 12th to April 29th and a 365-day solar calendar that included the rest of the 105 days. The August date began the new year for the Maya (and presumably the Teotihuacanos). The Sun Pyramid is the largest of the trio and the third-largest pyramid in the world. The Moon Pyramid is about 40 percent of the Sun Pyramid's size. Interestingly, 105 days is 40 percent of the 260-day sacred year.

The first pyramid a person encounters when entering the Avenue of the Dead from the south is the Temple of the Feathered Serpent. Although it is the smallest of the three pyramids, it is the most ornate and remarkable for its eye-catching sculptures. Dragon-like heads with feathered collars jut out at intervals from its talud-tablero layers.

The Feathered-Serpent Pyramid features two types of serpent heads on each level.
Arian Zwegers, Brussels, Belgium, CC BY 2.0
<https://creativecommons.org/licenses/by/2.0>, via Wikimedia Commons;
https://commons.wikimedia.org/wiki/File:Teotihuacan,_Citadel,_Temple_of_the_Feathe red_Serpent_(20686669345).jpg

These Feathered Serpent heads alternate with goggle-eyed, two-fanged heads, with each of the two types of heads weighing more than four tons. Scholars hotly debate the goggle-eyed creature's identity. Some think it is the Tlaloc-like god of the storm, who is known for his goggle eyes. However, bas-reliefs of reptilian bodies writhe along the walls, appearing to connect to each head. It might be a crocodile god, a rattlesnake god, or the fire serpent, which were all Mesoamerican deities.

Although its top layers are now severely weathered, the pyramid once stood almost one hundred feet tall, about the height of a ten-story building. Each side of its square base measures about sixty-five feet. The eyes of the serpents' heads probably had obsidian green glass in them that glittered in the sunlight. Today, the pyramid is a dull grey, but sixteen centuries ago, its façade gleamed with bright blue, red, gold, and green paint. The Teotihuacanos built the Feathered Serpent Pyramid between 150 to 200 CE.

The Feathered Serpent Pyramid sits within the Ciudadela ("Citadel"), a thirty-eight-acre sunken courtyard. On each side of the pyramid are palace-like structures, perhaps where royalty or priests lived. The enormous Ciudadela, which surrounded the Feathered Serpent Pyramid, provided plenty of space for massive outdoor gatherings to observe ceremonies. Around the perimeter of the Ciudadela are fifteen stepped platforms, perhaps used for sacrificial rituals or as observation posts. Archaeologists believe the Ciudadela was sunken so it could be filled with water periodically as a reenactment of the sacred mountain emerging from the sea at creation.

The Feathered Serpent Pyramid is obviously dedicated to the Feathered Serpent and his reptilian partner. Almost all Mesoamerican cultures worshiped the Feathered Serpent. In Olmec art, he seemed to represent fertility and growing things. In Maya mythology, he was Kukulkan, the Creator. The Toltecs and Aztecs called him Quetzalcoatl: the morning star and god of creation and the wind.

What about the goggle-eyed reptile that partners with the Feathered Serpent on the pyramid? The Maya had a crocodile deity they saw in the sky on clear, dark nights. Clouds of cosmic dust leave a long, dark, arching path called the "Dark Rift" through the Milky Way. To the Maya, the Dark Rift appeared to crawl through the sky like a crocodile. But it also seemed like a dark tunnel to the underworld, the path from the primordial womb. Could the reptile accompanying the Feathered Serpent on the pyramid be the "Dark Rift" crocodile? The reptile's identity may be related to a tunnel the length of a football field running under the Feathered Serpent Pyramid. The tunnel was dug about fifty to one hundred years before building the pyramid.

The Milky Way's Dark Rift
https://commons.wikimedia.org/wiki/File:Dark_Rift_2012.jpg

In 2003, a torrent of rain flooded Teotihuacan, opening a sinkhole at the base of the Feathered Serpent Pyramid. Archaeologist Sergio Gómez of Mexico's National Institute of Anthropology and History arrived the following day to examine the hole. He wasn't sure what he was looking at but knew it needed to be repaired to maintain the pyramid's integrity and the tourists' safety. He didn't expect to find anything in the hole. Still, he descended into the abyss with a rope tied around his waist and held by his colleagues.

When his feet finally touched the ground, he shone his flashlight around and realized he was in a manmade tunnel, not something carved by the weather. It had a ceiling, but massive stones blocked the passageway. Gómez knew that archaeologists had discovered a tunnel under the Pyramid of the Sun in 1971. And now, he'd found one under the Feathered Serpent Pyramid!

But Gómez knew he'd have to wait a while before discovering what treasures the tunnel held. "You can't just dive in and start tearing up earth. You have to have a clear hypothesis, and you have to get approval."[167]

---

[167] Shaer, "A Secret Tunnel."

With the site blocked off from tourists, Mexico's National Institute of Anthropology and History delivered a radar device. Gómez and his team set to work scanning what lay under the Ciudadela. By 2005, they completed a digital map that showed a 330-foot tunnel running under the Ciudadela to the center of the Feathered Serpent Pyramid. They submitted their findings to the Mexican government, requesting permission to dig.

Finally, in 2009, six years after initially finding the tunnel, Gómez got the authorization he sought. The process of digging through the forty-foot tunnel was excruciatingly slow. They had to dig by hand cautiously so as not to harm any artifacts. They also had to build scaffolding to prevent the tunnel from collapsing on them. Tons of earth were carefully removed as they uncovered human skin, jaguar and puma bones, amber balls, ceramics, jewelry, obsidian knives, and figurines, including a jaguar statue. Two robots assisted with the tunnel's final portion, which opened into a cross-shaped room.

Initially, Gómez thought the chamber might hold the tombs of great Teotihuacan kings. That's what the Aztecs and many archaeologists believed. Instead, Gómez found pools of mercury on the floor and iron pyrite (fool's gold) embedded in the floor, ceiling, and walls, emitting an eerie glow. The tunnel and the chamber at the end seemed to emulate the primordial Mesoamerican underworld, the cave of creation, where mankind rose out of the darkness.[168]

When one leaves the Feathered Serpent Temple and walks north on the Avenue of the Dead, the Pyramid of the Sun looms ahead, just to the right of the avenue. It is 246 feet high and has four layers. Its rectangular base measures 720 by 760 feet. Rather than coming to a point at the top, it has a flat layer on which a temple once stood. Viewed from above, it brings to mind a rectangular wedding cake with four layers.

---

[168] Shaer, "A Secret Tunnel."

The Pyramid of the Sun as viewed from the Avenue of the Dead.

The sides of the pyramid are smooth, with facing stones, and about 1,800 years ago, it would have been plastered with lime and perhaps painted with murals. A series of single and double staircases lead up the layers on the front of the pyramid, which faces west. The top offers a dramatic view of the entire city. A large platform in front of the pyramid would have been used for ceremonies.

Excavations in 1906 found children buried in a seated position at all four corners of the pyramid at each level. These child sacrifices led to speculation that the pyramid was dedicated to the Tlaloc-like God of the Storm, as the Aztecs sacrificed children to Tlaloc. But at that time, scholars had no evidence that the Teotihuacanos practiced the ritual killing of children to their goggle-eyed Storm God, nor did anything else point to that deity.

For the next seven decades, various teams dug tunnels under the pyramid without finding much of interest. Several archaeologists, including Rene Millon, who spearheaded the Teotihuacan Mapping Project, were sure that royal tombs lay under the pyramid. In 1971, a team discovered a tunnel on the Sun Pyramid's west side, leading a little over three hundred feet to four chambers extending out like a cloverleaf. These chambers had been looted in ancient times, probably by the Toltecs or Aztecs. All the looters left behind were pottery shards and flakes of obsidian.

But then, in 2011, archaeologists were thrilled to discover another tunnel. A team led by Saburo Sugiyama had been excavating since 2008. Their efforts unlocked several mysteries regarding the stages of the pyramid's construction, the functions of the tunnel, the meaning of the pyramid, and dedication offerings for the pyramid. The Aztecs had assumed that Teotihuacan's largest pyramid was dedicated to the sun, but was that the case?

Sugiyama's team concluded that the tunnel discovered in 1971 was manmade, not a lava tube, as once thought. They also found that the Sun Pyramid was built over three earlier temples, which the Teotihuacanos demolished to construct the final pyramid. Structure One of the earlier temples was not a pyramid but a walled building. Sugiyama's team found a newborn baby buried near Structure One. The infant was likely sacrificed when that temple was flattened before the construction of the existing Sun Pyramid. [169]

The team determined that the Teotihuacanos built the existing Sun Pyramid in one construction phase after placing more sacrifices in its foundation and fill structure. The archaeologists uncovered the partial skull of a toddler between one and two years old and a child between four to six years old. They also found offering caches with a large conch shell, obsidian blades, and an obsidian figurine. Eventually, they discovered another tunnel leading to an offering chamber, where animal bones, greenstone figurines, ceramics, pyrite, and more obsidian objects lay. Several exhilarating finds included eleven complete Tlaloc vessels, an exquisite green serpentine mask, and two greenstone figurines. Animal remains included an eagle that had recently eaten two rabbits, a puma skull and claws, and a wolf skull.

[169] Nawa Sugiyama, et al, "Inside the Sun Pyramid at Teotihuacan, Mexico: 2008–2011 Excavations and Preliminary Results," *Latin American Antiquity* 24, no. 4 (2013): 403–16. http://www.jstor.org/stable/23645621.

A Teotihuacan Tlaloc vessel of the God of the Storm.
Gary Todd, CC0, via Wikimedia Commons;
https://commons.wikimedia.org/wiki/File:Teotihuacan_Ceramic_Vessel_of_Storm_God_Tlaloc,_Valley_of_Mexico,_150_BC-750_AD.jpg

Sugiyama's team conducted new radiocarbon testing on the pyramid and its subterranean tunnel. These tests revealed the pyramid was built between 170 to 310 CE, about a century later than previously supposed. The Teotihuacanos built the tunnel between 140 to 240 CE. These new dates challenge the assumption that all three pyramids were constructed at about the same time.[170] The Teotihuacanos built the original Moon Pyramid around 100 CE and erected the Feathered Serpent Pyramid between 150 and 200 CE. They probably constructed the Sun Pyramid later. But the Moon Pyramid's renovations continued into 400, possibly even to 450 CE, well after the other two pyramids were completed.

What ceremonies did the Teotihuacanos celebrate at the Pyramid of the Sun? Even before they built the pyramid, they sacrificed children at the previous temples at its location. To which god did the Teotihuacanos dedicate the pyramid? Dr. Saburo Sugiyama believes that objects such as the Tlaloc vessels and child

---

[170] Sugiyama, "Inside the Sun Pyramid," 416-29.

sacrifice point to the pyramid's association with Teotihuacan's goggle-eyed god of the storm.

The last stop on the Avenue of the Dead's gradual uphill climb is the Pyramid of the Moon. Standing 141 feet tall with a rectangular base of 480 by 427 feet, this pyramid mirrors the Cerro Gordo Mountain looming behind it. The creation myth of most Mesoamericans was that people arose from the bowels of a sacred mountain, and Cerro Gordo is the highest mountain among those that encircle the Teotihuacan Valley.

Like the Pyramid of the Sun, its sloping sides are relatively smooth. Attached to the front of the pyramid is a five-layer platform with a wide central staircase. Construction on this pyramid began around 100 CE. It was initially a small pyramid, but it had six renovations over the next three and a half centuries. Each time, a new larger pyramid covered the previous structure until it reached its final size.

What deity does this temple/pyramid honor? Some anthropologists believe it is a temple to the Great Goddess of the underworld, water, and possibly creation. Others think it's not associated with a particular god but rather Teotihuacan's cosmology. As with the other two pyramids, the rituals at this pyramid included animal and human sacrifices, although no pre-adolescent children. In the successive layers of the ever-growing pyramid, archaeologists have uncovered the remains of jaguars and other wild cats, eagles, hawks, snakes, and humans. The Feathered Serpent Pyramid apparently had only one sacrificial event, but it involved the massacre of over two hundred people. In contrast, the builders of the Moon Pyramid offered several human sacrifices every fifty years or so as they enlarged the pyramid.

Pyramid of the Moon

Jorge Láscar from Australia, CC BY 2.0 <https://creativecommons.org/licenses/by/2.0>, via Wikimedia Commons; https://commons.wikimedia.org/wiki/File:Lascar_Pir%C3%A1mide_de_la_Luna_(Pyramid_of_the_Moon)_(4567206968).jpg

Saburo Sugiyama and Rubén Cabrera led excavations of the interior of the Moon Pyramid and its surrounding area from 1998 to 2004. Intriguingly, they did not unearth human sacrifices at the three earliest stages of construction in what is now the pyramid's inner core. Sugiyama believes Teotihuacan passed through a political and military transition when the third pyramid reconstruction occurred. This new layer, completed around 250 CE, was much larger than the first three. The dedication of this new pyramid involved sacrificing at least two humans. Researchers discovered one complete skeleton of a middle-aged, high-status man believed to be a war captive, as isotope analysis showed he wasn't from Teotihuacan. They also found a piece of another person's skull in the sacrificial pit, along with cougars, rattlesnakes, birds of prey, and shells.[171]

The Teotihuacanos renovated the Moon Pyramid a fourth time around 300 CE, using the talud-tablero architectural style on the pyramid and the Adosada platform in front. They increased the

[171] Saburo Sugiyama and Leonardo Luján, "Dedicatory Burial/Offering Complexes at the Moon Pyramid, Teotihuacan: A Preliminary Report of 1998-2004 Explorations." *Ancient Mesoamerica.* 18 (1)(2007): 127–146. doi:10.1017/S0956536107000065. JSTOR 26309326. S2CID 54787122.

distance from front to back by 340 feet. Two teenage boys, a young man, and a middle-aged man—all foreigners—were sacrificed and buried with the heads of pumas, wolves, a jaguar, and a hawk. In a separate sacrificial area, archaeologists found twelve decapitated sacrificial victims with their hands bound.

Around 350 CE, the Moon Pyramid had a fifth renovation, which enlarged its east-to-west size to 472 feet wide. This building project involved the violent sacrifice of seventeen middle-aged males. The offering pit contained only their skulls and remnants of the cloth stuffed in their mouths to gag them. Isotype analysis showed that none of them were native Teotihuacanos or long-term residents.[172]

In this fifth renovation, at the top of the pyramid, the Teotihuacanos offered a different and unusual sacrifice of three elderly men. Most of the skeletons of other sacrificial victims had their hands tied behind them, but these three men were sitting cross-legged, resting their hands on their legs. Two wore the chest ornaments of elite Maya and were buried with a golden eagle and two pumas. Their honorable burial indicates they were high-ranking men. Dr. Saburo Sugiyama believes this burial symbolizes an intriguing Maya-Teotihuacan connection:

"I think this is significant because, for the first time, we have data indicating a Maya ruling class connection at Teotihuacan, from the heart of one of the city's major monuments ... We have to study the objects and bones further, but the offerings strongly suggest a direct relation between the Teotihuacan ruling group and the Maya royal families ... In addition, they were found in a cross-legged seated position, which is very rarely, if ever, found in burials here. The position, however, can be seen in images in murals, sculptures, or figurines as priests, gods, or warriors in Teotihuacan and other related sites."[173]

---

[172] Christine D. White, et al, "Residential Histories of the Human Sacrifices at the Moon Pyramid, Teotihuacan: Evidence from Oxygen and Strontium Isotopes," *Ancient Mesoamerica* 18 (1) (2007): 159–72. http://www.jstor.org/stable/26309328.

[173] Arizona State University, "Ceremonial Burial At Moon Pyramid Shows Teotihuacan Rulers Had Mayan Connection," *Science Daily*, October 29, 2002.

The Moon Pyramid's sixth renovation took place around 400 CE, and there were no sacrificial burials found from this final building project. But what about tunnels? We know the Pyramid of the Sun and the Feathered Serpent Pyramid had tunnels under them. A 1990 geophysical investigation showed a tunnel running toward the Moon Pyramid. Subsequent electric and magnetic measurements indicated caves and multiple tunnels might lie under or near the Moon Pyramid.

In 2017, electrical resistivity tomography revealed a tunnel thirty-three feet underground leading from the plaza in front of the pyramid to a fifty-foot-wide chamber under the pyramid.[174] What lies buried in the secret room under the Pyramid of the Moon? That answer will have to wait until the archaeologists complete their investigation.

---

[174] Argote, D. L., et al, "Designing the Underworld in Teotihuacan: Cave Detection beneath the Moon Pyramid by ERT and ANT Surveys," *Journal of Archaeological Science*, 118, 105141 (2020). https://doi.org/10.1016/j.jas.2020.105141.

SECTION THREE:
TEOTIHUACAN'S
INFLUENCE ON
MESOAMERICA

Chapter 9: Relations with the Maya and the Zapotecs

In the mid-1930s, a football club in the western suburbs of Guatemala City decided to enlarge its practice field by carving into two modest embankments. Clank! A shovel hit something hard. A rock? As the worker began moving soil to dig it out, he realized it wasn't a rock. It was an ancient building! The minister of public education invited three renowned archaeologists to investigate.

Alfred Kidder, Jesse Jennings, and Edwin Shook began their careful excavations. They were thrilled to discover they were unearthing an ancient Maya city called Kaminaljuyu, meaning "hills of the dead" in the K'iche' Maya language. They uncovered pottery, architecture, shrines, and tomb goods. They were exhilarated to uncover items that displayed unmistakable Teotihuacan traits: ceramics, stone carvings, and talud-tablero architectural features dating from 200 to 500 CE.

What was the relationship between Teotihuacan in central Mexico and Kaminaljuyu in Guatemala? Did the Teotihuacanos conquer and inhabit Kaminaljuyu? As the archaeologists delved further, they realized the Teotihuacan artifacts didn't arrive suddenly but were gradually incorporated into the layers of Kaminaljuyu's site. The discoveries at mounds "A" and "B" had typical Maya characteristics at their lowest levels, but the two highest levels featured the talud-tablero on the pyramid slopes.

They were also covered with *piedrin*, a protective material made from crushed stone and water. It was commonly used in Teotihuacan. The tombs contained Pachuca green obsidian from Teotihuacan's mines at the Sierra de Las Navajas volcanic complex.[175]

This gradual emergence of Teotihuacan cultural features in Kaminaljuyu, blending with classic Maya artifacts, pointed to a peaceful social interaction, probably based on trade. No evidence suggests that the Teotihuacanos conquered and subjugated Kaminaljuyu. In Teotihuacan, numerous examples of Maya motifs exist alongside classic Teotihuacan art and architecture. The two civilizations probably enjoyed a mutually beneficial relationship.

Teotihuacan's history raises questions about how the other Mesoamericans of that time regarded Teotihuacan. Did they consider it an attractive economic hub and trade destination, as we might think of cities like Amsterdam, Guangzhou, Shanghai, or Tokyo? Or did they fear being swallowed up by its military machine? Were they awed by Teotihuacan's mammoth size and meticulous city planning? What factors pulled the Maya, Zapotecs, and other cultures to establish their enclaves within the cosmopolitan center?

Whether a political empire or a commercial one, Teotihuacan impacted most of the Mesoamerican region, even places that were over a month's journey away. Murals and stone stelae carved by the Maya record their interactions with the Teotihuacanos. Architecture in the Teotihuacan talud-tablero style is found throughout southern Mexico and extends down the Pacific and Gulf coasts into Guatemala. Did this represent military dominance or diplomatic emissaries renewing friendship ties to promote trade? This question remains a matter of debate among anthropologists.

Teotihuacan's role in Maya political development is unclear, but the two cultures enjoyed a strong trade relationship. Although Teotihuacan had numerous workshops producing all types of

---

[175] Edwin M. Shook and Alfred V. Kidder, "Mound E-III-3, K'aminaljuyu, Guatemala," in *Contributions to American Anthropology and History*, Vol. 9 (53) (1952): 33–127. Washington D.C.: Carnegie Institution of Washington.

pottery, they also imported Maya ceramics. Many Maya city-states held long-term interactions with Teotihuacan that endured for hundreds of years, especially the Petén region of southern Mexico bordering Belize and Guatemala.[176]

How far would you be willing to travel for chocolate? After the Olmecs figured out how to brew a chocolate drink from the cacao bean, the bean became a popular luxury around Mesoamerica for making a ritual drink. The Maya even used cacao beans as currency; money literally grew on trees! The most prized cacao beans came from the Soconusco region on the Pacific Ocean, close to Mexico's border with Guatemala and about six hundred miles from Teotihuacan.

Cacao trees, mountains, and quetzal birds of the rainforest are featured on some of Teotihuacan's pottery and murals, implying a solid link between Teotihuacan and Soconusco. Teotihuacan exchanged green obsidian with northern Guatemala's Pacific coastal region for jaguar pelts, cacao beans, and colorful bird plumes. The two areas also exchanged artistic innovations and religious ideas.[177]

The curiously named Plaza of Columns lies on the Avenue of the Dead's west side between the Pyramids of the Sun and the Moon. It does not have any columns; rather, it's a complex of three pyramids surrounding a large central plaza. Archaeologist Nawa Sugiyama's excavations at the Plaza of Columns, beginning in 2015, have uncovered Maya-style murals. The team also discovered a mixture of fine ceramics in both Maya and Teotihuacan styles. They believe it represents a grand feast between the Maya and Teotihuacanos at the dedication of the plaza's main pyramid (the fourth largest in Teotihuacan) between 300 to 350 CE.[178]

[176] Sarah C. Clayton, "Interregional Relationships in Mesoamerica: Interpreting Maya Ceramics at Teotihuacan," *Latin American Antiquity* 16, no. 4 (2005): 427. https://doi.org/10.2307/30042508.

[177] Kenneth G Hirth., David M. Carballo, and Barbara Arroyo, *Teotihuacan: The World Beyond the City* (Washington, D.C.: Dumbarton Oaks, 2020), 422-3.

[178] Lizzie Wade, "The Arrival of Strangers: New Evidence Points to a Clash Between Two Ancient Mesoamerican Cultures, Teotihuacan and the Maya," *Science* (February 27, 2020) https://www.science.org/content/article/astounding-new-finds-suggest-ancient-

Much of the Teotihuacanos' interactions with the Maya involved friendly trade and cultural exchange. However, the Teotihuacanos' fascination with the treasures from the Maya rainforests ultimately led to a military invasion of Guatemala and Honduras. The Maya city of Tikal in Guatemala is in the Petén region at the base of the Yucatán Peninsula between Mexico and Belize. Inscriptions in Tikal documented the entrance of armed Teotihuacanos in 378 CE.

Wouldn't an invasion have disrupted Teotihuacan's friendly trade relations with other Maya centers, though? The Maya cities sprawled over about 150,000 square miles in southern Mexico, Guatemala, Honduras, and Belize. They never had a unified empire; the city-states were independent. Thus, Teotihuacan could maintain a friendly trade relationship with some Maya cities while conquering and ruling others. A study of Tikal's written documents, archaeological remains, and artwork reveal a violent takeover in 378 CE.

Archaeologist David Stuart and Mayanist scholar Tatiana Proskouriakoff concurred that a Teotihuacan warlord killed the Maya king of Tikal, Chak Tok Ich'aak I (Jaguar Paw). The city's inscriptions say that a general named Siyaj K'ak' (Fire is Born) entered the city on the same day that Jaguar Paw died.[179] General Fire is Born probably served under the Teotihuacan King Spearthrower Owl (Jatz'om Kuy or Atlatl Cauac), who Maya inscriptions say reigned over Teotihuacan from 374 to 439 CE.[180]

One year after King Jaguar Paw's death (he was likely executed or killed in battle with the Teotihuacanos), Fire is Born installed Yax Nuun Ayiin (First Crocodile) as Tikal's new king. First Crocodile, son of Spearthrower Owl, ruled until he died in 404 CE. One portrait shows First Crocodile holding a Teotihuacan spear-thrower (an atlatl) and wearing a type of tasseled headdress commonly depicted in Teotihuacan murals. Although Maya art is usually realistic, some images of First Crocodile and Spearthrower

empire-may-be-hiding-plain-sight.

[179] Michael D. Coe, *The Maya (Ancient Peoples and Places Series)* (London and New York: Thames & Hudson, 1999), 90.

[180] Wade, "The Arrival of Strangers."

Owl in Tikal have the abstract, two-dimensional appearance of Teotihuacan art.

Yax Nuun Ayiin (First Crocodile) ruled Tikal from 379 to 404 CE.

Archaeologists found what they thought was First Crocodile's tomb under a pyramid in Tikal. Nine human sacrifices surrounded his body, and a cup inscribed "the cup of Spearthrower Owl's son" lay in the tomb. However, isotope analysis (which gives a picture of a person's diet throughout their lifetime) shows that the person buried in the tomb grew up in Tikal or nearby, not in Teotihuacan.

So, who was First Crocodile? Was he a Maya from nearby pretending to be a Teotihuacan prince? Or is the person in the tomb not First Crocodile? Perhaps First Crocodile was a Teotihuacan prince who grew up in Tikal for some reason; when he came of age, the Teotihuacanos dispatched the Maya king and crowned First Crocodile. All we know for sure is that the Maya believed him to be Spearthrower Owl's son and a Teotihuacan prince.

Anthropologists Edwin Román Ramírez and Stephen Houston published their lidar light detection study of Tikal in 2021. The lidar software revealed that what appeared to be a hill covered by jungle vines and trees was actually a temple. The team was astounded to find a replica of the Ciudadela complex in Teotihuacan encompassing the temple, except it was 30 percent smaller. The Tikal complex used the talud-tablero architecture and Teotihuacan-style incense burners.[181]

After First Crocodile died, his son, Siyaj Chan K'awiil (Storm Sky), became king of Tikal in 404 and ruled until he died in 456. General Fire is Born also defeated the city of Uaxactun, fifteen miles south of Tikal, founding a dynasty of kings of his own descendants in that city. In the next generation, K'inich Yax K'uk' Mo' (Great Sun, Quetzal-bird the First), who came from Tikal, established a new dynasty in Copán in Honduras. He was probably a descendant of First Crocodile, as inscriptions say he was a foreigner and that Teotihuacan ordained him as Copán's king.

The isotopic signature of the skeleton in Great Sun's tomb shows he lived in Tikal, which makes sense if he had grown up as Tikal's royal prince. Unlike DNA, which provides genetic information, isotope analysis gives information on where a person grew up and lived as an adult based on their diet. Moreover, artwork shows him wearing Teotihuacan-style clothing and with goggle eyes, like the Teotihuacan god of the storm. [182]

---

[181] Stephen Houston, et al, "A Teotihuacan Complex at the Classic Maya City of Tikal, Guatemala." *Antiquity* 95, no. 384 (2021): e32. doi:10.15184/aqy.2021.140.

[182] Wade, "The Arrival of Strangers."

A Copán incense burner representing Great Sun, Quetzal-bird the First.

DuendeThumb, CC BY-SA 3.0 <https://creativecommons.org/licenses/by-sa/3.0>, via Wikimedia Commons; https://commons.wikimedia.org/wiki/File:Yax_Kuk_Mo.jpg

Around the time of Tikal's 378 CE invasion, vandalized artwork in Teotihuacan hints at violence against Maya residents in Teotihuacan. Between 350 and 400 CE, the Teotihuacanos ripped Maya murals from the walls of the Plaza of Columns, scratched out the faces, broke the murals into pieces, and buried them deep underground. This destruction was close to the time that the Teotihuacanos sacrificed three elite and elderly Maya men at the Pyramid of the Moon. Around 350 CE, the amicable relationship between the Teotihuacanos and the resident Maya fell apart.

Sugiyama's team unearthed another dark find in the Plaza of the Columns area: a pit of burnt human bones of men, women, and children. They were either hacked to death or dismembered shortly after death. Who was massacred here, and why? Some of the skulls are flattened in the back, typical of Maya cranial shaping by binding infants' heads on a board. The Maya also wore jewelry in their teeth, and some of the skulls had holes bored in the teeth.[183]

Teotihuacan's relations with the Maya were complicated, but what about the Zapotecs? We know that emigrants from Oaxaca to Teotihuacan continued practicing their distinct customs and interacting with their homelands. The Teotihuacanos and Zapotecs enjoyed a robust trade, shared fundamental religious ideology, and exchanged artistic ideas and techniques.

Oaxaca lies south of Teotihuacan (with the Puebla region between the two) and spreads from the Pacific Coast to the Veracruz region. In Teotihuacan's Classic era, the Zapotecs were the dominant inhabitants of Oaxaca. Their mountaintop capital was Monte Albán (White Mountain), which grew to about twenty-five thousand people. Monte Albán was its Spanish name; the Zapotecs still living in the region when the Spaniards arrived called it Dani Baán or Danipaguache ("Sacred Mountain").

Teotihuacan had an outpost called Chingdu about sixty miles northwest, close to what would become Tollan (Tula), the future Toltec capital. Curiously, analysis of its artifacts indicated Chingdu had a mixed population of Zapotecs and Teotihuacanos, even though Chingdu was over three hundred miles north of Monte Albán. In the same area, the town of Holt Mehta also had a mixture of Zapotecs and Teotihuacanos. Why were the Zapotecs living so far from their homeland? They had a well-documented community in Teotihuacan. Did the Zapotecs and Teotihuacanos jointly colonize this region?

---

[183] Wade, "The Arrival of Strangers."

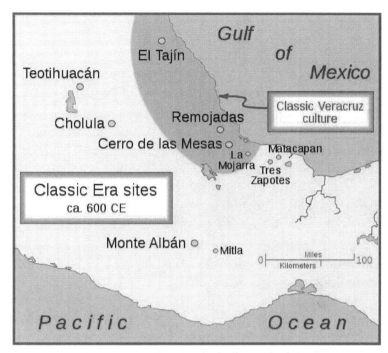

Monte Albán was about three hundred miles south of Teotihuacan.
Madman2001, CC BY-SA 3.0 <http://creativecommons.org/licenses/by-sa/3.0/>, via Wikimedia Commons; https://commons.wikimedia.org/wiki/File:Classic_sites_1.svg

A 2022 isotope study of human remains indicates that at least a few Teotihuacanos also lived in Monte Albán.[184] A Teotihuacan enclave in the Zapotec capital may have been part of its trade management system. Oaxaca had no known obsidian sources, so it was a highly desired import. Green obsidian articles mined from Teotihuacan's Pachuca mines made up 80 percent of all obsidian found in the Zapotec-controlled Rio Verde Valley in the Classic era. The Zapotec coastal region of Saltillo produced ornamental shells, a coveted item for the Teotihuacanos. Teotihuacan also imported cacao-bean appliques, cotton, and pottery, such as Gray Ware tripod vessels from Oaxaca. Around 250 CE, the coastal Zapotecs realigned their trade relationships with other regional powers to focus on Teotihuacan.[185]

---

[184] Isabel Casar, et al, "Monte Alban and Teotihuacan Connections: Can Stable Isotope Analysis of Bone and Enamel Detect Migration between Two Ancient Mesoamerican Urban Capitals?" *Archaeological and Anthropological Sciences.*

[185] Arthur A. Joyce, "Interregional Interaction and Social Development on the Oaxaca

As Teotihuacan engaged in thriving trade with the coastal Zapotecs and Monte Albán, the cultures also exchanged ideas, such as architectural styles, artwork, and decorative motifs. For example, the Zapotec monuments from the coastal area display symbols linked to Teotihuacan. Some scholars argue that Teotihuacan advanced its trade empire through strategic alliances but also, at times, through conquest and colonization. The Zapotecs developed hieroglyphic writing by 250 CE, and their monuments document the "arrival" of Teotihuacanos in Monte Albán. Yet they did not give information on what their arrival entailed. Did they come for trade or as emissaries representing Teotihuacan? Was it a single event? Or was this an invasion?

In 2002, anthropologist Marcus Winter proposed that Teotihuacan may have governed the Zapotec capital of Monte Albán in its IIIA period (200–500 CE) and that Teotihuacanos lived in the city in that era. Researchers have unearthed Teotihuacan artifacts in the Oaxaca coastal towns of Cerro de la Tortuga and Charco.[186] Anthropologist Arthur Joyce noted "disruptions" to densely settled Zapotec settlements in the Pacific Coast Rio Verde Valley. For instance, settlements moved to hilltops and built defensive walls, and some towns were burned or abruptly abandoned. He believes Teotihuacan forays may have caused the turmoil in the region.

Teotihuacan's relationships with the Maya and the Zapotecs centered around a desire for exotic goods like cacao beans, ornamental shells, and cotton. Although Teotihuacan ruled some Maya cities in Guatemala and possibly Honduras, it also engaged in trade relations with other Maya city-states in Mexico and Central America. The Zapotecs were robust trade partners with the Teotihuacanos and peacefully coexisted with them in Teotihuacan and the Tollan area. Teotihuacan possibly exercised some political control over parts of Oaxaca, but conclusive evidence is needed.

All three cultures shared similar deities and religious rituals, including animal and human sacrifice. As they interacted through

Coast," *Ancient Mesoamerica.* 4, no. 1 (1993): 67–84. http://www.jstor.org/stable/26307326.

[186] García-Des Lauriers and Murakami, *Teotihuacan and Early Classic Mesoamerica.*

trade, they benefited from exchanging ideas and technologies. Despite being the largest city in the Americas and ruling a vast trade empire, Teotihuacan never developed the writing level that the Maya and Zapotecs achieved. We only have the archaeological record and a few Maya and Zapotec inscriptions for information on Teotihuacan's history, religion, and politics.

Chapter 10: Influence over the Aztecs

For the Aztecs, Teotihuacan was where the gods came into being. It was the mystical place where a lowly god threw himself into a raging fire and became the sun, giving birth to the fifth and final creation of the world. When the Aztecs first gazed at the city, they must have been breathless in wonder. Never had they seen a city of this magnitude and order. Even though the city was crumbling, the towering pyramids and majestic temples triggered astonishment.

What happened in the six centuries between Teotihuacan's collapse and the Aztecs' arrival? In that time, the jungle reclaimed many Maya cities, some only now rediscovered through lidar imaging technology. But Teotihuacan's pyramids and ancient monuments stood over the semi-arid highland valley. It still stood long after the Aztec Empire rose and then fell to the Spaniards. Analysis of pottery by the Teotihuacan Mapping Project shows Teotihuacan once again became a vital city-state in the Aztec era, continuing after the Spaniards arrived.[187]

Teotihuacan was never entirely abandoned in the Epiclassic period (600–900 CE). After the collapse in 650 CE, a remnant of

---

[187]Christopher P. Garraty, "Aztec Teotihuacan: Political Processes at a Postclassic and Early Colonial City-State in the Basin of Mexico," *Latin American Antiquity* 17, no. 4 (2006): 36. https://doi.org/10.2307/25063064.

people continued to live in the city. It was still the only significant urban area in the Teotihuacan Valley, a sub-valley of the Basin of Mexico. The population slowly recovered in the Epiclassic period, with an estimated population of about thirty thousand by 900 CE. But political mastery over central Mexico had shifted. The new major players were the Toltec city of Tollan in the northwest and the Otomi city of Otompan (Xaltocan), about sixty miles east of Teotihuacan.[188]

Teotihuacan artwork in this era was eclectic, incorporating new styles into the traditional Teotihuacan motifs, suggesting a gradual shift in ethnicity. The Teotihuacan art continued to portray the Feathered Serpent and a mythical place of origin called Tollan. Tollan was the name of the Toltecs' nearby city, meaning "among the reeds," which some scholars believe was Teotihuacan's original name. Maya hieroglyphics called Teotihuacan "Puh" or "among the reeds."[189]

In the 8th century, successive waves of Nahuatl-speaking Chichimeca began invading the Teotihuacan Valley, eventually commanding dominance over the Basin of Mexico. The Chichimeca were fierce nomadic people from northwestern Mexico's harsh deserts with no cities and no written language. Abandoning their wandering ways, they settled in central Mexico's more welcoming environment. They established their first settlements on the borders of Teotihuacan influence.

The Aztecs claimed to be Chichimeca, but they also said they originally lived in Aztlán, a mysterious island city located on a large lake in northwestern Mexico. Their mythology said seven tribes came out of seven caves within a large mountain in the island's center. One by one, these seven Aztec kinsmen tribes left the island. They migrated south to central Mexico: the Xochimilca, Tlahuica, Acolhua, Tlaxcalteca, Tepaneca, Chalca, and Mexica. The last tribe to go was the Mexica, which eventually became the most powerful tribe and head of the Aztec Empire.

---

[188] Susan Toby Evans, "Aztec-period Political Organization in the Teotihuacan Valley: Otumba as a City-State," *Ancient Mesoamerica* 12, no. 1 (2001): 90. http://www.jstor.org/stable/26308189.

[189] Nichols, "Review of Teotihuacan," *Latin American Antiquity*, 335–36.

The Toltecs were a Chichimeca tribe that was not Aztec. Renowned for their artistry and craftsmanship, the Toltecs made their home in Tollan (Tula) around 700 CE, about sixty miles northwest of Teotihuacan, close to the Teotihuacan-Zapotec towns of Chingdu and Holt Mehta. An analysis of pottery designs shows that Tollan was under Teotihuacan's influence when the Toltecs arrived, but the Toltec culture took over. The Toltecs built a new Tollan (Tula Grande), which grew to about sixty thousand people and became the powerhouse of central Mexico.

Around the time of Teotihuacan's collapse, the Toltec king, Ixtlilcuechahua, began expanding Toltec territory, taking advantage of the power vacuum. About a century later, the priest-king Ce Acatl Topiltzin Quetzalcoatl ruled the Toltecs. His maternal grandparents, possibly from Teotihuacan, taught him to revere the Feathered Serpent or Quetzalcoatl. The king was so enamored with the deity that he took its name but outlawed the human sacrifice often associated with Quetzalcoatl.

After Topiltzin Quetzalcoatl ruled over the Toltecs as a wise king for many years, Tezcatlipoca, the smoke and mirrors god, tricked Topiltzin and his sister into drinking hallucinogens. The following morning, they woke up naked next to each other. Ashamed and humiliated, Topiltzin abdicated his throne and wandered aimlessly through Mexico, continually stabbing himself in a bloodletting ritual to atone for his sin.

When he reached the Gulf of Mexico, he built a raft and paddled out to sea, vowing to return to the same spot in the Year of One Reed. The Mesoamerican calendar followed a fifty-two-year cycle, with "one reed" being the first year of each cycle, "two reeds" the second year, and so on. Thus, when Hernán Cortés's ship arrived in 1519, it was a "one reed" year, beginning a new cycle. Some Mesoamericans thought Cortés was the great king Topiltzin Quetzalcoatl returning.

After Topiltzin Quetzalcoatl left, the Toltecs started practicing human sacrifice again. Conflict over this led to a brutal civil war, which decimated their population, leaving them vulnerable to invasion by other Chichimeca tribes. After attacking Chichimeca burned their pyramid and temple complex around 1150 CE, the Toltecs abandoned Tollan. Some resettled on Lake Texcoco's western bank at Chapultepec, a former Teotihuacan town. Others settled in the Yucatán Peninsula.

Meanwhile, from 900 to 1200 CE, the Teotihuacan Valley experienced a population surge as small villages sprang up. One of these villages was Otumba, ten miles east of Teotihuacan, settled by the Otomi people, who were possibly Chichimeca but not an Aztec tribe. Otumba grew into a powerful city that, centuries later, shook off Aztec control and ruled the northern Teotihuacan Valley. Otumba came to the Aztecs' aid against the Spanish but lost a decisive battle. After its people begged and received Cortés's forgiveness, Otumba continued as a strategic commercial center through the colonial era.

Another Nahuatl-speaking tribe, the Acolhua branch of the Aztecs, entered the Valley of Mexico around 1200 CE. They gained control of the city of Texcoco, about sixteen miles due south of Teotihuacan on Lake Texcoco. In the early 1300s, the Acolhua-Aztecs subdued Teotihuacan and incorporated it into the Acolhua confederacy. They integrated Teotihuacan and the upper Teotihuacan Valley into the city-state of Otumba, which was also under their control.

Four Aztec warriors from the Codex Mendoza, written around 1541.
https://commons.wikimedia.org/wiki/File:Four_Aztec_Warriors_in_Drawn_in_Codex_Mendoza.jpg

While the Acolhua were asserting power in the southern Teotihuacan Valley, the Otomi in the northern Teotihuacan Valley foothills established maguey farming estates on terraces. The Mesoamericans used maguey or agave fiber to make rope, fishnets, mats, and hammocks. They made paper from maguey, on which they painted their codices or pictorial histories. The maguey sap has antibiotic properties, and the Aztecs mixed it with salt to make wound compresses. The Toltecs and Aztecs made an alcoholic beverage called pulque from the maguey flower stems.

About the time the Toltecs fled Tollan, the Mexica-Aztecs, another Nahuatl-speaking tribe, left their island of Aztlán in northwestern Mexico and wandered through the cacti spines and poisonous lizards of the searing desert for a century. They said they descended from a deity or chief named Mixcoatl, who the Toltecs said was King Ce Acatl Topiltzin's father. They were close kin of the Acolhua-Aztecs and later allied with them to form the Aztec Triple Alliance. The Mexica-Aztec said they walked into Tollan around 1250 CE. They lived in the mostly deserted city for twenty years, absorbing the rich culture left behind and intermarrying with the few Toltecs still in the area.

The Mexica-Aztecs next made their way down into the Lake Texcoco region, passing through Teotihuacan on the way. Although stunned by the magnificent city, they did not linger as they had in Tollan. Instead, they continued south, where they would scratch their way to the top for control over the lake system and, ultimately, the entire Mexican Basin. After forming the Aztec Triple Alliance with two other Azteca-Chichimeca tribes, they created an empire in the early 1400s. They ruled central and southern Mexico until the Spaniards arrived about a century later.

In 1545 CE, Franciscan friar Bernardino de Sahagún began an ethnographic research study on Mesoamerica, interviewing elite-status Nahuatl-speaking men, mostly Aztec. The *Florentine Codex* (*Historia General de las Cosas de Nueva España*) contains his research in twelve books written in both Spanish and Nahuatl. Franciscan friars learned Nahuatl and converted it into the Latin alphabet (used for English and other western European languages).

When Sahagún asked the Aztecs what they knew about Teotihuacan, they told him,

"It was the burial place of rulers. For it is said: 'When we die, we do not truly die, because we are alive, because we are brought back to life, because we still live, because we awaken' ... Thus, the elders said: 'He who died became a god.'" [190]

Sahagún recorded that the Aztecs believed the first laws came into being in Teotihuacan. They also thought giants once lived in Teotihuacan, assuming ordinary men could not have built the great monuments:

"And so they built very large mounds to the Sun and the Moon, as if they were just like mountains. It is unbelievable when they say that these were made by hand, but at that time, giants still lived there."[191]

Aztec Emperor Moctezuma II (L) in the Florentine Codex.
https://commons.wikimedia.org/wiki/File:Pr%C3%ADncipe_Moctezuma_el_Joven_llegando_al_res cate_de_los_mercaderes_sitiados_en_Ayotlan,_en_el_folio_6r_del_libro_IX.png

The Aztecs considered Teotihuacan the epicenter of creation, giving the city the name we call it today, which meant "the place where the gods emerged." They were also intrigued by its model of city planning. They thought of Teotihuacan as the archetype for their city of Tenochtitlan, although the Aztec capital never approached the ancient metropolis's size and grandeur. The Aztecs revered the primeval Teotihuacanos who built the magnificent city.

The Aztec royalty made regular pilgrimages to Teotihuacan reportedly every twenty days during the reign of Moctezuma II,

---

[190] Fray Bernardino de Sahagún, *Historia General de las Cosas de Nueva España*," ed. Francisco del Paso y Troncoso (Madrid: Fototipia de Hauser y Menet, 1905), book 10, folio 142v-143.

[191] Sahagún, *Historia General*, book 10, folio 142v.

who was the emperor when Hernán Cortés invaded Mexico. The Aztec priests built altars and offered sacrifices to their sun god Huitzilopochtli at the foot of what they named the Pyramid of the Sun. They discovered one of the pyramid's hidden tunnels and explored its depths. They found exquisite ceramics and stunning stone masks, which they carried home to their capital city of Tenochtitlan and installed in their Templo Mayor.[192]

The Acolhua-Aztecs of Texcoco made Teotihuacan part of their own city-state. But it became an official city-state of its own in 1409, with the Acolhua prince Huetzin as its first Aztec *tlatoani* or king. Huetzin was of Toltec and Acolhua lineage but only reigned for nine years. The Tepaneca, another Aztec tribe, invaded the area, killed Huetzin, and took control of Teotihuacan. They installed Totomochtzin, a Tepaneca prince, as Teotihuacan's king in 1418.

The Tepaneca rule of Teotihuacan ended abruptly when three major Aztec city-states formed the Triple Alliance in 1427. Texcoco, Tenochtitlan, and Tlacopan joined forces to gain control of the Basin of Mexico, creating the Aztec Empire. Tlacopan was a minor player compared to the Mexica-Aztec of Tenochtitlan and the Acolhua-Aztec of Texcoco. Texcoco reclaimed Teotihuacan and most other city-states east of Lake Texcoco by 1434.

The Mexica-Aztecs forced the worship of their sun god Huitzilopochtli on all the city-states in the Aztec Empire. Aside from that, most city-states, including Teotihuacan, had relative independence. They could choose their own king and enjoy political stability, which led to profitable trade. They could worship their own gods as long as they made Huitzilopochtli the chief god. Teotihuacan had to pay tribute twice a year, which included cotton mantles, loincloths, skirts, and warrior outfits. The cotton probably came from Morelos, already woven into cloth, which Teotihuacanos sewed into garments. The tribute also included maguey syrup, chili peppers, honey, and limestone. Additionally, they provided a certain number of warriors for the empire's campaigns.[193]

---

[192] Robb, *Teotihuacan: City of Water*, 13.

[193] Evans, "Aztec-period Political Organization," 95.

Teotihuacan had its own *tlatoani* (king) but operated under the overlordship of the wise and long-lived Nezahualcoyotl, who transformed the Texcoco side of the Aztec Empire into a cultural center. Nezahualcoyotl was a poet, a seer, and an engineer. He developed brilliant irrigation innovations and collected *tlamatini*: astronomists, philosophers, sages, and scholars who sparked a cultural renaissance in Texcoco. Nezahualcoyotl worshiped Tloque Nahuaque, the unknown god and uncreated creator, and he hated human sacrifice. But the gory ritual continued regularly in the Mexica-Aztec capital city of Tenochtitlan.

Nezahualcoyotl, overlord of Teotihuacan.
https://commons.wikimedia.org/wiki/File:Nezahualcoyotl.jpg

As a self-governing city-state under the overlordship of the Acolhua-Aztecs of Texcoco, Teotihuacan enjoyed Acolhua social engineering strategies, interaction with other city-states in central Mexico, and heightened trade and access to materials. Teotihuacan had always been a multi-ethnic city and continued to have a blend of cultures. Pottery analysis shows that the Teotihuacanos of the Classic era were likely almost extinct. The Aztecs had a simplistic writing system and were meticulous record keepers yet wrote nothing about ancient Teotihuacan's history. It was apparently as much a mystery to them as it is to us.

The Aztecs controlled about fifty city-states in the Basin of Mexico, including Teotihuacan, by the time Cortés landed on Mexico's shores in 1519. The Aztecs built a wall around Teotihuacan's main ceremonial area, perhaps to protect it from looters or to restrict commoners from accessing the holy ground. The Teotihuacan Mapping Project found an abundance of Aztec pottery, showing the Aztecs lived in the residential part of Teotihuacan. An absence of Aztec pottery close to the pyramids indicates the center of the city likely stood empty except for ceremonial events by the Aztec royalty and priests. [194]

When the Spaniards arrived, about five thousand Aztecs lived inside Teotihuacan, governing about forty square miles of the Teotihuacan Valley's farmlands and villages with a total population of around fourteen thousand for the city-state. At that point, five other Aztec city-states existed in the Teotihuacan Valley, with a total population of about 130,000. That number would quickly plummet with the arrival of the conquistadors.

The Spaniards brought viral and bacterial diseases to which the Aztecs and other indigenous people had never been exposed: smallpox, measles, typhoid fever, and influenza. Waves of epidemics swept through Aztec cities, shattering the Basin of Mexico's population. In the first year after Cortés landed in Mexico, about 40 percent of the people of the Aztec capital of Tenochtitlan died of smallpox. Within fifty years, at least one-quarter of the Aztecs and other inhabitants of the Basin of Mexico perished from these diseases against which they had no acquired immunity.

After the Spaniards conquered the Aztecs in 1521, they organized their new administration. Teotihuacan became one of the four regional administrative centers of the former Acolhua regime. The Spaniards introduced horses and new technology, such as wheeled transport. Franciscan friars brought Catholicism and recorded the indigenous population's histories.

Sadly, within a century, disease, resettlement, and famine from a drought reduced the once-thriving indigenous population in the Teotihuacan Valley to only 10 percent of its former numbers.

---

[194] Garraty, "Aztec Teotihuacan," 365.

Meanwhile, multitudes of Spanish colonists arrived to displace the indigenous people. Teotihuacan had seen the rise and fall of multiple cultures; now, a new chapter began for the two-thousand-year-old city.

Conclusion

Much of Teotihuacan remains a mystery, yet it had a spectacular influence on Mesoamerica. Its growth into a vast and populous city and its breathtaking achievements set an example for other civilizations. Teotihuacan's significance as a religious and trade center and its role in the region's urbanization left its marks on history. We can find correlations to today's urban centers and learn from Teotihuacan's successes and failures.

How did Teotihuacan grow into the largest metropolis in the Americas and among the top ten in the world? The Teotihuacanos couldn't take all the credit, as nature played a part, with volcanoes driving people from their former cities. But Teotihuacan welcomed emigrants from near and far, establishing barrios for different tribal groups. Migrants could feel comfortable in neighborhoods among others of their culture and language while putting their specific skills into play in the city's remarkable assortment of workshops.

Teotihuacan also embarked on an innovative housing project for virtually the entire city, which was unprecedented for that time and even today. Its system of one-story apartment housing for over 100,000 people provided comfortable and orderly living conditions and stands as an example for urban planning today. For its early and middle history, everyone in the megacity had enough to eat, indicating successful irrigation and farming techniques.

Teotihuacan tended to do everything on a grand scale. When it was built, the Pyramid of the Sun was the highest in Mexico and the second-highest in Mesoamerica. Yet the Teotihuacanos constructed it without the wheel or beasts of burden. Its vast trade network spread over a radius of more than one thousand miles, from the Pacific Ocean to the Gulf coast and into Guatemala, Honduras, and Belize. It successfully managed its massive cosmopolitan milieu and produced breathtaking works of art: stunning temples, brilliant murals, exquisite pottery, and intriguing figurines.

Teotihuacan was Mesoamerica's most prominent religious center and served as a bustling trade hub for multiple cultures. It was the Basin of Mexico's premier worship center and drew pilgrims from around Mexico and Central America. Even after its fall, the Aztecs traveled there to offer sacrifices and pray at the Pyramid of the Sun. As a trade nucleus for Mesoamerica, it exported obsidian and other products produced in its many workshops while importing raw materials, luxury goods, and food for its population. Teotihuacan drew on its multi-ethnic population to cultivate friendly trade partners and enriched itself in the process.

Teotihuacan was the only urban center in the Teotihuacan Valley in its zenith. Still, it played a role in the urbanization of the larger area: the rest of the Mexican Basin and farther south in the Zapotec and Maya areas. It had a dynamic networking process and multitudes of people coming and going for trade and religious reasons. Teotihuacan served as a model of urban development and had a thriving economy with successful strategies to sustain its massive population.

What are the key takeaways from Teotihuacan's successful urbanization? How can we correlate the ancient metropolis to today's big cities? Let's think about the components that make a good city. The first would be strong and effective leadership. Anthropologist Cowgill was convinced that Teotihuacan had a dynamic and powerful ruler (or probably a series of strong monarchs) during its flurry of building pyramids and city housing. These leaders had a vision and the capacity to convince people to capture that vision and put it into play.

Once the construction projects were completed, Teotihuacan may have shifted to a leadership council that focused more on the collective issues of the people and not the city's glory. A collective leadership council would value its people's diversity while providing everyone with a decent quality of life. Such a council might be more engaged with the regular people and aware of their needs. Both types of leadership are essential to a thriving city today, depending on where the urban center is in its development and its specific challenges.

What can we learn from Teotihuacan about prospering in an urban lifestyle? Many city dwellers today feel isolated in the middle of a crowd, as they have no meaningful connections to others around them. That's why Teotihuacan's housing compounds were ingenious. They brought together small groups of around sixty or more people with kinship or ethnic links. In their "village," they were walled off from the city's bustle and noise. Everyone knew everyone else and was probably connected to the same workshop. They could grow pots of flowers and vegetables, the children could run safely in the sunshine, and there was camaraderie and mutual support.

Teotihuacan reminds us of the multiple benefits of knowing our world history. We glean ideas we can implement in our present and future through studying the past. It helps us realize there's not "one way" of doing things correctly. But we can also learn from the failures of the past. While we can't be entirely sure what happened during Teotihuacan's decline, the analysis of skeletons indicates that the city experienced a food shortage. Environmental changes may have slowed agricultural production, but the leadership apparently failed to deal with the problem.

The leaders could have reduced their population by establishing colonies in other parts of the Teotihuacan Valley or even farther away. Maybe that's what they did and why the population declined in the last century. They could have ramped up grain and dried fish imports from other regions. The near-starvation that the people experienced may have led to unrest and riots in the administrative and religious center of the city since the temples and palaces were burned. Multiple cities today are coping with protests and violence that threaten their existence. Teotihuacan may be an example of what *not* to do when faced with such urban challenges.

And yet, even though Teotihuacan "collapsed," it continued, at a reduced scale, through multiple changes in leadership and people in the Basin of Mexico. It watched the Toltecs rise and fall, and it was assimilated into the Aztec Empire. It became a regional administrative center in the Spanish colonial days but was almost obliterated by disease and famine. Today, Teotihuacan's history is integral to Mexico's identity and honor. Over four million visitors travel to the city every year to experience the remarkable legacy of Teotihuacan.

Here's another book by Enthralling History
that you might like

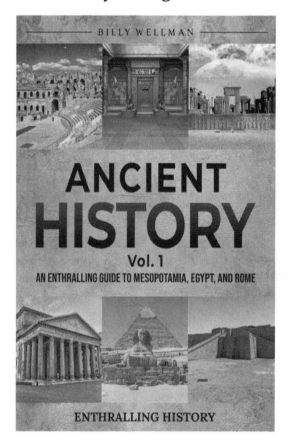

Free limited time bonus

Stop for a moment. We have a free bonus set up for you. The problem is this: we forget 90% of everything that we read after 7 days. Crazy fact, right? Here's the solution: we've created a printable, 1-page pdf summary for this book that you're reading now. All you have to do to get your free pdf summary is to go to the following website:

https://livetolearn.lpages.co/enthrallinghistory/

Once you do, it will be intuitive. Enjoy, and thank you!

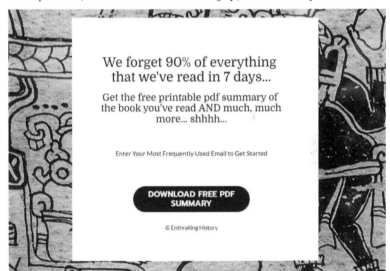

We forget 90% of everything that we've read in 7 days...

Get the free printable pdf summary of the book you've read AND much, much more... shhhh...

Enter Your Most Frequently Used Email to Get Started

DOWNLOAD FREE PDF SUMMARY

© Enthralling History

Bibliography

Bellamy, Kate. "On the External Relations of Purepecha: An Investigation into Classification, Contact and Patterns of Word Formation." Doctoral Theses, University of Leiden, 2018, https://www.lotpublications.nl/Documents/498_fulltext.pdf.

Berdan, Frances. *Aztecs of Central Mexico: An Imperial Society.* Belmont, CA, USA: Cengage Learning, April 28, 2004.

Bierhorst, John. *History and Mythology of the Aztecs: The Codex Chimalpopoca.* University of Arizona Press, June 1, 1998.

Blanton, Richard. "Prehispanic Settlement Patterns of the Ixtapalapa Peninsula Region, Mexico." PhD diss., University of Michigan, 1970.

Blanton, Richard. "Prehispanic Adaptation in the Ixtapalapa Region, Mexico." *Science,* 175 (4028) (1972):1317-26.

Burkhart, Louise M. "The Solar Christ in Nahuatl Doctrinal Texts of Early Colonial Mexico." *Ethnohistory,* 35, no. 3 (1988): 234-56. Accessed June 10, 2021. doi:10.2307/481801.

Carrasco, Pedro. *The Tenochca Empire of Ancient Mexico: The Triple Alliance of Tenochtitlan, Tetzcoco, and Tlacopan.* University of Oklahoma Press, March 1, 2011.

Clendinnen, Inga. *Aztecs: An Interpretation.* Cambridge University Press, July 28, 2014.

Coe, Michael D., Javier Urcid, Rex Koontz. *Mexico: From the Olmecs to the Aztecs.* Thames & Hudson, September 17, 2019.

Colston, Stephen A. "'No Longer Will There Be a Mexico:' Omens, Prophecies, and the Conquest of the Aztec Empire." *American Indian Quarterly,* 9, no. 3 (1985): 239-58. Accessed June 1, 2021.

doi:10.2307/1183828.

Cortés, Hernán. *Cartas y Relaciones de* Hernán *Cortés al Emperador Carlos V.* Edited by Pascual de Gayangos. Paris: A. Chaix, 1866. Microfilm.

Cruz, Isabel De La, Angélica González-Oliver, Brian M. Kemp, Juan A. Román, David Glenn Smith, and Alfonso Torre-Blanco. "Sex Identification of Children Sacrificed to the Ancient Aztec Rain Gods in Tlatelolco." *Current Anthropology* 49, no. 3 (2008): 519-26. Accessed June 10, 2021. doi:10.1086/587642.

Dewan, Leslie and Hosler, Dorothy. "Ancient Maritime Trade on Balsa Rafts: An Engineering Analysis." *Journal of Archaeological Research*, Vol. 64 (2008): 19-36.

Elzey, Wayne. "A Hill on a Land Surrounded by Water: An Aztec Story of Origin and Destiny." *History of Religions*, 31, no. 2 (1991):105-49. Accessed June 16, 2021. http://www.jstor.org/stable/1063021.

Hosler, Dorothy. "West Mexican Metallurgy: South and Central American Origins and West Mexican Transformations." *American Anthropologist*, Vol. 90, No. 4 (1988): 832-843.

Ioannidis, Alexander G., Javier Blanco-Portillo, and Andres Moreno-Estrada. "Native American Gene Flow into Polynesia Predating Easter Island Settlement." *Nature*, Vol. 583 (2020): 572-77.

Levy, Buddy. *Conquistador: Hernan Cortes, King Montezuma, and the Last Stand of the Aztecs.* New York: Bantam, July 28, 2009.

Lockhart, James. *The Nahuas after the Conquest: A Social and Cultural History of the Indians of Central Mexico, Sixteenth Through Eighteenth Centuries.* Stanford University Press, September 1, 1994.

Matthew, Laura E., Michel R. Oudijk. *Indian Conquistadors: Indigenous Allies in the Conquest of Mesoamerica.* University of Oklahoma Press, October 22, 2012.

Miller, Mary Ellen. *The Art of Mesoamerica: From Olmec to Aztec (World of Art).* Thames & Hudson, June 11, 2019.

Pohl, John, Adam Hook. *Aztecs and Conquistadores: The Spanish Invasion and the Collapse of the Aztec Empire.* Osprey Publishing, October 10, 2005.

Powis TG, A. Cyphers, N. W. Gaikwad, L. Grivetti, and K. Cheong. "Cacao Use and the San Lorenzo Olmec." *Proceedings of the National Academy of Sciences,* 108(21)(2011): 8595-600.

Smith, Michael E. *The Aztecs, 3rd Edition.* Wiley.com, December 27, 2011.

Strawn, Susan M., "Hand Spinning and Cotton in the Aztec Empire, as Revealed by the Codex Mendoza." *Textile Society of America Symposium Proceedings.* 5 (2002).

Thomas, Hugh. *Conquest: Cortes, Montezuma, and the Fall of Old Mexico.* Simon & Schuster, April 7, 1995.

Valentini, Philipp J. T. "The Olmecas and the Tultecas: A Study in Early Mexican Ethnology and History." *American Antiquarian Society,* (October 1882): pp. 209-30, https://www.americanantiquarian.org/proceedings/48003300.pdf .

David Freidel. A Forest of Kings: The Untold Story of the Ancient Maya. William Morrow Paperbacks; January 24, 1992.

Matthew Restall. Invading Guatemala: Spanish, Nahua, and Maya Accounts of the Conquest Wars. Penn State University Press; January 15, 2008.

Lawrence H. Feldman. Lost Shores, Forgotten Peoples: Spanish Explorations of the South East Maya Lowlands. Duke University Press Books; February 5, 2001.

David Drew. The Lost Chronicles of the Maya Kings. University of California Press; March 20, 2000.

Elliot M. Abrams. How the Maya Built Their World: Energetics and Ancient Architecture. University of Texas Press; June 4, 2010.

Simon Martin, Nikolai Grube. Chronicle of the Maya Kings and Queens: Deciphering The Dynasties of the Ancient Maya. Thames & Hudson; April 28, 2008.

Michael D. Coe, Stephen D. Houston. The Maya (Ancient Peoples and Places). Thames & Hudson; June 16, 2015.

Richard Diehl. Olmecs: America's First Civilization (Ancient Peoples & Places). Thames and Hudson; December 31, 2004.

Michael D. Coe. America's First Civilization. Discovering the Olmec. American Heritage Association / Smithsonian; January 1, 1968.

Robert M. Rosenswig. The Beginnings of Mesoamerican Civilization: Inter-Regional Interaction and the Olmec. Cambridge University Press; December 28, 2009.

Francisco Estrada-Belli. The First Maya Civilization: Ritual and Power Before the Classic Period. Routledge; December 20, 2010.

Sarah E. Jackson. Politics of the Maya Court: Hierarchy and Change in the Late Classic Period. University of Oklahoma Press. May 24, 2013.

Richard A. Diehl. *The Olmecs: America's First Civilization (Ancient Peoples and Places).* London: Thames & Hudson; November 1, 2005.

Michael D. Coe. Rex Koontz. *Mexico: From the Olmecs to the Aztecs (Ancient Peoples and Places)*. London and New York: Thames & Hudson; June 14, 2013.

Christopher A Pool. *Olmec archaeology and early Mesoamerica.* Cambridge and New York: Cambridge University Press, 2007.

Deborah L. Nichols. Christopher A. Pool. *The Oxford Handbook of Mesoamerican Archaeology.* Oxford University Press; September 24, 2012.

Douglas J. Kennett. *Archaic-Period Foragers and Farmers in Mesoamerica.* Sep 2012.

Rosemary A. Joyce. John S. Henderson. *Beginnings of Village Life in Eastern Mesoamerica.* Cambridge University Press; 20 January 2017.

Michael D. Coe. *Magnetic Exploration of the Olmec Civilization.* Yale University. January 1972(PDF online reproduction).

Karl A Taube. *Olmec Art.* Washington, D.C: Dumbarton Oaks Research Library and Collection; 2004.

Kathleen Berrin. (editor) Virginia M. Fields(editor). *Olmec: Colossal Masterworks of Ancient Mexico.* Yale University Press; October 26, 2010.

Mary Ellen Miller. *The Art of Mesoamerica (World of Art).* Thames & Hudson; September 10, 2012.

Christopher A. Pool(editor). *Settlement Archaeology and Political Economy at Tres Zapotes, Veracruz, Mexico (Monographs).* The Cotsen Institute of Archaeology Press; July 1, 2003.

Nigel Davies. The Toltecs, until the fall of Tula. University of Oklahoma Press; January 1, 1977.

Nigel Davies. The Toltec Heritage: From the Fall of Tula to the Rise of Tenochtitlan. University of Oklahoma Press; January 1, 1980.

Richard A. Diehl. Tula: The Toltec Capital of Ancient Mexico. New York: Thames & Hudson; November 1, 1983.

H. B. Nicholson. Topiltzin Quetzalcoatl: The Once and Future Lord of the Toltecs. University Press of Colorado; September 15, 2001.

Frank Díaz. The Gospel of the Toltecs: The Life and Teachings of Quetzalcoatl. Bear & Company; July 30, 2002.

Jeff Karl Kowalski. Cynthia Kristan-Graham. George J. Bey III. Twin Tollans: Chichén Itzá, Tula, and the Epiclassic to Early Postclassic Mesoamerican World, Revised Edition. Dumbarton Oaks Research Library and Collection; November 28, 2011.

Michael D. Coe, Stephen D. Houston. The Maya (Ancient Peoples and Places). Thames & Hudson; June 16, 2015.

Elliot M. Abrams. How the Maya Built Their World: Energetics and Ancient Architecture. University of Texas Press; June 4, 2010.

Argote, D. L., A. Tejero-Andrade, M. Cárdenas-Soto, G. Cifuentes-Nava, R. E. Chávez, E. Hernández-Quintero, A. García-Serrano, A., and V. Ortega. "Designing the Underworld in Teotihuacan: Cave Detection beneath the Moon Pyramid by ERT and ANT Surveys." *Journal of Archaeological Science*, 118, 105141 (2020). https://doi.org/10.1016/j.jas.2020.105141

Arizona State University. "Ceremonial Burial at Moon Pyramid Shows Teotihuacan Rulers Had Mayan Connection." *Science Daily*. October 29, 2002.

Braswell, Geoffrey E., ed. *The Maya and Teotihuacan: Reinterpreting Early Classic Interaction*. Austin: University of Texas Press, 2003.

Carballo, David M. "The Social Organization of Craft Production and Interregional Exchange at Teotihuacan." In *Merchants, Markets, and Exchange in the Pre-Columbian World*, ed. Kenneth D. Hirth, 113-140. Dumbarton Oaks Pre-Columbian Symposia and Colloquia, 2013. https://sites.bu.edu/patt-es/files/2014/10/Carballo2013_Merchants.pdf

Carballo, David M. "Urban Life on Teotihuacan's Periphery – New Research at the Tlajinga District." *Ancient Mesoamerica* 30, no. 1 (2019): 91–94. doi:10.1017/S0956536118000500.

Carballo, David M. *Urbanization and Religion in Ancient Central Mexico*. New York: Oxford University Press, 2016.

Casar, I., L. Márquez, and E. Cienfuegos. "Monte Alban and Teotihuacan Connections: Can Stable Isotope Analysis of Bone and Enamel Detect Migration between Two Ancient Mesoamerican Urban Capitals?" *Archaeological and Anthropological Sciences*

Clayton, Sarah C. "Interregional Relationships in Mesoamerica: Interpreting Maya Ceramics at Teotihuacan." *Latin American Antiquity* 16, no. 4 (2005): 427–48. https://doi.org/10.2307/30042508.

Coe, Michael D. *The Maya (Ancient Peoples and Places Series)*. London and New York: Thames & Hudson, 1999.

Coggins, Clemency Chase. "Creation Religion and the Numbers at Teotihuacan and Izapa." *RES: Anthropology and Aesthetics*, no. 29/30 (1996): 16–38. http://www.jstor.org/stable/20166942

Cowgill, George L. *Ancient Teotihuacan: Early Urbanism in Central Mexico (Case Studies in Early Societies)*. Cambridge: Cambridge University Press, 2015.

Cowgill, George L. "State and Society at Teotihuacan, Mexico." *Annual Review of Anthropology* 26 (1997): 129–61. http://www.jstor.org/stable/2952518.

Day, Jane Stevenson, Kristi Butterwick, and Robert B. Pickering. "Archaeological Interpretations of West Mexican Ceramic Art from the Late Preclassic Period: Three Figurine Projects." *Ancient Mesoamerica* 7, no. 1 (1996): 149–61. http://www.jstor.org/stable/26307287.

Demarest, Arthur. *Ancient Maya: The Rise and Fall of a Forest Civilization.* Cambridge: Cambridge University Press, 2004. ISBN 978-0-521-53390-4. OCLC 51438896

Department of the Arts of Africa, Oceania, and the Americas. "Teotihuacan." In *Heilbrunn Timeline of Art History.* New York: The Metropolitan Museum of Art, October 2001. http://www.metmuseum.org/toah/hd/teot/hd_teot.htm

Evans, Susan Toby. "Aztec-period Political Organization in the Teotihuacan Valley: Otumba as a City-State." Ancient Mesoamerica 12, no. 1 (2001): 89–100. http://www.jstor.org/stable/26308189

Follensbee, Billie J. A. "Fiber Technology and Weaving in Formative-Period Gulf Coast Cultures." *Ancient Mesoamerica* 19, no. 1 (2008): 87–110. http://www.jstor.org/stable/26309219

García-Des Lauriers, Claudia, ed. and Tatsuya Murakami, ed. *Teotihuacan and Early Classic Mesoamerica: Multiscalar Perspectives on Power, Identity, and Interregional Relations.* Louisville: University Press of Colorado, 2021.

Garraty, Christopher P. "Aztec Teotihuacan: Political Processes at a Postclassic and Early Colonial City-State in the Basin of Mexico." *Latin American Antiquity* 17, no. 4 (2006): 363–87. https://doi.org/10.2307/25063064

Grennes-Ravitz, Ronald A., and G. H. Coleman. "The Quintessential Role of Olmec in the Central Highlands of Mexico: A Refutation." *American Antiquity* 41, no. 2 (1976): 196–206. https://doi.org/10.2307/279172.

Gruner, Erina, and John Hodgson. "Precursor to Teotihuacan?" *Archaeology* 59, no. 2 (2006): 9–9. http://www.jstor.org/stable/41780063.

Hassig, Ross. *War and Society in Ancient Mesoamerica.* Berkeley: University of California Press, 1992.

Headrick, Annabeth. *The Teotihuacan Trinity: The Sociopolitical Structure of an Ancient Mesoamerican City (The William and Bettye Nowlin Series in Art, History, and Culture of the Western Hemisphere).* Austin: University of Texas Press, 2017.

Hirth, Kenneth G., David M. Carballo, and Barbara Arroyo. *Teotihuacan: The World Beyond the City.* Washington, D.C.: Dumbarton Oaks, 2020.

Houston, Stephen, Edwin Román Ramírez, Thomas G. Garrison, David Stuart, Héctor Escobedo Ayala, and Pamela Rosales. "A Teotihuacan Complex at the Classic Maya City of Tikal, Guatemala." *Antiquity 95,* no. 384 (2021): e32. doi:10.15184/aqy.2021.140.

Joyce, Arthur A. "Interregional Interaction and Social Development on the Oaxaca Coast." *Ancient Mesoamerica.* 4, no. 1 (1993): 67–84. http://www.jstor.org/stable/26307326

Lachniet, Matthew S., and Juan Pablo Bernal-Uruchurtu. "AD 550–600 Collapse at Teotihuacan: Testing Climatic Forcing from a 2400-Year Mesoamerican Rainfall Reconstruction," In *Megadrought and Collapse: From Early Agriculture to Angkor,* edited by Harvey Weiss, 183–204. New York: Oxford Academic, 2017. https://doi.org/10.1093/oso/9780199329199.003.0006.

"Mammoth Traps near Mexico City Are First Ever Found." *Mexico News Daily.* November 8, 2019. https://mexiconewsdaily.com/news/mammoth-traps-near-mexico-city-are-first-ever-found/

Manzanilla, Linda R. "Cooperation and Tensions in Multi-ethnic Corporate Societies Using Teotihuacan, Central Mexico, as a Case Study." *Proceedings of the National Academy of Sciences.* 112, no.30 (March 2015): 9210-15.

Moran, Barbara. "Lessons from Teo." *The Brink: Boston University,* 2015. https://www.bu.edu/articles/2015/archaeology-teotihuacan-mexico/

Nichols, Deborah L. "Review of Teotihuacan and the Development of Postclassic Mesoamerica, by Davíd Carrasco, Lindsay Jones, Scott Sessions, and Kenneth G. Hirth." *Latin American Antiquity 12,* no. 3 (2001): 334–36. https://doi.org/10.2307/971638

Pasztory, Esther. "Still Invisible: The Problem of the Aesthetics of Abstraction for Pre-Columbian Art and Its Implications for Other Cultures." *Anthropology and Aesthetics.* 104 (1990-1991): 19-20. https://doi.org/10.1086/RESvn1ms20166829

Pasztory, Esther. *Teotihuacan: An Experiment in Living.* Norman: University of Oklahoma Press, 1997.

Pre-Hispanic City of Teotihuacan. UNESCO: World Heritage Convention. https://whc.unesco.org/en/list/414

Reuters. "Riches of Artifacts under Pyramid Reveals Ancient Mexican Culture." *Daily Sabah*

Robb, Matthew, ed. *Teotihuacan: City of Water, City of Fire*. Berkeley: University of California Press, 2017.

Rodriguez, Maria Teresa Palomares. *The Oaxaca Barrio in Teotihuacan: Mortuary Customs and Ethnicity in Mesoamerica's Greatest Metropolis*. Carbondale: Southern Illinois University, 2013.

Sahagún, Fray Bernardino de. *Historia General de las Cosas de Nueva España*. Edited by Francisco del Paso y Troncoso. Madrid: Fototipia de Hauser y Menet, 1905.

Santley, Robert S., and Philip J. Arnold. "The Obsidian Trade to the Tuxtlas Region and Its Implications for the Prehistory of Southern Veracruz, Mexico." *Ancient Mesoamerica* 16, no. 2 (2005): 179–94. http://www.jstor.org/stable/26309178.

Shaer, Matthew. "A Secret Tunnel Found in Mexico May Finally Solve the Mysteries of Teotihuacán." *Smithsonian Magazine* (June 2016). https://www.smithsonianmag.com/history/discovery-secret-tunnel-mexico-solve-mysteries-teotihuacan-180959070/

Shook, Edwin M., and Alfred V. Kidder. "Mound E-III-3, K'aminaljuyu, Guatemala." In *Contributions to American Anthropology and History*, Vol. 9 (53) (1952): 33–127. Washington D.C.: Carnegie Institution of Washington.

Smith, Michael E., Abhishek Chatterjee, Angela C. Huster, Sierra Stewart, and Marion Forest. "Apartment Compounds, Households, and Population in the Ancient City of Teotihuacan, Mexico." Ancient Mesoamerica 30, no. 3 (2019): 399–418. doi:10.1017/S0956536118000573.

Somerville, A. D., N. Sugiyama, L. R. Manzanilla, and M. J. Schoeninger. "Animal Management at the Ancient Metropolis of Teotihuacan, Mexico: Stable Isotope Analysis of Leporid (Cottontail and Jackrabbit) Bone Mineral." PLoS One. 2016 Aug 17;11(8):e0159982. doi: 10.1371/journal.pone.0159982. PMID: 27532515; PMCID: PMC4988673.

Storey, Rebecca. "An Estimate of Mortality in a Pre-Columbian Urban Population." American Anthropologist 87, no. 3 (1985): 519–35. http://www.jstor.org/stable/678874

Storey, Rebecca. "Perinatal Mortality at Pre-Columbian Teotihuacan." *American Journal of Biological Anthropology*. 69, no. 4 (April 1986): 541-548.

Sugiyama, Nawa, Raúl Valadez, Gilberto Pérez, Bernardo Rodriguez, and Fabiola Torres. "Animal Management, Preparation and Sacrifice: Reconstructing Burial 6 at the Moon Pyramid, Teotihuacan, México."

Anthropozoologica, 48(2), 467-485, (1 December 2013).

Sugiyama, Nawa, Saburo Sugiyama, and Alejandro Sarabia. "Inside the Sun Pyramid at Teotihuacan, Mexico: 2008–2011 Excavations and Preliminary Results." Latin American Antiquity 24, no. 4 (2013): 403–32. http://www.jstor.org/stable/23645621.

Sugiyama, Saburo and Leonardo Luján. "Dedicatory Burial/Offering Complexes at the Moon Pyramid, Teotihuacan: A Preliminary Report of 1998-2004 Explorations." Ancient Mesoamerica. 18 (1): 127–146. doi:10.1017/S0956536107000065. JSTOR 26309326. S2CID 54787122.

Taube, Karl A. "The Teotihuacan Cave of Origin: The Iconography and Architecture of Emergence Mythology in Mesoamerica and the American Southwest." RES: Anthropology and Aesthetics, no. 12 (1986): 51–82. http://www.jstor.org/stable/20166753.

University of California - Riverside. "Modern Activities Follow the Contours of Ancient Teotihuacan: Lidar Mapping Study Reveals Vast Landscape Modifications That Still Influence Construction and Farming." ScienceDaily, September 20, 2021. www.sciencedaily.com/releases/2021/09/210920173156.htm

Venegas, Roberto. "Obsidian from Teotihuacan," *Historical Mexico.* https://historicalmx.org/items/show/78.

Von Winning, Hasso. "The Old Fire God and His Symbolism at Teotihuacan." *Indiana*, Vol. 4 (1977). https://doi.org/10.18441/ind.v4i0.7-61

Wade, Lizzie. "The Arrival of Strangers: New Evidence Points to a Clash Between Two Ancient Mesoamerican Cultures, Teotihuacan and the Maya." Science. February 27, 2020. https://www.science.org/content/article/astounding-new-finds-suggest-ancient-empire-may-be-hiding-plain-sight

White, Christine D., T. Douglas Price, and Fred J. Longstaffe. "Residential Histories of the Human Sacrifices at the Moon Pyramid, Teotihuacan: Evidence from Oxygen and Strontium Isotopes." *Ancient Mesoamerica* 18, no. 1 (2007): 159–72. http://www.jstor.org/stable/26309328

Made in the USA
Columbia, SC
02 October 2023

23779853R00391